VERMILION
GATE

D1347748

Aiping Mu aged six in Beijing, spring 1958

VERMILION GATE

Aiping Mu

LITTLE, BROWN AND COMPANY

A *Little, Brown* Book

First published in Great Britain in 2000
by Little, Brown and Company

Copyright © Aiping Mu 2000

The moral right of the author has been asserted.

All rights reserved.
No part of this publication may be reproduced, stored in
a retrieval system, or transmitted, in any form or by any
means, without the prior permission in writing of the
publisher, nor be otherwise circulated in any form of
binding or cover other than that in which it is published
and without a similar condition including this condition
being imposed on the subsequent purchaser.

A CIP catalogue record for this book is available
from the British Library

ISBN 0 316 64170 7

Typeset in Centaur by M Rules
Printed and bound in Great Britain by
Clays Ltd, St Ives plc

Little, Brown and Company (UK)
Brettenham House
Lancaster Place
London WC2E 7EN

Contents

Acknowledgements

Since my childhood, I have been familiar with an ancient Chinese idiom, 'Yin-shui-si-yuan,' which means when you drink water, think of its source – in other words, never forget where one's success comes from. My mother is the first person to receive my thanks. Her unstinting support to me has been a major source of my strength, courage and determination to survive the unthinkable past, and to overcome the difficulties while writing this book. Without my father's influence on my life, I would not be what I am today, and there would not be this book.

Volker Wille, the first reader of my book, made considerable contributions to my writing especially through his frank critiques and intelligent discussions with me. His encouragement and understanding helped me to keep my spirits up throughout the writing.

I feel fortunate to work with my agent, Peter Robinson of Curtis Brown, and Alan Samson, my editor at Little Brown and Company (UK). I treasured their wise advice about my writing, and was hugely impressed by their knowledge about modern China. I would also like to thank Steve Cox for his excellent editorial work, and Becky Smith for her efficiency.

Other members of my family, especially my siblings, also offered their support to my work, to whom I express my gratitude. My thanks go to many friends inside and outside China. A-bing, the first person who persuaded me to write this book, never gave up convincing me of this idea for nearly ten years before I was ready to start writing. Yansheng, who shared the hardship with me in the remote village of North Shaanxi three decades ago, and helped me in checking details of our past experiences. With the advice of Brian Turvey I was able to find a first-class agent and publisher, which ensured that my work was in safe hands from the very beginning. Professors Dennis Hawkes and Freda Hawkes, whose generosity and assistance to me were immeasurable especially during the most difficult years after I left China, were among many others to whom I would like to express my gratitude on this occasion.

This is a book about my own and my parents' lives in China in the twentieth-century. The events have passed and gone. Instead of tracing who should be responsible for the plight of my parents and myself in the past, I would rather show, through writing this book, that we are all products of the society that we live in.

Author's Note

Names of my parents and siblings are real, so are the public figures. Each of them begins with the family name, the personal name coming second, as it is the custom for Chinese. Other personal names are disguised.

Most of the Chinese names are spelled according to Pinyin, the phonetic romanization system to show pronunciation of Chinese characters. For example, my family name 'Mu' is pronounced 'Moo', and the pronunciation of my first name 'Aiping' is 'Iping'. I use 'Mao Zedong' instead of 'Mao Tse-tung', 'Zhou Enlai' for 'Chou En-lai' and 'Zhu De' for 'Chu Teh'.

Some other names in the book are translated into English instead of being transcribed phonetically. Under the Communist regime, women don't adopt husbands' family names after marriage.

Family Tree

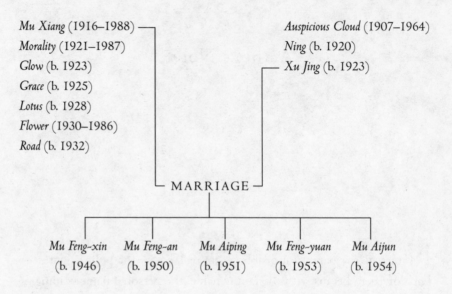

Mu Xiang (1916–1988) ——
Morality (1921–1987)
Glow (b. 1923)
Grace (b. 1925)
Lotus (b. 1928)
Flower (1930–1986)
Road (b. 1932)

Auspicious Cloud (1907–1964)
Ning (b. 1920)
—— Xu Jing (b. 1923)

└─ MARRIAGE ─┘

Mu Feng-xin   Mu Feng-an   Mu Aiping   Mu Feng-yuan   Mu Aijun
(b. 1946)   (b. 1950)   (b. 1951)   (b. 1953)   (b. 1954)

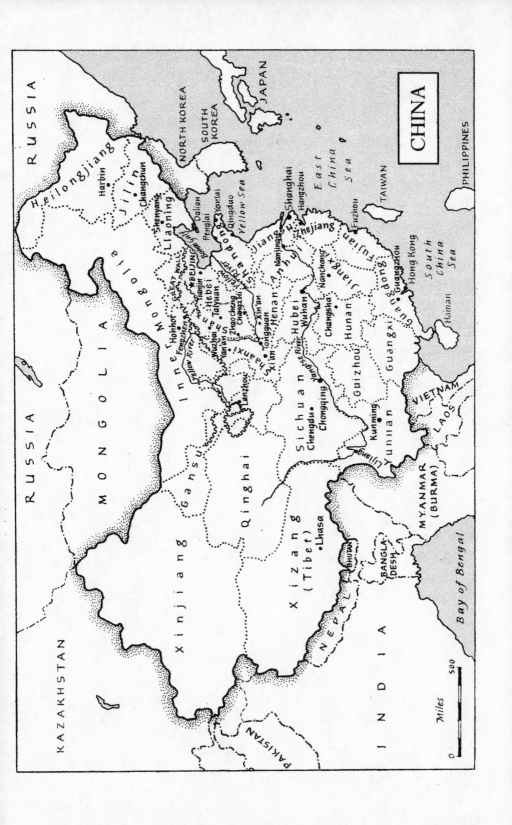

Part One
1916–1964

Red is the east, rises the sun;
China has brought forth a Mao Zedong.
For the people's happiness he works;
he is our great saviour.

from 'The East Is Red',
the most familiar song in my childhood

Chapter I

The East is Red:
Hard Times for New Arrivals

(1946–1951)

At dawn, the city of Beijing (in the West often spelt as Peking), the traditional 'northern capital', was bathed in rosy clouds. When the sun came out, golden glazed tiles on the heavy roofs of palaces, temples and pagodas glinted under the azure sky. In front of the magnificent Tian-an Men (Gate of Heavenly Peace) Rostrum in the centre of Beijing, a massive red flag with five golden stars, the national flag of the People's Republic of China, fluttered in the wind on top of a huge pole. It was 1 August 1951, the Communist Army Day. The streets of the Communist capital were full of slogans written in huge-size characters on brightly coloured paper: 'Long Live the Communist Party!', 'Long Live the People's Republic of China!', 'Long Live the People's Liberation Army!' (PLA). Nearly two years had passed since 1 October 1949 when Mao Zedong, Chairman of the Communist Party, stood on that Rostrum at the founding ceremony of the People's Republic and declared to a cheering crowd one third of a million strong: 'The Chinese people have stood up!' By now, the entire mainland of China was under

Communist control, and the country had started to recover from the three years of Civil War between the Communists and the Nationalists (Kuomintang), known in Communist history as the War of Liberation. For my family, the most significant improvement was that after six years of marriage, my parents eventually settled down in Beijing. In this year, my father was thirty-five years old and my mother was twenty-eight.

Around ten o'clock in the morning, my mother's labour started. 'Please contact my hospital if you don't hear from me by lunchtime,' she told her secretary before leaving for hospital. She had reached Beijing just a few months before, working for the North China Bureau of the Communist Party's Central Committee. Of the six regional bureaux under the Committee, the North China Bureau was in charge of the cities of Beijing and Tianjin plus a number of nearby provinces.

From the regional bureau down to local levels, there were and are Party committees in all governmental and non-governmental organizations. The smallest power unit of Party organization is the branch, which operates in workshops, villages, offices, schools or shops. Both in the Party committee and in the branch, the leader is the secretary. Key Party members often hold concurrent posts in committee and branch. From my mother's appearance at that time, it was hard to believe that this young woman with well-educated manners and a quiet smile was a Communist Party member of thirteen years' standing. Her post as senior policy researcher was equal in the Communist hierarchy to the rank of county governor.

My father was not around that day, as he was stationed with his troops in Hengshui, a county in Hebei province nearly 300 kilometres away from Beijing. His post as Political Commissar for a division was equal to that of a division commander in the PLA. From the beginning of the Communist revolution, it had been emphasized that the Party must control their military, a rule expressed in Chairman Mao's famous saying: 'The Party must command the gun, while the gun must never be allowed to command the Party.' Therefore, there were Party organizations at each level of the military. In those days my father was slim. The heavy features in his serious face made his physical appearance quite spectacular among Chinese. Since the system of military ranks was not adopted until 1955, the chief clue to my father's position came from his woollen army uniform, which was only provided to officers from the level of division commander and above, and from the fact that he was usually attended by at least one armed bodyguard.

Beijing is divided by crisscross streets which surround the Forbidden City, the former Imperial Palace. Off the main thoroughfares run count-less lanes called 'hutongs'. My mother's office was located in the Temple of Grace (Yuan-en Si) Hutong, a wealthy residential area in the eastern part of Beijing near the Forbidden City. Along both sides of each hutong, there were mud or plaster walls, several feet high, which screened the houses behind. Normally, each house comprised a compound with four rows of rooms around a courtyard – a style famous as the 'Beijing Si-he-yuan'. Dark grey was the basic colour of the walls and tiled roofs of houses in hutongs. It contrasted starkly with the magnificent colour of the nearby palace, with its dark red surrounding walls, 20 feet high, and golden glazed roof tiles.

It was quiet outside when my mother passed through the hutong. Along both sides, the gates of most houses were painted in vermilion or black with metal lions' heads biting on large rings. Most of the gates were tightly closed, indicating that each house behind the gate was occu-pied by one household only, a luxury available only for well-to-do families. Among ordinary people, it was common for several house-holds to share a compound. Normally, the front gates of such houses had lost the colour of the original paint, and were not shut even at night. What happened inside was easily visible from the street. In the morning, housewives gathered in the courtyard and lit small stoves with egg-shaped briquettes for cooking. In order to save fuel, ordinary households did not keep their stoves on at night except in winter, so that the whole city was full of the smell of burning firewood and coal until the later morning. In those days, the most common dress for housewives in Beijing was the plain cotton qipao, close-fitting, with a high neck and slit skirt, which is a classical costume for Chinese women. While waiting for the fire to get stronger, they brushed their teeth in the courtyard, gargling loudly then spitting on the ground. In Beijing, most families lacked any basic sanitary facilities at home, with no indoor toilet or running water.

My mother walked slowly to the nearest hospital, stopping from time to time till labour pangs subsided. At the end of the hutong, she was invited to get into an empty rickshaw by the puller, a strong young man. At that time, there were not many tramcars or buses in Beijing, and only a few could afford bicycles, so rickshaws were the major means of transport until the mid-1950s. On this hot morning, the puller took off his jacket, but still streamed with sweat having just delivered a passenger. My mother refused his offer. Since moving to Beijing, she had never tried rickshaws, as she always felt sorry for these poor men when she saw them pulling passengers and running through the streets. My mother's position in the Communist hierarchy entitled her to transport from her work unit, especially under these circumstances, but she did not request it.

It was close to lunchtime when my mother, lying in the hospital's bright delivery room, took her first glance at me, her newborn baby daughter. Her labour had gone smoothly, which was quite a relief after her struggles to give birth to my two elder brothers. Two days later, when being discharged from hospital, she decided to leave me behind for a while, rather than carry me all the way home on her own. She promised to send a nanny to pick me up, but her suggestion gave rise to strong suspicions among the hospital staff, since it was not unusual to see baby girls abandoned in those days, due to women's low status in Chinese society. Having recognized their doubts, my mother laughed:

'My daughter is the treasure of our family. How could I give her away?'

It was true. My parents already had two sons, and had longed for a girl. I was also the first child in the family that my father saw as a new-born baby. He came home on the following weekend, sat by my cot and caught each shade of feeling in my face. 'Look! This little girl takes after me so much,' he said to my mother with delight.

Under the Communist regime, it was common to give names with revolutionary implications to newborn babies. After the establishment of the People's Republic in 1949, the popular names had been 'Reconstruction of China' (Jian-guo), 'Victory' (Sheng-li) or 'Long March' (Chang-zheng). Seeing that I was born on Army Day, suggestions for my name included 'Establishment of the Military Forces' (Jian-jun) and 'The First of August' (Ba-yi). Since China's involvement in the Korean War in October 1950, names like 'Resisting America' (Kang-mei) or 'Supporting Korea' (Yuan-chao) had also become fashionable for both girls and boys. Several years later when I went to school, there were about half a dozen pupils in my year called either Resisting America or Supporting Korea. The Korean War also affected my family life, as my father's division was designated among the 'Chinese People's Volunteers' (CPV), the name that Chinese troops used in the Korean War, and was going to be assigned to Korea in the month after I came into the world. In order to commemorate this special event, I was named 'Aiping' (Loving Peace).

After the outbreak of the Korean War, an anti-America campaign was launched nationally by the Chinese government. Quoting an ancient saying that 'if the lips are gone, the teeth will be cold', it was said that the safety of China would be threatened if its neighbour Korea was controlled by the imperialists. All over China, slogans like 'Resisting American Aggression to Support Korea! Defending [our] Home and Country!' were displayed. Hundreds of thousands of youngsters were mobilized to join the CPV. Their departure ceremonies were often accompanied by stirring marches: 'Valiantly and spiritedly/ Striding over the Ya-lu River [boundary between China and Korea]/ Defending peace for our country . . .!'

According to the media, the CPV had won significant victories in Korea at the time when I was born. Up against the well-equipped American forces and their allies, on the other hand, the Communist troops also took heavy casualties, including a considerable loss of officers. At the end of 1950, the eldest son of Mao Zedong, Mao Anying, was killed in an American bombing raid while working for the Commander-in-Chief of the CPV in Korea. Nevertheless, my father accepted his assignment without hesitation. Ever since joining the Communist Party nineteen years before, he had dedicated his life to its cause, and obeyed its decisions without a second thought.

Before his departure, my father took many photographs of the family, and said to my mother: 'Please keep the negatives carefully. If I can not survive the war, they will be the only thing I leave for our children.' The photographs accompanied him throughout his time in Korea. 'The delicate little face of our baby daughter always appears in front of my eyes,' he wrote to my mother from Korea, 'she reminds me of our family which has encouraged me to cope with the brutal war.'

In Korea, my father's division was responsible for constructing and maintaining several Communist military airports which were frequently targeted by the American airforce. A major task was to remove the numerous time-bombs dropped by the American bombers every day. Lacking the proper equipment for bomb removal, the troops used simple tools to dig huge holes and expose the bombs, which each weighed 200 pounds. Each bomb was then pulled out with a rope by a work gang and eventually carried to a nearby river bank for final disposal. A number of soldiers were killed when bombs blew up during the removal operation. Later, the troops learned how to disable the timers in the bombs.

One day, my father's command post was completely destroyed by American shells. When he escaped outside, a piece of shrapnel whizzed past his head and then hit and felled a tree behind him. When everything was over, my father found the shrapnel that almost killed him, and said to his bodyguard: 'I will keep it for my children.' He kept that lump of dark metal until the end of his life, and showed it to me many times as I grew up.

In June 1952, shortly after my father returned to China with his division, he was transferred to Beijing and worked for the headquarters of the North China (Hua-bei) Military Region. That was the end of the long periods of separation which had repeatedly kept my parents apart ever since their marriage in August 1945. Having been through constant dangers and instability in his revolutionary career for the last twenty years, at long last my father could enjoy a peaceful and stable life with his beloved family. Coming back from his office, he liked spending time with me in the evenings. In order to cajole me away from my nanny, he brought sweets or fruits to please me. While working or resting in his study, he enjoyed having me toddling around and listening to me babbling. I became my father's favourite child.

When my parents' first child, my eldest brother, uttered his first cry, it was in a very different world from the one that greeted me. On 13 May 1946, just ten days before he was born, my mother had to retreat from Fengzhen, a city located in a Communist base area in Suiyuan province (part of Inner Mongolia after 1954), and now under military attacks from the Nationalist forces. It was the eve of a full-scale civil war between the Communists and Nationalists. The Sino-Japanese War, known as the War of Resistance Against Japan in China, had ended only nine months before. The mainland of China was under the Nationalist regime, but the Communists had established nineteen bases covering a total area of more than one million square kilometres. In order to take control of the whole country, the Nationalists planned an all-out offensive against the Communists. With his 4.3 million well-equipped troops, Chiang Kai-shek, President of the Nationalist government, was confident that the 1.2 million soldiers of the People's Liberation Army would be defeated within six months.

Riding a white horse, her heavily pregnant body covered by her baggy grey army uniform, my mother travelled on the rugged road along a chain of undulating hills which was the only route controlled by the Communists towards their rear in the northwest of Shanxi province. It was a journey of more than 300 kilometres from Fengzhen. She hardly noticed that the hills were changing to green as grass and shrubs started to grow in spring. Throughout the journey, she was preoccupied with thoughts of my father, who was still commanding his troops in the front line near Fengzhen. Since their wedding nine months before, this was the second time they had had to separate, and there was no knowing when or where they might see one another again.

Three months before, in February 1946, my mother arrived in Fengzhen, the nearest place to where her husband was stationed, from another Communist base area. In order to end their first separation, which had lasted for two months, she had applied for a job with the Fengzhen government, starting her trip as soon as she received the new appointment. Already pregnant with her first child, she tramped about 600 kilometres along the narrow mountain paths in the cold of winter, looking forward to being reunited with her husband in Fengzhen.

Since early 1946, many places in north China had changed hands several times between the Communist and the Nationalist forces. A place of strategic importance in the north of China, Fengzhen had just been taken over by the Communists when my mother arrived, but soon it was under attack. A fierce fight was imminent, and scared local residents fled as soon as possible. Inside the town there were rumours, assassinations and kidnaps of Communist officials, organized by active Nationalist agents. The room my mother rented was broken into several times, and Party documents stolen. Despite the dangerous situation his pregnant wife faced, my father was hardly ever around. Due to the tension at the front line, he only managed to visit my mother twice in Fengzhen during her four-month stay.

In March 1946, Commander He Long of the Communist Northwest Military Region, later to become Deputy Premier of China, arrived in Fengzhen inspecting troops in the front line. Seeing that some women officials were still around, he insisted that they must be sent to the rear immediately. My pregnant mother's name went to the top of the evacuation list, but she refused to leave. Since the late 1930s, both of my parents had lost touch with their families during the Sino-Japanese War. Once removed from her husband again, whom could she turn to for help and support? Nor could she bear the idea of leaving him behind in the front line of this brutal war. But my mother's objections were overruled, and she had to retreat to the rear. She started her long journey again shortly after Commander He Long's inspection.

To spare her from walking, my father provided my mother with a white horse and a groom, or rather half a groom! She could not believe her eyes when she first saw him. On his tiny body, a normal-sized army tunic reached like a baggy coat down to his knees. A pair of old shoes were bound to his feet with cord because they were too big to wear. The upper part of his childish face was completely overshadowed by the peak of his battered cap. Ignoring my mother's surprise, the little groom kept wiping his runny nose on his dirty sleeves. He was called Little Ninth (Xiao Jiuzi), the ninth child in his family, and he was only twelve years old. My mother had to swallow her disappointment. Little Ninth was all that the army could spare, and in any case she heard later that despite his youth, her new groom had been through many harsh experiences in his life. The son of a poor peasant family, he lost his mother at three. From the age of seven, he had to work for their landlord as a shepherd, and suffered beatings and starvation. The previous year, when my father's troops passed by his village, Little Ninth clung sobbing on to the tail of a soldier's horse and insisted that he had to join the Communist forces to fight for the poor. The soldier lifted him up, and the PLA had a new recruit.

With only Little Ninth for an escort, my mother travelled towards the Great Wall. Due to her pregnancy, they only managed 20–25 kilometres a day, and soon lagged far behind their retreating fellows. At night, they stayed in army service stations, staffed by about ten people, which were established along the routes controlled by the Communists. Located in rented village houses, they were responsible for moving supplies to the front and for providing travelling officials with accommodation and food. Seeing her heavily pregnant body, everyone they met on the way was concerned about her physical condition. The long journeys had drained her energy, and the future was uncertain both for herself and for her husband. But it was too dangerous for her to stop, as the Nationalist forces were approaching. Feeling the foetus stir inside her, she kept on repeating to herself: 'I will never give up!'

The area they travelled through is called 'Sai-wai' in China, meaning beyond (or to the north of) the Great Wall. It was known for its strong winds, bitter cold, barren land and remote location. Travelling along the endless undulating hills, they hardly met anyone else except when they passed through a few small villages. It was a desolate, lonely journey. Fortunately, Little Ninth was good company for my mother. He tended her horse with care and enjoyed singing cheerful songs: 'Riding a white horse, carrying a foreign gun, I am a smart fighter to the old Chiang [Chiang Kai-shek].' His childish voice echoed among remote hills and blended with birds' clear singing.

It was the tenth day of the journey. Shortly after starting off that morning, my mother's waters burst, and drenched her saddle. 'What has happened? My childbirth is not till next month.' She felt nervous: 'What can I do now?' Before midday, they had to stop at a village near the Great Wall. When they saw that her labour was coming, the villagers refused to let her a room. According to local custom, no woman, not even a close relative or married daughter, was allowed to give birth in their houses except for their own wives. Otherwise, it was said, their households would suffer in future. In desperation, Little Ninth found the village chief's wife, a sympathetic woman in her forties with an open mind. She rushed home from the field, loosed a large bundle of firewood from her back, and said to my mother: 'Please stay with me. Don't worry about the custom.'

Like those of many another families, the village chief's home was located in a few caves (yao-dong) cut into earthen cliffs, with bare floors, ceilings and walls. Each entrance was blocked by a two-piece wooden door. Small windows were covered by paper as glass was not available. Inside each cave, a huge 'kang', a platform mainly for sleeping, with a stove inside for heating and cooking, occupied more than half of the space. Most kangs in the village were built of earth because bricks, the proper material, were too expensive. Normally, the bare earthen top of the kang was covered by straw mats. In the daytime, a small table with short legs was placed in the middle on the kang, while bedding was rolled up and kept in a corner. Sitting cross-legged on the straw mats, people spent much of their spare time by the table, where they ate, and received visitors. In that harsh climate, heating was required from October to May, but fuel was scarce, so members of different generations had to share one cave in each household: parents slept with children and even with grandchildren on the same kang.

Having accepted my mother, the kind village woman started heating a second cave for her, but when the labour started, she panicked. The local folk midwife was away, and there were no medical services or basic sanitary equipment available. Although she herself had given birth several times before, the chief's wife had never helped anyone to deliver a baby. 'Elder sister, please help me!' my mother pleaded. When he heard her voice, Little Ninth stopped playing outside and rushed into the cave. At the sight of my mother's pale face, he sank to his knees in front of the village chief's wife, clung to her legs and screamed: 'Auntie, she is dying! Please save her life!'

'Wait outside, good boy! Be quiet please!'

Dismissed from the cave, Little Ninth couldn't stop screaming. As my mother's moaning grew louder, he hammered with his fists on the locked door. He broke the window paper and shouted to the people inside: ·

'Auntie, she is the wife of our Commander, please don't let her die! If you save her life, I will do everything for you!' The small quiet village was in an uproar. Curious villagers gathered and whispered to each other.

The village chief's wife decided to help. Inside the cave, a big earthenware vat with a broken edge was moved beside the kang. The woman poured ashes inside it, and told my mother: 'Please take off your trousers and sit on top of the vat.' She forced my mother to sit on the 'delivery seat'.

'Please don't move off it! We all had our babies like this.'

The hours that followed seemed endless. The labour was long and painful, and the vat's jagged edge tore her skin. Suddenly, a wail rose from the vat. 'Wa!' At the same time, my mother felt a sharp relief in her body. From the ashes in the vat, the woman fished a crying baby. Outside the cave, the villagers grew quiet. Little Ninth stopped screaming. 'It's a pupil!' the woman announced to the crowd. Since only boys were sent to school in that area, a pupil meant a male child. 'Congratulations!' came the sound of cheerful voices outside the cave.

Lying on the heated kang, my mother felt exhausted. Under her body, there was a thick layer of ash, which was in common use for absorbing blood during labour. 'Elder sister, please sterilize the scissors first!' my mother said before the woman cut her baby's umbilical cord. 'Don't worry, they're clean.' The women wiped the rusty scissors on the front of her threadbare jacket. After cutting the umbilical cord, she picked some dusty cotton wool from her winter jacket's padding, blew on it twice, then placed it on the baby's bleeding stomach. Later, my mother heard that among the woman's seven children, five had died of umbilical tetanus shortly after birth.

One hour after the birth, the afterbirth had not emerged. My mother kept on bleeding and the woman was alarmed. Drawing on her previous experiences, she instructed my mother to chew her own hair and served her various soups, made of different herbs and including soil from the cave's wall, which were normally used to stop women's bleeding at labour. When the afterbirth finally came out, my mother fell in a dead faint.

'Please keep sitting up and keep your eyes open!' The woman's voice was nervous. 'Otherwise, your brain would be blocked by your blood.'

My mother did not answer. She was too weak to move. This made the woman more anxious. Standing on top of the kang, she lifted my mother up and then kept her sitting upright for a long time.

When everything was over, it was evening. Under an oil-lamp's cheerful light, the whole family rejoiced for the newborn baby. On the door-knocker they tied a red scarf to celebrate the birth of a boy. The woman wrapped a thick towel around my mother's head to keep her warm, and then served her a pot of delicious chicken soup, which was a traditional recipe to help women to recover after giving birth.

'My elder sister, how can I repay you?' My mother's eyes were moist with tears, as she knew how valuable a hen was for this poor family.

'You should not mention it!' the woman replied. 'You and your husband are fighting for poor people. Without the Communist Party, we would still be starving.'

What she said was true. Since the Communists had taken control five years previously, land rents and taxes had fallen in this area. Most families finally had food enough to survive throughout the year, as they never had before.

At the kind woman's insistence, my mother remained in her home for a while. According to the local custom, in the first month after childbirth women must stay in bed for a complete rest, or risk damage to their health. After the birth, my mother suffered from postpartum anaemia, and remained very pale and weak. During the day, her hostess would not let her do anything, or even go outside, as it was said that cold air was harmful for women after childbirth. Her kang was heated, the broken window papers carefully repaired, and a heavy curtain with cotton wool padding fixed behind her door to keep out draughts. Every day, my mother was served five meals, which was a special treat to improve women's health after childbirth.

It was the season of spring ploughing and sowing, and the woman was already hard at work for her own household. Every day, from dawn to evening, she was busy cooking for her family, feeding pigs and chickens, grinding grain or working in the field. When Little Ninth offered help collecting fuel, she refused: 'Just you enjoy yourself, good boy!' So Little Ninth was like a happy hare running up and down hills with village children every day. Yet the woman insisted on looking after my mother's newborn baby herself at night. She got up as soon as he cried, and if there were too few nappies to change at night, she swapped her dry sleeping place for the baby's wet place. In those days, nappies were made of old clothes or worn-out bed sheets and reused until they were completely finished. Each morning, the woman carried a large pile of dirty nappies to the spring outside the village, and washed them in cold water. During bad weather, she dried nappies on top of the heated kang.

On the thirteenth day after the birth, the family organized a red-egg ceremony, the first celebration (xiao-man-yue) for my mother's new born baby. Due to a high infant mortality rate, superstitious villagers made no fuss about a new birth for a certain time, for fear that the news of childbirth would be passed to Hell and the vulnerable baby would be taken away by the king of Hell (Yan-wang-ye). On the thirteenth day, the baby was considered to be strong enough to survive. Several days before the ceremony, the couple had been extremely busy with the preparation, grinding glutinous millet and buying meat from the market. Boiled eggs were coloured red to be distributed to celebrate the new arrival. In the morning of that very day, their relatives and friends visited my mother with precious presents: chickens or fresh eggs. Later, a special feast was provided to visitors by the generous couple: deep-fried cakes made of glutinous millet, and stewed potatoes with pork, which were the best food available in that area.

Afterwards, the baby was brought to the guests, his first public appearance since birth. He was carefully wrapped in a piece of new, bright red fabric. On top of his hat, a small tiger head made of cotton fabric was a symbol of protection against devils for boys. 'What a hand-some little Communist!' everyone agreed.

Next morning, my mother started her journey again, together with her son and Little Ninth. She felt too much indebted to that kind family to bother them any longer, and the Nationalists were not far away. Lying on a stretcher, my mother was carried by two strong peasants, as she was too weak to ride the horse. In Wuzhai, a county in north-west Shanxi, they found the Communist prefectural government, and after two weeks' rest in an army service station my mother was assigned to the town of Wuzhai, with responsibility for training local Party officials. Little Ninth returned to the front line with her white horse. It was the eve of the Nationalists' all-out offensive against the Communist base areas, and there was a great demand for experienced Party officials. Being a dedicated Communist, the Party's interest had always come first for my mother, so she went to work before her full recovery, and found a wet-nurse for her newborn baby.

In those days, the Communists still lived on a special supply system (gong-ji-zhi), which prevailed until the early 1950s. No one received a salary. Instead, free accommodation, food, uniforms and transport were provided at a standard which reflected each one's position in the hier-archy. At that time, there were three general categories. A small number of 'leading cadres' officials occupied the top of the pyramid: these were the Party, government or military leaders of the Communist base areas. The second category, which my mother belonged to, comprised section directors in the Party organizations or government, and district gover-nors. The vast majority were on the lowest rung including junior officials and soldiers.

According to their status, meals were provided to each one by differ-ent canteens. The Small Canteens (xiao-zao) were for leading cadres and senior officers such as my father, and the Large Canteens (da-zao) for soldiers and junior officials. Food provision differed between them. For example, the ration was 2 kg of meat per head in the Small Canteens every month, but only 1 kg in the Large Canteens. The standard of food provision for the Middle-Sized Canteens (zhong-zao) where my mother had meals was between the two. All Communists, within or outside the military forces, wore the regulation baggy fatigues. For leading cadres and senior officers, they were made of fine cloth before the 1950s, while the rest wore coarse cloth. After each childbirth, officials of high or middle rank were entitled to a special supply for the baby, as well as for hiring a nanny or a wet-nurse, which was normally paid in grain or cloth or other materials. In those hard times, such provisions for child-rearing were seen as a sizeable income, and jokers remarked that whereas the living standard of a family with one child was like a poor peasant's, with two children it could match the standard of a well-to-do family, and with three it could rival that of a landlord's family.

Each month, my mother paid her baby's wet-nurse two decalitres of dry millet provided by the government, which was a handsome amount by local standards. The wet-nurse was a kind Christian woman, living in a small mud-brick house in town with her children, parents-in-law and unemployed husband. Due to difficulties finding lodgings for herself, my mother had to leave her baby to this poor family. Since local residents seldom washed themselves or changed their clothes, lice were unavoidable, and the baby was soon infested. My mother felt appalled, but she was left with little choice.

After my eldest brother's birth, the political situation changed rapidly. In June 1946, the Civil War broke out in full scale. Within a year, the Nationalists lost a quarter of their military forces, and their high military expenditure caused huge financial deficits and inflation. In the Nationalist areas, money could be devalued by half within a day. More and more people suffered from unemployment, exorbitant taxes and poverty. The Communists, on the other hand, led by Mao Zedong, were preparing to launch a strategic counteroffensive against the Nationalists. At this crucial time, they felt it necessary to improve their base areas further and gain stronger support from poor peasants, the vast majority of Chinese. From summer 1946, a series of land reforms set out to abolish the traditional feudal system of land ownership which had prevailed in Chinese society for thousands of years. Rich landowners in rural areas were the major targets. Under the new policy, those living entirely on the rent of their land for the past three years were labelled as landlords, and those whose lands were mainly cultivated by tenant peasants or hired labourers were classified as rich farmers. In rural China, these two categories constituted less than 10 per cent of the total population but owned more than three-quarters of the land. During the land reforms, their possessions were confiscated and then redistributed to poor peasants.

In spring 1947, my mother was assigned to a village as part of a work team conducting a trial of the new reforms for the county. With over 200 households, the village was known for its large size and the wealth of a small number of rich landowners. As soon as the trial started, my mother and her colleagues faced strong hostility from them. Under the strong political pressure, landlords and rich farmers seldom showed public resentment against the forthcoming changes, but at home, many kept detailed accounts secretly recording their lost possessions or the humiliations they suffered from peasants. It was expected that when the Nationalists returned in the near future, they would restore their wealth and retaliate for their sufferings. One evening, the leader of my mother's team was on his way to use an outdoor toilet on the outskirts of the village when he was stabbed in the back by a dagger. The fur overcoat which he had draped across his shoulders took most of the impact and saved his life. Afterwards, no one in the team was allowed to go out on their own.

The arrival of my mother and her colleagues also caused great confusion among poor peasants. Unused to change, many were not enthusiastic about the land reforms, fearing that they would be punished for their involvement if the Nationalists returned. Some felt that the confiscated possessions of the rich were ill-gotten wealth which they should not accept. A number of peasants had good relationships with their landlords and refused to take steps against them. During mobilization meetings for the reforms, many peasants either did not show up or never spoke.

Members of my mother's work team therefore decided to establish a 'Poor Peasants Committee', based on local grass-roots support. With help from the loyal peasants, Communist ideas were introduced to villagers. Every day, members of the team were engaged in house visits, meetings and political rallies. They told the peasants that the rich had always lived by exploiting the poor, and that kind of social system had to be changed completely. With the Communists prevailing in the Civil War, most villagers were gradually convinced that it was time to follow the Communists, and the trial was successfully completed.

After the trial, my mother was appointed governor of a district, an administrative level in between township and county. The location of her new job was several kilometres away from the town. The official policy was to divide her district into several areas where the land reforms would be launched one by one, to allow for close control and supervision throughout the process. However, more and more peasants were getting impatient. After the success of the trial, they recognized that the world had already changed, and were eager to take part in the reforms. Within a few days, the reforms broke out all over the district, and soon the district government lost control of the situation in many villages. During the chaos, many landowners were wrongly classified as landlords or rich farmers, even though they had never been involved in exploiting activities such as letting land or hiring labourers. They lost all of their possessions. During emotional rallies against the exploiting class, radical peasants started bullying and torturing the rich, hanging them on poles or beating them violently, especially when the rich refused to surrender their possessions.

For months, my mother hurried from village to village in her district trying to stop the chaos. At her insistence, many mistreated landowners had the accusing label of landlord or rich farmer removed, and their confiscated possessions returned. As for the violence inflicted on the rich, my mother emphasized that the Communists did not intend to destroy the exploiting class as individuals. After their possessions were taken away, they were expected to be thoroughly remoulded by supporting themselves through their own labour, so they should be treated with humanity. It was hard to placate the radical peasants, especially since what they did had been common in many other areas, but thanks to my mother's tireless efforts, the chaotic situation was resolved. However, the heavy workload delayed the recovery of her health. She remained pale and thin, and often felt dizzy.

Her job was demanding, travel was difficult, and she could only see her baby a few times a month. During each brief reunion, she tried her best to look after the baby, changing his clothes, picking lice off his tiny body, and singing lullabies. One day a disturbing message reached her: her toddler boy was begging in town with an old woman, the mother-in-law of his wet-nurse, whose family had been unexpectedly classified as a landlord's household. The trouble was caused by the wet-nurse's mother-in-law who had once been a pretty girl, known in her native village for her sharp tongue and intimate relationship with a rich man. After the man was categorized as landlord, resentful peasants took their opportunity. Since the only property she had was a small run-down house built of mud-bricks, she was labelled as an 'impoverished landlord', a member of the exploiting class in spite of being poor. When my mother rushed back, the family was in utter destitution, as all their belongings including the worn-out bedding and cooking utensils had been taken. The only thing left was their run-down house, which was no use to the peasants in her native village, far away from town. My poor brother looked filthy, and he cried of hunger all the time. The milk of his wet-nurse had stopped some time ago, and there was no food left in the family.

My mother wept with frustration. Since that village was not in her district, she could not interfere. Then what could she do for her poor boy? Right then, it was impossible to bring him along to her district. As a governor, she owed her time to tens of thousands of people. Her personal safety was also at risk, both from rich landowners who had lost everything in the land reforms, and from radical peasants whose violent activities she had checked. She thought of finding another wet-nurse, but the boy cried madly and would not be parted from the family. Before her duties claimed her again, the only thing my mother could do was to leave all her money to the wet-nurse, so that the family could start a small food stall in town to earn a living. After that, local residents often saw my brother, a malnourished little boy, sitting on a small wooden stool by a busy street accompanying a woman who was selling deep-fried millet cakes. In bad weather, it was hard to scrape a living. Sometimes my eldest brother was taught to steal food or fuel from the shops or neighbours, which helped the family to survive.

By autumn 1948, the Civil War had reached its final year. As the political situation improved, my parents' correspondence was getting regular, though the service was still slow. My father was deeply concerned about his family, but could offer no help. Since the outbreak of the war he had been commanding troops at the front, far away.

In winter 1948, my eldest brother fell ill with smallpox. Torn between grief and guilt, my mother rushed off to see her son, and found him covered with pustules which were terribly painful, and kept him crying from morning to night. He also suffered from serious diarrhoea. In that poor area there was no medicine to be had, and the only way to save his life was to improve his diet and living conditions. 'Why don't you give him to a childless family with decent conditions?' some sympathetic people suggested. My mother refused. Among the Communists, a number of couples she knew never saw their children again after such a separation, which included Mao Zedong and his former wife, He Zizhen. From the later 1920s to 1930s, He Zizhen gave birth to several children, but most had to be given away due to the chaos of wars, and were never found again.

For several tortured nights, my mother was sleepless, but at last she compelled a decision. With tears, she embraced her son and whispered: 'My little treasure, Mama has to give you away. Please forgive me! I will take you back as soon as we win the revolution.'

A few weeks later, a peasant couple called at the wet-nurse's home. They wanted to see the boy first before discussing adoption with my mother. In terror at leaving the family, the boy screamed and rolled on the ground while his wet-nurse burst into tears. Their mixed chorus shocked the whole neighbourhood. Soon a crowd gathered. Old women sobbed. 'Poor boy! His parents are abandoning him for the revolution. These Communists!' At the height of this outcry, two men in army uniforms arrived on horseback. The front one, in his early thirties, passed his horse to the younger companion and talked to the surrounding people. Suddenly, he ran into the house and swept the dusty boy from the earthen floor. With tears in his eyes, he announced: 'I'm the boy's father! I'm here to see my son.' This was the first time my father met his son. For this moment, he had waited for more than two years.

My father's troops were resting in Fengzhen after the Communists' victory in north China. When my mother's letter came with the appalling news about the boy, he set off at once to Wuzhai with his bodyguard. It was high time to end the days of separation. At the end of 1948, the eve of the birth of the People's Republic of China, my family went to Fengzhen together and enjoyed their first reunion. At my father's suggestion, the boy was named 'Feng-xin'. The name is made up of two characters: Feng, meaning 'plentiful', the generation name of my father's family, which was an essential part for a boy's name; and Xin, meaning 'new' – a new life in the coming republic. After a short break, my mother returned to her district to carry on the land reforms. Fengxin stayed behind with my father for a while, being cared for by a young soldier who had lost one leg in battle. Under treatment by the military surgeons, Feng-xin gradually recovered from his illness, but he never lost the pockmarks on his face.

My second brother was born in March 1950, five months after the birth of the Communist republic. By then, my mother had completed her work on land reforms, and had moved with Feng-xin to Guisui (the former name of Hohhot, today the provincial capital of Inner Mongolia), working as deputy director of the organization section for the Party provincial committee of Suiyuan. As the provincial capital of Suiyuan, Guisui had direct railway connections to Fengzhen. When the Civil War was going to end in early 1949, my parents expected that their family would soon be reunited, but in autumn 1949 my father was assigned to a special and dangerous mission: to reorganize the Nationalist troops whom he had fought throughout the Civil War when they were handed over to the Communists by their commander, General Fu Zuoyi. The long separation continued.

On 21 January 1949, General Fu Zuoyi, Commander in Chief of the Nationalist Forces 'for Suppressing Bandits' (the Communists) in north China, announced his decision to hand over Beijing city, the site of his headquarters, to the Communists. By then, the Nationalists had completely lost their military superiority, together with most areas to the north of the Yangtze River. For more than a month previously, General Fu and his quarter of a million troops were besieged by the triumphant PLA in Beijing city. The local community begged General Fu to stop fighting, so that China's most famous city could be saved from the flames of war. General Fu was a person of integrity, who had tried hard not to get involved in the Civil War. After long consideration, and intensive negotiations with the Communists, he decided to split with the Nationalist government, and handed over Beijing and his defending troops to his opponents.

On 3 February 1949, a grand ceremony was launched in Beijing to welcome the arrival in the city of the People's Liberation Army. The military parade was led by three armoured cars decorated colourfully like floats, with two portraits in front: Mao Zedong, chairman of the Communist Party, and Zhu De, Commander in Chief of the PLA. The troops passed proudly through the major thoroughfares, which were packed with cheerful crowds. Following the marching troops, many expressed their joy with popular rural folk dances, waving a long length of red silk attached to their waist. Their dances were accompanied by singing such as: 'How sunny it is in the liberated area!/ How happy are the people in the liberated area!/ Democratic government loves the people,/ We can never say enough about our gratitude to the Communist Party . . .'

In accordance with General Fu's agreement, his troops were free to decide about their future: whether or not to remain in the military forces and accept the reorganization. For those intending to return home, travel expenses were provided, together with a 'Certificate of Participating in the Peaceful Liberation of Beiping (former name of Beijing)'. With such a certificate, they were assured that they would be treated as well as ex-servicemen of the PLA. Under the Communist regime, General Fu's troops were to be reorganized as part of the PLA, which meant installing the Party's organization to lead the command system, and clearing out obstinate Nationalist supporters.

At first, my father was assigned as Deputy Political Commissar to one of General Fu's divisions in Suiyuan province, where Fu's power was based. Several months after Beijing's peaceful settlement, Suiyuan was also handed over to the Communists together with about 80,000 Nationalist troops stationed in the province. When the Political Commissar of my father's division failed to show up, possibly due to his fear of the intense antagonism among sections of the Nationalist troops, my father had to take charge of the reorganization on his own, and later was appointed as the Political Commissar. Much of the strong resentment he faced came from senior officers. They owed their careers to

General Fu, but it was not easy for them to accept the control of the Communists, their former enemy.

The troops' negative reaction towards the Communist reorganization was used by the hard-line Nationalist supporters who did not accept the collapse of Chiang Kai-shek's dynasty. Having failed to stop the peaceful settlement in Suiyuan, they played on the troops' resentment of being reorganized. In particular, the outbreak of the Korean War in 1950 boosted their hopes. Soon rumours were circulating that the Third World War was coming, and then the USA would help Chiang Kai-shek to return from his refuge in Taiwan. A certificate issued by the exiled regime appointed the Nationalist Army Commander, Lieutenant General Liu, as the new governor of the Suiyuan province. Almost every day, armed revolts took place in the troops, while a number of Communist officers assigned to the reorganization were assassinated. In my father's division, an entire regiment staged an armed revolt and fled to distant mountain areas to await the return of the Nationalist government.

Despite the dangers, my father was given only about a hundred Communist officers and not many soldiers to help to reorganize his division. After their arrival, his team members were assigned to different command levels. In the divisional headquarters, my father kept only about ten Communist officers and three bodyguards. In early 1950, a secret message started circulating among his troops, exhorting them to kill Mu Xiang (my father) before the mid-autumn festival. The coup was plotted by several senior Nationalist officers in his division, with the support of Lieutenant General Liu and the division's Deputy Commander. Lieutenant General Liu himself would often abuse my father even in his presence. His life was in constant danger, and his bodyguards worked three shifts round the clock. Two years later, he recalled in a written document:

Among the Party members, it was discussed whether we needed to withdraw, especially after the withdrawal of communist officers from two other divisions. I was asked every day for solutions by the officers I brought with me. I had no idea about what to do. But clearly, running away from the mission was not acceptable. Fortunately, it was the Party who provided me with the courage and strength. Eventually, I decided that we must carry on our mission until the last moment of our lives . . .

Due to this mission, my father was unable to return home when my mother's labour started unexpectedly in the early morning of 15 March 1950. Again it happened earlier than expected. Soon her contractions were getting stronger, but she could not find anyone to help. At home, there were only Feng-xin and his nanny. 'You must go to hospital immediately!' she was urged by the doctor who was called in later from the clinic of the Party's provincial committee where she worked. Unfortunately, none of the committee's vehicles were in. In desperation, my mother asked Feng-xin's nanny to hire two tricycles, the chief means of transport, one for herself and another for Feng-xin and the nanny, and they rushed to the provincial hospital. On the way, she wrapped herself in a thick quilt to keep warm as it was still cold and windy in Guisui, a city beyond the Great Wall. While the tricycle bumped noisily along the rough and dusty road, raising clouds of dust, my mother's labour became stronger and regular. Suddenly, she felt pangs in her belly. She put her hands into her trousers to stop it, but it was too late, a baby had slipped out before she reached the hospital. After the birth, my mother suffered postpartum bleeding again for more than two months. Considering my father's dangerous situation, she kept her illness quiet.

Two months later, my father attended a military conference of senior Communist officers in Guisui, and saw his second child for the first time. He named the baby boy 'Feng-an' – 'An' for 'tranquillity', in the hope of a peaceful future. The venue of his conference frequently came

under fire from die-hard Nationalist supporters. While waiting for her
husband at night, my mother worried about his safety, especially when
she heard shots in the distance.

Before she could fully recover, my mother had to return to her new
assignment of improving the Party's organization at county levels of the
province. Her frequent travels to the countryside made it hard to look
after two young children, so at my father's suggestion, Feng-xin was
sent to a boarding kindergarten which was run by the Party's provincial
committee, while Feng-an was sent to a wet-nurse in town two months
after his birth.

After Feng-xin's experiences, my mother found a family with reasonable living conditions for Feng-an. His wet-nurse's husband had been a
clerk for the Nationalist government. Unfortunately, the couple looked
down on my parents, a poor Communist couple who could only afford
the official allowance of two decalitres of dry millet monthly, and in
order to earn extra money, the wet-nurse took in another baby from a
former Nationalist officer's family without informing my mother. The
rich family paid them handsomely, so that their baby had the wet-nurse's
milk while Feng-an was fed with a gruel made of water and millet. The
resulting malnutrition damaged Feng-an's development. In the following
months, the family made various excuses when my mother got suspicious
about her baby's condition, until their trick was revealed to her by sympathetic neighbours. When she brought him home, Feng-an looked
terribly thin and weak.

Meanwhile, General Fu had been anxious about what was happening
to his troops in Suiyuan during the reorganization. He raised the situation with the Communists, who already knew about the connection
between the Nationalist Lieutenant General Liu and the exiled Chiang's
government. Shortly afterwards, senior Nationalist officers of the
troops, including army, division and brigade commanders, were invited
to Beijing by the North China Military Region for an official conference. At the end of a banquet, Liu and his two anti-Communist

colleagues were arrested, and subsequently imprisoned for their counter-revolutionary conspiracies.

Following the arrest of Lieutenant General Liu, the situation in my father's division stabilized. With his polite manner and educated background, he had already won over many Nationalist officers. With their help, political campaigns were launched to expose the intended coup among his troops and to arrest its major leaders. Gradually, the majority of officers recognized how strong the Communist regime was, and started to cooperate. During the campaigns, my father and his colleagues also introduced revolutionary ideals to the soldiers. Most of them came from poor peasant families and had been forced to join the Nationalist forces. Through political education, they soon became supporters of the Communists. By the end of 1950, my father's division had completed its reorganization. In the following year, shortly after I was born, it was assigned to Korea as part of the 'Chinese People's Volunteers'.

After my parents established their first home in Beijing in 1951, my widowed paternal grandmother joined our family from her home province. She could not believe her first sight of the two grandsons. Feng-xin looked sallow and emaciated, with a non-stop running nose, his little face covered by deep smallpox pockmarks. He also had a threadworm infestation around his anus, which he caught at his wet-nurse's home. At night when the parasites were active, he cried with discomfort. For several weeks, my grandmother washed his body and underwear with the liquid prescribed by doctors, until the problem was cured. At one year old, his brother Feng-an was still unable to stand up properly because of the damage to his physical development.

During the following years, my grandmother tried her best to improve the two boys' health with nutritious food. At table, Feng-xin was like a hungry tiger cub who stuffed himself till he could hardly stand. The fear of starvation still haunted him. On the other hand, Feng-an showed no interest in food at all apart from the gruel made of water and rice or millet that was the only stuff familiar to him.

My own experiences after birth were totally different. During the first six months, I was breast-fed by my mother every day. In accordance with the new regulation, she obtained eight weeks' maternity leave, and then was entitled to two hours' breast-feeding time per day for several months. I was also provided with free milk from the North China Bureau where my mother worked. On warm days, milkmen from the bureau's dairy farm often called on my family in the evenings with a bucket of spare milk: 'Would you like more milk? Otherwise, it will be wasted.' At that time, millions of Chinese could not even stand the smell of dairy products, and there was no cold storage available to keep milk either. It was a pleasure for my grandmother to watch me. As soon as one bottle was finished, I started crying impatiently until the next one was ready. Once my stomach was full, I would fall asleep in seconds. In a few years, I grew stronger than Feng-an. For a long time, people mistook him for my younger brother because he was so much smaller.

Chapter 2

Daughter of the Yellow River:
My Mother's Story

(1923–1934)

'Tell me a story, Mama! Tell me a story, Baba! The story about your revolution.' For many years, this was my favourite request to my parents. From my days as a plump toddler, I had recognized the links between my parents and 'Chairman Mao', the 'Communist Party', and 'revolution', which were the most familiar words I heard. After I went to school, my curiosity was boosted by my pride in being the daughter of a revolutionary couple.

In the early 1960s, my mother started her story. After lunch on a Sunday afternoon, the snowflakes started falling thick and fast while the fierce northwest wind rattled our windows and doors – signs of a typical Beijing winter's day. Inside my parents' study, my father was still working at his desk. Behind him, my mother and I sat huddled together on a comfortable sofa. That afternoon, my mother's story was frequently interrupted by my naive questions, such as 'Is the person good or bad?' In my simple mind as a little girl, there were only two categories of human being in the world: one belonged to the good people who supported our revolution, while the other comprised the 'bad eggs' (huai-dan) who were against the Communist Party. Ever since that afternoon, my mother's storytelling continued sporadically in her limited spare time until my childhood was over, and the peace of our lives was wrecked by political and social upheavals.

More than three decades after that afternoon, I have become a mature woman, but my enthusiasm for tracing my parents' past has never diminished. As we Chinese believe that 'every tree has its roots and every river has its source', my life is connected to my parents, and my character has been strongly influenced by them. No matter how many differences come between us, our blood comes from the same source. One day, a large parcel was delivered to me from Beijing, which was the memoir of my mother's life that she wrote for me at my request. From the very first lines, the pages held my eyes. I was captured, fascinated and thrilled by the stories she told, about the distant years, about the tales and legends of a generation whose dedication to Communism brought fundamental changes in China.

My mother was born in October 1923 near the lower reaches of the Yellow River, the second longest river in China. The name of her home county, Xin'an, meaning 'new' and 'tranquillity', also formed part of my two elder brothers' names. It expressed local people's expectation of a peaceful life, which unfortunately never came true. Located in an agricultural area of Henan province in central China, the county was historically known for its poverty and local governors' tyranny, described more than a thousand years ago in a famous poem 'Xin'an Official' (Xin'an-li) by Du Fu (712–770 AD, in the West often spelt as Tu Fu), the great classical poet of the Tang Dynasty. In my mother's childhood, her county was troubled by four disasters: flood, drought, a plague of locusts and Tang Enbo, the Nationalist general who governed the province.

In my mother's memory, the Yellow River was like a ferocious dragon which had caused countless nightmares for local people. The river's upper and middle reaches drained the world's biggest area of loess highlands, where soil erosion was serious. After a rainstorm, topsoil was carried away through gullies into tributaries and then into the river. The water was always mixed with mud and sand, which explained how the river got its name (in Chinese, this particular colour is called brown yellow). In the lower reaches, the river bed was built up metres above the ground as the soil transported by the water weighed 1,600 million tons a year. Over a period of 2,000 years in China's history, 26 major changes of course and more than 1,500 dyke breaches were recorded along the lower reaches. Powerless to control the river's action, local people could only offer sacrifices to the god of the river, begging for its mercy. But the response was frequent floods.

In my mother's county, drought was also common. Dry springs and summers scorched the crops under the burning sun, till the fields turned grey and the ground was full of cracks. For centuries, worshipping the Dragon King, who was supposed to produce rain, was one of the most important rituals along the Yellow River basin. Desperate peasants burned joss-sticks in his temples and then paraded in dusty village streets, often to the heavy sound of drums. Many decked with branches of willow round their heads in wreaths and prayed: 'Over the fields let the good rains fall. Oh Dragon King, come save us all! Come save us all!'

Even with favourable weather for crops, the peasants' expectation of a good harvest could be destroyed within hours by plagues of locusts, dark clouds flying towards the green fields. When they blotted out the bright blue sky, the rattle of their wings filled the air. In those days there were no pesticides. The peasants beat drums, wailed and waved colourful flags. They ran wildly around their fields to stop the locusts landing. Sometimes, dried plant leaves were burned to smoke out the insects. But nothing worked effectively. In a moment, the whole field could be covered by the hungry creatures. Watching green crop leaves wiped away, the frustrated peasants could do nothing but lament.

Nearly every year, there were famines in my mother's home county. The impoverishment was like a widespread pestilence in which more and more peasants lost their land and home. During the great famine of 1937, which was reported to have cost more than 10 million lives nationally, my mother's home province was one of the severely afflicted areas. In rural areas, daughters and wives from impoverished peasants' families were sold either to the local rich as slaves or concubines, or to cities as factory workers or prostitutes. Famished skeletal children roamed abroad, and corpses lay on the roads. Desperate peasants looted rich families' houses and robbed travellers. The small town where my mother's family lived was surrounded by a high brick wall. From time to time, all the gates in the wall were closed and blocked by huge earth-works for fear of the bandits' attack. The government kept increasing troops to protect the local rich. Exorbitant taxes were collected decades in advance. Peasants suffered, corrupt local officials prospered, but the bandits were never eliminated.

Every year, thousands of starving peasants poured on to the roads to flee from home: each man carried two baskets with a shoulder pole, one for a skinny baby and the other for his few possessions. He was followed by his shabbily dressed wife and teenage children. They begged their way far to Shaanxi province, a fertile area next to Henan, but many died en route.

My maternal grandfather's family, the Xus, were rich and influential in Xin'an. My great grandfather owned a considerable amount of fertile land outside the town, most of it rented out to peasants for cultivation. The rent was half of the crop, or sometimes an equivalent amount of cash. After paying rent and taxes, many peasants only had meagre incomes left. In a year of poor harvest, tenant peasants would run up debts, which were charged at high interest. Those who failed to pay their debts were forced either to sell everything they had or to provide free labour to their landlords working as domestic servants or coolies.

In the county, my grandfather's fourth cousin was a wealthy landlord and a powerful squire. His dark, rough skin, squat figure and rustic clothes made him look like a typical country bumpkin. His manner was so arrogant and rude that it was hard to believe his educated background. Yet each newly appointed magistrate had to pay an official call to his residence, as they knew that without his cooperation, no one could rule the county peacefully. In the words of a famous Chinese saying, 'the mighty dragon is no match for the native serpent'.

My mother was never fond of her father's fourth cousin, and still remembers how he interrupted her parents' ceremony for the completion of their mansion in her childhood. It was a beautiful autumn day. In front of the mansion's entrance, which was specially decorated with colourful streamers, a group of folk musicians performed cheerful music. Salvos of loud firecrackers went off, to drive out devils from the new building, with its three large courtyards, and to keep its residents safe. The guests were especially impressed by the elegant terracotta animals sitting at each end of the roof's ridges, including a crane, the symbol of longevity, and a Chinese unicorn, indicating luck and happiness.

Suddenly, my grandfather's fourth cousin appeared, but he had not come to congratulate my grandparents. With a spade in his hand, he kicked the front gate open and ran into the front yard, shouting to my frightened grandparents: 'How dare you destroy my good feng-shui?' By a tradition that still survives, the aspect and location of a house are supposed to have an influence on a family's fortune. Living next door to my grandparents, he could not tolerate the fact that his roof was slightly lower than theirs — a fact which no one had recognized. He demanded that the new house's roof must be lowered, or else he would give my grandparents a thrashing. My mother was terrified, the guests left quietly, and next day my grandparents started to have their newly built mansion reroofed.

Although he was born into a wealthy family, my grandfather's upbringing was not lucky at all. Shortly after his birth, his mother, a soft village woman, was abandoned by his father. She was repeatedly beaten by her husband because he was fond of another woman. Fearing for her life, my great grandmother took their son and left her husband's mansion quietly, with neither a share of family properties nor support for the new born baby, just like a bucket of water being poured out her husband's door. Considering the Xus' power, no-one said a word about the injustice. Afterwards, my great grandfather lived in luxury with his mistress who later became his concubine, while his estranged wife endured poverty with his son, living on her own spinning and sewing.

At a young age, my grandfather made a firm resolution: to build up his family's fortunes. Being an intelligent and hard-working man, he passed the imperial examination for selecting Mandarins at the end of the Qing Dynasty, which had been ruled by the Manchus since 1644, as it was the only way for poor people to change their social position. But in 1911 the Manchu empire collapsed, and this was the start of decades of civil war and anarchy in China. Dr Sun Yat-sen's short-lived republic gave way to a short-lived empire, and then to a collapse of central control. After 1916, three main military groups emerged, which were named after the provinces where their major leaders came from. The Wan (Anhui) Group, known as 'Wan-xi', and the Feng (Manchuria) Group, known as 'Feng-xi', gained support from Japan; the Zhi (Hebei) Group, known as 'Zhi-xi', was supported by Britain and America. Apart from these three groups, there were numerous lesser warlords, provincial or within each province, who set up local regimes like feudal states. Changes and shifts of power were common, and factional quarrels brought frequent wars. From 1912 to 1928, the republican cabinet set up by the warlords was replaced 47 times; the shortest lasted only a matter of days.

During that chaotic period, my maternal grandfather's political ambition crumbled, but he did become known in Xin'an as a respectable scholar, and attracted a number of well-to-do families who were looking for a son-in-law. He married my grandmother mainly because of the generous financial help promised by her father, a local landlord. A few years later, he himself became a wealthy landlord, owning dozens of hectares of fertile land and a mansion.

In all, my grandmother gave birth to eleven children, but only four survived. My grandfather named his only son 'Ding-yi', which meant 'to keep this one definitely'. Unfortunately, the boy died when my mother was five, and this left three girls, of whom my mother was the youngest. With no surviving son, my grandfather became a 'Jue-hu-tou', meaning head of a childless household, as daughters were not counted. Certainly, no one dared call him 'Jue-hu-tou' in his presence, for that would be offensive and cause him to lose face. All the same, his failure to have sons was regarded as an unforgivable defect because there would be no one in his family to keep up the sacrifices to ancestors. Behind his back, the gossips said that his having no sons must be a retribution against him, for the sins of either his ancestors or himself.

More seriously, losing the only son meant that my grandfather lost his heir, because women had no right of inheritance. Being over forty years old, and in poor health, my grandmother could not give birth again, so my grandfather came under heavy pressure from the Xus to adopt his nephew as his heir. Rather than that, he took a momentous and ultimately tragic decision. He told my weeping grandmother: 'I'm going to sell some land and buy a concubine. My mind won't change whether you agree or not.'

A few weeks later, a young girl from a remote village was carried by a donkey to my grandparents' house. The procedure she experienced was different from the normal practice associated with a formal wedding ceremony. There was no sedan chair to bring her to her bridegroom's house, no instruments playing or sumptuous feasts prepared. She was not even allowed to wear red, the typical wedding dress in China. A formal wedding ceremony required the bride and groom to kneel down shoulder to shoulder on a red cushion in front of the ancestors' memorial tablet in the family's central room, but this girl's lowly position had disqualified her for such a declaration of her marriage.

It seemed that the naive girl did not mind about her casual reception.

The matchmaker had told her that her husband was young and newly widowed, so that she would be a 'tian-fang', which meant 'a woman who comes to fill the empty bedroom of her bridegroom who is a widowed man'. For a peasant girl, nothing could be better than to marry a husband who was rich and young.

After her arrival, the girl was led straight to her wedding chamber. On the bed lay dates (zao), peanuts (sheng), longan fruits (gui) and melon seeds (zi). These four items, 'zao-sheng-gui-zi', happen to be identical in sound with the Chinese characters that make up the message: 'May you have honourable sons soon.' It was a traditional wish for a newly wedded couple in China.

The candlelight flickered, and a man came into the wedding chamber. Here was her husband, a man who was old enough to be her father! But there was worse news to follow. Next day, she met my grandmother at the dining table. Now she knew that she was not a wife, but only a concubine. But there was no way out: her parents had spent the betrothal price to pay their debts. Once having been a concubine, a woman had no chance to marry a decent man.

After the wedding, she kept to her room. The family showed no sympathy, and she could not leave the house on her own. At night, she had to cover her sorrow and do my grandfather's bidding. She missed her parents very much and begged for permission to visit them. My grandfather's answer was as cold as his face: 'Never! You were sold to me by your parents. I don't recognize them as my relatives.' The girl wept bitterly without a word. A few days later, in the room which used to be her wedding chamber, she hanged herself on a roof beam with a white scarf. Having heard the tragedy, my grandmother held my mother and sobbed: 'This is a woman's fate!'

The girl was buried in haste, as a concubine deserved. Far from showing sympathy for her tragedy, my grandfather worried that her family would sue him for her death. As it happened, not only did the girl's parents remain quiet about the death, they also sent their son to my grandfather as a coolie, carrying water, grinding grain and cleaning the courtyard for year after year. 'Why do poor people have no rights to protect themselves?' my mother could not help asking herself when she saw the silently working man: 'Why are women's lives worth nothing?'

Determined to have sons, my grandfather bought another woman whose late husband was a junior Nationalist officer. On arrival, she was heavily pregnant, and when she gave birth to a boy shortly afterwards, my grandfather declared the child his own and said: 'I don't care who his real father is. He is my son as long as he was born in my house.' But the baby died within a month, and again my grandfather resolved to sell more land and buy another concubine – this time a rural woman with a squat body, the traditional image of a good breeder. My mother and her sisters called the two concubines Aunt Wang and Aunt Dong.

After the concubines' arrival, my grandfather's mansion was divided into two main parts: his estranged wife lived in the back yard together with their two unmarried daughters, my mother and her elder sister Ning, while he occupied the front quarter with his concubines. Outside his windows grew beautiful flowers from spring to autumn, around an exquisite pavilion. There he would sit, reading his favourite classical poems and dreaming about his sons and grandsons.

At the beginning, my grandfather shared his bedroom with the two concubines and slept between them in one bed. Such an arrangement, which was regarded as a symbol of family harmony, was copied from his fourth cousin, who also had two concubines at home. However, these two women warred every day, and my grandfather had no peace at all. Later, he had to separate them into different bedrooms and took turns to sleep with each for three nights running. The one who had her master in her room was responsible for running the household while the other seethed and grumbled.

One summer's day, Aunt Wang disappeared, fed up with her life as a concubine. She gave the slip to Ning, who was sent by my grandfather to watch her, and escaped through a field of tall crops. Afterwards, my furious grandfather put up posters everywhere offering a large reward for capturing the runaway. A couple of months later, Aunt Wang was caught and returned.

After the concubines' arrival, my grandmother rarely saw her husband, not even at table, because he normally ate in the front quarter with his concubines. The back yard where she lived was a desolate space, with no laughter or happiness remaining, and spates of bitter tears about the fate of being a woman. Why was my mother not a boy? Why were women's lives controlled by men?

In the family, my grandmother's great sympathizer was her mother-in-law. When the concubines arrived, my great grandmother was nearing her eighties, and in poor health. She had been looked after by my grandmother for a long time. Due to painful experiences in the past, she utterly detested concubines, and never allowed them to forget it. Early each morning, the first thing she did was to shoo chickens into the yard outside their bedrooms. Standing by their windows, she started to scold the concubines. As she was hard of hearing, her voice was particularly raucous against the chorus of panicking chickens. Soon the whole household was awake, and my grandfather would dash outside to rage at his mother. This scene was played out almost every day, until the death of my great grandmother several years later.

At the age of six, Ning and my mother were sent to a local school, and hence became the first educated girls among the Xus. Since women were only expected to be housewives in those days, there was no point in schooling them, even in wealthy families. However, my grandfather was nearing his fifties. He had to consider the future of his longed-for, unborn sons. Ning and my mother were expected to help him to bring them up when he was old. My mother was delighted to be away from her dreary family. She enjoyed her studies, and my grandfather was impressed by her good reports. When she grew older, he started to show her his business. During a visit to one of his tenant peasant families, my mother was served with baked sweet potatoes by the kind housewife, and played with their children in the field. When the time came to leave, she burst into tears. Being a sensitive and quiet girl, she had taken to this poor and loving family. At home, she liked talking to the servants, because they were always warm and cheerful. As a little girl, she did not understand why there was such a striking contrast between her family and the peasants, luxury and poverty.

A few years later, Aunt Wang finally gave birth to a baby boy, to the great joy of my grandfather. Hundreds of red eggs were distributed to the local families, and many guests invited home. The sumptuous feasts lasted for several days. Afterwards, Aunt Wang regarded herself as a family heroine and became more arrogant to my grandmother and Aunt Dong because they had failed to give surviving sons. Aunt Dong's response was her powerful fists.

As his concubines' power struggles worsened, their frequent quarrels kept my grandfather busy. Many times, my mother and Ning were summoned from school by servants to find the front quarter in chaos, ruined flowers scattered on the ground, and the pavilion floor covered with broken sticks and glasses, while the concubines screamed and spat. As she watched her sister pleading with my grandfather and the concubines, my mother felt her heart turn cold and heavy, as if a huge stone lay across it. 'I must leave this feudal landlord family!' she said to herself. 'I hate this living in the dark!'

Chapter 3

A Single Spark could Start a Prairie Fire:
My Father's Story

(1916–1935)

The first I heard about my father's past was in my childhood, from my paternal grandmother. 'Your father never behaved like you when he was your age,' was her familiar saying to my siblings and me if we misbehaved, say by disturbing other people, or dawdling with our homework. When I did well in exams, her standard response was: 'You take after your father. He always came top at school.' There is a Chinese saying that 'one's own children are always the best', but I wonder how many mothers could be prouder of their child than my paternal grandmother, whose accounts of my father's past were never negative.

Many years later, I recognized how valuable her information was for me. Despite my curious questions, my father rarely mentioned his childhood. Like many senior Communists, he regarded the start of his revolutionary career as the point where his real life began. His personal stories always related to the Communist Party's history, and its role in changing China.

My father was born in June 1916 in Penglai, a coastal county of Shandong, the province where Confucius came from. Located on the northern end of the Shandong Peninsula, south of the Bohai Gulf, Penglai used to be an important strategic and trading port. It was said that the county was named more than two thousand years ago by Qin Shihuang, the first Chinese emperor, who built the Great Wall. To the north of the town was the famous Penglai Ge, an impressive building with a thousand years of history, standing on top of a steep cliff facing the sea. On rare occasions from spring to autumn, mirages could be observed from there. When the vast sea was covered by mist, suddenly an upside-down mountain emerged above the water, then turned into a grand city. Hazily, an image of busy streets appeared, with moving pedestrians and vehicles. When the sun came out from the clouds, the whole scene disappeared in seconds. On top of the cliff a group of ancient temples built hundreds of years ago, while Penglai was a busy trading port, honoured various gods such as the god and goddess of the sea.

When my father was born, Penglai had lost its former prosperity. Frequent wars among feudal warlords . . . with economic depression to drive many of its inhabitants to cross over the Bohai Gulf to Manchuria (present-day north-east China), where they found a living in the major trading ports along the coastline of the Liaodong Peninsula. Penglai people accounted for a considerable proportion of the population there, mainly working for various small businesses. Normally, men left their families behind in Penglai, and only came home for a short break around the Chinese New Year.

In terms of Chinese culture, my father's family, the Mus, could be an ideal model. When he was born there were four generations living together under the same roof, with more than twenty family members: my great grandparents, their sons, grandchildren and great grandchildren. My great grandfather, a retired livestock dealer, had eleven children, but only two sons survived, the eldest and the youngest, who was my paternal grandfather. During an epidemic many years ago, my great grandparents lost four young children within a month, which was not unusual in those days, so there was a large age gap (more than 20 years) between the surviving sons. When my grandfather married, his eldest brother already had grandchildren.

My grandfather worked as a salesman for a shop selling silk and cotton fabrics in town, while his eldest brother owned a small general store nearby. Family life for the Mus was marginally above subsistence level since their incomes were just enough to keep everyone warm and fed. In those days, marriage partners should be matched in social and economic status, so my grandfather married a local girl whose father was also a salesman, working away from home in Manchuria.

Life in my grandfather's family was dominated by traditional rules, and this is not surprising, because in the Confucian world-view the principle of managing a family was the same as that of administering a country. Therefore, each family member must occupy a certain position, suited to their gender, generation and age, and must follow certain rules. When my grandparents married, the top position in the Mu family hierarchy belonged to my great grandfather, the senior male member. He enjoyed the best food and the most comfortable room at home, and his instructions were obeyed by all family members. Next came the grown-up males, such as my grandfather, his eldest brother and nephews. Being bread-winners, they supported the entire family with their incomes, and were looked after at home with special care. At the bottom of the hierarchy were the women who performed the household chores together, and served the whole family every day.

In terms of domestic affairs, my great grandmother was the decision-maker. After her eldest son married, her family position improved: now she could allocate chores to her daughter-in-law, instead of doing them herself. At dinner, she could sit respectably at table with her husband and the family's bread-winners, instead of eating in the kitchen with the young children as she did before. Her experience realized the ultimate female dream expressed as 'becoming a mother-in-law after long years of suffering as a daughter-in-law'.

My grandmother won over her parents-in-law immediately after her wedding. The delicacy and charm of her physical appearance was in clear contrast with the looks of her sister-in-law, to whom my grandmother felt that life was very unfair. Soon my grandmother's efficiency in the house-hold impressed everyone. If it was not her turn in the kitchen, her mother-in-law would ask her: 'Please replace your sister-in-law for cook-ing today. She always leaves big fingerprints on the pancakes, and it puts your father-in-law off.' Her sister-in-law would ask her with tears in her eyes: 'Please help me to finish this blouse for our mother-in-law. I can't meet her standards.' As a gifted dressmaker, it was not hard for my grand-mother to help. When her young nephews and nieces asked her as a favour to make a pair of shoes or sew a shirt, she tried her best to help. She felt sorry that her sister-in-law was unable to dress her own children smartly.

'Being a daughter-in-law,' my grandmother said to me half a century later, 'I had to move around our house all day long for the endless chores, like a non-stop spinning top.' Her daily work started at dawn, cooking breakfast for the family, cleaning the house and then attending to her parents-in-law when they were washing and dressing. During her labours, she had to snatch a quiet moment to return to her own bed-room, where her husband was still in bed, waiting for hot water and clothes to be prepared. As his parents' youngest son, my grandfather hardly lifted a finger. If his wife did not put the chopsticks in his hand at the dining table, he would sit there facing his food and smoking quietly.

Two years after their wedding, my grandparents' first child, my father, was born. He was given the name 'Xiansong', which was made up of two characters: Xian, the generation name of his family; and 'song', meaning 'pine', an emblem of strength and firmness, ideal qualities for a Chinese man. In the following sixteen years, my grandmother gave birth to seven more children. The six who survived were Morality (my Second Uncle),

Glow (First Auntie), Grace (Second Auntie), Lotus (Third Auntie), Flower (Little Auntie) and Road (Little Uncle).

Despite the family's tight finances, my father was sent to school from the age of seven, in the expectation that with a proper education he could find a decent job in the future and hence support the family. My grandfather's decision was supported by his wife, who knew what it meant to be illiterate. Due to difficulties with keeping accounts, she had been cheated many times by shopkeepers. When her father worked in Manchuria, she had to ask people for help in reading and replying to his letters. In a small town like Penglai, there was no sense of privacy, so that details of their correspondence became the talk of the community. For the sake of her children's future, my grandmother was determined that not only boys but also girls must be educated.

Her decision to educate girls was opposed by many people, including her mother-in-law. For them, sending daughters to school was like throwing money away, because girls would eventually marry out, with no responsibility for their own parents in the future. In their town, the first modern school for girls, recently opened by Western missionaries, had been strongly attacked by the public for corrupting its pupils' minds. According to false rumours, the pupils behaved like whores, and the school's toilet was full of aborted babies. My grandmother was blamed for risking her daughters' future as well as the family's reputation, but she pooh-poohed the stories.

Due to her capability and her contribution to the household, my grandmother developed the confidence to manage her own family life. When First Auntie was five, my great grandmother started to bind her feet, despite the objection from my grandmother, who had had her own feet bound since childhood. Since the abolishment of the imperial system more than a decade before, feudal customs such as the compulsory pigtails worn by Chinese men under the Manchu rulers had gradually changed, but in provincial places like Penglai, the binding of women's feet was still an unwritten law. Every day, First Auntie's feet were bound by thick white cloth one metre long. The cloth was then sewn with small stitches so that she could not release it herself. Under the pressure of tight binding, her toes, apart from the big one, were pressed to the soles, which would stop her feet growing. It was expected that after several years of binding, both feet would earn the description of 'san-cun-jin-lian' ('three-inch golden lilies'), the classical beauty that women were supposed to show.

Tortured by the constant pains in her feet, First Auntie was unable to walk, eat or sleep. Her face turned pale and her moans were endless. My grandmother held the little girl and complained: 'Who made this horrible rule to bind women's feet? It's nonsense to change our healthy feet into the ugly shape of "three-inch golden lilies", and disable us from walking and standing properly. I won't let my girl suffer as I have!' In the evenings, she released the thick cloth on her daughter's feet. When the girl got up in the morning, she wrapped her feet gently again. From the girl's peaceful manner, my great grandmother recognized the ruse. 'I wonder whether you are smart or stupid,' she said to my grandmother. 'No decent family accepts a daughter-in-law with a pair of unbound feet. You must think about your Glow's future!' But despite her mother-in-law's pressure, my grandmother persisted. Several years later, foot-binding was stopped in her county. When First Auntie grew up, no man fancied marriage to a woman with bound feet. My grandmother's foresight saved her daughters' lives from ruin.

My grandparents' greatest pride was my father. Among relatives and neighbours, he was praised for being good-looking, gentle and quiet. Even as a little boy, he was seldom noisy or naughty. Economic depression forced the family to ration its food, and hungry children would quarrel for more to eat, but he never joined in, and his influence calmed his younger siblings.

At school, my father was a gifted and studious pupil, always first in his class. Soon he was favoured by the headmaster, Mr Jiang, a well-known scholar in Shandong province, who had qualified as a Mandarin towards the end of the Qing dynasty, and trained in Japan as a military officer. After his return to China, he refused to work for the warlord government, and devoted his life to education in his home county. At school, my father often received Mr Jiang's individual tutorials, which spurred his knowledge and interest in classical Chinese literature. At home, he hardly stopped reading before midnight. Sometimes he asked my great grandfather to wake him up at dawn, as the family could not afford an alarm clock. Then he started reading again.

During the last few years of my father's schooling, his county was troubled by fighting among the feudal warlords. The school campus was often taken over as a barracks, which disrupted its teachings. Later, my great grandfather passed away, and then the large family split up. In conformance to tradition, my great grandmother was supported by her eldest son's family, while my grandfather had to support his growing young family with his own meagre income. Life was getting harder for my grandparents, and when they could no longer afford their children's education, my father left school and began his self-education. He read all he could find in classical or contemporary Chinese and foreign literature, history, sciences and sociology. In provincial places like Penglai, there was no library available to the public, so he had to borrow private books from friends and relatives. In order to earn a call on their books, he did all sorts of unpaid jobs for the owners' families.

Some aspects of his extensive childhood reading left a permanent mark on my father. Decades later, my grandmother told me how he interrupted the family's 'farewell ceremony' for the kitchen god (Zao-wang-ye). In those days, there was a little board forming a shelf immediately above the cooking stove in the kitchen of each family. On it were placed the offerings to the kitchen god and his wife (Zao-wang-nai-nai), whose paper image was fastened just above. This divinity was supposed to guarantee that the family would have enough to eat. Once a year, the kitchen god was supposed to ascend to heaven and report to the god of heaven (Lao-tian-ye) about everything he had seen in the household. On the twenty-third of the twelfth month, the departing god and goddess were offered melon-shaped sweets so glutinous that in heaven their lips would stick together and prevent them from uttering a word. At the ceremony, my father, only a teenager, told his family that what they did was superstitious. To prove it, he read atheistic books out loud in front of the painting of the kitchen god, and then shared the sweets with his siblings before the ceremony was over. He also flouted many traditional customs, for instance by refusing to attend weddings or funerals. Although they could not understand his behaviour, my grand-parents were extremely tolerant to him, because they trusted and admired him.

In summer 1929, at the age of thirteen, my father was sent away from home to Dalian, a major city in Manchuria, to work as an appren-tice in a small shop. He was expected to learn some useful skills, and to be a salesman in the future, which was usual for men from his back-ground. The contract made him practically a child slave to the shop-owner, with neither payment nor holiday due for three years, and only board and lodging provided. Despite the many stories about mal-treatment of teenage apprentices, my grandparents had to promise to the shop-owner never to voice a complaint, no matter what happened to their son during his apprenticeship. To pay for my father's trip to Dalian, my grandmother sold some of the jewels that were part of her dowry. Although it was his first trip across the Bohai Gulf, my father did not enjoy it at all. The cramped old ferry was packed with shabbily dressed Shandong people who, like himself, were braving the journey to Manchuria to try to make a living in a strange place. Sitting on the ferry's deck alone, he stared into the distance, the vast sea and endless waves, as if they were going to engulf him. His mind was dominated by the sadness of leaving his family and school, and by despair about his future.

In the following year, my father's life was occupied by endless work and harsh orders. In addition to working as an apprentice in the shop, he also served the shop-owner's large family. In those days, there was no indoor toilet; my father had to rise at dawn and carry their heavy chamber pot to the street before the night-soil cart arrived. When the family got up, hot water and breakfast must be ready. At night while everyone was sleeping, my father was still busy cleaning rooms, fetching water from the well and throwing rubbish out. His food was their leftovers and his bed was the shop's counter. In the freezing cold of winter, he never had heating at night. Every day, he was scolded for being lazy and at fault, but was forbidden to answer back. What upset him most was that he had no chance to touch a book, and his life seemed so far away from the world of beautiful literature that he had loved at school.

My grandparents were anxious about my father's situation in Dalian. A year later, they borrowed some money and paid for his trip back home. In summer 1930, my father was enrolled in a teacher training college in Laiyang, about a hundred kilometres south of Penglai. The only institution run by the provincial government in Shandong Peninsula, the college offered good scholarships to students, so that its entrance examination was very competitive and the selection very tough. Even though my father had no time for preparation, he came eighth among all the candidates, so that he qualified to study with second-year students right away. His family was thrilled when the good news arrived, especially knowing that most graduates from this college were guaranteed teaching posts, and my father was happy to resume his studies. He expected to support his family in the future by working as a teacher, so that his siblings could go to school and his parents could have decent lives.

Before my father left, my grandmother borrowed money again and treated him to delicious dumplings, the traditional farewell meal for family members, or for the Chinese New Year. Surrounded by his cheerful children, my grandfather laughed from ear to ear at the sight of my father, the future family bread-winner. No one dreamed that my father's life would soon run in a totally different direction. From that college, he became a dedicated Communist, a risk that could easily cost his own life and endanger his family.

At a secret meeting in July 1921, the Chinese Communist Party was established with about fifty members in Shanghai, the largest industrial city in China. It promoted proletarian revolution, with the ultimate goal of abolishing the system of private capital ownership and achieving Communism in China. In the following years, they launched labour movements in many industrial cities, which were quickly repressed by the warlord government. In 1923, at the suggestion of the Communist International, the Party agreed to establish a united anti-imperialist and anti-feudalist front with the Nationalist Party led by Dr Sun Yat-sen. Both parties faced the same major enemies: the imperialists and the feudal warlords. It was not impossible for them to unite together. In January 1924, Dr Sun reorganized the Nationalist Party, invited Russian advisers to help with political and military affairs, and admitted Communists to the party. Communist historians date the launching of the Great Revolution from that time.

With Communist Party support, a Nationalist republican government was established at Dr Sun's base in Guangzhou, the provincial capital of Guangdong in the extreme south of China, to oppose the warlord government in Beijing. In summer 1926, the Nationalist Northern Expedition Army, commanded by Chiang Kai-shek, marched northwards from Guangdong. Within a few months, the Army put the warlords' main forces to rout and reached the Yangtze River, the longest river in China. On their way, the troops were welcomed by local people, especially peasants and industrial workers. The feudal warlord regime was coming to its end.

But the Great Revolution did not survive long. Inside the united front, power struggles intensified between the two political parties, especially after the death of Dr Sun Yat-sen in March 1925. Within the

Nationalist Party, the right wing had opposed cooperation with the Communists from the very beginning. The triumph of the Great Revolution also caused panic among the foreign powers. In order to maintain their privileges in China, they looked for a new ruler to replace the defeated warlords. By now, Chiang Kai-shek had gained enormous power within the Nationalists; he was a natural ally.

At the end of March 1927, the warlord government in Shanghai was overthrown by rebel industrial workers organized by Communist leaders such as Zhou Enlai. On 12 April 1927, Chiang Kai-shek staged a coup in Shanghai in which the rebels were disarmed, imprisoned or killed. Chiang Kai-shek's wanted list included many prominent Communists who had worked with him previously, among them Zhou Enlai. Zhou barely escaped with his life, and many of his comrades were arrested, brutally tortured and executed. Some months after Chiang Kai-shek's coup, all Russian advisers to the Nationalists were removed from their posts. In a short period, a series of similar coups took place in many cities, while most Communist organizations were destroyed. Thus, the first united front between the Communists and the Nationalists split up and the Great Revolution was over.

After the Shanghai coup, Chiang Kai-shek established his Nationalist government in Nanjing (in the West often spelt as Nanking), a city by the lower reaches of the Yangtze River. In the following years, he won support from various warlords. In 1928, the last president of the feudal warlord government, Marshal Zhang Zuolin, was assassinated by the Japanese, and Chiang became ruler of the entire country. Under the Nationalist policy that 'we would rather wrongly kill a thousand people than let one Communist escape', one third of a million people were executed in China within a year for being Communists or revolutionary activists. In his child-hood, my father frequently saw the heads of executed Communists hanging from flagpoles in his home town, as a deterrent to revolutionary activists.

But the Communists did not give up. On 1 August 1927, exactly twenty-four years before I was born, an armed insurrection started in

Nanchang, the provincial capital of Jiangxi. Major organizers included Zhou Enlai and other prominent Communist figures who later became members of the famous 'Ten Marshals' in the People's Republic, including Zhu De, He Long, Nie Rongzhen and Liu Bocheng. The insurrection was also regarded as heralding a new era of Communist armed struggle against the Nationalists – an era known to Communist historians as the Agrarian Revolutionary War. Later in Communist China, the first of August became Army Day.

From 1927 to 1929, more than a hundred armed insurrections took place against the Nationalists, organized by prominent Communists including Deng Xiaoping. In October 1927, Mao Zedong established the first Communist base area in the remote Jing-gang Shan mountain area of south China. The Communist forces were known as the Chinese Workers and Peasants Red Army. Summing up the Party's experiences and China's situation, in 1930 Mao Zedong wrote a famous article, 'A single spark can start a prairie fire', which underlined his revolutionary theory of establishing the Communist bases in rural areas first and then besieging and occupying cities. He pointed out that revolution would not win in China without support from the peasants who accounted for more than three-quarters of the total population.

While they developed their activities in rural areas, the Communists also started restoring their underground organization in the cities. In 1930, the first underground branch of the Communist Party in the Shandong Peninsula was established in Laiyang, where my father's college was based. When the Party decided to recruit members among students in 1931, my father was one of the earliest candidates. Through essays published in his college journals, he was known for his radical views. He was therefore approached by secret Communists working for the underground, including some senior students and his lecturer in economics, who became the Communist deputy governor of Shandong province a few decades later. On their advice, my father read widely among authors such as Marx, Lenin, Gorky and Lu Xun, a great modern

Chinese writer with left-wing views. Through his reading, he learned that the inequality he so much resented was the outcome of a social system that allowed the exploitation of man by man. The poor got poorer because the rich oppressed them. The *Communist Manifesto* convinced him that it was possible to change the social system, an idea that was unclear to him before. Gradually, he accepted that the best solution for China was to achieve Communism, as Russia had done.

At this time, the Communists had established a number of bases known as Soviet bases, most of them located in remote rural parts of southern China. Here, land was confiscated from the rich and then distributed to peasants, which was the earliest practice of land reforms. As a result, the Communists gained strong support from peasants. From winter 1930, the Soviet bases experienced Chiang Kai-shek's repeated encirclement campaigns, with millions of troops. Due to Chiang's blockade, salt, fuel, cloth, medicine and even matches became scarce and dear. The few Red Army troops were poorly equipped and undernourished. Many were ill, and the wounded hard to treat. Despite all this, by 1931 the forces commanded by Mao Zedong, with his guerrilla strategy, had defeated Chiang's three encirclement campaigns. The Red Army's victory boosted my father's expectation of social reforms. He started to consider what he should do for China.

On 18 September 1931, Japanese troops attacked Manchuria, in northeast China, while Chiang Kai-shek was still waging his campaign against the Red Army in the south. In March 1932, a Japanese-controlled state, Manchukuo, was established in Manchuria. The puppet governor was Puyi, China's last emperor, overthrown at the age of six in 1912 by Dr Sun Yat-sen's revolution. In March 1934, Puyi became the puppet emperor of the newly established Manchukuo Empire.

The Japanese invasion angered and pained my father. A region familiar all his life had been severed from China. He could not bear the tragedy that his Manchurian compatriots had suffered. Because he believed that everyone had a share of responsibility for the fate of his own country, he decided that he must give up all his own interests to save his nation, including his studies for a good future.

My father was deeply disappointed by Chiang Kai-shek's policy of continuing the anti-Communist war instead of resisting the Japanese. Chiang clung to his view that 'Before resisting foreign aggression, internal stability must be achieved.' A few months after the defeat of his fourth encirclement campaign against the Communists, Chiang Kai-shek launched his fifth campaign in October 1933. In the Nationalist areas, participants in the anti-Japanese movement were punished by beatings and jail. Posters warned the public: 'Don't mention national affairs', if they wanted to keep out of trouble. All the same, my father started to take part in the patriotic movements launched by the Communist underground. As a member of his college's 'Save the Nation Committee', he organized student anti-Japanese demonstrations, strikes and fundraising to support the defending Chinese troops.

In an account of his personal history which he provided to the Party authorities in December 1952, my father wrote:

One evening in Autumn 1932, I was called outside by Yibin, my best friend in college. He told me secretly that he wanted to recommend me to join the Communist Party. In the past, I had heard a lot about the Communists . . . and expected to join them one day. What I had not realized was that my best friend was a Communist. No wonder he was so knowledgeable and helpful to me . . .

My father was sixteen years old when he joined the Communists. On a quiet evening, he attended a secret ceremony in a student dormitory. When he arrived, the windows were carefully covered with bed-sheets so that nothing could be seen from outside. A candle was lit, and my father saw two sincere faces staring at him. One was Yibin, who had recommended him for membership. The other was a member of his underground branch, who was the only witness to the ceremony. On the wall, there was a paper flag of the Communist Party, a golden sickle and a hammer crossed on a bright red background, which stood for the revolution of peasants and industrial workers. My father was affected at once by the serious and exciting atmosphere. In front of the flag, he raised his right fist and spoke the solemn pledge: 'Sacrifice myself, obey the Party, strictly guard the Party's secrets, never betray the Party!' At the end of the brief ceremony, he felt his hands grasped firmly by the two men, and heard their emotional whispers: 'Welcome, comrade!'

Later that night, my father paced up and down on the college's sports ground, with tears in his eyes and a whirlwind of emotion in his heart. For a long time, he had felt like a kite with a broken string, without a direction for his future. From now on, a new life had started. He decided to follow the Communist Party until the end of his life. From that time on, my father was no longer a dedicated student, because most of his time was spent on activities such as attacking Chiang Kai-shek's civil war policy and organising anti-Japanese movements. Under the Party's instruction, he recruited a number of college mates as new members.

January 1931 saw the start of a period known to Chinese Communist historians as the 'Era of Wang Ming Left-adventurism', since the Party was controlled by Wang Ming and other Russian-trained Communists who believed that the only way to revolution was marked by the Russian experience. They looked down on Mao Zedong for his ignorance of true Marxism-Leninism, because he had not studied Marxism abroad. In their view, Mao's strategy of guerrilla warfare was an old-fashioned method fit only for bandits. They removed him from command of the Red Army, and ordered it to occupy major cities, on the Russian pattern, instead of improving the Communist bases in rural areas. This was supposed to produce a surge of revolutionary momentum and a rapid victory. A wave of activity was launched among industrial workers and students in the Nationalist areas, such as strikes, demonstrations, and even armed insurrections. Due to lack of preparation and support, most of these activities were crushed, and the Communist underground badly damaged.

Among my father and his fellows working for the Communist underground, these intra-party conflicts were unknown. Surrounded by the anti-Communist 'white terror', they felt that the Party was like their mother, the only source of courage and direction. As Party members, their only choice was to obey the Party's decisions.

During the Chinese New Year holiday in 1933, my father was invited to Yibin's parents' home in a village outside town, together with several other Communist students. The village was packed, due to a New Year fair. Pedlars sat on the ground and attracted customers with their loud cries and colourful displays: white eggs, green vegetables, red-shelled peanuts and golden yellow maize. The centre of the village was a large square, which was converted into an open-air theatre for traditional local operas. A huge crowd of peasants was enjoying the performance. Village children perched in the forks of trees around the square. In those days, such operas were the only entertainment that peasants could afford; the performers were normally amateurs, paid by the local community.

Suddenly, hundreds of white leaflets were flying above the crowd, like flakes of heavy snow. Yibin jumped on to the stage, and his deep voice rose in the square: 'Dear compatriots, the Japanese have occupied our Manchuria, China is in a crisis!' The leaflets kept falling from his comrades' hands. Curious peasants vied with each other in picking them up, some read aloud to their illiterate companions. Standing by Yibin, my father conducted the crowd to sing anti-Japanese songs and shouted patriotic slogans: 'Down with the Japanese imperialist!' and 'Stop civil war to resist the Japanese invasion!' Soon, the village square resounded with the peasants' voices.

These patriotic activities alerted the Nationalist local authority. In case of trouble, my father went into hiding for a few days in a remote village. In spring 1933, many students active in the anti-Japanese movement were expelled from the college, among them Yibin and other secret Communists. Due to his youth and excellent academic record, my father remained, so now he took charge of the Party's secret activities there. As he was closely watched by the authority, many students avoided him, and he had to find a cover for his political activities. Instead of making direct contact, if he wanted to contact a Communist student and that person was reading in the library, my father would punch him and run away, like a schoolboy playing a prank. With pretended fury, his victim would chase him into an empty toilet where their secret meeting took place.

Before the summer holiday in 1933, my father received a letter from the Party's Laiyang prefectural underground committee summoning him to an urgent meeting outside the college. It was examination time, and students were not allowed to leave the campus, but my father could not afford to miss this meeting. The sender was his only contact with his leader in the Communist underground. In those days, the Communists' secret activities were frequently cracked by the Nationalist authority. For the safety of the Party's organization, their regular communication would stop if my father missed this appointment.

After lunch, my father slipped out of his dormitory, crossed the sports ground and then passed through a wire entanglement surrounding the campus. The rendezvous was located in a field outside town which was covered by tall crops. There he received the Party's instructions for summer activities.

It was nearly dark when he returned. Outside his classroom, a frightened student stopped him: 'How dare you come back!' My father heard how his absence had caused an uproar. The Party's letter had been intercepted by the college's political instructor, a Nationalist official. Through the name of the sender, a former student expelled for his revolutionary activities, the political instructor recognized the purpose of the meeting. That afternoon, a snap roll-call had revealed my father's absence. The instructor announced immediately: 'Mu Xiansong is a Communist, the troublemaker of our college. Now everything is clear, we must punish him severely!' Shortly before my father returned to college, a Nationalist cavalry force was sent to the rendezvous to catch the participants.

Later that evening, my father was called to the political instructor's office on the ground floor of the main building. 'Where did you go this afternoon?' the instructor bellowed like an interrogating policeman. He placed a thick notepad on his desk and waited to write the answer down. 'An old college friend asked me to return his book immediately.' My father's answer was already prepared. 'You are my favourite student – young, intelligent, with a good future. Don't be used by other people.' The instructor used soft-soap tactics, angling for the Party's secret connections. Looking at the ceiling with an innocent manner, my father kept his mouth shut all the time.

Finally, the instructor lost his temper, threw his pen on the floor, and then struck the desk and poured out a stream of abuse. Straight away, my father jumped up from his seat, struck the desk too, and answered back. Their quarrel broke the quiet summer evening, and attracted many students who gathered outside the office and were fascinated to see the frustration of the arrogant political instructor in front of my father, a gentle and suave student. Being excited by my father's courage, they took the opportunity to boo and hoot at the arrogant instructor. The interrogation was suspended. 'Come back tomorrow!' my father was told. Like a triumphant soldier, he walked out of the instructor's office proudly.

In my father's dormitory, a Communist student was waiting for him anxiously. 'You must leave now! The situation is very dangerous for you.' My father asked him to send his luggage home and then left the campus immediately. A few days later, my grandparents were informed that my father had been expelled from the college for 'misconduct'. Fortunately, the Nationalist authority in Penglai did not bother my father very much, since they came under a different administration from Laiyang, where his college was based. When the commotion was over, my father returned home secretly.

My grandfather was scared by what happened, especially when he recognized that his son would not change his mind. 'Do you want to see our son lose his head?' he asked my grandmother. 'Please make him stop!' My grandmother had no idea about politics, but she trusted her eldest son. Ever since his childhood, he had never been drawn to adult misbehaviour. How could a man of such integrity turn his life to evil ways? She did not believe that the Communist Party that my father joined were bandits.

For my father, the summer of 1933 was particularly hard after his expulsion from the college. For a while, the Nationalist authority was in the ascendant, and revolutionary activities restricted. He thought of leaving home to join the Red Army in the Soviet bases, but the Communist underground instructed him to carry on working among students. Coincidentally, a letter arrived from his former Chinese lecturer in college, inviting him to resume his studies in the senior middle school where the lecturer worked. The school was in Jinan, the provincial capital of Shandong. In order to support their son, my grandparents borrowed more money from their relatives, but at the end of his first term my father was once again expelled for his revolutionary activities.

Afterwards, my father returned to Penglai, his home county, with another mission: to set up the Communist Party's first underground branch there. Since 1930, the Communists had failed several times to establish themselves in Penglai. Only months before, my father's predecessor, a schoolteacher, had gone on the run after his revolutionary activities were discovered. Learning from previous experiences, the first thing my father did was to establish a literary society in town, the 'Misty World' (Yan-chen Wen-xue She). It provided a cover for meeting educated young people regularly and exposing them to revolutionary ideals.

My father organized various activities in the society. Sometimes, they climbed precipitous cliffs to the famous Penglai Ge building, where shelling by Japanese warships completely destroyed a precious fresco during the first Sino-Japanese War of 1894–5. Overlooking the sea, my father and his fellows recited stirring classical poems written by great patriotic heroes such as Lu You, Yue Fei and Wen Tianxiang during the Song Dynasty (AD 960–1279). To the east of the cliff lay an ancient naval port called the 'Water City' (Shui-cheng), built six hundred years before as a headquarters of Chinese defences against Japanese pirates. Now it was often packed with refugees who fled in small boats from Japanese-occupied Manchuria. Grieved by their tragic experiences, under my father's guidance these passionate youngsters debated the future, read many books by famous left-wing authors such as Lu Xun and Guo Moro, and wrote patriotic articles. Later, some members of the society joined the Communist Party.

In 1934, my father was invited by the county's newspaper to edit a weekly literary supplement to be called the 'Misty World', in honour of his society's growing influence. His earliest novels, with themes opposed to the civil war and the Japanese invasion, were published there and made him known locally as a popular left-wing author. In 1935, the county authorities issued several serious warnings to my father's supplement on account of its political views. Later, when he had to resign from his post, circulation fell rapidly and eventually its publication ceased.

In October 1934, the Red Army started the Long March from south China after its defeat in Chiang Kai-shek's fifth encirclement campaign. From October 1933, a million Nationalist troops were sent to attack the Soviet bases, under the German General Hans von Seeckt, who headed Chiang's military advisory group with the approval of Adolf Hitler. This time, the Red Army discarded the hit-and-run strategies which had enabled Mao to defeat Chiang's previous campaigns. The Communist International had sent Li Teh (Otto Braun), another German military

adviser, to the Red Army. His strategy was to hold fast to each position
and launch frontal attacks against the powerful enemy, like using an egg
to smash a rock. It played into Chiang Kai-shek's hands, and years later
Li Teh admitted that Western methods of warfare did not always work
in China.

By the winter of 1934, the Red Army had been forced to abandon its
bases in the south and set out on its desperate, legendary journey northwards. On the way in January 1935, Mao Zedong took control of the
Communist Party and the Red Army in a historic conference in Zun-yi
city. The era of 'Wang Ming Left-adventurism' was over. During the four
years of Wang's leadership, according to Communist historians, the
Party lost nearly all of its underground organizations in the Nationalist
areas, and 90 per cent of the Red Army, as well as the Soviet bases. The
number of Party members fell from a third of a million to 40,000.

These intra-party conflicts were unknown to my father and his colleagues. After the Long March started, the Central Committee lost its
regular contact with the outside world as the Red Army trudged on for
month after month through desolate, uninhabited regions, pursued by
the Nationalist forces. For a long time, the news of changes in the
Communist leadership did not reach their underground organizations in
the Nationalist areas and the Communist International in Moscow.

In summer 1935, my father had an unexpected visitor at home. Sun
Ziping was a thin and sickly-looking scholar, the headmaster of a rural
school about 10 kilometres from town. Stories he had heard about my
father's revolutionary activities convinced him that he had found the gen-
uine Communist he had been looking for, and he invited my father to
teach at his school. In fact, there was no vacancy there, so Ziping contributed ten silver coins each month, which was half of his salary, to pay
his new assistant. Being seven years older than my father, Ziping looked
after him like a thoughtful elder brother. Living together in the same
room, he would tuck in the corners of the quilt at night to keep my
father warm.

The school was located in a picturesque village on the bank of a limpid river where they talked for hours on end. Ziping walked slowly because he suffered from tuberculosis of the backbone. Most of the time, he wore a long plain lined cotton gown and a scarf, which was common for educated people in those days, the equivalent for a respectable school headmaster of a man's suit and tie in the West. When my father was talking, Ziping's tall slim figure bent over him slightly while his deep eyes gazed at my father's face. Sometimes their conversation stopped when Ziping was greeted by local peasants. Although he came from a rich farmer's family, Ziping was deeply concerned about the future of China and his obligations to poor people. In his mind, my father was his revolutionary guide. A few months later, my father was delighted to recommend him for Party membership. About half a century later, he recalled that 'it was hard to describe Ziping's happiness' at the moment when he joined the Communist Party.

In autumn 1935, the main strength of the Red Army arrived in northwest China. After covering more than 12,000 kilometres in a single year, they had shaken off the Nationalist pursuit. When the Long March ended, only a few thousand Red Army members survived, about one in ten of the number a year before.

At the same time, the Communist underground gradually improved in my father's home county. In his school, Ziping recruited his younger brother and a servant, and a number of senior pupils were also selected secretly as candidates. Since some of the Party members were peasants who had never gone to school, my father often read the Party's documents to them or gave individual tutorials about Communism. By order of the Party, an armed insurrection was planned in the Shandong Peninsula. On 4 November 1935, the scheduled date, my father and Ziping were to bring their senior pupils to meet peasant rebels who were headed by another Party member. Then they would occupy the county town and capture weapons from the Nationalist troops. They expected to rally revolutionary forces and eventually bring them to join the Red Army.

The plan was ambitious and bold. In an area under Nationalist control, my father and his comrades were poorly equipped, with no support from outside. The Red Army was more than 1,000 kilometres away. But this was the Party's decision, and my father believed Mao Zedong's statement that a single spark, such as the Communists were, could start a revolutionary prairie fire in China. Full of excitement, he and the others started to prepare, training members of the Party's underground organizations, setting up a liaison network and collecting intelligence about the Nationalist troops. As a special exercise, he boxed a flagstone every day, so that his fists became rock-hard. Decades later, their power still amazed me.

On the last Sunday of October 1935, my father was busy marking exercises when an undercover Communist rushed into his office from another village. 'You must leave at once! Troops are on their way to catch you!' Due to their lack of experience, the authorities had got wind of the uprising. The provincial governor, General Han Fuqu, rushed several divisions to the Shandong Peninsula. Soon, the jails were packed with political prisoners. Every day there were brutal tortures and executions. There is no knowing how many people lost their lives during that period.

In my father's home county, a Nationalist brigade arrived. The commander was known by his nickname 'Peel off People's Skin Zhang' (Zhang-ba-pi), both for his love of extorting money from civilians, and because of the cruel tortures he inflicted on his prisoners. Zhang imposed martial law at once, and his troops started searching for Communists. It was said that during their searches, even a piece of red string could inculpate the owner, who faced arrest and even execution. As a major organizer of the insurrection, my father's name headed the wanted list. Where could he go? Who could help him to escape? He had no idea. There were Nationalist troops everywhere. Since the secret Communists he knew were either in jail or in hiding, he had lost all contact with the Party's underground. Eventually, a name came to his mind,

Xing Long, a former member of the 'Misty World Literature Society', who was living in Tianjin (in the West often spelt as Tientsin), a major industrial city in north China, near Beijing.

Before fleeing to Tianjin, my father went into hiding for a few days in a remote village. It was impossible for him to say goodbye to his family. When would he see them again? What would become of them? Over the past years, his revolutionary activities had caused constant anxiety and danger to his parents. As the eldest son, he felt especially guilty that he had never done anything to repay their love and generous support. He only hoped that one day they would understand that, as a Communist, he had to put the Party's interest first.

When he received my father's message announcing that he had to go away, my grandfather beat his breast. 'Is my son mad? Why does he give up a secure future as a respectable teacher and risk his life for the Communists?' My grandmother took off her gold earrings, the last remaining pieces of her dowry, which she had refused to sell on several occasions. She stared at them for a while, then turned her face to her daughter: 'Please take them to the pawnshop. We need money for your eldest brother's trip.'

Before he left, my father arranged a secret meeting with Ziping, whose political identity was still intact, and passed on their work plan for the future and the procedure for contacting the Communist underground. The meeting took place at dawn by a quiet road leading towards the neighbouring county. Disguised as a merchant, my father wore a long plain gown and a hat; his eyes were screened by spectacles. Tears ran down Ziping's face. Finally, he handed twenty silver coins to my father: 'My good brother, please take this with you, it's my salary for this month. I hope you have a safe journey. Do contact me as soon as you settle down.' My father replied: 'Please believe that a single spark can start a prairie fire. No one can stamp out the revolutionary flame, even though we lost this time. For the final victory of our revolution, we will never give in!'

Chapter 4

Along the Yellow River towards
the Loess Highlands:
My Mother's Story
(1934–1938)

In 1934, at the age of eleven, my mother was enrolled at a middle school in Luoyang, a city about 35 kilometres away from her home county. Away from her depressing family life, she felt as joyful as a songbird escaped from its cage, revelling in her freedom and in all the surprises of a great historic city. Well sited in the valley of the Luo River, a major tributary of the Yellow River, Luoyang was the capital of China under four dynasties from 781 BC to AD 904. An inquisitive girl was bound to be impressed by its associations with so many great names in China's history.

My mother's school was located in an ancient, massive building whose vermilion gate and high surrounding walls kept it safe from the outside world. In those days, only wealthy families could afford to educate their children – and especially their daughters – at middle school level. All the pupils boarded during term time, which cost my grandfather five silver coins each month, a sum equivalent to half a year's income for one of his tenant peasants.

In 1935, my mother's second year at school, a new headmistress, Madam Zhou, was appointed. She was in her early thirties. In striking contrast to the pupils' luxurious lifestyle, her appearance was simple, although she too came from a wealthy family. She always wore a plain cotton qipao, and her unadorned face, under short straight hair, showed determination and intelligence. What impressed my mother most was her great courage and her record of striving for women's emancipation and democracy.

Between 1915 and 1919, while their country was ruled by feudal warlords, Chinese intellectuals launched the first political and cultural movement in modern Chinese history. They promoted ideals of anti-imperialism and anti-feudalism, as well as disseminating the success of the Russian Revolution. Since her childhood, Madam Zhou had witnessed how miserably women were treated. She detested the prevailing social injustice and longed to change her own life in the future. She felt particularly inspired by the movement's slogan, 'Down with Confucianism!' – the first time in China's history that Confucianism was publicly challenged.

Around the beginning of the Christian Era, Confucianism, which was founded by Confucius about five centuries earlier and expounded by Mencius later, was officially adopted by Chinese emperors as the feudal ethical code. Ever since, Chinese thinking and behaviour had been dominated by its principles. Contacts between the sexes were restricted, for example, because 'men and women when giving and receiving things from one another, should not touch each other' (nan-nü-shou-shou-bu-qin). According to the three cardinal guides (san-gang), 'Ruler guides subject, father guides son, and husband guides wife'. Hence women should not order their own lives. Because it was said that 'of the three unfilial acts, leaving no issue is most grievous' (bu-xiao-you-san, wu-hou-wei-da), women without sons were often discriminated against by their families.

Being influenced by revolutionary ideals, Madam Zhou attributed the injustice that women had suffered to Confucianism, and started to rebel against the feudal dogmas. In the early 1920s, short hair for women was viewed as a badge of revolution. At school, Madam Zhou was the first pupil to cut her long hair. She was denied admission to the classroom. She was also refused entry to her parents' mansion, and the message from her father was: 'I will not accept you at home until your hair grows long enough.' Later, Madam Zhou shocked society again by ceasing to bind her feet. They started to grow again, but her toes never regained their natural position. At that time, women's feet in that condition were called 'reformist feet' (gai-zu-pai-jiao), because they were seen only among those with radical anti-feudal ideals.

In the late 1920s, while studying at the Women Teachers University in Beijing, Madam Zhou decided to end her unhappy marriage, arranged by her family. In those days, divorce was condemned for corrupting public morals and disgracing a family's reputation. Madam Zhou's scandalized father threatened that the family would break off relations and stop supporting her studies. In reply, she published two personal announcements on the same day in the same newspaper, one breaking off relations with her father, the other declaring a split from her husband. Afterwards, she financed her studies through part-time work. The story of Madam Zhou's life appealed enormously to my mother: she saw that it was possible to rebel against the feudal ethical code, and not to repeat her mother's experience.

My mother could not forget the story she heard from Madam Zhou about the 'Massacre of 18 March' in Beijing. On 12 March 1926, Japanese warships bombarded Dagu Fort by the Hai River, on the way to Tianjin city from the Bohai Gulf, killing more than ten of the Chinese servicemen who fought in self-defence. Afterwards, the Japanese made no apology for intruding into China's territory. Instead, and in league with other foreign powers, they demanded an apology from the Chinese government on the grounds of 'military provocation'.

This incident enraged the Chinese people, who had suffered enough from foreign insults. Since the Opium War between China and Britain in 1840, there had been hundreds of unequal treaties imposed on China by countries such as Britain, France, Russia and Japan. These foreign powers acquired International Settlements and concessions on Chinese territory, where their colonial rules were enforced, and ordinary Chinese often barred from public places. In many parks there were signs at the entrance such as 'No admission for Chinese or dogs'. For the sake of personal gain, the rulers of China collaborated with the invaders. The response of most Chinese was very different.

On 18 March 1926, Madam Zhou took part in a huge rally against Japanese imperialism in Tian-an Men Square in Beijing. Afterwards, two thousand demonstrators, most of them students, marched to the Residence of President Duan Qirui, a leading warlord of the Japanese-backed Wan Group. It was located in the Iron Lion (Tie-shi-zi) Hutong, where both ends were equipped with heavy metal gates.

When the demonstrators arrived, the entrance of the Residence was blocked by armed troops, as if grave danger threatened. While their representatives were negotiating with the troops about handing a petition to the President, all at once a fusillade of bullets swept the street, and many people fell. When the shocked crowd tried to break out, it found that the metal gates at both ends of the street had been locked, and there was no way to escape. More than forty civilians were killed, including Madam Zhou's university friend, Liu Hezhen and nearly 200 were wounded. Next day, Madam Zhou and her fellows found the naked bodies of Ms Liu and other demonstrators lying in front of the President's Residence. All their clothes had been stripped off by the brutal troops.

The massacre shocked the whole nation. It was called 'the darkest day in the Republic of China' in a famous article, 'In Memory Of Liu Hezhen', written by Lu Xun, the great writer who taught Madam Zhou at university. In my mother's Chinese class, pupils were taught this article by Madam Zhou, who explained that China was bullied by imperialists because the warlord government had betrayed their country for the sake of personal power and wealth.

Being a follower of Dr Sun Yat-sen, Madam Zhou did not join the Communist Party, but many of the teachers she employed were members of the Communist underground in the 1930s. During the next half-century, a number of them became high-ranking Communists in China.

In spite of pressure from the Nationalist-controlled educational authority, these Communist teachers tried their best to sow revolutionary seeds. In her Chinese class, my mother learned articles written by pro-Communist authors and read classical patriotic poems. Her teacher of philosophy taught Marxism and Leninism. In her music class, pupils sang stirring patriotic songs together. Many revolutionary books which were banned by the authority were secretly circulated among the pupils. My mother's favourite books included stories about the Russian Revolution and the Red Army in China. She was thrilled by the vision of a new world where the life looked bright and meaningful, and women were treated as equals.

In winter 1936, President Chiang Kai-shek arrived in Luoyang city for his birthday celebration. At my mother's school pupils were told that in the bitter cold, many fishermen were sent to the Yellow River to catch fresh carp, a famous delicacy, for Chiang's sumptuous banquet. In that season the many homeless beggars in Luoyang wrapped themselves in gunny-sacks to keep out the cold, and filled their empty stomachs with white clay. The pupils recalled a famous poem written by Du Fu in the Tang Dynasty more than a thousand years before: 'Behind the vermilion gates meat and wine go to waste, while out on the road lie the bones of those frozen to death.' My mother recognized that not only women but also poor people were the victims of social injustice. She felt ashamed to belong to a landlord family, and she came to accept that only the Communist Party was able to save China. It was they who fought against feudalism and imperialism, and they who proposed to establish a new society that would not tolerate poverty and injustice. Gradually, a decision came to my mother's mind: to follow the Communist Party, and to establish a new society in China. Among the pupils, her experience was not unusual. By the end of her third year in the middle school, a number of her senior schoolmates had secretly joined the Communist underground.

In December 1936, shortly after his banquet in Luoyang, Chiang Kai-shek went to Xi'an, the provincial capital of Shaanxi, famous today for the discovery of the magnificent terracotta army from the tomb of Qin Shihuang, the first Chinese emperor. The city's name meant 'peace in the west', but the purpose of Chiang's visit was to supervise military operations against the Red Army, who had just established a new base area in northwest China after their Long March. Chiang Kai-shek was not happy about the performances against the Communists of the Manchuria and the Northwest armies.

The Manchuria Army was commanded by Zhang Xueliang, known as the Young Marshal, then in his thirties. In 1928, his warlord father, Marshal Zhang Zuolin, had been killed by the Japanese after opposing their excessive demands in Manchuria, his power base. When he succeeded his father, the Young Marshal was regarded as the youngest ruler in the world, controlling a population of thirty million. His refusal to detach Manchuria from China, despite threats from Japan, gained him public popularity, and he was appointed Deputy Commander in Chief of the Nationalist forces. However, on 18 September 1931, when the Japanese attacked Manchuria, the Young Marshal withdrew his troops from Manchuria, reportedly under orders from Chiang Kai-shek, his trusted leader. For this action, he was blamed by the whole nation. Now, he and his troops were eager to drive the Japanese out of their home provinces, and had been promised support from the Nationalist government. What they received instead were instructions to fight against the Red Army, rather than to resist the Japanese.

Among the troops of the Northwest Army, the Communists had been influential over the last decade. Their commander, General Yang

Hucheng, had even offered important posts to secret Communists of high Party rank. The Northwest Army had little interest in pursuing 'Chiang's civil war'. Since 1935, the Japanese had extended their aggressive activities from Manchuria into the neighbouring area of Shaanxi. The Northwest Army felt ashamed that at this crucial moment they had to fight against the Red Army, and kill their fellow countrymen, instead of resisting the Japanese invasion.

Generally speaking, the Nationalist forces were an amalgam consisting of the Central Army, under Chiang Kai-shek's direct control, together with various subsidiary troops such as the Manchuria Army and the Northwest Army. The forces in the second category usually belonged to feudal warlords based in areas where Chiang Kai-shek's power could not reach directly. So Chiang's anti-Communist war strategy in northwest China was suspected as a conspiracy: by pushing his less compliant troops to fight against the detested Red Army, he himself, as the unengaged third party, stood to gain greater power.

In 1935, the Communist Party again proposed to establish a united front with the Nationalists to throw back the Japanese aggression. This plan appealed to many patriotic Nationalists and Chiang Kai-shek supporters, including the Young Marshal and General Yang. A number of senior officers had received letters from Mao Zedong and other senior Communists. Nationalist servicemen captured by the Red Army and won over by its friendly treatment and political propaganda spoke up for the proposals when released. Gradually, the relationship between the Red Army and the two Nationalist armies improved. High-level contacts increased, the Communists sent secret transmitter-receivers to the two Nationalist armies for regular communications, and the Young Marshal's private plane was able to fly between Xi'an and the Communist base. By April 1936, the Young Marshal and General Yang had achieved a secret cease-fire with the Red Army. Thereafter, the two belligerent parties along the front line put on an act of fighting by day, and gathered by night to sing patriotic songs.

How much Chiang knew is unclear, but he probably got wind of these developments through his active intelligence agents. On his arrival in Xi'an, he gave the Young Marshal and General Yang two choices: either agree to suppress the Red Army in the northwest, or make way for the Central Army. Neither was accepted. The two commanders pleaded, but Chiang Kai-shek was not to be persuaded. Eventually, they decided to change his mind by applying their military forces.

At dawn on 12 December 1936, the Residence of Chiang Kai-shek, a famous hot-springs resort outside Xi'an city, was encircled by the Manchuria Army. Chiang was captured, and brought to Xi'an city. Around the same time, his delegates and senior officials were also arrested by General Yang's troops in the city. With Chiang in custody, the two commanders issued a circular telegram addressed to the Nationalist government, various provincial leaders, and the Chinese people at large, urging all patriotic groups to establish an anti-Japanese united front.

All over China, the Xi'an Incident created a sensation. Inside the Nationalist government, the active pro-Japanese group wanted to crush the two commanders by military force. If Chiang Kai-shek was killed during the chaos, the pro-Japanese group would control the government, which would result in more conflicts, infighting, even a larger scale of civil war.

In this emergency, the Communist Party accepted the two commanders' request to mediate between them and Chiang Kai-shek. The Communist delegation assigned for this historical mission was headed by Zhou Enlai, the Party's deputy chairman, and a former colleague of Chiang's during the 1920s, under Sun Yat-sen. After the two parties split up in 1927, Zhou's head was priced at 80,000 silver coins by Nationalist 'Wanted' notices. Surprisingly, the Communists did not intend to kill Chiang Kai-shek, although he had been their chief enemy for ten years. For them, the priority was to unite and defend the nation: more fighting between themselves and the Nationalists would only help

Japan. After intensive negotiations, Chiang Kai-shek eventually agreed to stop the anti-Communist war to resist the Japanese invasion.

On 25 December 1936, the release of Chiang Kai-shek concluded the Xi'an Incident peacefully. In a sequence of events that remains a mystery, the Young Marshal accompanied Chiang Kai-shek back to Nanjing in his private plane. It may be that he wanted to repair Chiang's dignity as leader of the country. If so, he sacrificed himself to save Chiang's face. Without his own troops to protect him, the Young Marshal was arrested and held prisoner for decades by Chiang Kai-shek. In the late 1940s, he was taken to Taiwan before Chiang had to leave mainland China.

At my mother's school, pupils watched in suspense as the Xi'an Incident unfolded. After Chiang Kai-shek's arrest, the Nationalist government launched a furious propaganda campaign against the Young Marshal and General Yang, and censored information from Xi'an. Wild rumours filled the press. The Young Marshal was an agent of Japan, or even of Soviet Russia; the Manchuria and Northwest armies were bandits; their revolt had plunged Xi'an city into a hell of looting, rape and killing.

My mother attended an unforgettable class given by Hao Deqing, her Communist teacher. The first thing he did was to shut the windows and doors. As he looked back into his pupils' serious faces, his voice was deep and heavy. 'I must tell you that Zhang and Yang [the two commanders] are innocent! They are patriots! What they did was to try to save our country. China is in crisis! We should be ready to shed the last drop of our blood for our national liberation!' His pupils listened with their hearts on fire and their faces running with tears.

In June 1937, my mother finished her three years of study in junior middle school. On 7 July 1937, during her summer holiday, Japanese troops intruded into the suburbs of Beijing and the second Sino-Japanese War broke out. After that, Chiang Kai-shek finally agreed to establish an anti-Japanese united front with the Communists, and granted legal status to the Communist Party. The decade of armed confrontation between the Nationalists and the Communists known as the Agrarian Revolutionary War was officially over.

By the end of 1937, Nanjing city had fallen into Japanese hands and Chiang Kai-shek and his government had fled to Chongqing, a city by the upper reaches of the Yangtze River. Before the end of 1938, the Japanese had occupied most major cities and provinces along the prosperous coastal area of China. In the days after the war broke out, hundreds of thousands of refugees passed through my mother's county, many with babies crying to be fed, and many with eye-witness accounts of the brutal persecution inflicted by Japanese troops on innocent Chinese civilians.

In September 1937 my mother went to Kaifeng, the then capital of Henan province, for another three years of study in senior middle school, the final stage of secondary education in China. The Number One Kaifeng Girls' Middle School was regarded as the best institution for girls in the province. Its early graduates included radicals such as Deng Yinchao, wife of Zhou Enlai and a prominent leader in Communist China after 1949. However, my mother was disappointed to find that the school's pro-Nationalist authorities were still advising pupils 'Don't mention national affairs' and 'Save the country by concentrating on your studies' – in other words, stay away from the anti-Japanese movement. For her liberal mind, this atmosphere was suffocating after the revolutionary climate in Luoyang.

Soon after my mother's term started, a series of raids by the Japanese air force spread terror in Kaifeng. Late in 1937, her school decided to leave the city before it was occupied by the Japanese, but with China at the mercy of the invaders, no one knew a safe destination. Public feeling raged against Japan. In Kaifeng, there were frequent anti-Japanese demonstrations and fund-raising activities to support the defending Chinese troops. Students and pupils went to villages to launch patriotic activities among the peasants. At this turbulent time, my mother could no longer focus on her studies. She was not yet fifteen, but over the past years her mind had brimmed with revolutionary ideals through the influence of her Communist teachers. At this moment of national calamity, she felt it was her duty to fight for her country and people. When Ning, her elder sister, and some of her schoolmates decided to join the anti-Japanese forces, she followed without hesitation.

'Please don't leave me on my own!' my maternal grandmother pleaded, with tears in her eyes. There were only days to go before my mother left to join the anti-Japanese forces with Ning. It was the eve of the Chinese New Year, February 1938, only a few months after the outbreak of the war. The family was having a traditional New Year dinner – my maternal grandparents, Ning and my mother together with my grandfather's two concubines and their young children. A huge golden 'Luck' character (Fu) hung on the wall against a red background, the colour associated with happiness in China. The carefully selected menu such as 'Fourfold happiness meat balls', 'Happy and glorious sliced chicken' and 'Six happiness cakes', showed my grandfather's wishes for his family's future.

It was deadly quiet, the only sound was the fierce wind blowing outside the house. Sitting opposite her mother, my mother had no appetite for the banquet; she too was crying. Her eldest sister had married many years before, and Ning, who was three years older than my mother, had also left home to work as a teacher. As the youngest of her mother's surviving children, my mother had been the only companion in her lonely life. 'My dear mother, how will you survive after I leave?' The question jarred my mother's mind.

My grandfather did not say a word. Since the war broke out, the flood of refugees that passed through the county had left behind stories of atrocities committed by the Japanese Devils. The closer they came, the more intensely he feared for the safety of Ning and my mother, his two unmarried daughters. It would be a relief if the girls could leave home before the Japanese arrived. The forces they would join were commanded by a friend of the family, so my grandfather hoped to see them well looked after.

'Please let me go!' my mother cried. She could not bear to live in this depressing landlord family any more. 'I must start a new life and fight against the Japanese invasion!' she said to herself.

On the morning of my mother's departure, two days after the Chinese New Year, my grandmother could not help weeping as she followed her two daughters to the front gate. 'Please write as soon as you arrive,' she kept repeating, and asked Ning to take good care of my mother. My mother tried not to look at my grandmother's face, for fear that her will to leave home would succumb to her mother's sadness. On the way to the railway station outside town, they carried their elegant leather suitcases, packed with their favourite clothes, books, photographs and even some toys, as if going on holiday rather than to war. Behind them came my grandfather and a coolie who shouldered their bedding rolls.

The railway station was in chaos due to the huge number of refugees, some of them fugitives from the Japanese-occupied areas, but many others local residents desperate to escape before the Japanese arrived. The ticket office was packed with anxious crowds who were shouting and pushing each other in their haste to buy tickets. Before incoming trains had come to a stop, frantic crowds were fighting to board the overcrowded, overloaded carriages. After conferring with the station manager, my mother and Ning left their county in an open coal wagon. They travelled with about eighty other young people who were going to join the same anti-Japanese forces. In this group, there were only five girls, and my mother was the youngest. Before the train departed, she failed to say goodbye to her father. For years she had hated him for what he had done to the family. Now she did not know how to express her feelings towards him.

Their destination was Zhaocheng county in Shanxi, a neighbouring province of Henan. In those days, it was not an easy journey, as they had to cross the Yellow River from Tongguan, a small town in Shaanxi, another province about 200 kilometres away from my mother's home county. Due to Japanese air attacks, their train stopped frequently. Beside the railway line tramped the long stream of walking refugees who could not pay for transport, carrying their few belongings towards an unpredictable future. By the time they reached Tongguan, after two days of piercing wind in a wagon thick with coal dust, no face could be recognized. My mother's bright silk jacket, a New Year present from my grandmother, had turned black.

Standing on the south bank of the Yellow River outside Tongguan, my mother was amazed to see the mighty brown waves that rolled incessantly over a riverbed several kilometres wide. Raging waves and fierce winds made crossing impossible along many reaches of the river. At the crossing-point, my mother's face was battered by a strong wind laden with dust and sand, so that she had to squint at the far north bank of the river, the famous Fengling Ferry. A number of small open wooden boats crept towards her, each of them rowed by two strong men, one at each end. On each boat's tiny bow deck stood a shrine where a thicket of joss sticks and candles burned, praying the river god to grant a safe passage. My mother and her fellows were divided among several different boats carefully. What followed was like a nightmare, a baptism of fear for my mother. The river's roaring waters caught and tossed the little boat like a leaf in a storm, now suddenly thrown skywards, now dropped into the valleys of the brown breakers. My mother clung hard to Ning's hand and watched the boatmen struggle with the waves. She did not notice that her fingernails had torn her sister's skin.

Once across the Yellow River, my mother reached Shanxi province, and then took the train again to Zhaocheng. On her way to the local railway station, she and her companions visited a food stall, a single room with walls blackened by cooking smoke. The owner commended his menu, shouting in the local dialect which my mother had trouble understanding, and wiped a greasy table for them with an oily rag of an unrecognisable colour. Despite her empty stomach, my mother lost her appetite when the food came. The thick noodles reminded her of the disgusting roundworms she had seen illustrated in her textbooks. Mixed with a tasteless sauce, they were served in a dirty pottery bowl with a jagged rim. It was all so different from the fine food and careful service that she was used to before. 'Heavens!' she thought. 'This must be the roughest food in the world!' But she was wrong. In the years to come, when she sometimes made do with a diet of chaff and tree leaves, my mother always regretted having wasted precious food on that occasion.

The force my mother joined belonged to the Alliance of Sacrificing Ourselves to Save the Nation (Xi-meng Hui), an anti-Japanese organization controlled by the Communist Party. Its commander, Han Jun, was not only a friend of my mother's family but also a famous patriotic figure with a pro-Communist reputation. While a student in Beijing University, Han Jun was an active member of the anti-Japanese movement after Manchuria was occupied in 1931, and was then jailed by the Nationalists. During his imprisonment, he joined the Communist Party. After the Xi'an Incident in December 1936, he was released, and then assigned to Shanxi by the Party to establish resistance to the Japanese invasion. Shortly after the Sino-Japanese War broke out, Shanxi province became the front line of the war, which attracted an endless stream of patriotic youngsters from all over China.

Having arrived in the detachment headquarters in a village in Zhaocheng, my mother was surprised to meet Hao Deqing, the Communist teacher at her junior middle school in Luoyang, now serving as an officer. At that time, she did not know that Commander Han Jun and Mr Hao were Communists. Clashes were still occurring between the two political parties in China, even though their hostility had officially ceased, so most Communists had to keep on concealing their political identity in the Nationalist areas. My mother and her group were recruited into a training course run by the detachment, but actually organized by the Communist underground. It lasted six months, of which two-thirds was military training and the rest was political studies.

On arrival at the training course, newcomers were requested to change their appearance. My mother took off the bright clothes she had worn since leaving home, and put on the dark grey army uniform provided by the detachment. Her short hair was hidden beneath an army cap, her calves were wrapped in cotton puttees, her tunic fastened by a leather belt. Seeing each other in military uniform, my mother and her companions could not help cheering. 'Look! We've turned into fighters against the Japanese Devils!'

The next thing they were asked was to change their names. As members of resistance forces with a pro-Communist reputation, they needed to consider the safety of families left behind in Nationalist or Japanese-occupied areas, so much of their past must also be left behind. Among my mother's fellow recruits, it was fashionable to have new names with revolutionary implications. Some girls adopted their families' generation names, a practice reserved only for male children under the feudal code. A common change was to use a single character for one's first name, instead of the traditional two still widely adopted. My mother's given name of 'Ruilan', meaning 'auspicious orchid', was now replaced by 'Jing', meaning quietness and calm, which pointed to her personal character.

Life in the training course was ruled by iron discipline. Every day, the trainees got up at dawn and then sang the anthem of their detachment, which was based on the rousing tune of the 'Marseillaise', the French national anthem, but with a new lyric: 'We are young fighters against the Japanese invaders, we are the people's forces . . .' The 'Marseillaise' was popular with many senior Party members whose early revolutionary lives had been spent in France during the 1920s, such as Zhou Enlai and Deng Xiaoping.

During the political class, trainees sat on the ground in the open and took notes on their laps. Sometimes, they used their shoes as cushions to reduce the damp from the soil. They slept on beaten earth in rooms rented from villagers, with straw spread for a mattress. This life was harsh for a teenage girl brought up in luxury. One day, my mother found herself screaming for help in the canteen's kitchen, just because water was boiling and she did not know how to stop it. From day one, Ning had to help my mother even with washing her hair and clothes, jobs previously done by her mother or servants, as well as on sentry duty at night, because my mother was scared of the dark. Yet my mother never regretted her decision to leave home, for the new life she found here was full of enthusiasm, optimism and purpose. A few weeks later, some trainees quit the course and returned home, unable to cope with the hardship. My mother and Ning stayed on.

When her two daughters left, my grandmother felt desolate. She could not sleep and lost her taste for food. She worried most about her youngest daughter. How could a girl not yet fifteen survive the dangers and hardships of war? Every day, she stood by the front gate of the mansion, eagerly waiting for their letters, or looking at the end of the street as if the girls might suddenly appear. Two months later, a letter arrived from my mother and Ning. My overjoyed, illiterate grandmother could not wait for her husband to come home, and asked neighbours to read it for her. When she learned that her daughters were working for a small shop in Shanxi, she was deeply upset. 'They're bound to run out of money.' Poor grandmother, she did not know that her daughters could not tell her the truth. To protect their family, located in a Nationalist area, they followed their orders to hide the fact that they were working for a well-known pro-Communist organization.

My grandmother did not hear from her beloved daughters again for a long time. Their communications stopped when the Japanese attacked Zhaocheng in April 1938 and their formation had to retreat to Fenxi county, in the Lüliang mountains. For two weeks, they made their way along rugged mountain paths every night to avoid the frequent enemy air-raids. It was the first time in her life that my mother had attempted such a trek, and the ordeal was exhausting. Not only was she young, but she had never been sturdy. A serious illness ten years before had left her thin and pale, and liable to collapse even in her physical education class at school. Now she had to keep up with her unit, carrying all her kit. Before leaving, she parted reluctantly with most of the personal belongings she had brought from home. However, even the few items she had kept now felt like a dead weight on her back. Every step hurt, because both feet were a mass of blisters. She walked with a limp, panted for breath, and regularly dropped out. Ning coped well: she was a sporty young woman. After a few days, she even found a donkey for my mother to ride. But this did not help her very much. Uphill, she slid backwards on the donkey's bare back. Downhill, she would slide towards its neck. Poor Ning had to walk beside the donkey, and prop up my mother to keep her from falling. Although no one said a word against her, my mother felt utterly embarrassed and frustrated. After the march, she told herself: 'You're not a spoiled young lady any more. You must change yourself to be a piece of useful steel in the revolutionary struggle!'

Shortly before the retreat of my mother's unit, the Communist forces started to establish bases to fight behind the Japanese lines. They used their traditional techniques of guerrilla warfare to win back many rural areas. It was a successful strategy, because the Japanese could not possibly exert total control over the vast territory captured so quickly, except to hold railway lines and urban areas. As invaders, they did not know the ground, and they also faced strong hostility from most of the population. The Communists, on the other hand, were the natives who defended their own country and were supported by their own people. Within a year, they established more than a dozen anti-Japanese bases, while their forces increased from 50,000 to 180,000.

In summer 1938, the Communist Party decided to establish an anti-Japanese base in Zhaocheng, where my mother's detachment had been based before the occupation. Having completed their training course, my mother and Ning were assigned. The team they joined was headed by a regional director of the Alliance of Sacrificing Ourselves to Save the Nation, a post equivalent to local governor at that time. In September 1938, they started to march back from Fenxi to Zhaocheng, retracing the route of their retreat five months before. But this time, most of the areas they passed through were controlled by the Japanese. Soon after they set out, my mother contracted typhoid and suffered continuing high fever. On the journey, she was carried by a hired horse-drawn cart most of the time, for she was too weak to walk.

On their way back to Zhaocheng, the most dangerous task was to cross the Tong-Pu Railway line, a main rail connection between north and south China. Japanese surveillance made it impossible to approach it by day, so the crossing had to happen at night. In pitch-darkness, the rest of my mother's unit followed a local guide, a patriotic peasant, and crawled towards the line. My mother had to take cover behind a small nearby hill, lying in the horse-drawn cart and being looked after by Ning. Suddenly, a vast expanse to either side of the railway line was lit by the glare of searchlight beams. Everyone hugged the ground and lay still. The next few minutes seemed incredibly long as they held their breath and waited for the armed Japanese patrol to pass through. When it turned dark again, the silent group jumped up swiftly and launched themselves across the railway line. My mother's chasing cart jolted so wildly over the built-up roadbed that it nearly threw her out several times.

After the Zhaocheng base had been set up, my mother's illness lasted for several more weeks, owing to the poor diet and lack of medication. She remained pale and skinny for a long time, and lost her dark glossy hair for months. When she returned to duty, Ning came to say goodbye before leaving for a new job in Fenxi. She invited my mother to join her, but she replied: 'It's time for me to be independent, you don't have to look after me any more.'

My mother was appointed deputy director of the Education

Department in the Zhaocheng base's administration, the first job ever in her life. In a district that took in half of the county's territory, her chief responsibility was to improve primary school education. Most of the time, she was busy meeting local community leaders or government officials, and trying her hardest to impress them. Unfortunately, no one took a teenage girl very seriously, and sometimes they would scoff at her proposals. The Japanese were close, and when the heavy booming of their field-guns would startle my mother, some local people teased her: 'Are you afraid of the Japanese Devils? Why don't you go to the front line and fight?' She felt like telling them off, but wondered if anyone would listen.

In October 1938, an advertisement appeared on the local government notice board announcing that the Chinese People's Anti-Japanese Military and Political University was recruiting students. Her eye was especially caught by the university's location, Yan'an, a remote city in the loess highlands in north Shaanxi, where the Communists had established the capital of their republic after the Long March. Half a year earlier, north Shaanxi had become well known in China following the publication of Edgar Snow's book, *Red Star Over China*. In 1936, this American author had broken the Nationalist censorship to visit this area where the Communists had settled. As the first Western journalist to enter Red territory, he reported on his interviews with Communist leaders such as Mao Zedong, Zhou Enlai, He Long and Peng Dehui. After the publication of its Chinese edition, *Red Star Over China* had created a great sensation in the country, as the first in-depth account of the Communists. 'I must go to Yan'an!' My mother felt the pounding of her heart.

My mother's application to Yan'an was approved. In mid-October 1938 she started her journey, together with two young men, musicians from the local government's propaganda team, who wished to study music in Yan'an. On the map, the direct distance between Zhaocheng and their destination is about 200 kilometres, but in fact they had to make a roundabout journey along mountain paths to avoid the main roads which the Japanese controlled. This time my mother was determined to cope with the journey independently.

Once again, she had to cross the Tong-Pu Railway line. This time she was ready to fight to the last if they were found by the Japanese. On a moonlit night, she and their guide crawled quietly towards the railway line, like actors in a silent film. When they were close enough, they jumped up and started running. Suddenly, the silence was broken by a chorus of dogs barking from nearby villages. 'What's happened?' My mother panicked for a moment. 'Follow me!' The guide's voice was nervous too. In her hurry, my mother stumbled over the rail on top of the roadbed, and her momentum took her rolling all the way down the slope. Soon after that, she fell into a ditch full of muddy water. She was wet through, and her clothes and luggage were soaked and dirty, but none of that could stop her feeling happy, for she had faced a dangerous task by herself.

After crossing the line they walked westwards, covering twenty to thirty kilometres every day, trying to avoid the Japanese-occupied areas. Most of the places they passed through were sinks of poverty with appalling living conditions. Soon, my mother was crawling with lice caught from the villagers who housed them every night. The continual itching plagued her, but as there was not enough water to bathe or wash her clothes, the only thing she could do was to ask village women to pick the lice off her skin. Day after day, the walk went on. Her luggage dwindled as she threw away belongings that she had grown too tired to carry. Now and then a donkey-drawn cart would give her a lift or carry her bag for a while, but mostly there was no help at all. Yet despite all the hardship, her spirits stayed high. She was no stronger than she had been, and she suffered no less than on her first expedition half a year before, but this time she was going to Yan'an, a place of hope and brightness in her mind. During halts, she joked with the others, or sang her favourite songs to the playing of their mouth organs.

After more than a week they arrived in Yonghe county in west Shanxi, where they faced the Yellow River once again. Standing on its bank, my mother was struck dumb with fear of its sunken bed, deep swift current and churning surface, which drummed with a sound like ten thousand horses stampeding. It was far more frightful than the crossing of the river near Tongguan. The ferries here were open wooden boats, pointed at the ends like the shuttles of a traditional loom, with room for only eight passengers. The boatmen, aged between twenty and fifty, were stark naked, with solid muscles showing under tanned skin that gleamed in the sunlight. To this day, my mother remembers how embarrassed she felt at a sight she had never seen before. 'I closed my eyes, but there were also loud remarks full of swear-words and rough expressions that I had never dared think about.' But she did not blame them for their rudeness. Every day, these poor men had to risk their lives to fight the murderous river. After each crossing, their bodies streamed with sweat, so that being dressed would be not only uncomfortable but also harmful, as their bodies lost heat to their sodden clothing. As well as that, the only lifesaving appliance available was a few buoys made of sheepskin. If they fell into the water, clothes would drag them under.

When they set out, the oarsmen standing at each end started a sonorous work song to synchronize their movements, 'Hei-you! Hei-you!', while steering a course over waves ten metres high. Tortured by the brown breakers and wild winds, the old wooden frame of the small boat groaned out loud, 'Ga-zhi! Ga-zhi!', as if tearing to pieces. My mother shut her eyes and clung on, till suddenly the pitch and bump from the top of a high wave shook her loose, and she screamed for help, but a strong male passenger caught her arms. 'Don't move! Stay where you are!' the boatmen yelled.

Having crossed the Yellow River, my mother arrived in Yanchuan county, Shaanxi province. From here, she entered the Communist Central Base in northwest China, known as the Shaan-Gan-Ning Border Region from its location among the three provinces of Shaanxi, Gansu and Ningxia. In China, this base area is associated with its founder, Liu Zhidan, a 'Robin Hood' figure who came from a decent rural family in a county northwest of Yan'an, and joined the Communist Party in 1925. Liu Zhidan gave up all his family holdings for revolutionary activities, and was deeply loved by the poor but hated by the rich, with a huge price set on his head by the Nationalist authorities.

By 1932, Liu Zhidan had built up a powerful Communist force. His Soviet base in north Shaanxi provided a new home for Mao Zedong and his troops after the Long March. Unfortunately, my mother could not meet him in Yan'an. In 1936, before she left home, he died in battle at the age of thirty-four. Afterwards, Bao'an, the county where he was born, was renamed Zhidan.

At the moment she set foot on Red territory, my mother was excited beyond her describing. What she saw first was the fine autumn scenery of the loess highlands. The blue sky was as clear as a vast piece of plate glass. The rolling barren hills were bathed in golden sunlight, and made her think of pictures she had seen of mighty ocean waves. The breeze brought a voice singing folk songs, and then a flock of sheep appeared, drifting along the valley's narrow paths like clusters of white cloud. The shepherd wore a handmade white jacket and black trousers, with a long wide scarlet belt around his waist, made of thick cotton. Such a peaceful scene was in great contrast with what had come before it.

'How far are we from Yan'an?' She was eager to see the Red capital.

'About 150 li [75 kilometres], little comrade,' the shepherd replied with a smile.

The rest of the journey came as a joy to my mother. When they stopped she begged the peasants for stories about 'Old Liu' (an affectionate title for Liu Zhidan) and his Red Army, or the land revolution. At last she had found her longed-for dreamland.

After more than two weeks of non-stop travelling, my mother reached Yan'an. It was late afternoon. In front of the flaming sunset, an ancient pagoda towered over a high hill – a symbol of Yan'an now familiar among the Chinese people. Immediately forgetting her tiredness, my mother ran straight up the hill with her companions, and then looked around. Set in a valley and surrounded by rolling cliffs and barren hills, the town was not large, and consisted mainly of small one-storey houses with tiled grey roofs. Most of the streets were paved with large flagstones. Through opened doors, shop-owners displayed their goods to throngs of customers. Although Yan'an was not regarded as an affluent city in China, my mother was impressed by the scene. Since the outbreak of the Sino-Japanese War, more than a year before, it was the first time she had seen people living and working in peace and content-ment. On cliffs and hills outside the town were the rows of caves where most of the Communists in Yan'an were housed during the war. People dressed in the dark grey uniforms of the Communist forces passed in and out of the caves. At the foot of the pagoda hill, the Yan River wound through the valley. My mother dashed all the way to the river bank to wash her face and hands, then closed her eyes as she tasted the clear sweet water. 'I'm home now!' she said to herself.

Chapter 5

From an Exiled Revolutionary to Leader
of the Anti-Japanese Guerrilla Forces:
My Father's Story
(1935–1940)

In autumn 1935, after the defeat of his armed insurrection against the Nationalist government, my father escaped to Tianjin. He hardly ever talked about the journey, but I know that he fled first to Yantai, a coastal city in the Shandong Peninsula, and then crossed the Bohai Gulf by ferry. It took him more than a week, far longer than the actual travel time, because the Nationalist man-hunt forced him to lie low for a few days when leaving the peninsula.

Tianjin is about 100 kilometres away from Beijing, and 50 kilometres by river from the Bohai Gulf. Due to its convenient rail links to provinces in the south, as well as geographical closeness to the north and west of the country, the city had become one of the most important industrial and commercial centres in China, next to Shanghai. At that time, flour and cotton milling were the leading industries, with many factories owned by foreigners. The city was also the chief centre of the export trade in wool and fur. Like Shanghai, Tianjin became one of the 'treaty ports' decreed under the unequal treaties imposed on China by foreign powers since 1860. During my father's time, Britain, France, Italy and Japan still kept their concessions in the city. Following the Boxer Uprising in 1900, China's imperial government had to agree not to maintain Chinese troops on the route between Beijing and the Bohai Gulf, and to allow the Western allies and Japan to station troops in Tianjin, Beijing and elsewhere.

On his arrival, my father was shocked by the sharp contrast between the extreme wealth and poverty in the city. The foreign settlements were modern, with well-paved streets and handsome buildings. They were also homes to many former mandarins and generals of China's imperial government, as well as to various warlords. Puyi, China's last emperor, lived in the Japanese Concession for seven years after being overthrown by Dr Sun Yat-sen's revolution, until he was transferred to become the puppet ruler of Japanese-occupied Manchuria at the end of 1931.

The city's slum areas, where the majority of Chinese residents lived, were crammed with hovels built of straw and mud. In the absence of sanitary facilities and a sewerage system, these areas smelled foul throughout the year, and the stench was especially unbearable in summer. Malnourished children teemed on the streets. Barefoot and ragged, they tried to help their families to survive by begging or by scavenging through rubbish.

My father sought refuge with Xing Long, a former member of his 'Misty World Literature Society', but soon after that Xing Long had to leave Tianjin and join his parents, because he could not find a job. Left alone in a city where he knew no one and had no money, in order to survive he tried various temporary jobs, such as private tutoring for children of well-to-do families, but mostly he would set out a desk and two chairs in a main street of the slums and write letters for local people. Occasionally, he wrote short articles for local newspapers or magazines.

All this time he was seeking to get back in touch with the Communist organization. Although the insurrection had been crushed, his belief in revolution had not wavered. During his exile, he changed his name from 'Mu Xiansong' to 'Mu Xiang'. 'Xiang' was the abbreviation for Xiangtan, the home county of Mao Zedong, and to express such admiration for Mao was a dangerous gesture at a time when Tianjin was ruled by Nationalists and by foreign occupying powers, and the Communist Party was illegal. These were the days before the Sino-Japanese War broke out. The Anti-Japanese United Front lay two years in the future, and meanwhile people could face arrest, imprisonment and possibly death, merely for voicing pro-Communist views. Under the 'white terror', the Party organization had to remain underground, and made itself deliberately hard to contact.

In the autobiographical note my father wrote in December 1952 at the Party's request, he mentioned his feelings during his forced exile in Tianjin:

> I felt terribly lonely and depressed. I knew only a few factory workers in Tianjin, whom I met through Xing Long. I lived in a small room with one of the workers. Where could I find our Party in that vast sea of people in the city? . . . For about half a year, I was like a child who had lost his way. I felt that I had no other choice but to continue the revolution . . .

On 9 December 1935, just a few months after my father's arrival in Tianjin, over 6,000 students went on to the streets in Beijing, protesting against the Japanese invasion of China and calling on the Nationalist government to stop the civil war against the Communists. This heralded the '12.9 [9 December] Movement' famous in Chinese history. Armed police and troops suppressed the demonstration, and the number of students arrested or injured shocked the nation. Soon many major cities saw similar demonstrations. Tianjin was the site of several important universities, with a large student population, and for decades had been known for its key role in China's democratic movements. The active figures in the earlier days included Zhou Enlai and his wife, Madam Deng Yinchao. Now, as the '12.9 Movement' grew, thousands of students joined their Beijing counterparts and travelled to the south of China, launching the anti-Japanese campaign.

From the very beginning, my father took an active part in the student demonstrations in Tianjin, and sensed – quite rightly – that the movement must be led by the Communist Party. The Party's underground organization was soon impressed by his enthusiasm, as well as by the skills in running revolutionary activities developed through his previous student experience. But the rule of secrecy was strict: no one from the Party underground was allowed to disclose their political identity to him, because he had no way to prove his Party membership. He was treated as a pro-Communist activist and admitted to the Tianjin student union, a legal organization actually controlled by the Communist underground.

In summer 1936, my father was assigned by the student union to launch a patriotic campaign among peasants in the suburbs of Tianjin. First, he went to Wanglan village and established an evening school for peasants. Through this work, he soon won over the local community, and was put in charge of the village school. His growing influence in the locality enabled him to organize many patriotic activities, and he established a secret organization called the 'Society for Resisting Japan to Save Our Nation' among the peasants, as well as organising peasant resistance against the fiscal extortion imposed by the Nationalist authority. In this area, a major income for peasants came from salt production, but the business was monopolized by the government, which charged a heavy duty on transactions. Through my father's efforts, many peasants began to recognize that the heavy taxes and levies were unfair, and so refused to pay them. When armed police were sent to suppress this opposition, my father led the peasants to fight back and burn their vehicles.

It was during this period that my grandparents learned my father's whereabouts through Xing Long. My grandfather went straight to Tianjin, and spent several days trying to convince his eldest son to give up the idea of revolution. He was baffled by my father's behaviour. Since joining the Communists, he had sacrificed his personal life and endured unthinkable dangers and hardships. Yet here he was again, shabbily dressed and living like a poor peasant. Before taking charge of the school, he had no proper income at all, because all his time was spent on his revolutionary activities, and the Tianjin Student Union only paid for his food. Now that he did have an income, he donated most of it to patriotic activities. Knowing that his eldest son still worked for the Communists, my grandfather feared for his safety. 'Please come home with me,' he begged. 'Why risk your life?' But my father's mind remained unchanged. From the time he joined the Communists at the age of sixteen, no one and nothing could deter him.

In December 1936, as a result of the sensational Xi'an Incident, President Chiang Kai-shek agreed to stop the anti-Communist Civil War and to resist Japanese invasion. Immediately afterwards, my father was assigned to Taiyuan by the Communist Party's underground to participate in the anti-Japanese movement. His revolutionary activities in Wanglan village had finally revealed him as a Communist, and the local Nationalist authority had ordered his arrest. He could not remain in Tianjin.

Taiyuan is one of the major historic cities of northern China. It is the provincial capital of Shanxi, and lies about 400 kilometres southwest of Beijing. During my father's time, the city was surrounded by a wall about ten kilometres around. Two broad streets ran north and south and two to the east and west, connecting the eight gates and dividing the city into rectangles. Decades later, my father told me how impressed he was by the city's fine streets and ancient trees.

Shanxi had been ruled by General Yan Xishan, the warlord governor, after Sun Yat-sen's revolution in 1911. When Chiang Kai-shek established his Nationalist government in Nanjing after his coup against the Communists in 1927, Yan Xishan became one of the strongest warlords in China, controlling several provinces in the north with about a quarter of a million troops. He rapidly fell out with Chiang Kai-shek, because of their conflicting self-interests, and in 1930 he launched a war against Chiang in alliance with General Feng Yuxiang, another warlord based in the north of China. It lasted seven months, and mobilized over a million troops. When Chiang won the war, Yan Xishan had to flee to Manchuria and received support from the Japanese. In 1931, after Manchuria was occupied by Japan, he regained his rulership of Shanxi.

Now, as the Japanese made obvious preparations to occupy the north of China, which included Shanxi province, the General began to detach himself. In face of threats from both the Japanese and Chiang Kai-shek, he had to turn to the Communists, despite his previous hostility. Even before the Xi'an Incident, he had agreed to establish a united front with them against the Japanese aggression. At his invitation, the Party assigned a number of senior members to Taiyuan, under the leadership of Bo Yibo, later to become a statesman under the Communist regime. Bo Yibo was put in charge of the Alliance of Sacrificing Ourselves to Save the Nation, founded by Yan Xishan. Under Communist control, it developed rapidly. In early 1938, the formation that my mother joined belonged to the same organization.

On his arrival in Taiyuan, late in 1936, my father joined a training course run by the Alliance. Yan Xishan wanted to muster an extra 300,000 troops in the province, to counter the Japanese threat, and it fell to the Alliance to train the necessary personnel. As one of the earliest trainees, my father found that among his colleagues were young people not only from the province but also from many other parts of China, including major cities such as Beijing, Tianjin and Shanghai. The developments in Shanxi had attracted patriotic youngsters from all over China, and the Communists also assigned many members to work for the Alliance. It was on his training course that my father met a former leader in the Party's underground in Shandong Peninsula, who helped him to resume his Party membership.

During our conversations several decades later, I was struck by my father's passionate descriptions of the patriotic atmosphere in Taiyuan. In the Lantern Festival of 1937, two weeks after the Chinese New Year, about 10,000 people, one tenth of the city's population, took part in a demonstration organized by the Alliance. They all carried paper lanterns displaying anti-Japanese slogans. Never in the history of the province had the public responded so strongly to a political campaign.

My father, already a group leader, often brought his course mates to visit the city's residential areas, busy streets, factories or even the Nationalist troops' barracks. They sang patriotic songs to the crowds, such as 'On the Song-hua River':

My home is on the Song-hua River in Manchuria.
There are forests, coalmines,
and fields of soy-beans and sorghum all over the countryside . . .
From the 18th of September [1931], that tragic moment,
I fled away from my home town leaving behind the everlasting
    treasure.
Tramping, tramping,
every day, everywhere . . .
Dear father! Dear mother!
When may we return to our lovely home town?
When may we regain our everlasting treasure?

Very often their singing had to stop because both the choir and the audience were choked with sobs. After the singing, the emotional crowds gave back my father's shout of: 'Down with the Japanese imperialists!'

In July 1937, the month that the Sino-Japanese War broke out, my father completed his training and was assigned to represent the Alliance in a county on the outskirts of Taiyuan. As usual in that province, the Communist Party had no organization in place there, so as well as launching the anti-Japanese campaign, my father had orders to create one. In this he faced strong opposition from the Society of Justice (Gong-dao-tuan), an anti-Communist organization founded by General Yan Xishan and with branches all over the province, even at village level. For years this organization, based on the local rich and on government officials, had underpinned Yan Xishan's control of Shanxi. Its new function was to restrict the influence of the Communists within the Anti-Japanese United Front. In almost every county, the key political division now fell between the Society of Justice and the Communist-controlled Alliance.

During his mission, my father often found the Society of Justice taking action to bar peasants from supporting patriotic activities launched by the Alliance. Local government officials imposed higher taxes on poor peasants, supposedly for purposes such as buying military supplies for the anti-Japanese forces, but often to line their own pockets. My father found it hard to curb the hatred he felt for the corrupt officials and local tyrants whom earlier in his revolutionary career he had regarded as enemies, but now he had to work with them. As a Communist, he sincerely supported the Party's policy of cooperating with all possible social groups against the Japanese invasion, and he tried his best to rally their support.

By September 1937, Japanese troops had occupied north Shanxi, and were approaching Taiyuan. At this crucial time, Zhou Enlai, deputy-chairman of the Communist Party, arrived in the city. On behalf of the Party, he talked to General Yan Xishan about improving the United Front and conveyed messages to the Alliance. In a speech given at a conference of the Alliance, he declared: 'I hope that the Alliance will lead and organize to arm people in Shanxi against the Japanese invasion, to defend Shanxi, defend the north of China and defend the whole country!' It was the first time that my father had seen Zhou Enlai in person, and he was hugely impressed by the passion and sharpness he showed. After the conference, my father started to train Alliance activists in his county, in readiness for a guerrilla war. For the rest of his life, the autumn of 1937 remained a landmark in his mind.

On 8 November 1937, Taiyuan fell into Japanese hands, as did many other nearby towns and cities. Major railways and roads in the province were cut by the Japanese. Having fled to the south of Shanxi, General Yan Xishan found that most of the troops he had commanded for years had melted away after high-ranking officers abandoned the front line. In this emergency, Yan Xishan became more reliant on the Alliance and its guerrilla forces.

Three days after the occupation of Taiyuan, my father led his raw guerrilla force in its disciplined withdrawal to the mountain areas out-side Taiyuan. His troops were mostly members of the Communist Party or Alliance activists. They came from various backgrounds – school-teachers, students, peasants – and were poorly equipped. It was early winter. Villages in many areas they passed through had been reduced to rubble by Japanese air-raids, and the roads were filled with refugees who had seen their homes destroyed and family members killed.

But the most unbelievable sight was the terrible looting and violence inflicted on villagers and refugees by Yan Xishan's own troops. Many had turned into bandits, and tried to boost their strength by forcing people they captured to join them. Several times along their way to the moun-tain areas, the guerrilla forces almost became captives of these routed troops.

Following the Japanese occupation of Taiyuan, the Communist Party started to establish its own resistance bases in the north of China, fight-ing behind the enemy lines. Once Chiang Kai-shek had agreed to establish the Anti-Japanese United Front, the Communist forces, known as the Red Army, began to receive support from the Nationalist gov-ernment. The Red Army in north China was reorganized into the Eighth

Route Army, while those who had remained in the south and did not participate in the Long March became the New Fourth Army. The Communist forces also included various newly established guerrilla groups in other areas, such as the one my father founded.

My father's force was accepted by the provincial United Front, and named the Taiyuan Detachment. By then, its numbers had expanded to more than 1,000, so it was rated at the level of a regiment, and my father was appointed as Political Commissar, with a permanent armed body-guard. Sometimes, people confused the two men's roles. It was unthinkable that the detachment could have been founded and com-manded by a man only twenty-one years old, with a gentle manner.

My father was delighted when a former Red Army officer, a survivor of the Long March, was assigned to command his detachment. In my father's mind, a Red Army veteran was a revolutionary hero, and it was an honour to work with him. Commander Gao was much less impressed by his new colleague. While he himself was nearing his thirties, came from a peasant background and had only a limited education, my father was an educated urbanite, very young, and with no experience of com-manding troops or the guerrilla life. But despite his commander's reservations, my father behaved with respect, and gradually Commander Gao was moved by his manner and impressed by his ability. Within months, the two became good friends.

The Commander-in-Chief of the resistance forces in Shanxi was the Nationalist Lieutenant-General Xu Fanting, a veteran of Dr Sun Yat-sen's revolution in 1911. About two years before, in December 1935, he had shocked the whole nation by attempting hara-kiri inside Sun Yat-sen's Mausoleum in Nanjing, in an effort to shame Chiang Kai-shek into fighting against the Japanese invasion. Guards found him and rushed him to hospital, and hence his life was saved.

By the time the Xi'an Incident took place in December 1936, Xu Fanting had become an influential figure in the Northwest Army and had moved to Xi'an. He strongly supported the action. It was during this episode that Xu Fanting met Zhou Enlai, when he came to Xi'an to help to solve the crisis. Xu Fanting welcomed what he heard from Zhou Enlai about the Communist aim for an Anti-Japanese United Front. He came to believe that only the Communists were able to save China, and when the Japanese advanced into Shanxi he was influential in convincing General Yan Xishan to cooperate with the Communists. His special social position and connections made him a leading figure in the United Front throughout the Sino-Japanese War, which helped the Communists to control many anti-Japanese resistance forces in northern China. He died soon after the war, in 1947, at the age of fifty-five, having never fully recovered from the self-inflicted injury suffered in 1935. By his own wish, he was posthumously admitted as a member of the Communist Party. Mao Zedong, Zhu De, Zhou Enlai and other Communist leaders sent elegiac couplets or telegrams of condolence to mourn his death.

When he first met my father and Commander Gao in 1938, Lieutenant-General Xu Fanting told them: 'Although we've never met before, I've heard a lot about you. The enemy radio and newspapers are always announcing your deaths. Like the heroes of legend, you never lose your lives, no matter how many times your heads are cut off by enemy propaganda.'

By early 1938, my father's guerrilla force was famous in the mountain area in the west of Shanxi where it was based. In 1966, he visited this area again, for the first time since he left in 1940, and was treated like a living legend. When they heard about his return, local people lined the streets for miles to welcome him.

Despite the foundation of the Anti-Japanese United Front, power struggles between the Communists and the Nationalists had never stopped. When Chiang Kai-shek promoted the vision of 'one party and one leader' for China, his purpose was to restrict the increasing influence of the Communists. He also took steps to tighten control over all political activities in the Nationalist areas, and repeated military clashes between the two parties culminated in the blockade of the Communist bases.

General Yan Xishan was equally hostile to the growth of Communist influence in his province. By February 1938, he had lost most of his territory to the Japanese, and the bulk of his forces had collapsed. The Communists, by contrast, had established solid bases and continued to build up their forces. Although he held a leading position in the Anti-Japanese United Front in Shanxi province, Yan Xishan now had no power to control the Alliance and most of the newly established resistant forces. In summer 1938, addressing senior officers of his remaining forces, he informed them: 'Since the war broke out, we have lost almost everything, but the Eighth Route Army just keeps expanding. In addition, the Alliance and their forces have cooperated with the Communists and the Eighth Route Army. So where does that leave us in the future?' Under the general instructions he issued to reduce the size of the Communist-controlled resistance forces, my father's detachment was downgraded from regiment to battalion, and his rank from Political Commissar to Political Instructor.

From winter 1939 to spring 1940, conflicts within the United Front intensified, and Communist historians call this the period of the Nationalists' First Anti-Communist Campaign during the Sino-Japanese War. In December 1939, Yan Xishan launched military attacks against the Communist-controlled resistance forces with his remaining crack troops, aiming to drive the Communists out of his province. The first target of this action was the resistance forces stationed in the west of Shanxi, which included my father's troops. At the same time, these troops also faced the Japanese army, as well as harassment from local bandits based on Yan Xishan's routed troops.

Under these pressures, my father's troops went to ground in a remote mountain district in the northwest of the province, where some communities had been living in isolation for centuries. The Communist-controlled resistance forces suffered heavy casualties from their assortment of enemies, but they also faced internal troubles. Many officers formerly attached to the Nationalists started to collaborate with the outside anti-Communist powers, and tried to launch armed revolts. During the chaos, many Communist officers were assassinated or kidnapped. Supplies were another serious problem. Those previously agreed by Yan Xishan dwindled and stopped, and the new base area was known for its poverty. Many troops lacked warm winter clothes, and the sick and wounded could not be treated.

In that critical situation, prolonged mental strain and a heavy workload eventually took their toll on my father's health, and he fell ill with typhoid fever. For three days, he burned with fever and kept on losing consciousness. No modern drugs were available, the herbs prescribed by local folk doctors did not work, and his condition was deteriorating. As a last resort, Lieutenant-General Xu Fanting recommended a retired folk doctor, over eighty years old, to save my father's life, but his prescriptions failed to quell the fever. In desperation, he started to tell my father a story:

Many years ago, there was a wealthy landlord, who treated his baby boy, his only son, like a precious treasure. One day, the baby fell ill, and the doctors were helpless to cure him, but just when he looked certain to die, an old man arrived and promised that he could save the boy's life. 'How much grain is in store in your house?' the old man asked the landlord. 'Several hundred dans' [1 dan = 50 kilograms]. 'Please have all of it carried to the areas where poor people live, and then exchange the grain for lice from the poor, one sheng [= 1 litre] of grain for each louse. The more lice the better.' Forced by his love for his son, the landlord agreed, and spent his whole store of grain on a bag of lice. The ailing baby was then undressed, and placed in a manger with his arms and legs tied up. The old man opened the bag and poured all this swarm of lice into the manger. Soon, the baby's body was alive with these countless wriggling creatures, and likewise his face, his nose, his ears, his neck . . .

'Oh no, I'm gooseflesh all over!' my horrified father interrupted. All at once he was gushing with sweat. The old doctor touched his wet forehead, and sighed with relief: 'Well, my story is done, and your condition is improving.' When my father saw the purpose of the story, he was struck with admiration. Now that he was sweating, the fever subsided and he started to recover. In my childhood, this was a story he loved to tell.

One day my father was summoned to an official meeting, together with other senior officers of the resistance forces. Among the documents provided to each participant, he found a booklet, clumsily mimeographed, entitled *On Protracted War*, written by Mao Zedong and based on a seminar he gave in Yan'an in May 1938. As soon as he started reading, he could not take his eyes off the pages. Many years later, he recalled the flood of his excitement as he saw how many of the questions about the war that he had faced and found insoluble were answered in this booklet, along with other important issues that he had not even considered. By comparing the military and socio-economic resources of China and Japan, Mao pointed out that the Communists must give up any fantasy of quick success, and discussed the necessity for a protracted campaign of guerrilla warfare against the Japanese invasion. According to Mao, China would pass through three strategic stages: defence, which referred to the current situation, stalemate, and counterattack. No matter how much military superiority the Japanese showed now, the final victory must belong to China. 'It was as if I reached the top of a mountain and saw the panorama all around,' my father recalled. 'Through this booklet, I could foretell the direction the war would take, and see why we were facing such complicated situations at that time, and how we could deal with our problems.'

Straight away, my father set about organising his troops to study Mao Zedong's booklet. He had it reprinted and provided each platoon with a copy. In lulls between the fighting, he wrote further comments for his troops, and gave a series of seminars to his officers, based on his own study of Mao's ideas. Often he worked until dawn. Through his efforts, the troops absorbed the confidence, and the clear perspective about the war, that he himself had gained through studying Mao's booklet.

According to Communist historians, the guiding principles in handling the Nationalists' Anti-Communist Campaign derived from Mao Zedong's instruction that the priority was to preserve China's Anti-Japanese United Front. Yan Xishan was still influential in the north of China, and the Communists were reluctant to involve themselves in a civil war against him, especially while he stayed with the Front. A number of Communist leaders paid him visits, trying to convince him to stop his military actions against the Alliance, but he took no notice until his attacks were defeated by the Communist forces in early 1940. In February, two envoys delivered Mao Zedong's personal letter to Yan Xishan, appealing for a peaceful settlement. This time, Yan Xishan had no choice but to call a cease-fire. Around that time, other hostile actions launched by Chiang Kai-shek were also defeated, and so the First Anti-Communist Campaign was over. Although political struggles still went on, the Anti-Japanese United Front did not break up.

In summer 1940, my father's application to study in Yan'an was approved. He was accepted by the Academy of Military and Political Affairs, an institute established to train senior Communist military officers from the level of regimental commander. By then, the Communist base in northwest Shanxi had expanded fast, following the defeat of the Nationalists' Anti-Communist Campaign, in which my father and his troops played a key part. Later, it became part of the Jin-Sui base, a major Communist base during the Sino-Japanese War.

Chapter 6

Growing up in Yan'an:
My Mother in the Communist Capital
during the Sino-Japanese War

(1938–1942)

At the end of October 1938, my mother arrived in Yan'an, in the loess highlands, to study at the Chinese People's Anti-Japanese Military and Political University, founded in 1937 and known for short in Chinese as Kang-da. Ever since becoming the Red capital, Yan'an had been crammed with Communist officials and troops. The first Japanese air bombardment in winter 1938 nearly reduced the city to rubble, and created an acute shortage of housing. My mother's university occupied several earthen cliffs outside the town, where staff and students lived in rows of dug-out caves. In the previous year, students had had to excavate their accommodation while studying. Most of the caves were dug high on the hillside in order to avoid summer floods, and they averaged about 15–20 square metres in area. Conditions were primitive, with no electricity, tap-water or sewerage. The entrance was blocked by wooden doors and a small window fitted with a pane of paper, since glass was not available in Yan'an. At night, the glimmer of oil-lamps shining through rows and rows of paper windows made the cliffs twinkle in the dark.

In China, my mother's university was the most famous institution for training Communist personnel. Mao Zedong, the Communist leader since 1935, held a concurrent post as chairman of the university's education committee and lectured to students regularly. The university chancellor was Lin Biao, who became Mao's heir-apparent in the 1960s. The duration of each course varied from three months to one year, but normally it lasted from six to eight months. The two major courses taught were military affairs and politics, which my mother attended. Her subjects included history of social development, the Communist Party's ideology and organization, the Anti-Japanese United Front, and war strategy and tactics. The teaching was functional and practical, its contents based mainly on the Party's political requirements.

Before her enrolment, my mother spent a few days in the university's guest house. 'The place was like a busy fairground,' she recollected. Every day there were new arrivals. Like my mother, most of them had only lately joined the revolution. They came from all over China, some even from abroad, and their family background varied from peasants or industrial workers to the rich. Some came from the ruling class in China, such as Zhang Xuesi, younger brother of the Young Marshal Zhang Xueliang. No entrance examination or educational qualification was required, and the only document necessary was a reference letter from the local Communist organization in the area where the applicant came from.

My mother's first amazement was the enormous size of the university, which as well as the headquarters in Yan'an had other branches located in the major Communist bases. From 1937 to 1945, more than 100,000 students graduated, and were assigned to various posts in locations mainly decided by the Party. Hence it could happen that husband and wife, or fiancé and fiancée, were posted to different areas and did not see each other for years. For those sent to Nationalist or Japanese-occupied areas, the names used in Yan'an had to be changed. The security of the Party's underground required them to break contact with their

family and friends. No one complained. 'Obey the Party' was a fundamental rule for each member.

Most of the students were men, and there were only two classes for
women. When she first met her class, my mother was welcomed by a
group of friendly young women in army uniforms. In front of her new
classmates, she blushed for shyness as well as for her squalid appearance.
After the march to Yan'an, she had nothing left but the lice that infested
and continually plagued her, yet she could not replace the filthy rags she
wore because with her family out of reach she was penniless. Nor could
she obtain a new uniform until the following year, owing to the long
supply lines to Yan'an.

On the first evening, her classmates fetched a bucket of hot water
from the canteen – a big cave at the foot of a cliff, which had the sole
supply on the campus. They helped my mother to wash her hair and
body, then dressed her in their own clean clothes, from underwear to
uniform. Afterwards, they held up an oil-lamp to examine my mother's
face, and told her with a warm smile: 'What a smart little revolutionary
devil ["Xiao-gui" in Chinese – a term of endearment for a teenage
recruit] you are!'

As the youngest of her classmates, my mother was treated like a
little sister. To get rid of the lice, they washed her clothes and hair
again and again. Then when the lice disappeared she was troubled
again by sarcoptic mites and the terrible itching they caused. Every
evening, her classmates took turns to fetch hot water and help her to
bathe. When the doctor prescribed it, they applied sulphur ointment
to her skin, and then lighted hay in an empty cave to fumigate her
naked body for hours. It was dark outside, and a torch was a luxury in
Yan'an, so her classmates often fell while fetching water, especially
when the ground was under snow. Their buckets went rolling down the
cliff, the spilt hot water sometimes scalded them, and it frequently
took several trips to fetch enough hot water. When at last she recovered, after two months of treatment, her classmates clapped and

cheered: 'Hurrah for our victory!' Tears rose to her eyes, and her heart was warmed by love.

My mother shared a cave with nine classmates. In each cave, there was only a bare wooden desk for studying, and an earthen kang for sleeping, which gave each student half a metre's width. It was hard to find room again after visiting the toilet, so she must ease herself gently in between two deeply sleeping classmates. The female toilet, located on a higher level of the cliff, consisted of some holes dug in the ground and surrounded by straw mats that functioned as walls. In winter, the frozen Yan River looked like a crystal belt below, but the view gave no comfort to my mother as she stumbled up the slippery icy path. In summer when it rained, everything turned to mud, especially inside the roofless toilet. Each visit at night was an ordeal, because she was still scared of the dark. For quite a while she had to ask for company.

In Yan'an, climbing was a daily routine. For each meal, my mother went down and up between her cave, which was halfway up the cliff, to the canteen at its foot. Their dining area was a piece of open ground in front of the kitchen. When the weather was bad, they brought the food back to their quarters, one student clearing the way on the slippery path while her partner balanced two heavy buckets. My mother was rarely assigned to such an important duty, in case she fell and spilled the precious ration.

Their diet was poor and meagre, and based on millet, which was only used for feeding birds at home. Unpeeled potatoes boiled in a dark and tasteless sauce were the only dish available for most of the year; the sight made her sick. Sometimes, their food had gone mouldy and stank, but it was all there was and they had to eat it. Twice a month, a few pieces of meat, bean curd or egg were found in their dishes. To satisfy their craving, students invented a popular game, the imaginary feast, and competed to describe the delicious remembered flavours of their home town.

Most of the time, students attended lectures in the open air, as there were very few classrooms. Their writing equipment was self-made: a nib fixed into a pen-holder, usually a chopstick or twig; ink made of dark dyestuff with water. They sat on the ground and took notes on their laps. Summer was best for studying, being mostly warm and dry. The winter brought deep snows and bitter winds, and their clothes were too flimsy to protect them. They had no boots or overcoats, and their feet and ungloved hands became numbed and chilblained. After lectures, my mother often found that her ink was frozen in the bottle.

After the course started, my mother was elected as her class representative because she had the highest educational level. 'But I am the youngest,' she protested, 'and I have no revolutionary experience. How can I take on such an important responsibility?' It was her classmates' support that reassured her and fed her enthusiasm as she helped them to take lecture notes or revise their written work. At the end of the year, her class was praised by the university for its performance. Her confidence grew, and she felt lucky to have met so many nice people in her class, though later she discovered that every other class felt the same. 'How wonderful Yan'an is!' she said to herself. 'I must join the Communist Party!'

Here a problem arose. The rules required my mother to contact the Party's organization in the university to apply for membership. But membership remained confidential in the university, even in the Red capital itself, as a security measure in case graduates went to work in hostile areas. In December 1938, my mother was approached by Chen Po, a classmate who was already a secret Communist. Privately, they had discussed their attitudes towards the Party and the revolution. One day Chen Po suggested: 'Would you like to join the Communist Party with me? Shall we try to contact the organization?' My mother agreed at once, but how to make the contact? Chen Po replied with an understanding smile.

A few days later, my mother was overjoyed to hear that she had been accepted as a Communist, even though she was only fifteen – three years younger than the stipulated minimum age. 'Considering Comrade Xu Jing's good performance in the university and her mature revolutionary consciousness,' according to Chen Po's reference, 'it is worthwhile to make an exception . . .' My mother was bursting with pride, and longed to tell everyone that she had joined the revolutionary family, but the rules forbade it. So because she could not share her happiness openly she worked even harder to improve herself, amazing her classmates through the progress she made with everyday chores such as washing her clothes and cleaning the cave. Looking at my mother's cheerful face, they smiled and said: 'How wonderful! Our little revolutionary devil has grown up!'

By 1939, life in Yan'an was getting harder. The Communist Central Base, the Shaan-Gan-Ning Border Region where Yan'an is located, was known for its harsh climate and barren, hilly land, and the influx of Communists was bound to put a strain on its resources. During winter 1939 to spring 1940, repeated military clashes with the Nationalists culminated in the blockade of the Communist bases. Outside Yan'an, Chiang Kai-shek's troops occupied several counties, intending to attack the Red capital. People travelling to Yan'an to join the Communists faced imprisonment, even execution, if arrested.

Inside the Red capital, clothes, food, medicine and other necessities ran critically low. Students used salt as a substitute for toothpaste, and plant-ash to wash their hair and clothes. Winter clothing was issued in every second year, instead of yearly. In the hospital, patients underwent operations without anaesthesia, and mechanical pliers were used to pull teeth.

In order to break the economic blockade, Mao Zedong proposed his famous policy: 'through our own efforts to provide ample food and clothing'. In spring 1939, the university sent students and staff to reclaim uncultivated land in an outlying mountain area, and my mother was assigned to a team with people from other classes. Every day, they set out at dawn, carrying their simple lunch and heavy pickaxes. Their journey was only 10 kilometres, but the mountains outside Yan'an were dense with undergrowth, and it was hard going to reach the uncultivated land along the dales. If someone slipped and fell on the dewy grass, stones would go rolling down the cliffs, and frightened birds break cover. By the time they reached their destination, my mother was already out of breath and streaming with sweat.

First they lit bonfires, to clear the ground. The blaze and roar excited the young pioneers, and their cheering broke the silence of the empty cliffs and dales. The next task was to turn up the soil for planting. My mother stood with a long row of her teammates, hacking with her pickaxe at the ground, which was hard and dry and thick with plant roots. Most of the time, my mother's pickaxe rebounded as if from a rock, and left hardly a scratch. The pickaxe grew heavier as her arms grew weaker. Soon her male teammates had finished their work, but my mother lagged far behind, frustrated and running with sweat. 'Don't worry, Little Xu,' came the voice of their team chief, Zhong Yi. 'Please go easy and do what you can.' Then her teammates attacked the field from the opposite end, and so my mother's quota was completed.

After the first day's work, my mother's palms were blistered raw, her back and legs ached, and her whole body felt disjointed. Back in her cave in Yan'an, she collapsed onto the kang and did not stir till morning. But she kept going back, and gradually her labours toughened her body. By the end of the spring, she could manage half her quota on her own. In the autumn, these pioneers reaped their first harvest. For a couple of weeks, they cut the ripe millet with sickles, and humped it back to town on their backs. For ever after, my mother could not bear to see food wasted. I still remember that at home she would pick up rice spilled by her children on the table and eat it at once. In her mind, every grain meant blisters and aching backs. Her farming experiences taught her what hard lives countless millions of Chinese peasants had endured. She felt as if reborn into the proletariat, a different person from the one her birth had made her.

In July 1939, as proposed by Mao Zedong, the Chinese Women's University was established in Yan'an, the first institution for training women Communist cadres. Altogether about 1,000 students graduated, most of whom later held senior positions in Communist China, from government ministers to university chancellors. In the first year, the 500 students enrolled included those in the two female classes from the University of Resistance where my mother studied. Many of the students had been to school or university. There were also a few special classes for veterans of the Red Army or local women cadres, often illiterate or semi-literate, owing to their peasant background.

On a beautiful summer day, my mother arrived in the Women's University, together with her classmates from the University of Resistance. Dressed neatly in army uniforms, each girl carried a bedroll on her back, and had an olive-green cotton bag slung over the left shoulder. Their team chief was Madam Ding Xuesong, later to become China's first woman ambassador when appointed to the Netherlands in the 1970s.

The new university was located by the Yan River, near the pagoda hill. Months of work by hundreds of labourers had dug more than a hundred caves into a hillside, together with three classrooms and an assembly hall. Two armed women guards flanked the entrance. A smiling female officer took the newcomers on a tour around the campus. In each cave, there was a massive plank bed for eight to ten students sleeping together, instead of the earthen kang, which was a special treat for these girls. By the foot of a cliff, there was a simple shower room – a luxury in Yan'an. The campus rang with laughter and cheerful greetings. 'I like this place!' my mother thought.

On 20 July 1939, the campus was jubilant, waiting for the opening ceremony. The front gate was decorated with an arch of fresh branches and green leaves. To either side, spectacular red characters announced the university's motto: 'Hard work, plain living, high morality, and help for others'. On top of the entrance, there were portraits including Dr Sun Yat-sen, Mao Zedong and Chiang Kai-shek, as well as prominent figures in the international women's movement such as Clara Zitkin, Nadezhda Krupskaya and Soong Chingling (Madam Sun Yat-sen). Dressed in their best uniforms, my mother and her classmates stood by the entrance welcoming each guest.

The ceremony was held in the assembly hall of the Central Party School, as the university had no room for so many guests. It was scheduled at three o'clock in the afternoon, possibly because Mao Zedong, the guest of honour, normally worked at night and slept in the morning. After lunch, the assembly hall was crammed with cheerful students. Laughter and singing almost raised the roof. Suddenly, my mother heard a shout: 'Jiang Qing [Madam Mao]!' Outside the hall, a slim young woman had just arrived on horseback. She looked artistic in a smart white suit with stylish baggy trousers, and dark hair carefully tied in two short bunches. Jiang Qing had worked as an actress in Shanghai, and had married Mao Zedong soon after she reached Yan'an.

When Mao came on to the platform, the audience's shouting turned to thunderous applause. Among Communists, Mao was known for his casual style of dress. At the ceremony, he appeared in a well-worn grey uniform, with big dark patches on his trousers and his jacket pockets stuffed with books and newspapers. He wore no cap, and his long dark hair nearly covered his ears, which was unusual in Yan'an. Seeing him dressed so plainly, my mother thought: 'How equal it is between our leader and us!'

Mao sauntered on and waved to the audience. Following his tall figure came other leading Party officials such as Zhu De and Zhou Enlai, and delegates of the fighting forces such as Deng Xiaoping and Zhang Dingcheng. The audience sang the Internationale and the university's anthem, before listening to a speech from their chancellor,

Wang Ming, the former leader of the Communist Party, who had returned from Moscow at the end of 1937. Mao's speech came next. It was brief, but not easy to understand, especially for those who came from north China, owing to his strong Hunan accent – his home province. Fortunately, it was no problem for my mother, as she had heard him give lectures. Mao was in high spirits, no doubt pleased to see his project under way. At the end of his speech, he stubbed out his cigarette and raised his voice: 'The day that all Chinese women arise will be the time that the revolution triumphs!' His statement brought roars of applause.

There were many similarities between the courses taught in the Women's University and the University of Resistance, as they focused on political training and were given by famous theorists and senior Party members. One day a week, students focused on two selected subjects such as Accounting, Bookkeeping, Tailoring, Media Communication, Literature, Drama or Music. The foreign language courses included English, Russian, Japanese and Esperanto. The list of the lecturers in these selected subjects was like a *Who's Who* of contemporary China – names such as Xian Xinghai, who was regarded as 'China's Beethoven' and Madam Ding Ling, a famous woman writer. Their lecturer in Russian was Huang Zheng-guang, a Vietnamese Communist who had studied in Russia for many years. He returned to Vietnam years later, and became Minister of Education under the Communist regime. In no subject were there textbooks provided, except for a few printed sheets, so it was essential for students to take notes during lectures.

By the end of 1939, the Party had begun to operate openly inside the institutions in Yan'an, mainly because the Communists had strengthened their bases, and extended their influence in the Nationalist areas. In the Women's University, the Communist members met twice a week, which was upsetting for those excluded. At these meetings, my mother heard special lectures given by leaders such as Mao Zedong, Zhu De and

Zhou Enlai, and other senior members such as Liu Shaoqi, Deng
Xiaoping and Deng Yinchao (Madam Zhou). The major topics were
politics and the women's movement, with special emphasis on revolutionary integrity. Students were told, for example, how to work for the
Party's underground in enemy-occupied areas, how to cope with interrogation and torture if arrested, and how to keep the Party's secrets. One
lecture was on dealing with their love affairs correctly. It was said that
the key was to place the revolutionary cause and their private lives in the
proper order, in other words, to put the Party's interests first.

Life in the university was dominated by iron military rules and an
intensive schedule. A student's day started at half-past four in the morning and finished at eight in the evening. At midnight, they were woken
up by emergency alarms for war exercises. They had to dress and pack
their kit in the dark, then sling their bedrolls over their backs and spend
hours marching through valleys and climbing cliffs. For most it was a
very tough experience, especially because they slept in such crowded
conditions, and in their hurry they often grabbed someone else's shoes,
or donned the wrong clothes. But nothing could diminish the revolutionary passion and youthful spirit among these girls. Despite their
poor diet, most of them developed wiry figures, rosy cheeks, and a
bloom so much in contrast with the appearance of their male comrades
that jokers said that the millet in Yan'an was only good for girls.

In the Red capital, students at the Women's University enjoyed huge
popularity, mainly because women were so scarce in Yan'an: the total
ratio was about eighty men to one woman, or 18:1 at a conservative estimate. On top of that, nine out of ten Communists were single and
young. Most people, especially those who joined the revolution during
the Sino-Japanese War, were under thirty. Apart from the two universities where my mother studied, there were numerous institutions in
Yan'an, such as the Central Party School, the Academy of Marxist-
Leninist Studies, the Academy of Military and Political Affairs, and Lu
Xun Art College. But the Women's University was the first place where

so many young, educated Communist women had ever gathered. In the morning, the files of girls who ran down to the Yan River to wash, and sang as they ran, were like streams winding through the brown earth-covered cliffs. This magnificent scenery always drew many male observers, to admire from the opposite bank.

In the low-water seasons, the river's dried flood plain became a social thoroughfare, a Champs Élysées for Yan'an. After work, people would stroll there under the setting sun, and the students in my mother's university were always the centre of attention. Many had tailored their army uniforms to show off their slender figures. Some wore their army caps tilted at jaunty angles, or smart shoes pieced together from worn-out clothes, each with a bright woollen pom-pom on top. Among my mother's classmates, some of the more lively and outgoing girls soon had their circles of admirers, like moons in a halo of stars.

It did not take long for students in the Women's University to receive marriage proposals, whether from students, Communist officials or soldiers serving in Yan'an. Some had been married before, particularly among the 'Old Cadres' who had joined the revolution before the Sino-Japanese War, but it was not hard for them to remarry, and the Party organization was ready to approve their divorce and remarriage applications. Although no firm statistics are preserved, this was probably the first 'divorce wave' in Chinese Communist history. Many abandoned wives came from illiterate peasant backgrounds. Some were themselves 'Old Cadres'. Others were victims of the traditional marriage by arrangement, left behind to look after their children and parents-in-law after their husbands joined the revolution. During the 'divorce wave', the attitude of these remarried husbands was deplored as 'love the new [woman] and loathe the old [wife] – be fickle in affection'.

The Communist women's organization in Yan'an was unable to intervene, or to protect these abandoned wives. The 'Old Cadres', especially the Red Army veterans, were regarded as revolutionary heroes, and their behaviour largely tolerated. Many of them also held powerful positions, and could bring their personal influence to bear on the Party's views. More importantly, many of them had the backing of Mao Zedong for their loyalty during intra-party conflicts. In fact, Mao himself also took part in the 'divorce wave' when he left his Red Army wife, He Zizhen, who went through the Long March with him, and married Jiang Qing. Objectors were told that judgements on Party members should be based on their political integrity (da-jie) rather than the way they ran their personal lives (xiao-jie). Therefore, although in public the Party set a 'high standard of morality' for its members, Mao's pragmatism saved the political careers of numerous high officials whose divorce and remarriage might have harmed them.

In fact, many of my mother's fellow students were not interested in marrying 'Old Cadres', despite their standing in the Party. This was not a matter of age difference, since many of these men were only in their later twenties or early thirties. Rather, the gap lay in their educational backgrounds and personal interests. Some girls were disappointed when 'Old Cadre' admirers showed little interest in books that were popular in the Women's University, such as *Anna Karenina*. One officer rushed to the post office claiming a gift from his girlfriend, because her letter ended 'give you my kiss', and he with his little education did not know the Chinese character for 'kiss' (wen). Such stories were common in Yan'an. One of the girls in my mother's university made a list of her criteria for a husband which included a university degree and knowledge of several foreign languages. A few of her admirers were baffled – 'What? Several English languages?' To them, the only foreign language was English.

During that time, Yan'an was shocked by a sensational murder case. Huang Kegong was a former regimental commander in the Red Army and a veteran of the Long March. His victim was his former girlfriend, a young urban student from the Nationalist area. When she left him for another man with whom she had more in common, the furious officer shot her dead. Afterwards, the Party's Central Committee decided to convene a public hearing to announce his death sentence. Friends and supporters of Huang Kegong appealed for mercy, on the grounds of his contributions to the revolution, but the verdict did not change. Later, Mao Zedong explained that with the bullet that executed Huang the Party had retrieved its honour, and hence gained more support from the masses.

My mother did not marry in Yan'an. Her parents had arranged her engagement in the earlier days to a young man from her home county who had also joined the revolution and was stationed in another Communist base. This circumstance kept suitors at a distance.

In those days, married students normally lived in the university except at weekends, when they happily joined their husbands. Unmarried students like my mother also enjoyed the weekends, because they meant easier sleep in a less crowded bed. In those days, few had proper bedding, and people used their cotton army overcoats as duvets. Those who had a blanket to sleep on were viewed as very lucky by the majority who had nothing to cover their bare earthen kang or plank bed, so spare bedding left by the 'weekenders' softened the hardship of sleeping in unheated caves.

By early 1940, the Communist 359 Brigade had captured five counties to the northeast of Yan'an from the Nationalists. In this newly liberated area, most people knew nothing about the Communists, and some remaining Nationalist organizations were still influential. In order to help the Communist local government, the Central Committee decided to send cadres from Yan'an, and my mother was assigned to a team in Suide, the seat of government of the newly liberated area. During a four-day trip, she and eight classmates carried their luggage and walked for nearly 200 kilometres.

The first assignment my mother had was to draft an open letter for the local women's federation to support the Communist troops in the front line. Her writing impressed many senior officials and later was published in the local paper. Subsequently, she was appointed director of the publicity department in the local women's federation. Another duty was to run a women's magazine, which she did single-handed, as editor, compositor and circulation manager. But she wanted to do more. At the opening ceremony of the Women's University, Mao Zedong had told students: 'You must go to the front, village and factory, to organize the 225 million Chinese women resisting the Japanese invasion.' My mother was eager to follow his advice and work with poor peasant women.

At her request, she went to a poor village alone, to establish a Women's Federation for Saving the Nation. The remote locality was barren and dry, with no road for vehicle traffic. When she arrived on foot, a crowd of children tagged along, shouting: 'A woman Communist!' She got a cool reception from the village chief, but he agreed to find her somewhere to stay, and here the first problem came up. As it was the peasants she needed to approach, she turned down offers from the well-to-do families, but poor peasant houses lacked spare rooms. In order to save fuel, the entire household shared one kang at night – men, women and children all together – which was not suitable for a young woman visitor. Finally, my mother was reluctantly accepted by an old childless widow who lived in a shack.

For the villagers, a woman in army uniform was a mystery. They suspected a plot to recruit girls for the Communist forces, and did not welcome the idea, having suffered enough from troops in the past during the warlords' frequent quarrels and the Nationalist occupation. In any case, service women had a particularly low reputation, owing to the tradition that decent women did not leave home, either on their own or to work with men. Therefore, every family kept their girls locked up at home and tried to avoid my mother. In desperation, she realized that she must first convince the men about her reasons for contacting their women.

One evening, about fifty silent men gathered in a small room in a villager's house to hear my mother speak about the importance of women's participation in the anti-Japanese movement. While speaking, she sat on the edge of the kang that took up half the space in the room, as she was not used to the local peasants' habit of either squatting on the floor or sitting cross-legged on the kang. Following her speech, there was a stubborn silence, except for the sound of the audience sucking on their long-stemmed Chinese pipes. Again and again, she tried and failed to draw them out. In the gloom of the single oil-lamp and the reek of strong tobacco, her anxiety grew and her face started streaming with sweat. Suddenly, a man sidled up to her and began to pinch her thighs, forcing her to stop and back away. The audience sniggered. A few days later, she learned that the assault had been a test. Under the Nationalist occupation, the villagers had been told that the Communists intended to communize all private possessions, including wives and property, so all Communist women were sluts.

On the first night, my mother was questioned at length by her cold-faced landlady, who asked about her age, her home and family, even her marriage status. When my mother said that she had joined the revolution voluntarily, the old widow could not see why. And when she heard that the Communists paid no wages, she could not believe her ears: 'Impossible! Why work for nothing?' 'Because I want to fight against the Japanese invasion,' my mother answered.

Every day, my mother rose at dawn to carry water, collect fuel and feed the chickens for her landlady. In the evening, she helped with mashing the boiled black beans that were cooked again next day as a staple food. Her host was eventually won round, and told the villagers: 'She is a decent girl, hard-working and considerate. She comes here to help our women!' Gradually, women started talking to my mother and invited her to their homes.

Such contacts brought unthinkable difficulties. In this isolated area, electricity and tap-water were unheard-of. My mother caught lice again from her landlady, and there was no way to get rid of them, since medicine and even water was scarce. It was said that local residents only washed three times in their lifetime: after birth, before marriage and after death. Every day she had meals with different peasant families by arrangement of the village chief. For a long time, she ate mostly chaff and wild vegetables because semi-starvation was the norm. What struck her most was the appalling living conditions. In the summer, their houses teemed with flies. They covered her face, her hands and any other bare part of her body, invaded her food, and caused her food poisoning several times.

One day, a little boy shat on the earthen floor by the table where she was to eat. Due to the poverty, local children hardly ever used nappies, and did not even wear trousers until their teens. The boy's mother cleaned his anus with a small piece of stone, a substitute for toilet paper, and then she went straight on to prepare food for my mother without washing her hands. Afterwards, a dog was called to eat the shit, which was a customary practice. Between the slurping of the dog and the stink of the shit, my mother did not know how her meal was finished. But she blamed this backward lifestyle on the exploitation of the feudal landlords and foreign imperialists. As a Communist, she felt obliged to share the peasants' hardships to change their lives. Gradually, she became the women's trusted friend. She started to organize them, introducing revolutionary ideals, and a few months later the Women's Federation for Saving the Nation was established in that village.

During 1941–2, the Sino-Japanese War entered its most difficult period for the Chinese. The mounting Communist threat brought massive retaliation from the Japanese. In north China, they launched nearly 200 search-and-destroy operations against the Communists, while the infamous 'three-all policy' – burn all, kill all, loot all – was applied. Along the borders of the Communist base areas, they built deep trenches and high earthworks. Displaced civilians were resettled under concentration-camp conditions in 'zones under strengthened public order'. Faced with resistance, they deployed indiscriminate firepower, ruthlessly wiping out whole villages. In such operations inevitably women, children and the elderly were the primary victims.

At the same time, the relationship between the Communists and Nationalists deteriorated further. Chiang Kai-shek tightened his blockade on the Communist bases, and in January 1941, 9,000 members of the New Fourth Army, the Communist anti-Japanese forces in south China, fell into an ambush of 70,000 Nationalist troops in Anhui province. About 7,000 Communist troops were killed or captured. According to Communist historians, this incident was the peak of the Nationalists' Second Anti-Communist Campaign.

From 1940 to 1942, the number of Communist forces fell by nearly a quarter, and the population in their bases halved. In response, the Communists introduced a series of emergency policies to improve the United Front and gain peasant support. In order to ease the taxpayers' burden, they slimmed their administrative staff. In August 1941, the Women's University merged into Yan'an University. The most influential development was a campaign to improve the Communist organization. Known as 'the Rectification', it provided the prototype for subsequent political campaigns in the following decades. Apart from the outside factors, it derived from tensions within the Communist leadership between Mao Zedong and Wang Ming, the Chancellor of the Women's University.

Since his return from Moscow in November 1937, Wang Ming had challenged Mao's leadership, continuing the power struggle begun in the early 1930s between students returning from Russia and the peasant-based groups. Wang Ming had a high position in the Communist International, and was known for his close relationship with Stalin. After his return, his views put him on a collision course with the majority of the Party leadership. According to Mao, the Party must maintain its independence from the United Front. But Wang Ming promoted two slogans, 'Everything should go through the United Front' and 'Everyone should obey the United Front', which were believed to be copied from

France but not applicable to China. Wang Ming also disagreed both
with Mao's view that 'Political power grows out of the barrel of a gun'
and with the leading role played by the peasantry in China's revolution.
He denied the necessity of establishing Communist bases, and promoted regular large-scale warfare instead of guerrilla warfare.

In July 1938, a message reached Yan'an from the Communist
International showing support for Mao Zedong's leadership of the
Party and cautioning Wang Ming not to grapple for power with Mao.
Encouraged by this message, Mao and his supporters organized the
Sixth Plenary Session of the Sixth Central Committee in Yan'an to crit-
icize Wang Ming's mistakes. After that, Wang found his influence
sharply reduced.

However, to most Communists these intra-party conflicts were
unknown, as details were withheld. Since the outbreak of the war, Party
membership had grown from 40,000 in 1937 to 800,000 in 1942.
Among new members like my mother and her classmates, Wang Ming
enjoyed a reputation as the Party's leading Marxist-Leninist theorist. His
lectures were always packed by the time he arrived, with listeners from
every major institute and organization in Yan'an. They lasted several
hours, and he spoke without notes, quoting copiously from Marx,
Engels, Lenin and Stalin, with accurate page numbers. Caught in this
torrent of theory, most of the audience failed to recognize how much
his views differed from Mao Zedong's. The very title of Mao's pamphlet
On Protracted War conceded the short-term military superiority of the
Japanese, whereas a lecture given by Wang Ming in 1940 continued to
argue that a rapid win was possible. In her eagerness to equip her mind
with revolutionary ideas, my mother spent most of her spare time studying books recommended by her chancellor, and largely ignored Mao's
publications. For those with peasant backgrounds, on the other hand,
and therefore not exposed to Marxist-Leninist thought, it was equally
hard to recognize the two political lines.

On the eve of the Rectification Campaign, my mother returned to

Yan'an after her mission in Suide. Having passed her entrance examination, she was enrolled in one of the two senior classes at the Women's University for postgraduate studies at the end of 1940, the year before the university merged into Yan'an University. They consisted of about 100 postgraduates who were selected from Party members with good educational background and appropriate working experiences. Her classmates in Senior Class Two included Ye Qun, who later married Marshal Lin Biao. These postgraduates were expected to provide the leadership of the future women's movement in China.

In early 1941, the pre-Rectification Campaign was launched in Yan'an, to be followed by the Rectification in February 1942. To begin with, the major topics were current affairs, historical research and the application of Marxism-Leninism to China's revolution. Some of the basic texts were works by Mao, such as *Reconstructing Our Studies*, *On Investigation and Research* and *Improving the Party's Work Style*, which focused scathing criticism on a variety of errors inside the Party. But most of all he attacked the dogmatism inherent in studying the works of Marx, Engels, Lenin and Stalin in the abstract, regardless of their relevance to the Chinese revolution.

During the campaign, it was Wang Ming who was criticized as the number one dogmatist, and his prestige dissolved in Yan'an. It was the first my mother knew about the harm done to the Party in the 1930s under the leadership of her respected university chancellor. She felt glad to be warned against dogmatism, and started reading Mao's publications seriously.

By 1942, Mao Zedong had consolidated his grasp on the Communist leadership, and his writings and speeches were widely projected as the embodiment of the Party policy and spirit. This represented Mao's growing influence within China's revolutionary movement as architect of a successful guerrilla strategy and subsequently of the second United Front. In the historical tradition of Chinese rebel movements, it also reflected a deliberate effort to present a leader and personality as a rallying-point for the nation. From then on, my mother decided to have her revolutionary career guided by Mao's ideas, following him in her life and doing whatever he wished.

In August 1941, my mother was assigned to the General Office of the Central Committee in Yan'an, having completed her postgraduate studies. The secretariat where she worked was headed by Wang Shoudao, a veteran of the Long March who later became Vice-President of the People's Congress (Parliament) in Communist China. Among its four divisions, Division One was responsible for transmitting, receiving and translating the radiotelegrams that provided a major wartime link between the headquarters of the Communist Party and its bases and troops. Most of the staff were in their teens. Due to the confidential nature of their work, they lived and worked in a valley isolated from outside. Every day, the shoals of telegrams received included those from Nationalist or Japanese sources which were handed over by the Communist secret services or intercepted from the enemy's communications. Before being passed on for action, these telegrams were security-processed by Division Four, where my mother worked. Her job was to conceal the source of the information, alter the writing style and reorganize the paragraphs of the documents. The other two divisions dealt with everyday secretarial work such as printing and filing.

My mother's office was located on the ground floor of a two-storey building in Yang Hill, near the Women's University. Upstairs were offices and conference rooms for the Party leaders, but Mao Zedong normally worked from home, which was a nearby cave. Between his residence and the secretariat office ran a small plank bridge with no guards. Throughout the war, security for the Party leaders was rather casual in Yan'an. Sometimes, Mao or his colleagues would go strolling on their own, or stop for a chat in the street. Living above Mao's cave, my mother passed his door every day on her way to and from work. Very often, the oil-lamp shone all night in his window. In the morning, people tiptoed past his door. On warm afternoons she would see Mao working in front of his cave at a plain wooden desk.

In 1942, Western-style ballroom dancing was very popular in Yan'an. In their spare time, Mao and many other Communist leaders would often turn up at the dances organized by the Party's General Office. Dressed in threadbare army uniforms, they danced on a beaten earth floor to the music of an ancient gramophone – usually Russian revolutionary songs. Most of the females who came were young girls working in the General Office, including my mother. To her eye, Zhou Enlai was the most elegant dancer and the best-looking man, though he seldom appeared, owing to his work as the Communist representative in Chongqing, the war capital of the Nationalist government.

The fashion for dancing caused strong criticism in the Red capital. Wang Shiwei, my mother's former English teacher at middle school, known in Yan'an as an outspoken Communist writer with an acid pen, wrote in a sensational article that 'while in the front line troops fought the invaders with their blood, in the rear they were cavorting at dancing parties'. One evening while dancing with Zhu De, Commander in Chief of the Eighth Route Army, my mother asked him curiously: 'Why does the General Office still organize dancing parties after being criticized by Wang Shiwei?' Zhu De laughed, but he did not stop dancing. His movements were slow and precise, and he always kept his distance. Because he was so tall, he would bend over and extend his long arms in a posture like pushing a trolley. 'Wang Shiwei's article has been boosted by the Nationalists,' Zhu De told my mother. 'You can see whether what he said is good or not for our Party. We Communists are optimists, and always try to be relaxed. In between battles, we can sing or watch plays. So what is wrong with dancing?'

During these parties, Mao Zedong was normally accompanied by his wife, who taught him dancing step by step. One day, he stopped in front of my mother. 'Little devil, would you like to dance with me?' My mother blushed, partly out of natural shyness and partly because she was only a beginner at dancing. 'Don't worry! I'll teach you.' Mao understood her feelings and walked her to the centre of the hall. To my mother's surprise, it was not hard to follow his dancing. He moved slowly and relaxedly, as if strolling on an empty field. Sometimes he got the steps wrong, but never the rhythm. While they danced, Mao asked my mother her name, age, place of birth, job, and even her favourite reading. When she complained about the shortage of books in Yan'an, he said: 'Why don't you borrow books from my private library?' Before she could answer, he pulled a mock-serious face: 'Mind you, little devil, if you don't look after my books, I'll take back the offer.'

A few days later, my mother received two books from her first list, brought by one of Mao's private secretaries. One was *Anna Karenina*, the other a Russian revolutionary novel. Both were translated into Chinese and published before the Sino-Japanese War in Nationalist areas. On each title page there was a large character, 'Ping', written in red pencil all across the page. My mother recognized that these novels belonged to Mao's wife, Jiang Qing, and were signed with her stage name, Lan Ping.

In contrast to Mao's behaviour, Jiang Qing's was disappointing. Working as Mao's private secretary, she belonged to the same Party cell as my mother, whose fewer than ten members met at least once a week. During these meetings, Jiang Qing was either absent or upset the others by quarrelling with another member of Mao's private staff, Ye Zilong, who looked after Mao's daily life. One day, the meeting was completely disrupted by their row over Jiang Qing's proposal to arrange a dinner party for her toddler daughter's birthday, at the public expense. When Ye Zilong opposed her suggestion, and reminded her of the frugal conditions on Communist bases, Jiang Qing lost her temper and accused him of taking advantage of Mao's trust to deliberately undermine her. She also accused him of helping himself to gifts sent to Mao by governors of Communist bases. 'Don't make out you're innocent!' she yelled. 'What your children have at home is exactly the same as my child's. How can you afford so many smart clothes and all that bedding? Where did the stuff come from?'

Ye Zilong was part of Mao's inner circle. He took no notice of her words, and when Mao got to know about the row, he criticized his wife for her lavish lifestyle. With Mao's support, Ye Zilong did not fear Jiang Qing's hostility. Privately, he talked to colleagues about her notorious former life in Shanghai, and the sex scandals exposed by the local newspapers there, and praised Mao Zedong's two former wives, Yang Kaihui and He Zizhen, who were both viewed as heroines in the Party.

Mao Zedong had a passionate and romantic relationship with Yang Kaihui, daughter of his favourite professor. Their final separation started when Mao launched his armed insurrection against the Nationalists in 1927, and Yang Kaihui was left behind with their three young sons in Changsha, the capital of their home province. In 1930, she was arrested by the Nationalist authorities, together with her first son, Mao Anying. Having refused to betray her husband, she was cruelly tortured and later executed. Afterwards, their boys became street urchins for several years, starving and brutalized by the police. After the outbreak of the Sino-Japanese War, only two of the boys were found in Shanghai and sent to Yan'an by the Communist underground. The youngest, it was said, had already died. In 1950, Mao Anying, Mao's favourite son, was killed while serving with the Chinese People's Volunteers in Korea.

In the late 1920s, Mao met He Zizhen, a beautiful Red Army member, in Jing-gang Shan, his first rural base. During their ten years together, several children were born, but most had to be given away for adoption due to the wars, and were never found again. During the Long March, He Zizhen was severely injured while protecting a colleague wounded in a Nationalist air-raid. Later she went to Moscow for medical treatment, and it was then that Jiang Qing took up with Mao.

The Central Committee disapproved of Jiang Qing and her ambitions. In addition to her sexual reputation, there were also suspicions about her record while working for the Communist underground in

Shanghai before the war, when she was captured by the Nationalists. According to the Party's information, she had talked during her imprisonment, and since then had kept up close relationships with senior members of the Nationalist intelligence services. Such a woman would make a dangerous wife for the Party's leader. But although they had not known each other long, Jiang Qing had entirely won over Mao Zedong, so a compromise had to be reached. It was said that under pressure from the Communist leadership, she agreed a deal. She could become Madam Mao; in return, she must stay out of the Party's affairs, and not appear in public as the first lady.

To the staff in the General Office, Jiang Qing was rude and arrogant. She behaved towards colleagues, including those in senior positions and with greater revolutionary experience, like a hot-tempered mistress to her servants, either telling them off or ignoring them. Everyone tried to steer clear of her.

In July 1942, my mother left the General Office in Yan'an for the Jin-Sui Communist base, where her fiancé worked. The transfer was arranged by Lin Feng, the governor of the base, in order to end the young couple's long separation. When the time came to say goodbye to Yan'an, my mother's eyes were moist with tears. Four years before, she had arrived as a naive teenager with revolutionary dreams. When she left, she had grown into a mature and well-trained Communist with a firm belief. It was in Yan'an, the cradle of the Communists in China, that her life's new chapter began.

Chapter 7

Revolution and Romance:
My Parents' Marriage

(1942–1946)

Before she was ten, my mother's parents arranged her engagement to Guo Bing, who was born in the same year in the same county. During his infancy, Guo Bing had lost his father, and he was brought up by his uncle, an enlightened squire who ran a workshop in town teaching modern weaving techniques to local women. The earliest impressions that my mother had about Guo Bing's family came from stories about his eldest brother, who joined the Communist Party in the early 1920s. After Chiang Kai-shek's coup in 1927, he fled from home and left his wife behind. Although the two families were on good terms, my mother and Guo Bing never communicated either before or after their engagement, due to restrictions of contacts between people of different genders.

When my mother was enrolled in the county girls' school, Guo Bing went to the boys' school, and both were known as gifted pupils. In 1934, they joined the same middle school in Luoang, but studied on different campuses as there were no mixed classes. When their paths crossed, they felt awkward and passed on without a word, not knowing how to express their feelings. In their third year at the school, some girls in my mother's class started writing letters to fiancés or boyfriends, and my mother did the same, having heard from her teachers that Guo Bing was a noble-minded, hard-working boy. His written reply was brief, stating that he cared about nothing but study. Hurt by this snub, she did not write again.

In early 1938, they left home on the same day to join the anti-Japanese forces, but until my mother left Yan'an in 1942, there was no communication between them at all. For a long time, she did not even know whether Guo Bing was still alive or remained single. In July 1942, she arrived in Jin-Sui base, which covered part of Shanxi and Suiyuan provinces. She found that Guo Bing had become a respected Communist cadre, highly appreciated by the base leaders.

Their reunion took place one morning in the temporary guest quarters where my mother was put up in Jin-sui. The meeting was not exciting at all. When she opened her door, each of them saw a stranger, an adult formed by four years' separation. 'How are you, Comrade Xu Jing?' Guo Bing greeted my mother with a dry voice and a serious face. 'I am fine, thank you, Comrade Guo Bing,' she replied in the same formal manner while they shook hands, and felt relieved immediately. This was a fiancé whom she hardly knew and had not been in touch with. It would be awkward if he showed her affection, when her own was uncertain, but they both knew how to treat a comrade.

For a long time, I could not understand why my mother did not break her engagement to Guo Bing during their long separation, since they were not interested in each other. My mother's explanation was that it would hurt Guo Bing. Despite the gap between them, his existence had been part of her life, and she admired him. They had joined the revolution together, and both had devoted their lives to Communism. Perhaps they would get to know each other now. But the war took a different path. In the following six months, the Jin-Sui base suffered the Japanese mopping-up operation, enforced by the infamous 'three-all policy' of burning all, killing all and looting all. My mother and other women cadres were ordered back to a safer area, and Guo Bing remained in the front line.

In spring 1943, the situation improved and my mother was posted to Xingxian county, in north Shanxi province, where Guo Bing was director of the local Anti-Japanese United Front. She saw how kind and honest Guo Bing was, and he grew fond enough of her to suggest that they marry in the coming winter. It seems that no romantic passion broke through their natural reserve. Their only gesture to commemorate their marriage decision was a photo taken together in front of the blooming chrysanthemum planted by Guo Bing outside his room. In it, they stood shoulder to shoulder, neither smiling nor holding hands.

Unfortunately, my mother and Guo Bing were never able to marry. Shortly before their scheduled wedding day, Guo Bing was forced to cross a frozen river while making a tour of the county to organize anti-Japanese activities. As Guo Bing and his comrades stepped on the ice, it broke and they had to walk through ice-cold water with bare feet. The exposure did permanent damage, and soon he was paralysed. My mother rushed to visit him in hospital, but although he tried his best to make light of his condition, he could not hide how much he had suffered. In autumn 1944, she went to the hospital again, but this time it was for Guo Bing's funeral.

However, the loss of her fiancé was not the only ordeal my mother faced at that time. In January 1944, she was sent to the Jin-Sui base's Communist Party school to attend a conference. When she arrived, she was shocked to find out that instead of a conference she faced immediate internment. The school had been converted into a political concentration camp for Party members suspected of being Nationalist or Japanese spies. Because she was in prison, she was unable to make regular visits to see her sick fiancé before he died.

It was at the final stage of the Rectification Campaign that the Party's focus had shifted from political training to scrutiny of members' personal history. The process began in December 1942 with a spectacular case in Yan'an. Zhang Keqin, a nineteen-year-old student at a Communist cadre-training college, was arrested because: (1) he had joined the Party in 1937 in a Nationalist area; (2) his father, a Communist working for the underground, had not behaved 'properly' while jailed by the Nationalists; (3) he had voiced forthright criticism of his college leaders' work. During his imprisonment, Zhang was interrogated, tortured, and pressured by threats to confess to being a Nationalist spy.

The case was conceived and supervised by Kang Sheng, who was seen as the new Madam Mao's closest ally. Both of them came from Zhucheng county in Shandong province. During the 1930s, Kang Sheng had worked in Moscow as a delegate to the Communist International, where he was known as a supporter of Wang Ming, though not a part of his circle. The story goes that after his return from Moscow in 1937, he helped Jiang Qing to gain access to Mao Zedong in Yan'an, and so to become the Party's first lady. By way of Jiang's influence, this earned him Mao's favour for the rest of his life. In Chinese history, Kang Sheng's experience is familiar enough to carry the label 'Mei-ren-ji' meaning 'using a woman to ensnare a powerful man'.

By 1942, Kang Sheng was working with Mao in the Central Committee of Rectification Study. He also held the powerful post of Director of the Social and Intelligence Department of the Party's Central Committee – China's equivalent of the KGB. Following the political disgrace of Wang Ming during the Rectification Campaign, Kang Sheng felt insecure. He had bailed himself out by turning against Wang Ming, but if his record in Moscow came to light he would lose the trust of Mao Zedong, and with it his political ambitions. In order to divert attention from the Wang Ming episode, he raised the spectre of treason, having witnessed the Moscow trials of the 1930s. Hence the arrest of Zhang Keqin.

Having been forced to admit his 'guilt', Zhang Keqin was paraded around the Communist Central Base to talk about his experience of 'being reborn' from a Nationalist spy, for which Kang Sheng claimed credit. In July 1943, Kang Sheng gave his infamous speech in Yan'an entitled 'Rescuing those who take a wrong step in life'. The new stage of the Rectification Campaign was known as the Rescue Campaign. According to him, the Red capital had been threatened not only by outside military force but also by the horde of spies sent by both the Nationalists and the Japanese. There were hidden enemies everywhere. According to Kang Sheng's estimate, more than half of the Communists in Yan'an were either enemy spies or bad characters. Those not politically reliable should be rescued – in other words, arrested and interrogated. His precept that the more hidden enemies an organization unearthed, the more the campaign was achieving, led to some ludicrous consequences. In the Yan'an Guards Regiment, responsible for the public security of the Red capital, some 80 to 90 per cent of its personnel were classed as Nationalist agents. Even in the Secretariat of the Party's Central Committee, where my mother once worked, nearly a quarter of the staff were labelled as hidden enemies. Chaos descended, fuelled by the terror of arrests and interrogations.

After confessing their 'crimes', these new-found culprits were forced to invent more details of their counter-revolutionary organizations, such as their leaders or contacts. When senior Communists previously in charge of the Party's underground in Nationalist or Japanese-occupied areas also became victims, Kang Sheng labelled their former provincial networks as the 'Red-flag Party', working for the enemy under the revolutionary flag. Those with links to the 'Red-flag Party' were suspected as enemy agents, and required investigation. As the campaign snowballed, Party members from Nationalist or Japanese-occupied areas became its particular victims.

The Rescue Campaign marked the first major instance in China's Communist history when members with an intellectual background were persecuted. Inside the Party, it was usual to divide cadres into two main categories. Most were called (industrial) worker-peasant cadres — generally peasant youths with illiterate or semi-literate backgrounds, who often came from Red territories located in desolate rural areas and joined the revolution during the Communists' recruitment campaign. Throughout the armed struggle they were praised for their strong loyalty to Mao Zedong and deep attachment to the revolution. On the other hand, since the outbreak of the Sino-Japanese War there had been a growing influx of cadres, like my mother, from the Nationalist or Japanese occupied areas. These were the intellectual cadres, so called for their more educated backgrounds.

From time to time, the two groups had quarrelled. There was a history dating back to the 1920s of clashes between Mao Zedong and opponents who were either students returned from abroad or well-known scholars. Among the twelve founders of the Communist Party, it was said, Mao was the only one with a peasant background, and one of the few who stayed close to the peasantry during the course of the revolution. He himself once wrote that '(In the past), I felt that only educated people were clean. Through the revolution, I got to know workers, peasants and revolutionary soldiers, and . . . I recognised that the cleanest ones are workers and peasants, while these intellectuals are unclean . . .' (speech to the Forum on Literature and Art in Yan'an in 1942). This division gave Kang Sheng his opportunity. Even though he himself came from a Nationalist area and was seen as an intellectual, he was able to make political capital out of casting suspicion on to intellectual comrades who had always been loyal to Mao.

The Rescue Campaign soon spread from Yan'an to all other Communist bases. From autumn 1943, nearly all cadres in the Jin-Sui base who came from the Nationalist or Japanese occupied areas were sent to the concentration camp, including the non-Party members. The Jin-Sui Party School, where my mother was jailed, had to establish four extra branches to house the mass of suspects.

My mother was detained chiefly because the Communist underground in Henan, where she came from, was labelled as a 'Red-flag Party' front, but also because of her links with Wu Xiang, a prominent journalist who ran the Communist newspaper in the Jin-Sui base. Since first meeting my mother in Yan'an in 1939, he had become her admirer, and would send her letters, books, magazines, and sometimes even money. My mother appreciated him, but could not tell whether she loved him, so that she tried to treat him as a friend. Wu Xiang's professional contacts with the press in the Nationalist areas made him a regular and influential correspondent there, reporting on anti-Japanese activities in the Communist bases. To the Rescue Campaign, these were signs of a Nationalist spy, and he was one of the first arrested.

In the camp, prisoners were divided into groups of ten, controlled by worker-peasant cadres who acted as group chiefs, guards or interrogators. Other peasant Communists made up the 'shock brigade' whose task was to carry out intensive 'rescue' operations for 'incorrigibly obstinate' individuals. These uneducated cadres knew very little about life in the outside world, and Kang Sheng's instructions misled them. In their minds, areas occupied by the Nationalists or Japanese were so much in the grip of the 'white terror' that it was impossible for anybody but an enemy spy to cross over into Red territory.

For the political prisoners, the first experience was interrogation. My mother was expected to provide information about her connections with Nationalist fascist organizations whose names were actually unknown to most prisoners, including herself. When she first heard the charges against her, they came like a bolt from the blue. Ever since joining the revolution, she had completely rejected the exploiting social class to which her family belonged, and devoted herself to the Communist Party. When she came to Yan'an she was fifteen years old, with not a single Nationalist connection. Since then, she had made hardly any contact outside Red territory. What else could she do to prove her innocence?

But her pleas were denials of her 'guilt', and the method of 'rescue' was torture. Her head and body were hit by the armed guards with their rifle butts, and stoned by chiefs of the prisoner groups. Sometimes her interrogation lasted for more than twenty-four hours, with no break or food or drink for my mother, while the interrogators worked in shifts. In the winter, she was locked outside in heavy snow for a whole night, and nearly passed out in the freezing cold.

Under the intense psychological pressure and torture, most prisoners decided to comply and so made false confessions about their 'counter-revolutionary crimes'. They believed that the Party would rehabilitate them one day, and meanwhile the truth did them nothing but harm. This was the reasoning of the ancient Chinese saying that 'a clever fellow will get himself out of trouble by doing whatever is possible' (Hao-han-bu-chi-yan-qian-kui). As soon as they confessed their suffering stopped.

In order to pressure other prisoners who refused to lie, these 'confessors' were brought to mass rallies in the camp to introduce their 'rebirth' experiences. Standing on the platform, telling their fabricated stories, some shed tears and beat their breasts. Afterwards, officials conducted the chorus of 'Welcome the rebirth of our comrades!' and shook hands with the tearful penitents. Then each new 'reborn' person was invited to a feast to celebrate their 'confession' with wheat flour noodles, a luxury in those days. Unfortunately, they had to stay on in the camp. Kang Sheng's policy required them to atone for their crimes and the way to gain merit was to 'rescue' reluctant confessors. A high achiever in the 'rescue' operations could even earn the title of 'rescue hero'.

The next stage was for prisoners to raise their revolutionary consciousness through political introduction. For my mother, this experience matched her interrogation. As the only non-confessor in her group, and therefore an 'incorrigibly obstinate Nationalist spy', she faced strong hostility from her fellow prisoners. Apart from physical punishment, she frequently suffered starvation, because confessed 'rescue activists' used to spit in her precious food ration until she could not stomach it. She could not complain, because any such treatment was merely applying the Party's policy of 'leniency to those who admit their crimes and severity to those who refuse to'.

For my mother, the most unbearable feature of the political indoctrination was to listen to her fellow inmates reciting their 'crimes' committed as enemy agents, even though everyone knew that these were lies. According to Kang Sheng's doctrine, the more the prisoners denounced themselves, the more they proved their revolutionary zeal, and the less correction they required. Some painted themselves as black as Qin Hui from the Song Dynasty, the most infamous traitor in China's history. 'Why did they behave so ridiculously?' my mother asked herself. In her mind, a real Communist should stick to the truth. She would never sell her conscience and dignity for temporary comfort, and she felt sad that so many had succumbed. At the same time, it confused her that an honest person could be a victim of intra-party conflict. Her only support was her unconditional trust in the Communist Party. 'It will be over soon,' she told herself every day. 'I believe that the Party will rehabilitate me.'

Despite her isolation, my mother kept insisting that although she might not be a perfect Communist, she had always tried to act in the interests of the Party. When these claims resulted in more punishment, she could only fall back on silence, but this too was counted as opposing the Rescue Campaign. Her silence drove the leader of the Party branch in the camp, a veteran of the Long March, to shout: 'Xu Jing, how dare you be so arrogant!'

For many 'confessed' prisoners, the problem was coping with their own lies. A girl in my mother's group was tormented by her false confession. Every day she stood by the entrance to their cell, stared into the distance, tugged at the front of her jacket, and kept on repeating: 'There are two sets of stories about my personal history, one is true and the other is false.' Each time, her face was slapped by the group chief or guards, but she would not be quiet.

My mother's most grievous memory was the tragedy of a vulnerable young girl from her home province, whose first interrogation drove her into a deep depression. Perhaps she could not cope with the contrast between the new world she had dreamed of and the cruel reality of the camp. Only sporadic spitting interrupted her blank-faced silences. There was no medication for prisoners, and counselling was an unknown treatment. To witness the girl's decline was a slow nightmare. As a prisoner herself, my mother was not allowed to offer her help or even talk to her. Before the Rescue Campaign was over, the girl had passed away. Another girl tried to commit suicide by cutting her throat with a piece of broken glass. Her life was saved, but the damage destroyed her voice.

One day, my mother was brought to a rally where 'incorrigibly obstinate Nationalist spies' were pressured to admit their crimes. The venue was in a remote uninhabited valley which was now packed with political prisoners from all branches of the concentration camp. Above the platform, a giant slogan proclaimed: 'Leniency to those who admit their crimes and severity to those who refuse!' In front of the platform, a small group of men sat on the ground, surrounded by armed guards. These were the important incorrigibles, and major targets of the 'rescue' operation. My mother was not among them, but the sight of their suffering was expected to convert her, in line with the famous proverb: 'Kill the chicken to frighten the monkey' (Sha-ji-gei-hou-kan).

The rally started when an official mounted the platform and then led the vast audience to shout: 'Wu Xiang must admit his crime!' After the shouting, armed guards dragged Wu Xiang on to the platform. There he stood, with his head bowed and his face pale. Curious stares were turned on my mother, recalling the gossip about her relationship with Wu Xiang. She stared at her feet without a word. More names were called, and more people dragged into view. Sickened, my mother closed her eyes. Suddenly, another burst of shouting roared: 'Mu Xiang must admit his crime!' Mu Xiang and Wu Xiang, how could the names be so similar? Had my mother misheard? Identical first names, and surnames that rhymed? She felt so curious that she had to look up, so she was watching when a young man appeared on the platform. 'My first impression about him was his deep eyes and a nose with a high bridge in his serious face,' she told me many years later. And this was how my mother met my father.

My father arrived in the Jin-Sui base from Yan'an in autumn 1942, after two years' study at the Academy of Military and Political Affairs. He was no stranger to the base. Before being posted to Yan'an in 1940, he had been involved in establishing its territory. Now he was to work as an aide to Luo Guipo, a senior officer and for many years a key contributor to China's revolution in the areas of military, diplomatic and political affairs. As a Red Army commander before the Sino-Japanese War, Luo Guipo went through the Long March. In the 1950s, he was assigned to Vietnam as chief military adviser to President Ho Chi Minh, and was involved in the decisive battle of Dien Bien Phu. After serving as Vice Foreign Minister, he later became the provincial governor of Shanxi. For both men, it was a good working relationship. Luo Guipo valued my father for his education, ability and commitment, and often asked him to draft important documents. My father respected Luo both as a person and for his clarity of mind. His writing was unskilled, but without consulting notes he spoke so fluently about the topics he dealt with that the uncorrected transcript was almost ready for publication.

In 1943, my father's unexpected posting to a lectureship in the Jin-Sui Party School was the prelude to his imprisonment in the Rescue Campaign. Anybody who had worked for the Party's underground in the Nationalist areas before the Sino-Japanese War was an automatic suspect. In addition, a former colleague had falsely confessed to being a Nationalist spy, so that put my father in doubt. In fact, he had already been examined in Yan'an about the gap in his record caused by losing official contact for a year during his forced exile in 1935. The inquiry had cleared him, but nothing could help him now. He was arrested and jailed.

His position entitled him to 'rescue' by the 'shock brigade', and for fifty days he was interrogated every day, with the help of torture. 'At that time, he didn't look human,' my mother told me many years later. 'It was hard to believe that a person could be as skinny as he was.' But exactly what he endured remained a mystery, for he seldom mentioned it afterwards.

A few decades later, one of my classmates wrote an essay at school in praise of her father, a high-ranking Communist officer. In particular, she mentioned the many scars on his body left by injuries received while fighting against the Nationalists and the Japanese. Shortly afterwards, this naive girl was shocked to discover that the scars she had seen were actually marks of tortures suffered during the Rescue Campaign, the relics of systematic burning by cigarettes. For many years, it was rare for details of the Rescue Campaign to surface in the official literature. Since I grew up, facts leaked gradually through various sources have helped me to imagine what happened to my father.

Despite the interrogations and tortures, my father refused to make up nonsense about himself or others. During the political indoctrination, he remained silent. Sitting unseen in a corner of his cell, he wrote a series of vivid literary sketches about the ridiculous behaviour he observed among the 'confessed' and their 'rescuers'. After the campaign, he showed my mother some of these satiric sketches. Fortunately, no one ever caught him at work, or else he would have suffered for this subversion.

After that rally, my mother paid attention to my father. Every day, they met on the way to the canteen, but were forbidden to speak by their armed guards. The army uniform my father wore was frayed and dirty. He trod softly, with a crudely made pottery bowl tucked under his arm, and the peak of his cap pulled down over serious eyes. Sometimes, his nose and mouth were covered by an old gauze mask. He told my mother later that it helped him to cope with the humiliation and abuse. She heard on the grapevine about his work for Luo Guipo and his conduct in the camp. Gradually, she began to admire this young man.

There were some of the Party's leaders who criticized the Rescue Campaign from the very beginning. Zhou Enlai argued: 'I know the Party's underground in Sichun province very well through my own experiences, and I have never heard of this "Red Flag Party"! The injustice to their members should be corrected.' Mao Zedong once cautioned Kang Sheng: 'There must be something wrong in your work.' Later, he recommended that no cadre in need of 'rescue' was to be killed and the majority were not to be arrested. This was a policy totally different from the hard line adopted by Stalin during the Soviet purges of the 1930s. My parents considered that it saved many Communist lives, even though wholesale arrests still occurred. In August 1943, after Kang Sheng's notorious speech, a document issued by the Party's Central Committee condemned the extraction of confessions by compulsion during the Rescue Campaign, and the ordering of arrests, beatings and executions without conclusive evidence.

Kang Sheng pursued his policy. All Communist bases had to take orders from the 'Central Committee of Rectification Study', where he was second in command to Mao Zedong, and in charge of all routine affairs. Once he had convinced the administrators in the various bases that his directives were backed by Mao himself, only Mao could put a stop to the process. In autumn 1943, despite the changes called for in the Central Committee's document, the Rescue Campaign reached the Jin-Sui base and took hold of my parents.

Under pressure from the Party's Central Committee, the rehabilitation started in Yan'an in December 1943. About 90 per cent of political prisoners were declared innocent, and subsequently released and allowed back to work. A year later, Mao Zedong admitted the mistakes of the Rescue Campaign. Eventually he made a public apology to the victims of injustice, saying that as director of the Central Committee of Rectification Study he must shoulder all the blame for its excesses.

After that, Kang's image faded in Yan'an. After the Communist Party's Seventh Congress in 1945, although he retained his membership of the Politburo, he was stripped of his other powerful functions, such as heading China's version of the KGB. But secure in his friendship with Mao, he lost none of his arrogant ways, and denied his responsibilities for problems in the Rescue Campaign. After the rehabilitation, more than 100 Communist cadres stayed in jail in Yan'an as enemy spies, because their cases were controlled by Kang himself. When the Nationalists occupied Yan'an in 1947, after the Sino-Japanese War, these prisoners were taken to the bank of the Yellow River and secretly executed by order of Kang Sheng.

In the Jin-Sui base, the rehabilitation started in autumn 1944 and lasted for nearly a year. With Kang Sheng's policy rescinded, most of the charges were dropped. Now that the fantasy of the 'Red Flag Party' had vanished, many 'spies' recanted their confessions. The most awkward situation faced those who had victimized comrades. One prisoner said: 'My arrest was based on a report from one of my colleagues who said that I shouted the slogan "Long live the Nationalists" at a rally. In fact, what I shouted was "Long live the Communists". Now let me confront the person who framed me.'

The rehabilitation showed my parents again that it was right to trust their beloved Party. In their mind, what happened during the Rescue Campaign was like the case of children being wrongly blamed by their mother. Who could deny a mother's love? In the end, the Party would always treat them justly. A spring breeze of change dispelled the cloud of terror. The camp where my parents were jailed was abolished; all prisoners became trainees at the Jin-Sui Party School and then had their freedom restored.

In order to relax the tensions among the former prisoners, the school authority organized leisure activities. For the first time in her life, my mother performed a dance in public. It was her way to celebrate release after suffering, and joy after persecution. To her surprise, the performance was a popular success, and soon she was cast to sing and dance in a play called *Good Crops* staged by former prisoners. In the following months, they toured the entire Jin-Sui base. The high point came in a massive rally held in support of heroes in the war against Japan and attended by 10,000 people.

My mother was now a shining star, and after her appearances in several more new plays, the Communist cultural work troupe of the base tried to recruit her as a professional actress. But she turned the offer down. Acting had expressed her feelings of the moment: she did not want to make it a career. And although her fame brought admirers, she rarely accepted their gifts or invitations. 'Your mother was a marvellous performer,' her former colleagues told me many years later, 'but in those days she was also known as a cold and arrogant girl.'

In fact, she did not mean to be hurtful. She valued her comrades and friends, but love was different. In her mind, the ideal husband should be well educated, a dedicated Communist, and a man of integrity. On her way from Yan'an to the Jin-Sui base, she was given a lift by Zhu De, Commander in Chief of the Eighth Route Army. Almost every day, he sent off a letter to his wife in Yan'an, Kang Keqing, who was a famous veteran of the Red Army. My mother expected her future husband to be equally caring and affectionate.

Before the Chinese New Year in February 1945, trainees in the Jin-Sui Party School started their first holiday since their imprisonment two years previously. One evening, while on their way to an open-air theatre to see traditional opera performed by a local troupe, my mother and her female classmates met a group of male trainees which included my father. The two groups mingled to watch the show, and spent the evening in a light-hearted mood. My father was not an active talker but my mother felt his deep eyes turned towards her. It was nearly midnight, and the groups were exchanging good-nights before returning to their quarters in the village, when my mother heard a quiet voice call her name. It belonged to my father, who handed her a small piece of paper and then walked away in the moonlight.

The note was a love letter, and it faced her with a choice – Yes or No – that was all the more difficult to make because it was the first time in her life that she had had to make it for herself. By any standards, he had shown many of the qualities that my mother dreamed of in her ideal husband, and both were reserved by nature. His only defect was his size. At 1.60 metres in height, my mother was tall for a Chinese girl, while my father was only just taller than my mother. After several days of pondering, my mother's conclusion was: 'I should look for a man who is not only as good as him but also taller than him.' She told my father that she was not ready to talk about love at such a critical time. The conversation took place on their way to the canteen. Having heard my mother's reply, my father bowed his head and walked silently away.

A month later, she ran into him again in the same place. Apart from his eyes, most of my father's face was hidden behind a worn-out army cap and a dirty gauze mask, but she could tell that he was pale and dispirited. He told her that he was recovering from an illness, but soon she learned that his illness was the fruit of her refusal, which had deeply hurt his pride. His struggle to master his bitterness had brought on a fever, and with drugs in short supply a colleague had treated him with acupuncture and bloodletting.

For the first time in her life, my mother's heart was touched by the love that a man felt for her. After a sleepless night, she decided to accept my father as her boyfriend, and from then on their relationship grew fast. In his spare time, my father wrote play scripts for my mother to perform. He escorted her on her tours, and during the performance he looked after her costumes and luggage. When they came to a river, he would hoist her on his back and wade across, especially during her menstruation. (According to Chinese medical tradition, cold water could damage women's health during their period.) In return, my mother washed and mended his clothes, and stitched a new duvet for him with her own bedspreads when his old one wore out. Later, my father told her how pleased he had been when he found a trace of her menstrual blood on the new duvet. At night, he would touch the mark gently as if touching my mother's body.

In those days, sexual relationships before marriage were not common in China. Though deeply in love, my parents never overstepped the line. They still lived separately, sharing single-sex lodgings with colleagues. In the evenings, they met outside the village. Lying in the meadow, or strolling along the bank of the Yellow River, they enjoyed their heart-to-heart talks. One night, a prowling wolf interrupted their conversation, and my terrified mother threw herself into my father's arms. In the pitch-darkness, the wolf's eyes were moons of light, staring at the two unarmed young lovers as they clung to each other, not moving and barely breathing, like statues. They had heard in the past that a wolf would attack if you tried to run. In the contest of courage and strength between the two sides, finally it was the wolf who quit and ran away.

From that time on, my father started writing to my mother every day, whether they were able to see each other or not, usually a single sheet of paper with no greeting and no signature. When my mother asked why, his reply was an affectionate smile. She suddenly recognized his reason: their love had been beyond any usual form of address. His custom went on for several decades.

Through their close contact, my mother heard more about my father's personal history. His first affair had started in 1937, with a colleague in Taiyuan city, where he worked for the Communist underground. In 1940, she had married someone else after he left for Yan'an. There he had met quite a few of my mother's fellow students, but nothing had happened. In 1942, he and my mother had met by accident in Yan'an shortly before she left for Jin-Sui, and he was drawn at once to this well-educated young girl. In general, my mother's physical features did not match the classical image of beauty, such as a nose with a high bridge, large eyes and light skin, but her poise and quiet sweetness made her stand out. On evenings when she strolled by the river with her friends, he would follow in secret and listen to them talk. My mother never noticed him, since the river bank was crowded at that hour, and my father was too proud to approach a girl first. So after she vanished from the river bank, he had no way to trace her.

When the camp reunited them, early in 1944, my father thought their meeting must be fate. At the end of the Rescue Campaign, he joined the Communist committee in the Party School. He was put in charge of the rehabilitation of former political prisoners, and what he found out about my mother's behaviour during the campaign completely won him over.

At dawn on 15 August 1945, my parents and their colleagues were woken by delirious shouting. 'The Japanese have surrendered! The Japanese have surrendered!' The voice belonged to the Dean of the Party School, who had just received the news by telegram, and in his excitement had rushed out of his cave to pass it on, dressed only in his underpants. Straight away, the village burst out in celebration. The streets rang with cheering, singing and dancing, and every bowl and washbasin turned into a gong or drum. Everyone was in tears, the Communists and villagers, women, men and children, with feelings too strong to control.

For a while, my parents lost the words to speak their joy. Ever since the outbreak of the war, eight years ago, they had dreamed of this day. In order to achieve it, they had sacrificed their youth, and risked enormous dangers and hardships. To defeat the Japanese, tens of millions of Chinese had died. During the war, my mother grew up into a mature Communist and my father became a seasoned soldier. During the war, they also witnessed the enormous development of the Communist Party, its forces enlarged by struggle from 50,000 to over a million troops. Their territory had grown from a single base in the poor and drought-stricken corner of northwest China, the Shaan-Gan-Ning Border Region, to nineteen bases covering more than a million square kilometres. A quarter of China's inhabitants were now controlled by the Communists. My parents had been watching when the single spark of revolution had truly flared to become a prairie fire.

As soon as Japan capitulated, a new era started in China. Suddenly the Communist Party needed to send masses of cadres to work in the vast areas lately vacated by the Japanese. Every day the road outside the village was thronged with troops passing by on their way from Yan'an to Manchuria. Training in the Jin-Sui Party School finished immediately, and the former political prisoners were assigned to different posts. Soon the school was like a busy station, with travellers bound for many destinations. A short-lived 'marriage wave' took place, as people rushed to wed before they left. After the Rescue Campaign, many Communists with intellectual backgrounds had shed their pride in choosing marriage partners. Among the small number of educated female Party members, many were marrying worker-peasant cadres.

My parents accepted their assignment to Manchuria, over 1,000 kilometres away, and claimed 20 silver coins each as their travel expenses. Because they faced a difficult journey, with transportation scarce, they discarded most of their belongings. They also took a radical decision. Till now, they had planned on deferring their marriage. My mother was twenty-two, my father twenty-nine: they felt that they were too young. In any case, they wanted to save some money first, having earned none at all throughout the war. The prospect of the trip changed their minds. Once married, they could stay close and look after each other. They applied to the Party Committee, and the Dean gave permission, though because of the shortage of housing in the school it would happen when a cave became available.

On 20 August 1945, my parents' wedding took place. That morning, they moved in with their only possessions: two frayed duvets and a few clothes. The cave was located in a small village by the Yellow River, and the conditions were as primitive as any they had experienced, but on that day it looked special to my parents because it was their wedding chamber, and the first home they ever shared. In the afternoon, their simple wedding ceremony took place, and after it a dinner party to which nearly all remaining members of the Party School were invited. The only dish they served was fried fish caught fresh in the river, thanks to helpful colleagues. My cheerful parents dressed in spruce army uniforms, the best clothes available, each with a red tissue paper flower pinned to the tunic and made by themselves – the only decoration they could afford. And the frequent toasts that wished them a happy marriage were drunk in cold water, because alcohol was a luxury in the base. But it did not matter to a couple intoxicated with happiness.

After their wedding, my parents were surprised to learn that their assignments to Manchuria had been cancelled without consulting them: instead they were to remain in the Jin-Sui base. Later, they discovered that the director of the Communist News Agency (Xin-hua News Agency) in Jin-Sui had pulled strings to swap his post with my father's. Among the Party cadres, it was common knowledge that in Manchuria, as in other areas just vacated by the Japanese, promotion would come faster owing to the strong demand there for Communist personnel. My mother's mission to Manchuria was also cancelled, and her appointment left to be decided. My parents did not welcome the change, seeing that there was not much for them to do in the Jin-Sui base. But the Party had decided, and they had no choice but to obey.

Before moving in as director of the Communist News Agency in Jin-Sui, during his brief honeymoon my father was asked to oversee the closure of the Party School. For both of them, it was their first break since they joined the revolution. The school was nearly empty and the war was over. They could lie awake all night talking about their past experiences and future lives, and in the daytime they could stay in their cave conversing or reading together, and hardly leaving each other's side. They ate from the same bowl, drank from the same glass, walked hand in hand and sat shoulder to shoulder. Every day, my father sang Peking Opera for a while, self-accompanied on his jinghu, a two-stringed bowed

Chinese instrument. This was his favourite hobby. While a pupil in his home town, he would sneak into the local theatre after school to watch performances, because he could not afford a ticket. Years later, he still knew several classical operas by heart. During the honeymoon, he copied out the entire script of *Farewell My Concubine* (Ba-wang-bie-ji), and enjoyed teaching my mother to sing.

At the end of the Sino-Japanese War, tensions sharpened between the Nationalists and the Communists. On 11 August 1945, three days before Japan surrendered, Chiang Kai-shek issued a presidential order instructing the Communist forces to take no further military action against the Japanese or their Chinese puppet forces without the permission of his government. But the Communists had no intention of allowing Chiang Kai-shek to act as if he alone was responsible for the Japanese defeat. On 13 August 1945, Mao Zedong told the Party in Yan'an that if Chiang tried to override the Communists, their policy would be to make him fight for every inch of land. Victory against the outside enemy had speeded the countdown towards full-scale civil war.

In autumn 1945, Chiang Kai-shek gave secret orders to open a new campaign against the Communists. Over 1.5 million Nationalist troops were mobilized. From September to November 1945, the Nationalist General Fu Zuoyi in Suiyuan province launched his 100,000 troops in an all-out offensive against the Communist bases in north China.

By now, my father longed for a transfer. The place for an experienced military commander was out in the front line fighting against the enemy, not back in the rear, managing news. But though he looked hard for a post at his level, in the end the only door that opened was in the Sui-Mon region, which covered part of Suiyuan province and Inner Mongolia. In the face of the advance by General Fu, the Communist regional committee urged my father to come at once, and to bring a team of cadres from the Jin-Sui base.

In those days, the Sui-Mon region was the very last posting a cadre

would wish for. As part of the 'Sai-wai' (the lands beyond the Great
Wall), it was the place where prisoners were exiled in ancient times,
China's Siberia. In the late 1940s, it was still so poor that to own a flock
of sheep would be viewed as exceptional wealth. During the long winter,
even many local rich could not afford to heat a second bedroom, and the
entire family would sleep in the same room with their servants, coolies
or even guests. For the Communists, survival was particularly hard. The
sparse population could not support them either through taxes or
through confiscation, which required an affluent class with valuable
treasures in store. Perhaps this was why my father could still find a
vacancy. If so, he did not mind, because for him the Party's interests
always came first. He set out for Jining, then the capital city of Suiyuan
province, while my mother remained in Jin-Sui. She was pregnant with
her first child, and had just started work as director of the Communist
women's federation in a county.

In my father's autobiographical note, written in 1952, I found a brief
account of what he found:

> I arrived in a completely unfamiliar place . . . Sui-Mon was in
> chaos [due to Nationalist military attacks]. The cadres I brought
> with me were soon assigned to different jobs. In the end, I was kept
> by the Party committee of the Sui-Mon region, and took charge of
> mass work in Jining city. The arrangement was based on my past
> experience of working for the Communist underground in
> Nationalist-occupied areas . . . [Within a few days] I organized a
> trade union among barbers and took part in meetings with railway
> workers . . .

Soon after this, my father met a former superior who was now a
leader of the Communist troops in the region. 'Why are you here?' he
said to my father in surprise. 'You must come with me immediately. We're
desperate for experienced commanders.' However, the regional committee

refused to let my father go. Only when the army agreed to barter several officers in exchange for him could he resume his military career.

After the Sino-Japanese War, the previously separate Communist forces were renamed as the People's Liberation Army. My father's appointment was in Inner Mongolia, as Political Commissar for a cavalry detachment, the equivalent of regimental commander – the same rank he had held in Shanxi province, eight years before. He should have risen higher by now, but a number of factors had damaged his career. In particular, the Rescue Campaign disabled him during a period in the Sino-Japanese War when the rapid expansion of the Red armies brought a string of quick promotions to his colleagues.

In the Sui-Mon region, expansion was more difficult. The sparse population curbed recruitment, and supplies and ammunition cost money. During the civil war, the number of troops was cut, and their officers' ranks reduced, which was the reverse of what happened elsewhere. At one point, my father found that his newly appointed leader had been a soldier in the guerrilla force he himself had founded and commanded years before, at the start of the war against Japan. In his autobiographical note, he wrote:

> The war did not allow me to think about my own interests. Fortunately, the Party gave me strength. I cautioned myself that I must settle down with my job, and respect my new leader . . . During those brutal wars, we often commanded the troops together day and night . . . we became very close to each other . . . I felt pleased that I was able to overcome my selfishness.

In December 1945, my father and his escort set off on horseback to join his cavalry unit. In his autobiographical note, he mentioned that he could not ride a horse when first assigned, but much of his long journey ran through Nationalist territory, and no other transport would do. In the rush to leave, he had no time to collect warm clothes, but winter in

Inner Mongolia was unbelievably cold, especially when the wind blew from Siberia, and each day the frost bit harder. Halfway through their journey, the weather changed. Within minutes, a raging blizzard blotted out sky and land, as if to mark the end of the world. Local people called this the 'white feather whirlwind'. Eddies of snowflakes, heavy sand and dust blew everywhere. Voices shouted, horses neighed, but no one saw where. Soon, the sweat on my father's body turned into a sheath of ice. His thin army uniform, first wet with snow then frozen hard, crackled each time he moved. His army cap gave no protection. 'Suddenly, my ears swelled up like flaps of risen dough, and soon they were totally numb,' my father told me many years later, 'but I didn't dare touch them for fear they might drop off at any moment.'

This was the afternoon, and my father had not eaten since breakfast because food was in short supply. Now hunger and the blizzard drained his strength. He managed to call his team together, then passed out from exhaustion and cold. Anxious for the life of their leader, his escort made a run for the next village, where with help from local people they rubbed his skin with spirit in an unheated room until he came round, then fed him a huge bowl of hot soup made from ginger and brown sugar, which was a folk remedy to throw off the cold. Slowly his skin warmed. Before moving on, he followed the advice of local peasants and bought an uncured sheepskin coat, together with some pieces of hare fur, one to protect his groin, the others to keep his ears warm. With this simple protection, he came through the rest of the journey.

The cavalry unit that my father joined was rather like a guerrilla force, untrained and undisciplined. The troops were disliked in the locality because of behaviour such as refusing to pay for purchases or for damaging people's property. Three days after his arrival, a battalion revolted and went over to the Nationalist side. They planned to assassinate my father, but he got wind of the conspiracy, and managed to escape.

Instead of being deterred, he launched a programme of political training based on the 'Three Disciplines and Eight Notices' introduced by Mao Zedong as guidance for the Red Army before the Sino-Japanese War. At my father's instruction, a special team was set up to monitor the troops' behaviour and settle what they owed round about. Gradually, the relationship between troops and local residents improved. A number of peasants even volunteered to serve in the unit.

The commander of the cavalry detachment, a Red Army veteran with a poor educational background, did not conceal his disrespect for intellectual cadres. When my father arrived, the military budget barely stretched to basic ammunition and meagre rations, and the troops went unpaid for some time. Unlike the commander, whose luxurious meals were prepared by his own private kitchen, my father refused all privileges. He ate what his soldiers ate, and turned down the warm fox-fur jacket issued to high-ranking officers in favour of the cotton uniform worn by his juniors. In his mind, the more a senior officer consumed, the poorer the condition of the troops. When spring came, he tried to have the lining of his winter jacket made into a shirt, as he had no spare shirt. Local peasant women joked to his bodyguard: 'We have never seen such a poor master.' When the troops arrived in a new place, my father always made an official visit to the local governing body with his adjutant. Many times, the respectful reception focused on the officer clad in the fox-fur coat and cap, while my father in his everyday uniform was mistaken for the other man's bodyguard and ignored.

Thanks to my father, the standards of the unit quickly rose. His major principles when commanding troops were to introduce revolutionary ideas to its members and to enforce strict military discipline. As he raised the standards of his unit, he made sure he practised what he advocated; and soon he earned deep respect from his troops. Promotions followed after the outbreak of the civil war. By 1951, before I was born, he was assigned as Political Commissar to a division, the equivalent of a divisional commander. But rank did not alter his principles. For instance, after victories over the Nationalists he would never accept the trophies of war offered as gifts by his administrative officers.

A Chinese proverb says that 'when a man gets power, even his chickens and dogs rise to heaven' (Yi-ren-de-dao, ji-quan-sheng-tian). This rule of patronage did not hold true for my father's personal staff, following his promotion. For a long time, his bodyguards complained about the contrast between their own outdated weapons and the modern equipment owned by his colleagues' bodyguards. My father's reply was that they should be thankful for what they had, seeing what most of his troops had to make do with. This situation continued until many months later, when repeated victories gave them access to equipment captured from the Nationalist forces. After his troops seized Zuoyun, a large county in Inner Mongolia, my father was furious to learn that one of his bodyguards had bought a pair of pillows with embroidered cases. This was his troops' first station-ing in a city, and he did not want to see them corrupted by the lure of material wealth. The young man was criticized for his extravagant purchase, and placed in detention for several days. What my father did sounds heavy-handed, but he was highly respected by his troops, including his pri-vate staff. They admired him for setting the example of a real Communist.

My father's posting to the Sui-Mon region started a series of separa-tions that lasted till June 1952, when he returned from the Korean War and was posted in Beijing. By then, I, their third child, was close to one year old. During that period, whole years went by without their meet-ing, and this was very painful for a young couple deeply in love, who had been as inseparable as a body and its shadow during their honey-moon. Before he left Jin-Sui for the Sui-Mon region in 1945, my father worked about ten kilometres away from my mother, and both were given lodgings near their work. My mother was pregnant, my father worked long hours at the news agency, transport was scarce, but neither could bear to be parted. So almost every day, my mother travelled on foot between their two locations. By now she was suffering from morn-ing sickness, and for several weeks raw carrots were the only food she had, since she could not stomach cooked food and fresh fruit was too expensive. But no matter how much the journey tired her, it made my mother happy to see her husband every day.

Before my father left, my mother tried her best to mask her feelings, and prove she had the strength to face their unpredictable future. After saying goodbye, she wept until next day. Her husband was going to war, and their first child would be born in a few months' time. The life she faced was certain to be hard. Throughout the separation, they corresponded as much as they could. On the way to Sui-Mon, my father noticed a puddle in front of an army service station (one of the many reception centres set up during the Sino-Japanese and civil wars to provide travelling troops or individual service men with free accommodation, food and livestock), and immediately wrote to my mother warning her to be careful if ever she passed there. During the civil war, my father's life was constantly in danger. In order to keep my mother's letters and her photograph safe, he made himself a small leather bag that fitted on the belt he always wore. As he told my mother later, its contents would stay with him until the moment he died. In one battle, he and his troops were surrounded by Nationalist forces. He lost everything he had, including his horse, but the bag and its contents remained.

In fact, there was a possible remedy for my parents' separation. It was a common practice in the Party for the wives of senior officials to work for their husbands in sinecure jobs, to keep the couples together. In the Sui-Mon area, the army set up a camp in the rear for the families of senior officers, and offered to put my mother in charge of it, so that she could see her husband during lulls in the fighting. But my father turned down the suggestion. As a senior officer, he wanted to share the wartime hardships that his soldiers and junior officers endured. They both agreed that the Party's interests must come first, so it would be wrong for his wife to sacrifice her own revolutionary career merely for their temporary contentment. Both then and later on, he encouraged my mother to work independently, and never interfered in her favour. To this day, she is grateful to my father for his valuable moral support to her career.

Chapter 8

Under the Red Flag:
Stories of My Father's Family

(1935–1954)

Like most who worked and studied in Yan'an during the Sino-Japanese War, my mother discovered the scenery along the Yan River bank, and loved to stroll there. My father too spent time there, and on an autumn evening in 1940 his attention was captured by a group of young men dressed in Red Army uniforms and talking with the twang of the Shandong Peninsula where he came from. The accent took him by surprise, because it was a sound that he had rarely heard since going on the run in 1935 after the defeat of his armed insurrection. 'Comrades, do you come from the Shandong Peninsula?' he enquired.

'Ai-ya! Eldest brother, you're here!' A young man called out with an eager voice. His face seemed familiar, but my father simply could not place him. 'Eldest brother, it's me, Morality, your younger brother.' The young man's speech was choked with sobs. 'Where have you been all these years? We thought you'd been killed.' Tears ran down my father's face. He clung to his brother's hands and lost his words, 'overjoyed by the shock of our reunion', he recorded nearly half a century later.

Since my grandfather's visit in Tianjin in 1936, my father had never heard again from his family. At first he was a fugitive, forced into exile and wanted by the Nationalist authorities. Any attempt to get in touch might have risked his own and his family's safety. During the war with Japan, his home county was occupied by the invaders, which blocked communication even more. Deeply concerned about his family's fate, more recently he had tried many times to make contact, but none of his messages got through. Yet here, in the wastes of northwest China, he and his younger brother were reunited. It felt like a dream. Five years ago, he had left behind him a quiet teenager, fourteen years old. Now, a keen young Communist stood in front of him.

From then on, my father spent almost every Sunday with Second Uncle until autumn 1942, when he left Yan'an. The Yan River bank became their rendezvous. In sight of the ancient pagoda they talked about their revolutionary careers, their future hopes, and the plight of their family after my father left. When midnight came and neither wanted to stop, they would return to one cave or the other, to lie on a kang, sharing a single duvet, and talk till they both fell asleep.

At the age of nineteen, Second Uncle was already a Party member of two years' standing. After working as director of publicity for the first Communist government in his home county, he arrived in Yan'an in spring 1939, as part of a delegation reporting to the Party's Central Committee. Afterwards, he attended the Central Party School for a two-year training course. So much experience at such a young age seemed to promise him a bright future in the Communist hierarchy. Surprisingly, in autumn 1941 he decided to study music, and went to the famous Lu Xun College of Art, the only Communist art institute in Yan'an, to study singing and composing.

For his entrance examination, Second Uncle was interviewed by a panel that included Lü Ji, a composer who later became a leading figure in the musical world, and An Po, a famous composer and writer who was head of the Department of Music. The interview took place in their office, in a cave outside Yan'an. Opposite the window, a portrait of Lenin and several large sheets of music were pinned to the rough earthen wall by thorns of the wild jujube, since it was hard to get drawing pins in the Red capital.

'Why are you giving up your bright political career?' An Po asked Second Uncle. 'If you study acting, you'll only be an actor in the future; if you study composition, you'll only be a composer, whether you write one or a hundred pieces of good music in your life.' An Po told him frankly: 'This way, you will never be a powerful government servant, or gain the privileges that come with political position.' What he said was true. In China, even among the Communists, there was much higher status reserved for officials than for those engaged in art or literature.

'Since the proletariat need music to express their feelings in the revolutionary struggle,' Second Uncle replied passionately, 'I would like to devote the rest of my life to our proletarian art, and celebrating workers, peasants and soldiers.'

Though my father said little about the change in Second Uncle's career, he did not welcome it. He himself was a lover of literature and art, so he understood his brother's decision, but he also felt that any piece of good art work should stem from real life. As a full-time musician, Second Uncle would not gain the material experience of revolutionary struggle that might reinforce the fruitful career he wanted.

At that time, work in the college was strongly influenced by Western art, as most of the staff had trained either abroad or in Westernized institutions in urban China. Many had been prominent figures before they came to Yan'an, and were aiming to use their familiar medium on behalf of the revolution.

One summer night, my father was invited to watch a new production by Second Uncle and his colleagues of *Phoenix Nirvana*, a choral work based on the poem by Guo Moro, a famous contemporary. It quoted the myth of the phoenix to express the poet's admiration for revolutionaries. The temporary theatre was a church built by a Spanish missionary in the

1920s, which was the only Gothic building in Yan'an, its tall spire spectacular by day against the background of barren yellow earthen cliffs and blue sky. Two hours before the performance, the theatre was packed with soldiers, officers and local peasants who sat on the long wooden benches and kicked up a clamour of noise. Here in this desolate region, a visit to the theatre was like a festival.

Purple curtains opened gently. Under the light of several gas-lamps, my father saw his younger brother standing in the mixed choir. In front of them sat an orchestra equipped with Western instruments, most of them self-made. At the conductor's signal, a piece of passionate music started, but many in the audience kept on talking. Unused to Western conventions, they thought that the performance was like the prelude in traditional Chinese operas, a first call that audiences could ignore. Later, a foreign-trained bass made his entrance. It had been a joke in Yan'an that his voice was strong enough to shake the cliffs, but tonight the form and style of what he sang grated so harshly on people's ears that some complained: 'Why is he making such a din and stopping us from chatting?' After a soprano solo, some peasants shook their heads: 'What a pity such a pretty girl sounded like a donkey's bray!' My father also shook his head. It seemed that the attempt to adapt Western-style music for a revolutionary purpose was likely to offend a Chinese audience.

The Rectification Campaign launched in February 1942 caused havoc in Communist art circles. Some writers' work was condemned for attacking the Party. The saddest case was Wang Shiwei, my mother's former English teacher, whose outspoken articles criticising his leaders' work included his complaint about the dancing craze in the Red capital. He was picked up during the subsequent Rescue Campaign, jailed until 1947, and then executed secretly together with other political prisoners by order of Kang Sheng.

Another target was Ding Ling, a young woman writer famous since the 1920s. Her first husband, also a well-known writer, worked for the Communist underground in Shanghai. He was killed by the Nationalists in 1931, and Ding Ling was jailed. In 1936, she was rescued by the Communist underground and conveyed to Red territory. In March 1942, she published an article protesting against the biased treatment suffered by two women Communists during their divorce proceedings. Because their husbands were Communist officials, the Party had failed to protect them. Ding Ling was accused of exaggerating the dark side of life in Yan'an and therefore discrediting the Party. Fortunately she was rescued again, but this time by one person, Mao Zedong, when he decided that nevertheless, Ding Ling was still a comrade, and should not be treated as an enemy. So she avoided the fate of Wang Shiwei, as well as the persecution commonly endured during the Rescue Campaign by intellectual Communists like my parents.

Apparently, Mao was not happy about the artistic community in Yan'an, especially when it headlined internal problems or deferred to Western influence. In May 1942, he published his famous article, 'Speech to the Forum on Literature and Art in Yan'an', in a move that heralded reforms. For decades afterwards, this article was cited as the highest authority. Mao's theme was that revolutionary literature and art must serve workers, peasants and soldiers. Therefore writers, actors, musicians and artists should look to the villages, factories and armed forces for their subjects. After his speech, Mao went to the Lu Xun Art College to enlarge on his views. Standing on the college's outdoor basketball court, he told Second Uncle and his colleagues: 'If you do not know workers, peasants and soldiers, how can you serve them well? How do you produce work which is loved by them? Life is the only source of literary and artistic creation.' It was not long before the staff and students of the college were mobilized to go to villages or military units in order to learn their duties. Second Uncle was sent to a remote village located in the sparsely populated highlands of north Gasu province.

Second Uncle spent most of the next two years, till the end of the Sino-Japanese War, in the desolate villages of the highlands, and became good friends with the local peasants. In the daytime he worked in their fields. At night, he slept on the same kang. Through this close contact, he was moved by the resolute way they faced the hardships and poverty of their lives, and was also amazed by the wealth of folk literature and music he discovered. In the evenings, he visited villagers in their caves, and noted down folk songs and tales. One peasant friend delighted in collecting local colloquialisms. Very often, Second Uncle was woken up at midnight by some new find, and would scribble it down in the glimmer of an oil-lamp. The two grew so close that they embraced and wept when Second Uncle had to leave.

Under the guidance of Mao's speech, soon a number of new productions from the Lu Xun Art College were adapting popular folk music and dance to convey the Party's propaganda message. They caused a sensation in Yan'an, and some of them are regularly revived to this day such as the famous *The Girl with White Hair* (*Bai-mao-nü*), written as a folk opera by a group of Second Uncle's colleagues led by He Jingzhi, a future Vice-Minister of Culture.

The play tells the story of a young peasant girl called Happiness (Xi-er). One New Year's Eve her father, her only surviving relation, commits suicide after being forced to trade her to his landlord to pay his debts. Now Happiness has to work as a servant for the landlord, and is ill-treated by his mother and later raped by him. Before her master can sell her as a cast-off slave, she runs away to the mountains and lives there for years in isolation. Local people take her for a ghost, and are scared by her mysterious appearances. When Communist troops retrieve her at last, her dark hair has turned completely white. The moral is that only in the new society, under Communism, are poor people treated as human beings.

Measured by the size of its audiences and number of productions, *The Girl with White Hair* is possibly the most successful play in China's history. During the civil war in the late 1940s, it was a favourite with Communist cultural work troupes, put on in areas captured from the Nationalists to highlight the darkness of the old society and stir up resentment against the exploiting class. When the Land Reforms started, it was used to mobilize peasants to struggle against landlords. Red Army units saw it performed during lulls in the fighting against the Nationalists, usually in an open-air theatre decorated like a venue for a political rally. Above the stage, a huge red banner inscribed with black characters urged: 'Never forget the bitterness of class oppression! Remember our hatred of blood and tears!' The mass audience sat on the ground, and wept for the plight of Happiness and her father. The actors cast as the evil landlord were often stoned and sometimes even shot at by soldiers unable to contain their feelings. In the thick of battle, Red troops would shout: 'Revenge our Happiness! Down with the old society!'

Second Uncle told me that he made his commitment to Communism in winter 1936, several months before the outbreak of the Sino-Japanese War, when he was fifteen years old and studying in a teacher-training course in his home county. For the sons of poor families, this was the only way forward. Once past the competitive entrance examination, they could obtain scholarships which covered their fees and basic living expenses while studying.

One day, Second Uncle was asked to a meeting with Sun Ziping, my father's former colleague in the Communist underground. After the defeat of their armed insurrection in 1935, Ziping had continued to work in Penglai as headmaster of a rural school, as his cover had not been broken, so Second Uncle knew only that he was my father's trusted friend. When they met, Ziping told Second Uncle bluntly: 'The Japanese are coming soon, so there's no point continuing your studies. Please come to the countryside and join us. I'll find you a post in a village school.' Second Uncle agreed at once, as he had longed to do something useful for his country. The Xi'an Incident had lately made headline news all over China, and Ziping explained the Party's view that the priority must be to establish an Anti-Japanese United Front with the Nationalists. Lastly he enrolled Second Uncle in an organization called the 'Vanguard of Chinese Liberation', and warned him to keep his membership secret because the organization was controlled by the Communist Party.

When he realized that Ziping was a Communist, it came as a thrill to Second Uncle. Two years before, he had discovered the ideals of Communism through books recommended by my father before his exile. During one of their midnight conversations, my father revealed that he was a secret Communist, which shocked Second Uncle speechless for a while. His initial response was fear for my father's safety, but he came to admire the Communist ideals, and decided that one day he too would work to make the future brighter for poor people and for China.

Early in 1937, Second Uncle started work in a village school. Under Ziping's guidance, he threw himself into the anti-Japanese movement, and soon his school was bustling with patriotic activities. In the classrooms, wall-newspapers written by pupils praised the resistance against Japan. On the campus, posters with patriotic slogans lined the walls. What Second Uncle most enjoyed was performing patriotic songs with his pupil choir. After class, they would visit rural markets and even Nationalist barracks. After their performance, the large crowds that gathered to hear them sing patriotic songs such as 'On the Song-hua River' would follow Second Uncle to chant: 'Down with the Japanese imperialists!' or 'Stop the civil war and resist the Japanese invasion!'

At home, Second Uncle also taught patriotic songs to his teenage sisters, Glow and Grace (First and Second Auntie), which introduced the girls to revolutionary ideals. Grace was a cheerful girl, and wherever she went she loved to sing, but their father disapproved of their activities.

'Our stomachs are shrivelled with starvation, who feels like singing?' he asked them. 'You'll be arrested if the government hears your songs.' When Second Uncle explained that patriotic songs were one way to help unite the country against Japan, my grandfather objected: 'Can you fill your empty stomach and drive the Japanese away by singing?'

Second Uncle and his sisters did not blame their father for his doubts: they understood his situation. Only a year before, he had been the family's breadwinner, till the shop where he worked had closed down. Around that time, his elder brother had also lost his business, and later moved with his family to Manchuria, to seek a new start. My grandparents had stayed, reluctant to expose their young children to an area already occupied by the Japanese.

With economic depression and the threat of war, my grandfather could not find another job. In desperation, he tried different lines of work, such as peddling vanishing cream or hair oil to village women, but mostly, he came home disappointed as few could afford cosmetics. He kept losing weight, and was troubled by an endless cough. Though in his early forties, he became stooped and his dark hair turned to white. He looked like a man over sixty. When he became too weak to carry his goods, his small business had to stop. After that, the family lived mainly off my grandmother's sewing, helped by my two teenage aunts.

My grandfather had borrowed to buy his house. As soon as he lost his job, creditors flocked to the door in pursuit of his debts. Most were former colleagues or family relatives – in those days, mortgage services were arranged mainly through personal connections. Within months, nearly all of the family's possessions were sold or pawned, even their bedding, cooking utensils and my father's school textbooks. Finally, most of their house was taken over by their biggest creditors, my grandmother's younger sister and her merchant husband, who spared the Mu family a corner.

Before Second Uncle started teaching, the family was penniless. My grandmother managed to dress her children neatly by careful mending and washing, but very often they went without food. It was a torment to smell the meals cooked in the kitchen of my grandmother's younger sister, which used to be theirs, or to see her children pass by their door, nibbling sweets or cakes.

On Chinese New Year's Eve in early 1938, a few months after the outbreak of the Sino-Japanese War, Second Uncle came home from his village school with startling news: he was leaving at once to join a local guerrilla force newly set up by the Communists. My grandfather lay on the kang and wept. 'You are the family's only breadwinner, please think about the situation of your parents and younger siblings after you leave.' Second Uncle wept too. 'Dada, Mama, if the Japanese come to our county, none of us can live in peace. Please believe me, what I'm doing is in the interests of our family as well as our country.'

My grandmother stayed silent; she saw that her second son's path would follow his brother's, who might be dead for all she knew, as no one had heard from him since my grandfather's visit in 1936. 'Am I going to lose my second son too?' she asked herself quietly, and felt a sharp blade in her heart. She knew from past experience that Communists were stubborn: they could not be swayed from their ideals. Right now, her only wish was to cook a delicious New Year's dinner before her second son's departure. Ever since infancy, Second Uncle had suffered the malnutrition caused by poverty. Though already seventeen, he looked more like fourteen years old. If he had to go to war, and face an unpredictable future, today might be her last opportunity to make up for all the treats she could never afford. But her purse had been empty for days. She looked at the empty kitchen, and started to wail uncontrollably.

In May 1938, the guerrilla forces that Second Uncle belonged to as an officer defeated the Nationalist troops in his county, and occupied the town. As soon as the fight was over, my anxious grandmother and her two teenage girls went looking for her son. The empty streets still reeked of gunsmoke, and were littered with abandoned Nationalist uniforms and weapons. In front of the town hall, under a huge red flag that blew in the wind, Second Uncle was conducting his troops singing: 'Devils beheaded with broadswords!/ All fellow patriots,/ The day has come to fight against the Japanese invasion! . . .'

What an army it was! My grandmother could not believe her eyes. Troops dressed as shabbily as peasants, not even the officers in uniform, only a handful of old-fashioned rifles, but plenty of shiny broadswords, recently forged. With such crude weapons, it was amazing to have defeated well-equipped troops, and in fact the victory was eased by the crumbling morale of the Nationalist troops. With the Japanese approaching, their hold on the county was precarious, and now it was the Communists who would bear the brunt of the attack.

During his short break at home, Second Uncle told my grand-mother that he had secretly joined the Communist Party, with the support of Sun Ziping, who was a senior fellow leader. Three years before, it was my father who had recruited Ziping. My grandmother stopped Second Uncle's explanation. 'Your brother and Ziping are good people. I believe that you are doing the right thing for poor people and our country.'

In autumn 1938, the first Communist government took office in Penglai and chose my uncle, who was not yet eighteen, to head its Publicity Department. He became an instant celebrity in the county, kept busy with a stream of engagements such as staging anti-Japanese demonstrations, speaking at rallies, or conducting choirs for patriotic songs. With his encouragement, First and Second Aunties became activists too, and toured the county promoting resistance to Japan.

In September 1938 First Auntie, aged fifteen, left home for a military and political training course run by the Communists and recommended by Second Uncle – a journey of about 100 kilometres. 'Can you spend one more day at home?' my grandmother asked in tears when she first heard the news. Her daughter was to leave on the day of the Mid-Autumn Festival, by tradition a family occasion. But before First Auntie spoke, grandmother shook her head and told herself: 'How silly I am! The Japanese are coming, it's more important to protect our country than to celebrate festivals at home.' On that day, First Auntie started her revolutionary career. In order to safeguard her family, she changed her surname from 'Mu' to 'Wang'.

In early 1939, Second Uncle was sent to Yan'an as a member of a delegation from Shandong province, reporting to the Party's Central Committee. On its way to the Red capital, the mission clashed with blockading Nationalist troops, and suffered heavy casualties. When the news reached my grandfather, he wept for the loss of another son. No one could comfort him, because it was the last he ever heard of his second son.

Before he set out for Yan'an, Second Uncle took his younger sister, Grace (Second Auntie), on a visit to the Communist troops. 'Would you like to sing for the revolution?' he asked her. 'You're only thirteen, too young to do anything else here.' So Grace joined the Children's Troupe, which became famous in the region during the Sino-Japanese War. She followed the Communist guerrilla forces, and sang tirelessly for soldiers and peasants. At night, she crept close to the Japanese lines and sang patriotic songs to troops of the Chinese puppet army. This was her contribution to the Communist 'political offensive', psychological warfare waged to deter Chinese nationals from fighting for the Japanese. For this dangerous work, Second Auntie was praised as the 'golden voice of the Shandong Peninsula'.

Their children's activities brought my grandparents strong hostility from their local community, townspeople whose brutal image of a Communist came chiefly from Nationalist propaganda. They blamed my grandparents for their failure to discipline their children. As a result, my grandmother's younger sister came to the door and shouted: 'The Communists are bandits. Look at their shabby uniforms and ridiculous weapons! How can they beat the Japanese? You should marry your elder daughters to decent families, instead of letting them mix with soldiers every day and corrupt public morals.'

Most of the time, my grandfather held his tongue and kept to his small damp room. He found it hard to cope with social pressure. He had always cared deeply about his reputation, and felt shamed by his years of unemployment, which to him meant loss of face with the local community. The effect of his children's revolutionary activities was like adding frost to snow in winter. But my grandmother could not let the challenge pass. 'I believe the Communists are good people,' she retorted to her sister. 'They would never do evil. Let the future judge!'

Shortly after Second Uncle left for Yan'an, a Japanese force reached Penglai. After a violent clash with the invaders, the ill-armed Communist forces fell back into the distant countryside. Thousands of Japanese and Chinese troops (members of the Chinese puppet army) marched through the streets to celebrate their victory. In front of the town hall, the Japanese national flag was raised. Frightened residents hid at home and wondered what would happen next. Soon, a Chinese puppet government was established in the county, and started to take reprisals against families with Communist connections. The town was soon in chaos, caught in the terror of arrests, interrogations and executions.

Early one morning, my grandparents abandoned their home and left the town by stealth, together with their three young children. In recent times, the Mus had sprung into the public eye. Four of their children had joined the Communists, and my father and Second Uncle ranked high in the Party. The rest were in danger of their lives. My grandfather carried some clothes, bundled up in a sheet, and walked with my grandmother, Little Auntie, eight years old, and Little Uncle, who was six. My ten-year-old Third Auntie helped her parents to care for her younger brother and sister.

The family hoped to find refuge with the local Communist guerrilla forces, relying on Second Uncle's former colleagues. But where were they? No one could say, not even the local people. After each random hit-and-run attack, they disappeared. Since main roads and areas close to town were controlled by the Japanese, the place to look was further out, in the distant mountain areas where the Communists must be hiding. It was a desperate choice and an exhausting journey. By day, the family tramped along rugged mountain paths, and begged for food. On lucky nights, villagers took them in; if not, they slept outside, huddled together against the cold.

Nearly a month had gone by, when one afternoon an armed troop came in sight, hustling along a narrow mountain path, and moving so fast that in minutes it had reached the terrified family. What would happen if they were Japanese, or troops of the Chinese puppet army? My grandparents were too scared to meet their eyes, and quickened their pace to pass as soon as possible. Suddenly, a stunned voice broke the silence – 'Uncle, auntie, what are you doing here?' – and a startled young officer jumped down from his horse and took hold of my grandfather's hands. It was Xing Long, once a member of the 'Misty World Literature Society'. In 1935, he had sheltered my father in Tianjin. Now he had become a leader of the local Communist forces. After a raid on the Japanese, he and his guerrillas were heading for their base.

When my grandparents recognized Xing Long, they and their children could not stop their tears. Nor could Xing Long, seeing their shabby clothes and starving faces. 'Please come with us,' he said to my grandparents. 'I will look after you as if I were your own son.' From then on, the family became a special unit of the Communist forces. They met old colleagues of my father and Second Uncle, such as Sun Ziping, now a Communist leader in the Shandong Peninsula.

At that time, the Communists had established a small base area in Penglai, where the family stayed in the village of Li Gully, renting a room from local peasants. My grandfather was recruited as a military storekeeper, and though no job was found for my grandmother, she became the busiest person in the village. Her home was like an army point of call, always open for passing Communist officials and troops. For years, she hardly slept a whole night. When travellers arrived, she started cooking. While they rested at night, she would wash and mend their uniforms, or hunt lice in their clothes by the glow of an oil-lamp. Before they left at dawn, fresh food was waiting. When Ziping's wife, a Communist cadre, was in labour, my grandmother acted as a midwife. In the following months, she looked after the newborn baby.

One summer night, Li Gully was surprised and surrounded by enemy troops just as a group of Communist guerrillas was going to sleep in my grandparents' home. Alerted by shooting, the guerrillas grabbed my young aunts and uncle and ran for the hills outside the village. 'What are you doing?' my panicked grandfather cried to his wife, when she lagged behind to pick up some pistols and Party documents left behind by the guerrillas. 'You go ahead,' she said. 'I'll catch you up.' Within minutes, the attackers had blocked the main streets, and their voices rang outside. Carrying the documents and weapons, grandmother crept out by a back door and then hurried through back lanes towards the hills. By the village boundary, voices behind her shouted: 'Stop, or we'll fire!' She kept on running, though it was hard in the dark and her bound feet made her wish for wings, they hampered her so much. Within minutes, steps came close behind her, and she could hear the breaths of her pursuer. Even so, she kept her head and hid the pistols and documents underneath a stone, so that her captors only found two silver coins in her pocket – all the money she had – but nothing else. Under interrogation, she made out that she was a local villager panicked by the fight, and played the part so well that they released her.

Despite the risks and hardships, my grandmother loved her work. In her mind, it was the guerrillas who had rescued her family in distress. For the first time in their lives, they had enough food and warm clothes, and she wanted to repay their benefactors. 'We will never forget the kindness of the Communists to us,' she told her young children. During the war with Japan, countless Communist officials and troops in the Shandong Peninsula received her help and care. They called her 'Mother of the Guerrillas'. Years later, when many were senior officials, they still came to visit my grandmother in Beijing, calling her 'Auntie Mu'.

Starting in 1940, the Japanese clamped down hard on Communist bases, so my grandparents could no longer live in Li Gully. The next two years were the most critical phase of the war, when the family went on the run with the guerrillas in the remotest mountain areas. 'As soon as the Japanese rifles cracked outside,' my grandmother told me, 'I'd jump on a horse and follow the running guerrillas as fast as we could, till we gave the enemy the slip.' Little Uncle often said that he grew up in the panniers slung across the guerrilla's horse, because a lot of his childhood was spent there while evading the Japanese.

In 1942, the family arrived in a small seaside village in Penglai called North Forest Yard, located in a Japanese-occupied area. The move was forced. Due to increasing enemy attacks, the guerrilla forces could no longer look after them. However, in recent years the Communists had established close ties with the patriotic villagers, and the local leaders made regular secret contributions. On arrival, the family reminded themselves of Xing Long's warning: 'From now on, your surname is Li. Never let anyone know who you are.' The guerrilla forces had arranged for their regular support through the village fund, but no one could guarantee their safety in an area under Japanese occupation.

One autumn afternoon some months later, men of the Chinese puppet army burst into the single room that my grandparents rented in a villager's house. Only my grandmother and Little Auntie were at home. 'Are you the Mus?' they asked. 'Your sons and daughters are Communists.' A villager had betrayed them, tempted by a large reward offered for giving up Party members' relations. 'No, we are the Lis,' my grandmother said flatly, sitting on the kang, and continuing to sew a winter jacket for her daughter. The intruders dragged her to the floor, and started to beat her with their rifle butts. 'Don't be afraid, my girl!' grandmother shouted to her daughter, and Little Auntie ran out of the room and straight to the village chief's house crying for help. When she returned with her father and the other two children, her mother was gone and the family belongings were either smashed or looted. In the shambles of their empty home, they were struck dumb, until Little Uncle burst into tears: 'I want Mama!'

The news of my grandmother's arrest brought Sun Ziping straight to the village, despite the danger he faced in a Japanese-occupied area. He was determined to save her at any cost, and exerted his influence in the Peninsula to persuade the village chief and wealthy local squires to put up a large ransom for her release, and to lobby intensively with the occupying forces. The bid was successful, but my grandmother and her family had to go into hiding, staying in a cellar and fed by local villagers, until the Japanese round-up was over the following spring.

On 9 September 1945, the Japanese in China surrendered. By then, the whole of Penglai county had become Communist territory as part of their base in the Shandong Peninsula, and the family settled down in North Forest Yard, where they were loved and respected for their and their absent children's contribution to the war. In particular, my grand-mother became a local celebrity, among other things for her skilful cooking and expert tailoring, favoured especially on occasions such as weddings or birthday celebrations. She enjoyed being busy, and never charged for her work, delighted to repay the kind villagers who accepted and supported her family during their hardest times.

My grandfather had less to feel happy about. For an ordinary man, life was not complete without his children. Once the war was over, he had hoped to be reunited with all his sons and daughters, and spend his later years in the family circle. But the fate of his two elder sons remained a mystery: it was years since the family had heard from them.

For the two elder daughters who had also joined the Communists, it was their work that kept them away. And now he had to lose his younger children. The district was badly off for schools, and they had to attend a boarding institution in Huangxian, a neighbouring county. It was run by the local Communist government, and its pupils received free education with political and military training, but they came home only for summer and winter holidays. For the sake of his children's future, he consented, but the separation distressed him. How would the three of them cope with being parted from their parents for the first time? Their school was located in a poor village, with no street-lights and no indoor toilets. Would the girls go outside at night? Little Uncle was not a forward boy. Would he get enough to eat in the scramble for communal meals? Anxious for their welfare, he paid the school regular visits.

In April 1946, just two months after the winter holiday, my grand-father made another routine trip, this time carrying his children's summer clothes on his back, together with favourite treats like steamed buns made of wheat flour. He was longing to see them so much that he walked all day from North Forest Yard to Huangxian, and completely forgot his fatigue. Before going in, he decided to see his third daughter first, and ask her to take charge of all the food, in case the two younger ones might eat themselves sick. It was early evening, and some pupils were singing outside their dormitory, when one of them spotted my grandfather and immediately called out: 'Uncle Mu, Lotus [Third Auntie] has joined the Communist army.'

As if hit by a truncheon, my grandfather fell to the ground, and did not speak till Little Auntie came. She told him that Third Auntie had left two days before. It was the eve of the Civil War between the Communists and the Nationalists. A recruiting drive had visited the school, and she had joined up as a nurse for an army hospital. 'Dada,' Little Auntie tried to comfort her father, 'when she left she was wearing a huge red tissue flower on the front of her jacket. It was glorious!' 'My little girl,' grandfather muttered, 'do you know how a father feels when he loses his child again?'

After seeing his two remaining children, my grandfather refused the school's offer to put him up overnight and set off home, carrying the luggage and bedding left behind by Third Auntie. When he arrived, he fell on the kang without a word. From the sadness on his face and the sight of Third Auntie's belongings, grandmother knew what must have happened. 'When children grow up, it's not up to us to decide their future.' She tried to hide her pain and comfort him. 'Joining the Communist forces to fight for poor people is the right thing to do.' But grandfather made no reply. He had made up his mind: no matter what, he would keep his two youngest children at home.

'Your Mama and I are getting old, please don't leave us alone.' When the children came home for the summer holiday, my grandfather told them: 'After you finish school, I will ask your uncle Xing Long to find jobs for you locally, so that in future you can be good company for your aged parents.' 'Don't worry, Dada,' Little Auntie promised. 'I won't leave you and Mama.' Little Uncle showed the same determination. For the first time since Third Auntie's leaving school, my grandfather smiled.

In autumn 1946, the Communist government launched land reforms in Penglai. In return for their contribution to the revolution, the Mu family were given a large plot of fertile land which was then cultivated by local villagers. It was the official policy for villagers to provide services to families with absent members working for the Communists. The family also received a fine house, furniture and decent clothing, all confiscated from landlords. As soon as they moved in, my grandparents bought portraits of Mao Zedong and Zhu De and displayed them on their living-room wall. Without Chairman Mao and Commander-in-Chief Zhu, how else could they have lived in such a house? Afterwards, my grandfather's greatest joy was to allocate rooms for his children. 'The east-wing room is for Flower [Little

Auntie]. Road [Little Uncle] can stay with us in the main room in the holidays. He's too young to sleep on his own,' Grandfather brooded. 'You spoil your youngest son,' Grandmother liked to tease him.

'Is Uncle Mu in?' a voice enquired one day. It came from a young man carrying Little Auntie's bedding roll. 'Flower has left school and joined the Communists in south Shandong. I was asked to bring her things home.' The sight made my grandparents cling to each other and cry. Soon many villagers gathered and wept along with them. Some women sobbed: 'You shouldn't let your children leave you again.' Grandmother explained: 'My Lotus and Flower have been brought up by the Communists. How could I say No when they joined the revolution?'

A few months later, Little Uncle came home unexpectedly, but only to say goodbye. From winter 1946, Nationalist troops attacked the Shandong Peninsula base, and Little Uncle, aged fourteen, made up his mind to join the Communist forces, in the footsteps of his siblings. 'We won't have our children at home any more,' Grandmother said to him tearfully. My grandfather bottled up his sadness and talked to his son all night about the revolutionary careers of his elder sons and daughters. Next morning, he travelled nearly twenty kilometres with Little Uncle to the assembly place in town, walking in silence except for the rasp of his breath. When the troops set out, he followed after his youngest son until officers dissuaded him. And now it started snowing. In the distance, Little Uncle saw his father still standing on the crest of a hill, staring down at the column marching away on the road, his thin body coated in snowflakes already, like a snowman. Little Uncle faced forward again and could not check his tears.

My grandfather's health was failing. Soon after his youngest child left, he was gnawed by constant pain in his body, and his cough grew worse. Unable to sleep or eat most of the time, soon he became so weak and wasted that he could hardly stand up. Modern medical services had yet to appear in the region, but my grandparents were reluctant to appeal to their third daughter, who worked in a neighbouring county. 'Her army hospital had its hands full with our wounded soldiers,' grandmother told me many years later. 'How could we make a nuisance of ourselves?' So my grandfather's illness was never diagnosed. The only medication he received was various folk cures given by local villagers, such as plant roots and barks. Eventually, even the valuable camphorwood chest acquired during the land reforms was burnt to fumigate his legs and back. But nothing worked. Grandfather knew he was dying, and he longed to see his children again, but nobody came. The two elder sons had disappeared a long time ago. For their brothers and sisters, although most of them still worked in the Shandong Peninsula, to go home on leave was impossible in a phase of heavy Nationalist attacks.

'Please drink it.' My grandmother brought a decoction of herbs in a bowl. Her husband lay on the kang and did not answer. Teardrops brimmed from his closed eyes. Grandmother knew that he must be dreaming about his sons and daughters again. Sometimes he saw his eldest son in combat with Japanese troops on a battlefield, wounded and covered in blood, but fighting on. Grandfather cried out and ran to hold his son. When my grandmother woke him he was in a cold sweat and his face full of tears. One night, a thin young man with several children appeared in his dream and said to him: 'Dada, it's me, your second son. I've brought my children to visit you and Mama.' The children flocked around him. Seeing their rosy cheeks and hearing their sweet voices call him 'Grandpa', he laughed out loud. The door opened again and a group of young people came in. 'Dada,' they said in unison, 'we're home.' How wonderful! It was Glow, Grace, Lotus, Flower and Road! Straight away, grandfather called out: 'Mother, come here please! Our sons and daughters are home!' Suddenly, all of them vanished from his sight. 'Oh no! Please don't leave me alone!' He shouted and shouted until his eyes opened. It was midnight. The house was quiet and dark, and only his wife was with him, weeping silently. 'Where are you, my children?' he muttered. 'Come back please! Let me see you again!'

In April 1948, Third Auntie passed through Penglai on her way to a new post. Because of her father's illness, she had been granted compassionate leave — her first visit home for two years. The long walk to North Forest Yard was speeded by the prospect of seeing her parents again, and especially by the good news she had to tell them — her engagement to a kind young man, a doctor at her hospital, which was certain to please her sick father.

A few kilometres outside the village, Third Auntie met a local peasant. 'Lotus, you've come back too late,' he told her. 'Uncle Mu passed away last night.'

The message stunned Third Auntie. She completed her journey in a daze, and when she came to the house her legs gave way and would hardly carry her. Her first sight was my grandfather's body, lying in a coffin in the main room, surrounded by seven plain wooden sticks laid out on the ground. According to local custom, a dead adult must be mourned continually by his or her offspring until burial. They must dress completely in white, including their hats and shoes, and each must hold a specially made wooden stick with a strip of white paper twined round it: this was called the mourning stick. Without this ritual, the soul of the dead would not rest in peace. My poor grandfather, although you had raised seven children, none of them held the mourning stick at your death! Were you able to be in peace in the next world?

In front of the coffin, my grandmother clung to Third Auntie and sobbed: 'Your father's heart was broken by missing his sons and daughters too much.' During his final days, grandfather was often delirious, but still called the names of his sons and daughters. Over and over, he muttered: 'Where are my children? If I don't see them again, I won't close my eyes when I die.'

A few days after my grandfather's burial, Third Auntie had to return to her unit. Afterwards, Second Auntie spent time at home on maternity leave, keeping her lonely mother company. By this time, Second Auntie had married a Communist official and had just had a premature baby. Since it was impossible for her to look after the baby as well as fighting with her troop, she was granted a few months' leave. One day, a letter arrived from Re-hei in north China, its battered envelope evidence of a long passage through many hands. The moment she opened it, Second Auntie sang out with excitement. 'Mama, it's from my second brother! He's alive!' Since his leaving for Yan'an nine years before, it was the first the family had heard from Second Uncle. They learned that he had become director of a Communist cultural work troupe in Re-hei, and had built a happy family with a singer from his work troupe. Again and again, grandmother asked Second Auntie to read her son's letter, now laughing, now crying, as if going mad. Later, she took Second Auntie to the cemetery. She knelt at her husband's grave, and said: 'Old man, this is our second son's letter, and our two daughters also came home to see you. Why didn't you stay a little bit longer? Why didn't you wait to share the happiness of our family reunion?'

In summer 1949, the Communists took over Qingdao in the Shandong Peninsula, a famous summer resort and naval and industrial centre. (Today, Qingdao beers are sold worldwide in Chinese markets and restaurants.) First Auntie became leader of the city's Women's Federation, her husband chief of staff for the city government, and the city's first Communist governor was Xing Long. Soon after settling down, First Auntie invited my grandmother to live with her family, and hoped to see her live out her life in peace and comfort.

In China, Qingdao was known for its strong German influences. It had been the centre of the Kiaochow territory leased to Germany by the Imperial government from 1898 to 1914. The city was well laid out, with handsome buildings and well-lit streets. As high-ranking Party officials, First Auntie and her husband took over an elegant Western-style house in the city centre, with facilities such as piped water, flush toilet and central heating, which grandmother had never seen before. 'How spacious and solid these houses are!' She could not help expressing her amazement. 'Whatever goes on upstairs, even if people are chopping wood, no noise can be heard downstairs.' Since the family employed a nanny, it was the first time in my grandmother's life that she had no household chores to get on with, but happiness and comforts did not match. In October 1949, the Communists established their republic in China, and soon she was contacted by all her sons and daughters except for the eldest, my father. Was he still alive? Where was he? She could not stop thinking about him.

One evening early in 1951, a man came knocking at First Auntie's door and asked if she was in. 'She's still at work,' Grandmother answered through the closed door. At the sound of her voice, the visitor wept. 'Mama, it's me, your eldest son. I'm back!' At first, grandmother did not believe her ears, as the man's combination of Penglainese and Northern Chinese accents sounded strange. When she opened the door, a man in a woollen army uniform stood there with a little boy. Unable to speak, staring up at the man's face, suddenly she recognized her eldest son, whom she had not seen for sixteen years, and had missed every day.

Ever since the civil war had ended, my father had been searching for his family, but found that his inquiring letters either went unanswered or yielded nothing useful. Over the years, the family had moved several times, and changed their names, and no civil records were available. Before taking up his command in the Korean War, he had finally traced First Auntie and my grandmother through the Party's committee in Shandong province. This was his earliest chance to come, and he had brought his first child, my eldest brother Feng-xin.

In my family's photo album, there was a special picture which recorded Third Auntie's reunion with my father after their nineteen years of separation, together with her second brother (Second Uncle), whom she had not seen for sixteen years. The photo was taken in August 1954, when my family had settled in Beijing. By then, my father had risen to director of the Communist organization department, a major part of the Party's committee, for the North China Military Region. Responsibilities of the organization included recruitment of new Party members, job assignment, promotion or discipline of Party members. My grandmother had joined our family permanently, and I had a younger brother, Feng-yuan, who was only one year old. The name 'Yuan' recalled Suiyuan, where my parents had worked before.

In 1953, my family had moved to one of Beijing's most famous streets, Temple for Protecting the Nation Street (Hu-guo-si Da-jie), which lies in the northwest part of the city, within walking distance of the Forbidden City. Historical records date it back to the Yuan Dynasty (1271–1368), descendants of Genghis Khan. In the 1950s, the street was well known as the site of the new National Peking Opera House, known as the People's Theatre. Celebrities such as Dr Mei Lanfang, the great Peking Opera Master, lived there.

My family lived in a grand mansion that had once been the Korean Embassy and now belonged to the North China Military Region, as a residence for its senior officers. The spacious and solid one-storey house was completely modernized, but retained its original carved beams and painted rafters. All the rooms had beautiful tiled or wooden floors. During the long Beijing winter, free central heating kept us warm. In the hot and humid summer, it was cool and dry inside, with breezes wafting through the big wide-open windows. 'What a magical house!' our visitors always approved. For years, a cellar under the floor of my father's study inspired my imagination. Prompted by the revolutionary films I used to watch, I felt sure that it must once have been a dungeon where brave Communists were held captive by the Nationalists or the Japanese. I would tell tales about its make-believe history to entertain my friends.

Our courtyard was divided by gates or arches into several areas, and most of the ground was paved instead of grassed, like many houses in Beijing. In the spring, shrubs, flowers and several trees provided beautiful blooms and fragrance. In the middle of the main courtyard, an elegant fountain played. After school, I loved to sit and read on the smooth stone edge of its pool, in the shade of two flowering crab-apple trees, and nibble fried peanuts or sunflower seeds. During the following decades, my family moved around a lot as my parents' jobs required, but this house remains the most lovely and enchanting in my memory.

After the civil war, Third Auntie worked as a medical officer in Fuzhou Military Region in south China, where her husband administered all the army hospitals – a post equivalent to regimental commander. Before the reunion in Beijing, Second Uncle had brought his wife and children to stay with my parents for a while. They travelled from Shenyang, the provincial capital of Liaoning in Manchuria, where Second Uncle was now one of China's most successful new playwrights. Another who attended the reunion was Little Auntie. When my father first met her in 1951, after their long separation, she was commanding a signals station in the Jinan Military Region. Seeing that China's wars had wrecked her education, my father insisted on helping her to make good the loss. She was just over twenty years old, and still unmarried, so she was entitled to go for full-time education. At my father's request, the military authorities agreed to send her to the People's University in Beijing, which provided special foundation courses to Communist officials at that time. For their contribution to the revolution, these students were exempted from fees and kept the salaries paid in their previous posts.

Their work prevented the rest from joining the gathering, but fortunately they had managed to visit us before. First Auntie and her family were still in Qingdao. Second Auntie had given up her singing career after her first child was born in 1948, and worked as a section chief in the Communist government in Changzhou, an affluent city near Shanghai. Her husband was the city's first Communist governor. Little Uncle was unmarried, and worked in the Nanjing Military Region. When he joined the Communist forces at the age of fourteen, he was posted to the cultural work troupe, being too young to do anything else, and later become a skilful violinist.

The day that Third Auntie and her family were expected was extremely hot and humid. My parents went to meet them at Beijing railway station, but the train was delayed, and in those days there was no passenger information service, or public telephone, so there was nothing to be done except to go home and wait. Several hours later, the door opened and a young woman in uniform appeared, followed by her husband and a little girl. The sight struck my father and Second Uncle dumb. Though they had seen her recent photos, it was hard to connect this impressive young officer with the little sister whose image their memories had preserved.

Third Auntie also lost her voice. 'How can brothers and sisters not recognize each other?' Grandmother shook her head in tears, and then introduced her daughter to her sons. After their long separation, it was an utterly strange feeling for Third Auntie to call them 'eldest brother' and 'second brother', and when the words were out, everyone wept. A few decades later, she recalled: 'It was an unbelievably happy moment for us, and we just kept talking and talking. Our conversation was endless and our feelings were too strong to express . . .'

Next day, a photographer came to my home to take pictures of the reunion. Later, one photo was displayed in the studio window for a long time, and drew many people's attention. With half an eye, it was easy to tell that this was not an ordinary family. Among the standing adults, there were three army officers: my father, Third Auntie and her husband. Since the military ranking system had been discarded in China, it was impossible to place them, but my father's confident manner was his badge. The leather shoes Third Auntie's husband wore were supplied only to officers at the level of regimental commander or above. Apart from my grandmother, the style of dress worn by the other adults signified that they were Communist officials with good positions. In particular, the children's Western-style clothes were not at all usual in those days. Surrounded by her numerous descendants, my grandmother sat in the centre of the photo. The gold earrings she wore were my father's gift, in thanks for her unquestioning support when he fled home in 1935. In front of the group, a plump girl was held by my grandmother. Can you imagine who she was? It was me, three years old. Even years later, people still asked me: 'Are you the little girl in the middle of that impressive photo of a revolutionary family?'

Chapter 9

Thorough Remoulding:
Stories of My Mother's Family

(1938–1954)

In 1950, soon after the Communists founded their republic, my mother started looking for her family. Since joining the revolution in 1938, she had been cut off from home. During the wars, postal services often failed and mail to and from her was either lost or considerably delayed. The last letter she had from her father came in 1939, after she reached Yan'an. It was only a few lines long – his usual style – and told her briefly that everyone was all right at home. In reply, my mother told her parents that she was studying in the Red capital, but not that she had joined the Communist Party. From then on, communication stopped. It was now twelve years since she had left home. What had become of her parents? After such an age of social turmoil, did they still live at the same address? My mother sought to trace them through Ning, her elder sister, with whom she joined the anti-Japanese forces early in 1938.

When Ning and my mother parted in Zhaocheng, late in 1938, they completely lost touch with each other. In the following years, both worked in different Communist bases, separated by enemy-occupied territories; this made contact impossible. As one war succeeded another, their addresses changed with the shape of events, and there was no fixed point to aim at. Yet all through these years, my mother believed her sister was alive. In the absence of regular postal services, personal messages circulated verbally through friends, acquaintances or colleagues. If anything happened to Ning, the news would reach my mother sooner or later. But it never had.

Where was Ning if she was still alive? For my mother, it seemed an unthinkable task to look for her sister among a huge population in a vast country where registration records had broken down. However, for a Communist official, there was a practical option: to ask around the Party's provincial committees, which had charge of official appointments. Before long, my mother heard from Shanxi province that Ning was working there as a section director in the provincial committee. Ning told her in a letter that she was now a widow with young children. In 1948, during the civil war, her husband, a Communist brigade commander, had died in battle outside Linfen city while leading his troops to victory against the Nationalists. The battle was famous in the history of the People's Liberation Army, and in praise of their victory the Communist authorities later named the unit the 'Linfen Brigade'. When her husband died, Ning was pregnant with their second child, a daughter who was named Glory at birth. Their first child, a boy, was then two years old, and was later named South of Shanxi, after the area where his father was killed.

Unfortunately, Ning too had lost contact with their parents a long time ago. Both sisters were deeply concerned about their family's situation, and especially anxious for their mother. All these years later, the image still sharp in their minds was their mother, lonely and desolate, standing by the front gate and watching her daughters leave home. Since they had gone, how had she coped on her own? Under the Communist regime, what kind of treatment had their parents received as members of a wealthy landlord family? Because my mother's work spared her no time, it was Ning who first went home the following year. She found their father, but she was heartbroken to hear that their mother had passed away some years before.

'Your maternal grandmother was a victim of that feudal landlord family,' my mother told me many years later. What she said was true, but I also believe that her long separation from her two beloved daughters struck like a deadly blow in a miserable life.

When my mother and Ning said goodbye, their mother was left stranded in the drab back corner of her husband's mansion. Relatives in her parents' family lived far away. Her eldest daughter, Auspicious Cloud, was a drudge in her own home, married to a wealthy farmer and not only waiting on his large family, which included his parents and two brothers, but also cooking for coolies working on the family land. There was hardly anyone to visit my grandmother.

At home, grandmother was hounded every day by the two concubines. Though they fought between themselves, they shared the spite they showed towards their rival. My grandfather, on the other hand, cared more about pleasing his concubines than defending his wife. For him, Aunt Wang was the family heroine for giving birth to a son, while Aunt Dong, though she had only produced a girl, was still young and might give him another son. Therefore, the concubines overmatched my grandmother, and were entitled to more privileges. In the past, my grandfather had provided equal allowances to the concubines, after paying school fees for his two daughters, but my poor grandmother received nothing. After my mother and Ning joined the anti-Japanese forces, the concubines increased their demands. As soon as their master came home from a trip, they would frisk his pockets for money. Normally, the search succeeded and smiles would appear; if not, he would suffer their anger and cold faces. Sometimes, one concubine forestalled the other by taking his jacket away, while her rival chased her around the house, shouting and scolding. The show brought guffaws from my grandfather, and when the din invaded the back yard it made my grandmother's miserable life even harder to bear. But now that her daughters were gone there was no one to comfort her.

In 1940, Aunt Wang finally managed to escape from her master. She left her four-year-old son behind, and the family never saw her again. Afterwards, my furious grandfather blamed his wife rather than Aunt Dong, for making Aunt Wang feel unwelcome. Since Aunt Dong would have nothing to do with her enemy's child, my kind-hearted grandmother had to look after the boy, and treated him fondly, despite her long humiliation by his mother.

It was not easy to look after a young child again, considering that my grandmother was nearing her sixties and suffered from poor health. At first, the boy kept crying for his mother, especially at night, and badly missed her breast-feeding. (It was a common local custom for children of four or even older still to be breast-fed, as well as having solid food. This was not a nutritional requirement; the children used the nipple as a comforter before they went to sleep.) In the evening, grandmother would hold the boy for hours to calm him down, and let him suck at her milkless breasts. The boy would fall asleep, but it was agony for my grandmother to feel his sharp teeth gnaw her delicate nipples.

During the early 1940s, my grandmother's health began to fail. In her small town, there was no doctor with Western-style training, and in wartime there were other priorities for the practitioners of traditional medicine, so her only medication was herbal decoctions that did not work at all. Gradually, her whole body swelled up and her abdomen was bloated with liquid. Yet sick as she was, there was no one to visit her bedside except Auspicious Cloud, who came in her rare spare time. To my grandfather and Aunt Dong, it did not matter whether she lived or died. Their heartless treatment was more than my poor grandmother could bear. In her final days, she could not feed herself and had to be looked after by a full-time maid. One morning when the maid came to her bedroom, my grandmother had already passed away, and nobody knew when she died.

After the outbreak of the Sino-Japanese War in 1937, my mother's home county remained in Nationalist hands until spring 1944, when it came under the Japanese attack. Before the invaders took over, the Nationalist administration withdrew to the countryside and left the town in chaos. My maternal grandfather fled with his family, leaving his property in the care of my grandmother's former maid. His daughters' involvement in the anti-Japanese movement put his family in jeopardy under the Japanese occupation, but where could they go? The Japanese had blocked all major roads and railways. As an old-fashioned landlord, grandfather had no bank account, or even sufficient cash, as his wealth was based mainly on his land and house, as well as on a huge store of grain, which was the rent his tenant peasants paid. So even though they were lucky enough to elude the Japanese blockade, there were no assets they could draw on outside their home county.

At first, the family took refuge with a distant relative who lived about twenty kilometres away from town, but he could not afford to keep them very long. Eventually, my grandfather moved to a village sited near a piece of land he owned, which was a few kilometres outside town. They lived in some disused caves abandoned by his tenant peasants. It was a comedown from his luxury mansion, but the family's choices had narrowed to survival.

Grandfather did not expect to settle in the village, and in any case he could not be parted from the wealth he had spent most of his life accumulating. Before the Japanese took over, he made regular trips home on his own to keep an eye on his house and furniture and the storage of his grain. Gradually, his trips grew more frequent and his stay at home more prolonged. He had taken a fancy to my grandmother's former maid, who had stayed to take care of his property. A peasant's widow in her mid-thirties, with a little girl of her own, the woman had endured many years of poverty, and was desperately seeking security for herself and her daughter. She had reason to accept my grandfather's approaches, and soon she became his new concubine. Later, he invited all his cousins to a dinner in his mansion to announce the news, and then brought her back to his temporary lodgings in the village. Aunt Dong was furious, but this time there was no domestic warfare between his two concubines. The Japanese troops were approaching, and the uncertain future put off Aunt Dong from challenging her new opponent.

After the Japanese arrived in May 1944, they commandeered my grandfather's mansion to house their military headquarters in the county. Since the occupation took place towards the end of the war, the invaders never controlled most rural areas of the county, including the village where the family was living. My grandfather's fourth cousin was a powerful squire, and to help them maintain public order the Japanese selected him to head the local Peace Preservation Association, a puppet organization. When he pleaded illness, they sent a stretcher to his home, insisting that if he was too weak to walk they would carry him to the office of the Association. In desperation, he secretly contacted the county's Nationalist government-in-exile, asking for advice. They told him to accept the offer, but on condition that Japanese troops must stop raping and killing civilians and burning houses. His condition was accepted, but never observed.

One day, my grandfather's fourth cousin was forced to give a public speech at a mass rally to support the Japanese. Despite the bayonet held to his back by a Japanese soldier, he condemned the invaders' brutal tactics. 'We would rather die than be slaves without a country,' he announced. Fortunately, he was spared from certain execution by his interpreter, who left out parts of his speech in Japanese.

The Japanese occupation brought enormous changes into my grandfather's life. In the upheaval, most of his tenant peasants stopped delivering his customary share of their grain harvest, and wartime conditions were too dangerous for him to travel around his widely scattered holdings and collect the rent himself. Nor could he sell his land or his mansion to support himself, because he could not find a buyer. On top of that, his huge hoard of grain was confiscated by the Japanese to feed their troops. Now he was penniless, and soon he faced starvation, together with his two concubines and their young children. He was the only male adult in the family; the only way to support himself and them was by his own labour. So grandfather, in his sixties, had to revive his early life and work as a peasant again. I can imagine how hard that was for a man whose skills and toughness had mostly deserted him after his decades of life as a wealthy landlord. Sometimes his two concubines tried to help, but they too found it difficult to cope. Occasionally, some of his tenant peasants would come and lend a hand out of sympathy for his troubles.

Hard work staved off starvation, but there was no comparison between the family's past and present standard of living. In their county, the rich ate a diet based on wheat flour, but this had disappeared from grandfather's table. Instead, rough millet or maize, which were only for peasants, became their staple food. But although they had lost every one of the luxuries they had once enjoyed, the two concubines held on, though not out of loyalty to my grandfather, but rather because the war gave them nowhere else to go.

In August 1945, the war with Japan was over, but still my grandfather was unable to go home or to retrieve his property, as the county was caught up at once in the civil war between the Communist and the Nationalist forces. In 1947, the Communists finally gained control of the county. Under the new regime, my grandfather soon recognized that he could not hang on to his wealth. As an educated man, he was not unfamiliar with the Communist aim to abolish the old social system and the exploitation of man by man. Knowing about the land reforms already enacted in many Communist areas, he saw that there was no use in trying to revive his former status: from now on, people would have to live by their own labour. In a time of swift social change, his philosophy was not to stand against the tide. The safest choice was to forget about what he had lost and embrace his new position as a peasant, so he swallowed his tenants' refusal to pay rent, and kept quiet when the county's Communist government occupied his mansion as their offices.

In 1950, the land reforms reached his home county. All adults were allocated a class category – landlord, poor peasant, and so on – officially determined mainly by their economic status during the three years before the county was liberated by the Communists in 1947. This meant that my grandfather was classified as a landlord. Although he had lost his wealth and lived mainly on his own labour since 1944, unfortunately the shift in his economic status had taken place a few months less than the stipulated three years or more before the liberation. Another problem was that he was still receiving an occasional trickle of rent from his land, which had saved him from ruin during the occupation, but marked him as a landlord today.

On the other hand, for a man classified as a landlord the treatment my grandfather had was comparatively lenient. Partly, this was due to his past good treatment of his tenants, who were not inclined to publicly humiliate or hit out at him when convened by the Communists to denounce their landlord. He was also saved by his wise decision not to resist the land reforms, but instead to bend with the wind and surrender his property to the government unconditionally, apart from a piece of land to provide a living. But his chief protection was the record of his two revolutionary daughters. Ironically, their situation entitled my grandfather and his family to be treated as dependants of Communist officials by the local government. To help them work their land, the benefits they received included free labour, which came to the family like a gift of charcoal in snowy weather.

In contrast with my maternal grandfather's experiences, his fourth cousin had the worst luck of all the Xu family under the Communist regime. Shortly after the land reforms started, he was arrested on the charge of being a tyrant landlord. For having held office in the Peace Preservation Association under the Japanese occupation, he was also labelled as a traitor and collaborator. Unfortunately, he was unable to hire a lawyer, because the new regime had abolished the system of legal defence. In the local community, no one stood up for his resistance activities during the Sino-Japanese War. A so-called 'native serpent', he had incurred strong resentment among local people: a tyrant landlord rated as the most hardened of reactionary elements. After the Sino-Japanese War, he had received an inscribed plaque from Chiang Kai-shek, praising his anti-Japanese activities. The board hung on his living-room wall, with Chiang Kai-shek's inscription in huge golden characters: 'Bu-qu-bu-nao' (meaning 'Unyielding'). Under the Communist regime, however, such an honour further condemned him.

After the arrest of my grandfather's fourth cousin his possessions were confiscated, and he was frequently denounced for his crimes at huge rallies held to promote the land reforms. Dragged on to the platform by armed soldiers, he wore a tall cap made of white paper, which proclaimed in large black characters: 'Down with the despotic landlord', or 'Down with the traitor'. Very often, the angry crowd would stone him or spit in his pale face, but no matter what happened to him, he remained silent, bowing his head. For local people, these were unthinkable events. Not long ago, no one dared to breathe a word to his discredit. Now, everyone was free to stand against him. Society had really changed. Later, he was sentenced to death at a public trial, and executed immediately afterwards.

Grandfather did not feel too much sympathy for the troubles of his fourth cousin, whose domineering manner had also antagonized his relatives. In view of his previous behaviour in the local community, grandfather believed that his fate proved the ancient Chinese saying: 'Good will be rewarded with good, and evil with evil.' In fact, the only injustice grandfather complained of concerned the fate of his seventh cousin.

In the local community, his seventh cousin had a well-earned reputation as a wastrel. With his inherited fortune, he enjoyed a lavish lifestyle,
never did a stroke of real work, and did not even glance at his property.
His opium habit was like a bottomless pit into which most of his
money disappeared. Some time before the Japanese arrived, he had run
through all his money, and sold off his mansion and land to pay his
debts. When the county turned Communist in 1947, he and his wife
had been living in caves for more than three years in the same village
where my grandfather resided, supported by their grown-up sons who
worked as tenant peasants. So he was listed as a poor peasant during the
land reforms, and hence enjoyed the best outcome possible in the rural
world, being awarded land and a house which were confiscated from
landlords. 'This is not fair,' grandfather grumbled to my mother during
their first reunion. 'I paid my own way by working hard, and lived fru-
gally all my life, but now I'm treated as a landlord. In the past, my
seventh cousin was much richer than me with his inherited fortune. Just
because he squandered every penny before the liberation, he becomes a
poor peasant and gets land and a house again.'

In spring 1952, my maternal grandfather arrived in Beijing to visit our
family. Although it was his first trip to the capital, he did not tell my
mother in advance. Knowing how much she resented his treatment of
her mother in the past, he probably expected her to object to his visit. In
this he was partly correct, though my mother had other reasons not to
want to see him. My father had left for the Korean War several months
before, and since then she had been terribly busy dealing with her three
young children at home as well as her long hours at work. As a loyal
Party member, she also knew that the influx of relatives visiting officials
in Beijing was causing a nuisance to the government.

Soon after the establishment of the Communist republic, nearly all
officials in Beijing found their visiting relatives converging from all over
China. During the wars, many officials had suffered long separations

from their families, and now it was natural to wish to see them, especially for those too busy to have time to travel home. Then too, for many Chinese people it was the dream of a lifetime, which no one would think of missing, to enter the city where the emperors had lived for centuries. Under the prevailing supply system (gong-ji-zhi), parents or siblings of Communist officials were entitled to travel expenses, free accommodation and food during their visits, so before long this flood of privileged guests was putting a heavy strain on the resources available in Beijing. The scarcest of these was accommodation. In the few years since Beijing had become the capital of the Communist republic, a horde of officials and troops had invaded the city, causing serious housing problems. Officials were advised to reduce these family visits.

All the same, one sunny morning my maternal grandfather came knocking at the gate of my mother's office, the North China Bureau of the Party's Central Committee. It was located in an elegant three-storey house, built in the Western style several decades ago, and formerly Chiang Kai-shek's official residence in Beijing. When she received the unexpected news, my mother suspended her meeting and rushed to the porter's room where her father was waiting. It was fourteen years since she had seen him last, but she felt no rush of excitement. Instead, all sorts of questions that had never been resolved welled up in her mind again, and completely fragmented her feelings towards her father. How was she to treat him – a man who had given her life but had also caused such grief to her mother? Since joining the Party, she had accepted that it was the old social system rather than any individual that was to blame for her mother's plight, but now she found herself struggling to forgive him for what he had done in the past. In addition, she was in two minds about her attitude towards her father as a landlord, and therefore a member of an alien class. In theory, a Communist official had no choice except to stand with her Party and make a clean break with the class enemy. However, he was also her father, an old man who needed her support. As a human being, she felt an obligation towards him, even though she had never felt attached to him. It would also reduce the financial burden on the government if she made herself responsible for him.

My mother tried to collect herself when she entered the porter's room. 'Baba, you're here.' Her voice was quite composed, as if talking to someone she had been seeing every day. Despite the easy manner she assumed, her first impression shocked her after their long separation. He was close to his seventies, so it came as no surprise to see that he was now an old man with grey hair, and in any case the cast of his features was familiar. What did surprise her was the enormous changes caused by his economic fall. With his weather-beaten face and calloused hands, he looked like a typical peasant who had suffered years of hardship, a total contrast with the image in her memory of a wealthy landlord whose soft unblemished skin signalled a life of leisure. The landlord had dressed with style and elegance. The peasant's clothes were crudely made with coarse material.

Relatively, it was my grandfather who felt the greater shock. For a while, he was lost for words, unable to match the assured young official standing in front of him with the quiet schoolgirl of years ago, determined to resist the Japanese. But he quickly collected himself. Like my mother, he too was naturally quiet and reserved, so there were no tears shed or voices raised during their first reunion. In reply to his daughter's greeting, my grandfather sighed: 'Oh, I am really old.' Then quiet smiles relieved the tension between them. Apparently, they both tried to avoid the sensitive topic of the injuries done to my maternal grandmother, which seemed a good solution for my mother, as it helped her to control her resentment, and to maintain a zone of contact.

When she heard who was coming, my paternal grandmother prepared a delicious dinner to welcome him. Among officials' relatives, she was seen as an exceptionally lucky case, because she had been entitled to the Communist supply system for more than a decade, in honour of her children's contribution to the Party. The allowance was originally arranged by former colleagues of my father and Second Uncle in the Communist base of the Shandong Peninsula during the war with Japan. It granted her the same living standard as a Party official, and was later transferred to Qingdao, where she moved to live with First Auntie's family, and then to Beijing when she joined our family.

My mother always said that without her mother-in-law she could not imagine how she would have brought up her children and coped with her challenging career at the same time. In the early 1950s, a puritanical lifestyle still prevailed among Communist officials. During the week, many had to work in the evenings, and could not go home at night. Except at weekends, my mother slept in her office and ate in the office canteen at the Bureau's expense. After his return from the Korean War, when he was transferred to the headquarters of the Beijing Military Region, my father lived at home, which was a privilege for senior officers, but he still had meals in his canteen. My siblings and I were looked after by nannies at home before the age of three, and then were sent to government boarding institutions. However, life would never be easy for a family with young children if the mother was away most of the time, no matter how much help they were due. After I was born, a second nanny was provided to look after me, because my second brother, Feng-an, was only one and a half years old, too young to board. Soon, squabbles broke out between the two nannies, and several times my mother had to come home from work to sort them out. Eventually, my paternal grandmother decided to keep one nanny only for Feng-an, and she minded me herself for a long time, which was fine for me because the special care she offered was more than any nanny could provide, and soon I was a strong and lively baby.

My maternal grandfather relished his daughter's happy family life and visited us regularly during his stay. By official regulations, he was entitled to spend a month in Beijing, the stipulated maximum in a year, as a guest of the North China Bureau. The lodgings he occupied were packed with relations of the Bureau's officials. During the day, they were assigned coaches and guides for free sightseeing tours to famous sites such as the Forbidden City, the Great Wall and many former imperial gardens or ancient temples. In the evenings, they could go to the theatre or the cinema for nothing. 'Sounds like a package holiday,' I joked to my mother when she described the visit many years later.

'How lucky Beijingers are!' My maternal grandfather could not help voicing his envy at the easy lifestyle in Beijing. For him, the capital was a paradise on earth, where rice and wheat flour were everyday foods, and no one faced the wind, rain or sun every day to scrape a living, as peasants had to do. Even compared with life as a wealthy country landlord, nothing could rival the city.

At the end of her father's visit, when my mother realized that he hoped to join our family in Beijing, she argued against it. First of all, his own family still lived in the village and depended on him. Since the new marriage law adopted in 1950, traditional polygamy had been abolished, but it was very difficult for his two concubines to find somewhere else to live. They were both in their forties, they lacked the skills to earn a separate living, and the children they had with my grandfather were still young. As a result, the local authorities were bound to tolerate their presence in his household. This situation lasted several years, until Aunt Dong's daughter invited her mother to join her own family after her marriage.

Another major obstacle to grandfather's wish was the rules in force to limit the access of officials' relatives to the government supply system in Beijing. As a Communist official, my mother had no salary herself. Instead, she relied on the free accommodation, food, uniforms, transport and childcare provided by the Party. Under this supply system, she could not afford to keep her father. It was a common practice for Communist officials to install their parents at home to look after their young children, and to maintain them with the government allowance for nannies. But this was not an option for maternal grandfather, because he could not manage housework. He was nearing his seventies, his hard life in recent years had sapped his health, and sooner or later it would be he who needed daily care. Clearly his presence would put a strain on our family, and especially on my paternal grandmother, who had joined us for good and was running the household. My mother also knew that the mere idea of giving a home to her father would exasperate my father and his siblings. None of them would tolerate the prospect of their honourable revolutionary mother having to wait on an ageing former landlord.

In fact, her father's position as a landlord made his request even harder to accept. After the land reforms, landlords were expected to rehabilitate themselves through compulsory labour, under the eye of poor peasants in their native villages. That was the Party's policy, but it was common knowledge that a number of high officials took their former landlord parents or parents-in-law under their own roofs, and spared them from the hard village lives that they deserved. My conscientious father detested this behaviour, which undermined the Party's policy, so it was out of the question for him to do the same. My mother shared his view. Her experiences during the intra-Party conflict had taught her how badly her father's landlord background could affect her situation, especially during the regular cycle of political campaigns. For example, she would be accused of not making a clean break with her landlord father, or failing to stand by the Party. In the past – for instance during the Rescue Campaign – only she had been accountable for her political problems. Now that she was married, with a happy family, she had to consider the outcome for her husband and children if anything happened to her.

My disappointed grandfather left Beijing for his village. When I heard his story many years later, I wondered how he saw it in the end. For years he had tried to safeguard the family fortune, and the only plan that came to him was to have sons as heirs. To reach that goal, he ruined his wife's and his concubines' lives, and drove his daughters to forsake their home and rebel against the class he belonged to. Under the

Communist regime, he had to let go of his fortune, even though he had managed to father sons. In his old age, even his own daughter did not want him. Soon after his first visit, he wrote to my mother bewailing the hardships in his life. From then on, she started to send him money that she saved from her small allowance provided by the North China Bureau, where she worked.

In 1955, the supply system (gong-ji-zhi) for Communist officials was replaced by a salary system based on a scale of thirty grades. As the head of the Party and chief of state, Mao Zedong was entitled to Grade I, the apex of the pyramid. My mother's initial rank was Grade 13, which was equivalent to a county governor. Her salary was over 150 yuan per month, which was exceptionally high, seeing that the average income of officials was less than 40 yuan. Several years later she was promoted to Grade 12, on a par with the governor of a prefecture or city, and her salary rose to 170 yuan. In 1982, she received her final rise to Grade 11. In China, those who achieved Grade 1–13 were regarded as high officials. Of the hundreds of thousands of officials in each province, only a few thousand reached this level. My father's position in the army counted as Grade 9, which carried a salary of 340 yuan per month. Officials in his grade or above were very rare, perhaps only tens of thousands in a population of more than 1 billion today.

By definition, the Party's decisions were final, and in every organization the same applied to the grade assigned in the salary scale. The grade for officials was set mainly on the basis of their previous revolutionary experience and current position – the recipient was not consulted. When the decision was announced in my mother's office, nobody argued, because any complaint would be viewed as scrambling for personal power and profit, and exhibiting a lack of revolutionary consciousness.

As well as their excellent salaries, my parents were also entitled to all sorts of extra benefits such as chauffeur-driven cars, soft seats on trains or free aeroplane tickets when travelling, and a private telephone at home. Their health care was provided by departments reserved for high officials. If they needed to go to hospital, there were special units where each patient could occupy an entire room with first-class care, instead of staying in overcrowded wards with other patients. Since there were more government organizations in Beijing than in any other part of China, privileged resources, and especially accommodation, were less generous and in shorter supply than in the provinces at the same grade. My mother was entitled to an apartment with four rooms, which was a lot more space than the average for staff in her office. Since the army had provided my family with a larger house, she did not make a claim.

Out of her salary, my mother sent her father at least 25 yuan a month until his death in the late 1960s. For my siblings and me, our image of our maternal grandfather was vague. During his first visit, I was only a few months old. When he came again a few years later, I was already at a boarding institution and away from home most of the time. After his second visit, his health gave way, and he did not visit us again. But in the following years, my mother never took any of her children to visit him. In her mind, she was tied by birth to her landlord father, but she would try her best to save her children from being bracketed with a family from the exploiting class.

Chapter 10

Dynasts and Their Children:
My Privileged Childhood in Beijing
(1954–1964)

In September 1954, after my third birthday, I was sent to a boarding kindergarten in Beijing which was part of the Beijing Ba-yi School, famous until the late 1960s as China's largest and most prestigious educational institution. My schoolmates included Mao Zedong's daughter, Zhou Enlai's nephew and niece (Zhou had no children of his own), and the children of vice-premiers such as Deng Pufang (Deng Xiaoping's elder son), government ministers and the governors of many provinces. When the military ranking system was introduced into China in 1955, only pupils whose parents held the rank of colonel or above were qualified to attend, and there were marshals and many generals among the pupils' fathers. During the 1950s and 1960s, the school also admitted a number of foreign pupils whose families were close friends of the Chinese government, among them members of the royal family of Laos. In high official circles, it was not unusual for families to send their children away from home at a young age. When I went there, my eldest brother, Feng-xin, was already in the primary school, and my second brother, Feng-an, had just transferred to the kindergarten from another institution. Two years later my younger brother, Feng-yuan, joined us at the age of three.

The school was established in 1947, during the civil war, for the children of senior Communist officers who were mostly in the front line fighting the Nationalists, and whose wives had jobs in Communist bases. In those days, the institution was known as the Rongzhen Primary School, after its founder, Marshal Nie Rongzhen, commander of the Jin-Cha-Ji base where the school was located. This base covered large areas of Shanxi, Cha-er and Hebei provinces in north China. Marshal Nie Rongzhen's daughter was one of the earliest graduates.

During the war, the institution consisted of a kindergarten and a primary school, which between them housed several hundred children ranging from babies of a few months to teenagers. At this time it was normal that children of the Communist high officials had no chance to receive regular education, so my school had to accept some teenagers as they had little education. Many of the children had backgrounds as harsh as Feng-xin's, and for similar reasons. There was no campus in those days: children and staff stayed in rented peasants' houses. The headmaster and most of the teachers were Communist officers, and the children were maintained by the army, so the school was rather like a military institution. Being separated from their parents by the war, the children were deeply attached to the staff, and addressed them as 'uncle' or 'auntie'. This close relationship became a school tradition and lasted for several decades afterwards.

In those days, the school had to keep on the move as the fighting shifted. In winter 1948, it made an emergency retreat from Hebei to a remote mountain area in the nearby Shanxi province. On their forced journey, pupils over ten had to manage the mountain paths on foot, many with their luggage on their backs. The younger ones either travelled in horse-drawn carts, or were carried by members of the staff. It was said that the school's cook, a strong man, had a young child perched on his shoulders during the march, and each of his arms held a toddler. The headmaster who commanded the retreat carried a kindergarten baby. They were frequently strafed or bombed by the Nationalist air force, so their usual tactic was to lie low in valleys by day, and carry on walking at night. When the bombers droned overhead, the children would scream: 'Huai-dan ["bad eggs"], you just wait! We'll shoot you down when we grow up!'

Early in 1949, the school moved to Beijing on the heels of the Communist takeover there, and soon it became popular among high-ranking Communists in the country, as many had just started their families. When regulations issued under the new republic prohibited the naming of public organizations or places after Party leaders, the name was changed to Beijing Ba-yi School. (Ba-yi means the First of August, the National Army Day; coincidentally, also my birthday.) At that time, it came under the jurisdiction of the Beijing Military Region, with a huge annual budget. By then, the forces of the People's Liberation Army were broadly divided into eight large military regions, each with about a third of a million troops. When the new ranking system for Communist officials was adopted in the early 1950s, the school's leaders were counted as Grade 12 or 13, since all of them were senior officers in the PLA and veteran Party members. Their grades placed them higher than most local governors in the same district. As the capital of the Communist republic, Beijing was a municipality directly under the central government, equal in status to a province, and each of its districts equal to a provincial prefecture. Though located in the Haidian district, our school did not answer to the local education authority.

When I joined the Ba-yi School in 1954, the campus had been settled in Haidian, a northwest suburb of Beijing, located in an area particularly favoured by the imperial and aristocratic families of the Qing Dynasty, who built many grand retreats there, including the famous Imperial Summer Palace. When Beijing city was plagued in summer by scorching heat and high humidity, Haidian enjoyed cool air and gentle breezes. During the winter, the Western Hill that lay beyond the suburb was often covered in snow, and looked like a huge silver dragon sleeping under the blue sky.

In those days the enormous school campus covered nearly 100 hectares and occupied most of one side of a long street. Inside the surrounding high stone wall, the services provided ranged from everyday facilities such as canteens, hairdressers and a laundry, to a vehicle unit, a film projection team, and a full-sized hospital with about fifty beds and a team of first-class paediatricians and dentists. The hospital had its own laboratory, X-ray room, pharmacy, physiotherapy room and operating theatre. In the school's small zoo, pupils could see monkeys, deer, foxes, peacocks and various other birds. It was said that an aged horse in the zoo had survived the Long March with the Red Army. Away from the campus, the school owned several farms whose large workforce produced milk, meat, rice and fruit for the pupils' consumption.

At the age of three, my only memory of my first day at school is the heavy traffic massed around the campus and the unusual security. Until the late 1970s, Beijing was seen in the West as a city without cars. In those days, private transport was non-existent for the vast majority of Chinese, and few could afford a taxi or any other hired transport, so most vehicles were provided by the government or army for the use of their staff. That afternoon when I arrived with my parents and elder brothers, several streets near the campus were already packed with chauffeur-driven cars, minibuses and coaches, all of them official. The pupils they delivered were accompanied by their parents, some with their family nannies or bodyguards. Passengers in the gleaming vehicles were shielded from curious eyes by shirred gauze curtains. When I first went abroad in 1984, I was surprised to find there were no curtains on the back windows of cars!

Each of the several car parks on our campus had room for hundreds of children to play, but now they were crowded with vehicles whose make and size spoke clearly about the passenger's status or connections within the Communist hierarchy. Among government ministers, for example, Russian-produced limousines were common in the late 1950s. Marshals or vice-premiers merited a more sophisticated and larger model of limousine which was also of Soviet make. At the end or beginning of term, it was said that at least half of the cars in Beijing could be seen in Ba-yi in a day.

On the day I arrived, I saw a tall man in a neat Mao-style suit standing by the school's front gate and beaming as he greeted new arrivals. This was the school's headmaster. According to my parents, I took it fairly well when they left me. I cried a lot, but unlike many other newcomers I did not cling to their legs and scream for home. Their absence had been normal all my life; perhaps I had grown used to separation.

The kindergarten was located in a former summer palace built in the eighteenth century by a prince of the Qing Dynasty and used by the family for generations. After the collapse of the imperial system, the family's massive debts compelled them to sign it away, and it passed into the hands of the Le family, whose traditional pharmacy business, known as Tong-ren Tang, served the imperial family in the Qing Dynasty, and is famous today among Chinese all over the world, with branches in many Western capitals. When they heard that our school had its eye on the palace, the Le family asked only a symbolic price, 1,500 bolts of plain cotton cloth, which was far less than the value of the palace, the plants or the land. According to Le Songsheng, the head of the family, it was their pleasure to contribute to an educational institution that would train the children of the revolution.

The entire palace was surrounded by extensive rockery hills several metres high, which shut it off from the rest of the campus. An impressive arch spanned the immense vermilion gate. In feudal China, the vermilion gate was a symbol of social position, and only the imperial, noble or mandarin families had vermilion lacquered gates for their houses. Outside the gate, a pair of huge, majestic lions, carved in white marble, stood guard. Behind it, a scattered array of one-storey buildings stood in their different courtyards, which were also divided by rockeries or high stone walls. The buildings were tall, solid and spacious, with carved beams and colourfully painted rafters. They looked like those in the Imperial Summer Palace, except their tiles. In the days of the emperors, only they were permitted to have golden glazed tiles on their roofs; for everybody else, the tiles had to be grey. Before I came, the palace had been completely modernized, with flush lavatories, central heating and running hot water – rare luxuries in those days, even in Beijing.

For ages, I could not help losing my way in that maze of walled and open spaces. Much of my time there was spent on the first courtyard, where a group of grand buildings, either standing on top of a rock formation or surrounded by long verandas which were also decorated with carved beams and colourfully painted rafters, had originally been ceremonial halls, and in one case a theatre. Like many other palaces and grand mansions in Beijing, all buildings here were single storey only. Most of these buildings were divided into several huge rooms by hardwood partitions carved throughout with lifelike flowers, plants and animals. The building I lived in housed about a hundred children, but it did not feel crowded at all. Before going to sleep, I loved to stare from my bed at the beautiful carvings, and tell myself fairy tales to match them.

In the palace, spring was my favourite season. I still remember the sweet singing of birds that woke me up at dawn. As soon as the morning bell sounded, I ran from the dormitory and was drunk in a moment on the fresh air scented with breaths of blossom. Behind our group of buildings, a large garden with exotic flowers and rare trees was elaborately tended by the school gardeners. One of them was the kind Grandpa Kang, who had served the Imperial family as a gardener in the last years of the Qing Dynasty. By now he had no teeth left, but whenever he saw us his wrinkled face would open in a smile. We spent long hours playing outside, watching goldfish glide in a vast garden pool, or scurrying over the stone bridge that led across the pool to an exquisite pavilion in the centre.

By any standard, life in the Ba-yi School was a paradise, one that no ordinary Chinese could imagine. But for me and my siblings it was not the place to be: we longed for home. Apart from the winter and summer holidays, we spent only two days a month at home, from Saturday afternoon to Sunday afternoon on alternate weekends called the 'big weekends' – the others were the 'small weekends'. At night in my first year, I would sit up for hours in my cot in the kindergarten dormitory, and cry for my paternal grandmother, the closest person in my life. Feng-yuan, my younger brother, cried less than me, but he expressed his homesickness by picking at his padded quilt before he fell asleep. He needed new bedding more often than anyone else in my family. One day, my father popped in on his way to a meeting, and spent a short while with his children in the school's boardroom. When he was leaving, Feng-an, my second brother, hid beneath a small table for a long time, and would not come out. Eventually, the school staff and my father had to pull him out, and my father was nearly late for his next meeting.

Feng-xin, my eldest brother, was the fiercest rebel during our earlier days at Ba-yi School. At the end of each 'big weekend', my siblings and I and other pupils from nearby streets were always collected by a special coach provided by the Beijing Military Region where my father worked. The moment the coach pulled up outside our house, Feng-xin would start crying and shouting, demanding to stay at home. He regularly had to be carried to the coach by my father's personal assistant and bodyguard, trailed by his embarrassed parents. On the following day, the two poor men always complained about their aching backs and arms. When the next 'big weekend' came round, on the other hand, Feng-xin sometimes refused to leave school, because he had grown attached to his classmates.

At the end of December 1954, I came home for a 'big weekend' and saw a newborn baby lying on my grandmother's bed. 'Who is she? Where is she from?' I asked. 'You've got a little sister,' said my grandmother with a teasing smile. 'We found her for you in a rubbish bin outside the house.' My mother and I met so rarely that I had not noticed her pregnancy, and I swallowed the story at once. Later, I discovered that a number of my classmates were told similar stories after their mothers gave birth. My little sister was named 'Aijun', where 'jun' means noble character. I hardly saw her as a baby, because I had so little time at home, but nor was I close to my other siblings. Although we lived so long on the same campus, our paths rarely crossed. Children in different years had their own quarters to live, study and play, except for occasional gatherings in the assembly hall, or tournaments in the main sports ground. The effect was that attachments flagged among us as we grew up. At home, my grandmother complained that we were fonder of our schoolfriends than of each other, and I cannot summon much to prove her wrong.

In kindergarten, I was viewed as a gifted child. The teachers' reports often made comments such as: 'Aiping has showed an excellent under-standing and memory in absorbing new knowledge. In her class, she is a popular story-teller.' By the age of five, I was a kindergarten star, and topped the bill as a solo dancer on special occasions such as parents' meetings or national festivals. To people who praised my performance, my father would proudly reply: 'My daughter takes after her mother.' My mother's blushes quickly turned to smiles.

A few years after I went to primary school, the kindergarten closed, as most children in the Communist high official families had grown up and my school only accepted children from these families. (It was very difficult for younger officers to join the highest ranks.) By then a junior middle school was running, so that pupils could continue to study until the age of fifteen. The kindergarten was later converted into sleeping quarters for all the female pupils. From then on it was rare to see a man in the former palace, because male staff and boys were forbidden.

Wrapped in this privileged cocoon from the age of three, and mixing with no one but the children of other high official families, I had no notion of the lives of ordinary people. The pupils knew each other not only by their own names but often by those of their parents, especially their fathers. In our Chinese textbook at primary school, there was a story about a famous battle during the Long March, when the brave Red Army fought for control of a bridge over the Dadu River. The daughter of the hero of the story – now a three-star army general – was sitting in the classroom next to ours. Another textbook story was about Dr Norman Bethune, a Canadian medical volunteer who died of blood poisoning in north China while working for the Communist forces during the Sino-Japanese War. Mao Zedong's article, 'In Memory of Bethune', which praised the spirit of international communism, later became one of the three most famous Maoist homilies, and made Bethune a household name in China. When we learned his story at school, our faces turned spontaneously to a classmate whose soldier father had worked with Dr Bethune and appeared in the text. In my mind as a naive girl, the Communist republic was created by our parents.

In spring 1960, my second year at primary school, I was selected to join the Young Pioneers. The Communist republic created a three-tiered system of political organizations: the Young Pioneers recruited children from the age of nine, the Communist Youth League from fifteen, while the minimum set for full Party membership was eighteen. Not till years later did I realize what this system implied: it enabled the Party to control people's lives from an early age and hence to entrench its regime. But at that time I was overjoyed to be recruited. I had been told already that I must work hard in the future to take up the cause of the proletarian revolution. Joining the Young Pioneers meant that I had made the first step towards the great ideal. It made me especially proud to be one of the first group chosen in my year, even though I still had a few months to go to my ninth birthday. The teachers made the choice, chiefly on the basis of our academic records and behaviour.

'Please take good care of your application form,' my mother kept telling me when I brought the news home. The details required included information about the political background of the applicant's parents, and the reason for applying. Some years before, Feng-xin had used the form to wipe his bottom when the school lavatory ran out of paper. This action was regarded as an insult to the dignity of the Young Pioneers, so grave that he was criticized in class and his membership was postponed for several months.

On a sunny Saturday morning, I and the other new Young Pioneers took the oath of admission in a special ceremony held in the school assembly hall. By the time we arrived, the hall was packed with about 1,000 cheerful pupils. A huge portrait of Chairman Mao hung against a red backdrop on the platform, surrounded by potted flowers in full bloom which filled the air with fragrance. Our names were announced, and we ran to the platform from our seats at the front of the hall, in a roar of applause. My face was burning with excitement. I had performed here many times before, but never felt as proud as that moment. Suddenly, trumpets blared and rousing drumbeats sounded. At the main entrance a band appeared, dressed in snow-white shirts and dark blue trousers, each wearing a bright red scarf, the symbol of the Young Pioneers. They marched down the aisles in two columns, following huge red banners, and came to a halt at the platform, greeted by thunderous cheers.

'Red scarves award to new Young Pioneers.' A team of senior Young Pioneers came on to the platform, each one holding a new red scarf. In minutes, a boy stopped in front of me. Although I had never spoken to him, I knew that he was two years older than me, and his father was a general, a veteran of the Long March.

'Congratulations, Wa-wa-men ["babies"]!' The headmaster started with his favourite endearment to his pupils. 'You are the successors to the cause of the proletarian revolution. I expect you to become pillars of the state, and our school to become the cradle of marshals and generals. In the future, you will take over the revolutionary responsibility from your parents . . .'

At the end of the ceremony, feelings ran high in the hall. In front of Mao's portrait and the red banners of the Young Pioneers, we all stood up and raised our right fists. 'Be prepared to strive for the cause of Communism!' A Young Pioneer leader issued a solemn pledge. 'Be prepared at any time!' Along with all the rest, I answered loudly, shaking with excitement. This was my first solemn vow, and it thrilled me to take it. The red scarf weighed on my shoulders as if they were carrying the historic mission of the proletariat.

Even as a toddler, I longed to know what my parents did, that kept them so absent from my life. 'What do you do at work?' I asked when I came home from kindergarten. 'Do you listen to Snow White or Pinocchio stories too, and play games with little friends?' To begin with, my naive questions would make my parents laugh, but a gradual change followed my transfer to primary school. 'Why is your military rank lower than some of my schoolmates' fathers' when they joined the revolution after you?' I asked one day. 'I joined the revolution to help poor people, not to advance myself,' he replied, then chided me: 'It is not good to compare your parents' positions with other people's.'

The system of military ranks introduced in Red China in 1955 was almost a direct copy of the Soviet army's. The lowest rank was second lieutenant (shao-wei). Apart from the top rank of marshal (yuan-shuai), there were four different levels in each rank. Generals were divided into major or one-star general (shao-jiang), lieutenant or two-star general (zhong-jiang), general or three-star general (shang-jiang) and senior or four-star general (da-jiang). Among several million soldiers, there were only ten marshals appointed, and about a thousand generals. The rank was decided by the Party, mainly in consideration of previous revolutionary experience and current position.

In the Ba-yi School, our parents' revolutionary careers were a subject often raised among the pupils, and taught me many basic lessons about Communist history in China. For example, I heard that one girl's father had earned his rank of two-star general because he had been with Chairman Mao in the Jing-gang Shan mountain area, the first

Communist base established in 1927, and was one of the very few officers surviving from those days. One boy's father with a similar length of service held a rank of only four-star colonel. I heard that this was due mainly to his performance in a famous battle at the end of the civil war in the later 1940s, when as a deputy commander he left his front-line post at a crucial moment, and several regiments were destroyed. Mao was so angry that he told the man's commander: 'Don't choose him for any job in the next ten years.'

Despite my father's criticism, I still wanted to know what had happened to his career. What made me feel especially curious was the fact that although his starting rank of senior colonel (da-xiao) was at the high end of the colonel grade, some of my schoolmates' fathers who had joined the revolution later and held similar positions had been appointed one-star generals.

I heard later that the treatment my father received reflected his lack of appropriate experience either in the Red Army, the Communist forces before the Sino-Japanese War, or in the Long March. Among the first PLA generals, this was regarded as a crucial qualification. The reason sounded unconvincing to me. During that period, it was the Party's orders to stay in the Nationalist areas that prevented my father from joining the Red Army. When the Long March started in 1934, he had been an active member of the Communist underground for years. Working under the Nationalist 'white terror', he risked his life all the time for the revolution. After 1937, he had established a guerrilla force in Japanese-occupied territory, and then brought it to the Communist base.

Another bar to my father's progress was that his position in the army when the Communists took power in 1949 was equivalent to a divisional deputy commander, not a commander. Here too he was damaged by factors beyond his control, such as his imprisonment for being an intellectual during the Rescue Campaign of the 1940s. On the eve of the civil war, he followed his orders again. Sidelined unfairly in the desolate Sui-Mon region, he lost the opportunity for rapid promotion that others gained by working in affluent Manchuria. When the war ended, there was no chance to make good the damage to his career.

Many years later, I realized that my father's fate stemmed mainly from his lack of political connections. In the army there were a number of factions known as the mountain stronghold (shan-tou), after the source of their political power. With the right connections, it was said, an officer could shoot up like a plant fed with chemical fertilizer. In the Beijing Military Region where my father worked, for example, most senior posts went either to veterans of the Long March, or to men who had joined the Communist forces in the Jin-Cha-Ji Base during the Sino-Japanese War. My father came from Jin-Sui, a different base, and had no experience in the Red Army, so he had no link with any of the mountain strongholds. He did not care about connections, because he believed what Chairman Mao said: 'We hail from all corners of the country and have joined together for a common revolutionary goal.' However, it turned out that an outsider's interests could be overlooked, and with so few vacancies available for the rank of general, his chance became too slim.

'I really think that you deserve a higher rank than senior colonel,' one of his chiefs told my father after the ceremony held to award the new ranks. On top of his considerable revolutionary experience, my father was well known among senior officers in the region for his ability and political integrity. It was suggested that his position would improve if he lobbied for himself, but he took no notice, and made no complaint. His initial military rank entitled him to a salary equivalent to Grade 9 in the official scale. A few years later, as a political gesture to reduce their privileges, the salaries of officials between Grades 1–10 were frozen as were their chances of an upgrade, so my father never had a pay raise until the end of his life.

In 1964, my father was promoted to major-general, which was one of few such cases after the initial award in 1955. In honour of his promotion, he was issued with a brand-new uniform, bright blue and made of fine woollen serge, the best material available. In my memory, the uniform was always relegated to a corner of my parents' wardrobe, together with my father's numerous medals, which he hardly ever wore. In editions of the *Biographical Notes on Marshals and Generals of the People's Liberation Army* published several decades later, my father is unusual for appearing without his dress uniform, because he never sat for such a photo in his life.

One of the few extra privileges that followed my father's promotion was the provision of a chef, the second of our full-time household staff. He was in his mid-thirties; my siblings and I called him Uncle Zhong. The orderly who already worked for our family was a young soldier whose duties included cleaning and shopping. Since the 1950s, the provision of private staffs had been available only to a small number of high officials. With his new rank, my father's food rations also improved. When he travelled, a bodyguard came with him. For our family, a chauffeur-driven car was always ready.

Among my fellow pupils, such privileges were not unusual: many of them enjoyed a similar lifestyle at home. The real difference, I discovered, was in the position of our mothers, the wives of high officials. Many had joined the revolution during the wars but had stopped work after their marriages. They either quit their jobs to become housewives or held sinecures, and so lived on their husbands' patronage. In contrast, my mother had risen high in her career without making use of my father's position.

In 1958, when the Ministry of Education was looking for senior staff for universities, my mother applied for a transfer. At that time, she was heading the office of liaison with Russian advisers in the Ministry of Water Conservancy and Power. By the terms of treaties signed during their 'honeymoon' period in the 1950s, many experts from the USSR came to China as professional advisers working in various fields. In her ministry, their involvement included the design and construction of hydroelectric power stations all over China, and my mother's frequent trips to these locations made it difficult to care for a family of five young children. She was also concerned about her lack of professional or practical qualifications in the industry. The field of education was familiar and congenial after her experiences during the Sino-Japanese War, and working in a university would broaden her own education.

My mother's application was soon accepted. When high officials changed their jobs, it was usual to ask them what position and location they would prefer, but her reply was brief: 'I obey the Party's decision.' In March 1958, she was appointed concurrently as personnel director and director of the general office of the Party committee (a role similar to secretary-general in Western organizations) in the Forestry University, one of Beijing's famous 'eight universities'. Three years later, at the age of thirty-eight, she was promoted to vice-secretary of the university Party committee, the equivalent of vice-chancellor. Under the Communist regime, organizations such as institutions, enterprises or factories came under parallel government and Party control. As vice-secretary of the university Party committee, for example, my mother's authority included approving staff appointments and monitoring standards of performance. At that time, hardly any women held the highest positions in Chinese universities. My mother was the youngest, and one of a tiny minority of women in the whole country to be ranked at Grade 12 or above. Among wives of senior officers in the Beijing Military Region, she was one of the few who received the highest salary with the highest independent social status.

In my childhood, I was proud of my mother's status both as a high official and as the wife of a high official. Every year, on the anniversary of the People's Republic, the 1st of October, my parents were often invited as special guests to the celebrations held in Tian-an Men Square, which was a great honour for Chinese. They left home separately in chauffeur-driven cars, one provided to my father by the Beijing Military Region, the other to my mother by her university. When I watched the event through documentary films or TV, my heart always swelled. I saw

Chairman Mao standing on the rostrum over a sea of flags and flowers, reviewing the military parade and waving to the cheerful crowd. I knew that my parents sat just in front of Mao in the reviewing stands. I also knew that my mother was one of the handful of women guests of honour, invited entirely for her own achievements.

Another proud occasion was the publication in 1962 of my father's first novel, *Autumn in Jinyang* (Jinyang was the ancient name of Taiyuan, the provincial capital of Shanxi), inspired by an unexpected meeting there in spring 1953 with a former member of his guerrilla forces in the Sino-Japanese War. All sorts of buried details and lost feelings revived as they looked back on their past and cherished the memory of colleagues who had sacrificed their lives. From then on, peace left my father's soul. Memories surfaced like fountains, and the faces of passionate young revolutionaries, his comrades during the war, crowded his dreams. At last he decided that for the martyrs and for future generations he must resurrect his past. By 1959, he had written a draft of nearly a million words, and called it *The Billows*. *Autumn in Jinyang*, published as volume one, ran to nearly half a million words and almost 600 pages. It told the story of a group of young Communist intellectuals in Taiyuan at the start of the Sino-Japanese War, the unforgettable autumn of 1937.

While he was writing, my father was backed by the authorities of the Beijing Military Region, and a number of influential figures such as Zhou Yang, the Party's deputy chief of propaganda. There was keen competition to publish it among several of the largest national publishers in Beijing, who offered big advances and kept inviting my father to dinners, outings or the opera. But he was unmoved by this treatment. Out of his loyalty to the military, he signed the contract from the publishing house of the People's Liberation Army, although they did not offer the best deal.

The novel became an immediate bestseller in China and was quickly and repeatedly reprinted. Critics admired its style and use of language. In the same year, the book was broadcast nationally by the Central

People's Radio Station of China, in a version adapted by Dong Xing-ji, a famous actor from the Beijing People's Art Theatre. For several months, a peak-hour audience of hundreds of millions listened to my father's stories. Many people asked me: 'Is your father Guo Song? Is your mother Lan Rong?' – these were the leading male and female characters. I remember letters forwarded by the publisher arriving at our house in huge gunny-sacks. Readers absorbed by the fates of the leading characters wrote to express their feelings and to ask about future stories. Later, the book was selected as an 'excellent novel' by the General Political Department of the Military Forces, which was one of the few national literature awards in China. In the following years, a number of major film studios approached my father about adapting his book as a film. The famous Beijing Film Studio was the most enthusiastic, but had to shelve the project after he turned down several adaptations.

I still remember how proud I felt when I showed the novel to my classmates. In the past, I had kept quiet about my parents' intellectual backgrounds, and especially my father's, as it was unusual among senior officers. Since most of China's veteran revolutionaries came from poor and therefore uneducated families, lack of education came to signify the right family background and class origin for revolutionaries. I also heard that Mao Zedong had repeatedly criticized intellectual Party members as 'petty bourgeois', and strongly favoured worker-peasant cadres. Intellectual Party members were told to behave like cautious dogs, and tuck their tails between their legs. In other words, a good education could amount to a black mark on the record of a Communist cadre. When my classmates referred to their fathers as 'uneducated persons' (da-lao-cu) with pride, I felt pity for the defect in my father. But things seemed to change when his novel came to school. They looked at his name on the beautiful jacket, and said how much they envied me for having such a wonderful father.

'Your father must have made a fortune from his book,' people supposed. In fact, how much he earned remained a mystery to me for a long

time, as our parents never told us about it. Before the book was published in 1962, China had abolished the royalty system, so my father
received a single payment, based on the number of words. But for any
Chinese, the amount he received was considerable – 6,000 yuan, which
was roughly a whole year's salary for Mao Zedong, at the top of the
scale. With my mother's agreement, my father decided to donate most of
his income from the novel, 5,000 yuan, to their beloved Communist
Party. Since personal cheques were non-existent, my mother had to
withdraw the sum in cash. Having filled her handbag with notes, she
astonished the staff at the bank by informing them that all the money
was to go straight to the Party's organization.

The only purchase paid for by my father's book was a black-and-
white TV set, bought chiefly to entertain my grandmother, who was
bored by her idle life at home. In 1962, the first TV station in China
had just been established in Beijing. Our set was produced in Tianjin by
the only factory in the whole country. Despite the horrendous cost of
nearly 1,000 yuan, its quality was very disappointing. Several weeks
later, the volume failed, and from then on the set needed frequent
repairs. In those days, there was only one repair shop in Beijing or in
China as a whole. Most of the staff were quite young, and they usually
made deliveries by bicycle. According to them, there were only a couple
of hundred television sets among a population of several million. Beijing
was the only city in China able to receive television programmes, and
most of the private owners were high officials, including many of my
schoolmates' families.

Even without my father's novels, since both of my parents were high on
the salary scale, my family's income was large by Chinese standards. In
those days, senior officers' families had very few living expenses. Under
the salary system, they were still entitled to many free services, including
water, electricity and telephone, while others – such as housing and
medication – cost only nominal amounts. In 1962, our family moved

from my favourite place, Temple for Protecting the Nation Street, to the north of the city, outside the Gate of Virtue and Triumph (De-sheng-men). Our new house had six bedrooms, and luxuries such as sofas, carpets, beds with soft mattresses, and a hot-water bath, at a rent of about 20 yuan a month. Most of it came free from the army, including the dining and living rooms, my parents' bedroom and study, and accommodation for an orderly. The total boarding fees for their five children came to 60 yuan per month, which was more than a university graduate earned, but only a fraction of my father's wages. For senior officers' families, the major expense was food and clothes.

Most of my parents' income was spent on my father's book collection, which was based on Chinese classical literature and history. He started it in 1952, after we settled in Beijing. For nearly a thousand years, under various names, Beijing has been the capital of China, with only brief intervals elsewhere. Historically, the imperial family, nobles, great families and distinguished scholars kept extensive collections of classical art. The fall of these families with the collapse of the Qing Dynasty started a booming trade in classical art and antiquities, whose two main centres by the early 1950s were Liulichang (Beijing's most famous antique shopping street), southwest of Tian-an Men Square, and Peace in the East Bazaar (Dong-an Shi-chang), in Wangfujing, east of the Forbidden City.

My father's favourite place was Peace in the East Bazaar, a vast one-storey building divided by many intestinal corridors, narrow and dark, where crowded rows of little shops sold all sorts of everyday items. The book market clustered in a corner of the building, each store a small room of about 10 square metres, and stacked from floor to ceiling with shelves loaded with old and new books or magazines. Many of the books were traditional Chinese thread-bound editions, whose missing covers and discoloured pages were signs of long journeys through history. At the entrance to each store, the quiet owner stood or sat behind a dark desk by a big abacus, and greeted his customers with a smile. Normally, these owners dressed in Chinese-style cotton jackets and baggy trousers, tied at the end with a dark cotton band. Their hand-made shoes – always clean, with black uppers and thick white soles – were the kind known as 'cloth shoes with a thousand layers of soles' (qian-ceng-di bu-xie). In the early 1950s, few could afford books. Under the prevailing supply system, my parents had only a small cash allowance, and my father's collection started slowly.

In the late 1950s, the onset of nationalization merged these small private bookstores into one large state-run company, the 'China Bookstore' (Zhong-guo Shu-dian), based on Liulichang. This gave the government a monopoly over the trade in second-hand books published before 1949, and the right to make private purchases was restricted to a small number of high officials and senior professional people, because classical Chinese culture was regarded as an unhealthy remnant of feudalism. By that time, my family's finances had soared after the introduction of the salary system, and now that my father was free to buy, his collection grew fast.

My father had been an ardent lover of classical culture since his child-hood. During the wars, stationed in back-country places, battered books and old newspapers found in abandoned houses became his treasure and occupied much of what luggage he had. He once gave up his finest pos-session, a heavy woollen coat captured from the Japanese and issued to senior officers only, in exchange for a book by Lu Xun. This book accom-panied him until 1942, when as a precaution before a clash with the invaders he wrapped it carefully in oil-paper and buried it in a remote valley. He never had the chance to reclaim it, but when he came across a copy of the same book in Beijing in the 1950s, he had a special box made for it, covered in dark blue cotton, with the title embroidered in red.

The second-hand booksellers of Beijing knew my father as one of their few serious customers, and a thoughtful friend. Most of the assis-tants in the China Bookstore had formerly owned their own shops. They seldom had much education, due to their poor family back-grounds, and nationalization left them badly off. Their coarse clothes made them look like peasants. Yet my father considered them national heroes, the saviours of China's cultural heritage. Due to their efforts, and their lifetimes of knowledge, many priceless ancient books and paintings were discovered, and rescued from recycling as waste paper. In the 1950s, one of these assistants wrote a study of Chinese bibliography that is now an essential reference book for librarians and researchers. Another salesman could date the provenance of any ancient and rare edition as far back as the Song Dynasty (960–1279 AD). Most of these men were on close terms with a range of famous scholars and distinguished personages who were regular customers. My father enjoyed their company, picked their brains, and paid attention to their anecdotes about the history of rare editions. He made himself an expert on rare and second-hand editions of classical literature and history.

In those days, the China Bookstore had nationwide sources to draw upon. When new stock arrived, the staff kept books my father might want to see, and if he was too busy they delivered them. Sometimes a string of flatbed tricycles halted outside our home, all of them loaded with books, which my father could choose from before they went on the market. This privileged treatment was only available to a few select customers, such as Qian Xingchun, a prominent dramatist and veteran Communist known by his pen-name, A-ying. He became my father's best friend. The privileged customers also included Kang Sheng, the author of the infamous Rescue Campaign in the 1940s. Now he had become an important political figure in China, responsible for cultural and educational affairs.

By the early 1960s, my father's collection had annexed our house, so that Feng-xin had to sleep in the dining room while my sister and I shared a bedroom with our grandmother. My father's book bills varied from a few hundred to over a thousand yuan per month, which was a considerable sum even for my family, and compelled my parents to make economies. For a long time, my father never bought any decent clothes, and had his old army uniforms dyed blue for civilian wear. When first invited to attend the anniversary celebrations held in Tian-an Men Square, my mother found that she had nothing suitable to wear. In our childhood, my siblings and I had hardly any pocket money. Since the Ba-yi School stopped providing pupils with uniforms after the mid-1950s, we were often embarrassed by the cheap and threadbare clothes we got from home. In those days, I longed for a new pair of socks to replace my usual supply of uncomfortable mended ones.

At home, the most familiar image of my grandmother was her endlessly patching and mending, with her head tilted low in concentration, and her presbyopic glasses slipping down the bridge of her nose. I often used to help her thread the needle. In 1961, my mother bought a sewing-machine, which made the work much easier. All the same, our neighbours' nannies would look at all the patches on our clothes, and ask our grandmother: 'How can your family be so poor?' Because of our tight budget, most of our food was bought at a reduced price in the sale.

'It's crazy to spend all your money on books,' my grandmother urged to my mother. 'You should stop him.' My mother's response was a smile. She knew how much books mattered to her husband. With nothing but his school education, he could never have published his novel. In any case, reading was also a joy to her, and she loved to visit bookshops with my father. As high officials, my parents were secure. Compared with their salaries, their costs of living were extremely low. Individuals did not pay income tax, and under the Communist regime the property market was abolished, so what else could they do with their money? Her salary was enough to maintain the whole family. Why should she not support her husband's mission, and give him the freedom to save their country's cultural heritage?

In his spare time, my father liked taking me to visit the China Bookstore, hidden away behind high brick walls in an immense one-storey mansion with several large courtyards. Most of the rooms were huge and crammed with books, but not with customers — to visit the place took special permission that no ordinary citizen could obtain. Inside the main hall, my father was always greeted by a salesman in his late thirties, who specialized in servicing him and Kang Sheng. 'Chunhua!' I remember my father's cheerful voice when he called the salesman's name. Chunhua arranged for my father to borrow some rare editions from Kang Sheng, who would seldom let his prizes out of his sight, but when he offered to introduce them my father refused. He had not forgiven Kang Sheng for his role in the Rescue Campaign, and besides, both of my parents hated to curry favour with the powerful, because it smacked too much of the old bureaucratic mentality that the new regime should disown.

Normally, my father's searches took him several hours. In summer, the rooms were terribly hot and humid, and his nonstop waving of a folding paper fan did not save him from streaming with sweat. In winter, the cavernous rooms dwarfed the single coal stove that they each contained, and he had to make dashes to warm himself. Before his own search started, he always found some books to recommend to me – mostly classical novels and history books, meant to teach me the art of patience. I remember reading the Chinese translation of Marco Polo, and feeling amazed by the picture of ancient China as seen through a Westerner's eyes. After spending some time reading in the stillness of the rooms, I enjoyed exploring treasures that ranged from ancient books published hundreds of years ago to modern publications published before 1949 and banned by the government because their contents were regarded as anti-Communist or pornographic. My most interesting discoveries were Chinese translations of recent bestsellers in the West, available only to privileged readers, and most of them published without the consent of the authors. When we finally emerged, I always felt thirsty and tired, and my stomach was rumbling with hunger, but my delighted father carried another huge armful of books.

As my father's collection grew, he devoted more and more of his spare time to its upkeep. When he brought new items home, first he would wrap the covers in special tailored jackets, which were thin and almost transparent, to protect them from damage, leaving the print and decoration clearly visible through the delicate wrapping paper. The process of restoring damaged volumes was terribly time-consuming. Since it was too expensive to pay specialists, my father learned the skills through watching experts at work in second-hand bookshops in Liulichang. Some books he bought were heavily damaged and had many pages stuck together. After unbinding the books, he soaked the pages in water in our bathtub, then teased them apart with a long needle, dried them, and thoroughly pressed them under a heavy stone. When the repaired pages were resewn with silk thread, a completely new book was created. The final step was to follow the Chinese tradition and give the book its own special box, made by my father from cotton cloth and thick paper. During school holidays, my siblings and I were often conscripted to assist. I still recall my father's happy face, gazing at his immaculate re-creations like a mother watching her newborn baby.

After the mid-1950s, the puritanical lifestyle of Communist officials was gradually replaced by a more normal family life. But my mother still lived in the small apartment provided by her office, and came home only on Wednesdays and weekends, which was unusual among my parents' colleagues. She was following through my father's suggestion that they should dedicate some of their spare time to improving their education. For several years, they both studied Russian, using a standard history of the Soviet Bolsheviks. At weekends, they checked each other's progress and discussed the latest problems in their studies. In order to improve his writing skills, my father read widely in classical and modern literature. His favourite lair for reading was a chilly little cell that had once been a storeroom. It had no radiator, and in winter he would sit there till midnight with his books, wearing a hat, warm boots and an overcoat. From 1958 to the early 1960s, when he was assigned by Marshal Nie Rongzhen to head a team compiling the history of the Communist forces in north China, he worked with prominent writers such as Deng Tuo and Wei Wei. The numerous essays on political science that he published in the military newspapers and journals were based on his working reports. This was unusual among the senior officers, as many relied on assistants for writing at length.

To escape the Beijing heat, in summer many of my father's colleagues would spend their family holidays in Beidaihe, on the Bohai Gulf, a favourite resort town with the Party elites. But the only time I went to Beidaihe was in 1959, when my father and his team had to work throughout the summer for Marshal Nie Rongzhen, who was there with his family. As far as I can remember, my parents never took any of the free holidays provided annually for senior officers and their families.

As a lover of classical culture, my father expected his children to become writers, or students of literature or history, which contradicted what we learned at school: that the Party's objective was to train heirs to the proletarian revolution. On holidays, each child had to practise calligraphy. To draw at least 50 Chinese characters every day using the traditional writing brush took us more than an hour. In Chinese society, calligraphy was a key skill for scholars and officials, a pointer to their educational background. Without the proper training in the art, people would be slighted for their poor education, no matter how capable and knowledgeable they were. Unfortunately, I was never keen to practise, as it bored me too easily, so my father often criticized my work. On the other hand Feng-an, my second brother, showed a precocious talent for calligraphy and painting, and his meticulous patience always amazed me.

Encouraged by my father, I started collecting series of books about China, and world culture, history and geography, which were issued by a prestigious national publisher (Shang-wu-yin-shu-guan) from the early 1960s. Soon I had over 100 titles — my first ever steps through the gate of the palace of art, which led me to great Chinese poets such as Li Bai, Du Fu and Bai Juyi (in the West often spelt as Li Po, Tu Fu and Po Chu-I) of the Tang Dynasty (618–907 AD) as well as to the magical power of Dante, Shakespeare, Goethe and others. It was reading these series that gave me my elementary education in literature, history and geography. In particular, I learned not only the chief events in several thousand years of Chinese history, but also what happened in other parts of the world, which we did not learn at primary school. Using knowledge picked up from these series, years later at middle school I often spotted errors that vexed or embarrassed my teachers. When they complained to my parents, I was criticized for rudeness and arrogance.

Feng-xin, my eldest brother, had a passion for science that started at primary school. He impressed his teachers by his ability to assemble transistor radios on his own, and to see him turn a small soapbox into an elegant case for a radio was like watching a conjuror perform. Unfortunately, his interest in science displeased my father, who saw no career for his children outside literature or history. On school holidays or 'big weekends', Feng-xin had to hide his work and tools beneath his duvet when my father came home, otherwise he would see it all locked away in my father's desk. But Feng-xin held out against this pressure, and began to steal money from my grandmother to buy more tools and spares. In 1959, in his first year at middle school, he broke the school rules by reading his favourite transistor radio manual in Russian class. In those days, Russian was the only foreign language taught in most middle schools, but Feng-xin disliked it. When the manual was confiscated, he lost his temper, jumped out of his seat, and grappled with his teacher to retrieve it. He was banned from the classroom next day.

My parents were ashamed of Feng-xin's behaviour, for they had asked their children to be polite, modest and honest. But their busy schedules made it hard for them to talk to us regularly, because my mother lived mainly at her university, and my father used to go to his study as soon as he came back from work. Weekends were their precious time together, when they hardly left each other's side. To their colleagues, they were a deeply affectionate couple. In this situation, it was our paternal grand-mother who became the centre of our home life. When we came back from school, the first place we went was her room. If anyone needed help, they turned to her. The warmth of her arms cheered my heart,

especially when she patted my head and murmured 'This girl!' Back
from outdoors one winter's day, Feng-an slipped his cold hands inside
her jacket to warm them on her body, the way we all did. 'You're going
to be a man soon,' Grandmother pretended to grumble. 'Remember
never to touch a woman's body through her clothes, or you'll be for it!'
In the holidays, we followed her around like little tails. 'Why don't you
go to your parents?' she said when they were home, but my three brothers seldom ventured close.

Among his colleagues and relatives, my father was known for his stern
discipline at home, as he believed in the traditional saying that 'It is a bad
father who rears but does not discipline his children.' Among his own siblings, a major deterrent was to threaten their young children: 'I'll tell your
Eldest Uncle.' Even my naughtiest cousins would succumb, though most
of them had hardly met my father, and lived in different parts of China.

In my family, the strict demands made on my siblings and me were
based on Confucian ethics, which ordained obedience to parents, especially to fathers. My father often laid the law down at dinner time, as it
was one of the rare occasions when his mind was not fixed on his work.
He could make any of us cry, and the rest feel intensely uncomfortable,
but no one at the table dared to say a word for the victim, for fear of
being next. 'Why don't you let them finish eating?' But if our mother did
protest against his methods she was failing to maintain a united front,
and had to keep quiet later on. So dinner with our father could petrify
us all, as we never knew what we had coming. If he got to the dining
room first, every child stayed outside as long as possible. If he came last
the liveliness dissolved when he appeared. During the meal no one
spoke, because that was forbidden. When he finally left the room, we
broke out talking or laughing, teasing or fighting again, as if coming
back to life.

Another tribunal was his study, where he would sit for hours behind
his desk with no expression, condemning his children's mistakes or misbehaviour. We stood there and must not offer a word, except to say 'Yes'

or 'I'll never do it again'. Afterwards, the guilty were often required to make written confessions criticising their bad behaviour. We had to obey, but we did not always agree, and least of all Feng-xin, my eldest brother and a teenage rebel. His domestic education from my father consisted of being repeatedly told off, confined to his room or even beaten.

In the winter holiday of 1963, on the eve of the Chinese New Year, Feng-xin's school report arrived, with only a 'pass' grade in several subjects. His growing resentment of my father's harsh discipline had hampered his studies, especially on the side of the arts. The grade my father expected from his children had to be excellent. He flew into a rage, and shamed his son in front of all the family. But this was too much for a boy of seventeen, and some time next morning Feng-xin left home in silence. Beijing was a world of ice and snow, and he had no money. Where was he? How could he survive? My parents feared for his safety. Each day after work they walked the city streets, but could not find him.

Three days later, my grandmother was woken up at dawn by a quiet knocking on our back door. There was Feng-xin, sitting on the ground, looking pale and weak. Since leaving us, he had spent his days mostly hanging around in Tian-an Men Square, and his nights huddled in a big concrete pipe by a roadside. Freezing cold and hunger had forced him back home. 'Please be kind to him from now on,' Grandmother pleaded to my father.

Being my father's favourite child, I was kept at home most of the time during holidays and weekends. If my mother was away, I kept him company when he was working in his study. He rarely spoke there, so after finishing the long stints of drawing or reading that he set me, I had to amuse myself. In pre-school days, my favourite game was imitating the mannerisms of high officials seen in newsreels. Standing with my hands clasped behind my back, I delivered a solemn address to an imagined conference: 'How do you do, comrades! Here in our great socialist country, the revolutionary situation is excellent . . .' It always drew a laugh from my father, before he returned to his work.

After I started school, my father was more reluctant to let me play outside. To his mind, a well brought-up girl should be quiet and hard-working, so most of my spare time should be spent on reading, calligraphy or helping with the housework. Before the age of ten, I started to learn classical poems from him, one for each weekend at home. It pleased him that I could recite a new poem after hearing him read it only once. He also introduced me to drama and the Peking Opera, by taking me to the theatre or playing records at home. I was surprised to learn that many famous singers playing female roles in the Peking Opera were actually male. It took me a while to be convinced, especially when I heard the high sweet register of their voices, and saw their absolutely feminine manner.

Initially, I thought that my father's special strictness towards me was unreasonable. In holiday time I wanted to go out and enjoy myself like other girls my age, and it was hard to be cooped up. As an ordinary schoolgirl, I was not equipped to appreciate the complex ancient stories and stylized performance of the Peking Opera, and preferred to watch a children's film instead. Yet my disobedience would bring angry condemnations of my 'wild behaviour' for playing out of doors, or my ignorance of classical Chinese culture. Since I was the only one among his children who dared to answer him back, my stubbornness was particularly vexing, and normally resulted in a beating. 'Silly girl,' my grandmother tried to advise me, 'just admit you were wrong and then it will all be over.' But what was wrong with what I did? Instead of giving way, I stood up for myself, and argued till the beating was over. 'Perhaps I shouldn't have fed you so much cow's milk when you were a baby,' my grandmother said, 'and then you wouldn't have such a cow's temper.' (In Chinese culture, a cow or ox is a symbol of stubbornness.)

My father's punishments affronted me. Several times, I promised myself never to speak to him again after a beating, but then he would come and talk, and express his regret, and I would unbend. Sometimes, he brought me sweets or books, which was very unusual for a man who hardly ever gave presents to other family members. 'Beating shows parents' fondness for their children, and shouting shows their love' (da-shi-qin, ma-shi-ai): Grandmother tried to win me round by quoting the famous Chinese saying. In her view, my father's authority as head of the family should never be defied, neither by his children nor even by herself. After her husband's death, it was her duty to obey her darling eldest son.

Unlike Feng-xin, I eventually embraced my father's passion for classical Chinese culture. At the age of ten, I wrote my first poem, which followed the example of my classmate, the youngest daughter of Xie Juezai, who was Director of China's Supreme People's Court. In my class, she was regarded as a gifted pupil and we liked to share each other's interests. The poem resembled a short nursery rhyme, four lines long. Its title, 'Red flowers turn towards the sun', showed my admiration as a red (revolutionary) flower for Chairman Mao, the sun in our hearts. When he read the poem during the following 'big weekend', my father approved, and started to teach me the rules and forms of classical poetic composition, but my phase of writing poetry did not last long, as I soon turned to novels and history. With my father's collection to browse in, my interests and writing skills improved. My essays were singled out for praise, and some were read out in front of my class, or even the whole school.

Apart from Feng-xin and me, there was not much friction between my father and the rest of his children. As I recall, Feng-an and Feng-yuan tended to be quiet both at home and at school, and hardly did anything that specially pleased or specially riled my parents. Aijun was Grandmother's pet. Reproof made her cry, and brought Grandmother quickly to the rescue, which saved her from all sorts of troubles at home. As she grew up, the restrictions my father set for me did not affect her, so she had more freedom than I did, and enjoyed more leisure activities on holidays.

Chapter 11

Mysteries of My Relatives and Friends:
The Great Leap Forward, Famine and
Intra-Party Conflicts

(1958–1964)

Early in 1960, when he was fourteen, Feng-xin sat at school dinner and mumbled: 'Since the Great Leap Forward, we've stopped getting those tasty steamed buns made of wheat flour.' His remark was overheard by a teacher, and was interpreted as opposing the Great Leap Forward launched by Chairman Mao. Questioned by school security, Feng-xin admitted that he had heard his grandmother say the same at home, so it came to the attention of the Beijing Military Region that my grandmother had attacked the Great Leap Forward – a charge serious enough to get the offender jailed or sent to a labour camp. A few days later, the Party secretary-general of the regional headquarters popped into my father's office. 'Please tell your mother to mind what she says,' he asked my father. 'Don't worry, we trust you, and don't believe your mother is a counter-revolutionary.' So had it not been for my father's political position, Feng-xin's casual remark would have caused grave political troubles for my grandmother and perhaps the whole family. 'Never tell anyone outside the family about things you hear at home,' my parents warned their children afterwards.

In fact, what Feng-xin said was true. In 1958, the Great Leap Forward launched Mao's ambitious plan for China's industrial output to overtake Britain's within two or three years, and the USA's in ten years. China would create the Communist society, a paradise on earth, with ample food and clothing for all. Mao's call had a powerful impact. The Chinese people never forget their past experience of being humiliated and bullied by the big powers. It would boost their national pride to show the world a new China performing economic miracles. This vision of abundance appealed most of all to peasants who had endured poverty and hunger for generations. During the wars, the Chinese had seen what miracles the Communists could do. With crude and simple weapons, their army had triumphed over well-equipped Japanese invaders and American-backed Nationalist troops. Within a few decades, revolution in China had grown from a single spark to a prairie fire. Considering the Communists' achievements, why doubt their economic capability? The Great Leap Forward began in a surge of enthusiasm. Now two years had passed, and everyone – even a teenager like Feng-xin – could see what a crisis had resulted.

From 1959, a terrible famine descended on the country. As the capital city, Beijing was the last place affected. From 1960, the monthly food ration was cut to just over 10 kg of grain for an adult in Beijing, most of it supplied as coarse maize flour. Rice, wheat flour, meat, fish, eggs and cooking oil were rarely seen, and fresh vegetables rationed to less than a hundred grams a day. At dawn, there were long queues outside each food store, whose limited supplies quickly left shoppers with empty hands and hungry stomachs. Occasionally, a few items remained on the shelves, but they were only for display. Failing to solve the crisis, the government appealed for the people to tighten their belts.

One day, my mother attended an official conference of two thousand senior Communists gathered in the Great Hall of the People in Beijing. The keynote speaker, a county governor, was invited to present his experience of filling empty stomachs with limited food. One method was 're-steaming rice': you take cooked rice and steam it in more water, to increase its volume. Another method was to reduce the size of bowls to make it seem as if the food was going further. Obviously none of these palliative tricks could cure starvation. In desperation, people even in Beijing ate anything that could fill their empty stomachs, such as tree leaves, bark and grass. To supplement their diet, many people grew chlorella in human urine at home. I never tried the stuff myself, but it was said to taste really disgusting. Soon, oedema and hepatitis were epidemic in the country – effects of malnutrition.

My mother was one of the 'sugar and bean officials' – those whose seniority entitled them to an extra monthly supply during the famine, which included 500 grams each of sugar, soy-beans and eggs plus 250 grams of cooking oil. As a military man, my father's food ration was larger than a civilian's, and he too received additional supplies for his rank. Their work still required them to eat at their office canteens, and they brought most of their extra rations home to make up my grandmother's poor diet.

In 1958, when my younger sister Aijun was three years old, she entered boarding kindergarten at the Beijing Ba-yi School. My parents wanted to keep a nanny at home, but Grandmother refused. She prided herself on her housework, and no one else would do. Besides, in a time of severe food shortages a nanny would burden our family. Most female domestic workers came from rural areas and were not entitled to an official food ration, so their employers had to provide for them.

At school holidays or 'big weekends', my siblings and I always brought our own food coupons home, otherwise the food would not go round. With her poor arithmetic, it was a real headache for my grandmother to count the big pile of coupons for everything from rice to meat, cooking oil, and even for different fresh vegetables. In the end, she would give up and ask us to sort out the problem. In order to treat us all equally, she began to ration food at each meal, just as she had when raising her family in the past. In China, the Lunar New Year is traditionally the occasion for a sumptuous family feast. In the early 1960s, even on New Year's Eve my family dined on coarse maize flour and a small portion of vegetables pickled in brine. In order to prepare dumplings for one meal, a traditional New Year's delicacy, the whole family had to save wheat flour and meat for weeks.

During the famine, even the Ba-yi School, with all its privileges, had to lower its standard of living. Though no one suffered starvation or malnutrition, the previously customary wheat flour, rice, meat, fish and eggs disappeared from our tables. For a long time, one of our few occasional luxuries was the meat of Mongolian gazelles. The Beijing Military Region sent hunting expeditions to the Mongolian highlands to provide meat for themselves, senior officers and pupils in my school. It was a disaster for these innocent creatures to be slaughtered in their hundreds of thousands by military motorcades invading the vast prairie where they had lived and bred for centuries. Since then, the population has declined enormously, and the Mongolian gazelle has disappeared from many areas of China where they once used to thrive.

I never enjoyed their meat, and nor did many other pupils. Its texture was tough, the taste was strange, and even the thought of its aftertaste makes me feel sick to this day. 'Sinful!' said my grandmother when I grumbled. 'You should feel lucky to have meat these days.' My father gave cuts of gazelle meat to some of the assistants in the China Bookstore, as well as food coupons spared from his personal supply. Afterwards, he was told how precious his gifts had been for these starving families.

Pupils at the Ba-yi School unused to coarse food and small portions started to wonder what had happened, and why. Due to their families' political positions, many had little fear of complaining, but ordinary people risked reprisals if they traced the food crisis to errors in Party policy, such as the Great Leap Forward. When the famine started, the official line was to blame it on exceptionally severe natural disasters such as drought or flooding. Later, it was also attributed to Premier Nikita Khrushchev of the Soviet Union, who withdrew Soviet experts and assistance from China in 1960 in a move that marked the end of the 'honeymoon' period between the two socialist powers. We were told that despite our current difficulties the Soviet Union also demanded repayment from China, and that much of our grain, meat and eggs went there.

My grandmother was not convinced by the official propaganda: 'There was no natural disaster in many areas of the Shandong Peninsula, but people are still starving,' she said. When Feng-xin got into trouble for the remark he made at school, her response was: 'Why does the Communist Party stop people from telling the truth?'

The rural situation was no secret to my parents. When the Great Leap Forward was launched, agriculture became the first target for transformation, and one of the key ideas promoted was to apply Mao's famous 'people's war' strategy to farming. The order went out to 'make a five-year plan and use an ocean of labour forces to deep-plough land'. Mao's enormous personal prestige compelled leading officials and provincial governors to bow to whatever he said, so his order was propagated as a top priority all over the country at each administrative level. Marshalled by local cadres, millions of peasants gathered in the fields and dug deep around the clock. There was no scientific supervision, and no standard set to guide the work, apart from the maxim that the deeper the land was dug, the higher the tide of socialist rural construction. No one must raise a different voice. In such a climate, land could be dug four metres deep. In principle, Mao's idea might have made sense, seeing that fairly deep ploughing has been used to good effect, but in this case the technique did great damage, which many peasants blamed on their local cadres.

In autumn 1958, my father accompanied a group of senior military advisers from the Soviet Union on a visit to Xushui, a county in Hebei province not far away from Beijing. A piece of high-yield land there was thick with wheat so densely planted that they supported a school-aged boy standing on top. Around the plot, several electric fans blew air to prevent the plants from rotting. It was estimated that the yield from the plot would be 15 tons per mu (1 mu = $\frac{1}{15}$ hectares), over thirty times higher than from the most fertile land in a good year in the county. Such miracles had been repeatedly reported by the Chinese media, and shown to hundreds of thousands of visitors all over the country. Xushui's miracle exhilarated Mao, and he started considering what else peasants could do, since they were now producing more food than they could possibly eat. On his tour to Xushui, shortly after my father's visit, he suggested that peasants could cut their working hours by half, now that there was no need to work full-time, and spend the other half of their working hours acquiring new knowledge or enjoying entertainments.

When my father arrived with his guests, the land was encircled by red flags, as well as by loudspeakers that broadcast stirring music. The Russian Generals looked on in silence, but their strong doubts were clear in their faces. Though the local cadres talked on and on, to describe their experiences of creating miracles, the visitors left without a word. On their way back to Beijing, the chief of the Russian delegation said to my father privately: 'What happened in Xushui is dangerous. During Stalin's campaign of collectivization, the same things happened in our country, and severe starvation resulted.' My father was not convinced either, but Party discipline forbade him to criticize official policies in front of foreign visitors. A few months later, Xushui's high-yield miracle was exposed as a fabrication. On the orders of the local governor, just before harvest time peasants had transplanted crops from several plots of land to a single plot. Most of the crops did not survive to harvest because of the late transplantation and excessive density, but no one, not even the decision-makers, was held responsible.

Despite the fabrication, nationwide publicity paid tribute to Xushui for its rapid progress towards the Communist society. In August 1958, it was announced that all peasants in the county now belonged to the People's Commune, a model of collective organization spawned by the Great Leap Forward. According to a fantastic plan drafted by the Party authority in Xushui, the county would start its transition from socialism to Communism within a year, and would enter the Communist society by 1963. Any opponent to the plan, whether a local cadre or a peasant, would be branded as a counter-revolutionary and suffer public humiliation in mass rallies. As a transitional step to Communism, the salaries of Communist cadres were abolished, along with the income earned by peasants. Instead, everyone in the county, from birth to death, would receive all the necessities of life from the People's Commune, dispensed on the principle of equality. In villages, massive canteens produced free meals for all families, while cooking at home became outlawed.

'The People's Commune is great,' Mao rejoiced. He considered it as an embryonic form of Communism. Through the communes, peasants were expected to be militarized in organization and collectivized in daily life. Eventually the family, the basic unit of society, would be abolished in rural China. The entire countryside would be like a massive military camp, where everyone spoke in the same tone and acted in the same way. An ecstatic report in the *People's Daily* declared: 'In the near future, the People's Commune of Xushui will bring its members to the most wonderful paradise in human history, to the days of "from each according to his ability, to each according to his needs".'

Driven by Mao, what became known as a 'storm of communization' swept across rural China. It was said that in a township in south China, a leader of the Party committee proclaimed in a mass rally that next month the socialist system in the area would end and Communism would begin. Chaos came after the rally. Peasants too impatient to wait for the birth of Communism started to ransack the local shops, and

then to grab neighbours' possessions. With no more private ownership – which was what the Communist system meant to them – they
thought that everything should be communized, including food, clothes,
houses and money.

During the 'storm of communization', peasants put much less energy
into working for the collective economy than for themselves, because the
rewards were the same no matter how much or how little they worked,
and no one bothered to take care of the collective property. The most
painful experience was eating at the mass canteens, which were supposed to liberate women from daily cooking and hence to increase their
productivity and improve the quality of life. The outcome was just the
reverse. With no electricity or modern domestic appliances in most
parts of China, preparing food was very labour-intensive in rural areas,
and ranged from milling grain to carrying water, collecting fuel, cutting
firewood and chopping vegetables. Therefore, as much as half of a village's labour power could be tied up in running the canteen. Misled by
the propaganda, peasants assumed that a life of abundance had begun,
and they could eat their fill. Every day, the canteens of Xushui served
four main dishes and a bowl of soup for lunch as well as for supper – a
sumptuous meal, beyond the reach even of most landlord families before
the revolution. It did not take long before all of a village's food reserve
was consumed.

One day, Second Uncle arrived unexpectedly to visit my grandmother.
'Please use this for anything you fancy, don't hang on to it,' he said, and
passed her 500 yuan, which was a lot of money in those days. During
the 'storm of communization', a spate of rumours spread. Urban communes were soon to be established. Private ownership would be
abolished and individual families would not exist. All town-dwellers
would eat in mass canteens and sleep in public dormitories. No one
could guess the near future, not even senior Communist officials like my
parents and Second Uncle. Caught by the panic, he decided to let his
mother spend part of his savings before they disappeared. 'Are you

mad?' My grandmother dismissed her son's concern. 'You're a Communist high official, not a landlord. Why should your money be confiscated?' She refused to spend all the money and banked it instead.

Soon after Second Uncle's visit, the local authority opened a children's day nursery next door to our house, which was a trial for launching the People's Commune in Beijing. All the staff were untrained housewives, and the nursery was based on their own pre-school-age children. Posters on the walls and windows of each room displayed slogans such as 'Women can hold half of the sky' and 'The People's Commune is great', quoted from Mao. Right from the start, my grandmother became a regular visitor, as she knew some of the staff, and enjoyed being helpful. Soon she discovered that children whose mothers were on duty there were often better fed than the others, and received more attention. This preferential treatment led to quarrels, and within months the nursery had closed down.

A few months after Xushui's senseless plan was adopted, the county ran out of money, and its pledges to the people came to nothing. By November 1958, Mao had removed the spotlight from Xushui. But by then it was too late. During the 'storm of communization', the peasants had lost nearly everything, even their cooking utensils and food reserves. Rural areas were taxed on a percentage of their output, so Xushui's false claims of high yields incurred high taxes, and many places lost so much of their true output that they could not feed their own inhabitants. Starting in 1959, more and more peasants began to go hungry in China. When the famine ended three years later, no one knew how many deaths it had caused. One estimate put the number of deaths in rural China at 23 million.

Shortly before the famine, my mother started her job at Beijing Forestry University. One day, she was given an urgent assignment: to obtain a large sheet of steel plate for use in constructing the university's furnace. Obviously, the assignment was not her responsibility but she accepted it. It was at the height of the Great Leap Forward, when Chairman

Mao had shifted his focus from agriculture to industry, and made steel his top priority.

The target was for China to double its previous year's output of steel in 1958. Mao's confidence had been boosted by the progress of the Great Leap Forward in rural areas, but to reinforce his scheme he imposed an iron discipline on the officials responsible for steel production. If a factory failed to meet its quota, its managers, and even the local governors or Party leaders, would be demoted, dismissed, or even expelled from the Party. Again, Mao applied his 'people's war' strategy by mobilising the whole nation to realize his ambition.

In autumn 1958, many rural areas faced promising harvests, but a shortage of able-bodied labourers. The entire country was one vast steel-workshop strewn with primitive furnaces. People were forced to contribute their household possessions made of iron or steel – pots, pans, knives, even locks torn from doors. When the furnaces ran out of coal, trees and even furniture became fuel. Peasants were conscripted from the fields to work on backyard furnaces. They slaved to the point of exhaustion to bring about the economic miracles promised by Mao. But what came out of the furnaces was useless, and the scheme to boost steel production had catastrophic consequences, especially for China's peasants. With too few labourers working the fields, many crops were left to rot in the ground, which was another major factor in the famine that broke out the following year.

My mother was never convinced that building makeshift furnaces was the answer to increasing steel production, but the Party's decision was final, and she felt sorry for the official saddled with the task in her university. Once the scheme had started, all of the fifty or so higher educational institutions in Beijing had to make weekly reports to the Municipal Party Committee about their steel production, which was carried out by students and staff using furnaces they built themselves. Those who lagged behind the others, or fell short of their quotas, would face charges.

For help with her task, my mother went to Qinghua University, which she knew had some large steel plates in store. She and the vice-chancellor had joined the revolution together in 1938, and he arranged for her to borrow a large sheet of steel plate. She signed a receipt for the loan, but both of them knew that it was just a scrap of paper. The Party had called out for steel. Since the steel plate my mother borrowed would be used to build a furnace, how could the lender ask for it back?

In contrast to the frenzy of the Great Leap Forward, in my mother's university the atmosphere seemed cheerless. The campus was almost deserted, and only one furnace was built. This gloom did not express disaffection – no one would dare – but a major crisis faced the university. With orders to leave Beijing for rural areas, most of the students and teaching staff had been posted to the remote countryside.

In July 1958, during the summer holiday, the university had an unexpected visit from Kang Sheng, Deputy Director of the Cultural and Educational Committee of the Party's Central Committee. Most of the senior staff, including my mother, were away. Sitting in the university boardroom, he listened with a frown to the extremely deferential account of their work given by the university Chancellor and his colleagues, till suddenly his voice rose in anger: 'What? A first degree course lasts for four years? What a waste to let students take so long, just learning to dig holes to plant trees!' Further details only enraged him further: 'Forty-five minutes for a class is too long! There's no need to let students learn basic theory in their field.'

Kang Sheng's remarks came as no surprise. Since the start of the Great Leap Forward, he had scoured the country inspecting universities, colleges and schools. Wherever he went, he behaved with the same intolerant arrogance, determined to attack the established educational system. It was high time to start the Great Leap Forward in education, he insisted, and that meant reducing the length of courses. He liked to claim that a three-year college course could be completed in a year, or possibly even ten days. Few dared to argue with him.

In the boardroom of my mother's university, the atmosphere was tense after Kang Sheng's tirade. Then at the end of his visit there was a further setback when the sight of a beautiful man-made lake inside the campus caused him to fly into a rage with the Chancellor and his colleagues. 'Ridiculous! Instead of locating your university in the mountains, you stay in the city and build artificial lakes and hills.'

In August 1958, after his inspection of my mother's university, Kang Sheng attended a plenary conference of the Politburo convened by Mao Zedong in Beidaihe. Under the Communist regime, the Politburo is the inner core of the Party leadership, its principal policy-making body. This conference took a number of major decisions. It officially introduced the People's Commune in rural areas, and adopted the ambitious goal of overtaking Britain in steel production within two or three years – key moves in the Great Leap Forward. A document issued at the conference called for educational institutions dealing with agriculture and forestry to move to rural areas participating in the Great Leap Forward. Courses must be shortened, and their students and staff re-educated by peasants in the countryside. These decisions were strongly influenced by Kang Sheng, the major policy-maker on education, and a member of the Politburo.

Kang Sheng's behaviour grieved and antagonized the staff of my mother's university. It was hard to believe that a man so conspicuously ill-informed could be making policy for the Party and for the nation. Forestry was a scientific subject that needed proper conditions of study, yet in rural China there was no access to transport, communications and library services, and in many areas not even to bare necessities such as electricity and tap water. How could a university train students there, conduct research, or keep contact with other institutions? Not only must academic standards fall, but everyday work would be crippled. What imagined benefit would compensate for the enormous cost involved, and the total dislocation of the lives of students, staff and their families?

But Kang Sheng's ideas were now law, and had to be dealt with. A solution came from the university Chancellor, an 'intellectual cadre' who had joined the Communist Party in the 1930s while working in Nationalist territory as a professor with attainments in forestry. During the Great Leap Forward, he was concurrently Vice-Minister of Forestry in the central government. 'Let's defer the relocation for the moment,' he advised, 'and send students and staff to the countryside first.' With the strong support of the university Party leader, his proposal was accepted, and the university saved from losing its campus in Beijing.

After the summer vacation of 1958, most students and teaching staff were dispatched to rural districts scattered over several provinces, where their major task was labouring. Due to the remote location and lack of communication, they were cut off from outside, and teaching stopped. Their only source of regular information was the university bulletin that my mother edited in Beijing. Early next year the university declared its failure to find a new location outside Beijing, and recalled all its students and staff. Gradually, normal teaching resumed. Soon after that, both the Chancellor and the secretary of the university Party committee were dismissed, mainly for having disobeyed Kang Sheng.

During my childhood, a family mystery obscured the plight both of my mother's father and of her eldest sister, Auspicious Cloud. I knew very little about them, except that they were still alive. What they looked like, I had no chance to learn. Auspicious Cloud never paid us a visit before her death in the early 1960s, and I was too young to remember anything when my maternal grandfather came in the early fifties. Even today, I have never seen a photograph of either.

After the salary system was introduced for Communist officials in the early 1950s, my maternal grandfather asked Ning if he could live with her family permanently. Since his visit to Beijing, his rapidly failing health had made it harder for him to cope with the harsh life in his village. By then Ning had moved to Lanzhou, the provincial capital of Gansu, on the ancient Silk Road, and was heading the construction section of the Lanzhou Railway Bureau. Ning had no parents-in-law living with her, and with her good salary and my mother's regular support there were no financial snags, so my maternal grandfather took up permanent residence with Ning's family, and left his last wife, my maternal grandmother's former maid, to remain with her children in their village.

Later, Auspicious Cloud also joined Ning's family, together with her only son. My mother supported him too, and from the late 1950s she also financed both his education and that of her half-brother, Aunt Wang's son, whom my maternal grandmother cared for after his own mother ran away during the Sino-Japanese War. With her financial support, the two young men were able to graduate from university.

As the wife of a wealthy farmer, Auspicious Cloud had lost all her family possessions during the land reforms in 1950, apart from her jewellery, which she managed to bury underneath the earthen floor of her outdoor lavatory. Ever since moving to Lanzhou, she had longed to regain her hidden treasures especially since she had no income herself, and in 1958 she thought that her chance had come. With the peasants kept busy producing steel and absorbed in the Great Leap Forward, she hoped for more freedom of movement when she returned to her village, and sure enough, her quiet return attracted no attention. Around midnight, she crept back to the spot. She found the jewellery, but the noise of her digging alerted some people nearby, and she was discovered. Even so, she managed to give them the slip, and set off for Lanzhou, nearly a thousand kilometres away. There her luck ran out. The local authority traced her to Lanzhou, brought her back to her village, and confiscated her treasures. Afterwards, she was placed under the surveillance of local peasants for a long time.

Under the new regime, all Chinese were classified as rural or as urban residents. Peasants were expected to live on their own produce, only town-dwellers had access to the food-rationing system, and few were allowed to change from rural to urban. Although he lived with Ning's family for several years, my maternal grandfather was unable to get his village resident's card transferred to the city of Lanzhou, which suffered much worse than Beijing when the famine came. The effect on his health was destructive. Trapped in the rural class, he could add nothing to the limited ration granted to Ning and her young children, and with everybody starving, there was little to spare. As a big man with a large appetite, he could not bear the constant hunger, and often went scavenging for left-over vegetable leaves and roots in rubbish bins, and boiled them to eat. Malnutrition soon caused serious oedema, in those days treatable only with soy-bean flour, which therefore became a real luxury, much in demand all over China, and unobtainable in Lanzhou. Eventually, my mother found some in Beijing, prescribed by doctors in her university clinic, but by now the damage had been done. After the famine, he became terribly forgetful and weak, and could not even reach the corner shop on his own.

When the famine started, my parents helped Ning to move her two children from Lanzhou to Beijing. The boy, South of Shanxi, joined our school, while the girl, Glory, went to Shi-yi, another privileged institution. In those days of starvation, it was particularly hard to find a vacancy in such privileged havens. Many provincial governors, and generals based outside Beijing, queued to send their children to a school that guaranteed good rations to its pupils. 'This boy is the only son of the Commander of the Linfen Brigade who sacrificed his life for our Party during the war,' my father informed our headmaster. 'If the school is full, I'm willing to vacate one of my own children's places for him, as his welfare matters more than theirs.' The headmaster was moved by what he said, and accepted South of Shanxi unconditionally.

Having found school places for Ning's children, my father also helped them to secure financial grants from the army's General Political Department, which agreed to support them both until their educations were completed. Only the children of parents who had died during the wars as senior officers were entitled to these terms.

One Sunday morning during a 'big weekend' in winter 1959, a letter arrived at our house from Second Uncle in Shenyang. 'Please read it for me,' my delighted grandmother asked Little Auntie, who was visiting her that weekend. The letter was addressed to my father, but it was quite usual for his siblings to do that with letters intended both for him and for their mother. To hear them read out was a treat, because she did not often see most of her children, who lived far away from Beijing, and whose work kept them too busy to visit their mother except on official missions such as attending government conferences.

'Eldest brother, I have to tell you some unfortunate news about what has happened to me recently, but please don't let our mother know anything about it . . .' Little Auntie's reading stopped and she turned pale. 'What's happened to your second brother?' Grandmother's anxious voice caught my attention as I was playing with Aijun. The room fell deadly quiet for a moment, then Little Auntie dashed to see my parents in their study with her face bathed in tears. Grandmother was left behind on tenterhooks, and finally she decided to break the suspense. I followed her to the study, and was shocked by the sight of my father's face streaming with tears. No one would answer my grandmother's inquiries, Little Auntie was choked with sobs, and my parents were silent. 'What happened to Second Uncle?' I went back to school that night with the mystery unsolved.

In my mind, Second Uncle was a brilliant writer driven by revolutionary passions. In 1950, his play *Dyke*, a story about peasants fighting a flood in Liaoning province, caused a sensation in Manchuria. Soon it was showing in theatres all over China, and Premier Zhou Enlai praised it when he met Second Uncle after a performance. In 1956, another play, *Firedamp*, based on the lives of two generations of miners, received an award for the best new play at the First National Drama Festival in

Beijing. At the suggestion of Cao Yu, the founder of modern Chinese drama, *Firedamp* was further revised and improved with a new title, *Two Weddings*, which brought national acclaim to Second Uncle. After its première by the Beijing People's Art Theatre, *Two Weddings* was listed on top of theatrical programmes everywhere in the country. Later it became a successful film, *The Changed World*. By his mid-thirties, Second Uncle was one of the rising stars of Chinese drama, known to the public by his pen-name, 'Kefu'.

As well as plays, Second Uncle wrote many widely published essays, some criticizing bureaucratic practices, but most conveying his approach to dramatic theory or performance. During the same period, he also held concurrent posts as vice-chairman of the associations of writers and dramatists in his province. In 1958 he founded and edited a periodical, *Young Writers*, and gained support from Shen Yanbing, who under his pen-name, Mao Dun, was a distinguished non-Communist writer and China's Minister of Culture. In less than two years, its circulation reached a quarter of a million. Under Second Uncle's guidance, a flock of unknown young authors developed their writing careers. When some became famous decades later, they made a point of thanking Second Uncle for his support in the dedications of their novels and plays.

One of Second Uncle's most glorious experiences was his visit to the German Democratic Republic (East Germany) in summer 1959, as a member of a Chinese writers' delegation. For the vast majority of Chinese in those days, an overseas trip was like a journey to another planet. 'My Second Uncle is going abroad!' I told my classmates proudly, knowing how rare this was in any family. During his short visit, Second Uncle felt inspired to write, and produced numerous articles and poems praising the landscape and expressing his admiration for the industrious German people.

Shortly after Second Uncle's return from Germany, a new political campaign was launched in China, aimed at 'rightist opportunists' and originating from another plenary session of the enlarged Politburo

convened by Mao in July 1959 in Lushan. One participant there was
Marshal Peng Dehuai, the Defence Minister and Vice-Premier, and a veteran of the Long March. He was worried by some effects of the Great
Leap Forward, and wanted to talk to Mao about correcting mistakes.
Unfortunately, Mao was resting when Marshal Peng called, so instead he
delivered a private letter. It was thoughtful and restrained, and it did not
blame any one person for the country's problems, or deny the gains
achieved by the Great Leap Forward, but it enraged Chairman Mao, who
brooked no voice that differed from his own. Mao was quick to retaliate.
He denounced Marshal Peng and accused him of planning to 'sabotage
the proletariat'. During the next few weeks, the conference was turned into
a forum for denouncing 'rightist opportunists', the label attached to
Marshal Peng and a handful of open supporters. Though many shared the
Marshal's views in private, few people dared to offend Mao. As a result,
Marshal Peng was dismissed from his post and placed under house-arrest.

In autumn 1959, when senior officials in his province were summoned to a conference called to mobilize an 'anti-rightist opportunists'
campaign, Second Uncle asked for leave of absence owing to high
demand for his work. Although he had been a professional writer for
several years, he still rated as a high official – paid at Grade 11 on the
salary scale – due mainly to his earlier revolutionary record and current
status in the cultural field. He never dreamed that his absence from the
conference would result in a personal disaster.

In the association of writers where Second Uncle worked, the campaign was led by Zhang. He was no stranger to our family. In 1938 his
wife was one of the five girls who joined the revolution with my mother.
During the Rectification Campaign of the 1940s, Zhang was a prisoner
in the same camp as my parents. In the 1950s he became director of the
Literature and Art Division in the Propaganda Department of the
provincial Party headquarters. But Zhang had trouble publishing his
work, which was criticized as clumsy by editors including Second Uncle.
He therefore nursed a grudge, and when Second Uncle failed to attend

the conference, he diagnosed reluctance to denounce Peng Dehuai, and reported him to the provincial Party committee.

What hurt Second Uncle most was the betrayal of his close friend Liang, a writer in his association whom he had got to know in Yan'an during the Sino-Japanese War, and who now came forward to expose and denounce his counter-revolutionary views. The details he provided came mainly from their private conversations, wildly exaggerated into anti-Party evidence. But Second Uncle's troubles did not stop there: his opponents were soon joined by Steel, one of the young writers whose work he had supervised, but found fault with his lack of dedication. To sever their connection, and dispel the threat of guilt by association, Steel accused Second Uncle of forming an anti-Party alliance among young writers and claimed to be one of its victims.

In Second Uncle, the campaign in his province had unearthed a major target. Early in 1960, shortly after the mobilization conference, another conference aimed at the province's 'rightist opportunists' was held in Shenyang. It was attended by hundreds of leading officials in the field of the arts, and lasted for nearly two months. (Under the Communist regime, it was common for conferences called to tackle intra-Party conflicts to be lengthy operations.) Second Uncle had to attend daily meetings or rallies to confess his anti-Party activities or listen to speeches denouncing him. In the conference hall, big-character posters censured his counter-revolutionary 'crimes'. One key piece of evidence was his purchase of a chicken from peasants during the famine – an action seen as opposing the Great Leap Forward. After the conference, a large reprint of his popular essays, termed 'poisonous weeds' for propagating anti-Party views in the 'garden of socialist art and literature', was distributed to officials all over the province for denunciation. His award-winning play, *Two Weddings*, was also condemned for ignoring the class struggle in Chinese society.

During the Shenyang Conference, most participants were sympathetic to Second Uncle, but no voice spoke up for him. While the campaign was raging, its course was unpredictable; defending an 'anti-Party element' was a risk that no one dared to take. Forbidden to speak for himself, he fell back on silence. When his other young writers were accused of belonging to his so-called anti-Party alliance, he refused to provide evidence against them, which redoubled the pressure on himself. It was a time of agony, undeserved and inescapable. He told my father later that he spent many sleepless nights roaming Shenyang city, close to madness.

Once branded as an 'anti-Party element', Second Uncle was dismissed from his posts. His magazine, *Young Writers*, ceased publication, he was demoted from Grade 11 to 13 on the salary scale, and a few months later he was consigned to a factory in Dalian, in Manchuria, to work as a manual labourer. But Second Uncle was not the only victim of the drive against 'rightist opportunists': more than three million people, most of them Party members or officials, suffered similar fates. In winter 1960, he and his family were evicted from their apartment in the magnificent Marshal Mansion in Shenyang, the former residence of China's last warlord president, Marshal Zhang Zuoling. In Dalian, a single room had to accommodate himself, his wife and their four teenage sons. Meanwhile his enemy, Zhang, was promoted to deputy chief of propaganda in the province.

For a long time, my parents kept us in the dark about Second Uncle's plight. Like anyone else with painful experiences of intra-Party conflict, they had always been guarded with their comments, especially on political issues. After the problems caused by Feng-xin's careless comment at school, they became even more discreet in front of the family, in case their words might reach the wrong ears. One day early in 1962 I showed my father a novel I had just finished reading. He pointed to the author's name and said: 'That is the man who persecuted your Second Uncle.' It was the first clue I had to the mystery of Second Uncle's plight, and the role of a writer named Liang.

Because they worked in different organizations, my parents had no political leverage to exert on Second Uncle's case. It deeply frustrated my father that he could not save his innocent brother, but he wrote to him at least once a week, trying to boost his morale and citing his own experiences during the Rectification Campaign in the 1940s to urge him not to give up hope. He quoted Chairman Mao's saying that 'we must have faith in the masses and we must have faith in the Party' to persuade Second Uncle that no matter what happened to him, in the end the Party would treat him with justice.

In March 1962, my parents took me to Beijing railway station on a weekend to meet Second Uncle, who was on his way back to Dalian after a visit to Guangzhou. Since his political disgrace more than two years before, it was the first time he had visited our family. As soon as the train stopped, out jumped Second Uncle, dressed in a smart Mao-style suit in silvery grey, and smiling all over his face. That weekend, he spent most of his time talking to my parents in their study, his cheerful voice and laugh clearly audible outside. 'What's happened to Second Uncle now?' I wondered.

The event that Second Uncle had just attended is known in Chinese history as the Guangzhou Conference, organized by the Ministry of Culture and the National Association of Dramatists. On 2 March 1962, addressing the conference on behalf of the Party Central Committee, Premier Zhou Enlai stated that intellectuals were part of the revolutionary alliance in China. A few days later, this statement was enlarged on by Marshal Chen Yi, China's vice-premier and foreign minister. In his speech to the conference, Marshal Chen rejected the accusation of 'bourgeois intellectuals' which had been levelled at millions of writers, scientific workers, doctors and anyone else with a professional or academic background. They had suffered from discrimination as virtual aliens to the regime. Now the slur must give way to the respected title of 'working people's intellectuals'. When the Marshal took off his hat in salutation to his audience, his frank speech was interrupted by prolonged applause and thunderous cheers.

Like everyone else at the conference, Second Uncle was moved to tears when he heard the new title of 'working people's intellectuals'. 'What an ironic fate for Second Uncle!' was my thought when I first heard his story many years later. From the age of fifteen, he had devoted his life to his beloved Party and people. After a quarter of a century, all he received was his outcast status in the People's Republic he fought to create by sacrificing everything he had, including his youth, his career and his responsibilities to his own parents.

The speeches by Premier Zhou and Marshal Chen rekindled Second Uncle's hopes. In the previous year, Mao had admitted that the purges of 'rightist opportunists' had gone too far. In Liaoning, Second Uncle's plight had won the sympathy of many officials. After a document issued by the Party Central Committee called for rehabilitation in China, his own was proposed, and argued at length. A political conference convened by the provincial Party's propaganda headquarters and the Department of Culture debated strenuously whether his essays were 'poisonous weeds', but strong objections from powerful opponents such as Zhang and Liang stifled the initial attempt to rescue him.

After the Guangzhou Conference, Deng Xiaoping, the Party's general secretary, took steps to speed up the rate of rehabilitation. The Secretariat headed by Deng was responsible for the day-to-day work of the Central Committee and Politburo. Now he had the further task of reviewing cases in the 'rightist opportunists' campaign. Within months, millions of people were exonerated, which was good news for Second Uncle and his supporters. In autumn 1962, Second Uncle's case was brought to Zhou Yang, the deputy chief of propaganda, in charge of cultural affairs in China. Zhou was the former vice-chancellor of Lu Xun Art College in Yan'an, where Second Uncle worked during the war. The two men spoke together in Dalian, during a private meeting arranged by An Po, the Party's chief of propaganda in the province. He too had worked for Lu Xun College, and recruited Second Uncle in 1941. 'I've read all your essays and couldn't find any anti-Party evidence,' Zhou Yang told Second Uncle. 'They are not poisonous weeds. I'd like to read more such elegant writing in future.' Zhou was a powerful figure, so Second Uncle's opponents could not risk blocking his rehabilitation a second time. Soon afterwards, the designation of 'anti-Party element' was withdrawn, and the decision to demote him rescinded.

At the end of a 'big weekend' in winter 1962, there was a boisterous mood in the boarding girls' division of the Ba-yi School. After a break at home, we were eager to exchange the latest off-campus gossip. But my friend An-an looked anxious. 'Promise you won't tell anyone.' We had found a quiet corner. 'I swear by Chairman Mao I'll keep your secret,' I promised my friend, using the pupils' most solemn form of pledge. 'This afternoon, Venerable Dong [Vice-President Dong Biwu] came to see my father at home, on behalf of the Party's Central Committee. I've just heard that my father has committed mistakes.' For high officials, committing mistakes implied serious political troubles. Now I understood why the name of An-an's father, Vice-Premier Xi Zhongxun, had dropped out of the news for a while. In the past, I had shared my friend's pride when her father's name was mentioned on high-profile national occasions.

The trouble stemmed from Xi Zhongxun's involvement in a novel called *Liu Zhidan*, tales of the 'Robin Hood' Communist leader who died in 1936 while leading his Red Army troops against the Nationalists. In Communist history, it was regarded as a great step in China's revolution that Liu Zhidan, founder of the Shaan-Gan Soviet base, provided a new home for Mao Zedong and his Red Army after the Long March. Since An-an's father was Liu Zhidan's former colleague, and a leader of the Shaan-Gan base, the author, Liu's sister-in-law, asked for his comments. In summer 1962, newspapers and magazines started to serialize the novel. Quite unexpectedly, it became a focus of intra-Party conflict.

During August to September 1962, Mao Zedong convened a pre-conference of the Tenth Plenum of the Party's Eighth Central Committee, where the novel was attacked for 'using the name of Liu

Zhidan to praise Gao Gang'. Vice-chairman of the Communist government in the early 1950s, Gao Gang was charged with forming an anti-Party alliance, and committed suicide in 1954 after being purged. The novel was branded as an attempt to rehabilitate Gao Gang, included as another leader of the Shaan-Gan Soviet base and a colleague of Liu Zhidan. An-an's father was accused of backing the so-called plot.

In his speech at the Tenth Plenum, Mao quoted a statement by Kang Sheng: 'To utilize novels to engage in anti-Party activities is a big invention.' The case against An-an's father headed the conference agenda, and when a special team was set up to investigate his counter-revolutionary activities, Kang Sheng took command. An-an's father's political disgrace lasted until 1980. While it went on, he suffered exile, house arrest and many years in prison. Kang Sheng's 'investigation' hounded hundreds of Communist officials, including relations of Liu Zhidan, for their involvement in the 'Xi Zhongxun anti-Party plot'. Many lost their lives as a result.

At the Tenth Plenum, another major victim was Marshal Peng Dehuai, China's former defence minister, who had been in political disgrace since 1959. When cases in the 'rightist opportunists' campaign were reviewed in 1962, the Marshal's repeated appeals for his own rehabilitation were rejected by order of Mao. Instead, he faced more accusations, such as conspiring to usurp the Party's leadership, and colluding with foreign countries to overthrow the Communist regime. The Marshal was denounced again, and placed under further investigation.

After the summer holiday in 1963, a newcomer joined our class. Though I had never met her before, her name, Elifila, was familiar. As the youngest child of a famous family, a number of pupils had mentioned her, and An-an knew her through family connections. Elifila's father, Baorhan, was Vice-President of the Chinese People's Political Consultative Conference (CPPCC), established just before the birth of the People's Republic to provide leading intellectuals and scientists, artists and actors, as well as members of the non-Communist 'democratic parties', with a platform and an element of power. Under the Communist system, the CPPCC ranks level with the National People's Congress (NPC), China's Parliament, and the leaders of both organizations have equal status.

Unlike the great majority of high officials, Baorhan was Uygur, a Muslim ethnic group inhabiting the Xinjiang Uygur Autonomous Region of northwest China along the ancient Silk Road, which accounts for one-sixth of China's total territory. His wife too was not Han, as most Chinese are, but Tartar, a tiny Muslim group in Xinjiang with a total population of a few thousand. For Han Chinese, there was something exotic and beautiful in Elifila, whose deep eye sockets and straighter nose reflected the ancient Arab heritage of her region. In those days, foreigners were rarely seen in China. Very often, she was surrounded and followed by curious crowds when she went walking in Beijing.

I was hugely impressed by the education that Elifila had received. In the 1950s, foreign languages were not part of the primary school's curriculum, but as well as fluent Uygur and Chinese she had a good grasp of Russian, which she had learned at a special school in Beijing for the children of Russian advisers during the Sino-Soviet 'honeymoon' period. The private piano lessons that she had started from an early age were unusual among Chinese children. Especially among parents from worker-peasant cadre backgrounds, the instrument stood for a tainted Western bourgeois culture. In any case, few families could even afford to buy a piano in those days. In China, the Uygur are famous for their dancing and singing, and Elifila soon impressed the class with her performances. Before very long, we had become inseparable friends. In our spare time, I would keep her company when she practised the piano in the music room, and she enjoyed teaching me Uygur dancing. After the lights-out bell, pupils were often quick to fall asleep in the dark dormitories, but Elifila and I liked to visit each other's beds. Lying side by side, we whispered together till midnight. As she was two years older, in private she called me 'younger sister', which was a joy for me, because I have no kindred elder sister.

One night, Elifila lay beside me, humming a haunting tune. 'I'll tell you a secret,' she whispered. 'Not long ago, 60,000 people from Xinjiang fled to the Soviet Union over the border. They composed that song to tell about the sorrow they feel for leaving their homeland and losing my father as their leader.'

Through talk among the pupils, I knew that because he was the most influential political figure in his region, her father was nicknamed the 'King of Xinjiang'. Baorhan had joined the Bolsheviks in his youth, and involved himself in defending the autonomy of local ethnic groups under the Han Chinese-based central governments. After the Sino-Japanese War, the Nationalists appointed him to govern Xinjiang. In September 1949, after Chiang Kai-shek fled to Taiwan, Baorhan handed over Xinjiang to the Communists, and hence retained his post as governor. In the early 1960s, he moved to Beijing with his family, to take up his post as Vice-President of the CPPCC. Under the Communist regime, everything was run by the Party, so the CPPCC was regarded as a figurehead body, powerless in practice, and even the National People's Congress was seen as a rubber-stamp. It was said that Baorhan was moved mainly to weaken his influence among the ethnic groups in Xinjiang.

Historically, their ethnic make-up and common border created close links between Xinjiang and the central Asian part of the former Soviet Union. For various reasons, the relationship between Xinjiang's ethnic groups and the central governments in China has been complicated, sensitive and subtle. A Uygur-led separatist movement launched earlier this century aimed to make Xinjiang an independent nation named Eastern Turkistan. After the Sino-Soviet split in 1960, resentment of Beijing grew stronger among Xinjiang's ethnic groups. Baorhan's removal did not relieve the tension, and Elifila was right about the mass exodus that fled the region in spring 1962.

I could feel the tears Elifila shed that night, and although I had virtually no idea about the complicated ethnic issues in Xinjiang, she was my best friend and I wanted to share her sorrow. On my visits to her home, I was hugely impressed by her father's gentle, cultured manner. Besides his political achievements, Baorhan was also a well-known writer, and his play *The Roar of Flaming Mountain* had recently been applauded in Beijing. I adored him, and was not surprised that his people felt the same.

By 1963, the Sino-Soviet conflict was public knowledge in China. In politics classes, we were told that the Soviet Union was not a real socialist country any more. The Party created by Lenin had abandoned the basic principles of Marxism; its revisionist line had restored the capitalist class. For the Chinese people, the Soviet Union was no longer an 'Elder Brother', but a new foe camped on our north and northwest frontier. Southward, the country faced a threat from an old enemy, the Nationalist government in Taiwan. With US support, Chiang Kai-shek had never given up hope of returning to the mainland by force. Along the southwest frontier, armed clashes with India took place. Mao Zedong told the country that there was an 'international anti-Chinese cantata' intending to destroy the Communist regime in China, which was led by John F. Kennedy, Nikita Khrushchev and Jawaharlal Nehru. Marshal Tito of Yugoslavia was also to blame, because he was the first leader among the socialist countries who had turned his party to revisionism.

In recent years, leading politicians in the USA had forecast that a peaceful evolution from socialism to capitalism would take place in the Communist countries, and concern for the future caused Mao to take precautions in the present, following the failure of the Great Leap Forward and the subsequent famine. He felt that his policies were questioned, and his authority challenged, not only by Marshal Peng Dehuai but also by other senior figures with reform ideas. For example, widespread trials took place of a new economic system known as 'setting farm output quotas for each household' (bao-chan-dao-hu), which went some way towards restoring the rural economy because it linked people's income to their work, and stimulated local agricultural initiatives. Among the Party's leaders, there was growing support for introducing the new system to rural China alongside the current collective system. It was expressed in Deng Xiaoping's famous saying that 'it doesn't matter if a cat is black or white, as long as it catches mice'. Mao was furious about the proposed new system, since the People's Commune came from him. By 1962, the chief promoters of the reform had been axed from their posts, accused of taking the capitalist road, while their supporters such as Deng Xiaoping were criticized.

At the Tenth Plenum of the Party's Eighth Central Committee in 1962, Mao developed his famous theory about class struggle under socialism, determined to defend his own authority. The Plenum's Communiqué expressed his view that 'throughout the historical transition from capitalism to communism, struggles exist between the proletarian and capitalist classes, and between the socialist and capitalist roads.' According to this theory, the intra-Party conflicts were evidence of class struggle. In the purges that followed, many of those who disagreed with Mao were branded as agents of the capitalist class, and therefore enemies both of the Party and of the Chinese nation.

Part Two
1964-1977

The Four Seas are rising, clouds and waters raging,
The Five Continents are rocking, wind and thunder roaring.
Our force is irresistible,
Away with all pests!

Extract from 'Reply to Comrade Guo Moruo,
to the tune of Man Jiang Hong',
composed by Mao Zedong on
9 January 1963

Chapter 12

The Gale is Raging and the Storm
is about to Break:
On the Eve of the Cultural Revolution
(1964–April 1966)

In July 1964, not long before my thirteenth birthday, I finished my primary education at Ba-yi School. By then, the school had been handed over to the municipal educational authority in Beijing, by agreement between the military and the State education and finance ministries. It was said that the move would be good for both the school and the armed forces. Since there had not been a war on China's territory for a long time, senior officers could enjoy a stable family life and look after their own children, so there was no more need for the military to run its own educational facilities. In the years that followed the transfer, the school retained the status of a privileged boarding institution for the children of Communist high officials.

My decision to leave Ba-yi School for my secondary education was fairly unusual, since most of my classmates would remain for another three years until they completed junior middle school. As I grew up, I had gradually recognized that a different life existed outside the walls of the campus I had entered when I was three. During my final year, a number of seminars were organized to inform us about the non-privileged schools in the unknown world outside. Through them, I found how little I had learned about society, since most people I knew came from inside the circle of the political and military elites. Pupils of our age elsewhere could travel to school on their own or go shopping for their families, while we still lived under careful supervision and had all necessary services provided. I had no idea what privileges we had at Ba-yi School. Instead, I thought how lucky children were in ordinary families, who enjoyed such independence in their lives, and I wanted to know them.

Early in 1962, when we moved to outside the Gate of Virtue and Triumph, my father had been appointed Deputy Political Commissar of the armoured forces in the Beijing Military Region, a post equivalent to Deputy Army Commander. Only a few of the eight large military regions in China had armoured forces, and about half of these were located in the military region controlled by my father's headquarters. After the move, a minibus service provided by the armoured forces enabled my siblings and me to go home every weekend instead of every other weekend, together with the children of my father's colleagues. By the age of eleven, I had got into the habit of walking home from school on Saturday afternoons, and used to invite one or two neighbouring girls to join me. Those were my earliest independent expeditions, and I made the most of them, especially in spring and autumn, the best seasons in Beijing.

In my memory, the sky seemed vast and clear as we left the campus, and the sun shone unusually bright. From our school in northwest Beijing, we walked to our homes partly by way of the northern section of the Third Ring Road, nowadays enormously expanded, with massive traffic bridges arcing across, and high-rise buildings lining both its sides like cliffs along a narrow valley where traffic streams from dawn to midnight. But in the early 1960s, the new Third Ring Road was rather like a country road skirting the city, narrow, dusty and empty. To either side, fields growing vegetables and other crops filled the air with their sweet scent and the aroma of the earth. Sometimes, the clop of hoofs on the metalled road broke the silence, and then a dawdling horse-drawn cart appeared, carrying dung to the fields or fresh vegetables to the city. A peasant in an old straw hat sat at the front, and occasionally cracked his whip in the air. I was fascinated by the scenery, so different from the landscape of Ba-yi.

My decision to leave the school was supported by my parents. The call of their work made it convenient to board us out, but they had grown concerned about the effects on their children of having them grow up in such a privileged cocoon. Having heard criticisms made about the arrogance of children from high official families, it pleased them to see me look forward to studying with children from ordinary families.

In Ba-yi School, pupils were normally given places in junior middle school after completing their primary education, regardless of their academic record. My new plan put me under pressure: I must achieve a good result in the all-Beijing entrance examination, which included maths and Chinese. But my teachers were confident, and my fellow pupils saw me as an intelligent, hard-working girl with a gift for the liberal arts. In those days, pupils were not informed about their examination results, but at the end of the summer 1964 I received an enrolment letter from the Number Two Middle School attached to Beijing Normal University, a leading school that specialized in the liberal arts.

Like most institutions of secondary education in China, my new school had two sections: junior and senior. In 1963, a special trial class had been established in the senior middle school, which took pupils from the whole municipality who graduated from junior middle school with excellent results in liberal arts in the all-Beijing entrance examination. In these special classes, pupils completed their courses for senior middle school in two years instead of the prevailing three.

Unfortunately, the trial was interrupted when the Cultural Revolution was launched in 1966, so only pupils from the original class were able to complete their studies. Many of these went on to enter top universities such as the famous Beijing University, and some of the former pupils from the class became well-known writers in the 1980s.

My new school was located in the north of the city, within walking distance from my home. The campus faced Beijing Normal University, a prestigious teacher-training institution. When I arrived, the school seemed cramped compared with what I was used to. Standing by the front gate, I could see the back wall of the campus. The place felt tiny, like one small corner of my former school. Certainly, there were no exquisite pavilions or grand buildings, nor gardens with exotic flowers and rare trees. The classrooms were dark, and crammed with fairly shabby desks and chairs. Although I expected a difference, the contrast was startling. It was my first experience of an educational institution without privileged social status; I did not know that the state of my new school was well above the norm in Beijing.

Soon after the first term started, my disappointment dissolved in the flood of new impressions. Here, a large number of the teachers were graduates of Beijing Normal University. Compared with the staff at Ba-yi, many seemed quite naive about China's politics, but this was not surprising, seeing how little contact they had with the world I knew, the circle of the political and military elites. At the same time, their professional knowledge and gentle behaviour made their classes a pleasure. Regardless of their gender, many were respectfully addressed as 'Mr', especially those in senior positions, which sounded quite old-fashioned and was unheard-of in my former school. It reminded me of the traditional atmosphere described in books about China's educational institutions in the old days. Since the birth of the Communist republic in 1949, honorific titles like Sir and Madam, or Mr, Mrs and Miss, had been replaced by the unisex Comrade. At school and even in university, the term 'teacher' was adopted as the proper address for almost all members of staff, including those who did not teach, such as administrators. Years later, I attended an English training course in a university where my lecturer, Mrs Wood, was often addressed as 'Teacher Wood' by students.

In the new surroundings, I was also amazed by the initiative and enthusiasm that pupils invested in all sorts of activities outside class, most of them self-organized, though supported by the school authority. As one of the tallest girls in my year, I was enlisted in the basketball team, and started regular training, but sport did not attract me, and I quit after just a few sessions. Afterwards, I was chosen by a dance group preparing for the celebrations in Tian-an Men Square on the coming anniversary of the Communist republic. All of the others belonged to the senior middle school, so I was envied by many in my year. For my school work and outside activities, I was elected captain of the Young Pioneers, in charge of recreational and sports activities for my class. It was the second highest rank in the organization, and was signalled by a badge with two red stripes on a square white background, worn on the left sleeve of my jacket. My life was getting busy, but I loved it, because it made me feel grown up, and it was fulfilling to find my abilities respected.

Another reward in the new school was to be able to come home every day. Most of my siblings were still at Ba-yi. When they left home on Sunday afternoon, I said goodbye and thought how lucky I was not to live away from home any more. After supper, my father liked to take me strolling in the neighbourhood, which we enjoyed in different ways, me like a cheerful bird, prattling about the day's events, my father mostly quiet, except to answer my questions. Today, I understand that these evening strolls might have been a perfect relaxation for my father, while my endless chatter was like a pleasant therapy that diverted him out of his tiredness after a long day at work.

It took me a while to realize that the lifestyle I was used to was foreign to most of my classmates, because they came from non-official families, none of them entitled to the privileges we had. For example, most pupils brought packed lunches and ate in their classrooms. As soon as I opened my lunchbox, classmates flocked round and licked their lips. 'What a delicious smell! Like food from a restaurant.' This came as a surprise to me, as the food I brought was very ordinary by the standards of my family and the Ba-yi School. It was based on rice or steamed wheat-flour buns, and fried vegetables with a few scraps of meat. But for many pupils, lunch was just a small portion of vegetables pickled in brine, together with fist-sized conical lumps of steamed maize flour, called 'Wo-tou-er' in Beijing, a food so coarse and tasteless that I would never touch it except in the three famine years. After the famine, food rations had improved in Beijing as the economy revived. By 1964, citizens were getting enough to eat, but the allowance was still based on maize flour, classed as coarse grain, whereas the small quota of rice and wheat flour was called fine grain. Each household received just 1 kg of eggs per month, plus 0.5 kg of meat per head and 250 g of cooking oil. Rations of other items such as fish and sugar were small and sporadic. However, my father and his colleagues were kept supplied all year with extras mainly produced on farms run by the armoured forces. So my everyday diet was a luxury that most of my classmates could only enjoy on special occasions such as the Chinese New Year.

This contrast in lifestyles weighed on my mind. At home, I asked Uncle Zhong to prepare the same food for my lunch as my classmates had. 'Silly girl,' he laughed at first, and then shook his head. 'Please don't make me extra work!' As a chef, Uncle Zhong took great care of my family's diet, and especially my father's, since his job was to keep him in good health. If he accepted my request he would have to work to two different standards; when he refused, my only option was to board in the school canteen, which served equal shares for all, based on the ration. Shortages of space and catering staff meant that there was always a long queue of applicants, and the chance of a place was especially slim for a first-year pupil like me, but at my request my mother visited my teacher and explained my wish to share an equal lifestyle with the others. My teacher was first surprised and then moved by my determination. With her help, I was eventually granted full board in the canteen from my second term.

The school canteen was a large hall packed with square wooden tables, most of them missing their original paint. There were no chairs or benches, so we stood at the tables to eat, which was a new experience for me. Some weeks into the term, my anxious grandmother told me that I had lost weight, and blamed it on my change of diet. After that, she made sure that there was always some food kept for me in the kitchen when I returned home, but I resisted the temptation, for fear that my will to bear hardships would be weakened if I yielded. Every weekday morning I had to arrive at school before half-past seven for breakfast, and could not leave till six, after supper. As there were no direct bus services, the long Beijing winter bit hard. To block the bitter cold, on my walks to school and back I always wrapped up in a big woollen shawl, thick clothes and a heavy overcoat, and covered my nose and mouth with a white gauze mask. With all this protection, I still froze stiff on the half-hour's journey through the dark of early morning, made on an empty stomach. After supper, it was dark again when I faced the howling wind on my way home. But I never regretted my decision to eat at school, for it let me share a non-privileged life with my new classmates.

One day, a classmate called Jasmine invited me to her home. She was the second child of a large family with five siblings, all of them kept by her father, who worked for a construction company in Beijing. She told me proudly that on the salary scale for industrial workers her father was entitled to Grade 8, which was the highest level. His monthly salary, together with bonus, was close to 100 yuan.

Most of the street where Jasmine lived consisted of a big factory that turned out heating radiators. It was manned by convict labour, and enclosed behind high brick walls topped by barbed wire. Metal dust hung in the air. It clogged my hair and covered my clothes and shoes. On my way there, I saw prisoners crossing the street. With unkempt hair and dirty faces, they walked silently though a narrow lane formed by two lines of armed soldiers. Several long rows of sheds at the end of the street were the homes of nearly a hundred families, including Jasmine's.

Like most of their neighbours, Jasmine's family lived in a room of less than 20 square metres, without running water or central heating. A massive plank bed resting on long wooden benches occupied nearly half the space. Her four younger brothers — three in primary school and one toddler — shared it with their parents. By the door, a narrow plank bed belonged to Jasmine and her elder sister, a pupil in senior middle school. The few sticks of worn-out furniture included a chest of drawers, a small table with short legs, and several small wooden stools. In good weather, Jasmine's mother cooked on a small stove outside their room. Otherwise, she had to cook indoors, between the beds.

Lacking an indoor lavatory, the family used a chamber-pot at night. In the morning, they queued outside public toilet latrines located in every row of sheds, each of them visited by dozens of households. Here there were no flushing facilities. Long planks placed along the wall opposite the window were pierced by a row of rectangular narrow holes, and the user squatted down over the deep cesspit underneath. In the summer, flies and maggots swarmed. When the pit was full, the human wastes were dug out by labourers and loaded into large wooden barrels, to be carried on their backs or shoulders and decanted into a container on a dung-cart parked on the street. In Jasmine's home, there was no mistaking the mixed smell of excrement and urine drifting from a public lavatory several doors away.

In answer to my surprise, Jasmine told me that her family's living conditions were not uncommon among our fellow pupils. She did not complain, but I was really shocked by what I saw. For the first time in my life I realized the striking gap in living conditions between people in the small circle I came from and the majority. One day I asked my mother:

'Why do we need a chef and an orderly? Is it fair on them?' My mother's first response was: 'Who told you this?' When she heard it was my own idea, she said: 'You'll find out when you grow up.'

For my parents, what I felt was nothing new. The regime gave extensive privileges to high officials, especially in the military. The area outside the Gate of Virtue and Triumph where we moved in 1962 was the residential quarter for senior officers in the armoured forces, and it was common there for families to have the land around their houses converted into private plots, where their personal staffs grew crops such as peanuts, soy-beans, sweet potatoes and corn on their behalf. While the famine continued, my parents simply followed our neighbours' example with hardly a thought. This privilege caused strong criticism among the junior or mid-ranking officers who lived in another section of the compound, mostly in crowded conditions, and with no private plots to subsidize their diet. It was also alleged that senior officers' families were treating their private staffs the way landlords treated farm labourers in the old days.

Wounded by this criticism, my father decided to give up the allotment. When spring came, all the plots but ours were covered by green seedlings. Uncle Zhong and our family orderly kept on telling my grandmother: 'What a shame to let the plot go to waste! Please let us plant something.' For them, my father's decision seemed pointless since none of his colleagues took his view. Without the allotment, on the other hand, they lost their chance to share the harvest with us. When my father left Beijing for a long official trip, they eventually talked my grandmother round and started to cultivate the plot. When he came home he was furious, and insisted on their pulling up the seedlings at once.

My parents also made a point of keeping privilege out of their children's lives. When travelling to and from the Ba-yi School, my siblings and I never took the chauffeur-driven cars provided to both of our parents. For a long time, my father did not allow us to wear woollen pullovers or cardigans: 'I never had such clothes in my childhood!' When he saw his children wearing new clothes, he often blamed my mother for spoiling us, so they had to be taken away and given to relatives. As I recall, we never went to any of the social clubs reserved for senior officers and their families.

In the new school, I tried to keep my family background quiet, since my parents had warned us not to show off their positions. Despite the privileged status of our family, they said, we were the same as anybody else. If we wanted a good future, the answer was to work hard, not to rely on their influence.

Despite their aversion, however, there was little my parents could do about their privileges. If my father rejected his entitlement as an army general, his administrative officers would wonder what was wrong with their work, and then fear for their jobs. As it was, my parents always required us to appreciate the services we received, and never to give our private staff an order. We always called them 'uncle', the respectful address for an elder, even though the orderly was only a few years older than Feng-xin. As a result, we earned a reputation for good manners among the headquarters' staff. To my father's colleagues, on the other hand, his efforts seemed odd and wrong-headed, and hardly any followed his example.

In summer 1965, Feng-xin finished senior middle school, and enrolled at the Military Engineering University in Harbin, Manchuria, established in the early 1950s, and famous in China for attracting top-flight students from senior official families. Its former chancellor was Senior General Chen Geng, who died in 1961 while serving as China's deputy defence minister. The graduates included a nephew of Mao Zedong and a daughter of Marshal Lin Biao. One of Feng-xin's classmates later became Deng Xiaoping's son-in-law. By the time Feng-xin left school, my father had given up pushing him to study the arts. All the same, his record of work was patchy, and threw some doubt on whether he could reach the standard required by such a prestigious institution in the all-China entrance examination. But Feng-xin had made up his mind. During his final year at middle school, he worked very hard, and eventually achieved his ambition, to the great pride of my parents.

On Feng-xin's departure day, I joined my parents to take him to the main Beijing railway station. When we arrived, the huge car park was packed with chauffeur-driven cars, and the concourse teeming with keyed-up young people of Feng-xin's age, many with parents escorted by bodyguards or chauffeurs. Cheerful voices clamoured Feng-xin's name, while my parents greeted various old acquaintances. All of these parents' faces beamed with pride. Fired by the atmosphere, I told myself that some day I must equal my brother's success.

Since I started middle school, the theme of class struggle had grown into a nationwide campaign. 'Never forget the class struggle' was a slogan universally displayed. It provided the title for an influential play called *Never Forget*, which showed how the former owner of a grocery shop set out to challenge the Communist regime by introducing her working-class son-in-law to features of the 'bourgeois lifestyle', such as smoking and wearing smart suits. The play was promoted all over the country, and performed by nearly every troupe and theatre. Later, it was adapted as a film that the whole of our school was organized to watch, to enhance our political indoctrination. Actually, I quite enjoyed the character of the former grocer who was the villain of the play, and found my feeling shared by many friends. As compared with other characters in the film, she seemed direct and witty, and her language colloquial and forceful. Many of her sayings went into common parlance at the time.

Gradually, the theme of class struggle became a major part of the curriculum. Sometimes, poor peasants or industrial workers came to speak, and poured out their grievances against the old society. In our combined assembly and dining hall, all tables were cleared out for 'speak-bitterness' sessions. Above the platform, a slogan written in huge black characters against a red background urged: 'Never forget the bitterness of class oppression! Remember our hatred of blood and tears!' The listening audience was quiet, except for its sobs of compassion. At the end of each session, an organizer led the crowd in chanting angry slogans against the evil enemy.

These class-struggle lessons disturbed me. I hated the bloodsucking landlords described in the stories. On the other hand, it was hard for me to picture my maternal grandfather in such a light. In my childhood, I had always been told to respect the senior members of my family, who surely included my maternal grandfather, even though I never had a chance to know him. Nor did this picture fit the landlords in the North Forest Yard village where my paternal grandparents took refuge during the Sino-Japanese War. Without their generous ransom to the occupation army, my grandmother might have been killed in captivity. However, my confusion made me feel guilty, especially when I recognized that the idea in my mind disagreed with Chairman Mao, so I tried to suppress the conflicts, and accepted what I was told.

In our Chinese class, we were asked to write essays detailing instances of class struggle found in our daily lives. It was not an easy assignment, since we had virtually no idea of what to say, but no one was excused, as this would betray a lack of political consciousness. One day, the pupils in my class were invited to the Beijing Film Studio as extras for a children's film. As we set out, we noticed that the teacher who escorted us had had his hair cut specially for the occasion, in order to look smart in front of film stars and directors. Afterwards the teacher, just out of university, was accused in several essays written by my classmates of having succumbed to bourgeois ideology, since only people from the exploiting class paid special attention to appearance. Later, the poor young man had to make a self-criticism in front of our class about his leaning to the 'bourgeois life style', and asked us to forgive his 'wrong behaviour'.

In the early 1960s, my family started to receive regular visits on Sunday afternoons from an unexpected caller who was neither our relative nor family friend. She was our next-door neighbour, the wife of Major-General Tang, Political Commissar of the armoured forces in the Beijing Military Region, and her children also attended Ba-yi School. Madam Tang was over forty, quite tall for a woman of her generation, with a strong body and dark skin. What struck us most was her loquacity. From the moment she passed our doorstep, the gush of her words and the blare of her giggles could go on for hours. One of her keenest interests was in the families of high-ranking military figures such as marshals and four- or three-star generals. Since my mother knew some of their wives from her time in Yan'an, Madam Tang lapped up details of these women's personal hobbies or interests.

While she was talking, Madam Tang's hands were busy knitting — articles such as cardigans, pullovers and sleeveless sweaters. Apparently she would strike up an acquaintance with the wives of senior officers, whom she met at the theatre or in one of the privileged social clubs, then offer to knit something for them. Later she would deliver the item in person, sometimes in company with her husband. Since most of the military leaders were originally from south China, where dog meat was eaten, Madam Tang and her husband had some armoured units raise dogs to provide their families with free meat. Later, I heard that the couple also entertained the children of military leaders, who were also pupils at Ba-yi School, by giving them access to military training facilities to practise their driving or shooting. This was surprising to me, since my parents did no favours to any of our schoolmates, whatever their fathers' positions.

It seemed that Madam Tang's favours paid off. One day she told my parents that during her recent visit to Madam Ye Qun, the wife of Marshal Lin Biao, she had been invited to Ye Qun's private room, to choose what clothes she fancied from her wardrobe. Only a few months ago, Madam Tang had told my parents that she had never met Ye Qun, and asked my mother what she looked like.

What surprised me most was Madam Tang's attacks on the family of another neighbour, Major-General Shao, commander of the armoured forces, whose children also attended Ba-yi School. I knew that Shao had completed the Long March, and was one of the founders of the Communist armoured forces in China. During the Sino-Japanese War, his wife had joined the Communists, and spent her time in Yan'an. To listen to Madam Tang, however, you would think that both had degenerated into new bourgeois elements, infecting their children too. In particular, she had it in for Shao's eldest child, a girl called Eastern Dawn, who was the same age as Feng-xin. Many of her claims were hard to believe.

My parents disregarded these complaints, especially since they themselves had no wish for influence gained by courting powerful figures. During Madam Tang's visits, they tried to speak with reticent politeness. When she stood up to leave, I sensed their immediate relief. After one of her visits, I asked my mother curiously: 'Is it true that Eastern Dawn behaves so terribly?' My mother's reply was stiff: 'Mind your own business.' Later, my father called me into his study and said: 'There are many things in the world that you won't understand till you grow up. Please take no notice of what you heard today.'

I did not know then that the headquarters of the armoured forces had been troubled for years by feuding among the leadership, which dated back to the mid-1950s, when Madam Tang fell out with Madam Shao. Since both were mid-ranking officers in their husbands' headquarters, the relationship decayed between their higher-ranking husbands. Although both women were later transferred to civilian jobs elsewhere, the two couples did not make up. When Mao Zedong launched the Anti-Rightist Campaign in 1957, Madam Shao, then vice-principal of a technical college in Beijing, was labelled as a 'Bourgeois Rightist', removed from her post and dispatched to a labour camp far away from home. During that campaign, more than half a million people in China suffered similar fates. Most of their plights were caused by their criticism of the Party's policies, bureaucracy or official corruption, made at the Party's own request at the start of the campaign. Major-General Shao came under heavy Party pressure to divorce his wife, but he refused, and tried to rescue her from the labour camp. The outcome was political disgrace, and later removal from his post. In 1965, the case of Major-General Shao was used as a warning by the military, to show how he fell captive to the class enemy – his 'Bourgeois Rightist' wife.

My father was trusted by major leaders of the Beijing Military Region, and when he took up his post in the armoured forces he was expected to help to quell or curb the feuding. Through previous experience, he was not unfamiliar with infighting among Communist high officials, and loathed those who schemed to harm their colleagues. By the time he arrived at headquarters, it was already clear that Tang had brought down Shao, but my father stonewalled during Madam Tang's visits when she tried to enlist his support.

In private with my mother, my father expressed his sympathy for Major-General Shao and his wife, but he was helpless to save them, because no one could redeem Madam Shao from the brand of 'Bourgeois Rightist'. More than thirty years later I saw my father's working notes, which recorded his disagreement with Tang's persecution. 'Tang intends to push Shao out . . .' he wrote. '[The authority of] the military region instructs [us] to help Shao correct his mistakes in a friendly way . . . I follow the instruction . . . which tends to vex [Tang and his cohorts] . . . It seems that Tang is playing a double game . . .'

Madam Tang's Sunday visits tailed off, and by 1965 they had stopped. In that year, my father was promoted to Political Commissar of the armoured forces, replacing Major-General Tang, who was to be posted as Political Commissar to a provincial military region. Promotion stemmed mainly from services rendered to the Party, gauged by the length of Party standing, known as 'Lun-zi-pai-bei'. Tang was three years older than my father. He became a Party member in 1933, a year later than my father, but his revolutionary experience started in 1930, one year earlier. He joined the Red Army in a Soviet base in south China, where he came from, and endured the Long March. In view of their similar records, my father's prospective promotion was nothing out of the ordinary. His previous work at the headquarters of the Beijing Military Region had impressed his superiors with his ability and political integrity.

But Tang was unhappy, especially because his new post was outside Beijing and his new rank no higher than before. In those days, it was an unwritten law that transfers from Beijing to the provinces often carried promotion. Tang's case was interpreted as a move by the Beijing Military Region to stop the endless infighting among leaders of the armoured forces. His instinctive response was to blame his disappointment on my father, his successor. Here he was mistaken. Under the Communist regime, jobs were not advertised, and promotion or transfer was up to the Party to decide, at a higher level. For senior posts in the Beijing Military Region, the crucial decision-making body was a small standing committee inside that military region's Party committee and superior authority, and consisting of the military region's Commander and Political Commissar, and their deputies. In China, standing committees operate at all levels from the Politburo downwards; they act as a kind of 'inner cabinet' and ultimate decision-making body. My father's new post was a strictly official decision. He did not apply and did not pull strings for promotion.

Tang was determined not to leave the armoured forces. He and his wife lobbied hard among their network of military connections, and his transfer was withdrawn, which meant that he retained his post while my father remained as Deputy Political Commissar. No explanation reached my father, nor could he possibly question these unexpected changes, knowing that under the new hierarchy a word from a single powerful figure could reverse an official decision. Shortly after this incident, my father wrote in his working notes: 'Tang refused his transfer . . . I try my best to stay on good terms with him, though he intends to remove me' (from the armoured forces). Clearly, my father's position was awkward, and he had been cast as Tang's new rival.

Meanwhile, Mao was displaying his distrust of China's established administration. In his view, not only had the Communists lost control of one third of their organizations at various levels, they also faced a multitude of agents of the capitalist class, as well as counter-revolutionary revisionists who lurked in the Party, government and military. Through Mao's speeches, the term 'capitalist-roaders' soon became familiar: it meant those who held power in the Party but were hostile to socialism, covert enemies inside the revolutionary camp. At the same time, Mao was distancing himself from Liu Shaoqi, the Party's No. 2. In 1959, Liu had become the Chairman of the Republic, when Mao resigned that post and retained only the chairmanship of the Party. By the end of 1964, Mao was attacking him publicly, and repeatedly warning senior officials: 'What will you do if there are revisionists inside the Party's Central Committee?'

As the top-level conflicts intensified, a number of new political figures took up active roles at Mao's side, among them his wife, Jiang Qing. It was said that she resented Wang Guangmei, Liu Shaoqi's much younger wife, and made no secret of it. Wang Guangmei came from a wealthy entrepreneur family in Beijing, and was educated at a university founded by Western missionaries before she joined the Communists in the mid-1940s. On visits abroad with her husband in the early 1960s, she dressed with style, made easy conversation, and performed well as China's first lady, which further galled Jiang Qing, who was forbidden to claim the limelight, or to influence Mao's policies, by the conditions imposed in Yan'an before their marriage.

But the new political climate created openings for Jiang Qing, and she was backed by Kang Sheng. She said some years later that her role at first was as a sentry in the cultural and ideological field, reporting to Mao about new trends. Years later, it turned out that she and Mao were already living separate lives at that time, and that Mao had many affairs, but his wife's political ambition served his purpose, because she was loyal, and he distrusted his colleagues. From then on, there is no doubting the influence of Jiang Qing and Kang Sheng on Mao's assaults in the sphere of art and literature.

'In many [cultural] organizations, very little has been achieved so far in socialist transformation,' wrote Mao in December 1963. 'Isn't it absurd that many Communists are enthusiastic about promoting feudal and capitalist art, but not socialist art?' In another influential comment, Mao complained that during the previous fifteen years, most of the literature and art organizations, their publications, and by and large their personnel, had failed to carry out the Party's policies. As a result, many prominent artistic and literary figures were denounced for their 'anti-socialist' work, and many leaders of the related professional organizations lost their jobs.

In summer 1964, a national festival of modern revolutionary Peking Opera took place in Beijing, organized by the Ministry of Culture. In previous years, Mao had objected that Peking Opera, enormously popular in China, was still based on historical stories or folk tales passed down for hundreds of years, and often conveying traditional themes such as filial duty, the chastity of widows, or loyalty to emperors. In one famous comment, he protested that Peking Opera sang only of emperors, kings, generals and beauties. At the festival, twenty-eight Peking Opera troupes from all over China staged thirty-seven new productions, based mainly on stories about the Communist revolution. In order to communicate revolutionary feeling, traditional styles and forms were radically changed. In the modern revolutionary plays, male singers no longer played female roles.

The festival was heavily publicized. Mao attended several of the new productions, and Premier Zhou Enlai gave an important speech about the Party's line in the field of art and literature. A spate of talks and articles praised modern revolutionary Peking Opera as a landmark in cultural reform. The festival marked a turning-point in Jiang Qing's political career, her public début as a pioneer cultural reformer, and 'bearer of the revolutionary standard in art'.

From then on, operas based on traditional plots were banned. The Communist revolution became the dominant topic, not only in Peking Opera but also in modern drama or other forms of opera with different provincial origins. For my grandmother, this was a mortifying change. To hear or watch Peking Opera had been one of the joys of her life. As an illiterate person, she delighted in its traditional plots, which illuminated China's history and culture, and she loved its classic elegance in performance.

In the early 1950s, my grandmother's favourite place was the open-air theatre in the centuries-old fair held every month at the Temple for Protecting the Nation, which stood in our street. During the fair, the temple yard was packed from daybreak with people from all over Beijing who came to sell, browse, barter, perform or look on. There were street magicians, wrestlers, Kung-fu adepts, or acrobatics done by children or monkeys and goats. Inside the open-air theatre, surrounded by canvas walls, the pulse of gongs and drums reached into the distance, and always drew large crowds. The cheap admission fees – a few fens per adult, free for a child – were bargains for my grandmother before the salary system was introduced for Communist officials. On the beaten ground of the theatre, dozens of thick narrow planks on piles of bricks provided seating. During the performance, people could come and go as they pleased. While they enjoyed the opera, the audience also chatted to each other, or nibbled fried peanuts or sunflower seeds, and discarded the shells. The oddest thing to my eye was the appearance on stage of the leading actors' servant, known as 'gen-bao', which was an old-fashioned custom, rarely seen in other theatres. If the part required the actor to kneel, a silent man dressed in a dark Chinese-style jacket would deliver a small cotton mat to keep his costume clean on the earthen floor, and then collect it quietly after use. Another service was to bring on a small pot of tea from time to time, so that the actor could drink when he felt thirsty.

When Aijun, the youngest in my family, was sent to boarding kindergarten at Ba-yi School in 1958, the temple fair had already been banned. After that, my grandmother started going to the People's Theatre, the National Peking Opera House, which was also located in our street. By then, she could afford the expense. On top of her income from my parents, a considerable amount of pocket money came from my father's siblings. But despite her prosperity she still wanted a discount on her tickets. After supper, she liked to wait for bargains outside the theatre, along with many other elderly local fans. As she discovered, these fellow fans were not very fussy about the location of their seats. During the performance, they liked to close their eyes and concentrate on listening. Sometimes they hummed with the singing quietly, absorbed in their own world. From the new friends she made, my grandmother learned how to appreciate the different styles of opera performance. Later on, she always said that this was the time of her life, with so many chances to enjoy China's finest Peking Opera singers.

After we moved far away from the People's Theatre in 1962, my grandmother had to make do with watching operas on television or listening on the radio. But now her favourite classics disappeared, and she disliked the modern revolutionary Peking Opera from the start. 'What a performance!' she complained, and then switched off the television. 'The stage is full of characters dressed like beggars and milling around with hoes, hammers or rifles in their hands.' Having heard the revolutionary operas on the radio, she shook her head: 'Oh no! That is screaming, not singing.' When she happened upon her opera-going friends they too would lament that nothing was worth listening to these days. Sometimes, she looked at her collection of tickets from the past, and said to herself: 'Lucky that Mei Lanfang [the great Peking Opera virtuoso] passed away several years ago, or his heart would be broken.'

I sympathized with Grandmother's complaints, because I too was fond of the traditional repertoire. At that particular time, I was eager to hear my father's views about the new trends in art and literature, considering his own involvement as a writer and through personal connections. To my surprise, he fended off my queries, and my parents seemed more serious than before. At home, we stopped listening to our records of traditional Peking Opera, and the pleasant evening strolls with my father were growing more rare.

Mao was intent on replacing his chosen heir, Chairman Liu Shaoqi, and his eye fell on Marshal Lin Biao, who had succeeded Marshal Peng Dehuai as China's defence minister in 1959. Early in 1962, the Party's Central Committee convened what has since become known as the 'Conference of seven thousand cadres'. Over seven thousand officials, from central government down to county level, gathered in Beijing to discuss the problems created by the failure of the Great Leap Forward. In public, Mao welcomed the criticisms made there about Party policy, and admitted some responsibility for the Party's mistakes. But according to Jiang Qing some years later, at heart he resented what was said. In particular, he was furious when Liu Shaoqi concluded that the famine was 70 per cent man-made – caused by mistaken Party policies – and only 30 per cent a product of natural disasters. In absolute contrast, Lin Biao argued that the Great Leap Forward had failed, and the famine erupted, because officials had not followed Mao's instructions: Mao Zedong's thought was always correct. In recent years, Lin Biao had gone out of his way to preach the cult of Mao to the military. No praise was too extravagant. He insisted that 'every sentence of Mao's is the truth, and one sentence of his is more powerful than ten thousand [from anyone else]'. In the words of Lin Biao, 'the thought of Mao Zedong has achieved the peak of Marxism-Leninism in our time'.

In 1963, Mao called on the whole nation to learn from the People's Liberation Army, which had blazed the trail for the cult of Mao. Mao studies flooded the country. In our school, indoctrination began to permeate pupils' lives. Special seminars focused on Mao's works, or Party documents. In our Chinese classes, propaganda overshadowed classical literature, and that made me bored. At the age of thirteen, with a passion for literature and art, I had little interest in politics, or in Mao's philosophy and theory.

Today, I recognize that my indifference stemmed partly from my background. Despite the political climate, my parents made no space for the cult of Mao at home, which was unusual at that time. Until 1965, there was not even a portrait of Mao Zedong in our house. Many of the rooms were decorated with fine art that included paintings by great traditional masters such as Zheng Banqiao, in the Qing Dynasty, and Qi Baishi (who was born at the very end of the Qing Dynasty, but is associated with the post-Qing era). The artistic atmosphere always surprised our visitors, at a time when many displayed only Mao's portrait, his calligraphy work, or revolutionary slogans on the walls of their homes. Relatives and family friends warned that it was dangerous to show such an open fondness for feudal or bourgeois culture, instead of conveying their love for Chairman Mao, but for some time my parents took no notice. To them, Mao was certainly a great leader of the Party and the whole nation. On the other hand, as Communists they could not endorse the cult of Mao: it was too reminiscent of the Soviet experience under Stalin. Although we never discussed politics at home, I could sense their apprehension, so I always felt uncomfortable with the fulsome praise of Mao served up by the media and at school. Yet this feeling also scared me. I blamed myself for my disaffection, and tried my best to do as I was told.

Another headache for me was military training, which was mostly provided in PE classes. As a teenaged girl, I had little interest in any activity connected with fighting, but now I had to carry a dummy rifle, and practise bayonet fighting every week. As we lunged at the targets, imagined as imperialists, revisionists or counter-revolutionaries, we had to let out murderous shouts – 'Sha!' ('Kill!') – which made the hair stand up on the nape of my neck. 'Where's your strength?' the instructor shouted. 'Your moves looked as soft as boiled noodles. How could you kill the enemy if we were on a real battlefield?' It was shaming to be scolded in front of my classmates, but no matter how hard I tried, my performance never made the grade, simply because I could not overcome my mental block. Sometimes we practised crawling on the school's dusty sports ground, as our training had to be lifelike, and when we closed in on enemy positions in wartime, our clothes and skin would be equally exposed. Afterwards, it always upset me to find my clothes grimy or torn.

Among the pupils, it was getting fashionable for those who could obtain it to wear khaki combat gear. Some even walked barefoot to school, which they saw as carrying on the glorious tradition of plain living set by the Communists and the PLA. For me, the barefoot style went too far, but combat gear accorded with Chairman Mao's famous poem: 'China's daughters have aspiring minds/ They love their battle dress, not silks and satins.' Also, it appealed to a teenager like me to depart from convention. Unfortunately, none of my father's gear would fit. Since his return from Korea in 1952, he had gradually put on weight, and was no longer slim. The summer uniform jacket I eventually cadged was still too big, even worn on top of my padded winter jacket, and like other pupils' finds it was also old and faded, but that did not matter, because I could sense the deep envy my fellow students felt. In those days, it was impossible to buy military uniforms on the market, so for those with no connection to the military it was a style to dream of.

In 1965, the system of military ranks was abolished. Ever since the Great Leap Forward, Mao Zedong had argued against it, saying that without it 'our troops still defeated Chiang Kai-shek and the Japanese. When we fought the Americans, we did not have the system either.' In his view, rank was associated with the 'bourgeois privileges' that had to be abolished as part of the measures to prevent the drift from socialism back to capitalism in China. From then on, all those on active service only wore two red collar tabs on their uniforms. The major badge of status was the number of pockets on their jackets, which was four for officers but two for the rest. Ironically, the families of generals like my father retained their privileges, from houses to chauffeur-driven cars and private staff.

In February 1966, signs of a new political alliance appeared when Lin Biao invited Jiang Qing to convene a forum on literature and art in Shanghai, attended by members of the armed forces who worked in those fields. (In the Communist military forces, it is a tradition for organizations such as 'cultural work troupes' to dispense political propaganda through art or entertainment.) In her speech, Jiang Qing claimed that a black political line, the foe of Chairman Mao's revolutionary line, had taken hold of China's art and literature. Although she held no office in the Party, her speech soon entered general circulation as an official document of the Central Committee. In Lin Biao's flattering judgement, she was not only very capable politically but also an expert in the cultural field. The upshot was that more films, novels and plays were denounced by the official media as 'poisonous weeds', hostile to Chairman Mao's line. Works with revolutionary themes were not exempt if they failed to meet Jiang Qing's taste.

This turbulent climate was a gift to Major-General Tang. No rival of his had been safe in the past, and my parents knew that sooner or later he would seize his chance to move against my father, seen as his main political opponent. My father's novel made him especially vulnerable. Jiang Qing disliked it, because it told the story of a group of young Communists with intellectual backgrounds, whereas her theory dictated that in revolutionary art only industrial workers, peasants or soldiers should be the heroes. My family's private collection of books could also incriminate my father, on the charge – in those days indefensible for a Communist officer – of being a lover of feudal and bourgeois culture.

Though troubled about their family's future, my parents did not tell us of their fears, though it was hard to find a smile on their faces, and my favourite source of reading dried up because they wanted to keep their collections as secret as possible. We were forbidden to invite friends home or to visit any other families, and my father warned my grand-mother not to talk to the neighbours or to our family staff, in case her words should be twisted and used against him.

For my grandmother, my parents' caution was hard to understand. Her warm heart made her popular with neighbours wherever she lived, and she got on very well with our private staff. Unable to read or write, talk was a vital means of communication. If it stopped, how else was she to entertain herself, especially now that her favourite classical Peking Operas were banned? The house was too big and too quiet when work or studies took the rest of the family away for so much of the time, and she had to keep her distance from Uncle Zhong and the orderly.

Feeling terribly lonely, and bored with so little to do, my grand-mother longed to return to North Forest Yard village, where she still kept a house. Living among these honest peasants, she always felt safe and relaxed. 'Now, I'm living like a prisoner,' she complained. 'I'd rather have an ordinary life than live in privilege but not free.' But my father and his siblings resisted. She was over seventy years old, and they were con-cerned that the harsh village life would be too much for her, especially since none of them lived close to their home county and could not look after her regularly. In the end, they promised my grandmother that as soon as the trouble blew over she and my parents would go back and spend some time in the village.

Despite my parents' worries, there was little my father could do to improve his chances. As a dedicated Communist, he always went where the Party directed, so he would not think of asking for a transfer, let alone of resigning from his post, which was certain to be interpreted as an act of protest against the Party's authority. And even if he could arrange a transfer, Tang would not forgo his opportunity. In the present political climate, he would pursue him wherever he worked. The only solution was for my father to drop out of sight for a while. In early

1966, having been granted six months' leave by the Beijing Military Region, he went to Taiyuan, the provincial capital of Shanxi, to work on the rest of his novel. There had been a strong demand from readers for the sequel, and his publisher had pressed him to complete it.

My father set out in the hope that by summer's end the political climate would improve, and with it his own situation. Like everybody else, my parents had no idea that the recent events in China were only the prelude to a political campaign waged on a scale without precedent in history. The Great Proletarian Cultural Revolution, launched by Chairman Mao Zedong, was to last throughout the next ten years.

Chapter 13

'True Gold Fears No Fire':
The Eruption of the Cultural Revolution

(May–September 1966)

On 8 May 1966, two items led the morning radio news. They were based on articles – 'Open Fire on the Anti-Party and Anti-Socialist Black Line' and 'Sharpen Our Vigilance, Tell the True from the False' – published that day respectively in the *Liberation Army Daily*, the official voice of the military, and *Brightness* (*Guang-ming-ri-bao*), the Party's newspaper for intellectuals, denouncing Deng Tuo, secretary of the Municipal Communist Party Committee in Beijing, for his counter-revolutionary activities. In particular, they attacked his popular series, 'Evening Talks on Yen Mountain', published in the popular *Beijing Evening Post* some years before. Another target was a well-known column, 'Notes From A Three-Family Village', published in the early 1960s in the magazine and newspaper run by the Municipal Party Committee. As well as Deng Tuo, the column's co-authors included Wu Han, Vice-Mayor of Beijing Municipality and a leading historian of the Ming Dynasty, and Liao Mosha, Director of the United Front Work Department in the Municipal Party Committee. Deng Tuo was accused of heading a gang of three to damage the Party and socialism in their writing.

The publication of the two articles, both of them written under pseudonyms, was a bomb exploded over China. By order of the Party, they were reprinted nationwide by other newspapers, magazines and journals, accompanied and followed by a barrage of further attacks. Every day, the media featured reports of the indignation felt by the masses against Deng Tuo and his two accomplices for their anti-Party and anti-socialist activities. To see such slashing attacks and sensational publicity directed against distinguished Communist intellectuals was so unusual that to many it signalled a major political storm.

When I heard the broadcast my heart sank at once, because Deng Tuo was a friend of my father. As members of the team invited by Marshal Nie Rongzhen at the end of the 1950s to compile the history of the Communist forces, my father had charge of the day-to-day work, while Deng Tuo read and revised the completed drafts. For my father, it was a pleasure to work with Deng Tuo, a scholar with a national reputation, but cooperative and considerate towards his colleagues. During the early 1960s, his journalism brought him countless readers, and his calligraphy was exhibited and admired in major Beijing galleries such as the famous 'Rong-bao-zhai' in Liulichang Street.

On that morning, as usual our house was quiet and empty. My mother was in Taiyuan, visiting my father, and all my siblings were either at school or in university. I walked into our living-room, where a piece of calligraphy by Deng Tuo hung on the wall, a copy of his poem dedicated to my father after the publication of *Autumn in Jinyang*.

Recollecting the rise of the national salvation movement,
Going down in the annals of history with the unforgettable past,
Portraying the land ablaze with revolutionary flames,
Extolling the autumn in Jinyang for thousands of years.

Since Deng Tuo's poem was so prominently displayed in our house, his connection with my father was no secret. While the radio condemned him, and I gazed at his beautiful calligraphy, I felt I was caught in a nightmare, a sensation I had never experienced before. How could Deng Tuo, the talented author and acclaimed calligrapher, suddenly become the enemy of the whole nation? Why would Deng Tuo, my father's close friend and a respected high official, turn against the Party and the system he had fought for? In particular, I felt panicked by the thought that my father might be involved. 'Impossible!' I told myself. 'Baba is the most loyal and devoted Communist that I have ever seen.'

After I left for school that morning, my grandmother went on listening to the radio, and could not make out what was going on. Eventually, she popped into the kitchen and asked Uncle Zhong: 'Does a tiny village with only three families deserve so much attention, even if they opposed the Communist Party?' 'There are three top cadres opposing Chairman Mao through their writings,' answered Uncle Zhong. 'The whole nation must come down on them to defend our Party and Chairman Mao.' Grandmother found this message hard to swallow, as she had some years before in the case of Marshal Peng Dehuai, the disgraced defence minister. During the wars, Marshal Peng had been a household name, a major leader of the Communist forces. If he had been an enemy, as was alleged, why risk his life going through the Long March and commanding troops against the Japanese and the Nationalists? My grandmother was never convinced by his 'anti-Party crimes'. Now that three more 'top cadres' were being accused, her doubts revived. 'After the famine, the common people are only just getting enough to eat, and the quarrels start again,' she said to me in private that night. 'When can we all enjoy a peaceful life, with no more quarrels?'

The campaign against Deng Tuo and his two companions was the opening salvo of the Cultural Revolution, ordered by Jiang Qing and her radical cohorts, and backed by Mao Zedong. Six months before, their first round had been fired. On 10 November 1965, the Shanghai news-paper *Wen Hui Bao* had published a long attack by a radical young polemicist, Yao Wen-yuan, on a recent play called *Hai Rui Dismissed from Office*, a Peking Opera about a famous honest mandarin of the Ming Dynasty. The play was by Wu Han, later to be one of Deng Tuo's fellow accused. Yao Wen-yuan called it a 'huge poisonous weed', an attempt to rehabilitate Marshal Peng Dehuai. His critique was supported by Mao, and its arguments developed in secret on Jiang Qing's initiative over a period of nearly ten months in Shanghai, where her cohorts were in charge. Hence the vast majority of the Politburo were taken by surprise when the article was published.

Yao Wen-yuan's article antagonized much of the political elite, and especially Peng Zhen, mayor of Beijing, Politburo member, executive secretary of the Party's secretariat, and vice-president of the National People's Congress. Other opponents included Vice-Premier Lu Ding-yi, the Party's chief of propaganda, and Zhou Yang, the deputy chief of propaganda, Second Uncle's saviour some years before. For them, Wu Han was a trusted friend and colleague, a distinguished scholar, and ready to learn from Mao. In the past, Mao himself had praised Hai Rui, and encouraged historians to write about him, which was what had inspired Wu Han to write his play in 1960. In 1961, the play had been well received in Beijing.

But what Peng Zhen and his fellows did not know was that Mao's view of Wu Han's play had completely changed, largely under the influ-ence of Jiang Qing and Kang Sheng. In recent years, there had been growing sympathy in the Party for the plight of Marshal Peng Dehuai, and Mao saw possible parallels between Hai Rui four centuries ago and Peng Dehuai in the present: both of them honest and principled officials holding vital positions, devoted to their country and loyal to their lead-ers, both of them dismissed from their posts. Eventually, Mao became convinced that to resurrect the fall of Hai Rui acted as a coded criticism of his dismissing Marshal Peng.

Not knowing the background of Yao Wen-yuan's article, Peng Zhen and his colleagues refused Jiang Qing's demand to mount a campaign against Wu Han's play. She had no formal status; senior Party officials disliked and despised her; without her husband, she was no one. It was only after Premier Zhou Enlai conveyed the orders of the Party's Central Committee that Yao Wen-yuan's article eventually appeared in national newspapers such as the *People's Daily*, the mouthpiece of the Communist Party, and the *Beijing Daily*, the voice of the Municipal Party Committee. Nevertheless, Peng Zhen continued to defend Wu Han's political innocence even during his meetings with Mao.

Mao's resentment grew stronger against Peng Zhen and his colleagues, the more it emerged that his leadership was under serious challenge in the Party. He complained that the Municipal Party Committee in Beijing had become a separate kingdom ruled by Peng Zhen, and so impenetrable that not even Mao himself was able to scan its affairs. The propaganda department of the Central Committee was turning into a 'Palace of Hell', and the 'King of Hell' had to be overthrown. On May Day 1966, Peng Zhen did not appear at the national celebration in Tian-an Men Square, an occasion he had always chaired previously as mayor of Beijing. To the whole nation, this signalled his political disgrace.

A few days later, an enlarged meeting of the Politburo opened in Beijing by order of Mao, and was attended by Jiang Qing and a number of her henchmen, including those lately brought to public attention through their indictments of Deng Tuo and his fellows. This was very irregular, because they did not sit on the Central Committee, and had no right to attend the conference. A major item on the agenda was to denounce the 'Anti-Party Clique of Peng Zhen, Luo Ruiqing, Lu Ding-yi and Yang Shangkun'. As a result, these four leading figures in the Party, government and army were dismissed from their posts.

After the conference, the Party's Central Committee announced the establishment of the Central Cultural Revolution Small Group, headed by the left-wing theorist Chen Boda, and advised by Kang Sheng. Jiang Qing was first deputy director, and other members included major allies of hers such as Yao Wen-yuan. Working under Mao's direct control, they functioned as the supreme headquarters commanding the Cultural Revolution. Broadly speaking, they aimed to depose and replace the administration established since 1949, because Mao now distrusted its leaders. Their first moves included seizing control of the *People's Daily*, previously the voice of the Party's propaganda department. After the takeover, a spectacular change was the appearance on the masthead of a daily quotation from Mao's works.

Following the disgrace of Peng Zhen, Mao set his sights on the Municipal Party Committee in Beijing, condemned as Peng's independent kingdom. So the first salvo of the Cultural Revolution was the broadcasts on 8 May 1966 whose chief victims were Deng Tuo and his two associates, close colleagues of Peng Zhen.

On the afternoon of Deng Tuo's broadcast downfall, an unexpected visitor came to my house. She was a former pupil at Ba-yi School, known then as Junior Duan, and now in her first year at university. Some years before, she and I had been quite close. Sometimes she would visit me at home, and when she spoke to my father, it was often to admire his book collection. In recent years our contact had declined, mainly because – unknown to me – her father, Senior Duan, the deputy chief of staff in the armoured forces, had joined Tang's camp against my father. Finding me out when she called cannot have surprised her, since she came during school hours, but she went straight to our living-room, took out a pen and notebook, and jotted down the text of Deng Tuo's poem. Mission completed, she left at once, with no explanation to my astonished grandmother.

That evening, when I heard about the visit, I only thought how odd it was. Since my parents had kept us in the dark about the infighting at the top of the armoured forces, I had no clue about the girl's intention, or the plight my father faced. 'What do we do with Deng Tuo's poem?' asked my grandmother. 'Let's wait for Baba and Mama to decide,' I suggested. 'Mama will be back from Taiyuan next week.' In the house, it was forbidden to alter my parents' arrangements. Next morning, my father's assistant dropped in, and urged my grandmother to take down Deng Tuo's tribute at once: 'It will only make trouble for Deputy Political Commissar Mu if it stays.'

On 13 May 1966, my father was summoned to Beijing urgently from Taiyuan, and walked straight into trouble. His diary for 14 May reads: 'Attended meeting of the [Party] standing committee [of the armoured forces], where I was put in charge of Cultural Revolution matters. Went to office of the writing team [compiling the history of the Communist forces] . . . to discuss Deng Tuo's problems and his influence on the work.' On top of this, he was also enlisted to prepare a report to Marshal Nie Rongzhen, on behalf of the team, concerning Deng Tuo's function in the writing. Two days after his return, he noted: 'I was told that Senior Duan abused me in a meeting before my return from Taiyuan, and Madam Tang attacked me in public.' On 24 May: 'Jing [my mother] heard that staff [in the armoured forces] have been prompted to file complaints against me with General Staff Headquarters.' On 1 June: 'I was requested to provide a statement about my attitudes towards the Cultural Revolution to the Party Committee of the Beijing Military Region . . .' On 14 June: 'I was urged again to provide the statement . . . and finished it by midnight. Feeling terribly unhappy about the request. Obviously, Tang and his wife intend to persecute me.'

On 25 June 1966, a conference called by the Party committee of the armoured forces comprised senior officers whose troops were controlled by my father's headquarters. Their subject was the documents issued by the recently concluded enlarged meeting of the Politburo, but the proceedings soon became a trial, with my father the principal target, denounced as a member of the reactionary gang of Deng Tuo. The prosecution was spearheaded by Tang and his core of supporters at headquarters, who agitated hard, both in private and in open session, to inflame opinion against my father and drum up support for their accusations.

As evidence of guilt, my father was accused of having held eight secret meetings with Deng Tuo since returning to Beijing. (In fact, Deng Tuo had committed suicide before my father left Taiyuan, but the official censorship suppressed the information.) My father's novel was condemned for opposing Chairman Mao's revolutionary line, and the love affairs among the major characters labelled as expressions of bourgeois emotion, which presented revolutionaries in a bad light. His published essays were taken as further evidence of his conflict with Mao Zedong Thought.

My father noted on the first day of the conference: '. . . a considerable amount of evidence has already been gathered against me. I heard that they have talked to people who worked for me in the past, and collected my remarks during meetings with readers of my novel, my broadcast writings and published essays. It seems that the campaign has been meticulously prepared.' Later, my father heard that before the conference, Senior Duan collected a heap of records from the China Book Store, detailing purchases made by my father since 1962, which yielded Tang a list of more than 100 'poisonous weeds' in my father's collection.

For most who attended the conference, there was nothing new about political strife among leaders of the armoured forces, as many had seen Tang at work before. People felt sympathy for my father, and some expressed their doubts about the evidence presented by Tang's camp. But since my father's friendship with Deng Tuo was widely known, it was not easy to stand up and vouch for his innocence, and for those in doubt, the wiser course was to side with Tang. Some also feared his powerful position in the armoured forces and his personal connection – widely publicized by himself and his wife – with various leading military figures. Since Tang seemed untouchable, it made no sense to speak for his opponent. More and more people tried to keep their distance, and did not even dare to greet him when they met during the conference, or at headquarters, for fear of getting involved in his troubles.

My father's diary for 28 June 1966 reads: 'Not allowed to attend any group session [of the conference]. Told to prepare a confession [about his "serious political problems"]. Next day, his access to the conference bulletin was denied, and he was requested to report to Tang in advance when contacting colleagues on his side. Held in this virtual quarantine, he had very little scope for self-defence. And almost every day he was to confess his errors to his fellow officers. More than three decades later, I read the text of one of these statements, entitled 'Confession of my bourgeois individualism':

> My hobby of book collecting is a consequence of bourgeois edu-
> cation, not the taste of the [industrial] workers and peasants . . . I
> have always been determined to be a real Communist, and tried my
> best to resist many kinds of behaviour caused by bourgeois indi-
> vidualism, such as scrambling for political power and personal
> profit and corruption . . . But now, I have to admit that my moti-
> vation was incorrect, as I cared more about my personal reputation
> than the interests of the proletariat . . . I have always looked for-
> ward to a peaceful and relaxing environment, so that we could
> achieve more in our work. Now I admit that the error of my
> thought is not realistic as it opposed Chairman Mao's instructions
> for class struggle . . .

During the conference, my mother's university was informed about my father's situation. Since the disgrace of Peng Zhen, my mother had been attacked in her university for her links with the Municipal Party Committee, so the message poured fuel on the flames. When he heard about Tang's ambush on his wife, my father could no longer contain his anger, but what could he do? After Mao's call to arms against Deng Tuo, his overt friend, he had no way to shield himself or his wife from their opponents. He felt like a caged animal who watched as his family was injured, while himself awaiting slaughter. In his frustration, he shut himself up in his study, and choked on his tears.

Despite her own misfortunes, my mother was alarmed for her husband. In recent years, he had suffered from high blood pressure, combined with angina caused by coronary heart disease. As well as taking regular medication, he had to stay calm and relaxed. Plainly so much anger and frustration must damage his health. During that time, my mother tried to come home every day and keep him company. One day, she suggested that they should visit Beihai Park, the former imperial garden, a favourite family haunt in the 1950s, as it was just two streets from where we lived. Beihai, 'North Lake', occupies the north part of the complex called Sanhai, 'Three Lakes', centuries old, and located northwest of the Forbidden City, within the territory of the former Imperial City. Under the Communist regime, only Beihai is open to visitors, for a small fee. The rest of Sanhai – known as Zhongnanhai, 'Middle and South Lakes' – was occupied by Mao and other Party leaders at that time, as their private residences and offices.

It was late afternoon when my parents arrived. The scenery of the former imperial garden was just as enchanting as before, and the air was filled with fragrance. Sitting on a long wooden bench, they stared at the calm lake in front of them, and the great White Pagoda that stands on a high green hill in the middle of the Jaden Islet at the other end. The early summer breeze carried the laughter of children playing around the elegant Pavilion of Five Dragons, near where my parents sat. Inside the peace of Beihai, it was hard to imagine the whole of China quaking with turbulence. After a long spell of silence, my father muttered: 'It seems that they are fully prepared to damage me this time.' 'True gold fears no fire,' my mother replied. 'The Party's higher authority will defend your innocence. They are clear about your relationship with Deng Tuo.' Later, my parents learned that their visit to the park had been recorded by Tang and his agents as one of their 'secret meetings' with Deng Tuo.

By 'higher authority' my mother meant the leaders of the Beijing Military Region. In order to proceed against my father, Tang had to obtain their approval, which could not be taken for granted. With his high-level army connections, he had emerged intact from his previous vendettas, but this time his superiors were less gullible. Whereas they knew my father for his ability, commitment and political integrity, they knew Tang for his intrigues against colleagues. So far, only a few leading military figures had been picked on during the national denunciation campaign, after being attacked by Mao himself and his radical followers. In the whole Beijing Military Region, no senior officer had been affected. The authority had to be cautious in dealing with Tang's accusations against my father, as it was one of the earliest cases they faced.

When the 'trial' began against my father, the work team assigned to the armoured forces from the military region headquarters was headed by Lieutenant-General Kong Haiqing, the regional deputy commander. After a spell of investigation, he made several public speeches stating his conclusion that there was no political involvement in my father's personal relationship with Deng Tuo. If there were problems in Mu Xiang's published essays, what they proved was that his grasp of Mao's thought was not good enough. Since no one dared to claim that their own grasp *was* good enough, Lieutenant-General Kong had cleverly neutralized this part of Tang's allegations. According to Lieutenant-General Kong, my father's novel was not a 'poisonous weed', and had been endorsed by the authorities of the Beijing Military Region, who would take a dim view of its detractors. As for the attacks on my father's hobby of reading and collecting literature and history books, Lieutenant-General Kong argued that it was not wrong to read them, as long as the reader was able to differentiate between the 'fragrant flowers' and 'poisonous weeds', those with revolutionary or counter-revolutionary contents.

My father's diary for 30 June 1966 reads: 'Kong encouraged me to stand up for myself. At the afternoon meeting . . . Tang and his cohorts looked triumphant listening to strong attacks against me. But Kong's closing speech criticized the hostile atmosphere. He cautioned everyone to beware of the personal spite behind the scenes . . . I could not quell my tears as I heard Kong supported me.'

Swayed by Lieutenant-General Kong, the majority agreed my father's innocence. Tang and his clique had to withdraw their charges. The 'trial' lasted more than two weeks. On 9 July 1966 it closed, and so did the first campaign against my father. On that day, my father's diary recorded: 'I feel terrible. In an anxious state of mind. Thinking of the conspiracies of Tang and his cohorts against me, I am in a towering rage.'

In May 1966, by order of Mao Zedong, the Municipal Party Committee in Beijing was reshuffled and the so-called independent kingdom of Peng Zhen destroyed. Soon after that, my mother attended the first official conference convened by the new municipal leader in the famous Beijing Hotel. Like my mother, the other participants were also Party leaders working for the Municipal Committee, whose positions were equivalent to prefectural governor or higher. (At that time, my mother's university was under dual control by the Municipal Party Committee in Beijing and the Ministry of Forestry.) The main business was to study the documents issued by the recently concluded enlarged meeting of the Politburo, and the conference was expected to last for at least two months.

Of all the documents they studied, what shocked my mother most was the speech by Lin Biao. Apart from his fanatical preaching of the cult of Mao, he focused on the counter-revolutionary coups which he claimed were being plotted by agents of the capitalist class and bourgeois revisionists inside the Party leadership. He warned how dangerous the crisis was, and instanced many cases of coups, especially palace coups, ancient and modern, in China and elsewhere. 'There were a lot of tortoise eggs [the term for "bastards" in Chinese],' Lin Biao warned, 'who tried to kill us, so we must down them first!' My mother was astonished by his language, so much cruder than his gentle public image would suggest.

Others at the conference shared my mother's incredulous response, but it was hard to question Lin Biao's message, because he was strongly backed by Mao Zedong, and perceived as speaking for him. Faced with no choice but to accept what he asserted, they were bound to feel deeply concerned for China's future. Most of the participants had joined the Communist Party in wartime, and had risked their lives fighting the Nationalists and the Japanese. Having followed Chairman Mao to create a new socialist China, who would tolerate its downfall, and see the capitalist system restored? At this critical moment, to defend their great leader and the Red regime was an absolute duty. At the plenary sessions, my mother joined the emotional crowd in chants of: 'Defend Chairman Mao with our blood and lives!' 'Be ready to die in defence of the Party's Central Committee!'

But whom should a brave defender fight? At this conference, she was briefed about the 'Anti-Party Clique of Peng Zhen, Luo Ruiqing, Lu Ding-yi and Yang Shangkun', which she found hard to believe in. To her, these four subversives were respected public figures, well known for their key parts in the Communist revolution. She even knew some of them personally. Now they were charged with conspiracy to overthrow the Communist regime. Never during her revolutionary career had intra-Party conflict grown so virulent, and she was watching from close to the centre of the whirlpool. Over the past six months, many good friends and acquaintances high in municipal and government circles had been branded as enemies of China. How could this happen? Yet in all her confusion, she could confide in no one, for fear that her remarks would be interpreted as supporting the reactionary gangs and fragmenting the revolutionary centre built around Chairman Mao.

On 1 June 1966, another fire was set in the Cultural Revolution when the national media gave massive publicity to a big-character poster appeared on the wall of the Beijing university campus which accused the leadership of Beijing University of sabotaging the Cultural Revolution. Throughout the Cultural Revolution, big-character posters were pasted all over the country. The main use of these posters was to attack leading figures of the country's establishment who had lost Mao's support. The posters were big and eye-catching so that it was easy for a large crowd to read them in public. This particular poster was written by staff members of Beijing University, headed by Nie Yuanzi, Party branch secretary in the department of philosophy, acting by secret request of Kang Sheng. The poster also attacked Song Shuo, director of the former municipal education authority, who was attending the Beijing Hotel Conference that day, and had no warning of this sudden ambush. Soon afterwards, Song Shuo disappeared from the conference.

'How wonderful the first Marxist-Leninist poster in the whole country is!' Mao rejoiced. With his approval, a front-page article in the *People's Daily*, written by an unnamed 'commentator', appealed to the whole nation to fight resolutely against the reactionary gangs, 'no matter how high their members' positions are, how senior in the Party they have been'.

Soon afterwards, the leadership of Beijing University collapsed. More and more students and staff plunged into the Cultural Revolution, classrooms emptied, and eventually all teaching was replaced by 'Si-da' – speaking out freely, holding great debates and writing big-character posters, major activities in the period to come. The university soon became the hub of the Cultural Revolution for all of China. All day long, the nearby streets were solid with vehicles and bicycles, as visitors converged from all over Beijing. Throughout the campus colourful posters and slogans covered not only the inside and outside walls, but also the temporary billboards that lined the major roads. Most of the texts backed Nie Yuanzi and her colleagues. Excited visitors stood in front of the posters and jotted down the contents in their notebooks, ready to turn these cutting edges of new political experience against their own authorities elsewhere. The location of Nie Yuanzi's first poster always pulled the crowd. A table placed against the wall provided a temporary platform where people queued to voice their will to rebel against the capitalist-roaders. When Nie Yuanzi appeared, cheering admirers flocked in their hundreds and thousands to chant their support.

What happened in China during the Cultural Revolution was unprecedented in human history. The young were promoted to rebel against the old, subordinates to question and denounce those in authority. Known as 'rebels', these people in fact represented Mao and his radical followers' wishes and were employed to destroy the country's establishment, which Mao himself no longer trusted. During the following ten years, people – regardless of their social positions – could become political prisoners overnight, and tens of millions of urbanites were dispatched to the remote countryside to endure hard labour. Teaching in educational institutions stopped for years, and China became a vast desert of culture because most literature and entertainments were banned. The whole country was often in a state of anarchy where violence and vandalism ruled.

The storm of publicity for Nie Yuanzi's poster stirred the whole nation to rebel against the current administration. From then on, my mother's conference was more and more disrupted as events overtook it. Many participants were intercepted on their way home by activist rebels – usually their colleagues or students – who hauled them in front of mass rallies staged at any time from dawn until midnight, to be denounced on various charges. As a result, many were not allowed back to the conference, and a sharp decline in attendance overshadowed the proceedings and dismayed the remaining participants. At the end of each day, as people took leave of each other, no one knew whether they would be able to meet again tomorrow. When participants arrived in the morning, it was not unusual for their chauffeur-driven cars to carry slogans on the doors or back windows put there by the rebels and proclaiming messages such as 'Down with the capitalist-roader X [the passenger's name]' – slanders that they were helpless to remove.

Despite the security provided by the municipal government, the venue was invaded almost daily by rebels hunting leaders to denounce. Normally, the captives were hustled outside with their hands tied behind them, and loaded on to the back of waiting trucks. A hush would fall on the conference. No one, not even the organizers, was able to stop the abductions.

Eventually, even the manager of the Beijing Hotel where the conference took place was denounced, by his own staff. Branded as a counter-revolutionary monster and demon, he was sentenced to compulsory labour under the supervision of radical waiters, cleaners and porters. One day my mother saw him at the hotel entrance, sweeping the floor with a big broom, wearing a conical white paper cap, nearly a metre high, inscribed with offensive slogans against him, written in big black characters. His body was covered by a huge kraft paper jacket with more abusive slogans.

During the conference my mother spent most nights at the Beijing Hotel, to avoid commuting, and tried to stay in touch with her university. One evening when phoning her secretary, she heard that her campus too had been turned upside-down, following in the footsteps of other universities. As she spoke to my mother, the secretary was crouching behind the office door, and whispering into the phone. In the background my mother heard the clamour of a crowd mixed with revolutionary music broadcast by loudspeakers outside.

In recent days, a number of staff and students at her university had visited Beijing University, which was only a few streets away. Now they had imported what they had learned there. Teaching had stopped by demand of the rebels, and already the campus was flooded with big-character posters and slogans which promoted the Cultural Revolution or denounced the capitalist-roaders in the university. Some texts condemned my mother as a member of Deng Tuo's reactionary gang, a

notion spread by Tang and his crew during their campaign against my
father.

By late June 1966, my mother's conference had collapsed with no
conclusion, because most of the participants, including the organizers,
had been caught in the hail of accusations. By then, Lieutenant-General
Kong had sent investigators to the university to clarify my parents' relationship with Deng Tuo, but on her return she found that many people
tried to avoid her, and some did not dare even to greet her. Soon, more
hostile slogans and posters appeared, again incriminating her as an
accomplice of Peng Zhen. Most of the university leadership knew that
the former Municipal Party Committee had promoted my mother several years before because she was a capable and principled official.
Although many details mentioned in the posters were untrue, my mother
also wondered how the rebels knew so much about her political background, and about the conflicts among the university leaders. Most of
the rebels were junior staff or students, and had virtually no access to
these circles. In self-defence, to clarify the facts, my mother wrote a
number of big-character posters. A few days later, another crop of
posters went up, written by the same accusers. They revealed that it was
Cao Lian, the vice-chancellor, who had prompted them to write against
my mother, and provided all the details, true and false.

From previous experience with Cao Lian, my mother was not totally
surprised. He had taken up his post in 1959, when he transferred from
the military forces. By then, both the chancellor and the secretary of the
university Party committee had run into political trouble, due mainly to
their resisting Kang Sheng's order to relocate the campus during the
Great Leap Forward. My mother had hoped that the arrival of Cao
Lian, a veteran Communist active since the mid-1930s, would
strengthen the leadership, but she was soon disappointed by his passion
for working against his colleagues. Since the chancellor and the university Party leader were bound to be sacked before long, Cao Lian saw his
chance to seize one of the two top posts, and through it control of the

university. He was furious when the two vacancies were eventually filled by outside candidates, appointed by authority of the Ministry of Forestry, particularly because the new secretary of the university Party committee was his junior in length of revolutionary service. Cao Lian resented his new leaders, and plotted to remove them, and anybody else in his way.

Many years later my mother told me that Cao Lian's schemes had shown more ambition than sense. Simply because of his veteran status, he saw himself as the chief authority in the university, and confused his thuggish manner with soldierly directness. His tantrums and public bullying made him unpopular among his colleagues. One of his tricks was sending forged university documents or anonymous letters to the higher authorities with false accusations against those he disliked, but their style was so plainly off-key that it flaunted its author's identity. His well-earned reputation as a troublemaker did him no good with the Ministry of Forestry or the established Municipal Party Committee in Beijing, but to his academic colleagues he was a splitting headache, since no one could cope with his attitude. Those who refused to comply, he regarded as opponents and constantly harassed, with the result that everyone, including my mother, did their best to keep out of his way.

During Cao Lian's campaign against his colleagues, however, my mother could not always escape attention. As one of the university leaders, she never supported his tricks, and considered them unworthy of a veteran Communist and senior Party official. Just like my father, she had a natural dislike for those who schemed to undermine their colleagues. Several times, Cao Lian's plots misfired when my mother looked into these cases, and judged them on truth and principle. For this, he never forgave her. Some years before, when she was promoted to vice-secretary of the university Party committee, only Cao Lian had opposed it. He also told tall stories to the staff, such as 'I wanted you promoted but Xu Jing refused.' Those who fell for these lies were recruits against my mother. To relieve this situation, in 1964 my mother applied for a year's leave, as my father did in 1966, intending to write the book about her life which she had had in mind for many years. Her application failed because the Municipal Party Committee relied on her to help to solve the divisions in the university leadership.

When the rebels first organized in my mother's university, some of the major figures were Cao Lian's hangers-on. Weihe was a labourer employed in the nursery garden, who had kept his job even after it turned out that he had been stealing and selling university equipment. Under Cao Lian's protection, he had managed to escape any punishment. For some years he had done no work, pleading illness, but continued to be paid, and was often seen in Cao Lian's private plot, planting or watering vegetables. Weihe's other occupation was aiming a stream of letters at the Party's Central Committee or the State Council with fake accusations against those who were handling his case, or were seen as opposing Cao Lian. Despite his notorious record, no one questioned Weihe's credentials when he joined the rebel organization. As a manual worker and former soldier in the People's Liberation Army, he belonged to the most revolutionary class in Chinese society. He focused first on Madam Lu Wen, the personnel director, a Party member since 1938, and no friend of Cao Lian. Weihe led an action group that invaded her home and stuck a lavatory waste basket on her head, wrapped in a sheet of white paper proclaiming: 'Down with the counter-revolutionary and bourgeois revisionist Lu Wen.'

Cao Lian showed no embarrassment after his smear against my mother was exposed, but plotted more false charges. In a mass rally attended by the university staff and students, he stood with my mother on the platform and testified: 'Xu Jing got special training from the former Beijing Municipal Party Committee before being sent to our university as a spy.' His new lie was as clumsy as the old one, but what really shocked my mother was the intervention by Ji Xian, secretary of the university Party committee: 'Of the five university leaders, only Xu Jing was appointed by the former Municipal Party Committee. The rest of us were sent by the Ministry of Forestry.' Ji Xian then supported Cao Lian's lie: 'Xu Jing has acted as an agent of the former Municipal authority. She often took notes on everything that happened at the university, and passed the details on to them regularly.'

For a moment, my mother could not believe what she was hearing. She had always respected Ji Xian as the university's top leader, much to the disgust of Cao Lian, who had even spread rumours of their having an affair. Ji Xian's false testimony fired up the rebels against her. During previous wrangles among the university leaders, Ji Xian had been bullied into submission by Cao Lian, and had turned a blind eye to his mischief-making. For the sake of a quiet life, he even gave up his own interests to meet Cao Lian's demands, causing many colleagues to despise him as a coward, unable to stand on his own feet. In the heat of the Cultural Revolution, with leaders called into question all over the country, Ji Xian feared what the rebels might do to him, especially when controlled by Cao Lian, who had never liked him. His solution was to divert the rebels' attention, using my mother as his scapegoat through her connection with the former Beijing Municipal Party Committee.

The 'evidence' of the university's two major leaders made it impossible for my mother to convince the rebels of her political innocence. She became a focus of their criticism, while Cao Lian was viewed as the authentic Maoist representative among the university leaders. Backed by his henchmen in the rebel organization, he also promoted and exploited his glorious political background. In terms of class origin, the son of a poor peasant family was bound to outrank the daughter of a landlord. Among the students, his service as an officer during the revolution gave him a hero's image.

According to Cao Lian, as the one true revolutionary in the university leadership he had been systematically victimized by my mother and her counter-revolutionary cronies, who were determined to unseat him. Impressed by his background, many naive students rallied to his flag. Before the rebels seized power from the university authorities, Cao Lian had already won them over through his generous support, as when he provided equipment to set up their own radio network, at the university's expense. Ji Xian was in the clear. In return for his services, he was later classified as one of the only two 'Revolutionary Leftists' among the university leaders, placed second to Cao Lian on a list produced by the rebel organization. My mother, the only woman among the leaders, was labelled as a 'Bourgeois Rightist'.

One morning, my mother was forced to take part in a demonstration. Escorted by rebels who banged on gongs and drums, she and the university chancellor, Mr Kui, had to parade around the campus, each of them carrying a plaster statue or bust in their arms. Originally, these beautiful art works had been used as models for sketching by horticultural students to improve their artistic skills (they were mainly copies of famous works of art such as Venus de Milo); now they were evidence of the bourgeois revisionist line of education introduced by my mother and her associates. Since Mao had expressed a dislike of flowers and grass, horticulture had been attacked as a subject favoured only by the non-proletarian classes, and useless to industrial workers, peasants and soldiers. Behind them trailed a horde of staff and students, strung out in several long files, while an organizer led them to shout slogans. When she heard 'Down with the counter-revolutionaries and bourgeois revisionists Peng Zhen and Xu Jing!', my mother thought sarcastically: 'Heavens! What an honour to have my name appear in the same slogan as Peng Zhen's!'

The demonstration shook the university. Drawn by the din of gongs and drums, and the roar of the demonstrators, more and more people lined the chosen route to see their leaders humiliated in public, for the first time in their lives. In many familiar faces, my mother sensed shock, doubt or sympathy, but no one dared to express their feelings publicly, and others refused to meet her eye. All at once her way was blocked by Chancellor Kui, who seemed to lose balance and stumble. Kui was in his early sixties, and had been seriously ill for some time, but the ordeal could not be escaped. A student just behind him kept shouting at him to hurry up, but his condition was worsening fast, and he had to be taken to lie down. At lunchtime he was rushed to Beijing Union Hospital, China's first institution of Western medicine, established early this century with funds donated by the Rockefeller Foundation, and renowned for its excellence. But now it was too late. Chancellor Kui remained in hospital until he died there two months later.

In my father's diary for 13 August 1966 he recorded: 'She [my mother] felt depressed by what she suffered from the rebels. I encourage her to be stronger.' On 22 August: 'Midnight, the rain came down in sheets. Jing came home with her hair cut up in a mess [by the rebels in a denunciation rally against her]. All morning till the early afternoon she was taken around the campus, condemned as a capitalist-roader. In the evening, she was denounced again in a rally and her head covered in a huge paper cap . . . My angina is getting terrible . . .' Two days later: 'At home, we hear an uproar from Beijing Normal University [several streets away from our home] where a denunciation rally is attacking their chancellor . . . Jing has tried to put up with her plight, but today she burst into tears. She has suffered more than she could bear . . .' On 1 September: 'Jing wept again and seems quite fragile. She has thought of death [by committing suicide]. I tried my best to comfort her.' On the following day: 'Jing did not come home till midnight. I felt terribly worried about her and feared that one day, I might not be able to see her again . . .'

Chapter 14

Chairman Mao's Revolutionary Path-Breaker:
I Become One of the Earliest Red Guards

(June–September 1966)

In early June 1966, I came to school one morning and sensed an unusual atmosphere. A whole lot of eye-catching slogans had appeared on the outside walls, written in huge characters on coloured paper. 'Cut classes and take part in revolution!' 'Down with the capitalist-roaders in our school!' The large crowds standing in front of the slogans included many teachers, who said nothing and looked grave. Pupils talked or whispered, voicing their confusion, curiosity or even excitement. From a distance, I saw many more pupils, mostly from the senior middle school, running in and out of different buildings wearing solemn expressions, as if with sacred errands to perform. Minutes later, a number emerged and rushed towards the crowd. They put up more slogans and posters, with similar messages.

When the bell rang for school, not many pupils obeyed. I sat in the classroom with a handful of classmates while the tumult continued outside, and wondered what came next. The building itself was quiet, apart from some footsteps hurrying through the empty corridor, but our teacher did not turn up. Suddenly, a boy looked in and shouted: 'What are you waiting for? Come and join the rally and debate!'

The site of the rally was a strip of ground between the huge main teaching building and the dining hall, a valley between steep cliffs, jammed solid with pupils and staff. Standing on an island in the crowd formed by a table-tennis table acting as a temporary platform, a final-year pupil was finishing her speech, hoarsely shouting slogans through a microphone. 'Be ready to die in defence of Chairman Mao's revolutionary line!' 'Uncover the capitalist-roaders in our school!'

The rally was organized and the speech-making dominated by pupils in the senior middle school rather than by the school authority, and it soon became clear that the elected villain was Jiang Pei, secretary of the school Party branch. To me this seemed unthinkable. Jiang Pei was in his early forties, a powerful figure, and deeply respected. He had started his career in his twenties, and supported the Communist Party when the Nationalists still ruled. In the past, I had enjoyed listening to his humorous, knowledgeable speeches in the school's assemblies, so different from the dull style of other indoctrination authorities. Now, all of a sudden, Jiang Pei was branded as the No. I capitalist-roader in our school.

Jiang Pei was accused in his absence of being an agent of the capitalist class, peddling the bourgeois revisionist line of education. In particular, he had promoted special trial classes in the liberal arts. By poisoning innocent pupils' minds with feudalist, capitalist and revisionist ideas, he had tried to turn them into a bourgeois intellectual elite. Our school had been selected for the trial by the former municipal educational authority – proof of a counter-revolutionary connection with the former Municipal Party Committee. Other accusations included his preference for bourgeois intellectuals – in other words, well qualified teachers with professional attainments.

The rally continued all day, but it was hardly a debate, since only a few spoke up for the school authorities, and those who did were often hissed off the platform midway through their speeches, and the microphone snatched from their hands. 'Shut up, you bourgeois royalists!' The heckling drowned their voices as the mood grew more bad-tempered and the rally more chaotic. For a while, no single speaker could be heard, and there was a free-for-all to reach the platform. Eventually, a final-year pupil jumped up. He seized the microphone and started to read a quotation from Mao Zedong's recent letter to Lin Biao, hot from big-character posters in Beijing University: 'The term of education must be shortened, and a revolution launched in the educational field. The fact of having bourgeois intellectuals run our educational institutions must cease.' His reading was answered by thunderous cheers and applause, while the few 'bourgeois royalists' lost their voices.

Following the issue of Nie Yuanzi's big-character poster two days before, many senior pupils at our school had visited Beijing University to learn from its revolutionary experiences. It was not difficult to start the fire of the Cultural Revolution on our campus. Spurred on by the official media, more and more pupils longed to strike a blow against the school authorities, and their craving to fight the class enemy was tinder waiting for a spark.

After the rally, almost every school official was denounced, and teaching stopped. When the pupils staged further rallies, they ended in further chaos. The campus teemed with slogans and big-character posters. In the early morning, its quietness was often broken by revolutionary music played by the pupils' own brass band, followed by broadcast indictments of the capitalist-roaders, interspersed with more revolutionary music piped through loudspeakers till late evening. Soon, senior pupils started to organize the juniors to join in. We were told that apart from Jiang Pei, the No. I capitalist-roader in our school, there were many more hidden class enemies who should be uncovered by the revolutionary masses. But where were they? No one could say. For more than ten years, China had been staging political campaigns, and those singled out as class enemies had been expelled from the educational field.

In our school, it was hard to find anyone with a suspect political record. Eventually, the focus of my class turned to Yu Zhen, our Chinese teacher.

In the past, there had been gossip at school about Yu Zhen's eccentric personality and lifestyle. Though in his thirties, he was single, which was rare and drew attention. At work, he dressed neatly, wore clean shirts, and kept his thick dark hair well groomed, whereas most of his male colleagues paid little attention to their appearance. Except when teaching, Yu Zhen rarely spoke. Having no home in Beijing, he lived and slept in a small dark room in a corner of the staff office building. His odd behaviour always reminded me of a solitary mole in a cartoon film, but the more he tried to hide from the public, the more he drew others' attention. Various rumours claimed that Yu Zhen came from a wealthy business family in Shanghai, and that his unsociable personality was the mark left by a short-lived love affair many years ago. Someone else guessed that it might be political reasons that made him so inscrutable – he might be a survivor of the Anti-Rightist Campaign of 1957, and almost branded as a Bourgeois Rightist then. But no one I knew had any solid facts about his background.

Despite all the gossip, I was captivated by Yu Zhen's deep knowledge of Chinese language and literature. Listening to his teaching, I found to my surprise that his eyes could flash affectionately behind the dark-framed spectacles, and his voice become intense. What astonished me most was his beautiful left-handed writing. (His right hand was missing, which was another cause of campus speculation.) Under my father's influence, I believed that skill in calligraphy measured a person's education, which was an extra reason to respect Yu Zhen.

Yu Zhen's denunciation, prompted by his former pupils, now in the senior middle school, was based on little more than hearsay, but that was enough in the prevailing mood. All over the campus, big-character posters and slogans condemned Yu Zhen as a 'mouthpiece of the capitalist class'. One poster asked him 'Where on earth are you trying to lead your pupils?', which referred to his singing a Western love song at a party arranged by his pupils a few years ago, and thereby infecting their minds with bourgeois ideas. Smart clothes and combed hair were corroborating signs of an absolute bourgeois intellectual. But no matter how slashing the attacks, Yu Zhen never said a word in self-defence. Perhaps he believed that in times without justice, silence was the best way to survive.

In my class, I was elected to draft big-character posters, because I had a way with words. Faced with that role, my responses were divided. Recently, I had felt like a fallen leaf, blown by the campus gale till I was lost. As if the world had changed, all the rules and principles that guided me before had been destroyed. From now on, our only guidance was to follow where Chairman Mao pointed. When I first heard his call to fight the capitalist-roaders, I was excited. Always proud of my family background, I pictured myself under a huge red flag, defending Chairman Mao's revolutionary headquarters shoulder to shoulder with my parents, and felt absolutely glorious. At the same time I also felt confused, since it was unthinkable to convert familiar figures like Jiang Pei and Yu Zhen into rabid class enemies. Eventually, it was my faith in Chairman Mao that convinced me to oppose my teacher. Despite all my efforts, however, my words failed to sharpen the campaign: I could not create forceful posters. And soon, my role was over.

As the anarchy swept over Beijing, President Liu Shaoqi, who handled the routine business of the Party Central Committee, contacted Mao Zedong for urgent orders. With Mao's approval, the Central Committee instructed the newly established Municipal Party Committee to send work teams to all universities and middle schools in Beijing, the places most affected by the recent convulsions. The work team that came to our school in late June 1966 was staffed mainly by personnel from the Central Cadre Training School of China's Communist Youth League. They were greeted with joy. Some of the staff and pupils even wept.

From then on, the work team took over from the school Party branch and controlled all activities of the Cultural Revolution. In the revolutionary committee that replaced the school's administration, the majority of members were those pupils from the senior middle school who had led the first resistance in the school.

At the end of June 1966, I was assigned by the revolutionary committee to help a senior girl named Ever-red to take over the school health centre. It did not seem too hard a mission, since the centre consisted of a small room, some basic equipment, and a small supply of medicine. Its only staff was a middle-aged nurse who had already been informed about the takeover. She handed everything to us and then left quietly. At this point in our mission, we realized that neither one of her successors had any medical knowledge, or any idea of what the work involved. Alerted to our problem, the school's new authority replied that under Chairman Mao's guidance, revolutionary path-breakers like ourselves could achieve miracles. This meant not only seizing power from the capitalist-roaders and the bourgeois intellectuals, but also running the school ourselves.

Despite this keen encouragement, however, our frustration remained, so at last, in desperation, we asked for help from the Military Hospital No. 262, located right next to the school. In support of the Cultural Revolution, the hospital authority organized a special free training programme for Ever-red and me, an experience I thoroughly enjoyed, as I loved to learn anything practical and was pleased to gain another chance to study, even though I had no idea what the future held for me, or what I would do with the knowledge. I also liked our two supervisors. One was a male doctor in his early thirties whose gentle manner and handsome looks won me over immediately. The other was a caring nurse who taught me necessary skills step by step, and patiently. Ever-red was less eager to be taught. Very often, I found myself the only trainee, while she was campaigning at school.

Normally, I trained in the morning, and then practised in the health centre in the afternoon or evening, to apply what I had learned. As the political campaign developed in our school, more pupils stayed on until midnight, attending rallies, debates or other meetings. Fortunately, most of my patients' ailments were not serious, as they normally suffered from colds, minor injuries, or even sore throats from too much shouting. If there was any case I could not handle, my supervisors would come right over to help. Part of my work was assisting Ever-red to give first aid at the school rallies. Now that summer had arrived, there were several occasions when speakers collapsed in the heat of their emotions, so these duties could be stressful, especially when the rallies turned to chaos. My frequent appearances in public soon made me a familiar figure at school. To people who did not know my name, I was 'the girl with two big braids'.

Due to my medical work, I became distanced from the political campaign at school, but the plight of our school leaders set me wondering what would happen to my parents during the Cultural Revolution. At that time, I had virtually no idea that they were already in trouble, but I knew that their positions laid them open to attack. In particular, I worried about my mother, as universities had become the most turbulent places in China. Then there was my father's friendship with Deng Tuo, and his passion for the classical arts. What could I do if they were branded capitalist-roaders? This was a painful question, but I might have to face it at any time. If it happened, my world would collapse, the sky would fall. If they were brought to denunciation rallies and treated as my school leaders had been treated, with their hands twisted behind their backs and their heads forced down to the ground to show their guilt, while the slogans accused them . . . Oh no! I could not entertain the thought. Ever since I could remember, my parents had been the pride of my life. To me, their names meant dignity and glory. I loved them dearly and would never let them be humiliated.

At the same time, another voice spoke in my mind: 'You are Chairman Mao's revolutionary path-breaker. At any time, you must stand by the Party alone, not by your parents.' This was the voice of authority, not to be challenged, but it faced me with conflicts that were frustrating and mentally exhausting. Sometimes, I really wanted to cry out loud, but I did not do so. No matter how disturbed I became, there was no one I could confide in about my parents' political troubles, for fear that I would be tainted at school and disqualified from fighting for Chairman Mao. At home, I did not dare to be open with my parents because I did not want to hurt them. Besides, it was not usual in my family for parents and children to share their thoughts and feelings, and since the start of the Cultural Revolution my parents had had even less to say than before.

During this period, I became close to Mighty China, a pupil in the senior middle school. We first met when he inspected our work in the health centre as a member of the school revolutionary committee. As I recall, the day had started badly. The sky was grey, and my feeling was blue. When the slim figure of Mighty China appeared at the door, I felt a sudden brightness in the room. I recognize now that my initial impression was based mainly on his pleasant appearance. He dressed neatly. He was the only boy I knew at school with a clean collar and wristbands on his shirt, and his gentle manner contrasted with the rough and arrogant appearance favoured by the leading rebels. When I heard that he came from the special liberal arts class, I even envied him, because I knew that only star pupils in the all-Beijing entrance examination could join.

After the first meeting, Mighty China found regular pretexts to return, and I soon sensed his interest. Later, he told me that I was the first girl in his life who attracted him immediately. As we got to know each other better, our conversations became more personal. He told me that his parents too were veteran Communists, and had been working abroad for China's secret intelligence services. For years, he and his siblings had lived in various boarding institutions in Beijing, seeing their parents only on a few occasions when they returned from their work abroad.

When Mighty China told me that he had read my father's novel, I did not press for his opinion. Since the novel had offended Jiang Qing, my pride in my father's achievement had turned to anxiety about his political safety. But when Mighty China asked what was troubling me, I eventually told him. Tears came to my eyes, and that made him hug me and gently pat my back, which was the first time in all my fourteen years that any male except my father had touched me in such a comforting way. He helped me to brush tears from my face, and told me seriously: 'I worry too, about my parents' political situation when they're working abroad – whether they would betray our country if they were arrested. In our lives, there are so many things beyond our control. But what we must know is that if our parents were to do anything harmful to our Party and Chairman Mao, then we should make a clean break with them.' Although his advice was not new, the conversation came as a relief, for at least I had found a sympathetic ear. Before he went, Mighty China took my hands and asked: 'Would you like to be my little sister? I'd love to have a sister as clever and pretty as you are.' I jumped at his suggestion. He was three years older than me, and I felt more attached to him than to any of my brothers.

As we grew closer, we met more often at the health centre, usually late in the evening when most of our work was done. Mighty China was a good listener with an encouraging smile, always ready with advice about my problems. Sometimes we talked till midnight, when it was too late for me to walk home, so he would stay all night to keep me company, instead of returning to his dormitory on the campus. During my childhood, I was told that going out alone in the dark was not safe for a girl. At the start of the Cultural Revolution, we also believed that 'class enemies' would attack us. As the health centre had no bed or blankets available, we slept side by side on the bare concrete floor, with newspapers spread underneath us, and wearing as much as possible to keep warm. Sometimes, Ever-red or a few other pupils also joined us, and the floor was divided in two, one half for the girls, the other for the boys.

At the time, it was not uncommon for pupils to stay till morning. By order of the revolutionary committee, pupils operated a rota to guard the school in case of sabotage by the class enemy, so many worked the night shift. There were also enthusiasts whose rebellious activities kept them till after the buses stopped running. After a long busy day, exhausted pupils found a classroom or an empty office and slept in their clothes on the floor or on makeshift beds built using desks or chairs. Although boys and girls did not mind sharing rooms, I never heard that anything sexual occurred, and romantic feelings would have been hard to express in those crowded surroundings, with so many ears to hear. As well as that, the fever of the Cultural Revolution had such a grip on most pupils' emotions that the growth of our adolescent sexual feeling was largely suppressed or diverted. Yet even with hindsight I can never be sure what Mighty China felt, as he hugged or kissed me sometimes in the dark, when there was no one else around. They were brief and gentle gestures, especially pleasant in a sleepy mood.

One morning in late July 1966, my training was interrupted by a traffic accident outside the hospital, as my supervisors hurried to assist. The casualty was a student from a university in west Beijing. She was semi-conscious and her face was covered in blood. As soon as she came round, she urged her male companion: 'Hurry up! Please take the message from the Central Cultural Revolution Small Group to our university comrades! Don't bother about me!' Her attitude reminded me of the portrayals of revolutionary heroines in propaganda films and plays, but I did not believe she was play-acting. In those days, it was natural for the younger generation to mimic their revolutionary heroes. Later, I heard that the two students represented a group opposed to the work team in their university. Having just won support from Jiang Qing's radical aides, the two excited students were cycling fast to bring the news when the girl had her smash with a bus.

By then, more and more work teams faced strong opposition at the city's universities. As outsiders pitchforked into chaotic situations, many even became involved in factional infighting among students and staff. Guidelines were introduced by the Party Central Committee, headed by Liu Shaoqi, but these restrictions on rebellious activities only caused more clashes between work teams and rebels. In mid-July, Mao Zedong began to accuse the work teams of blocking the masses' participation in the Cultural Revolution. He blamed Liu Shaoqi, even though the decision to intervene had been approved by Mao himself. At the same time, Mao's radical disciples such as Jiang Qing and Kang Sheng stepped up their activities, speaking at mass rallies, or meetings of university students and staff, in support of actions taken against work teams. Soon, the teams lost control in many universities, and some were expelled.

Liu Shaoqi was baffled. Speaking at a conference in the Great Hall of the People on 29 July, he admitted: 'How to conduct the Cultural Revolution? You have no clear idea, nor do I. You have asked me what the revolution is like. I honestly don't know, and nor I think do many other comrades in the Party's Central Committee and the work teams.' It was true. The majority of Communist officials, including my parents, did not realize that Mao no longer trusted China's existing administration, and intended to destroy it. Liu Shaoqi, Chairman of the People's Republic, could no longer rely on Mao's support.

At the end of July 1966, Mao Zedong gave orders for all the teams working in educational institutions in Beijing to withdraw. Although the work team in our school was not unpopular, large slogans had sprouted all over the campus, demanding 'Work team, get out of our school!' and 'Down with the slaughter of revolutionary path-breakers!' After that, the rebel pupils took over the school.

One morning, Ever-red arrived in the health centre looking grim. 'What did you do last night with Mighty China?' she asked me, ignoring my greeting. Pupils close to us had grown suspicious about the relationship between Mighty China and me. Early that morning, one of them had turned up at dawn while Mighty China and I were sound

asleep on our own. He saw through the window that we were lying side
by side, fully clothed, with my head resting on Mighty China's outstretched forearm – more comfortable than a pile of books. Apparently
the boy had gathered some schoolmates to look, and photographed us
sleeping through the window.

Under Ever-red's interrogation, I described my friendship with
Mighty China, eager to respond to the growing seriousness on her face.
'I swear by Chairman Mao that I respect Mighty China like his younger
sister, and he cares for me like my elder brother.' 'Ridiculous!' Her harsh
voice made me shiver. 'We are Chairman Mao's revolutionary path-
breakers, and the only relationship among us should be comradeship.' I
learned that, because my bourgeois ideas had seduced me into an
'immoral' relationship with Mighty China, I was barred from the health
centre and my medical training would cease.

After that morning, I never saw Mighty China again as I tried my best
to avoid him in the campus. I heard later that he was expelled from the
revolutionary committee. For a while, the rebel leaders tried to hush up
our case to protect the reputation of the revolutionary path-breakers.
Later, when power struggles broke out among the leaders themselves,
opponents of his group accused Mighty China of 'shameful and indecent
conduct' with an unnamed girl. From then on, the story began to come
back to me, loaded with fictitious details, and the campus buzzed with
gossip about the mystery girl's identity.

In early August 1966, some members of the former revolutionary committee established the Red Guard organization in my school, and it
soon took control. The movement had been founded only a few weeks
before, by pupils from middle schools in Beijing. A big-character poster
written by a group of Red Guards from a middle school announced that
the old world must be smashed completely, and heaven and earth turned
upside down. These young fanatics believed that the more chaotic the
situation became, the greater the victory for the Cultural Revolution. On

I August, Mao Zedong wrote them a personal letter praising their spirit of rebellion and saying that it was right to rebel against reaction. The letter was immediately made public by big-character posters, displayed all over Beijing. Within a few days, Red Guard organizations were set up in every middle school by the pupils themselves, and later among university students.

The movement was founded and initially led by pupils from high official families. As most senior Communists did not establish their families until the later 1940s, many of their children were still in middle school when the Cultural Revolution started. Proud of their backgrounds, these rebellious teenagers claimed that their recruits must come from among the 'five red' classes – namely industrial worker, poor peasant, lower-middle peasant, revolutionary official and revolutionary soldier. They took up the famous saying that 'When the father is a hero, the son must be a true man', and added the corollary that 'When the father is a reactionary, the son must be a bastard.' Many saw themselves as members of a privileged group with a vanguard role. As they were born to the red, they claimed to be better qualified than anyone else to guard the red regime founded by their parents.

For several weeks, the 'theory of bloodline' caused endless debates in my school, and in many other schools and universities in Beijing, mainly between pupils from official families and their opponents. At the end of each rally, the platform was often occupied by fanatical Red Guards. They used 'son of a bitch' to describe any pupil whose family belonged to the 'five black' classes, namely landlord, rich farmer, reactionary, bad element and Bourgeois Rightist. Soon, two broad camps emerged in my school: the high and mighty Red Guards, and those with the misfortune to descend from the 'five black' classes.

Without applying, I was recruited as one of the earliest Red Guards in my school, simply because of my parents' positions. However, my suspect relationship with Mighty China, which was known to the leadership of the organization, kept me out of the inner circle. In the following days, my task was to guard our campus, working with other Red Guards in three shifts. Each of us was issued with a weapon, normally a heavy wooden club or a model rifle, used previously in physical training classes. All the school's property was now controlled by the rebel pupils, and was used to serve their purposes.

At first, I took my new post seriously, as we were warned that the hidden class enemies would try hard to sabotage the Cultural Revolution. But I soon got bored, especially on night duty, since nothing ever happened. The school was a Red Guard domain, where teaching was forgotten. When I popped into the library one day, I could not believe what I saw. Bookshelves had been overturned, books strewn around on the floor. Many windows were broken, or left open to the wind and rain. A lot of books and magazines were badly damaged, with covers or pages missing, and many more had been pilfered by students, but nobody dared to protest. Frustrated by this waste of time, I started to fall asleep on duty, or missed my night shift altogether, which annoyed my colleagues. When they complained, I promised to improve, but I failed to keep my promise.

On 17 August, a thrilling message reached us. Early next morning, Chairman Mao intended to review the Red Guards in Tian-an Men Square. That night, many of us stayed at school, as we planned to meet on campus around midnight before setting out for the rally. The prospect of meeting our great leader kept us awake all night long, and when someone started singing a Red Army song dedicated to Mao Zedong, many voices joined in the chorus:

> Looking up at the Plough in the sky,
> Cherishing Mao Zedong in my heart.
> The direction is clear when thinking of you in the darkness,
> If I lost my way, the thought of you lights the road . . .

At dawn we arrived in Tian-an Men Square, after walking for hours, and joined more than a million cheerful Red Guards, most of them middle school pupils or university students in Beijing. Many were dressed in the same style: untidy khaki combat gear and cap. Nearly everyone wore a crimson armband on their left upper arm, with 'Red Guard' inscribed in bright yellow. All carried the famous 'little red book', the *Quotations from Chairman Mao*, in their right hand. (In the single year of 1967, the bright red, plastic-bound booklet had a print-run of almost 200 million copies.) Under the red sky of dawn, every face around me beamed with excitement and joy, and the square resounded with revolutionary songs and cheers. A bright sun rose in the east, and the rostrum where Mao would appear looked unbelievably magnificent. Overwhelmed by these surroundings, and inspired by our historic mission as Chairman Mao's revolutionary path-breakers, I felt that my life was full of hope and pride.

Suddenly, the loudspeakers played the first familiar notes of 'The East is Red', the signal for Mao Zedong's arrival. Before the rally started, Mao appeared unexpectedly at the front of the square to meet the crowds. Dressed in a creased soldier's uniform with a military cap, he emerged from the grand vermilion gate of the rostrum. Beaming with pleasure, he shook outstretched hands and waved his cap. 'Long live Chairman Mao!' Shouting and cheers broke out, and little red books waved by a million hands formed a billowing ocean. In the frantic atmosphere, I followed the others, running madly towards the rostrum, shouting slogans and waving the little red book. Though I had not slept or eaten, my fatigue and hunger vanished, but no matter how hard I tried, I could not find a path to see Mao clearly — our group was placed too far from the rostrum. Around me, many sobbed with emotion as they constantly chanted Mao's name. Some did not realize that they were running or leaping into the air with bare feet, after losing their shoes in the commotion.

After the rally, which was heavily publicized, the nation started to notice changes among the Party leaders. Lin Biao made his first conspicuous public appearance standing next to Mao Zedong as the Party's vice-chairman. In contrast, Liu Shaoqi's precedence among the Party leaders was downgraded from second, next to Mao, to eighth.

Through the rally on 18 August 1966, Mao showed his public support for the Red Guard movement, enlisting militant youth in a leading political role, his personal task force. As he allowed a pupil girl to fix a Red Guard armband on his arm, Mao deplored her name, 'Bin-bin', because it meant 'refined and gentle'. 'Be forceful!' (Yao-wu-ma!) he told her. Later it was reported in the media that Bin-bin had changed her name to 'Yao-wu'. Soon other names such as 'Wen-ge' (Cultural Revolution), 'Hong-wei' (Red Guard) or 'Xiang-dong' (Towards Mao Zedong) also grew fashionable all over the country. Speaking at the rally, Lin Biao called on the whole nation to support the Red Guards for their revolutionary spirit and their achievement in 'smashing the Four Olds' (old ideas, old culture, old customs and old habits). The Red Guard movement quickly swept the country.

Even before the rally, Beijingers had been shocked by the Red Guard's violence and vandalism. From mid-August, thousands of fanatical Red Guards, most of them middle school pupils, took to the streets every day, attacking everything that they associated with the 'Four Olds'. Armed with scissors, they cut any permed or long hair that they saw – the revolutionary hair style had to be straight, and not below shoulder level. People who wore jeans or any other close-fitting trousers, bourgeois style, were stopped and had their trousers split up to the knees or sometimes the hips. By order of the Red Guards, many streets received new revolutionary names – 'East Is Red Avenue' instead of the famous 'Eternal Peace Avenue' in the city centre; and 'Anti-Imperialist Road' and 'Anti-Revisionist Road' in the former Legation Quarter. Many shops and companies had to give up their successful trademarks and adopt names like 'Workers-Peasant-Soldier' or 'Ever Red'. My school was renamed 'Anti-Japanese Military School', showing the Red Guards' admiration for the Chinese People's Anti-Japanese Military and Political University that my mother attended in wartime Yan'an.

At the same time, local residents were ordered to surrender the 'Four Olds' in their homes – antiques, books, paintings, jewels or clothes of 'bourgeois' type, such as women's high-heeled shoes – or else their homes would be raided. By then, it was normal for the Red Guards to ransack households considered as suspicious, in search of counter-revolutionary evidence.

Many historic sites were wrecked: former palaces, temples, pagodas and ancient tombs. Museums and galleries were raided. How many precious paintings and books were torn up or burnt to ashes, how many magnificent sculptures shattered? It is hard to know even today. Later, I heard how some priceless historical objects had survived. Just before the Red Guards arrived, the entrances to target buildings were blocked by their staff with huge revolutionary slogans and portraits of Mao Zedong. The vandals were foiled, since tearing down slogans and portraits of Mao Zedong was regarded as a counter-revolutionary offence. It was said that the Forbidden City owed its survival mainly to troops urgently dispatched by Premier Zhou Enlai.

Whatever happened, the Red Guard was untouchable, because these teenagers were backed by Chairman Mao, and he had said that destruction must precede construction. During the chaos Xie Fuzhi, the minister of public security and one of Mao's leading radical followers, also instructed the municipal police authority that they should cooperate with the Red Guards. Fortified by their virtual immunity, and drawing on Mao's famous saying that revolution should not be conducted in a gentle and cultivated manner, many of them believed that the more grossly they behaved, the greater their revolutionary prestige. When they spoke, they made sure to use swear words. Soon, their touchy and unpredictable temper was known as 'the rebel mood'.

In late August, I was part of a group sent by my organization to support a joint operation staged by Red Guards from several middle schools. Our objective was the famous South Cathedral, in the centre of Beijing, which is mentioned in many travel books about the city. Before the Cultural Revolution, I often passed it on my way to the China Book Store with my father. Through him, I knew that the cathedral was built by an Italian missionary at the beginning of the seventeenth century, one of the earliest Catholic institution in the whole country. I was impressed by its solid surrounding walls and the front gate built in the Chinese style, which helped to keep out the Boxer attacks in 1900. Under the Communist regime, the cathedral was approved as one of the few places of worship allowed to the small number of foreign diplomats in Beijing. When we arrived in the evening, the entire cathedral, including its huge compound, had fallen into the Red Guards' hands. With the support of the Central Cultural Revolution Small Group and the police authority, nearly all churches, temples and mosques in Beijing were invaded or occupied by the Red Guards, who regarded religion as spiritual opium against Marxism-Leninism and Mao Zedong Thought. By the end of August, the last remaining Western clergy in Beijing, some Catholic nuns who ran a primary school, had been deported.

Our job was to keep watch on the clergymen now held captive in their own bedrooms, located in a one-storey building in a corner of the compound, where they had to keep their lights on all night long. Through their uncurtained windows, it was easy to see what was going on inside. Several times, Red Guards would pass through the courtyard on their way to report on their searches. 'There are strange sounds coming from the cathedral hall! It must be enemy spies using a transmitter!' The news made everybody nervous, as if we were surrounded by lurking enemies – Western imperialist spies under their robes, which was the way we saw the clergy. We had been told that churches and cathedrals were centres for imperialist cultural infiltration and intelligence gathering. Half an hour later, a small team returned from a thorough search of the hall. 'False alarm,' they said. 'We found nothing.'

On my first ever visit to a church, I was curious to learn how threateningly the clergymen behaved, but all I saw was their closed faces and silent manner. Before midnight, some Red Guards invaded an old priest's room. 'Old fogey!' they sneered. 'Are you still trying to cheat people with your God?' No reply. Again and again, they asked the question, but the old priest sat still in his armchair. Through his open window, I saw his short white hair, closed eyes and peaceful face. Years later, I realized that he must have been praying. By command of the interrogators, a young priest in his early thirties was brought in later, and spoke to the old man. 'Please don't be stubborn,' he pleaded awkwardly. 'I don't believe in God any more. It's all a swindle.' Still no reply. Irritated by the old priest's silence, a boy interrogator picked up a porcelain statuette of Jesus Christ from his desk and threw it on the tiled floor, where it shattered. 'Look! I've smashed your God!' snarled the boy. The noise caused the old man to open his eyes. 'Father, forgive him!' he said, staring out into the night. His interrogators howled with laughter. 'Who believes in your God?' the boy retorted. 'I don't need forgiveness!' 'Do you really want to go to hell?' Those were the last words I heard the old priest speak.

When my duty ended at midnight, the interrogation was still going. I spent the rest of the night with scores of Red Guards in a large room behind the front gate, commandeered as a temporary dormitory. Lying on the tiled floor, dog-tired but fully clothed, I failed to sleep. I could not help thinking of the old priest's placid face, and his voice: 'Do you really want to go to hell?' Before dawn, a thunderstorm started, and I thought of my grandmother's saying that thunder was the angry voice of Heaven, a warning to sinners on earth. I never took notice before, but now I felt scared by the thunder. Perhaps I was not a fearless revolutionary path-breaker after all.

At dawn when the thunderstorm stopped, I left the cathedral, and never entered another Christian place of worship in China. I heard afterwards that during that stormy night, several older captives passed away. When I wondered if the old priest was among them, my feelings were always mixed with grief and guilt, as I had to take some of the blame.

A few days later, in a meeting at school, my attention was caught by a gold watch worn by another Red Guard. In those days, a watch was a luxury. Even the cheapest would cost a few months' wages. This one was an expensive Western brand, and it seemed familiar. When he saw my curiosity, the boy told me proudly: 'I got it from Baorhan.' On the previous day, a group of Red Guards from my school had raided the house where my best friend, Elifila, lived. Her father, Baorhan, was accused of spying for the Soviet Union, mainly because of his past Bolshevik connections. During the raid, most of her family's belongings were taken, including Baorhan's watch. In front of his family and staff, Baorhan was humiliated and brutalized. It was said that Baorhan's wife tried to commit suicide after the raid.

Until that meeting, none of this had reached me. Although we went to different middle schools, we still saw each other regularly. A few weeks before the raid, I had spent a weekend with my beloved friend Elifila and her family. When she told me in secret that her father had been criticized by the Party Central Committee for his handling of the ethnic problems in the Xinjiang Uygur Autonomous Region, I had made light of her worries. With little idea about the complicated ethnic issues and the implications of the intra-Party conflict, I supposed that he would be safe from harm, considering that his position was equivalent to a head of state. But now, all of a sudden, her father and whole family were in jeopardy, and nothing could protect them, not even the heavy security outside their house. Most unthinkably, the intruders came from the organization that I belonged to!

Faced with Baorhan's gold watch, I was speechless and my heart sank sharply. Enough was enough! I left the meeting to avoid hearing more details about the plight of Elifila and her family, and felt frustrated that I could not help them. For years afterwards, I wondered if I should investigate what happened to them, but never had the courage to try, for fear of learning more than I could bear. Through a former Ba-yi classmate, I heard how sad Elifila felt that I broke contact, as she still regarded me as her best friend.

After that weekend stay in the hectic summer of 1966, the only time

I saw Elifila again was in the early 1980s. By then, the Cultural Revolution was over and her father was back in office. One day, I visited the venue of the annual plenum of the Chinese People's Political Consultative Conference, where Baorhan worked as Vice-President. Inside the building I glimpsed Elifila and her father, surrounded by journalists, officials and celebrities. From a distance, Baorhan looked transformed, with hair completely white and an aged face. Elifila was a mature woman and caring daughter who supported her father as they walked. As soon as I recognized them, I took cover behind the crowd. After all that had happened, I did not know how to face them again. In 1989, when Baorhan's obituary appeared on the front page of the *People's Daily*, I was already in Britain. My first thought was to contact Elifila, but again I failed to do so. It was too difficult to express the complicated feelings which had accumulated in the years between.

Meanwhile, my parents were heartbroken by the Red Guards' whole behaviour, and especially by the damage inflicted on China's historical and cultural heritage in the name of 'smashing the Four Olds'. Obviously, my parents did not welcome the Cultural Revolution, and disliked the barbaric Red Guards from the start. In particular, it mortified my father to see me, his favourite child, joining their ranks, after years of sharing his interests. But there was little my parents could do. They knew that I was out of their control, given that these rebellious teenagers were supported by Mao himself. In view of their own political circumstances, on the other hand, they had to quell their anger in my presence, and avoid the risk of clashes, otherwise the story might leak through our private staff, and lay my parents open to the charge of banning their children from the Cultural Revolution. So the only thing they did was to muffle my crazy moods. Whatever I did at school, they declined their approval.

Unfortunately, I did not see where my parents stood, and felt disappointed by their cold reception. Like many young people in those days, my mind was set on being a revolutionary path-breaker for Chairman

Mao. When I first joined the Red Guards in early August, I took on an urgent assignment – locating khaki combat gear – as my family connection with the military was common knowledge. For Red Guards of the 'Anti-Japanese Military School', I was told, combat gear was particularly vital. I provided all the gear I had been given by my father, but it was not enough, so I went to his headquarters for help. At that time, it was not unusual for the Red Guards to be issued with military equipment, including vehicles with drivers, by members with military connections, who gained credit for their contribution to the Cultural Revolution. With my father absent on a mission, the administrative officer received my request and asked the security guards to lend me twenty of their outfits – thereby, he said, showing their support for the revolutionary path-breakers of Chairman Mao.

On the day he came home, my father was furious, and rang me at school to demand the return of all the clothing. 'How dare you interfere with our soldiers' welfare!' His angry condemnation scared me. 'You just wanted to show off your family background! You have abused my position!' But it was not easy to obey him. From the very beginning, the Red Guard was a loose organization with no fixed rules and plans. Most of the time, my companions were scattered all over Beijing on their different activities, so it was impossible to track down all the gear straight away. Nor did I get much sympathy for my predicament from the organization, because my father's response put him on a collision course with the prevailing power. Some of my fellows grumbled that my father was making a fuss over nothing, and should be supporting our revolutionary activities unconditionally, like everybody else.

The delay enraged my father all the more, so to keep out of trouble I avoided going home, and slept in my classroom for a while. My sweaty clothes smelled dreadful in the summer heat and humidity, as I had nothing to change into, and prickly heat soon made my skin itch unbearably. But the worst headache came from my father's daily reminders, either by phone or by sending our private staff to my school. Finally, he made a series of evening visits to the school, and talked to leading members of my organization. Under his pressure, the uniforms were eventually collected and returned.

After this incident, our relationship began to deteriorate. As if turning into a stranger, he seldom spoke or smiled, which only increased my resentment. It was Chairman Mao who inspired us, so how could I be at fault? But I could not find sympathy at home. Though my mother mostly stayed in her university, in our limited contacts I sensed that she shared my father's view. Eventually, even my grandmother started to criticize me. As a Red Guard, I had my hair cut short and straight, which upset her very much. She had always been proud of my long, thick, shining hair, and loved to comb it. 'Silly girl!' she snapped, at the sight of my revolutionary crop. 'You have no sense of what's good for you!' My reply was: 'Granny, this is the Cultural Revolution! You've got to give up your old ideas.' She shook her head, and said no more.

The adults in my family turned against me mainly because of my supposed involvement in the Red Guards' activities, but in fact I was not interested in 'smashing the Four Olds', and always felt sad when I witnessed or even heard tell about vandalism. As my father's daughter, I was deeply attached to China's historical and cultural heritage, and did not have the heart to do them damage. In addition, the leadership tended to exclude me from their plans, in the shadow of my relationship with Mighty China, so my role in the Red Guards' activities was confined to a few episodes such as that unforgettable night in the South Cathedral.

When I arrived at school one afternoon, I found the campus in a ferment, with a number of eye-catching posters plastered on the walls. 'Debts of blood must be paid in blood!', 'Punish the counter-revolutionary murderer mercilessly!' In a corner of the sports ground, pupils swarmed around a temporary prison known as the 'cowshed', used by the Red Guards for holding counter-revolutionary prisoners, the so-called monsters and demons. From a distance, I had heard noises coming from it – physical torture, verbal abuse, and the moans of victims – that made my hair stand on end. I had never been inside the 'cowshed', but occasionally saw the prisoners outside, among them Jiang Pei, the school Party secretary, and a number of my teachers including Yu Zhen. Usually they had huge abusive placards hung around their necks. One side of their heads was shaved, in the humiliating style called 'Yin-yang head', symbolizing their status as monsters and demons.

Through talk outside the 'cowshed', I heard that a few hours previously a fellow Red Guard had been attacked and injured. My organization had announced its intention of staging a public trial of the 'murderer' next morning in the city's largest football stadium, Beijing Workers' Stadium, and expected an audience of more than one hundred thousand. Thousands of leaflets were being distributed all over the city to invite revolutionary comrades, leaders of the Central Cultural Revolution Small Group and the Party's municipal committee to attend.

The 'murderer', a boy of eighteen, was a pupil from our school, whose home had been raided that morning by a group of Red Guards, also from our school. When they accused his mother, Madam Fang, vice-chancellor in a school for Communist cadres, of being a capitalist-roader, a row broke out, and quickly turned into a fight. The furious boy picked up a kitchen knife and stabbed one intruder in the shoulder – an act of resistance interpreted as sabotaging the Cultural Revolution. By demand of the intruders, the boy was arrested by the police. Accused of colluding in the crime, Madam Fang was brought to our school, and had been suffering torture in the 'cowshed' ever since. Later that afternoon, she was rushed to hospital, her swollen face bruised and her torn clothes sodden with water and blood. It was said that her interrogators had lashed her continually with their belts, drenching her body in cold water each time she blacked out, till she failed to come round.

When Madam Fang had gone, the interrogators started to torture other prisoners, mad with rage, and spoiling to avenge their injured comrade. Soon, two more unconscious prisoners were rushed to hospital separately on flatbed tricycles pedalled by pupils. Both had their heads and bodies covered by sheets, with only their bruised arms and bare feet protruding. I recognized one as Jiang Pei by the sound of his moaning, and the other as Yu Zhen by his handless right arm. Later, I heard that all three had died that very day.

That night, leading members of my organization received an urgent invitation to meet Premier Zhou Enlai, who was alarmed about the growing violence in the Red Guard movement. Since the rally in Tian-an Men Square on 18 August, main streets in Beijing had been covered with frightening slogans such as 'Long Live the Red Terror!', and a plague of vandalism, house raids, interrogations, tortures and imprisonments had broken out. Nearly all the Party's municipal organs had been paralysed, their offices taken over by Red Guards, and their leaders denounced. Premier Zhou was left almost alone to lead a small team dealing with the turmoil. During the Cultural Revolution, Mao left Zhou unscathed because he needed his loyalty and obedience, and his ability to keep things ticking over. Premier Zhou was required to guarantee basic supplies for people's lives, and to safeguard the country's damaged economy. He also frequently had to counter the spreading violence, like a fire brigade chief in a drought. News of the brutality committed at our school soon became the talk of Beijing, and Premier Zhou realized that a public trial would further inflame the Red Guards' mood, and that savagery and chaos risked running out of control.

At midnight Premier Zhou received the Red Guard leaders of my school. During that period, it was not unusual for him to work around the clock, but despite his tiredness I heard later that he was extremely patient in his efforts to prevent the scheduled trial. For a world-famous negotiator, it must have been a strange experience to have to persuade these stubborn and excitable teenagers to change their minds. For hours, he listened intently, easing the atmosphere by making occasional jokes and praising their revolutionary spirit. He made no criticism of the decision to hold a public trial, but promised that he fully supported the rebels, and would instruct the police authority to deal seriously with the case. When his suggestion was eventually accepted, he looked very relieved.

A few days later, my father showed me the text of a recent speech by Premier Zhou about the political situation, in which he mentioned the trouble the projected trial had caused him. At my father's request, I explained the whole story. 'Madam Fang is a respectable Communist!' My father was deeply grieved by her death. 'I used to know her once.' In the 1950s, he had dealt with her divorce case (her husband was a senior officer of the Beijing Military Region) on the Party's behalf. He recalled Madam Fang as a capable and independent woman. Like my mother, she had joined the Party very young, and became one of the few women in all China to hold senior positions under the Communist regime. After her divorce, she had brought up her children on her own. 'Why did you beat her to death?' my father kept asking, beside himself with anger, though I had explained that I was not involved in her death.

At the same time, my parents also blamed me for the tragic deaths of Jiang Pei and Yu Zhen, although I explained my innocence. 'How did you have the heart to kill your own school leader and teacher?' my father glared. 'Red Guards, indeed! Criminals, that's what you are!' To them, I could not possibly be justified, because I belonged to the organization that committed the murders.

In fact, I was already shocked by the promotion of violence as a political weapon. The last few weeks had been a nightmare for me. After that bloody afternoon, I felt sick for days, and the Red Guard armband reminded me of those bleeding, senseless bodies. It was my first sight of death, and I was terrified by the brutality that took three lives in a single afternoon on my campus. 'What is the Cultural

Revolution for?' I started to ask myself. But except for political propaganda, no answer came. I began to think more about my parents' advice, and was getting less enthusiastic about the Red Guard's activities.

On 1 September 1966, I left Beijing for south China together with sixteen other Red Guards from my school, launching a national scheme known as 'big links' (da-chuan-lian), when groups of Red Guards travelled the country to exchange rebellious experience. The scheme was backed by Mao, who intended to use the Red Guards to overthrow provincial authorities he no longer trusted. With Mao's approval, all participants were entitled to free transport, accommodation and food while travelling. Our school dispatched the earliest groups. Before setting out, we made careful preparations, with leaders appointed and rules and regulations defined. We were told that our mission was to foster revolution throughout China, just as the Red Army had done during the Long March. With the provincial people, we must mind our behaviour and protect our revolutionary reputation. Later, I discovered that our preparation had been very unusual: most participants in the project had enjoyed much more freedom of action.

Our first destination was Changsha, the provincial capital of Hunan, where Mao Zedong came from. It was like a pilgrimage to visit places connected to Mao's earlier revolutionary career. I remember our excitement looking across at Orange Island, in the middle of the Xiang River. Spontaneously, we broke into one of Mao's famous poems: 'Alone I stand in the autumn cold/ On the tip of Orange Island,/ The Xiang River flowing northward;/ I see a thousand hills flushed crimson . . .'

Compared with the chaos of Beijing, Changsha seemed peaceful. Its rebels had only just organized themselves, and had not yet seized power from the provincial authority. Only a handful of Beijing Red Guards had yet arrived, so their influence was still limited. Regarded as envoys of Mao, we were welcomed by local rebels eager to receive our support and revolutionary experience. Local officials also gave us a generous welcome, and endorsed all our activities, in the hope of a quiet life. They contributed all services free of charge, such as printing and distributing leaflets to the public to announce our arrival and advertise our mission. On our visit to Mao's home village, Shaoshan, a few hours' drive from Changsha, a comfortable coach was provided. An official reception greeted us at the entrance to the village, with a huge crowd, red flags, a clamour of gongs and drums, and revolutionary music broadcast by loudspeakers. At lunchtime, we were invited to a feast in the sumptuous village hotel, specially built for entertaining Mao and the Party's high officials.

By the time we left Changsha in mid-September, millions of free-travelling Red Guards had flooded the country to 'exchange revolutionary experiences'. Rebellious organizations sprang up all over the provinces, based mainly on university students and industrial workers, and attacked local authorities. On our subsequent trips to Guangzhou and Shanghai, there was no more VIP treatment. Like everyone else we were put into student accommodation, and ate in university canteens. But I did not mind the change. From the beginning, I was pleased to escape from my painful situation in Beijing, and enjoyed my first ever trip to the south of China. Delighted by the beautiful natural scenery and historic sites, I showed more interest in sightseeing than in kindling revolution. Instead of frantically struggling against class enemies and capitalist-roaders, I spent more time chatting with new acquaintances drawn to my cheerful nature, sociable manner and good upbringing. By now, I no longer felt guilty for lacking revolutionary consciousness and enthusiasm, as I began to appreciate the goodness in the world.

On 18 September, the day after we arrived in Shanghai, the members of my group called an evening meeting whose main purpose was to denounce me for 'being imbued with bourgeois ideas'. Until that moment, I had not realized that in less than twenty days' travelling, I had made so many enemies. At the meeting, I was attacked for expressing interests in feudal and bourgeois culture, for instance by praising Ulanova, the greatest of Soviet ballerinas, while conversing with a passenger on the train. In the early 1950s, Ulanova visited Beijing during the brief honeymoon period with China, and gave a performance in the Zhongnanhai complex, where the residences of Mao Zedong and other Party leaders were located. My father saw her dance, and in the following years he often told me how enthralled he had been by her wonderful performance. In my group, only a few had ever heard of Ulanova, and that counted as additional evidence against me. My forwardness in contacting male Red Guards or passengers suggested to some of my companions that I was going to repeat the mistake they had heard about with Mighty China.

At first I was stunned – I had never been denounced before – but I instantly denied these charges. In particular, I explained that there was no 'immoral relationship' with Mighty China. But no one paid attention, and instead I faced more accusations, aimed at my morals and behaviour. When the meeting turned into a bitter quarrel between my fellows and me, I left them furiously. For hours, I wandered in the strange dark streets nearby, and wept at my unjust treatment, but my misery left all of them unmoved. At last, they decided that I was unfit to share their revolutionary mission, and refused my request to travel on my own, or to join other groups I had made friends with on the journey.

Next day, I was put onto the first train back to Beijing, escorted by two fellow Red Guards whose assignment was to prevent my escaping on the way or committing more 'mistakes'. Nearly a whole day's journey spent under close surveillance was an absolutely humiliating experience, since it resembled the treatment applied to class enemies. In protest, I refused to talk or eat. When we reached Beijing at dawn, I left the two escorts without a word, and went straight home. From then on, I decided to quit the Red Guard altogether.

Chapter 15

'Baba, Mama, Please Hold On!':
My Parents Become Political Prisoners

(September 1966–1968)

When I came home again in September 1966, millions of Red Guards from all over China were 'guests of Chairman Mao' in the capital. As the 'big links' scheme expanded, most of the country's railway system was dedicated to these youngsters' missions. Beijing's main railway station swarmed all the time with hundreds of thousands of free travellers. On every platform dense crowds fought their way in or out of the bursting carriages through doors and windows. All trains were unbelievably overloaded, some holding more than double their capacity, with even the lavatories, luggage racks, and spaces between or under the seats filled by passengers.

On 13 September 1966, my father noted: 'I was assigned to head a team to look after Red Guards from the provinces. The order from on top was: "This is a serious political assignment that needs handling without any slip-ups."' To deal with millions of provincial Red Guards in the capital, a special office was established, under Premier Zhou Enlai. Military forces were mobilized to help because Party and government

offices were almost paralysed, and they also took care of delivering the
Red Guards to attend rallies and parades in front of Mao. In the three
months following the first rally in Tian-an Men Square in August, Mao
Zedong reviewed the Red Guards seven more times, as more than 11
million young pilgrims came from all over China.

The constant massive influx of young travellers put my father under
enormous pressure. His diary for 27 September 1966 records the arrival
of more than 3,000 Red Guards from Shanghai, and on 8 November:
'More than 5,000 Red Guards arrived today [from the provinces].' A
week later: 'Attended a meeting convened by Premier Zhou, who urged
us to accept greater numbers of provincial Red Guards . . .'

On arrival, these Red Guards were billeted in temporary hostels in
and around the city, usually in schools or universities, at a time when
most students, pupils and even many staff were on free trips all over
China. In general, conditions were very basic: three meals a day, and a
single blanket for bedding. The dormitories were converted classrooms,
offices and assembly halls, always overcrowded, often with only
makeshift wooden platforms or straw-covered cement floors to sleep on.
Yet despite the discomforts, nothing could dull the excitement of young
people dazzled by their first ever chance to see Beijing. While waiting for
Mao's inspection, they explored the city with their free access to buses,
as well as to places of entertainment. I still recall the scenes in that turbulent era, the city teeming in every street and lane with the cheerful
youth of China's first Red generation, speaking with every possible
accent. On 12 November 1966, my father recorded: 'Jing left her university at three o'clock but did not get home till half-past eight at night.
She was stuck in the bus station for three hours as the buses were full of
provincial Red Guards.'

Each time Mao held a review, my father and his colleagues were kept
busy all night, since the notice they received could be less than twenty-
four hours. Mao never worked to a well-planned schedule, and did
everything, even when reviewing millions of Red Guards, on the spur of

the moment. November was particularly strenuous, because three of Mao's reviews took place that month. My father's diary for the 11th reads: 'Got up at three in the morning to organize the Red Guards to attend today's review . . . At half-past two in the afternoon, Chairman Mao arrived . . . The review was over by four o'clock.' On 25 November, immediately after another review of over a million Red Guards, the diary records: 'Working overnight to organize Chairman Mao's review for tomorrow.'

During this complex task, my father still faced his own political problems. Until late 1966, the Party did not allow the military to participate in 'Si-da' – airing views fully, staging debates and writing big-character posters, such major activities during the Cultural Revolution. The strategic threat from enemies such as the USA and the Soviet Union made it essential to keep the armed forces secure. But Jiang Qing and her allies disagreed. On several occasions, they asked: 'Why don't the forces denounce their own capitalist-roaders?' Jiang Qing was backed by Lin Biao, who saw his chance to get rid of political rivals inside the military. On 3 November 1966, my father noted: 'Si-da starts in the armed forces in December, when I will face three possibilities: (1) harassed again until I am dismissed from office and expelled from the Party; (2) outcome inconclusive; (3) the whole truth to come out.'

Another worry was the safety of his private collection of books and paintings, since most of them already counted as 'Four Olds'. Fortunately, our house was located in the same compound as my father's headquarters, so any intruding Red Guards were intercepted at the gate. But this protection had its limits. My father's diary for 28 August 1966 reads: 'Five Red Guards from Beijing Forestry University called to deliver their orders . . . Jing is to do compulsory labour, supervised by the revolutionary masses. By half-past seven tomorrow morning, she must report to their organization. I met them at the gate and signed for the order on Jing's behalf. They then asked: "Have you got any antiques at home? We need to check up." I stopped them: "It's all in order under military regulations." ... [Afterwards] I hastened to hide our important letters and the drafts of my novels ...'

Late in October 1966, my family moved to the western suburbs of Beijing, by the beautiful Western Hill, following the move of the entire headquarters of the Beijing Military Region. For my parents, this meant exposing their hidden collection to prying eyes. To prevent this, for months in advance they spent most of their spare time packing their books and paintings into small parcels that needed more than ten kilos of string and a huge amount of brown paper. After the move they chose the most valuable items – rare books and priceless paintings – and transferred them by stealth to the attic, which was the only safe place available. The semi-detached house that we lived in shared a common attic with our neighbour, so before shifting anything my parents sent their children to scavenge building materials. At night, my mother mixed concrete in the bathroom and then passed it into the attic, where my father built a brick dividing wall. All this was done in secret. Even we children did not know what was going on. I only remember my father's pale face during that time, and frequent medication because his health was further damaged by deep anxiety and a heavy workload.

On 15 October 1966, when inspecting troops in Zhang Jiakou, north-west of Beijing, my father collapsed and was rushed to hospital, suffering from pneumonia. Later, he recorded that day in his diary: 'It seemed that I was at my last gasp. Asked Little Dong [his bodyguard] to read Chairman Mao's quotation about revolutionary heroism for me by my sickbed. As I listened, my eyes were brimming with tears. I thought that I must grit my teeth to overcome the illness as I have so much to do in my life ...'

In early 1967, my father heard that his best friend, A-ying, had run into political trouble cooked up mainly by Jiang Qing, because of what he knew about her scandalous career in Shanghai in the early 1930s. A-ying's priceless collection of books, paintings and antiquities was well known in Beijing. Chen Boda, head of the Central Cultural Revolution Small Group, had it loaded into several lorries and delivered to his own residence, which reminded my father that he himself had more to contend with than the vandalism of the Red Guards. Only a year before, he had promised that if China went to war he would help in transferring A-ying's collection to a safe place. Now, even his own collection was at risk.

Since June 1966, my two elder brothers had been engaged in the Cultural Revolution at their school or university. My two younger siblings, Feng-yuan and Aijun, were sent home, considered too young as primary school pupils to take part in rebellious activities. After I joined them, I found that we had nothing to do all day. All our favourite literature and entertainments were banned, and I could not touch my parents' collection. Sick of hysterical propaganda, and bored stiff with idleness, I missed the lifestyle which had been wrecked two months before. The breakdown in schooling baffled my grandmother. 'What can you do in the future if you don't study now?' she lamented.

After I returned home, my father kept on treating me as a stranger, still angry about my involvement in the Red Guards' mischief. I resented this treatment, and started to say so, which sometimes earned me a beating. One day, I screamed: 'You're not supposed to beat me! Chairman Mao said stop resorting to violence.' As the Cultural Revolution took on a momentum of its own, the rebels began to splinter into factions that all claimed allegiance to Mao, but squabbled for power among themselves, while individuals shifted between groups in a bid for personal gain. Mao himself deplored this confusion, as it damaged his campaign to remove his political rivals. Reacting to the rebels' power struggles, he ordered them to 'resort to verbal struggle instead of violence'.

After I quoted Mao in self-defence, my parents took me seriously, and asked me to understand them. It was the first I heard about the political struggles in the armoured forces headquarters and my mother's university. By now, I was not entirely surprised by my parents' problems, but nothing could dent my faith that they were true Communists. What disconcerted me was that the source of their troubles was colleagues, many of whom I had addressed as 'uncle' or 'auntie'. Almost all my father's opponents were our neighbours. Their children were my former schoolmates. What made them pick on my parents, their comrades and colleagues? I could not understand. All I knew was that from now on I had to keep my distance both from them and from their families.

On the morning of 23 January 1967, our house was quiet as usual. My younger siblings were out with friends and my parents were at work. I was chatting with my grandmother when we heard sounds of heavy footsteps and two soldiers opened the living-room door. Ignoring my questions, they took away our telephone and left. Before I could investigate, Aijun came home, ashen-faced. 'Baba has been put up to face a denunciation rally outside his headquarters' office!' she said, gasping for breath.

The previous month, my father had started a new assignment at Beijing University, in charge of several hundred soldiers keeping order. Increasingly, the tensions among the rebel organizations, many of them from universities, were leading to violence and social unrest. Every day, the main streets of Beijing displayed more slogans and big-character posters publicising massacres or murders nationwide. To exercise control, Mao had to lean more often on the military, and my father's assignment to the university was a test case. Unfortunately, it did not work out. It was Mao himself who had encouraged the rebels to destroy the Party machine and the national administration: the chaos was his. Empowered by him and by his radical followers, they were fearless.

When I heard Aijun's news, I ran straight to the office block, which was several hundred metres away. From a distance, I saw the huge car park in front of it thronged with people, and heard a loudspeaker voice conducting them in slogans such as 'Down with the counter-revolutionary Mu Xiang!' Armed guards stopped me at the entrance, and would not hear my pleas to see my father. Soon after I got home, a squad of rebels burst into our house uninvited. I recognized a number of junior officers and soldiers from my father's headquarters, but now they showed none of the kindness and politeness I was used to. 'We're here to seal up your father's black lair!' said one. 'I don't understand what you mean.' I stood in their way on the staircase. 'There's no black lair in our house.' They did not bother to argue, but rushed upstairs with strips of gummed paper that they stuck over the doorframes to my parents' study, private library and bedroom, sealing them shut. I kept protesting until my grandmother stopped me. If I annoyed these intruders, she feared for my safety. 'Please come down with me,' she called when she tottered upstairs. 'Don't say another word.'

In January 1967, the tide of rebel power was rising all over China, as Party organizations and leaderships from provincial down to grass-roots level were replaced by the newly established revolutionary committees, made up of leading rebel figures and representative 'revolutionary cadres'. As this developed, the stability inside the armed forces began to crumble. In the Beijing Military Region, a number of rebel organizations sprang up within days, many with belligerent revolutionary names such as 'The East Is Red Contingent' or 'The Proletarian Revolutionary Rebels'. One organization was called 'Millions Strong Mighty Army', even though it had a total membership of one. Backed by Jiang Qing and Lin Biao, rebels arrested their Military Region's commander, the three-star General Yang Yong, who had commanded the Chinese People's Volunteers during the Korean War in the early 1950s. The Political Commissar, Lieutenant-General Liao Hansheng, also became their prisoner. This further weakened my father, because Yang Yong and Liao Hansheng were known as his supporters.

In 1967, 'Si-da' was launched in the headquarters of the armoured forces, which violated instructions issued by the Military Commission of the Party's Central Committee. In order to maintain the stability of the armed forces during the Cultural Revolution, it had been made clear that troops at army level [equivalent to my father's HQ] or below were not to practise 'Si-da'. But major leaders of the Party committee of the armoured

forces failed to obey this order. Without approval ... they launched
'Si-da' at their headquarters ...

Excerpt from Document No. 935 (1978) of
the Armoured Forces Party Committee
in the Beijing Military Region

In the early morning of 23 January 1967, my father received a telephone call from Tang, the Political Commissar and leader of the Party
committee of the armoured forces. 'The revolutionary masses have organized in our headquarters,' said Tang. 'They want you brought back for
denunciation.' To prevent more public chaos, my father returned from
Beijing University of his own accord. He knew that it was impossible to
escape, since there was no safety anywhere in the country, and even if there
had been, he did not want to leave his family and his collections behind.
When he left his office on the university campus, he saw that an officer,
one of Tang's followers, was talking in secret to his chauffeur and bodyguard. From that moment on, he knew that he was already a prisoner.

About a hundred metres from the front gate of the compound, armed
guards stopped his car and ordered him out. A massive crowd had gathered in front of the office block, many holding portraits of Chairman
Mao or waving red flags. They came rushing to the gate, shouting slogans against my father. Soon they had him surrounded, and were tearing
off the two red fabric tabs from his collar, implying that a suspected
counter-revolutionary was not qualified to be a member of the People's
Liberation Army. They threw his warm fur cap, specially made for army
generals, to the ground, and replaced it with a conical white paper cap,
about a metre high, with a slogan proclaiming: 'Down with the counter-
revolutionary Mu Xiang!' Wearing the abusive 'high cap', he was taken
straight to a pre-arranged rally for denunciation. From that day, he
became a prisoner in his own headquarters – the only one.

During that afternoon, I went out again and again to look for my
father. When I finally saw him it was almost evening, and he was

undergoing his last public humiliation of the day. Surrounded by taunt-ing rebels, he was staggering along, with his hands held clamped behind his body by two strong men, after being compelled to walk for hours between the two headquarters of the Beijing Military Region and the armoured forces. The more he stumbled the more his 'high cap' wobbled: he looked exhausted. 'Go home, please!' he said when saw me. 'Look after your grandmother and younger siblings! Look after our home!' Oh, what I saw in his eyes! The anger, pain and confusion, and the physical and emotional suffering! I would never forget that moment. In his eyes, I also recognized his trust and expectation, which made me feel that I had grown up. Tears ran down my face, but before I could speak they had hustled him off to the cell they had prepared for him. Gazing at his receding figure, I shouted: 'Baba, please hold on!' At that moment, this was all the support I had to offer.

Later, I took Aijun to the local bus-stop to wait for my mother coming home. The moment she saw us, she knew. Later, I heard that my parents had already foreseen this day. A month before, they had found the orderly newly assigned to our family trying several times to sneak into their study and private library, recently put out of bounds. Detecting his intentions, they decided that it was time to discharge all our family's private staff, including the chef. After that, I started to learn cooking from my grandmother.

After New Year 1967, my grandmother had been sent to stay with Little Auntie, my father's only sibling in Beijing. As mid-ranking officials in the Municipal Security Bureau, she and her husband would not be denounced as 'capitalist-roaders', so their home should be safe if any-thing happened to my family. Grandmother's unusual visit soon raised suspicions among Little Auntie's neighbours. One day, her children's nanny asked her: 'Is it true that your eldest son and his wife are in polit-ical trouble?' Grandmother went straight back home. 'I don't want to be a refugee,' she told my father. 'How could I be away when you and your wife are in trouble?'

On the weekend before my father's arrest, Madam Tang seemed particularly active in visiting officers' families in the compound. Discerning her purpose, my parents did not have the heart to let us know what was coming for my father. Now when she met us, my mother said: 'You know that many of your schoolmates' fathers have already been arrested. This is common during political campaigns.' At home, my grandmother wept. 'How could my son be charged with opposing Chairman Mao?' she asked my mother. 'He has devoted himself to the revolution since he was fifteen! Seeing how he is treated today, who wants to join the Communists in future?'

On the evening after my father's arrest, my mother managed to visit him briefly thanks to a sympathetic guard, and he warned her to move their personal papers somewhere safe, especially his diary of several decades and drafts of several novels. Around two o'clock at night, when everyone was sleeping, she crept upstairs in her bare feet. She did not turn a light on, in case of watchers. The problem was to enter their rooms without damaging the strips of paper used to seal the doors. Under the moonlight, she spent a long time soaking them bit by bit before peeling them off. When she finally got in, she found that most of the relevant files had been removed, including his diary, but she had no time to worry, as the raiders could return at any time. Sitting on the stairs, she used the warmth of her hands to dry the paper strips, before smoothing them carefully back.

When I woke up before dawn, I found my mother sitting in the dark in front of the kitchen boiler, with her face lit up by the flames. She looked exhausted. 'These are your father's letters to me during the war, which I've kept ever since.' She pointed to a thick pile of paper, carefully tied, before feeding it into the fire. 'This is the fruit of your father's painstaking work, about half a million words.' She showed me the only draft novel of my father's that the intruders had not found. 'But I can't let it reach the rebels' hands, or it would make more trouble for your father.' She watched the draft turn to ashes, tears shining on her face.

At daybreak, my mother had to catch the first bus so as to arrive in time for compulsory labour, on pain of punishment. When the rebels in her university learned of my father's arrest, my mother was not allowed home except at weekends.

At the end of January, Feng-an returned home. During clashes among Red Guard factions at Ba-yi School, he and some others were attacked, and he was badly beaten up. He was too kind and gentle to love feuding, and I was delighted when he decided to quit these school activities, because now we could look after the family together in this emergency.

After my father's arrest, rebels raided several high-ranking officers' houses, but ours suffered most, as searches came almost every day. The main target was our upstairs rooms, the so-called black lairs, as the collection was too extensive to be shifted straight away. During their visits, the family was forced to remain downstairs. Before they left, they carefully sealed the doors all over again. Listening to the noises up above, I felt as if sharp knives were cutting my heart. So many 'Four Olds' had been destroyed by the Cultural Revolution, and I feared for the precious books and paintings. 'The collection is Baba's life,' I said to my grandmother, 'and now it's all going to be destroyed.' But though I longed to get rid of the intruders, I was helpless to affect them: they could do as they pleased. Time after time I scurried upstairs in a rage, desperate to stop them doing damage. 'You're not supposed to smoke in my parents' study and private library! Please be careful when you touch the books and paintings! They are a cultural heritage of our country.'

In between raids, I visited my father every day. His cell was a small dark room in a corner of the compound, completely sunless, because the only window was boarded over from outside. Inside the cell, the walls were papered from floor to ceiling with slogans against him, written in huge characters. During the day, he was out for most of the time, paraded for denunciations and public humiliations, even once when he was ill with a high temperature. In the evenings, he was forced to clean toilets or wash floors in the barracks kitchen and canteen of the headquarters' accommodation block. Issued with no equipment, he had to kneel down and wipe the dirty floors with a wet rag. It was a difficult job for a man who had suffered from pain in his knee-joints for years, and soon he was panting for breath and streaming with sweat. Despite the rebels' warnings and threats, I pitched in to help out with his work, so that he could finish early and rest.

With the rebels always around during my visits, my father and I had hardly any chance to talk in private, but I managed to smuggle letters between him and my mother, who was forbidden to visit. One day, he passed me a letter appealing for help to the Party Committee of the Beijing Military Region. When we delivered it to the regional head-quarters, Feng-an and I were met by the adjutant to Lieutenant-General Zheng Weishan, who was on my father's side. Since the arrest of General Yang Yong, Zheng had been acting commander of the Military Region. When he passed me Zheng's supporting message to my father, the adju-tant apologized that his chief had urgent business and could not meet us. Later, I learned that during that period, Zheng Weishan was also under attack by rebels at his headquarters, so that his hands were tied.

From the day of my father's arrest, countless big-character posters and slogans invaded his headquarters' compound, smearing him with fabricated accusations trumped up by Tang and his people. Through the big-character posters, his personal diary was made public, in versions fantastically distorted as counter-revolutionary evidence against him. Since neither of my parents was allowed to see the big-character posters, my siblings and I started collecting information for them, which enabled my father to write in self-defence. When the rebels refused to provide him with large sheets of paper, my father had to write 'small-character' posters on A4-sized paper that Feng-an and I smuggled in. When he was forbidden to put them up, we did it for him.

My father's writings always drew crowds as soon as they appeared, and were copied into many readers' notebooks. Under their influence, more and more people began to suspect the truthfulness of his accusers. I also sensed a general enjoyment of my father's well-written articles, which were so unlike his opponents' clumsy lies. Despite the gloomy political climate, bursts of laughter greeted his sarcastic demolition of the bogus case against him.

One morning when I was busy jotting down information from the big-character posters near the office block, a rude voice barked: 'Tell your counter-revolutionary father to stop writing polemics against me! I am an uneducated person from a poor peasant family! Unlike him, a proper son of the landlord capitalist class, always spreading poisonous ideas in his writing!' The grumbler was Senior Colonel Mercy Ocean, Deputy Director of the armoured forces Political Department previously overseen by my father. I came across him first on a winter evening several years before, when he sent my father a whole lot of delicious oranges from his home county in south China. At the time I felt grateful, because fresh oranges were rare in Beijing. But now, that thoughtful uncle Mercy Ocean had emerged as one of Tang's major allies. His favourite lie was that my father came from a rich landlord family.

At first I was stunned by Mercy Ocean's bullying. I never dreamed that a senior officer like him could publicly humiliate a teenage girl to express his resentment of her father. My upbringing made it hard to talk back to an adult, as it was seen as rudeness in a child. Soon, a crowd was gathering round us, attracted by his shouting. While I stood shocked and silent, his voice grew louder and his words more uncontrolled. As if pushed to the edge of a cliff, suddenly I had no choice left except to fight. 'My father is not a counter-revolutionary!' My body was trembling while I shouted. 'Why are you persecuting my father?' Mercy Ocean's words ran out. He was as startled as the crowd, which only stared when I walked off, trying hard to quell my tears. I desperately wanted to cry, and to shout with rage against the humiliation and injustice that my family and I had suffered, but I did not want my father's enemy to see my tears.

On the following day, my father wrote a special 'small-character' poster protesting against Mercy Ocean's behaviour. 'How could you bully my teenage daughter . . .?', he wrote. 'Do you have any self-respect left to stand up again in front of the others? You don't measure up to my girl!' The poster created a sensation. Years later, I met some of my father's former staff who could still quote sentences from it. This incident also made me known at headquarters as a fighter for my father. Shortly afterwards, on my way home from visiting my father, I heard a quiet voice call in the dark. It came from my father's assistant, who had been waiting by the road with his letter to my father. In it, he provided some information and praised me as an 'unusually brave girl'.

The Chinese New Year of 1967 produced no festive mood in my family. My father was still in jail, and my mother had to perform her compulsory labour even on New Year's day. On that day, my grandmother and I were woken up before dawn by noises in front of our house. We found two lines of a couplet abusing my father pasted up on either side of our front door. Each character of my father's name was written upside-down in black ink with a red cross over it – a style used in the old days to announce the sentence of death on a prisoner, but now adopted by the rebels to humiliate their victims. Although unable to read the couplet, it horrified my grandmother to see the stark black characters on white paper – a style denoting misfortune and disaster. In China, New Year's day is a special occasion when only good wishes must appear, because the day's events predict the coming year, and all messages must be written on red paper, the lucky colour. 'Oh no!' The blood drained from Grandmother's face. 'This is to curse us!'

Before we finished breakfast, we heard over the loudspeaker outside that a rally had started to denounce my father. In order to support him, I tried to attend the occasions when he was denounced, so Aijun and I rushed straight to the venue, the headquarters' huge assembly hall. From the entrance, I saw my father standing on the platform, wearing the 'high cap' on his head. Round his neck hung an outsize cardboard model of his novel, *Autumn in Jinyang*, with a red cross above the title, displaying the 'poisonous weed' he had produced. His arms were twisted behind him by two young men who kept wrenching them upwards and forcing his head down towards the floor. During the Cultural Revolution, the resulting posture was known as the 'jet-plane position', and was often inflicted on victims at denunciation rallies. Among the many physical punishments my father suffered, this was his most dreaded experience, as the strain on his back and arms quickly became intolerable. From a distance, I saw how he struggled to keep his balance, and shook uncontrollably. Suddenly, another young man appeared on the platform and started beating and kicking him. As if driven by irresistible power, I ran towards the platform, blanking out everything else, but halfway down the aisle I was stopped when an organizer jumped down from the platform, grabbed hold of me, and hustled me and Aijun out of the hall. He locked the door behind us, and though I banged on the door and sobbed 'Stop beating my father! Let me in!', no one replied. From then on, I was banned from attending the rallies.

Meanwhile, many military headquarters were taken over by rebels inside or outside the armed forces, who removed confidential documents and looted weapons. Many senior officers also became targets, and one of the victims was Marshal He Long, my father's commander during the civil war. It was said that Lin Biao had disliked him ever since the Sino-Japanese War, and that their wives, who had both studied at the Women's University in Yan'an with my mother, did not get on. By order of Jiang Qing, now allied with Lin Biao, the marshal's residence was raided. Though Premier Zhou Enlai tried to shield them, He Long and his wife were later arrested by troops under Lin Biao's control. During his imprisonment, the poor diet and lack of medication wrecked his health. In June 1969, he died from a massive overdose of liquid glucose, administered to counteract a diabetic coma. Another victim was Peng Dehuai, the disgraced former defence minister. At the end of 1966, he was kidnapped by rebellious students, and imprisoned until his death in 1974. Under the torment of interrogations and denunciation rallies, his ribs were fractured by intensive beating and kicking, and his hands, arms and back severely damaged by the strain of the 'jet-plane position'.

As the chaos spread, senior commanders in safe positions complained that China would soon run out of control if stability was not restored in the armed forces. On 28 January 1967, Mao approved a document drafted on their initiative, the 'Eight Directives of the Military Commission of the Party's Central Committee', which was issued as a guideline to the military. The directives again ruled out 'Si-da', and ordered all 'prisoners' jailed by the rebels to be released immediately. Other activities banned inside the armed forces included unauthorized house raids and all forms of physical punishment or public humiliation, such as the 'jet-plane position' or the 'high cap'.

After the directives appeared, my father's imprisonment, physical punishments and public humiliations continued for another month. When informed of his release on 1 March, his first reaction after nearly forty days in prison was to demand to know why he had been arrested in the first place. Far from replying, the rebels condemned his demand as in breach of the 'Eight Directives'. However, soon after that all the rebel organizations in my father's headquarters were disbanded in accordance with the directives.

My father was reinstated in his former office, and our telephone reconnected, but my parents would no longer take any private staff into our home. At my father's insistence, I had started to learn to cook for the whole family, which was hard at first for an unskilled and inexperienced teenager. Like many households in north China, our staple breakfast food was a porridge made of rice and water, which took about an hour to cook. Since my father had to eat breakfast at seven, I had to get up by half-past five to light the coal-burning stove. Sometimes I went back to bed after putting the pot on the stove, for I was too tempted by my warm bed, especially in winter, and often the porridge boiled over. Several times, the fire almost went out. But I gradually became a competent cook, and I learned to keep our house clean and tidy, which I had not done before.

When files removed from home were returned, my father found only one draft of one of his novels. The rest, and most of the diary he had kept for several decades, were never retrieved. A considerable number of his books and paintings had also gone missing, and were beyond his reach. In the following months, many former rebels visited my father or even talked to me to express grief for what they had done to us, and blamed themselves for being used by Tang and his cohorts. My father's response was very lenient, even to those who had tortured him. 'They're still young,' he said, seeing my anger. 'Everyone makes mistakes.' But that did not mean that he forgave what had happened. When he met Lieutenant-General Zheng Weishan later, he asked for justice from the leaders of the Beijing Military Region for the injuries he had suffered. But the reply was: 'Forget about asking for justice. We know who you are, and you know yourself. That is it!' It seemed that Tang was still untouchable.

In spring 1967, the Party committee at my father's headquarters held a plenary conference to discuss problems caused by 'Si-da'. As the days passed, my father's face darkened again, and I sensed that his ordeal was not over. Once he looked particularly angry when he came home, and asked Aijun what dealings she had had with Mercy Ocean's daughter lately. That day, Mercy Ocean had shown a piece of rock to the conference, and accused my sister Aijun of bullying his daughter. 'My little girl was nearly killed by Mu Aijun with this stone,' he wailed. 'As a poor peasant's son, I suffered enough from evil landlords in the old society. I can't let my children be persecuted by the landlords' children!' The assault had been ordered by my father, he alleged, a worthy son of the landlord capitalist class. Aijun was upset, and denied the accusation. A few days before, she and a group of children had thrown pebbles at each other in play, but she had not even noticed whether Mercy Ocean's daughter was there, and had no knowledge of anyone being hurt. After this incident, my siblings and I became more cautious with other children.

It was 4 December 1967. My mother had left at dawn, and when I got up I saw a note on the dining table: 'Please ask granny for some food coupons, and bring them to me tomorrow.' Next day I arrived in her university dormitory, which she shared with Auntie Summer, a middle-aged lecturer incriminated by her involvement in an organization run by the Nationalists, as a schoolgirl thirty years before. It was lunchtime, but no one was there, and what surprised me more was that all my mother's belongings, even her bedding, had disappeared. The door opened, and Auntie Summer came in. 'Please don't ask me where your mother is.' She looked anxious when she answered my question. 'You'd better ask the university revolutionary committee.'

In the committee's office I was met by a plump female student, a rebel activist. 'Your mother was arrested yesterday as a Nationalist spy,' she scowled. 'You must make a clean break with her!' My pleas to see my mother were refused, and no one would tell me where she was. I left the office in tears, and heard the campus loudspeakers bellow: 'Celebrate the arrest of the bastard Nationalist spy Xu Jing! Long live the Great Proletarian Cultural Revolution!' Many years later, my mother recalled what happened:

> I was having my supper in the canteen when the loudspeakers announced: 'The revolutionary masses must exercise dictatorship over the bastard Nationalist spy Xu Jing.' That meant the start of my imprisonment. The news didn't panic me, because I was braced for this moment. As I was told, I moved my belongings to the cell. Before I finished unpacking, Weihe walked in. Sitting cross-legged on the only chair, with a cigarette dangling from his lips, he said to me triumphantly: 'You must know that Cao Lian is vice-director of the revolutionary committee [as a 'revolutionary cadre'], and I am also a member of the committee [as one of the 'revolutionary masses']. So now your political problems are our affair. Do you still intend to oppose Cao Lian?' Suddenly he jumped up from his chair with

glaring eyes, and hauled me to a corner of the cell by my collar. He grabbed my neck with one hand, and started slapping my face with the other, and shouting: 'This is what you get for opposing Cao Lian!' The beating went on so long that my face got terribly swollen, and a number of my teeth were loosened and ached terribly. In the following days, I had great trouble eating solid food ...

During the heavy interrogations that followed, no one mentioned the spying allegations which had justified my mother's arrest. Instead, the questions focused on her opposition to Cao Lian. By that time, the rebels at her university had split into two main groups, the 'Cao Lian Loyalists' and the 'Cao Lian Opponents'. Although the loyalists were still in power, the number of opponents was growing, and because they wanted him replaced on the revolutionary committee, he and his allies feared that my mother might be chosen to represent the 'revolutionary cadres'. It was to stop this happening that they found a pretext for arresting my mother.

My mother's record at the university gave Cao Lian and his followers too little ammunition, so they resorted to the accusation made against her during the Rectification Campaign in the early 1940s, despite her having been completely cleared. This time the trick worked better. After my mother's arrest, her supporters were silenced, because it was impossible to dig up evidence in a case more than two decades old, particularly when the relevant documents, previously contained in the Party's confidential file, were now in the hands of Cao Lian. During a meeting of Cao Lian's opponents, some rebels suggested that it was better to keep their distance from my mother, considering the charges against her.

The news of my mother's arrest stunned my father. Knowing the nature of Cao Lian and his lieutenants, he was alarmed for her safety, and feared that this time she might not survive their persecution. He could not sleep, lost his appetite, and was soon suffering from raised blood pressure and frequent chest pains. Despite his anxiety, however, he had to avoid direct contact with the rebels in her university, as it would only make things worse for them both. Desperate to know where she was, he turned to a former colleague in the 1950s, now Political Commissar of the Beijing Garrison Command, who told him that she was a prisoner on her campus. From then on, my father sent Feng-an and me to the university revolutionary committee almost every day, to ask for permission to visit her. 'Please find out if your Mama is still alive,' he said. Each time we came home defeated, I could not bear to meet my father's eyes, and the deep frustration they expressed.

In January 1968, back at her university, Feng-an and I spotted our mother from a distance, escorted by two female guards. We shadowed them, and finally located her cell: a small dark ground-floor room, with the only window boarded over, as my father's had been. In the room opposite her cell, four guards did duty around the clock. We came back around six o'clock next morning, bringing her a letter from my father and some food. It was still dark outside, and the loudspeakers blared loud revolutionary music to wake people up. When the guards returned to their room, and my mother was let out to use the lavatory and fetch water, we slipped into the cell. On her return, it shocked her to see us. She shut the door immediately, and tried to push us into the built-in wardrobe, but it was too small. 'My children, how did you get in?' she whispered, and slipped a piece of paper into my hand. 'Please give this to Baba and tell him I'm all right.' Our meeting only lasted a few minutes. Feng-an and I had to leave her before the door was locked again, or our presence discovered.

In her letter to my father, my mother suggested a secret means of contact. At least twice a month, posing as a university student, I visited the building where she was held. In the lavatory that she was allowed to use, I exchanged letters for my parents by wedging them into a space on the top edge of a stand-up urinal, as it had been a men's lavatory before. The letters were screwed up in layers of old newspaper, just like balls of waste paper, so that no one would be curious if they saw them.

It was not very hard to look the part. In those days, the style of dress was much the same all over, with the shapeless jacket and dark blue or olive-green trousers. At the age of sixteen, I was already taller than many female university students. But during the first few months I was terribly scared: I had never done anything more dangerous than acting as my parents' secret messenger. Any unexpected sound or eye-contact, and I readily broke out in a cold sweat, fearing a hostile approach, or a fault in my disguise. My visits to the revolutionary committee had made my face familiar to several people. Did they see me? Was I being followed? If I was caught, my mother would be deeper in trouble, and our line of communication would be cut. The fear played on my nerves, and sometimes my panic almost ran out of control.

One day, after exchanging the letters, I suddenly saw my mother emerge from a cubicle in the lavatory. Even after our long separation, however, we did not dare to show our feelings, or even to go near each other, in case our secret meeting was somehow found. 'How is everyone at home?' asked Mother quietly, after making sure that we were alone. But as soon as she spoke I heard footsteps in the corridor, and felt scared. 'Someone's coming, Mama!' I whispered. When a woman walked in, my mother was already on her way out with my father's letter in her pocket, and I was washing my hands, both of us strangers. My face in the window pane looked grey.

During that period, Feng-an behaved incredibly fearlessly. Every now and then, a note was slipped under the door of my mother's cell, and she recognized his handwriting. One note used Mao Zedong's famous quotation: 'Be resolute, fear no sacrifice and surmount every difficulty to win victory.' One day, the revolutionary committee passed her some dried noodles sent from home. Soon afterwards, another note appeared: 'Don't eat the noodles! Be careful!' The warning was my father's; he was worried that the food might be poisoned along the way. Several times, Feng-an slipped into my mother's cell again to deliver food. One afternoon she returned from outside and was amazed to see him creep out from underneath her bed, where he had hidden to wait for her. But this time he was trapped, as the door was locked behind my mother. After a short conversation, she started knocking on her door and shouting that she needed to go to the lavatory urgently. After they let her out, Feng-an slipped away.

As the first prisoner held at her university, my mother was brought to more denunciation rallies than anyone else. For hours at a time, from early morning till late evening, she was displayed on platforms, routinely contorted into the 'jet-plane position', beaten and kicked. When they knocked her down, they stood her up again, and the torture resumed. Often, Cao Lian would sit on the stage in a prominent position, conspicuously in charge. Several times when the rally was over, my mother had to run the gauntlet between strong men swinging heavy clubs, who beat her till her face ran with blood. Once, her front teeth were completely caved in by the clubs, and her forehead was a single haematoma. Doctors at the university clinic were so alarmed by the injury that they wanted her urgently taken to hospital, but the torturers refused. Denied all medication, she had to prop up the damaged teeth herself, and use cold water to rinse her bleeding mouth. Afterwards, her mouth was dreadfully swollen by severe inflammation of the gums, and the bumps on her forehead never went away.

During that period, my mother feared that her health might be permanently ruined. Apart from the beatings, she suffered particularly from the hours spent wrenched into the 'jet-plane position'. 'There was constant biting pain in my arms, shoulders and back,' she recollected. 'Soon, I was dripping sweat even in the frozen cold, but my screaming always led to more torture.' After a day of torment, it was all she could do to stand up straight, or to turn over in bed. In the frozen cold of winter, her cell was icy and her bedding damp with mildew, because the radiator was deliberately damaged and Weihe poured water in her bed. Very often, it was too cold to sleep at night, and she sat on her bed and huddled in her clothes. To cope with the endless dark and cold, sometimes she sang to herself: 'The sun is rising, and the sun is shining.'

I often think how inventive the rebels were in humiliating as well as torturing their victims during the Cultural Revolution. At the rallies, they daubed my mother's face with black ink, to signal her membership of the 'black counter-revolutionary gang'. Once, she was paraded together with Madam Lu Wen, the university's personnel director, and Madam Dew, a department head guilty mainly of public support for my mother. Pinioned side by side in the 'jet-plane position', the three – Cao Lian's most hated women in the university – were forced to wear their best coats inside out, as captives of bourgeois ideology. Supposedly, smart clothes like theirs were only worn by members of the exploiting class. This idea was inspired by a previous denunciation rally against Wang Guangmei, wife of China's disgraced President Liu Shaoqi, held in April 1967 at Qinghua University, supported by Jiang Qing and her allies, and attended by over a third of a million people. On the platform, Wang was forced to wear a necklace of table tennis balls, as a punishment for her bourgeois lifestyle. A few years before, when Wang Guangmei accompanied her husband on state visits to foreign countries, her fashionable wardrobe had drawn national attention, and the bitter jealousy of Jiang Qing.

During my mother's imprisonment, it was the deep love between my parents that gave her the courage and hope to survive. 'In my mind, he [my father] was the whole world, so I had to survive, not only to clarify my innocence but also to bring us back together in the future,' she wrote later. 'One night, he appeared in my dream, waiting for me in the narrow storeroom under the staircase of the building. He hugged me for a long time, and then touched my hair gently and stared at my face with deep affection. "You've suffered so much!" he said, and put my favourite sweets in my mouth. Feeling comforted by his affection, I smiled back at him and completely forgot my suffering. "You're still as handsome as ever," I started joking. Soon, both of us burst out laughing. Suddenly, he disappeared, and I was woken up by the guards banging on my door to stop me laughing.'

Each time she received food smuggled in from home, my mother was touched by the preparation. The fried peanuts were shelled, and the cooked chicken boneless and finely sliced, to leave no traces. She knew it must be my father's idea. On sleepless nights, she would read his letters, or write to tell him everything she felt. My mother could only ask for writing materials from the guards when she was forced to write confessions about her 'crimes'. Letters became her only comfort. 'Living in darkness, I did not know where Chairman Mao was, and my only unfailing support came from Mu Xiang's letters,' she wrote in her memoir. 'For me, his letters were precious possessions. Each character and sentence carried more weight than anything else. Through reading them, I could keep up my hope for the future.' All the letters were hidden in a wardrobe full of waste paper left by the Red Guards.

With her powerful will to survive, my mother came to terms with the daily tortures and humiliation. At first she always felt she might soil herself each time her captors kicked open her door to take her to a denunciation rally, another session of unpredictable suffering, but it did not take long to regain her self-control. She quickly discovered how ridiculous the allegations used to denounce her were – always the same fabrications. But whatever the charges, she had no right to defend herself. 'They just waste time repeating nonsense,' she always thought at the rallies.

On the day before the Chinese New Year in 1968, my father sent me to the university revolutionary committee again to apply to visit my mother. On behalf of the family, I brought some clothes and food and wanted to wish her 'Happy New Year'. All day I sat in their office, sometimes in tears, with nothing to eat or drink. I begged them again and again, but no one replied. When it was getting dark outside, people in the office started leaving, and exchanging New Year wishes. 'Hurry up!' some cheerful voices called from the corridor. 'Let's make dumplings for the New Year celebration!' I was reminded of the festive atmosphere at home on New Year's Eve, destroyed by the Cultural Revolution. In the past, my siblings and I always sat around a large table on New Year's Eve together with my mother, grandmother and sometimes even my father, to make dumplings for the New Year's family feast. We joked while we folded portions of delicious stuffing into thin rounds of dough, laughing and cheering as row after row of dumplings appeared on the table, like an army of perky soldiers. In my memory, this was the tastiest food of all the year, because of the joy we put into making it.

The office was about to be closed when some rebels finally approached me. 'We won't let you see your mother unless you agree to denounce her as a counter-revolutionary.' 'Never!' I flared. 'My mother is a great Communist and I'm proud of her!' 'Get out of here you bitch!' they screamed, then pushed me out of the office and would not let me in again.

Still holding the presents, I cried bitterly. I wanted to see my mother! What would I say to my family? In the cold winter evening, I roamed around the empty campus till the sight of my mother's boarded window pulled me into the building without a second thought. Two guards stopped me in the corridor and ordered me out straight away, but suddenly I heard a sound from my mother's cell, and there was her face behind the transom window above the locked door! She told me years later that because the rebels were busy with their own preparations they locked her in her cell all day, with nothing but some stale steamed buns to eat. She could not help thinking of her family: 'What are they doing right now?' This was the second New Year running spent apart from my father, with one of them in prison. When she heard my voice outside, her emotions took over, and she stood on the cell's single chair to reach the window. 'Mama, I'm here!' 'Aiping, please go home! Be careful!' We wept and called from our separate sides of the door.

On the afternoon of 14 March 1968 my father returned unexpectedly early from work and went straight to his room without a word. Shortly afterwards, two soldiers arrived and seized our telephone again. I knew from their rude behaviour that something was wrong. Later, I heard that Tang had summoned him urgently and told him: 'By decision of the Party Committee in the Beijing Military Region, you are suspended from office to confess your problems.' 'What problems do I have to confess?' 'You know it yourself,' Tang replied. This time my father was placed under house arrest.

Over the previous year, a case known as the 'Renegade clique of sixty-one' had shocked the nation. Those involved included Vice-Premier Bo Yibo and a number of central government ministers and provincial governors. The case dated back to 1936–7 when China faced Japanese aggression and there was a great demand for Party cadres. Shortly before the Japanese occupied Beijing, Liu Shaoqi, the Communist leader in North China, decided with Party approval to rescue sixty-one senior Party members held for some years in a Nationalist jail in Beijing, who would otherwise be killed by the Japanese invaders. On their release, the prisoners had to accept the Nationalist condition of putting their names to 'Anti-Communist Declarations' which were then published in the press. No one was blamed for signing the announcements, as it was done by order of the Party. Now, thirty years after the event, the case was used by Kang Sheng, Jiang Qing and their crew to persecute opponents. On their instructions, the rebel students accused the sixty-one of being a renegade clique headed by Liu Shaoqi, and many were arrested. Inspired by this 'revolutionary victory', rebel fanatics rampaged around China, hunting down more senior Party renegades.

To Tang and his allies, this turn of events offered another stick to beat my father. Unlike most senior officers, he had not joined the Red Army in his early career, but worked underground in Nationalist areas, which laid him open to the charge of renegade if he had ever been jailed in the process. To their disappointment, he had never been arrested. Their only exhibit came from my father's novel: they assumed that the story of Guo Song, the leading male character, was based on the author's experiences. In the book, Guo Song is captured briefly by troops under General Yan Xishan, the warlord governor of Shanxi province. From this clue, they deduced that my father had been captured at the beginning of the Sino-Japanese War, and this formed part of the 'evidence' to brand him as a renegade.

After elaborate preparations, they concocted another story: that my father was a 'fake Communist'. In his home county, the only surviving witness of the secret oath he took on joining the Party was Yibin, who had sponsored him for membership in 1932. Agents of my father's opponents traced Yibin and told him: 'Mu Xiang is a counter-revolutionary. Think what a crime you committed if you recruited him!' The poor man was now a timid peasant. Intimidated by their threats, he denied having recruited my father. Since the Communist underground could hardly store its records in Nationalist areas, and communications were kept secret and based on one-way contact only, my father could find no document and no other witness to prove his credentials. Confirmation for the lie came from the loss of contact with the Communist underground during his year's forced exile after the failed insurrection in 1935. Despite the positive testimonials provided by his former colleagues and leaders, it was alleged that he had never resumed his Party membership, even if he was able to prove that he had joined.

Using these brand-new accusations, the Tang faction moved to suspend my father from his duties. By then, the Standing Committee inside the Beijing Military Region's Party Committee had been reshuffled, and a number of my father's strong supporters politically disgraced. After intense lobbying, Tang's proposal to disgrace my father was adopted by the military region, and later approved by the Military Commission of the Party's Central Committee. What shocked me was that this time my father's enemies were joined by his Chief of Staff, Senior Colonel Ge, who had backed him during his spell in prison and whose children were also former pupils of the Ba-yi school. According to my father, Ge was paying him back for refusing to help him overthrow Major-General Ren, the commander of the armoured forces, whose post Ge wanted.

A special team was set up to look into my father's case, headed by Ge and staffed by his trusted officers. Their aim was to prove the case against my father, regardless of the truth – a procedure inflicted on many disgraced officials during the Cultural Revolution. In the following years, team members travelled all over China to accumulate false evidence, by means such as bullying Yibin. They also visited libraries and archives, searching for my father's name on the published 'Anti-Communist Declarations'. I heard later that they checked files and newspapers dating back to the early 1920s, when my father was a child.

While under house arrest, my father was frequently interrogated by the investigation team, who sought his confession to being a 'fake Party member' and abused him as 'a sinner stained with the blood of revolutionary martyrs'. During interrogations he often suffered from chest pains, but found no mercy for his cardiac condition. One day when he left for further interrogation at one o'clock in the afternoon, it worried my grandmother to see him looking so pale. At her request, I bought fresh vegetables and meat, and helped her to prepare my father's favourite supper, won ton soup. From five o'clock onwards, Grandmother kept an eye on the road through our front window, but could not find my father among the crowd returning home from work. An hour passed. Several hours passed. The water had boiled again and again, but my father did not come.

When midnight came, Grandmother sent us to bed and sat up watching. It was dark outside, and the huge compound was empty. From our house on a hilltop, she saw that the only lighted window in the distance was on the second floor of the massive office block, which she knew was the office of the investigation team. Staring at the window, she could not help wondering what was happening to her son behind it. The ticking of the clock became the dripping of his blood. Tormented by the feeling, she sobbed as she roamed around the house, until she saw the portrait of Mao Zedong on the wall. 'Please save my son, Chairman Mao!' she begged. 'I promise you that he has never done anything wrong. He was only fifteen when he followed you and joined the revolution. It was under his influence that all his siblings joined the Party and we became a revolutionary family. Please stop them persecuting my son, Chairman Mao!'

Around four o'clock that night, Grandmother woke Feng-an and me.

'Your father's still not home,' she told us anxiously. 'Please find out what has happened to him!' We ran our fastest, and as soon as we entered the empty office block, we heard harsh voices bellowing. In their office, our father had collapsed. Forced to sit on a chair, hemmed in by screaming interrogators, he was slumped against the wall, grey in the face and lips. Since the previous afternoon, the interrogators had been working in shifts, while my father had no break, food, drink or medication. When I took his hands, they felt so cold that I burst into tears, for fear that he was no longer alive. 'What have you been doing to my father?' Feng-an cried. 'Are you human beings?' Without their permission, we helped my father out of the room. One interrogator dashed out into the corridor. 'Mu Xiang!' he shouted. 'You'd better look out if you cause your children to sabotage the Cultural Revolution again!' The shouting made my father's body shudder more violently. 'You are not Communists! You are fascists!' After those words, he passed out and fell to the floor.

With both our parents prisoners, it was more and more risky for Feng-an and me to help keep them in contact. If we were caught, there was no telling what might happen to the family. In desperation, my father turned to Madam Dew, who was one of my mother's supporters at the university. I first heard her name in summer 1967, before my mother's arrest, when the university rebels raided her apartment and our house on the same day. Madam Dew's family lived in a building in central Beijing owned by the Communist Party's Central Office, where her husband was a senior figure in the private staff of Marshal Zhu De, Chairman of China's Parliament. Security was tight there, because many other residents held similar posts. For example, Madam Dew's next-door neighbour worked for Premier Zhou Enlai. The raid on her apartment was reported at once to Premier Zhou, who ordered the immediate return of everything taken.

Shortly before he lost his freedom again, my father had taken me to call on Madam Dew to discuss my mother's situation. Her warm reception on our first visit convinced us that she was a trustworthy person, brave enough to help us. From spring 1968 I started to meet her at weekends, picking up news about my mother.

One weekday, Madam Dew's youngest son, a junior middle school pupil called Drizzle, came to find me at school with an urgent message from his mother. 'Please act at once to rescue Auntie Xu Jing, or she could soon be beaten to death.' When I reached my father, he covered his face with his hands and was silent, trembling with frustration. Oh Baba, I would rather you cried out. I could not bear your silent trembling. Later he called Feng-an and me again. 'My children!' he said in tears. 'Now you are the only ones I can ask for help!'

On behalf of my parents, Feng-an and I visited the Central Cultural Revolution Small Group and the Party Central Committee many times to appeal for help. Since the Central Committee's headquarters were located in Zhongnanhai, heavily guarded and never opened to the public, we could make no direct contact. Each time, we had to leave my father's letter with the armed guards by the entrance, and no answer ever came. By then, the Central Cultural Revolution Small Group had established a reception department located in Zhongshan Park, the south-west corner of the Forbidden City. On my first visit, I arrived alone at dawn, as I had heard that the department was terribly busy every day. To my surprise, a huge crowd was already waiting outside the park's closed vermilion gate, and more and more kept coming. During that period, masses of people arrived every day from all over China to visit the Cultural Revolution Authority, trying to save themselves or their families. The silent crowd around me looked like refugees, mostly exhausted and shabbily dressed. Some carried injuries on their heads or bodies, some had their babies with them, all looked pale and tired. Standing or sitting on the ground, we waited patiently in the hope of justice and support.

When the department finally opened, I was lucky enough to be the first visitor to one of the many offices, where a middle-aged man dressed like an officer but not necessarily a serviceman sat behind an outsize desk. In those days, many of the officials who worked for the Central Cultural Revolution Small Group or the Party Central Committee liked to be seen in military uniform. Aware of my presence, he did not greet me or look up, too busy tidying his desk. As I waited for attention, I tried to look detached about his manner, in case he took offence. As long as he could help to save my parents, I would tolerate any amount of mistreatment.

At last he raised his head. 'What is your problem?' His voice and expression were cold. 'Please save my parents!' My tears ran as soon as I spoke. While he listened, he took notes but asked no questions. When I finished, his first disapproving response was: 'You must take a proper attitude to your parents' political problems.' 'Please believe me! My parents are innocent,' I explained, 'but they have been victimized . . .' 'You should not say that!' he interrupted. 'You must trust our Party and the revolutionary masses!' A few minutes later, I was dismissed, with nothing to show for my visit, or any expression of sympathy or comfort. Although I was assured that my request would be passed to the Cultural Revolution Authority, no good ever resulted for my parents.

Chapter 16

A Clouded Life:
Daughter of 'Counter-Revolutionaries'
and 'Delinquent Teenager'
(September 1966–November 1968)

Being sent back from Shanghai in September 1966 completely ruined my reputation at school. My 'shameful conduct' during the trip was soon the talk of the campus, with imagined details added. At the same time, my identity as the girl mixed up with Mighty China was no longer a secret. As if no one could remember the circumstances of those nights spent at school the previous summer, when they heard that I had 'slept' with Mighty China, everyone now believed that I had sex with him.

Traditionally, women's involvement in sexual relationships outside marriage was strongly condemned in China. History had taught me about the plight of unchaste women, and the cruel punishments inflicted under the feudal system, from public humiliation to drowning. During the Cultural Revolution, ironically, the traditional attitudes did not change. Those labelled as 'loose women' were regarded as evildoers. Targeted alongside the 'capitalist-roaders', they were publicly denounced, or sentenced to compulsory labour under the eye of the revolutionary masses. Many had their heads shaved in the humiliating 'Yin-yang' style, and each had a pair of worn shoes hung round her neck, because the term 'worn shoes' stands for 'loose women' in Chinese. During the Red Guards' activities in 'Smashing up the Four Olds', there were many cases when women accused of adultery were stoned by children or spat on in public by neighbours, colleagues or other willing denouncers, with no right to justify or protect themselves.

I had no idea what it would mean to be cast in the first sex scandal in my school since the Cultural Revolution. When I returned to the campus now and then, I felt very uncomfortable. Hardly anyone would raise the case directly, but I sensed how much gossip had gone on behind my back. Talking to schoolmates, I often felt curiosity, suspicion or even spite behind their awkward manners, but I decided not to justify myself. After my experiences during the 'big links' trip, I was afraid that no one, not even my friends, would listen to me, and the more I explained the further the stories would run. Unable to stop the gossip, I had to learn to live with it. For a proud girl with a sensitive nature, it was a dreadful experience. In wintertime, I often covered my nose and mouth with a large gauze mask when I returned to the campus, as a shield against the pressure. I tried to go as little as I could.

For a long time, I feared that I might be pregnant, although I had never had sex, because I heard that women could get pregnant after any close physical contact with men. During my final year at Ba-yi School, girls in my class would often jump about after leaving crowded buses, because they thought that this would prevent pregnancy after such close proximity with men. I watched the shape of my belly with anxiety, fearing that a foetus might be inside, despite my regular menstrual cycle.

At home, I never mentioned the gossip. Like many other families in China, our personal feelings about sex and love were a taboo never to be talked about at home. It was unthinkable to let anyone else, even my parents, know what had happened. I was also concerned that my parents and grandmother would not accept my friendship with Mighty China. Though sex was not involved, I recognized that our behaviour had

crossed the line of social tolerance. That was enough to ruin a girl's reputation, as I knew, with the possible consequence of being ostracized by
her family and by the community at large. No longer viewed as a decent
person, she would struggle to find a husband, which would further
shame her family. In my mind, my home was the only oasis left where I
could find warmth and love. I valued the trust and respect that I enjoyed
there, and since disclosure would wound my family, I felt I had no
choice but to keep quiet.

Shortly before my father's first arrest in January 1967, I met a boy
from my school who was visiting our neighbour, and knew from his cold
manner what would come next. Soon afterwards, the neighbourhood
buzzed with gossip. During the Cultural Revolution, sex scandals
became a favourite talking-point. More and more people had their lives
absorbed in constant campaigning, and were desperate for any diversion.
Over the last few months, I had made acquaintance with several girls
around my age in our neighbourhood, the residential quarter for senior
officers in the armoured forces. We often visited each other's homes, and
I knew that their fathers were not in collusion with Tang. When we first
used to meet, they seemed to admire my knowledge and intelligence.
Now they were more interested in condemning 'impure' girls, the ones
with damaged reputations. Sometimes their mothers joined in, and from
their hints and sarcastic remarks it was clear that it was me they were
condemning. Later, I heard that one of the girls even spread rumours
that I tried to seduce her elder brother, whom I only met briefly and
never in private. The neighbourhood atmosphere became almost as
unpleasant as the one I faced at school. But there was nothing I could do.
Once a girl was associated with a sex scandal, there was no way to
restore her reputation. To lessen the pressure, I started to distance myself
from them, and stayed indoors as much as I could.

I was particularly concerned that Tang and his allies would use the
hostile gossip to hurt my father. Some years before, I had seen how
Madam Tang spread slurs about Eastern Dawn, the teenage daughter

of Major-General Shao, whose condemnation for admitting the 'bour-geois lifestyle' into his family was partly based on gossip against his daughter. It seemed very likely to me that Tang and his wife would use the same device against my father, as I believed that the gossip was bound to reach them. So each time the loudspeakers crackled in the compound, I tensed in expectation of hearing my name brought into some 'sex scandal' on Tang's initiative. On my way to see the big-charac-ter posters every day, I always prayed not to be mentioned.

What would I do if it happened? I had no idea. Sometimes I thought that I should escape into the mountains to become a Buddhist nun and live in isolation, as girls did in the old days, when hope was lost and life was disillusion. In such a self-exile, I too could find peace again, far from political strife and social pressure. Unfortunately, this was a nebulous idea, as religious activities were banned and temples smashed or closed. Since the Red Guards' exploits in 'Smashing up the Four Olds', monks and nuns had been forced to resume the secular life. Perhaps I should commit suicide as the social humiliation and my family's disappointment grew too much to bear. If the gossip made things worse for my father, the guilt would be more than I could endure. But what would happen to my parents if I died or fled? Would my disappearance or death save my family from the disgrace I caused them? I could not convince myself. At that time, my father was still imprisoned and my mother also under pres-sure. As their main go-between, I had to think about my responsibility to the whole family. Day after day, I was deeply disturbed but could not talk to anyone.

Since my leaving the Red Guard, enormous changes had affected the rebellious organizations in China. By the end of 1966, university stu-dents had became a key weapon for Mao's radical followers in the intra-Party conflict, and this antagonized Red Guards in the middle schools of Beijing. Only months before, these younger rebels had starred as Chairman Mao's revolutionary path-breakers. Now, suddenly, they were out of favour. As the Cultural Revolution drove on, more and more Red Guard leaders and activists in the middle schools found that they no longer belonged to the glorious 'five red' classes. With the political disgrace of parents formerly in power in the old administration, suddenly their social status slid from the altitude of high official families to the depths of the discredited 'five black' classes. Fellow students whose families had stayed out of trouble felt their own futures in jeopardy. Having grown up in privileged backgrounds, many could not deal with what had happened to themselves, their families or their friends, and felt utterly betrayed.

In December 1966, an organization known as 'Lian-dong' (Joint Action Committee of the Capital's Red Guards) was established by self-styled 'veteran Red Guards' from Beijing's middle schools, the earliest members of the movement. Its target was the Cultural Revolution, and in particular Mao's chief radical followers such as Jiang Qing, Chen Boda and Xie Fuzhi. By now, the truth about Jiang Qing's notorious past was beginning to emerge, and many 'veterans' traced the persecution suffered by their own or their close friends' families back to her and her confederates.

On behalf of the Cultural Revolution Authority, Mao's radical followers quickly declared the Joint Action Committee (JAC) a counter-revolutionary organization, a front for the so-called bourgeois headquarters inside the Party, headed by Liu Shaoqi, China's disgraced president. By order of Jiang Qing and her allies, the committee was threatened with arrest and imprisonment, and many of its members arrested, which provoked stronger protests. It was common in those days to see groups of these 'veteran Red Guards' running like mad along the city's main streets, or whizzing around Tian-an Men Square on bicycles, with the JAC's name displayed on crimson armbands, and chanting passionate slogans – 'Stop persecuting veterans of the revolution!' 'The Central Cultural Revolution Small Group has driven us to revolt!' Another favourite slogan was 'We cherish Yang Kaihui!' (Mao's first wife, killed by the Nationalists in 1930). This was aimed at Jiang Qing, famously jealous of Mao's romantic relationship with his first wife. The demonstrators made several attempts to invade the Ministry of Public Security, China's police headquarters, demanding their comrades' release, which caused more arrests each time.

In late January 1967 a number of Beijing middle schools, including Ba-yi, were raided as suspected strongholds of the Joint Action Committee. It was lucky that Feng-an, who had also joined the JAC, had come home the day before the operation. He heard later that the school's whole campus was surrounded by over thirty thousand members of rebellious organizations mobilized from nearby universities. The handful of Feng-an's comrades who remained at school that day were taken completely by surprise. Cornered and violently beaten by opponents wielding clubs, they feared for their lives, and could only keep shouting 'Long live Chairman Mao!' to protect themselves. More than thirty pupils were arrested, and the Ba-yi School suffered incalculable damage. The largest privileged educational institution in China never regained its previous unique status.

One day, I heard from a classmate that her younger brother, a primary school pupil, had been arrested while cycling past Beijing Railway Station, and later suffered a brutal beating. A few days before, rumours had circulated that Liu Shaoqi had died of ill-treatment, and the police authority had been alerted that the JAC planned to stage protest activities. Knowing nothing about the situation, the poor boy went out with friends wearing a winter cap with a loose white lining that stuck out from underneath like a white band, and the police drew the false conclusion that he was wearing mourning for Liu Shaoqi. The story reminded me of a practice common under the Nationalist regime, when people could go to jail if they wore a red scarf, or anything red, as red was the colour of revolution. Decades had passed, the dynasty had changed, but the same thing had happened again.

In April 1967, Mao Zedong ordered the release of all the arrested members of the JAC. His reasons excited speculation. Some suggested that he was determined to keep a balance among the various political forces. The violent suppression of the JAC had brought strong protests from senior members of the Party and the government, especially since many of their children were involved with it, and it could be that Mao refused to take the blame for what his radical followers were doing. It was also said that Mao was acting on the advice of Premier Zhou Enlai.

On 22 April 1967, an emotional meeting took place in the Great Hall of the People between Premier Zhou and over a hundred newly released members of the Joint Action Committee. The Premier's teenage guests were shabbily dressed, unkempt and unwashed. It was said that when he arrived they stood up and burst out crying or shouting, like children telling their troubles to their parents. Zhou Enlai looked very sad, and his eyes filled with tears. At one point he comforted a boy whose mother, a senior member of the Premier's private office, had been driven to suicide by Jiang Qing's persecution. After her death, Jiang Qing had continued to spread false accusations. 'Please don't be too upset,' Premier Zhou said to the boy. 'I know both of your parents well. You are the child of our Party and people . . .' Among others that Zhou Enlai spoke to was the son of China's Vice-Chairman Dong Biwu. Some months before, pressure from the Cultural Revolutionary Authority had forced Dong to jail his own son, a leading 'veteran Red Guard'. It was said that when his son came home, Dong Biwu told him: 'You actually took my place in prison!' He believed that his son had been made a scapegoat in the radical Maoists' campaign against their rivals.

In March 1968, my mother was made to join the 'Lao-gai-dui' (team for self-reform through compulsory labour) run by the revolutionary committee in her university. At that time, these teams were being set up all over China. Hers contained a number of senior colleagues charged with being capitalist-roaders or counter-revolutionaries. Of course, Cao Lian was not among them, secure as vice-director of the revolutionary committee. Nor was Ji Xian, the former secretary of the university Party committee – a position known in China as 'first hand'. His was an exceptionally lucky case. Unlike most of the 'first hands' in Chinese universities, he was not branded as a 'capitalist-roader' by the Cultural Revolution, and hence avoided persecution. He owed his safety chiefly to currying favour with Cao Lian and the rebels, for instance by giving false evidence against my mother. A number of professors and lecturers were sentenced to join the forced labour team, accused of crimes such as exerting a reactionary influence, but what really surprised my mother was that her teammates also included students, some of them former members of the university Red Guard. One student was charged with treason, because he had tried to escape to North Korea by illegally crossing the border, reportedly dismayed by the chaos raging in China since the Cultural Revolution.

By order of the revolutionary committee, every day at eight o'clock my mother had to attend the morning roll-call held in the university nursery garden. But this was exactly the time when she was supposed to report to the investigators dealing with her case. Clearly, it was impossible to obey both orders, especially since the two locations were about two kilometres apart and she had no transport available. With typical intolerance, her request to change the schedule was refused. The investigators' office was close to her cell. All she could do was to go there every morning before eight o'clock and suffer the usual abuse. By then it was already half-past eight, and she set off to the nursery garden, running all the way and arriving out of breath. Despite her explanations, she then faced shouting and violent beating from the nursery garden workers who now commanded the forced-labour team. Often her spectacles were knocked to the ground and damaged, and because she had been very shortsighted for most of her life, and was lost without her spectacles, she had to rely on her teammates to gather up the pieces, and then stick them back together with adhesive plaster, or use string to hold them on.

To abet their own brutality, some of the workers also encouraged ignorant children to bully my mother. On her way back to the campus, she was often trailed by teenage boys with catapults. The hail of stones forced her to run away, and to shield her bleeding head with her bare arms, while the workers watched and laughed at her distress. Since my mother had never done anything to offend them, it seems that the main reason for these manual workers' eagerness to harm her was to please Cao Lian and his partisans, who now controlled the university. These workers' jobs were hard, and they were lured by the hope of promotion, higher wages, or a switch to jobs with better working conditions. My mother became their chief victim because she was seen as Cao Lian's major opponent.

Despite all her maltreatment, forced labour brought changes that my mother welcomed. The beautiful natural surroundings cheered her up and strengthened her will to survive. Though still locked up at night, she no longer lived in isolation. Working with teammates every day, she felt heartened by their friendship and support. Before the Cultural Revolution, she had been kept too busy as a leader of the university to have much personal contact with her staff or students. Now, their shared fate had cemented them together.

On my mother's first day of forced labour, Madam Lu Wen, her fellow worker, came and touched her swollen face, and the huge bruise on her forehead, with deep sympathy. In the afternoon, she slipped her a small package of tea leaves and whispered: 'I hear that chewing tea leaves is good for healing damaged teeth after beating.' At this act of affection, my mother was lost for words. Since her arrest four months before, it was the first chance she had had to feel supported by her colleagues. At that time Lu Wen, like most other members of the team, was still allowed home every day, so she often brought snacks to my mother, knowing what a poor diet she received. 'You must keep yourself fit,' Lu Wen said. 'We need to struggle against their persecution, and to see the day that they are driven out.'

Among all her teammates, my mother felt particularly sorry for Madam Dew, who was paying the price for supporting her, but Dew insisted: 'You mustn't blame yourself for what has happened. What I've done was to stick to the truth, which is my principle, and I'll never regret it.' During that period, I visited Madam Dew in her home regularly. She helped me to send food parcels to my mother, and to exchange my parents' letters, so as to reduce my secret missions to the university.

Members of the forced labour team could be summoned at any time to be denounced, and my mother most of all. 'I am amazed by your mother's courage,' Madam Dew told me several times. 'When leaving for the denunciation rallies, she is always calm and shows no fear.' My mother was equally impressed by Madam Dew's toughness and character. One day she returned from a denunciation rally and described one event to her work mates with a wry humour. 'What luck I had today – a marvellous bargain!' At the rally, she had been photographed while pinioned in the 'jet-plane position' on the platform. Slung round her neck, a notice written on a huge sheet of thick cardboard shouted: 'Down with the counter-revolutionary Dew!' At that time, the university revolutionary committee was assembling a collection called 'One Hundred Ridiculous Pictures', a favourite device with the rebels to humiliate their victims. Madam Dew told her work mates: 'I had my photo taken for nothing. Where else could I find such a bargain?'

Unlike Madam Dew, Mr Lee, another team member forced to pose for photographs at the same rally, did not report to the nursery garden afterwards. On the following day, my mother heard that he had committed suicide by hanging himself. Before the Cultural Revolution, Lee had run the university research department, and had supervised the nursery garden where Weihe worked. When Weihe was penalized for stealing, it was Lee whom he particularly blamed, claiming that he had picked on a manual worker and veteran of the People's Liberation Army – a title that Weihe exploited. Now, Weihe was a leading figure in the rebel organization, with the power to get even. From Lee's personal

Party dossier, previously confidential, the rebels learned that during the Sino-Japanese War, acting under duress, the teenage Lee's grandfather had taken him to kowtow to members of the Japanese army, together with other local villagers. When he joined the Communists later, Lee reported this incident, and was told that he would not be held responsible for what happened. But now, a quarter of a century later, Weihe used the story to accuse Lee of being a traitor, and made him another of the university's victims.

One evening shortly before his death, Lee had several ribs fractured by beatings at a denunciation rally, but he was forbidden to go to hospital, and was forced back to work by Weihe the following morning. When he returned to the nursery garden, the poor man crept around, bent double with pain, and terribly pale. The rest of the team helped him to finish his work, and their sympathy caused him to break down. 'You are not guilty at all. Don't be afraid of them!' my mother and Madam Dew tried to reassure him. Lee sobbed with grief. 'Cao Lian and Weihe are in the revolutionary committee. They have me completely in their power. How can I survive their persecution?' Lee was a harmless man, and reserved by nature, not equipped to cope with continual persecution. Soon, his mental condition was failing. Each time the loudspeakers announced that he was summoned for denunciation, his body shook and he fell to the ground, holding his feet and sobbing. In the end, he lost all his hope to survive, and decided to take his own life, leaving behind his wife and two young children.

When working in the nursery garden, my mother's attention was often attracted by cars that passed with army number plates. 'Is Mu Xiang coming to rescue me?' she always asked herself. When she could, she would stand by the road and tell herself: 'He might pass here on his way to inspect his troops. I must let him see that I'm still alive.' She missed him badly. Without him, she could not imagine how she would survive her ordeal.

One night, a few weeks after my father's persecution had resumed, my mother was roused from her cell and taken for interrogation to a room on the top floor of a high-rise block, which they had never used before. A huge wooden frame stood in front of the window, with a dangling noose in the middle, like a gallows. On the walls to each side of the window, big slogans written in fresh black ink advertised 'Leniency to those who admit their crimes and severity to those who refuse!' and 'Death is the only way out for those who continue resisting!' The pitiless faces of the interrogators made my mother wonder whether her life was about to end in this room. Perhaps she would be hanged on the gallows tonight, and tomorrow they would report her suicide. During the Cultural Revolution, many victims died under questioning, and the murderers had no fear of being charged.

My mother was forced to face the wall, and wrenched into the 'jet-plane position' again, with her arms grappled behind her. 'There's no escape,' she told herself. 'Just wait and see.' If they killed her now, her sharpest regret would be not to have had a chance to say goodbye to her beloved husband, children and mother-in-law.

'You must make a clean break with Mu Xiang!' When she heard an interrogator shout these words, my mother realized that her husband was in trouble again, and the purpose of this interrogation was to force her to inform against him. She refused to cooperate, and insisted that her husband was a real Communist, incapable of harming the Party.

After that night, my mother's worries centred on my father. He was a proud and sensitive person who suffered from coronary heart disease. She was afraid that the anger he was certain to feel about these renewed accusations would further damage his health. At night, she started having dreadful nightmares, scenes of seeing my father tortured. She wept and screamed over his unconscious and bloodstained body, till the guards came to pound on her door and wake her up, furious about having their own sleep disturbed.

In September 1968, my mother and other members of the forced labour team were transferred to the 'cowshed' just established by the revolutionary committee. It occupied one corner of a student dormitory block, divided from the rest of the building by a newly built wall in the corridor on each floor. By day, the only entrance to the 'cowshed' was kept guarded. From evening till early morning, it was locked from outside. I always wondered what would happen if there was a fire at night, since the prisoners had no way to get out. For most of the new captives, the move was a disaster, because now they lost their freedom to go home. One day, my mother heard that Lu Wen's home had been burgled. She shared it with her teenage son, who was left on his own in her absence. Later, Lu Wen discovered that a considerable sum of money had been stolen.

In the 'cowshed', my mother also met some newcomers. One was a young junior lecturer jailed for a slip of the tongue made at a rally called to denounce capitalist-roaders. The girl had been ordered to give an address, but she was not used to public speaking, and suffered from terrible nerves. Part of her task was to lead the audience in chanting revolutionary slogans, but when the time came to shout 'Down with Liu Shaoqi!', what came out of her mouth was 'Down with Chairman Mao!' She was arrested at once for her counter-revolutionary crime, and sent straight to the 'cowshed'. In front of the inmates, she often sobbed: 'I have always loved Chairman Mao, and never forgotten what the Communist Party has done for me . . .'

The 'cowshed' routine required all prisoners to recite 'the plea of guilty' several times a day, before each meal and before their compulsory labour. It was written by the rebels, and started: 'We are sinners towards the people. We have committed monstrous crimes . . .' After the recitation, everyone had to speak their own name, preceded by the title of 'sinner'. My mother detested this humiliating exercise. 'I am not guilty at all!' she reminded herself every time. 'I have given my life to Communism. Only Chiang Kai-shek and the Nationalists would see me as a sinner.' Her feeling was shared by her companions, who usually tried to skimp the compulsory plea. One day, Lu Wen was caught in the act, and the guard ordered her to repeat the ugly statement out loud. When she refused, she was made to stand outside for hours in the bitter winter cold, and bow her head to the statue of Chairman Mao.

Imprisoned in the 'cowshed', Madam Dew could no longer help my errands for my parents, so I took my mother's suggestion and started to meet her secretly again. We usually met during her lunch breaks, when she was not closely watched on her way back to work. Our rendezvous was a quiet wooded hill between the campus and the nursery garden, where we made our exchange, talked for a moment, and hurried off in different directions. Unfortunately, one of our meetings was spotted by a labourer, and reported to the revolutionary committee. My mother was interrogated and beaten, but she denied everything. After that, she was not allowed near the hill unescorted, and our meetings got harder and more irregular.

Yet despite my mother's suffering, there were benefits in moving to the 'cowshed'. First, the long strain of solitary confinement was over, since she now lived with several other inmates. Normally, only the hardest cases were kept in cells. And then, the denunciation process against her was tailing off and eventually stopped. My mother had been living on a prisoner's allowance of 20 yuan per month, replacing her salary of over 170 yuan, which was enough for only a basic diet. Now the allowance rose to 70 yuan, which meant better food. These improvements came mainly because the revolutionary committee had by then almost lost its powerful position in the university.

On 26 August 1968, Mao Zedong's latest instruction appeared in the *People's Daily*: 'To every place where intellectuals gather, either educational institutions or elsewhere, [industrial] workers and the People's Liberation Army should be sent, to break the monopoly of the intellectuals and occupy these independent kingdoms. The workers' teams must remain in the educational institutions . . . to lead them for ever. In rural areas, schools must be managed by the workers' most reliable allies, namely poor or lower-middle peasants.' After that, Workers' and People's Liberation Army Propaganda Teams of Mao Zedong

Thought arrived in the schools, colleges and universities of Beijing, where they aimed to restore order.

The Propaganda Teams assigned to my mother's university consisted of dozens of workers from factories in Beijing, and over a hundred naval officers and sailors. On the day they arrived, my mother and Madam Lu Wen were sent to collect human excrement and urine from the campus. They were given a large cart carrying six barrels, and told to deliver thirty barrels of manure to the nursery garden in the morning. The campus manure pit was covered by a heavy metal lid, its edges rusted to the surrounding frame. No matter how hard they tried, my mother and Lu Wen failed to raise it. Eventually, a passing member of the Workers' Propaganda Team helped them to prise up the heavy lid. By the time it was done, he was panting. 'This job was done by strong male workers in the past,' Lu Wen told the man. 'I'm getting on for sixty, and not in good health. How can they treat me like this?' It seemed that the man understood, but he left without a word.

When my mother and Lu Wen were digging human waste out of the deep manure pit, they could not help spattering their clothes, shoes, hands, and even their faces. But there was no time to wash or change. Failure to complete their thirty barrels brought verbal abuse, beatings or loss of food. When pushing the loaded cart to the nursery garden, they had to be very careful, as the rules required them not to spill a drop from the uncovered barrels on their way. On one occasion they ran into two young officers from the PLA Propaganda Team. Encouraged by their previous contact with the sympathetic worker, they ventured to introduce themselves. 'We have no political defects at all!' the two women pleaded. 'Please verify our innocence!' The officers listened, and promised that the Propaganda Teams would treat their cases fairly.

Shortly after their arrival, the two Propaganda Teams began to take charge of the university, pushing aside the revolutionary committee based on Cao Lian's supporters. The newcomers were not involved in the university's internal battles. With no personal resentments against the prisoners in the 'cowshed', they had no cause to mistreat them, and this put a block on the rebels' denunciation activities. One day, a member of the Workers' Propaganda Team, a kind old man, told my mother quietly: 'Please don't always argue with the rebels! We know you're innocent, but it will take some time to rehabilitate you.'

In October 1968, we received a letter from my mother through the post, the first since her imprisonment ten months before. The message was brief – a request for winter clothes. When we delivered them, Feng-an and I were allowed to see her for a while, and she asked us to buy new shirts and woollen sweaters for my father. In the past, she had shopped for his clothes herself. My father's response was that he would not buy any new clothes until she returned, and could act as she had before. Touched by his reply, my mother got hold of some wool and learned from fellow prisoners to knit sweaters for her family. During that period, all her letters were censored, and our meetings watched, but despite these restrictions we welcomed the improvements. I was relieved to be spared those secret missions to my mother.

Meanwhile, there was no improvement for my father. Despite the strain on his heart, interrogations continued as before. When he was too weak to walk, his inquisitors would enter our house at will to badger and accuse him. Without knocking on the door, they rushed straight to his bedroom, ignoring the family's protests. If they found the door locked from inside, they banged or kicked until it opened. Day and night, we lived in fear of their brutal invasions, and the terror of the experience has never left me. Ever since then, I often shout with fright when startled by knocks on the door or nearby voices.

One day, Feng-an stopped the intruders by the staircase. 'I hope you know how to behave when you visit people's homes,' he said, trying to master his rage. One of them answered: 'We're not here to visit your family, but to interrogate Mu Xiang, a counter-revolutionary.' 'My son is no counter-revolutionary.' My grandmother appeared. 'I am his mother.

I know he has given his life to the revolution, and left home for sixteen years to fight the Nationalists and Japanese. How dare you accuse him? Where were you when my son risked his life to join the Communists?' 'Mind what you say!' the intruders threatened. 'We know you attacked the Great Leap Forward in 1960. Only your son's position saved you from being counted as a Bourgeois Rightist!'

In July 1968, we heard that Major-General Tang and Senior Colonel Ge, my father's chief opponents, had been removed from their posts and arrested. At first, I could hardly believe it. Who dared to challenge Tang? As far as I knew, he was unbeaten in his political encounters. Ge too had proved himself a dangerous enemy. Over the last few months, the two seemed to have consolidated their grip on the armoured forces. Now, all of a sudden, it was broken. Later, I heard that their downfall stemmed from their personal connections with General Yang Chengwu, acting Chief of the General Staff, who had been purged several months before.

I have no way of knowing who organized the campaign against Tang and Ge, as my family had no inside information. The story we heard from several sources was that Major-General Ren, commander of the armoured forces, played a hand. Ge had had his eye on that position, so it was very likely that he would use the tactics against Ren that had worked with my father. To protect himself, Ren needed to strike first. Another key figure was said to be Colonel Long, director of the political department, once under my father's command. Both Ren and Long had objected to Tang's treatment of my father, and during the 'Si-da' phase in January 1967, they were hauled into several sessions to be denounced side by side with my father. As well as supporting my father, Ren was also condemned for his association with Senior General Xu Guangda, his disgraced former boss. Another charge levelled at Long was 'political theft' (Zheng-zhi-ba-shou), meaning political opportunism. In his current post, he already held a higher position than men – like Senior Colonel Mercy Ocean – who were senior to him in length of Party service and grade on the salary scale. His opponents ascribed his promotion to his craving for personal gain.

Whether or not this account was true, one thing seemed clear: the disgrace of Tang and Ge removed a powerful threat to Major-General Ren. Colonel Long soon became acting political commissar of the armoured forces, in succession to Tang. The two men now controlled the reshuffled Party Standing Committee of the armoured forces.

Like the rest of my family, when I heard what had happened to Tang and Ge I assumed that my father's ordeal would soon be over, as Major-General Ren and Colonel Long were known to have supported him before. During 'Si-da', when Ren was taken ill after suffering denunci-ations, Aijun and I visited him secretly and brought him some food on behalf of my then imprisoned father. Lying in bed in his empty house, Ren looked pale and lonely. He had separated from his wife long ago, and his children were not around. I did not know how he felt about our visit, but I hoped he recalled it with gratitude. It came at a time when his political troubles made him practically untouchable. Ren should know too that without my father's refusal to cooperate with Ge in the first place, he himself, not my father, might have been Ge's first victim. In my mind, Long was a close and trusted colleague of my father, who when he came to our home in the past had talked to other family members in a polite and thoughtful way. He used to tell my mother: 'I come from Henan province too. If you fancy any specialities from our home town, do let me know. I would be pleased to help.' It was these good impressions that made me feel so positive that both of them would treat my father fairly. I even expected them to visit him at home as before.

Weeks passed, and nothing happened. My father did not hear from Ren and Long, nor did they come to see him, though neither lived far from our house. My father avoided the subject, but I could sense his growing anxiety. In the day, he often watched from the upstairs windows through his wartime binoculars. In the evening, he paced around his rooms – a routine exercise during his imprisonment. His heavy breathing and restless movement always reminded me of caged tigers seen at the zoo. Eventually, he was informed that the reconstituted Party Standing Committee of the armoured forces had decided to proceed with his case. It grieved him to realize that under the new leadership of Ren and Long, his ordeal would go on.

I have often wondered since then why Ren and Long changed their tune at that crucial moment. On 1 July 1966, when the Cultural Revolution had just started, my father referred in his diary to a speech that Ren gave at an official conference. 'Ren said that the allegation against me [from Tang and his allies] lacked proof . . .' he wrote. 'But he also criticized me for being too different from the others, for instance reading too much and hence being strongly influenced by old art and literature, and having too little in common with [industrial] workers and peasants . . .' Three decades later, reading his journal gave me the feeling that my father was seen as an outsider among the senior officers even by his then supporters. Among the PLA generals, most came from peasant backgrounds, whereas my father was from an urban area with an intellectual background. In addition, he showed no intention of giving up his passion for art and literature, nor did he try to change so as to be more like a worker-peasant cadre, as Chairman Mao instructed. Certainly, these features did not appeal to many of his colleagues or bosses, but it was hard to believe that this would be reason enough for Ren to turn against my father. Perhaps the more likely conjecture is that during the political storms, everyone felt equally insecure, and Ren was simply not prepared to risk his political career on a man who was considered an outsider.

For Long's second thoughts, a possible motive that my family heard afterwards was his own political ambitions. After Tang's political disgrace, my father was seen as Long's major rival for the post of political commissar, at least two grades higher than Long's current position. Under normal circumstances, the two grades could take the rest of a working lifetime to achieve. My father had already been promoted to replace Tang before the Cultural Revolution: it was only Tang's obstruction that prevented him. So Long would know the likely outcome if my father was rehabilitated. In terms of their revolutionary experience, grades and abilities, he could not hope to compete with my father for promotion.

But these are speculations, impossible to verify without consulting Ren and Long themselves. They remained quiet about their motives, and I have no individual contact with either.

In July 1969, we heard that Colonel Long was promoted to Political Commissar of the armoured forces. A year later, he was promoted again, to deputy director of the Political Department in the Beijing Military Region. In the 1980s, he became Political Commissar for one of China's large military regions. In the early 1970s, Major-General Ren, commander of the armoured forces, was promoted to deputy Commander of the Beijing Military Region. Their previous posts were filled by two officers from a division under my father's headquarters.

Following the decision not to close my father's case, more problems arrived. One of them was new charges against his novel, which centred on the activities of the Alliance of Sacrificing Ourselves to Save the Nation, well known for its resistance during the Sino-Japanese War, but now accused as a counter-revolutionary organization. Its leader, Vice-Premier Bo Yibo, was under arrest as a ringleader of the so-called 'Renegade clique of sixty-one', and my father came under pressure to admit that his novel had been written by command of Bo Yibo, to enhance his public image in combatting Chairman Mao. To prove his innocence, my father combed the *Selected Works of Mao Zedong* and collected all Mao's positive remarks about the Alliance. But this did not save him. He could not undo the damage caused to Bo Yibo and the Alliance by Mao's radical followers, nor was he allowed to defend himself. A decade later, when he completed the tetralogy of *The Billows*, he wrote in the epilogue that during the Cultural Revolution 'numerous comrades [veteran Communists associated with the Alliance] were identified as particular characters in *Autumn in Jinyang*, and hence suffered penalties such as suspension from their jobs, demotion or banishment.'

One day, Aijun came in from outside looking sad. 'Mimi said her parents won't let her play with me again, because of our parents' political problems.' My little sister's misery upset me, as I knew that the girl next door was the only friend she had left. Since my father's house arrest, few people in the compound dared to contact us, and our visitors from outside were checked by armed guards at the entrance. Without official permission, no one was allowed to visit us, not even relatives or the children's friends.

I knew how Aijun felt. The gossip about my morals had made me a virtual outcast, and even before my father's first spell in prison, more than a year before, some of our neighbours' children had expressed their unwillingness to speak to the daughter of a political suspect. For a long time, my only company in the compound was a girl around my age whose father was an officer in my father's headquarters. As both of our schools were in town, we often met on my occasional trips to school, and I was getting to know her. One evening when I called at her home, she took me outside in a panic. 'Please don't contact me again!' she said. 'My father is furious about our friendship. He was told that it isn't our being close that matters, but it shows his personal support for your father.' I left her in peace, and did not blame her or her father, but on my way home I wept tears of pain and anger. As the daughter of 'counter-revolutionaries', I had no right even to make a friend! Why must our family suffer so much? When would our ordeals be over?

After Beijing became the Red capital, numerous administrative and residential compounds were established in and around the city, to house both government offices and their staff and families. Many of these enclaves, and especially the military kind, were like independent kingdoms as measured by their huge area, heavy security, and variety of services. The armoured forces compound, for example, provided shops, clinics, public baths, hairdressers and a swimming pool, as well as several staff canteens and guest hostels. The headquarters also ran a kindergarten and a primary school, and organized regular free entertainments such as films or plays.

From mid-1968, many military compounds grew quiet and empty. Most of their officers' middle school children had joined the armed forces, even though a lot of them were under eighteen, the stipulated minimum age. In those days, this was viewed as the best solution for students whose schools or universities no longer functioned. In the prevailing chaos, there were few jobs available anywhere, but in case of war with China's enemies a huge military budget kept the size of its forces expanding, and they became almost the only source of new employment. Due to the rise of Lin Biao, the defence minister, the military forces also occupied a powerful position in Chinese society, with higher social status.

But for the children of senior officers, much of the recruitment was organized through the back door, especially for girls, because the openings were limited. To the vast majority of families who lacked these military connections, the back door was closed. The children of 'counter-revolutionaries', like my siblings and me, were also excluded. By the time Tang and Ge were disgraced, their children had already been recruited, so my father became the only officer in the armoured forces whose children lost the privilege of employment – a precious opportunity.

This made our neighbourhood uncomfortable to live in, because it always reminded me of my misfortune as compared with the families around us. Soon, many of the new recruits started to return home for holidays. These teenage soldiers from senior officer families enjoyed all kinds of special treatment, such as choosing where to be posted and what kind of work to be given. They also got more time off duty than an ordinary recruit. When our neighbours' children came home on leave, their parents loved to show them off to friends and relatives. Smart in their uniforms, these teenagers, and especially the girls, caught attention wherever they went, as their appearance advertised good luck and social status. I resented these cheerful visitors, with their visible sense of superiority. They revelled quite openly in their privileged positions and bright futures. Where was my future? I could not help asking, as I began to recognize that it was already damaged by my parents' misfortunes. My family was outside the privileged circle. I was no longer a proud 'Red princess', and my life had turned in a totally different direction from those I grew up with. To avoid these surroundings, I was less and less inclined to go out.

During that period, the political mood intensified. Every day, people had to perform at least two compulsory rituals of loyalty to Mao: 'Zao-qing-shi' ('requesting instructions in the morning') and 'Wan-hui-bao' ('reporting in the evening'). In classrooms, factories, offices, barracks and many private homes, they had to stand and face Mao's portrait, holding the *Quotations from Chairman Mao* in their right hand. Normally, the ritual began with singing 'The East is Red'. Before reading from the *Quotations*, a cheerleader shouted: 'We wish our great leader, great teacher, great commander and great helmsman Chairman Mao a long, long life!', and the others had to brandish the little red book and chorus: 'A long, long life! A long, long life! A long, long life!' Pupils from primary schools were sent out into the streets to read from Mao to passersby. Shop assistants had to say 'Long life to Chairman Mao!' before they served each customer. To answer the telephone, the approved opening greeting was Mao's famous quotation, 'Serve the people'. In response, the caller must answer 'Whole-heartedly' before starting the conversation. Little Auntie told me that one day, two colleagues sat in the public lavatory and recited Mao's quotations like 'Be resolute, fear no sacrifice and surmount every difficulty to win victory' to encourage each other to defecate.

Residents of Beijing were disturbed by the frequent reports of widespread violence caused by feuding among the rebels. Aiming to develop their fighting capability, rebel organizations often sent delegations to observe the clashes in other institutions or factories, and their weapons included rocket-launchers and cannons. A fight in the famous Xi-dan department store resulted in a whole year's closure because of the damage caused by vandalism and looting. The brother of one of my schoolmates suffered a frightful experience. While he was undergoing an urgent operation in hospital, a quarrel broke out among the attending surgeons, anaesthetists and nurses, divided about the opposed rebel factions there. The operation was interrupted for nearly half an hour, leaving the boy's abdominal cavity exposed.

For all those middle school pupils who had no chance to enjoy the privilege of military service, on the other hand, life became stale. Their short-lived performances at the centre of China's political stage now lay in the past, and unrewarded. Many, including the 'veteran Red Guards' of the Joint Action Committee, felt let down by the Cultural Revolution. But what could they do to revive their idle lives? Nothing remained – no education, no entertainment, and no hope for their futures. One day, I heard that local pupils organized a contest between two city districts – a championship for crickets, which drew enthusiastic crowds to watch insects fight insects. Black markets emerged for exchanging Chairman Mao badges, and some pupils I knew became expert traders. Since it was forbidden to sell the badges, business was done by barter. Over the last few years, almost 2 billion Mao badges had been produced, in an incredible variety of designs and materials. These badges were often used by the rebels as gifts to their allies, friends and relations. One large badge I saw could almost cover an adult's chest but was amazingly light, because it was made of an alloy used only for aircraft in the past. I was told that this particular one required at least fifty ordinary badges in exchange.

Along Wangfujing Avenue, east of the Forbidden City, the busiest shopping street in Beijing, large crowds of teenagers gathered every day, most of them boys. They sat on the high metal railings, or stood alongside them, chatting and sharing cigarettes. If a passerby caught their attention, they would start shouting, booing or hooting. Their style of dress set the trend for the city's teenagers, and was still based on loose-fitting khaki combat gear. The Mao-style suit in navy blue was also in fashion, called 'government blue'. Through the opened buttons of the collar, a white shirt often showed. Their favourite shoes included the 'Hui-li' brand of heavy white trainers, produced in Shanghai. Many of the boys liked to wear sunglasses even on cloudy days and in the evening.

One of their topics of discussion was the latest fighting between different teenage gangs, whose divisions were often based on their members' family background, such as between official and non-official families. Further subdivisions signified factors such as the area or compound they lived in, or the school they attended. The children of officials – even the many officials now in political trouble – still felt superior, and referred to those from ordinary families as 'Pi-zi' ('riffraff'). In the frequent clashes among gangs, the main weapons included kitchen knives and cable-wire locks for bicycles. The sight of a pack of teenage boys cycling past with a din of bells told local residents that a fight was coming somewhere, but no one dared to stop them and the police often turned a blind eye. Among the hundreds of thousands of teenage boys in Beijing, the boldest, strongest gang fighters were regarded as heroes, with the same enormous popularity enjoyed today by pop singers and football stars.

When teenage boys talked about a girl, they gave marks for her looks like school examiners. One hundred per cent meant absolutely beautiful; less than sixty per cent meant ugly. By then, having a girlfriend was no longer unusual for many boys, and they liked to parade their high-scoring girlfriends. Among gang members, the fashion was to find their girls through 'pai', meaning pursuit, generally on the street, as there was nowhere else to socialize.

One day, I found myself pursued. Several tall young men in modish dress came up behind me, and kept asking: 'Shall we make friends?' I tried not to look or reply, for fear of attracting or provoking them. 'Are you listening?' They were getting impatient. 'What's your name? Where do you live? What school do you go to?' I quickened my pace, but did not know where to go. In the following hour, I just switched from one bus to another around central Beijing, desperate to lose my pursuers, and not to let them know where I lived or went to school. Eventually, they got fed up. 'Stupid!' they said before they left me. 'Don't know what's good for you!' When I came home, I looked terribly pale and felt clammy with sweat.

Some girls accepted these approaches and became involved with teenage gangs. Normally, they liked to dress in similar style to their boyfriends. Their hair was tied in two short bunches at the back, instead of on either side of the head in the usual way. Among teenagers in Beijing, these girls were attacked for being 'piao-er', meaning flighty. At home, they could face scolding, beating or even detention, by scandalized parents, but no matter how much punishment they suffered, many refused to give in, and still hung around in public with their boyfriends and other gang members.

Obviously, teenagers around my age had entered the phase of adolescent sexual feeling, although it was rather belated. The books that tended to circulate in secret were novels that featured descriptions of love or sex. The relevant pages often looked worn and smudged from repeated reading. But as far as I knew, sex was still rare for teenagers, even in the gangs, despite their reputations. As the first generation brought up under the Communist regime, we had absorbed a mixture of Communist propaganda, which disapproved of personal emotions, and feudal dogma, which outlawed the subject of sex. Therefore we had no access to accurate information, or even an opportunity to talk about the subject openly. Sex remained largely a mystery. Outside marriage it was sinful. Girls must be cautious not to lose their virginity.

At the end of August 1968, all middle school pupils in Beijing were summoned back to school to take part in a project called 'Resuming classes and practising revolution' (fu-ke nao-ge-ming), launched by the combined Workers' and PLA Propaganda Teams of Mao Zedong

Thought. Now that the country's old administration had been almost replaced by the new revolutionary committee, students were no longer needed as shock-troops in intra-Party warfare. In fact, the endless feuding among rebel organizations, coupled with teenage delinquent behaviour, had created a national crisis. After the chaos they had caused, confining China's students to their campuses was viewed as an essential step towards restoring the country's stability.

Back at school, however, I found that no classes took place. Instead, most of our time was consumed by tedious indoctrination – the works of Chairman Mao, or official documents – and military training. Later, I learned that Senior Colonel Mercy Ocean, my father's enemy, who had bullied me in public early in 1967, was now in charge of all the PLA Propaganda Teams assigned to the West District where my school was located, and had made several inspections of the school. I also heard that in one plenary session a leading member of the Propaganda Team had condemned me in my absence for 'harbouring counter-revolutionary parents'. My constant absences sent many rumours flying. One day, a schoolmate I met on a bus asked me about my recent imprisonment, apparently common knowledge among many people. According to some 'witnesses', I had been arrested in town and sent to jail for shouting counter-revolutionary slogans.

September brought extravagant preparations for celebrating the First of October, China's National Day. Under the Communist regime, such preparations are not unfamiliar for local residents: they take place routinely before large ceremonial events. Residents were mobilized to clean the streets, and to remove the thick veneer of posters and slogans. Along the city's main streets, many buildings were repainted on the outside, or decorated with red flags or coloured lights. For weeks around the National Day, Tian-an Men Square bloomed with potted flowers. Official channels made sure that shops and markets were much better supplied with goods than during the rest of the year. But for the city authorities, a higher priority was to restore and maintain public order, which involved clamping down on class enemies. Those perceived as active opponents of the Communist Party often faced arrest, detention or deportation from Beijing. This year, the authorities also targeted teenage delinquents.

In early September, schools were ordered to set up special camps for delinquents on their premises, and I heard that my name had been listed to attend. 'Why me?' I thought in disbelief. 'I've never stolen anything, or been involved with gangs.' Unfortunately, what I heard was true, and several days later I was instructed to report to the camp. I burst into tears. The injustice and humiliation were more than I could bear. Once labelled as a delinquent, I would have no way to clear my name. They might as well have stamped it on my face. How could I manage my life after this? What would happen if my family found out . . . ?

'Tell me, please!' I asked the appointed leader, a final-year pupil. 'Why should I be sent to the camp?' His reply was cold and brief: 'Don't ask me! You know what you did.' At last, I realized that the cause of my trouble was the gossip about my relationship with Mighty China. This was unjust – whatever I had done with him, it had nothing to do with delinquency. And even if it had, why should I be the only one to be punished? During our brief relationship more than two years ago, I had been a naive girl, not yet fifteen, while Mighty China, three years my senior, was almost an adult. Yet he was not assigned to the camp. Clearly, it was not his age that saved him, though he was no longer a teenager. In the camp, I saw several pupils around his age, mostly connected with gangs. Wasn't it because I was a female that I had been singled out to be punished – for a fictitious offence – whereas Mighty China, as a man, could be forgiven?

My plea for justice was ignored. Instead, I was told that if I refused to attend the camp, I would be picked up at home, which really scared me. At any costs, my family must not know, as there had been enough disasters in our lives. All I could do was to swallow the injustice.

The camp was a nightmare that lasted for several weeks. When they appeared on the campus, the 'delinquents', about twenty altogether, always drew great attention from the pupils, and the three female offenders most of all. The other two girls in the camp were accused of hanging around with boys. The crowds would whisper as we passed. Some even pointed their fingers, or sneered as they stared. To avoid these encounters, I often avoided going to the canteen for lunch, or using the lavatory. But when I came home, I had to pretend that nothing had happened, and keep my father and grandmother company.

During the day, the 'delinquents' were normally kept inside a room in a corner of the campus, either listening to reprimands from school officials, or making compulsory 'confessions' about their 'crimes', which meant spelling out their social and historical background. In other words, our ordeal required us to submit to all the charges made against us, and then connect them to social and political factors. For offenders who made compulsory 'confessions' during the Cultural Revolution, this was not an unfamiliar experience. A statement made by one boy shoplifter began: 'Chairman Mao taught us "never to forget the class struggle".' It went on to say that during the life-and-death struggle between two lines – the revolutionary and the counter-revolutionary – he had failed to take a firm proletarian stand, and succumbed to the class enemy's attacks with sugar-coated bullets. This showed how the capitalist class always tried to lure the younger generation away from the proletarian class.

When the camp closed, all the 'delinquents' had to admit their guilt in front of all their classmates and then beg forgiveness from the revolutionary masses. Despite official pressure, I strove not to let myself down in my 'confession', using the term 'mistake' to refer to what happened with Mighty China. Throughout that episode, I felt terribly bitter about the injustice I suffered, and being powerless to protect myself. My classmates made no objection to my 'confession', as none of them knew the truth.

After my experiences in the camp, I no longer respected my school. Gossip and injustice had made my life hell there, and I could not wait to leave.

Chapter 17

Cave Life, Starvation and Hard Labour: My 'Re-education' in the Loess Highlands

(December 1968–September 1969)

In the evening of 21 December 1968, Chinese radio reported a decree from Chairman Mao: 'It is essential that school-leavers go to rural areas to be re-educated by poor and lower-middle peasants . . .' Next day the story made headlines in the *People's Daily*. When I first heard it, I was on my way home by bus. Over a passenger's radio, the newscaster's voice sounded cold and demanding. Nobody spoke. In the faint light, I saw everyone around me looking serious.

Shortly after the broadcast, various orchestrated activities took place. Since the start of the Cultural Revolution, each time Mao issued a new order the routine was for the main streets of Beijing to be packed with hundreds of thousands of residents, mobilized for propaganda performances. Marching towards Tian-an Men Square, the crowds carried red flags or huge banners urging 'Respond with resolution to Chairman Mao's call!' or 'Long live the great and wise Communist Party of China!' Cheerleaders conducted them in chanting revolutionary slogans, often to a thunder of gongs and drums, or the bray of brass bands. I watched the celebrations on TV, and felt sad for the participants, as I knew what the new decree meant to most of their families.

Chairman Mao was showing his public support for a new national scheme launched several months previously, which aimed to send middle-school pupils to the countryside, as more than 10 million were stuck in either junior or senior middle schools. Although none had completed the courses cut short by the Cultural Revolution, they were now regarded as graduates, ready to leave. There was no prospect of further education, since universities had stopped teaching, and little chance of employment. In recent months, pupils at my school had been mobilized to take part in the scheme. We were told that participation would be voluntary, but at the same time it was made clear that for school-leavers in the cities, the only choice was to be re-educated by peasants in rural settlements where we were expected to spend the rest of our lives. Acting on orders, the school authorities tried to make sure that no pupil was exempt from the scheme, except in the case of only children. Since then, pupils had been notified of various possible destinations, scattered among rural areas in northern China, many of them distinguished by their remote location, harsh climate, sparse population and backward development.

For Feng-an and me, there seemed no choice but to take part in the scheme. In the past, I had desperately wanted to leave school, but now I needed to think about the consequences if we were exiled from Beijing. Our parents were still imprisoned, and we were my father's only link with my mother and the outside. Unfortunately, there was no alternative. Without official permission, we could not simply quit school, stay at home, and hence evade the scheme. For a while, we managed to stave off mobilization by not attending school. On the day after Mao's new decree was announced, my father received a message from the investigation team dealing with his case, which informed him that his children must respond to Chairman Mao's call. From that moment, he recognized that it was impossible for him to keep Feng-an and me at home any longer.

In fact, I was already under enormous pressure at school. Since October, our campus had emptied as pupils left for their rural settlements, so the few who remained became the focus of the mobilization drive. The central authorities were losing patience with the small number of holdouts, and hence coerced their families through their schools or neighbourhood committees. In urban areas, these committees, each of them based on several streets, wielded enormous local power. Most of their members were housewives or pensioners who showed a strong sense of communal responsibility, but tended to throw their weight around, and cause headaches for local residents, when implementing Party policies.

It was said that reluctant school-leavers could see their families invaded by noisy crowds sent by the school or local authority. With a din of gongs and drums, the unwelcome visitors announced to the assembled neighbours that the children of the family had agreed to go to the countryside – which was of course untrue. The families therefore faced embarrassment and pressure, which caused many to push their children to surrender themselves. These stories made me fear what might happen if this tactic was used against my family. Considering the influence of Mercy Ocean over the PLA Propaganda Team in my school, I had no hope of mercy. If my resistance continued, my parents would be accused of sabotaging the scheme, and hence face more political trouble.

Eventually, Feng-an and I had to agree to go to the countryside. Considering my painful situation in my school, I asked to join Feng-an and other pupils at Ba-Yi School, which was later accepted. After the raid in January 1967, Ba-yi had been denounced as a typical 'Bourgeois Aristocratic School'. By now, pupils in the primary school, including my younger siblings, had been transferred to schools near their homes. In the middle schools, pupils with parents untainted politically had joined the armed forces and evaded rural exile. Most of those left belonged to other families in political trouble, and we found a lot in common.

From Ba-yi School, I learned that the only locality available for us was

Yanchuan county – not an unfamiliar name, as it was there that my mother first entered the Communist Central Base during the Sino-Japanese War. It lies in the mountains northeast of Yan'an, the Communist capital where both my parents lived during the war. 'Is there any other settlement available?' my father asked when I told him. 'Yanchuan is a very poor county. I hear that even today, many local people are still penniless, and often suffer from starvation.' Indeed, the north of Shaanxi province was regarded by pupils as the most undesirable region of settlement, despite its former revolutionary glories. During previous months, most of the localities provided had been in relatively more prosperous areas, and many pupils had been recruited by the production and construction corps run by the military, where they could at least receive a small regular salary and adequate food. But by this time, the choices had almost run out.

Before our departure, my father tried to take Feng-an and me to town to buy some warm clothes, since our mother was still detained. He himself was still under house arrest, but on this special occasion he expected some compassion to be shown. He was mistaken. As soon as we reached the bus stop outside the compound, a squad of soldiers came to intercept him. His plea for compassion was ignored, and in the end Feng-an and I had to do all the preparation ourselves. It was the first time in my life that I went clothes shopping on my own. While choosing an overcoat in a department store, I did not realize that I had left my purse on the counter until the assistant picked it up. 'Why didn't you come with your parents?' she asked, and shook her head.

The morning that Feng-an and I left home is pinned in my memory. It was a cold winter day on 13th January 1969. At dawn, I heard my father's footsteps, already awake and walking around upstairs. Later at breakfast, he seemed to have aged overnight, and his eyes were red. Years later, he told me that he did not sleep that night, after his long conversation with us both. The table was hushed, except for my grandmother. 'Try to eat more, children,' she said tearfully, and kept our bowls filled up with her special dumplings. 'I wonder when you'll have our home-made food again.' Sitting in front of the delicious dumplings, I had no appetite, and felt choked by the heavy atmosphere. Knowing that my father was staring at me, I lowered my head to avoid eye contact, for fear of losing control and starting to wail. Eventually, it was time to say goodbye. Standing by the living room door of our house like a statue, my father was silent. Tears ran down his face. Being a prisoner, he was not allowed to see his children off at the railway station, nor was my mother. I clung to him and wept. I did not know when I could return, or how my parents would survive without us.

The main Beijing railway station was enormously crowded. That day, special trains had been put on to deliver pupils to their rural settlements. The platform was thronged with departing pupils and their families, and many were weeping. Little Auntie and her husband managed to see us off, together with Feng-yuan and Aijun. I could not quell my tears. 'Everything will be okay, child,' Little Auntie tried to comfort me, but soon we were sobbing together.

No one there knew that part of my sadness had another cause. When preparing for the countryside, I had persuaded two girls at my own middle school to join me in the same village, as pupils were allowed to group together. The prospect of an unknown distant place had made me very insecure and anxious, and because our upbringing had created no close bonds between my siblings and me, my brother's company was not enough to ease my fears. So I looked to my school friends for company. As it was years since I had left Ba-yi, hardly anyone there was familiar, apart from Feng-an. The two girls at my school were among the few I saw as friends, since they had treated me kindly throughout my troubles. I was not sure whether or not they believed the gossip, but I felt sure that they would never do me harm.

At the beginning, everything went smoothly. The two girls welcomed my suggestion, since they had no other obvious partners, and their parents approved the arrangement. Then on the day before we left I visited

My mother in the Communist Jin-Sui base in 1943, during the Sino-Japanese War, shortly before she became a political prisoner.

My father (left) with his bodyguard in Jining, 1946, during the Civil War.

My parents and Little Auntie (left), my father's youngest sister in Beijing, 1952.

My father (second from left) and his bodyguards, in the Korean War in winter, 1951 just after I was born.

Little Auntie and me in Beijing, 1953. Both of us were wearing a black armband on the left arm, as it was during the time of national mourning for the death of Stalin in China.

Students of the Women's University in Yan'an during their 'washing time' by the Yan River, 1940. Everyone wore army uniforms.

LEFT A class in session at the Women's University in Yan'an, 1940.
RIGHT Chairman Mao addressing a meeting at the Chinese People's Anti-Japanese Military and Political University in Yan'an, 1939.

The family reunion in 1954, taken in the courtyard of my family home in Beijing. I am in the centre, in front of my paternal grandmother.

The row behind me (from left): Second Uncle's two elder sons, paternal grandmother, Feng Xin and Feng-an.

The back row (from left): Third Auntie's husband, Second Uncle, Third Auntie with her daughter, Second Uncle's wife with her younger son, my mother with Feng-Yuan, my father, Little Auntie.

Chairman Mao meets pupils from my school, the Ba-yi school, in 1952 in his residence in Zhongnanhai, Beijing.

The headmaster of my school reporting his work to Chairman Mao in Zhongnanhai, Beijing, 1952.

Aged five in the courtyard of my family home in Beijing. The fountain in the background was my favourite as a child.

A family photograph taken in 1956 (from left): Feng-an, Aijun and me in the front, and Feng-Yuan and Feng-Xin at the back.

Aged six in Beijing.

In the Summer Palace in Beijing, 1959.

My father in his
study in Beijing,
1963.

My father chatting with soldiers and officers when inspecting troops in a suburb of
Beijing, 1964.

Elifila (left), my best school friend, and me in Beijing in 1964. Two years later, when the Cultural Revolution started, I became a Red Guard. Elifila's home was raided by my fellow rebels, because her father, Baorhan, a senior statesman, was persecuted.

My parents in Jinci, Taiyuan, 1966, while my father was writing his second novel. A few weeks later, he was summoned to Beijing and his nine-year ordeal of political persecution began.

During the Cultural Revolution, similar political rallies or demonstrations were held frequently all over China.

The crowds await the latest 'big character' posters pasted up by the Red Guards during the Cultural Revolution.

The cover of my father's award-winning novel, *Autumn in Jinyang*, published in Beijing, 1962.

One of the confessions my father was forced to submit in the early 1970s concerning his so-called 'crimes'. It was over 30 pages in four major parts. My father wrote: "Through the novel, which was widely sold throughout the whole country, bourgeois ideology was spread among readers. To a certain extent, it poisoned people's minds and largely damaged the Party's cause . . . I will accept all necessary punishments from the Party and the masses."

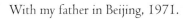
With my father in Beijing, 1971.

In Changzhi, Shanxi, 1972.

Performing "The Red Lantern", Madam Mao's favourite revolutionary Peking Opera, in Changzhi, 1972. I am the fourth from right.

Practising acupuncture with my colleague (right) in 1973. (This photograph was published in a number of newspapers, including *The People's Daily*.)

Giving a presentation during Mao's national campaign of 'Denouncing Lin Biao and Confucius', Changzhi, 1974. The Cultural Revolution with its endless political campaigns made political indoctrination a compulsory routine in people's lives.

My parents, Aijun and me (left at the back) in Beijing, 1973. My father's face reveals his state of mind during the last few years I saw him.

Me with the wounded and a colleague after the cease-fire of the Sino-Vietnam War in 1979. I am on the right at the back.

TOP Meeting Deng Xiaoping at Tianchi (Heaven Lake) on top of the Changbai Mountain, 1983. I (left, at front) was working for the State Family Planning Commission.

LEFT Little Mountain (left) with his cousin Little South, in Beijing, 1986.

BELOW In 1986 my father visited his home-country, Penglai, for the first time since he left in 1935. He died less than two years after the trip.

In Yorkshire, UK in 1993.

On my return to Beijing in 1996, I visited the former palace where I lived in the Ba-yi School during my childhood.

their homes, which were quite close to each other. They had asked me to help them pack their luggage. So I was stunned to hear from both of them that they were unable to join me because of strong objections from their parents, who in the last few days had listened to gossip about me, relayed by colleagues or neighbours with children at our school. In particular, it shocked their parents that I had attended the camp for delinquents. 'Why let your daughter go with Mu Aiping, a girl with a bad reputation?' they were asked. Faced with my friends' embarrassment, I felt that the way ahead had collapsed, as if hit by an earthquake. I had lost my last hope of support in an uncertain future. One girl's mother was scared by my distress, and tried to comfort me, but the message remained: her daughter could not go with me. The other girl's parents did not bother to see me at all.

After two days of travel, our train stopped at Tongchuan, a small town north of Xi'an city. Next day we had to carry on by truck, as Tongchuan was the end of the line. When our motorcade entered Yan'an, it was already late afternoon, the time of my mother's first arrival, thirty years before. The moment we stopped, I rushed to the famous pagoda and the Yan River, so vivid in my parents' stories, and many other pupils did the same. It was the low-water season, and the river was like a shallow stream and many parts were covered with ice. A number of huge flat stones forded the river-bed in front of me, and as they jumped across them I heard some pupils reciting: 'With white towel and scarlet belt/ Our dear people crossed the Yan River to welcome us . . .' – lines from a poem called 'Returning to Yan'an', which we learned at school. The author was He Jingzhi, who had been Second Uncle's colleague in Yan'an when he wrote his famous play, *The Girl with White Hair*. The poem expressed his excitement when he returned to Yan'an after the Communists came to power.

In great contrast to the mood of my parents and their wartime comrades, I was not at all excited by Yan'an. Having grown up in Beijing, I was used to its imperial surroundings, and that made it hard to appreciate what I saw. After the wars, many areas in the north of Shaanxi province remained poor and undeveloped, so to me Yan'an looked incredibly small and remote. Most of its dusty streets were lined with small, dilapidated houses. At night, the city was dark, for lack of street-lights. Suddenly, I was bursting with frustration. Oh, let me go! Right now! I could not stand even another second so far from home! My parents were still imprisoned, and I should not leave caring for the family to my grandmother and younger siblings! Thirty years earlier, Yan'an was a vision for hundreds of thousands of Chinese, like my parents, who sought a bright future for themselves and their country. But now, what was I here for? This was no choice of mine!

Past Yan'an, the journey got harder. Next morning soon after we left, the temperature dropped sharply and the wind rose. Our canvas-topped trucks were useless to keep out the cold, and because there were no seats provided, we had to stand or sit on the freezing metal floor. Most of the time, my whole body was numb with cold, as if the warm clothes I was wearing were made of thin paper. The large gauze mask that covered my face froze solid from my breath, except for small areas over my mouth and nostrils. When the trucks stopped for short breaks, we could hardly recognize each other beneath our thick layers of brown dust. As in most parts of the loess highlands, the roads were unmetalled, and vehicles raised plumes of brown dust, but the further we travelled, the fewer the signs of life. For hours at a time, we saw no villages, or any other vehicles or people. As the succeeding valleys grew narrower, I sometimes thought that our truck was going to get squeezed by the rolling cliffs and barren hills, never to move again.

Before evening, our convoy split into separate groups, each with several trucks and about a hundred pupils and their luggage, that then went off in different directions. After hours of bumping along the road, at last we stopped, and at once heard music blare and voices shout: 'Welcome school-leavers sent from Beijing by Chairman Mao!' My first impression was their strange local accent. The music was played by several 'suo-nas', a traditional instrument like a horn, and sounded breathy and often out of tune. By the light of several gas-lamps, I saw a large crowd of smiling peasants. Soon they surrounded us, and some local girls started to gaze at our clothes and whisper to each other. After four days of travelling, we had arrived in Wen'anyi Town, the administrative centre of the people's commune. From here, the whole group split again, and each small group went to its own destination. The small village of Liangjia He, where Feng-an and I were to settle, with six other pupils, lay in the mountains about 10 kilometres away from Wen'anyi.

The mountain path, winding between endless cliffs and hills, was so narrow that in places even a small wheelbarrow could hardly scrape through. So all our luggage, including heavy suitcases and bedding rolls, was carried by strong peasants from the village. In our torches' bobbing light, we tried to follow, but it was difficult. The frozen path was terribly slippery and full of bumps and hollows. With our plastic-soled shoes, we tottered like learners on skates. 'How far to the village now?' we kept asking. 'Not very far.' The peasants did not look at us, but walked ahead with our luggage on their backs.

Eventually, we came to a small flat ground on a hillside. Before I made out our surroundings, a door was opened at the other end. 'You're home,' someone said, and now I saw a deep narrow cave. Inside it, a small kerosene lamp provided a flickering light that shone on earthen walls and a small paper-covered window. A huge kang with rough earthen surfaces for sleeping occupied two-thirds of the cave. The few pieces of furniture included a small desk and four crudely made, unpainted stools. From now on, I would be sharing this cave with three other girls, while Feng-an and three other boys lived next door. All eight shared an extra cave as a kitchen. Official policy tended to assign girls and boys in equal numbers to each village, to balance the ratio of marriage partners.

My letters from Liangjia He:

20 January 1969
Baba,

. . . Our village forms a production brigade. Based on residential areas, it is divided into two production teams: the Liangjia He Front, where we live, and the Liangjia He Rear. Each team comprises about 100 inhabitants with around 20 households. Inside the village, there is not a single street or house. All the villagers live in caves scattered on barren hillsides along both sides of several narrow valleys. On the evening we arrived, I could not believe that we were already inside the village till I heard dogs barking nearby.

What's happening in our lives now is an absolutely new experience for everyone. Our caves are located by the entrance to the village, above a small spring which is the only water supply for the entire Liangjia He Front. Every day, we take turns to fetch water for drinking, cooking and washing. The two wooden buckets are so heavy that I have trouble even to carry them empty on a shoulder-pole . . . Most areas in the county, including our commune, have no electricity, tap water or sanitation. The caves we live in were previously used as storerooms, and are damp and terribly cold, and the stove to heat our kang is out of order. When we get up in the morning, we often find the water in our washbowls frozen. Often the wind blows snowflakes through gaps in our cave's wooden door, and they drift on the earthen floor. In particular, it is difficult for us to cope with the long winter night. Standing in the yard outside, I only see endless darkness surrounding me. Apart from the sound of wind, everywhere is quiet, even the dogs stop barking, as if we were at the end of the world.

. . . Since supper, all the girls have been sitting on the kang, with duvets round our legs to keep warm. I am writing this letter by the light of a small kerosene lamp, while the other girls listen to the radio. The radio brought by one of them from home has fascinated the villagers, and so has our clock, as they are the only ones in the entire Liangjia He Front . . . Every day, village children come to knock on our door asking to see and touch the radio and clock, and listen to their sound . . .

Of the three girls in my cave, I only knew one before. Her name is Beijing-Korea, in memory of her father going to the Korean War as a senior Chinese officer. Her father, Major-General Li, was a Red Army veteran and went through the Long March. You must have met him, because he also worked in the Beijing Military Region in the 1950s. Last year he was found dead in his bedroom, after being denounced as a counter-revolutionary in mass rallies . . . Beijing-Korea said that her father had suffered from serious coronary heart disease for a long time, so the rebels' actions eventually took his life. Her father's tragedy immediately reminded me of your situation. Baba, please take good care of yourself! Whatever happens, don't get too angry, please, or else your health will be further damaged.

In Liangjia He, I also know some boys from Ba-yi School. One is the younger brother of An-an, my friend in primary school. This boy is only fifteen. Their father, Vice-Premier Xi Zhongxun, has been in political trouble since 1962, and is now imprisoned. I found that Xi Zhongxun is a household name here . . . because he was a founder of the Shaan-Gan Soviet Base, so his son's arrival has created a sensation among local people.

. . . It is said that years ago, Wen'anyi was a busy town in northern Shaanxi province, where couriers changed horses or rested, but now there is no public transport and the whole town looks quiet and empty, apart from market days, which come about three times a month. The only main street is narrow, with a small post office, a tiny bank, and a few small shops selling household goods or food, which are the only facilities available for scores of villages in the whole commune. Once a week, the only postman visits our village to fetch and deliver the mail . . .

4 February 1969
Baba,
Village life doesn't seem busy at the moment. In winter, not much happens in the fields. At night, the peasants like to meet in someone's home and chat together. Women sit cross legged on the kang, busy stitching soles for cloth shoes while they gossip. The villagers always wear hand-made shoes, as it's too expensive to buy them from shops. I find their shoes much handier than our plastic-soled ones, especially when walking on mountain paths. It is always interesting to see how skilful these women are. Without any drawing, they stitch soles in beautiful neat patterns . . . But the funniest thing for us is seeing men knit. When we started laughing, the villagers were surprised, because in this area knitting is seen as a job for men. The wool is home-made and poor quality. Apart from the natural colour, some of it is dyed bright orange-red . . .

We joined village gatherings several times. It is much warmer in their caves, especially as their kangs are well heated and the doors and windows close-fitting. The hosts are very friendly . . . But what put us off about the gatherings was the thick tobacco smoke in their caves, as many men keep puffing their long-stemmed pipes most of the time. There is no fresh air at all, so often we choke and our eyes stream. We also discovered that lice are very common, as the villagers hardly bath or wash their hair all year long, or change their clothes regularly. It seems that most of them cannot afford a change of clothes, or even underwear, and water and fuel are so precious here. During these gatherings, every cave is packed . . . Through close body contact, it is very easy to pass lice around. Our worry about these problems has made us stop joining their gatherings.

The peasants like calling us 'Beijing children', 'Beijing girls' or 'Beijing boys', and treat us kindly. Recently, several families sent us bowls of pickled cabbage or carrots, knowing that we have no vegetables to eat. In this area, fresh vegetables are very rare and expensive all winter, so these pickles are precious even for the local families. When we thanked them for their generosity, they replied: 'Your parents in cave would be sad if we didn't look after you.' Local people always use 'in cave' instead of 'at home' . . . Several times, women have held our hands and cried. 'Poor children, to be so far from your parents, and suffer hardships here.'

28 February 1969
Baba,
It was the first time I've been away from home for the Spring Festival [the Chinese New Year], and I miss you all terribly . . .

Spring Festival here was very quiet, not even a sound of fire-crackers. I was told that in the past, celebrations could last for nearly a month, and towns and villages often rang with gongs and drums, or cheerful music played by local folk musicians. In those days, peasants dressed up in their best clothes, and were busy light-ing firecrackers or watching folk dances or operas. Since the Cultural Revolution, all these activities have been banned, because they were the 'Four Olds'. According to official instructions, vil-lagers were supposed to hold a revolutionary festival this year by working in the fields every day, but the chief of our production team ignored it, since no job needs urgently doing at the moment.

One evening before the Spring Festival, we tried to talk to our friend Liu You-you, whose father was the headmaster of Ba-yi School. Her village is several kilometres away. Since there is no telephone service and we didn't want to travel in the dark, we con-tacted her through the land-line network. In this area, almost every household has a small speaker connected to the network, which is run by the county authority to broadcast official messages. These speakers also enable local people to talk to each other. After the official broadcasting time, we stood on our kang with our mouths close to the dusty speaker and tried our best to shout: 'Liu You-you, how are you?' After several minutes of shouting, we eventually heard You-you's reply, which sounded extremely remote and muffled. We shouted ourselves hoarse, so did You-you, but didn't hear anything clearly apart from our names. Next day, many villagers imitated our shouting to tease us, since our voices reached all the speakers in the network!

A young chap nicknamed Monkey Boy likes showing off his knowledge about the national political situation, and enjoys topics such as class struggle. Since we came here, he is the only one who is always watching us or telling us off, as if he was our boss. In fact, he is not much older than us, and returned home as a school-leaver not long ago. Monkey Boy's father heads our production team, and his family belongs to the powerful Liang clan, which makes up by far the majority of the villagers. That's why our village is named Liangjia He [meaning 'River of the Liang Family'] . . .

On our arrival the villagers treated us with noodles, which was the best food they could provide. Afterwards, Monkey Boy complained to the local people's commune and to the county administration, saying that this treatment conflicted with Party policy. According to him, we should have been given a 'bitterness meal' made of inedible stuff like chaff or bran. That way, we would know what poor peasants had to eat in the old society. He also complained that the hardship we experienced was too little . . . I do not believe he meant to bully us. Rather, he wanted to show his authority, and enjoy his position as a member of the poor and lower-middle peasants now responsible for re-educating us.

One evening, we were invited to the production team's plenary meeting to elect a model member of the people's commune. Our nomination was Old Sixth, a quiet young shepherd in the production team, whose hard work and kindness have impressed us very much. To our surprise, no one responded, apart from Monkey Boy grumbling: 'Don't be silly! Old Sixth is a rich farmer. He's not eligible to be a model member!' Later, we heard that during the land reforms nearly thirty years ago, Old Sixth's father was classified as the only rich farmer in the Liangjia He Front. Due to extreme poverty among the local people, it was impossible to find a landlord in the entire village. The major grounds for Old Sixth's father's plight were that he owned a flock of sheep, which made him outstandingly 'wealthy', since most of the villagers were penniless. So Old Sixth had been treated as a member of a rich farmer family since his childhood.

30 March 1969
Baba,
After the Spring Festival, many households in our village begin to go hungry, and live on dried tree leaves or even millet straw or husk. Almost every year there is a famine in spring, but it normally starts in March and lasts till new crops are harvested in May. Since last year's harvest was particularly bad, many families had little left to eat by late February. We heard that our people's commune has issued passes to let peasants travel, so that they can beg in the south or the cities before the spring ploughing starts, and save the limited food for their wives, children or elderly parents at home.

Our life is also getting tougher. By the rules, each of us receives 10 yuan per month as living allowance from the government during the first year. The money has to pay for 20 kilograms of the cereal ration, mainly millet, maize and sorghum, and 250 grams of the cooking oil ration. What is left after that is so little that we have to limit our use of kerosene lamps at night. Since the Spring Festival, villagers cannot afford to give us vegetables, and we seldom taste meat, eggs or oil. But the poorer our diet the bigger our stomachs, so the cereal ration is not enough at all. To increase the amount, we try to live on soup instead of solid food, boiling cereals with a lot of water. At every meal, the gruel doled out to everyone is enough to fill a small washbowl, and I always finish everything within a few minutes, but soon after eating we feel hungry again and long for something else to eat. How I fancy a wo-tou-er [steamed buns made of rough unleavened maize-flour], the food I disliked so much at home! Among the various chaffs or brans we have tried recently, sorghum husks are relatively eatable, apart from the resulting constipation.

Recently, we were called unexpectedly to Wen'anyi for an urgent plenary meeting of the school-leavers from Beijing, organized by the people's commune. No advance information was provided about the agenda, and no absences were allowed. On our way to the meeting, each of us was escorted by at least one local peasant, even to go to the lavatory. The venue was a spacious courtyard surrounded by four rows of one-storey houses, offices of the people's commune. On arrival, I saw soldiers lying prone behind machine-guns mounted on the roofs of the houses. This reminded me of the official warning that no participant must bring even a fruit-knife to the meeting.

It seemed that most of the participants were not worried by this strange situation. This was our first full meeting, and everyone was busy greeting or looking for friends or ex-schoolmates from other villages. A group of teenage boys dressed in fashionable army overcoats and smart leather boots was particularly active. They chattered loudly and showed off smoking cigarettes. I heard that they were members of a gang from the Beijing Middle School No. 57, now in the same people's commune as us.

None of us knew that the plenary meeting was actually a public trial. As soon as it started, an officer appeared on the platform and announced that two leading gang members from Middle School No. 57 were to be arrested immediately. Everyone was stunned, including the gang members themselves. Within seconds, two boys were handcuffed by fully armed soldiers, and then dragged on to the platform. Through the speakers who followed, we heard that recently a violent fight had taken place in the village where the two young gangsters lived. At midnight, armed with kitchen knives, they forced their way into a cave occupied by opponents from the same school. One of their victims' legs was badly cut. The incident shocked the county authorities and peasants, especially when afterwards they heard rumours about what happened in Beijing. For example, it was said that some boys were very skilful thieves because they trained by picking small bits of soap out of water. So it was almost impossible to tell when they lifted wallets from people's pockets. For fear that similar violence or other crimes would happen here too, the authorities decided to hold a public trial as a deterrent . . .

Before Feng-an and I left home, my father asked us to write to him regularly, and insisted on knowing the true situation in our rural settlement. During his endless imprisonment, he read our letters again and again, and sometimes hit his bed at night and wept with frustration. Although he already had some knowledge about the situation in northern Shaanxi, what he learned from us still appalled him. It was more than a quarter of a century since he had left Yan'an, and the region seemed locked in its poverty. As a Communist, he felt guilty that the Party had done so little to repay the local people for their unstinting support for the revolution. As a father, he felt grieved by the harsh lives his children had to endure.

During that period, my father wrote to us almost once a week, trying his best to send us his support. When he heard that the cold dry weather caused chillblains on my ankles, he suggested covering them with warm mashed potatoes, which was a folk remedy he used during the war. Several of the food parcels we received from home contained parched flour made by my father himself, and all of the contents, such as wheat flour, cooking oil and sugar, were saved from the family's ration. From his experiences during the Korean War, he told us that parched flour was an ideal food supplement, especially since we had little fuel even for cooking. Just by mixing the flour with boiling water, we could make a bowl of thick tasty soup to fill our stomachs. He also encouraged me to keep a diary, and send it to him regularly. 'I will keep your writing for you,' he wrote to me. 'You will know how valuable it is later on.'

Soon after Feng-an and I left home, it was the turn of my younger brother, Feng-yuan, to go to the countryside. Like everyone else in their age group, although my two younger siblings' education was halted by the Cultural Revolution, both of them had 'graduated' from primary school and entered middle school. Now, pupils in Feng-yuan's year were regarded as school-leavers, and their choices were the same as ours had been. Due to our parents' political problems, he too stood no chance of recruitment by the armed forces, so his only prospect was to go to the countryside.

But this time, my father decided not to let Feng-yuan go. Through Feng-an and me, he knew what the countryside would mean. Also, my younger brother had played a vital role in keeping my parents in contact now that Feng-an and I had gone. In order to stay at home, Feng-yuan made various excuses to his school authorities, such as his duty to care for my aged grandmother. To mention his responsibility for my imprisoned parents would only make things worse. Not long ago, he was denounced at a rally organised by his school authority due to my parents' political troubles. For the son of counter-revolutionaries, it would be impossible to be exempted from consignment to the countryside. Feng-yuan's request was refused, and my family was visited repeatedly by staff from his school, officers from the armoured forces and members of the local neighbourhood committee, who tried to harass him into going. In desperation, my father had to send him into hiding with relatives.

During spring 1969, only Aijun was able to be at home with my father and grandmother. Through my father's letters, I learned how fast she had grown up. In my mind, my little sister was my grandmother's pet and relied on her elder siblings. Now, she spontaneously took on tasks such as shopping, cooking and running errands for my father. The first time she made won ton soup took her almost a whole afternoon, since she insisted on having no help. In the past she had often been timid, and hesitated to follow when I had to face our parents' persecutors. Now, she visited our mother on her own, and became my father's only link with outside.

It was the evening of 22nd March 1969 when my father heard Aijun's whoop of excitement: 'Baba, Mama is home!' Years later, my mother recalled that moment: 'Your father came rushing downstairs. His face was terribly pale, and he held my hands and cried. "Home at last! At long last, you're home alive! How desperately we've waited!" I lost control, and couldn't speak, and burst out crying too . . .'

My mother's release made way for a forthcoming political event, the Communist Party's Ninth Congress, scheduled for 1–24 April 1969. By then, the old administration in each province had been replaced by the new revolutionary committees, the source of incredible power for Mao's radical followers. It seemed that Mao Zedong had achieved his goal: to unseat the colleagues he no longer trusted. Through the Ninth Congress, he intended to confirm and consolidate the Party's new leadership.

Prior to the congress, the Workers' and PLA Propaganda Teams of Mao Zedong Thought started to inspect the 'cowsheds' in each institution, with orders to release those prisoners whose arrests were based on inadequate evidence. Soon, the 'cowshed' in my mother's university was empty, because none of the prisoners had valid charges against them. From now on, my mother could go home every day, but release did not mean rehabilitation, and her hard labour went on as before. In all her life, the journey home from the 'cowshed' was the longest she had ever experienced. After more than a year of imprisonment, it felt strange not to be under close control and surveillance, out in the streets and on buses.

All the way back, her mind had one idea: 'My imprisonment is over. Now I can go home!'

When she finally reached our compound, my mother was stopped at the front entrance by armed guards who knew of her imprisonment and suspected that she had escaped. For almost three hours, she was shut in a small room just a few hundred metres from our house, while the guards contacted officers in charge of my father's case, and they consulted leaders of the PLA Propaganda Team in my mother's university. Evening had come, before they confirmed her release. When I heard she was free, I felt enormously relieved. I knew what their reunion meant to my parents, and that their ordeals were not over.

The Ninth Party Congress was cryptically organized. Even for most Party members, there was no advance announcement about the date or venue. When delegates arrived in Beijing, they were taken straight to their lodgings, and not allowed to contact outsiders. During the congress, participants reached the venue, the Great Hall of the People, by secret entrances, leaving no outside trace of the event. Photos published later showed the seating arrangements on the platform. Left of Mao Zedong sat Lin Biao, Kang Sheng, Jiang Qing and their major allies brought to power by the Cultural Revolution. On his right sat the remaining members of the old administration, headed by Premier Zhou Enlai. As the overlord of the economy, Zhou managed to save a handful of vice-Premiers and ministers from political destruction to assist his work. To a large extent, it was the efforts of Premier Zhou and his assistants that staved off economic collapse during the long period of chaos.

Like most Chinese, my parents knew nothing at all about the congress until the communiqué was broadcast later. The revised Party constitution confirmed Mao Zedong's status as Party leader, and Lin Biao's as Mao's chosen successor. 'Oh no!' said my father to my mother, in disbelief. 'This is to legalize the feudal system in our Party's constitution!' In my parents' view of Communism, there should be no guarantee for anyone to be the Party's lifelong leader, let alone to appoint his successor. And they were deeply disappointed to find that more than half of the Politburo members now came from the camps of Lin Biao or Jiang Qing, Mao's radical followers.

'How could Jiang Qing and Ye Qun [Lin Biao's wife] qualify as Politburo members?' said my mother: 'After they married, they both cashed in on their husbands' positions, and did hardly any work for many years. Ever since I first met them in Yan'an, they have been notoriously arrogant and narrow-minded. But now, Jiang Qing controls the Central Cultural Revolution Small Group, and Ye Qun carries weight over the Cultural Revolution in the armed forces. Then there's Kang Sheng, who's now number five in the leadership, and all those other Politburo members who only care about persecuting others for their own gain. Sooner or later, our country will be ruined in their hands!'

My father spent many sleepless nights poring over the communiqué and the reshuffled Politburo list. Sometimes, he could not control his tears. 'This is the end of the Communists! I joined the revolution in my teens, but not for this kind of Communist Party! With these evil people in power, we can't expect justice for ourselves, and there's no hope for the country . . .'

Then he reached for comfort. 'But we must believe that no one can rewrite history. Eventually, history will prove us innocent.' In response to my mother's sense of outrage at their having no right to speak the truth, he appealed to philosophical principles. 'Let's trust the dialectic! Things will rebound the other way when they become extreme, so the more damage these evil people have done to the country, the closer they are to their end. We just wait and see!'

In my village, the peasants showed little interest in the Ninth Party Congress; the vital aim for them was to fend off starvation. When the weather got warmer, they prospected for edible wild plants and tree-leaves in the valleys. The earliest plants to appear were wild garlic.

Copying the villagers, we dug out the delicate plants and mixed them with salt as salad. Tender elm-leaves, prized for their sweet taste and smooth texture, were usually mixed with maize or sorghum flour and then steamed as a staple food, so it was hard to find an elm with leaves. Shortly after the elm-leaves, flowers of some local wild plants started blooming, and became another staple food. Later, we heard that flowers of these plants were often used as pig food in favourable years. Among other plants and tree-leaves we tried, most tasted bitter or were tough, but we had to eat anything available, because of our hunger, and to fuel our hard work in the fields.

As the famine continued, spring ploughing and sowing began. Since collectivization in the late 1950s, land and most productive resources such as machinery and livestock were owned by the production team, which organized the peasants' work collectively. Each morning, before the sun rose over the surrounding cliffs, the team chief woke us with shouts of: 'Go and climb the mountains', which was the local idiom for going farming, since most of the land was scattered among hills and cliffs. Half an hour later, we and a crowd of labourers followed the chief or other production team leaders on our way to work, mostly along narrow mountain paths, with a pickaxe on our shoulders. The furthest land was almost two hours' walk. On some steep paths, I could easily touch the ground in front without bending over. Soon I was breathless and exhausted, and so were the other Beijing girls.

During the following months, I often suffered from painful blisters that could cover half the soles of my feet. None of us had climbed before. Worse, our stomachs were still empty. In order to save food, we followed the peasants' routine and had only two meals a day, which left nothing to eat before starting. After about two hours' work, it was always cheering when at last a strong labourer appeared on the mountain path, carrying a large basket and a wooden bucket on a shoulder pole. Inside the basket, there was packaged food wrapped in small pieces of towel, collected from the various families. Workers on the land were often treated with better food than the rest of their family, but even then it was still based on a few steamed buns. The bucket contained hot drink provided by each household, a mixture of water and a little bit of millet. This meagre ration only kept us going for another few hours, but we had to work till early afternoon before returning to our caves for the second meal. On the way back, my legs tired, and I was often faint with hunger. I can think of nothing more miserable than hard labour on an empty stomach!

Compared with the peasants, we normally lived on less and poorer food. As new arrivals, we were not entitled to a private plot. Since collectivization, each household was allocated a small piece of land whose produce it could keep. As it was difficult to live on working for the production team, their own plots gave vital subsistence. But for us, the only subsistence was food parcels sent from home, which cost a lot to send, and were too few to spare us from starvation.

What really shocked me was that planting here was still done in the primitive way of many centuries past, with no help at all from modern technology. In fact, even the use of livestock was not possible. Our production team could not afford a single horse or mule, and the few donkeys they owned were kept busy grinding or milling crops. From ploughing to harvest, almost everything was done by manpower.

It was hard to explain lowland scenery to local people, since most of them had never left the mountains. Wherever we went to work, endless barren hills and cliffs surrounded us. Apart from a few small pieces of land, the colour was brown. Plants, especially trees, were rarely seen outside villages. When giving directions, local people would sometimes say: 'Just head for the next tree.' This could keep you going for hours on end, because there were so few trees in any direction. Fuel was always scarce. A girl in my cave fell from a cliff when out collecting fuel, and suffered from concussion and an injured back. It was said that many hills and cliffs had been covered with vegetation until a few decades ago, when Mao had promoted his famous policy, 'through our own efforts to provide ample food and clothing for ourselves', in order to break the economic blockade imposed by Chiang Kai-shek on the Communist Central Base. Shrubs, trees and other wild plants were cut or burnt to clear more land for crops, as my mother and her comrades did in Yan'an. The result was soil erosion, and worsening floods in summer. Among the hills and cliffs, we often saw gaping pits caused by flash floods. If no rain fell, which was the usual condition, the area suffered from drought, because it had no irrigation. And once the land was sowed, there was hardly any watering done, or fertilizer added, so the climate was a vital factor which determined every year's harvest.

I began to recognize that there was more to the villagers' poverty than harsh natural conditions and lack of technology, because harvests were not uncommon on the villagers' private plots, where the crops were well looked after and grew sturdy, in clear contrast to conditions on the collective land. The peasants showed a lack of initiative where there was no direct connection between their income and their work.

Under the collective system in rural China, the production team settled the unit of income shared among team members. The peasants' work was measured in 'gong-fen', work-points, whose allocation was initially decided by the combined members of the production team, based mainly on the labourer's age, gender, physical condition and agricultural skills. In general, adult male labourers, defined as the able-bodied labour force, earned ten work-points per work-day. Women, teenagers and the old, regarded as semi-able bodied, earned less. For example, it was six work-points a day for the Beijing boys, and five for the girls. After one's standard work-point entitlement was fixed, it was hard to change apart from age-related alteration. Assuming that the peasants went to work, each would be awarded work-points by a production team official. The more work-points peasants received, the higher their income, no matter whether they worked hard or not.

Official propaganda often stressed the vigorous commitment shown by peasants working for the socialist collectives. I had imagined our work against a background of cheerful revolutionary songs and bright red flags – the orthodox picture of socialist rural society. The truth was a startling contrast. When they arrived on the land, most peasants dawdled. Often they sat together on the ground, chatting or smoking until they were stopped by cadres of the production team. The first meal of the day was followed by a long break. A few hours later came a second break, 'time to smoke a pipe', as the villagers claimed. But each time, 'to smoke a pipe' lasted at least one and a half hours, while the women sat stitching their cloth shoes, and the men roamed the nearby hills in search of fuel, herbs or edible wild plants. Again, no one resumed their work on the land without prompting by the cadres. Even then, many people took no trouble with their work, and expected to go home as early as possible, so as to spend more time on their family plots. As fellow villagers, there was little the cadres could do. They were elected by the villagers, and they too lived by earning work-points, not on government salaries. So if they pushed their team members too hard, they would become unpopular, and might even lose their positions in the next election.

In spring, Feng-an suffered pains in his back, probably the consequence of sleeping in a cold damp cave. He also had sinus problems, which made it difficult to carry on farming, especially when the daily climb to work made him pant for breath. Among the school-leavers from Beijing, many also succumbed to problems such as an epidemic of diarrhoea and skin rash. Luckily, I stayed healthy.

The people's commune approved my brother's application to return to Beijing, because he could not be treated locally. A special office had been created at each administrative level to handle the cases of urban school-leavers settled in the countryside. As the lowest administrative body in rural areas, the people's commune exercised enormous power over our lives. Without its permission, none of us could leave. Feng-an's departure did not affect me too much. Since our arrival, we had led separate lives. I hoped to go home on holiday after the autumn harvest. In the meantime, I was keen to earn more work-points so as to support myself next year.

When Feng-an left, most of the land had turned green. And then the buckwheat was harvested, the local diet improved, and the famine was finally over. When the corn-cobs fattened, the peasants got nervous, and stood guard to protect the crop from theft. The villagers thought that eating young sweet-corn was an unforgivable waste, and always kept the crops growing until they were ripe enough to mill flour. Sometimes, their reaction to pilfering could be ugly. Unaware of the crime they were committing, some Beijing girls from a neighbouring valley once picked a few sweet-corns as they passed, and were caught by the peasants on duty. Their furious shouts and threats of violence terrified the girls.

Summer came. Now it was time to harvest wheat, the most popular crop in northern China. For several days, we were busy reaping the crop with sickles and tying the sheaves with cord. The return journey was hard, since we had to carry the heavy bundles on our backs through hilly country, but the harvest made everybody cheerful. The most interesting job for me was threshing. The outdoor threshing floor lay in the middle of our village, so we did not have to climb to go to work. I was particularly fascinated by the method. Two groups of labourers stood in line face to face, with the crop spread between them. Each thresher held a 'lianjia', a wooden implement with a long moving arm on top. One group stepped forward and flailed the hinged arms to thresh, while the other group retreated, and then vice versa. Each group moved in step, and made a 'cha-cha' sound in time with the threshing. It was like a powerful dance. But soon I found that it was not an easy task to stay in unison, step after step. After a whole day's threshing, my arms, shoulders, legs and back ached unbearably. During this season, sunshine was crucial, because the crops must dry fast, and so was the wind, or else the chaff could not be winnowed. Unfortunately, they did not often coincide, and when the wind did not come, the peasants would chorus into the distance, 'Wu-wu-wu . . .', to imitate its blowing, hoping to summon it to rise.

After the harvest, each villager was allocated only about 25 kilos of wheat, a small proportion of the total. Every year, our production team had to deliver most of the harvest to the government to meet the agricultural tax or sell at the officially fixed price. But I heard no complaints from the peasants. Perhaps they were inured to it. When they tasted the first meals made from the newly harvested wheat flour, happiness showed on every face. Children hung on to huge white steamed buns with small grubby fingers, and nibbled while they played outside their caves. In working hours, the usual silence was often broken by cheerful folk songs. One peasant nicknamed Blacksmith was a good singer whose fine strong voice carried beautifully in the barren surroundings. I could not understand most of the lyrics as they were based on local dialect, but sometimes women working by me would blush and laugh, and call him to shut up. Seeing me curious, they told me: 'You're too young, and not supposed to know. He's a naughty man.' Later, I heard that he sang about love and sex, for instance the strong sexual passion felt by a young woman in her widowhood, with detailed erotic descriptions.

After the wheat harvest, the county's touring film show arrived. They came once a year to most villages in the county, and showed mostly propaganda, but their arrival brought an instant festive air, a rare opportunity to glimpse real pictures of the outside world. Before sunset, the threshing floor, converted into a temporary outdoor cinema, was already packed with villagers, many of them dressed in their best clothes. When the portable generator got going, I was amazed to see how bright an electric light was, since my eyes were now used to the oil-lamp's glimmer at night. Though the programme hardly varied, some lads in my village trailed the projection team all around the commune, together with a crowd from other villages, watching the same films again and again. Every day, they walked for hours along the mountain paths, and came home after midnight.

Before the summer ended, a pair of blind folk story-tellers visited Liangjia He. They were not employed by the government, and lived on what they earned by performing. I never knew how they managed to travel among the endless hills and cliffs with their instruments and luggage. Normally, the story-tellers remained in each location for several days, and were housed by local families.

When I went to their first performance, held in the evening in the cave where they slept at night, they sat by the kang at a low table, dressed like villagers and wearing no make-up. On the table, an oil-lamp flickered. As there was little room inside the cave, many in the audience sat in the moonlight in the yard outside, watching and listening through the open door. When the story-tellers started to play their simple stringed instruments, the noisy crowd grew quiet. Soon I felt something touch my heart. It was the music, the deep tone with its passion and power! Sometimes it sounded familiar and reminded me of the peasants' folk-songs. Sometimes I just wanted to cry. It was like a key that opened the lock of my emotions, and I longed to express the loneliness, anger and pain of recent years.

Throughout their performance, the two played instruments to accompany their stories, whose contents were rather disappointing, as they drew on propaganda material. Later, I heard that the Cultural Revolution had forced them to replace the old stories with revolutionary lyrics. But they managed to retain the traditional folk music to accompany their stories.

I was immensely moved by the village's recovery from famine, which showed me how strong human beings could be. Indeed, it was dismaying to settle in this poor and distant area for the rest of our lives, but since there was no other choice we had to survive with the peasants' positive attitudes. I also gained great strength from my father's letters. Encouraged by his writing, I tried to ignore the cruelty of fortune, and to enjoy our life. In the evenings, I told my companions stories from books I had read at home. The most popular was Emily Brontë's *Wuthering Heights*, which I was asked to repeat several times. Heathcliff's desperate cries, the wild winds, the remote and lonely hills . . . they were surroundings we knew. At the end of the story, we were often in tears.

My cooking skills also made me friends, and for that I had my father's past discipline to thank.

Among the villagers, I was viewed as a sensitive girl with a pleasant nature. They also respected my hard work in the fields, as I strove to earn more work-points. In accordance with government policy, from next year on we would lose our living allowance, so I had to be self-supporting soon. Due to my parents' influence since childhood, I did not want to rely on anyone else financially. In nearby villages, I was 'that jiong-yan-yan nü-zi' ('pretty girl' in local terms). Some local girls liked to copy my speech or walk, due I suppose to their admiration for urban and educated girls. As girls in this area rarely went to school, and had little contact with the outside world, they felt intensely curious about anything or anyone new. Out in the fields, any stranger would catch their attention, and they watched them out of sight. 'Our girls have seen so little of the world!' the older villagers sympathized.

All my local friends were village girls around my age. Most had 'found their mother-in-law's family', which meant becoming engaged in local terms, and had their weddings planned for years ahead. Through family agreements, they were normally engaged to local boys in their early teens, and in the period before the wedding they received regular gifts in cash and kind from their fiancés and future parents-in-law. For peasants, it was essential to finance their sons' marriage in this long-term way, since support from their sons and daughters-in-law was the major source of old-age security. The costs incurred were a necessary investment. Before their sons' weddings, parents tried their best to please their future daughters-in-law, in case they should break their engagements. As a result, my village girlfriends were relatively better dressed than most other villagers. Some even went to the fields wearing delicate shoes, because they had no other opportunity to show off the gifts from their prospective families.

But for many boys, the major way to buy themselves new clothing was through collecting herbs, as most of their families' spare money went to their fiancées. It was a dangerous task, because herbs often grew on steep cliffs. After working all summer, the money they earned from selling herbs to the county's pharmaceutical company might just be enough for a shirt or a pair of trousers. Some of the Beijing boys joked: 'Why don't you mix some weeds with the herbs you sell, since the herbs are so hard to collect? No one would know.' 'It would be a sin if we did,' they replied.

In the autumn, I found that my year of hard work had earned me only about 20 yuan in total. The first income in my life brought me no joy, because the amount was less than a month's food and pocket money allowance for a military recruit. Starting next year, the government food ration would stop, and we would have to subsist on the shares due to us from the production team, as every local peasant did. But the crop allocated to each villager was only about 100 kilos altogether, which predicted a famine next spring. My dream of self-support was completely destroyed.

Chapter 18

Beyond the Clouds:
I Escape from the Loess Highlands;
My Mother Expelled to China's
Southwest Frontier

(September 1969–November 1970)

In mid-September 1969, I received a telegram: 'Mother is critically ill, please return home immediately.' In fact, my mother was not ill, and the telegram was my idea. Leave to go home was more and more restricted, even for a short holiday, as part of official measures to stop school-leavers fleeing their rural settlements, so a common tactic was to plead serious illness in the family, or other urgent family matters.

My experiences in the village had taught me how difficult it was to make a living there, no matter how hard I worked, and my future looked gloomy. In order to survive, some exiled Beijing girls married peasants, for the sake of local support. Certainly, this was not my intention. I was too young to get married, and not ready to spend the rest of my life in the mountains. My home was in Beijing, and my family needed me. After my mother's release, I desperately wanted to know how my parents were getting on.

After Feng-an's return, my parents were more worried for my welfare, and urged me to come back as soon as possible. All sorts of stories and rumours had been circulating in Beijing about the plight of school-leavers in the countryside, as hundreds of thousands of families had their children sent away, and strong complaints eventually reached Premier Zhou Enlai. It was said that he was particularly shocked by the appalling conditions in the Yan'an region, and lamented: 'We should feel guilty about the people of the old liberated area.' On his instructions, in summer 1969 a special team was assigned to investigate social and economic problems in the Yan'an region on behalf of the Party's Central Committee. The team member who visited my village was a young schoolteacher from Beijing, who talked with us for hours, taking detailed notes, but nothing happened after she left.

On the pretext of visiting my 'sick' mother, I applied for permission to return home. So did another Beijing girl from a neighbouring village, whose nickname was Little Rooster because she often wore green trousers and a red jacket. She received a telegram warning of 'urgent family matters' from her parents, diplomats before the Cultural Revolution, now just released from a labour camp. Clearly, the local officials did not credit our reasons, which were familiar in their office, but we got what we wanted. Perhaps they recognized that it was impossible to keep the school-leavers pinned down. Even without permission, many desperate teenagers still made their way home by taking detours through remote areas to avoid surveillance. Some even risked their lives to cross the Yellow River on small rafts made of sheepskin. If the rafts overturned they would drown. I also believe that many local officials sympathized with us. As long as our excuses made sense, they did not hesitate to provide us with travel documents. By the end of 1969, most school-leavers from Ba-yi School in our commune had returned to Beijing.

During my last days in Liangjia He, I was kept busy by villagers' farewell visits. From morning until evening, visitors knocked on my door bringing gifts of boiled eggs, or steamed buns made of precious wheat flour, or even unripe apples from their trees, if they could not find anything else. They said things like: 'Poor girl, you've suffered so much in our village, didn't even have enough to eat!' or 'I'm so glad that you'll be back with your parents soon.' Some also asked: 'When will we see you again?' Obviously, they did not expect me to return. The villagers had not welcomed us at first, because it was difficult enough to scrape a living. But they had no other choice, since dispatching school-leavers to the countryside was Chairman Mao's decision which they had to obey. After our arrival, they often expressed their doubt that we would stay. But now that I was leaving, they could not help expressing their affection.

These gestures brought tears to my eyes, as I knew how much the gift of food meant to them. In the past, I had longed for this moment. Now it was hard to say goodbye to these kind villagers, especially since I knew that I was unlikely to return. But how would I survive in Beijing? What could I do in the future? Just then, I had no idea, except for resolving that once in Beijing I would try my best to make the separation permanent. I might not be able to achieve it, and be forced to return after a spell at home, but I would try and try until I succeeded. And many of my companions shared this attitude. When I said goodbye to them, many gave understanding smiles before replying: 'See you in Beijing soon.'

I left Liangjia He at dawn, with Little Rooster. At my parents' request, I brought all our luggage with me, including the suitcase and bedding left behind by Feng-an. Most of our belongings were newly made or bought just before we left Beijing. From our village, we had to walk a whole day to the nearest bus station in Yanchuan county town, mostly along mountain paths. The production team provided a donkey to carry my luggage, and the team's vice-chief volunteered to guide it.

They said in the village that the vice-chief had been really handsome when he was young, and a fine singer. Now, in his late forties, his face was lined and I never heard him sing. Over the year, he had often helped us to carry our heavy pickaxes on our way to work, or arranged for us to carry smaller loads back from the harvest. When his wife cooked delicious food, she often sent their children to bring some to us. One dark evening soon after the famine, he knocked on our door, carrying two pumpkins. 'It's a shame you've had no vegetables to eat for so long,' he said. 'I picked the first pumpkins for you on the quiet, from the production team's land. This is the first time in my life I've stolen something, but what else could I do? Right now, I can't find you any ripe pumpkins in my family plot.'

When we arrived in the county town, it was already close to evening. The next bus left in the morning, so we had to find overnight lodgings. When we left Beijing the previous winter, our father had given 50 yuan each to Feng-an and me, and both of us had saved the money for an emergency or for going home. Before saying goodbye to the vice-chief, I insisted on inviting him for a meal in a small local restaurant, knowing that he had to walk all the way back tonight. By helping me today, he had lost the day's income. I also felt greatly indebted to him for his kindness over the year, and there might not be another opportunity to express my gratitude. But he refused the invitation: 'Don't waste your money, girl. My wife had prepared enough steamed buns to keep me going. Today's journey is nothing for us sufferers.' (The local people often referred to themselves as sufferers – 'shoukuren'.)

The 'bus' to Yan'an was a truck. As the weather was warm, the passenger platform was uncovered and we could enjoy the scenery, which made the trip more pleasant than last winter's. Most passengers were local peasants, and almost every man had a long rectangular bag across one shoulder, made of coarse sackcloth, with a central opening. Inside it was food and other stuff for travelling. Some passengers were on their way to visit relatives, with gifts of live chickens.

By the time we reached Yan'an, the only bus running to our next destination had gone, so our first errand was to queue for next day's tickets. In China, passengers could buy tickets only for trips that started from where they were. The journey to Beijing took nearly a week, and we had to keep changing, so queues became a daily routine. In Yan'an, we saw crowds of Beijing school-leavers, most of them on the run from their rural settlements. The government blockade seemed particularly tight, and we had to show our travel certificates when buying tickets or checking in to lodgings. We heard that local hostels were often raided at night by the police, who detained unlicensed travellers and sent them back to their settlements.

To find accommodation overnight, again we queued for several hours, before sharing a room of about 20 square metres with almost 20 guests, crammed into three huge plank beds along the walls. Each sleeper had just enough space to lie down. Before I fell asleep, a group of girls arrived, and one of them blurted to her friends: 'Look! It's Mu Aiping!' I closed my eyes at once, pretending to sleep. They were former pupils at my middle school. Some hours before, I had spotted and avoided them in town. Since leaving Beijing, I had decided to break contact with most ex-pupils from the school, and try to forget my humiliations there.

Our next destination was Tongchuan, the railway terminus. When we arrived from Yan'an, it was late afternoon. Soon the last train would be leaving. The small square in front of the railway station was filled with passengers, but no one was allowed inside until a few minutes before departure time. When the gate eventually opened, the huge crowd just burst through and charged towards the train. Soon the engine started to get up steam, but I was still outside the station, surrounded by my luggage. There was no trolley available, and I could not load the suitcases and bedrolls in time, even with Little Rooster's help. In desperation, I paid several local boys to help, but when I finally managed to board a carriage, the boys behind me disappeared, and so did the luggage. The platform still thronged, and the carriages bulging. 'Help me, please!' I screamed in desperation, fearing that I would never get my luggage back, but I did not know who could help me, and my voice was drowned in the uproar. At the last moment, a young man near me noticed my frustration and offered to help. He fought his way out of the carriage, and eventually found the boys at the end of the platform. They had lost me in the chaos, and did not know what to do. Now, with the young man's help, they passed the suitcases and bedrolls one by one through a carriage window, as all the doors were blocked by passengers. By the time we got everything in, the train was moving.

When I finally returned, my family had its first reunion since the Cultural Revolution started more than three years before. My eldest brother, Feng-xin, was home on holiday. By now, university students also faced 'graduation' with uncertain futures, and Feng-xin's fate would be decided next year. Feng-yuan also came home from hiding. His school had not given up trying to force him away. But the authorities had difficulties keeping up the pressure on him, as they were also involved in many other school matters. My parents' trials went on. My mother's hard labour continued every day, and the only concession to my father was allowing him to leave the compound without applying for permission in advance.

By the end of 1969, almost all the neighbourhood girls around my age were attending medical universities run by the armed forces, as higher education began to revive. Since joining the forces in 1968, these girls had worked as medical orderlies or in other unskilled jobs. Like all our generation, their middle-school education had been halted by the Cultural Revolution. But now, educational qualifications were not called for by the universities, and the entrance examination had been abolished. Hence, only the family's political background counted, and the student's personal record in the Cultural Revolution. To satisfy the Party's educational reform policies, the entrant's background must come from (industrial) workers, peasants or members of the armed forces – they were known as 'worker-peasant-soldier students'. For a number of girls I knew, all it took was a telephone call or letter from their fathers, or a family connection to the university authorities. While at university, 'worker-peasant-soldier students' received free education with a living allowance, or a full salary if they were officers. Those who attended the earliest medical courses during the Cultural Revolution studied for only two years, instead of the previous five. There was hardly any examination during their courses, nor later when they qualified as doctors.

In the neighbourhood, we were the only family that still had all its children at home, because we had no chance of work or further education. As far as I know, Feng-an and I were the only children, among all the officer families in my father's headquarters, who were expelled to the countryside. Now we became illegal residents. Once our brief holidays were over, we were not entitled to remain in Beijing. In those days the local authorities often mobilized neighbourhood committees to sniff out such offenders and force them back to their settlements. Every day, I lived in fear of a knock on our door. My father was also pressured by officers from the armed forces to send his children back to the rural settlements. He did not say 'no', but always found excuses to keep us. Since Feng-an and I were not entitled to State rations, our long stay caused the family to go short. In the winter of 1969, we only managed to eat twice a day. In order to supplement our diet, my parents taught us to make bean curd, a skill they learned in wartime in Yan'an. The bean residue, the rough and tasteless stuff that was normally used for feeding pigs, became part of our staple diet.

It seemed to my parents that the only way to improve things for Feng-an and me would be to relocate us to Penglai, my father's home county. Before we left for resettlement, we had been required to surrender our urban residency cards, and that made us rural residents, forbidden to transfer back to Beijing or to any other urban part of China. At that time, it was getting common for school-leavers to resettle in the rural areas that their parents originally came from, usually in better economic and living conditions than those assigned by the government. Clearly, we could not move to my mother's home county, as our connection with my maternal grandfather would mean being treated as a landlord's family. Shortly before the Cultural Revolution, Auntie Ning had been transferred to Beijing, and brought my maternal grandfather with her. Although the two families lived in the same city, my mother never took us or our father to visit him. Later on, my grandfather was expelled from Beijing as a former landlord, and went to live in his home village with his last wife, my maternal grandmother's former maid. He died a few years later. But in Penglai the Mus were known as a revolutionary family, and my grandmother still kept her house in North Forest Yard.

In October 1969, Feng-an visited Penglai, but found that we could not meet the conditions for new settlers set by the local authority. Since my father and all his siblings had left home during the wars to join the Communists, we no longer had close relatives there. The only relatives left were my grandmother's two younger siblings and their families. Thirty years before, her younger sister's husband had been a wealthy merchant. Now he had lost his wealth. Though he was over eighty, he still worked for the production team. 'What would my wife and I eat if I stopped working on the land?' he said, in response to Feng-an's surprise. Due to its good geographical location and climate, residents in Penglai had not experienced starvation for a long time, except in the nationwide famine of the late 1950s, but the peasants still lacked money, and the collectives were unable to support the aged.

Relatives in Penglai complained that my father had forgotten his home county: 'It's been almost forty years since your father left, and he has never returned.' Before the Cultural Revolution, a number of high officials originally from Penglai had returned for short visits that often became sensational events, due to their positions in central or provincial government. Local governors stopped working to escort them, and extra police turned out for their security. These visits reinforced their local influence, especially since many tried to help the county by using their political influence. In turn, their relatives enjoyed favours from the local authority. But my father disliked the self-advertisement of what the Chinese call 'yi-jin-huan-xiang' – 'returning to home town robed in embroidered silk'. He did not want to interfere with local officials, or to show off his rank in his home town, nor did he encourage his family to exploit his position, as that would conflict with his Communist beliefs. So he had deliberately avoided visiting Penglai, much as he longed to see his home town again. Now that he was in political trouble, and had no pull with the local government, no one dared to help his children's relocation.

Our family reunion was the first long period that my siblings and I had spent together, and it was not a comfortable experience. Since I was three, we had been separated most of the time, with little chance to develop our relationship. Now, the family was shadowed by my parents' political troubles, with discrimination from outside, and we all faced uncertain futures. When my frustration burned, I could not talk to my siblings, simply because I was not used to it. The one I could talk to personally was my father, but I did not want to hurt him by exposing my feelings. As pressures built up, I got easily depressed and short-tempered, which often led to rows with the others.

To make things worse, the gossip and rumours that haunted me at middle school had now infiltrated my family. A few years ago, Feng-xin had heard the stories through his friends. He told my parents, and though their immediate response was disbelief, they felt obliged to know the truth and asked me repeatedly about my contacts with male fellow pupils. I realized what had happened, and denied having 'slept' with anyone. But now, the topic was revived. Feng-an had heard the gossip from schoolmates in our rural settlement, and before my return the whole story was openly discussed among my siblings. My grandmother refused to believe it — 'I don't think Ping-zi [my nick-name] is like that' — but I faced more awkward questions from my parents. Though my reply remained unchanged, I avoided Mighty China's name, or giving a detailed account, because I was not sure that my parents would understand me. Also, I never mentioned my split with my Red Guard comrades in Shanghai during the 'big links' trip in 1966, or my ordeal in the school camp, as both were too painful even to think about again.

On 18 October 1969, the 'No. 1 Directive of Vice-Chairman Lin Biao' ordered 'the entire military forces into urgent combat readiness to inten-sify preparations for war and to guard against enemy surprise attacks . . .'. Around that time, it was a common view inside the Party that a world-wide war was imminent, with China a major target. As the Vietnam War continued, the well-equipped American forces there were seen as a threat to China's south frontier. On the northeast frontier in particular, armed clashes with Soviet troops came to a head in 1969. Following the direc-tive, northern China, including Beijing, was put on immediate alert against a Soviet invasion.

In Beijing, residents were mobilized to construct underground defence works everywhere. During this massive project, frequent casual-ties occurred when poor technical supervision caused tunnels to collapse. In our compound, a horde of troops arrived, and worked round the clock to build air-raid shelters for the headquarters. Pupils in Aijun's middle school were sent to demolish the ancient city wall and the West Gate, in order to provide bricks for the underground defences. Beside them were armies of labourers from local factories, shops, government offices or other schools. The magnificent city wall and the West Gate were built in the Yuan Dynasty in the thirteenth century. For centuries, they had repulsed attacks from various invaders. Now, in just a few weeks, everything was demolished. When he heard the news, my father shook his head: 'Criminal!'

More than a decade later, the No. 1 Directive was condemned officially as a conspiracy mounted by Lin Biao and his allies against their
political rivals. Soon after it was issued, many 'counter-revolutionaries'
were expelled from Beijing, including some families of pupils at Ba-yi
School. One of them was a friend of Feng-an's, a boy whose father,
Lieutenant-General Wang Shangrong, was deputy chief of the General
Staff. It was said that his plight derived mainly from his ties to Marshal
Peng Dehuai, the disgraced former defence minister. When Feng-an
went to say goodbye, the boy's father was still imprisoned, and his
mother in distress. The family had not been informed of their forced
destination, and had no idea when they might see the general again. With
only a few days' notice, it was impossible for Madam Wang to organize
the move. When Feng-an and other schoolmates offered their help, she
broke down.

During the application of Lin Biao's No. 1 Directive, the chief
victim was Liu Shaoqi, China's disgraced president. The previous year,
he had been nationally denounced on fabricated charges as a 'traitor,
secret enemy agent and blackleg'. The Party Central Committee also
voted to deprive him of his membership for ever, and to dismiss him
from all of his posts inside or outside the Party. For two years, Liu
Shaoqi had been locked in a cell in Beijing, cut off from his family and
the world. Constant humiliation and maltreatment had left him mentally confused and too weak even to leave his bed. But little care was
provided, doctors and nurses had orders to denounce him each time
before treating him, and his medication was inadequate. Before being
expelled from Beijing during the 'evacuation', Liu Shaoqi was already
close to death. He had been reduced to a skeleton and his body was
covered with bedsores. Unable to speak, he managed to object to his
expulsion by turning his face away from the written order. His refusal
did not save him. A few weeks later, Liu Shaoqi died naked in his
prison cell in Kaifeng. Without informing his family, his body was cremated quietly under a false name.

Around that time, my family heard of the tragic death of Sun Ziping, my father's former colleague in the Communist underground in 1935. Since 1957, Ziping had worked as Party secretary and deputy director for the Institute of Maritime Studies, run by the State Committee of Science and located in Qingdao. While preparing this book, I came across an official document written by the Revolutionary Committee of his institute on 29 December 1970, more than two years after his death:

At the start of the Cultural Revolution, some leading figures of the institute's former revolutionary committee . . . sought to vent their personal spite against Comrade Sun Ziping. With fabricated accusations, they hoodwinked and deceived part of the masses . . . During a long period, Comrade Sun Ziping suffered constant cruel violence. For example, some time before he had been diagnosed with bone tuberculosis in his back, but during denunciation activities he was forced to keep bending towards the ground, and the unbearable pain in his back often caused him to shake. Sometimes, he had to ask to kneel instead of bending over, and when this was refused he suffered more beating and verbal abuse.

. . . On the afternoon of 20 July [1968], he was told: 'You must admit your crimes honestly! Don't follow the way of your wife [she too was persecuted] by alienating herself from the people [meaning committing suicide]!' He was shocked by the news . . . On the following day, he started to sort out his belongings, and wrote a suicide note to his son at night. On 22 July, he left his cell by noon, pretending to wash his clothes, and did not return. Later, he was found dead by hanging [on a tree].

In his suicide note, Ziping expressed his chagrin about his suffering at the rebels' hands, and his deep sorrow for his wife. Several years later, my father saw his note and wept. For a long time, my family tried to keep the tragic news from my grandmother, whose deep attachment to the couple dated from the Sino-Japanese War. When she finally learned of their deaths, she could not restrain her grief and anger. 'Why should Ziping and his wife be persecuted to death? The best people I ever knew in the world!' she sobbed bitterly. 'Now that so many good veteran Communists are being persecuted, I wonder who feels happiest. In the past, millions of silver coins were offered for the heads of these Communist leaders by the Nationalists, the Japanese or the American Devils. But now, these enemies have got their wish without paying a penny or using a single bullet!'

As long as I could remember, Sun Ziping was a familiar name through wartime stories told by my grandmother, uncles and aunties. Shortly before the Cultural Revolution, he paid us a visit, which was the only time I met him. I was impressed by his gentle manner and warm smile, and especially his deep eyes, so calm that I thought this tall, thin, quiet uncle must live in a peaceful dream. I wish there were a world after death where I could meet Ziping again. On behalf of my family, I would like to comfort his broken heart and tell him how much he was loved. Dear Uncle Ziping, when you risked your life to join the Communists and offered yourself for the good of our nation, did you expect to leave the world so tragically? For your kindness to others and your contribution to the Party and the country, the treatment you deserved should have been limitlessly better!

Early in the Cultural Revolution, another friend of my father's, a university chancellor in Guangzhou, also took his life under persecution. In the year before his death, when he came to dinner, no one could have dreamed of such a future. During the Cultural Revolution, high officials accounted for only a fraction of those who died of persecution; the victims also included many well-known artists, writers, actors, sportsmen, distinguished scholars and doctors, as well as ordinary people. Once in Beijing, a man whose job was clearing human wastes from public lavatories was praised by Liu Shaoqi, China's then President, as a national model worker. As a result, he too was marked down for denunciation and violence, and did not survive it.

In late October 1969, my mother came home with unexpected news – most universities in Beijing must be evacuated to the provinces immediately, as part of implementing Lin Biao's No. 1 Directive. Within a few days, many universities were already on their way, but the move was not so easy for my mother's university. During the Great Leap Forward, Kang Sheng had insisted that the university must move to forested mountain areas. In China, the largest forest zone was in Manchuria, close to China's northeastern frontier, but that was not an option, because the area was already in combat readiness. In any case, Manchuria had its own established forestry university, and need not accept another. Eventually, her university opted for Yunnan province, on the southwest frontier, which had the second largest forest resources in China.

When he heard about the new location, my father was devastated. 'Oh no!' he said to my mother. 'Yunnan is a remote place, known for being beyond the clouds, where prisoners were exiled in the old days. Once you're there, neither I nor the children could see you again. I'd rather see you jailed in Beijing than sent to Yunnan.' In particular, he was concerned that if China was in fact invaded, then the family would lose contact and she might not be able to return. My mother agreed with him, but she had no choice. The Propaganda Team leaders refused her application to remain – 'If you and other university leaders did not go to Yunnan, how could the university carry on struggling-denouncing-reforming?' Since my mother was not rehabilitated, she was still subject to denunciation.

From the very beginning, the Workers' and PLA Propaganda Teams insisted that the whole staff must move to Yunnan, along with their families, young and old. My mother managed to keep her family in Beijing, because my father was a soldier and exempt. There was no allowance granted for the move. Each member of staff received several lengths of plank, the university's only contribution, enough to make a single packing case. The university also issued official letters authorizing staff evacuees to buy a few essential items such as a suitcase or travel bag, rubber overshoes or a piece of plastic sheet, which were rationed by the government.

Off the campus, there was a residential area where most of the staff lived with their families. Before moving, each household was in chaos because they had to shed as many belongings as possible. There was limited space for luggage on the journey, and they had to give up their quarters in Beijing. Also, no one had any idea of the nature or location of their future housing. For many, a painful experience was to abandon private collections of academic literature accumulated over many years. Some professors' valuable collections included rare editions of books in their field, or volumes of their research notes. But now, everything was sold at waste-paper prices, because no one could store all they had.

No matter what a nuisance the move was, few dared to complain, for fear of being accused of opposing Lin Biao's directive. In clear contrast, the students, especially the rebels, were determined to boycott the operation as soon as they learned that they too had to move to Yunnan. Not long before, they had accused my mother and some of her colleagues of flouting Kang Sheng's instructions in 1958 by keeping the university in Beijing, to keep up their cosy urban lifestyle. Now, when the countryside threatened, these 'revolutionary rebels' tried to cling to Beijing.

In early November 1969 the first convoy, mostly of students, was scheduled to start for Yunnan. The government supplied a special train, but the students refused to leave the campus, despite urging from the university authorities. After a whole day's fruitless negotiations, the leaders of the Propaganda Teams had to appeal to Premier Zhou Enlai.

His answer was clear: all students must leave for Yunnan. When they reached their first stop in Kunming city, the provincial capital of Yunnan, the students tried again to pull out. The plan was for the university to be dispersed, because the provincial authorities could not accommodate the several thousand newcomers in one place. Instead, they were assigned to ten different forest regions scattered across the province's territory, about two-thirds the size of France. But the students refused to proceed from Kunming, and demanded to be sent straight back to Beijing. During several days of confusion, a number did manage to return. Finding persuasion unsuccessful, the provincial authorities had to resort to force. These formidable youngsters were therefore coerced into boarding waiting vehicles, and resumed their journey escorted by troops.

My mother understood the students' reaction, since she knew that they were anxious about their futures. At that time, only a small number of students 'graduated'. Had it not been for the Cultural Revolution, the rest of them, enrolled during 1963–5, should also have completed their four-year courses. Now, there was no point in their retaining student status, especially since most students lived at their families' expense. But what would their futures hold? For more than three years, they had learned nothing about their subjects. Those in the most junior year had studied for only a couple of months when the Cultural Revolution started. Once in Yunnan, the university was going to be split, and no one – including members of the Propaganda Teams – had any idea whether teaching would resume, or how students would graduate. Even if they were all allowed to 'graduate', where would they work? Under the Communist regime, graduates were assigned to jobs provided by the government. They had to accept what they were offered, with little chance for personal choice. Most of these students came from north China, and the move they faced might compel them to settle somewhere far from their families, because graduates were often allocated to jobs in or close to the province that housed their university.

My mother's departure was set for 4 December 1969, which was exactly two years after her arrest. This train too was arranged by the government, with every carriage packed with luggage, no sleeping berths available, and only narrow seats for the passengers, including old people and children. It took almost three days from Beijing to Kunming, with a few stops on the way. From there, the passengers continued by truck to various destinations. After another day's travel, my mother and several hundred members of her university arrived at the headquarters of Qingshui Jiang Forest Region in the southeast of the province, about 100 kilometres away from the border with Vietnam. But this was not the end of their journey. From there, they were further divided into many small groups, and then posted to different work areas in the region, wherever the local authority had room for them. Much the same happened in the other nine forest regions, so that the several thousand university members were spread over nearly a hundred locations in the province.

My mother's destination lay in a remote mountain area. Apart from a few local forest workers, the contingent from Beijing saw hardly anyone else. Of the handful of villages in the whole mountain area, the nearest was several kilometres away, and most inhabitants were ethnic minorities who spoke their own language and knew hardly any Chinese. For many of the new arrivals, the remoteness seemed overwhelming. In the following months, some of the older relations died, and their families had to burn the bodies on bonfires, as the only way to dispose of them. With no railway or bus services available, the only transport for local people was the trucks that appeared at intervals to haul timber, and could also carry one or two passengers sitting next to the driver. Without these trucks, the mail would not have functioned. Postmen received the warmest welcome, since they brought messages from families or friends. Sometimes the trucks did not come for weeks at a time, as when the mountain roads were damaged by floods. Afterwards, piles of letters came at once.

In my mother's group, there were about thirty students with less than ten members of staff, including several professors. All of them lived in makeshift wooden huts, which were shared by several people or a family. In the subtropical climate, mosquitoes were active all year round, so everyone had to sleep inside a small mosquito net. On clear nights, the moon and stars shone in through the gaps in their boarded roofs. When it was raining, some of it found these crevices, and a piece of plastic sheet had to be fixed over the top of each mosquito net.

My mother and her companions were detailed to work as labourers, chiefly maintaining local roads. Every day, they followed two local forest labourers, and tramped the hills with shovels repairing roads. But the students refused to do any work, preoccupied with their uncertain futures. They spent much of their time in their huts, playing cards, sleeping or reading. Some of them embarked on close relationships.

In Yunnan, the members of the PLA Propaganda Team who were still supervising the university's affairs had less power to discipline the students, and could not answer questions about their futures. Nor could they cope with the problems of running the university in its new location. So they steered clear of students and staff, and waited to transfer their duties to another Propaganda Team assigned by the Kunming Military Region. In May 1970, after nearly six months' labouring in the mountains, my mother and her companions were informed about the arrival of the university's new leadership, the Yunnan PLA Propaganda Team, and the university reunion to be held in Lijiang city, in the northwest of the province.

After my mother left, we tried to conceal the news from inquisitive neighbours, in order to save her resident's card in Beijing. She ignored the official instruction to transfer her card to Yunnan, which would make it harder to return to Beijing. At home, my grandmother was often in tears when she was mentioned. When mail arrived, the first thing my father did was to look for my mother's letters, though they tended to minimize her hardships, so as not to worry her family. I still remember her descriptions of local customs. From Qingshui Jiang Forest Region, she wrote:

> The local residents are based on the Miao and Sha peoples [ethnic minorities]. Miao women's costumes are amazingly beautiful. Each one wears a short, close-fitting jacket, with a long, wide, pleated matching skirt. The materials are based on homespun, unbleached linen, and the hems are richly embroidered . . . The Shas [a branch of the Zhuang] like to wear black, and women even dye their teeth black. Every adult wears a robe, and a length of thick cloth for a head-dress, also in black . . .

After she moved to Lijiang, she wrote:

> In this region, the Naxi people [another ethnic minority] live in communities. The Naxis' own civilization goes back a long way. In the feudal dynasties, a number of Naxi scholars were chosen as Zhuang-yuan [first in the highest imperial examinations]. In this century, many Naxi people have travelled abroad to study . . . The Naxis are also called the 'Kingdom of Women', because women are the major working force even in planting or construction work . . . Naxi girls like to show what heavy loads of crops or fuel they can carry on their backs. Generally, each one can manage 100–150 kg at a time. Walking behind these heavily loaded women, I can hardly see their heads or feet, the load is so huge. But Naxi men are rarely seen doing such jobs, since many work in the non-agricultural sector with little involvement in hard labour. It is said that once at home, they enjoy looking after children or relaxing on their warm kangs while their wives toil outside . . .

A few months after my mother left, my father was informed that he was to be 'evacuated' to a remote mountain area in Hebei province. His request to bring one of his children was rejected. Considering his uncertain future and poor health, he asked Feng-an and me to assume responsibility for the family. Fortunately, the decision was reversed at the last moment, after sympathetic staff from the clinic of the armoured forces had made repeated appeals to the authorities, warning them that the move would endanger his life.

From early 1971, my father's special food allowance, available to senior officers from the level of major-general, was stopped. Our family was also excluded from many headquarters welfare services. Throughout the year, the farms run by the armoured forces produced regular supplies of products such as rice, cooking oil, meat and fruit. Under food rationing, this heavily subsidized provision was seen as a basic necessity. In the past, supplies had always been delivered to our house, or collected by our family's private staff. After my father's disgrace, my siblings and I had to go to the headquarters' storehouse, and queue to collect the supply. But now, we were often turned away. When she saw us come home empty-handed, my grandmother often repeated the Chinese saying: 'When a wall is about to collapse, everyone gives it a shove.'

In May 1970, my father was instructed to give up our house to a newly appointed Chief of Staff. I knew this would happen sooner or later. Former schoolmates whose parents were under a cloud commonly saw their families forced to move out of their houses, as well as having telephones cut off. But my father too had foreseen the event. Several months before, he had enlisted my brothers to help make containers for the family collection. Almost every day, his diary follows his progress. On 20 January 1970: 'Bought a saw. Preparing planks to make wooden containers. For several days, I have been suffering from angina.' Next day: 'Converted three large bookshelves into three containers . . . Bought gunny-sacks for books, each one costs 4–5 yuan.' Two days later: 'Sawed one thick plank into two thin pieces. Very difficult.' On 19 February: 'Made three containers . . . Converted an old kitchen cupboard into a container.' Two days later: 'Still slicing up planks . . . Bought four cardboard boxes, one large and three small. Bought nails.' On 8 April: 'Sawed up a tree trunk [collected by my brothers from outside] to make containers . . .' On 18 April: 'Planed planks all day with a borrowed plane. Feeling exhausted . . .'

During that period, our house was like a carpentry workshop, noisy with sawing and hammering, carpeted with sawdust. When my father dismantled his immaculate bookshelves, I could see his hands shaking. He must have felt agonized, as I knew how much he prized them. My job was to help him load the countless books into their various containers, as well as old magazines, newspapers and paintings. The work was time-consuming, especially since my father wanted everything just so.

Most of our moving activities took place at night, so as not to draw attention. There was no help from the armoured forces – not even a vehicle provided. For several nights, while people in the compound were asleep, my brothers and Little Auntie's husband, who was the only help we had, carried each packed container downstairs, and then to a handcart outside. The containers were terribly heavy, so that the process took time. As they pulled and pushed the laden handcart, my brothers and Little Auntie's husband were always panting for breath and streaming with sweat. Not till we moved did my siblings and I discover the cache in the attic where many particular treasures had waited for years.

The quarters we moved to were located in an area of the compound where mid-ranking and junior staff and their families occupied several large apartment blocks with basic conditions. It was a struggle for my grandmother to use the squat toilet. With her bound feet, she tended to overbalance when she parted her legs and tried to squat. There were no private bathrooms, and we had to use the public shower-house provided by the army, which had limited opening hours and was terribly crowded. Very often, there were hundreds of people jostling for use of a very few shower heads.

We now had four small rooms in two ground-floor flats, with less than half the space that we were used to. One room was piled from floor to ceiling with packing cases full of books and paintings. The rest went into my father's room; with too little space for furniture, he slept on top of the cases. Since these home-made containers were all shapes and sizes, and no mattress was available, his 'bed' was uneven and very uncomfortable. His desk was a single plank that spanned two cases, and his seat was a smaller case. The other two rooms, crammed with beds for the rest of the family, also functioned as our living room and dining room.

Meanwhile, there were signs of improvement in my father's political position. The team assigned to his case had recently been reorganized. Some members who had treated my father particularly badly were replaced by officers not allied to his enemies. In 1970, he was instructed to submit a political confession, which was seen as a signal of rehabilitation. At that time, rehabilitated victims of political persecution had first to accept a verdict stating: 'There are some grounds for it [the persecution], but investigation reveals no evidence.' No one was blamed for the persecution, but the victims had to admit to 'problems' to support the 'grounds'. My father was told that his confession must be approved by the headquarters Party membership – not only officers and soldiers but chefs and drivers too. Most importantly, his confession needed to satisfy the Party Committee of the armoured forces. Then his rehabilitation must be approved by the Party Committee of the Beijing Military Region, the General Political Department of the armed forces, and the Military Commission of the Party's Central Committee.

At first, my father refused: 'I have nothing to confess! The whole case against me is a fabrication.' This was seen as attacking the Cultural Revolution, which became an extra problem to confess to. If not, he would never be rehabilitated. Faced with these terms, my father was forced to concede, and to put up a smokescreen of lies in his confession.

More than a quarter of a century later, I saw one of the early versions, over thirty pages long. The first part dealt with the 'serious political problems' of his novel, such as not praising Chairman Mao's leadership, and focusing the story on a group of young Communist intellectuals, when according to Jiang Qing's theory, only industrial workers, peasants or soldiers should play major roles in a work of revolutionary literature. 'The novel expressed many of the feelings of the petty bourgeoisie [which was Mao's criticism of the intellectual cadres],' my father wrote, 'especially through love affairs between some major characters . . . bourgeois ideology was spread among its readers, which to some extent poisoned people's minds, and generally harmed the Party's cause. This is the most serious crime that I committed. I will accept all necessary punishments from the Party and the masses.'

In the next two parts of his confession, my father tried to clarify the allegations about his early career, and the details of joining the Party. 'I have always had confidence in my memory,' he wrote, 'but now I have no corroboration . . . There was no formal procedure when I joined, nor any official written record [by the rules of the Communist underground]. What happened was person to person . . .'

Lastly he dealt with the major reason for his 'serious political problems'. He had to take the blame for not using Chairman Mao's thought in word and deed, and also to attribute his problems to his family background as well as the feudal and bourgeois influences on his mind. In terms of Mao's theory of social class, my father came from a poor urban family of the petty bourgeoisie, not from the more revolutionary industrial workers and peasants.

From then on, my father spent months and years recasting and revising his 'confession'. Again and again, he was told that he had not made enough admissions. It seemed that his rehabilitation was still beyond the horizon.

During the following years, I asked my mother why Father's rehabilitation took so long. 'It's always easier to persecute a person than to rehabilitate one,' she said. 'In particular, your father could not receive backing from his superiors once the former leadership of the Beijing Military Region had been disgraced. Also, I think that his case was not handled by entirely disinterested people.' What she meant was that if my father was reinstated, some leading officers who had the power to approve his rehabilitation might feel their own positions threatened, as they could not match his revolutionary qualifications and capability. 'To make things worse,' my mother continued, 'your father's rehabilitation always faced strong objections from those who were involved in persecuting him and still held powerful positions in the armoured forces.'

After we left our house, the nervous strain grew on my father. Several times, he lost his temper when told to revise his 'confession' again. 'Enough is enough!' he snapped at his examiners. 'After two years' investigation, what political problems have been found? What else do I need to admit?' Such outbursts did not help his situation. Later, some sympathetic officers visited him in secret. 'Everyone knows that you're innocent,' they said. 'But without going through the procedure, you won't be rehabilitated. Please think about the future of your children.' This last point silenced my father. Due to his political troubles, Feng-an and I had endured hardships and exile from home, and Feng-yuan too faced a future without hope. In a few months, Feng-xin would 'graduate' from university. If there was no progress in my father's case, he would be labelled as one of the '[politically] educable sons and daughters', meaning children of politically disgraced officials, a 'second class' confined to inferior jobs. For the sake of his children, my father must continue his 'confession'.

Several times during that period, I found my father weeping on his own. His smoking – almost stopped some years ago on his doctors' advice – was now so heavy that I often choked to tears in his small room. Sometimes, he gave way to superstition. Once when I broke a Thermos flask, his face turned pale: 'I'll have a disaster today!' As it happened, that day he was summoned by the investigation team, and given a hard time. When he ate pears, he refused to share with us, because the words for 'sharing a pear', fe-li, sound the same as the word for 'separation'. It seemed that my father had changed dramatically from the dauntless figure I remembered.

Today, I often think that I should have given my father more care during that dreadful period, especially since my mother could not. In most of the four years since the Cultural Revolution began, my parents had been separated by their various imprisonments, and now my mother was expelled from Beijing. These long separations must have been incredibly hard for a loving couple. As a teenager, I was not fully aware of my father's pain, frustration and loneliness, and I also had pressures of my own. Confronted with endless disasters, I often felt at the end of my endurance, and longed for smiles, happiness and peace in our lives.

After my mother went to Yunnan, my father spent an enormous amount of time talking to Feng-an and me, sometimes long past midnight. It was then that I heard stories about his revolutionary career, and his romance with my mother. When we came to my parents' current situation, I mentioned their lack of political connections, which left them vulnerable to their opponents. As far as I knew, they had never curried favour as people like Tang and his wife had done.

'Your mother and I don't approve of flattering powerful figures,' my father replied. 'It's true that we've known many through our revolutionary careers, but as Communists, we firmly believe that we should rely on the Party organization rather than on personal connections.' Right from the start of their troubles, friends and sympathizers kept on urging my parents to seek help through connections such as Jiang Qing and Ye

Qun. For these powerful figures, my parents' rehabilitation would only take a word. But my parents disliked this idea. Apart from sticking to their principles and believing that truth would prevail, they never trusted Jiang Qing, Ye Qun or any of their allies.

Under my father's supervision, I started reading the family's collection of literature intensively. Through him, I learned about the genius of Charles Dickens in revealing aspects of Victorian society, such as the plight of orphans and the widespread poverty endured. His long reading list also included many Russian authors such as Tolstoy, Gogol and Pushkin, who were favourites of my father. Each time, I had to see that my hands were clean, in case his books got dirty. Also, I was not allowed to fold any page or leave a single mark. Determined to improve myself intellectually, I soaked up everything he recommended, and tried to memorize what he said. Another activity that fascinated me was my father's demonstration of changing the patterns of some famous Chinese classical poems by reorganizing the words, which inspired my interest in verbal skills. Our reading activities created an oasis where our souls were released from the system of political persecution.

When autumn came, my father liked taking me to visit old Beijing — former palaces, imperial gardens or temples. We also looked for historic sites mentioned in my reading. One day, we spent hours in the former palace of Prince Gong of the Qing Dynasty, supposedly the setting of a famous classic epic I had just read, *A Dream of Red Mansions*, written in the eighteenth century by Cao Xueqin. Following the collapse of his aristocratic family during court conflicts, Cao Xueqin suffered from poverty most of his life. The novel describes the rise and fall of an aristocratic family, and can be read as a condensed history of feudal society in China. Generations have shed tears over its tragic love story between the young prince Jia Baoyu and his cousin Lin Daiyu. Under the Communist regime, a major part of the former palace was converted into accommodation for government officials, so it was able to survive Red Guard attacks in the recent past.

While walking around hutongs in the city, my father told me that 'hutong' was ancient Mongol for 'well', which showed the strong influence of Mongol culture in Beijing. The city was the capital when China was ruled by descendants of Genghis Khan in the Yuan Dynasty (AD 1271–1368). In ancient times, people tended to live close to wells to guarantee fresh water, and lanes with houses originally built around wells were called 'hutongs'. In the Qing dynasty, there were nearly 1,000 hutongs in Beijing. When our family first settled there, my parents were fascinated by the lives of ordinary families in hutongs. After decades of war and social upheaval, they felt fulfilled to see how peacefully people lived in the newborn People's Republic.

During the early 1950s, many families in Beijing loved to drink fresh jasmine tea before doing anything else in the morning; it was a well-known passion. After tea, housewives were ready for their shopping, which always came to find them. From morning till evening, hawkers plied their wares door to door with different cries and sounds. After the vegetable vendor left, the housewives came out again when they heard the clack of the cooking-oil vendor with his wooden clappers and oily apron. He parked his wheelbarrow, and opened the lids of his various jars. 'Sesame oil, hand-pressed in small millstones! One drop is tasty enough to flavour a plate of salad!' The knife-sharpener cried 'Any knives or scissors to sharpen?', and jingled a bunch of small metal scraps in one hand. Each knife-sharpener carried a long wooden bench on his shoulder, one end mounted with a large grindstone, the other used to sit on while he worked. After grinding, they tried the blade with their right thumbs. Amazingly, they never cut themselves.

I was fascinated by what I saw and heard when touring the city with my father. Since most of my childhood was spent inside the high wall surrounding Ba-yi School, I knew little about the way people lived in Beijing. When I left that privileged cocoon in the mid-1960s, the city had changed a great deal. Following nationalization in the late 1950s, most hawkers disappeared, and residents had to rely on the limited number of local shops run by the government. Now, as the Cultural Revolution advanced, my father's description of ordinary people's lives sounded like a distant dream.

During this period, my siblings were busy at home. With my father's support, Feng-an started painting and learning English. He loved the Impressionists and copied their paintings every day. Feng-yuan developed a passion for science, just like Feng-xin in middle school.

Like many more in Chinese universities, Feng-xin and his fellow students had been living almost idly for years. They had lost interest in the Cultural Revolution, but there was no teaching available. Laboratories and libraries were smashed, books and equipment damaged or removed. Each year, Feng-xin stayed home for several months. While in Beijing, he borrowed some classical music records from his friends, and played them for us on an electric gramophone. It was my first introduction to great Western masterpieces such as Tchaikovsky's *Swan Lake*. Another favourite piece of music for us was the beautiful *Butterfly Lovers' Violin Concerto*, composed by Ho Zhan Hao and Chen Kang. Since all of these works were banned as 'bourgeois' or 'feudal', we had to close all doors and windows, and turn the volume very low, in case our pleasures came to outside ears.

In summer 1970, Feng-xin 'graduated' from university, and received a job assignment clouded by our parents' political problems, a small factory located in a remote county in Hebei province. Accepting the offer would require him to register as a local resident first, which would make it very difficult to transfer his resident's card back to Beijing.

For the sake of his children's future, my father made many appeals to the armoured forces. He still had supporters or sympathizers at various levels among the headquarters' staff, and some were in charge of personnel and conscription. Since my father had started his 'confession', they claimed that his problems were no longer 'contradictions between ourselves and the enemy' – in other words, he was not hostile to the Party. As a result, Feng-xin eventually enlisted in a division controlled by the armoured forces, instead of accepting the factory assignment. Since his enlistment took place in Beijing, he retained the option of returning to the capital after demobilization. During the annual conscription the previous winter, Aijun had already left home at the age of fifteen, and worked as a medical orderly for an army hospital in the suburb of Beijing. Thanks to my father's supporters, it was agreed that by the end of 1970 Feng-an, Feng-yuan and I would also be recruited to the army.

Chapter 19

Singer for Madam Mao's
Revolutionary Peking Opera:
My First Job in the Armed Forces

(November 1970–April 1972)

'The 12th of November 1970 is the day of your enlistment,' my father wrote to me a few days after I joined the army. 'You must remember this particular date for the rest of your life . . .'. In a subsequent letter, he wrote: 'It is very fortunate that you enlisted this year, thanks to those helpful uncles [my father's supporters in the armoured forces]. I hear that the military authorities have given orders to stop recruiting female soldiers . . . You must work hard, no matter what kind of job you are assigned to. That is the only way for us to repay the help we received.' On 20 December 1970, my mother wrote from Yunnan: 'You obviously know how difficult your enlistment was! How much these good comrades have helped us!'

On 12 November 1970, just a few days after learning of the chance of enlistment, I left home to join up in a hurry. Since my enlistment was arranged through his supporters, my father was concerned that any delay might cause hitches. If his opponents got wind of it, the whole arrangement would be blocked, and its promoters accused of violating regulations. But if it came out after my enlistment, I could not be so easily expelled. Despite the standing orders, many girls were still being recruited through their families' military connections, so if anyone moved to expel me, my father and his supporters could seek to defend me by questioning these high-profile cases, in which many armoured forces leaders were involved. In their own self-interest, my father's opponents would not risk too much fuss.

I left Beijing by train for Shacheng county in Hebei province, north of the Great Wall, where my posting was to a military base responsible for repairing armoured vehicles, and directly under the Equipment Department in my father's headquarters. 'It seems that everyone here knows you,' I wrote to him during my first week. 'Last night, my room-mates asked who my father is, and whether he is the author of *Autumn in Jinyang*. I tried to evade their questions, but they said that all the base staff know about it . . .' Walking to work or to the staff canteen, I was often stopped by strangers who greeted me kindly or claimed to know my family or my father. It was a warm experience. After our years of persecution and discrimination, I was pleased to find my father still secure in people's hearts. But the close attention also disturbed me. Several times, I was embarrassed by people publicly showing off their knowledge of the tough discipline my father imposed at home.

'When it comes to questions about me, you'd better not say much, or just plead ignorance,' my father advised. 'You must write at least once a week, and I will do the same to you . . . Indeed, I have thousands and thousands of words of advice, which are hard to put into writing.' Even without his urging, I knew how vulnerable my situation was. It was against the rules for me to join up from Beijing, as both Feng-an and I had lost our city residency by going to the rural settlement. But even if we returned to our village, we still did not qualify for enlistment. The rules required urban school-leavers to spend at least three years in their rural settlements before finding employment or enlisting. But joining the forces from our settlement was never advisable for Feng-an and me, as we would have to return to our village after our eventual discharge, with no right to re-register as permanent residents in Beijing.

Considering my parents' situation, I knew that if anyone made trouble about my enlistment, I could not expect much protection. Also, I had to be very careful when making comments about my surroundings, or expressing my personal feelings, or even making jokes, in case the words got back to any powerful figure in my father's headquarters who might turn them against my father and me. Despite the good will of my father's supporters, I was also handicapped by my parents' problems, since they had not been rehabilitated. For members of the armed forces, family political background was vital in determining job assignments and promotions, so unlike many others I knew, I expected no privileged treatment. For me, the only way to a good future was through hard work.

'Comrades often ask if I'm ill, since I look so thin and pale,' I wrote to my father in late November 1970. 'So they try to arrange lighter work for me, but I always turn the offers down. One day, we went to the local railway station to unload steel ingots [the material for making caterpillar treads]. It was bitterly cold. First, we had to push the freight wagon for several hundred metres to get it close to the platform. The ingots were piled all anyhow, and each one weighed nearly 20 kg. With comrades in my group, I picked them up one by one, and passed them to the others waiting outside. Soon, my back ached terribly. Several times, I almost fell over when lifting the heavy ingots, but I refused to take a break before my comrades and carried on working by gritting my teeth, determined to keep up. In the end all of us, including strong male soldiers, were exhausted. On the way back to the base, I found that several of my fingers were raw and bleeding . . .'

For my parents and myself, the major concern was my job assignment. Since the Cultural Revolution, my father had given up the idea that his children must have careers in literature or in other related subjects, as there were so many political complications involved. My parents expected me to work in an army clinic or hospital, a placement much in demand with female soldiers, because it meant the opportunity to receive medical training in future. A major requirement for entering medical school as a 'worker-peasant-soldier student' was one or two years of working experience in a medical institution, regardless of the nature of the job. In fact, there were not many suitable jobs for girls in the armed forces, despite the mass of new recruits in recent years. When I arrived, there were about thirty female soldiers among a thousand staff. All of these girls had enlisted last year, usually from officers' families. Most were assigned to the workshop repairing optical equipment for armoured vehicles. My father's supporters, who included a senior officer in the Equipment Department, had promised him that I would be allocated to the base's small clinic.

On arrival, I was put into the Telecommunications Squad first, pending my job assignment. For more than two weeks nothing happened, and I spent my time on political indoctrination and hard manual work. In the meantime, a new recruit of about my age arrived, and went straight to the already overstaffed clinic. She worked as a medical orderly first, and then was sent to a well-known hospital in Beijing to train as a medical doctor. Later, I heard that her great uncle was Marshal Lin Biao.

'Dear Baba, I have unexpected news,' I wrote on 30 November 1970. 'Yesterday afternoon, I was finally informed about my job assignment – singer for the modern revolutionary Peking Opera . . .'

Since the Cultural Revolution, all theatrical productions and films had been banned, apart from eight 'model revolutionary plays' which had Jiang Qing's support and included six 'modern revolutionary Peking Operas' and two 'modern revolutionary ballets'. Hence, this was known as the era of 'eight plays for eight hundred million people' (the total population at that time). In 1970, Jiang Qing launched a campaign to further promote these 'model revolutionary plays' throughout the country, enhancing her status in the Cultural Revolution. On the initiative of her close ally, Marshal Lin Biao, the armed forces played a key role. For a while, almost all sectors above division level established their own troupes, known as Literature and Art Propaganda Teams of Mao Zedong Thought. Each major military region was instructed to organize its own theatrical festival the following year, based mainly on the 'model revolutionary plays'.

Clearly, not many of the Literature and Art Propaganda Teams were able to stage 'modern revolutionary ballets'. China had only a handful of ballet schools, and their work had been suspended for several years, as in other educational institutions, so it was impossible to recruit enough dancers. But it *was* possible to stage the 'modern revolutionary Peking Operas', since only a few leading roles called for trained voices. Unlike Western operas, there was no chorus or large orchestra required. The modern revolutionary operas were therefore chosen by almost all the new Propaganda Teams. With official approval, many formations started recruiting 'literature and art soldiers', including many urban school-leavers from rural settlements, who because they had singing or instrumental skills were not obliged to serve out their term in the country, and did not need 'correct' family backgrounds or powerful connections. It soon became fashionable for parents in Beijing to pay for their young children to take singing or music lessons, hoping that they too might become 'literature and art soldiers' in future, and hence avoid the countryside.

In the autumn before my enlistment, my father and I had met two junior officers in a street in Beijing. They worked for the Equipment Department, and told us that they were looking for 'literature and art soldiers' for its Propaganda Team, soon to be established. As they talked to my father, they kept looking me up and down, which made me uncomfortable. After arriving in the base, I learned that one of the officers was Ganshi [junior political officer] Chang, and that his major task was to set up the Literature and Art Propaganda Team that would be stationed there. When we talked, he kept asking if I could sing, as he did with a number of my colleagues. My answer was always the same: 'I can't sing at all.' Indeed, it is difficult for anyone to sing Peking Opera without the proper training, because of the extremely high notes it demands. As well as singing, performers also require great skills in acrobatic dancing. Normally, training for Peking Opera singers should start at the age of six or seven. At nineteen, I felt that it was too late for me to learn. But despite my lack of both talent and interest, now I was enrolled in Jiang Qing's 'modern revolutionary Peking Opera'.

'I really don't want to work for the Literature and Art Propaganda Team,' I wrote to my father. 'I'm not qualified as a singer . . . The [Telecommunications] Squad chief lobbied the base leadership to keep me in her squad, as she appreciates me very much. But the answer was that I had been selected by the Deputy Political Commissar and Ganshi Chang, and my job assignment was a joint department decision. Since no one can change the decision, I have no choice but to obey it . . .'

My parents too were disappointed. At primary school, I was twice selected by the Dance Department of the PLA Art College, one of China's most prestigious institutions in its field. My parents turned both offers down – they did not see acting as an appropriate career. But this time there was little they could do. Their circumstances forced them to keep quiet, otherwise they would be blamed for opposing Jiang Qing's cultural campaign. Now that my three brothers and I had joined the army this year, my father was also reluctant to ask his supporters for extra favours. For those they had already provided, some of them already faced criticism at headquarters. So my parents encouraged me in their letters to approach this job assignment as a new challenge. The only consolation was that from now on, I would count as a 'literature and art soldier', if anyone disputed my enlistment.

On 25 December 1970, Feng-an and Feng-yuan were enlisted in the military, also with the help of my father's supporters, and joined two different divisions of a field army stationed in Shanxi province. As it was not connected to my father's headquarters, its leaders had no first-hand knowledge of my parents, but the official verdict was that they were still in political disgrace, and this made things harder for my brothers, for at least I was living among people who knew my father's history and treated me with sympathy. Feng-an's first posting was to an artillery battalion, while Feng-yuan was in the infantry, about 100 kilometres away. Their units were stationed in poor villages and lived in billets rented from local peasants. Life was harsh, like nothing my younger brother had experienced, and he wrote to my father about the freezing cold and poor conditions in his lodgings. For a long time, he worked as a labourer on his unit's farm. Very often, he had no fresh vegetables to eat, and the rice served by the army canteen was either burnt or only half-cooked.

During the annual conscription in winter 1970, my father also tried to help a number of my cousins whose parents were discredited. Second Uncle was the first of his siblings to fall foul of the Cultural Revolution when the Party's provincial newspaper denounced him as a counter-revolutionary in July 1966. By then Zhou Yang, the Party's deputy propaganda chief, who had rescued Second Uncle from political disgrace in 1962, was already under attack. Later, the Vice-Premier and Marshal Chen Yi were also purged. At the famous Guangzhou Conference in 1962, Second Uncle was deeply moved by Marshal Chen's sensational speech that paid tribute to his intellectual audience and was seen at first as an omen favouring Second Uncle's rehabilitation. Now, because his case was linked to Zhou Yang and Marshal Chen Yi, Second Uncle suffered strenuous public denunciation in his province. In 1968, his three sons had to leave home for different rural settlements after 'graduating' from middle schools, and he was sent to a back-country farm, far away from his family. For two years he lived on a meagre diet, forced to do hard manual labour every day. As he recalled years later, he often felt as if his bones had been pulled out of joint. Late in 1969, Second Uncle was transferred to a village to live as a peasant with his wife and youngest son, but the three elder boys, pinned to their settlements, were not allowed to join them.

First Auntie and her husband also suffered. Before the Cultural

Revolution they had moved to Hangzhou city, the provincial capital of Zhejiang, following their appointments as vice-chancellors for two different universities there. In the late 1960s, big-character posters branded them as 'counter-revolutionaries'. In 1968, their four children in middle schools were dispatched to Manchuria, thousands of kilometres from home, and worked as farm labourers for production and construction corps run by the army.

When I travelled home from my village in autumn 1969, I stopped at Xi'an city to visit Second Auntie and her family, and found that her husband had been under arrest for some time as a 'capitalist-roader'. Since the early 1960s, he had worked in Xi'an as deputy executive manager for one of China's largest aircraft companies. After his arrest, the family had to cede most of their flat to two other company families, retaining only two small rooms. Two of their children had also been sent to the countryside.

The most unspeakable case was Glory, daughter of my mother's second sister Ning, whose enlistment was approved in mid-1968 when the armed forces started recruiting girls. Her father's role as commander of the famous Linfen Brigade, killed in action by the Nationalists, entitled her to various benefits which included the privilege of enlistment. Just when she was about to join her unit, the appointment was cancelled, because her father was now accused of being a member of the 'Renegade clique of sixty-one' – the same charge brought against my father by Tang and Ge in 1968. Suddenly her father was downgraded from revolutionary martyr to 'counter-revolutionary renegade', and she along with him, even though he died before she was born. There was no way out but the countryside, and the army stopped her financial support.

In winter 1968, Glory came to say goodbye to my family before leaving for her rural settlement. My father assured her: 'Please don't believe the accusations made against your father. He was a revolutionary hero, you should be proud of him!' Due to these accusations, Glory's elder brother, South of Shanxi, was sent to a remote farm run by the army after he graduated from a military university, to work as a labourer. A few years later, when he was demobilized, he was assigned to factory work in Beijing.

'Glory and her mother came to see me today,' my father wrote to me on 15 November 1970, three days after I joined the army. 'I wrote four personal letters to senior officers of the provincial military region in Shanxi, and two more to senior officers in No. 69 Field Army [all of them former colleagues] . . . Glory can contact these people to ask about the prospects for enlistment . . . I spent a long time talking to Glory . . . I encouraged her again and again, trying to cheer her up . . .' On 10 December 1970 he wrote: 'Two of First Auntie's boys arrived yesterday from Manchuria . . . I went straight to see Uncle Chen [a former colleague in the 1950s], but he has no notion how to help the boys [to join the army]. Finally, it occurred to him that an acquaintance of his, vice-commander of a provincial military region in Manchuria, was in Beijing currently. He promised to contact his acquaintance, but was unsure about the result.'

For more than a month after I left home, my father mentioned in each of his letters how hard he was trying to help the children of my troubled uncles and aunties, and how difficult it was. Having no more help to expect from the armoured forces, he turned to friends and former colleagues elsewhere. One of them was Major-General Shao, former commander of the armoured forces and another of Tang's opponents, politically disgraced in 1965 but later appointed deputy commander of the Shanxi provincial military region, when the fear of war revalued sheer experience. At that time it was an unwritten law that rehabilitated officials were often downgraded in their new positions, and this happened to Major-General Shao, but he contrived to have Glory recruited by his region. By the end of 1970, Second Uncle's three boys had enlisted. Two were accepted by forces under my father's friend, the political commissar of a field army in north Hebei province. Another political commissar friend placed one of Second Auntie's boys in

Shaanxi province. The toughest cases were First Auntie's four children. Military regulations required them to gain approval to enlist from their production and construction corps in Manchuria. Their failure to obtain it made it hard for my father to help through his personal connections. In desperation, they went to Fuzhou, in the southeast, to appeal to Third Auntie's husband, a senior officer in the Fuzhou Military Region, who managed to have most of them accepted by the region.

The 'model revolutionary play' put on by our Literature and Art Propaganda Team was *The Red Lantern*, one of the most influential modern revolutionary Peking operas, whose arias are still familiar among hundreds of millions of Chinese. The story takes place in Manchuria during the Japanese occupation in 1940, and involves three generations who work for the Communist underground. The leading roles are Granny Li, an old housewife, Yuhe, a middle-aged railway worker, and Tiemei (Iron Plum), a girl of seventeen. For years, the three have lived as a family. On a mission to deliver a secret code to the guerrilla forces, they are arrested by the Japanese, and Granny Li and Yuhe are executed. Shortly before the execution, Iron Plum is amazed to hear from Granny Li that the three are completely unrelated. In 1923, when Iron Plum was a baby, her revolutionary parents were killed by the warlord government, along with Granny Li's husband, a Communist colleague of her parents and Yuhe. Afterwards, the three survivors lived as a family of three generations, and Granny Li and Yuhe kept working for the underground. After the death of Granny Li and Yuhe, Iron Plum manages to escape and eventually delivers the code to its destination. The red lantern is a signal lantern for railway workers, and works as a symbol of the revolution.

'Two days ago, Ganshi Chang and Political Instructor Xia asked me again if I can play the part of Virtuous Lotus [Hui-lian],' I wrote to my father on 8 December 1970. In the opera, Virtuous Lotus is the major female supporting role with a small singing part. 'I replied that I have never sung any opera in my whole life, or had any voice training either. They said that my physical appearance is good, so I must work hard to train my voice, and will soon be playing Virtuous Lotus . . . Baba, I don't like acting at all. I can't sing. I can't wait to leave the Propaganda Team . . .'

Three days later: 'Today is Sunday and our rehearsal starts . . . Two members of the Shacheng Hebei Opera Troupe [a local company] have been invited to supervise our training [mainly in dancing].' (During that time, companies working in the various provincial operatic traditions were also limited to adapting the 'model revolutionary plays'.) 'After breakfast, I joined the others to do the splits, jumps and other basic dancing training, and to learn the chorus dances. Since I didn't have much practice for my back and legs before, I have to work harder than the others. Soon, my back and legs are aching and I'm pouring with sweat . . . Compared with the others, I'm terribly clumsy, and didn't even know how to hold a rifle [in the guerrilla chorus dance] . . .'

                                                                    Shacheng

20 December 1970

Dear Baba,

I didn't have time to answer earlier. Every morning is spent train-ing or rehearsing. In the afternoons, I'm busy preparing costumes or props for the opera . . . Last Sunday [the only day off] I helped comrades to hand-wash their dirty clothes in the morning, and then helped my group leader preparing props again in the after-noon. In the evening, the Propaganda Team held a plenary meeting while the team leaders and Ganshi Chang gave further instructions about our work. All of them were dissatisfied with our progress, and asked us to work harder with revolutionary and 'death-defying' spirit . . . On 25 January, we will perform for staff at your head-quarters. Since the meeting, we've been terribly busy . . . This evening, our rehearsal went on till midnight again. I'm writing this letter after all that . . .

It has been decided that I am to play a guerrilla in the last scene, the one who appears on stage as soon as the curtains open. I will then dance with Iron Plum and other guerrillas to celebrate the revolutionary victory . . . I find it quite difficult to play my part, so I spend more time on dancing practice than the others . . . Since I can't do the splits properly, I asked my group members for help. Lying with one leg flat on the floor, I have the other leg constantly pushed towards my face. The method is called 'splitting up legs', and is used by trainees in the Shacheng Hebei Opera Troupe. During the splitting, the pain in my legs is like electric shocks. Sometimes my clothes are completely soaked in sweat . . .

On 24 December 1970, I wrote to my father again: 'Two days ago, I was asked again to learn the Virtuous Lotus role. It was said that apart from my good physical appearance, my deportment on stage is very good. I finished learning the Virtuous Lotus part in a few hours, which impressed everyone . . . But I still can't sing properly. When singing, I don't know how to breathe without showing it in my face. I have to work very hard to improve my singing and acting skills . . . Baba, you know about Peking Opera, please give me some ideas on improving my singing! . . .'

A week later: 'These days we always get to bed after midnight . . . My eyes are getting swollen, red and terribly sore. Maybe it's due to lack of sleep . . . According to our trainers from the Shacheng Hebei Opera Troupe, our voice training method is wrong, especially since we are not accompanied by an instrument such as the jinghu [Peking Opera fiddle]. If we don't change our training method, our voices will be damaged . . .' We never had a professional coach, so we just followed the lead singers to exercise our voices. 'My voice has been hoarse recently, which must be caused by the wrong way of training . . . Last night I was asked to rehearse Virtuous Lotus's part on stage . . . the first time my performance was accompanied by the orchestra. I forced myself to finish rehearsing the part. My performance was dreadful! I was so nervous, and my singing often got out of tune . . .'

In my letter of 23 January 1971: 'A musician from the Beijing Film Studio Philharmonic Orchestra arrived recently to supervise the orchestra rehearsals . . . A few days ago, he asked me if I could play Iron Plum, because my appearance is good, especially because of my physical resemblance to Liu Changyu [a famous singer whose performance of Iron Plum was favoured by Jiang Qing] . . . From what he said, I realized that it was mainly for my appearance that I was chosen. The musician suggested inviting a professional coach to help my voice training. Similar suggestions were made by some leaders of the Equipment Department and my Propaganda Team. I politely declined them all, as I now believe that it is impossible for me to be trained as a Peking Opera singer. In recent dress rehearsals, I was praised again for my physical resemblance to Liu Changyu on stage. In fact, my face is rounder, but it was said that with the stage make-up, the difference hardly shows. Concerning all this praise, reactions from our leaders, including Ganshi Chang, now seemed unenthusiastic. They replied that no matter how good my physical appearance is, it is useless for the opera, simply because I can't sing . . .'

On 23 December 1970, my father wrote: 'In two days' time [when Feng-an and Feng-yuan joined the army], there will be only your grandmother, Little Red and me left at home.' Little Red was Little Auntie's younger son, who was only seven. The year before, his parents had been consigned to a labour camp outside Beijing, where they lived separately in segregated dormitories, and were only allowed home once a month for a short break. In these circumstances, they had to send their younger son to our house. Their first son was about ten years old, and severely disabled since birth. As his parents were away, he was sent to his father's home county in Hebei province to be cared for by relatives.

When my siblings and I were gone, my father felt more and more cut off. Used to a busy fruitful life, he struggled to cope with the loss of meaning. It seemed he was forgotten by the world, with no job and hardly any visitors. Once in a while, members of the investigation team returned to re-revise his confession, and often tried his temper again. A person in disgrace was forbidden to read official documents or attend official meetings, activities once central to his life. Through the media, which was full of propaganda, it was difficult to know what was going on inside and outside China. He felt desperately isolated, and would travel around Beijing by bus to visit friends or former colleagues still in power, who could keep him in touch with China and the world. Often his trip was fruitless, because he could not give notice of his visits. Our home had lost its two telephone lines, and because Beijing suffered from a shortage of telephones, and prospective customers required official approval from their workplaces, it was impossible for my family to obtain one. Most of the books in his collections remained packed, since there was nowhere to put them. Now that his children were gone, there was no one to help him to locate books by shifting the heavy containers. Living all day with his books, he could not read them. Years later, he told my mother that during that period, he felt lost in a waste of desert, with no way to get out.

Driven by loneliness, my father spent a lot of time exploring the areas near the compound, which happened to include one of Beijing's most famous cemeteries, established before the People's Republic and named 'Happy Land [Futian] Cemetery'. People buried there included many celebrities from recent history, as well as foreigners. It became his most frequently visited place, and he spent hours there trying to decipher inscriptions on its shattered gravestones, mostly destroyed by the Red Guards. One day he found fragments of a beautifully written classical poem, which moved him deeply, as it expressed a husband's love for his wife. He combed the area for days, searching for the missing parts of the poem among the many other ruined gravestones scattered all over the cemetery. Unfortunately, he never retrieved the whole version. In the deserted cemetery, my father felt that he could regain his peace of mind, and forget the social chaos, and the persecution he had suffered. Reading the inscriptions warmed his injured heart with the love and emotions of human beings. Sometimes he stood among the graves and stared for hours at the blue sky. 'When will our country and people find peace again?' he asked himself. 'When will my ordeal be over?'

On 2 March 1971, my father wrote: 'Two weeks ago, Grandmother became critically ill. At first, her blood pressure rose to 250/150. After emergency treatment, her blood pressure fell, but then she came down with tracheitis and serious asthma. For several days, she could not eat or drink. After ten days of taking antibiotics, she is getting better . . . Several days ago, Little Auntie took some days off and came to help me, but soon both she and Little Red were running high temperatures and so had to go to bed too. Now, everyone is recovered . . . I insisted that Grandmother must stay in bed for another ten days, in case of a relapse, while I continued to look after her . . . During that time, I did not feel well either, so I started taking antibiotics myself, which seemed to work, as I did not run a temperature. But I still suffered from a sore throat . . .'

After my siblings and I left home, everyday life got harder for my family. One immediate problem was shopping for food. There were only a few shops available locally, and long queues were common. In the past, food shopping had been done by my siblings and me, but now my grandmother had to take it on. Close to her eighties, and with bound feet, all this queuing and carrying was a major task. When winter came, she easily caught cold, which often developed into tracheitis and asthma. At that time, families in the compound had been issued with gas cookers, as part of the headquarters' welfare arrangements. We were debarred from these – the only family in the compound that still used coal for cooking. Gas cookers had only just been introduced in China, and could not be bought on the market. Ever since the change, we had had to walk several kilometres to the nearest coal merchant, because it had stopped making deliveries to the compound for only one customer. Now, on their own, there was no question of my father or grandmother carrying coal supplies for several kilometres, especially with no transport available any more. Very often, they had to wait for Little Auntie and her husband to return to Beijing for their monthly break, and ask them for help.

On 16 March 1971, my father wrote: 'Ten days ago, my blood pressure suddenly rose to 180/130, and I felt too dizzy even to sit down. After doctors' emergency treatment, I felt better . . .' By the time I received this letter, my father had already been taken to hospital after a relapse. Since my grandmother was still unwell, Little Auntie was called back again. Two days later she had to return to her labour camp. Her repeated absences had caused criticism, and she was forbidden to care for her mother and son. In desperation, she appealed to her siblings by telegram. Second Auntie arrived to replace her, and stayed for about three weeks, before Third Auntie came from Fuzhou to take her place.

It was the end of April when Second Uncle came to replace Third Auntie from the village he was expelled to – their first meeting since the unforgettable family reunion in August 1954. My father was still in hospital, and Grandmother still confined to bed. Many years later Third Auntie recalled that moment: 'As soon as I saw him, the tears ran down my face like pearls from a broken necklace. He was so thin and emaciated, and his face so lined. His hair had turned grey, and his clothes were worn and patched . . .' Lying in her sickbed, my grandmother wept: 'My poor boy, you joined the revolution since childhood, and followed the Communists and Chairman Mao to fight for poor people. How could you be accused of being a counter-revolutionary?' Second Uncle held her hands and promised that some day things would change. During his stay, she kept pleading: 'Please tell your children, if they want a peaceful life, never to be interested in writing. Just think what has happened to you and your elder brother!' Second Uncle stayed for only a few weeks, as his movements were officially restricted. After he left, he sent his youngest son, Little Fourth, to look after my grandmother and Little Red.

On 5 April 1971 my father wrote: 'During your ten days' stay in Beijing [touring with my Propaganda Team], you visited me in hospital four times. It showed that your mind is full of worries about me. I also longed to see you, but on the other hand I did not want you to travel so much. It was so far for you to travel to the hospital. Each time, you left me in a hurry with no time for food. On your return, you had to face complaints from colleagues. Several times, I also had other visitors, so that I did not have enough time to talk to you. Each time I said good-bye, I felt as if I might not see you again . . . In fact, you should not worry too much about me, as it does not help. When you return to your base, don't always think of coming back to see me again. You must con-centrate on your work.'

When touring in Beijing, I tried to take as many chances as possible to visit my father in hospital, which caused criticism among some col-leagues because the rules set limits on visiting our families while on tour. All members of my group were girls, and since most of them came from Beijing, my frequent visits to my father were seen as a privilege. I heard later that each time I left for the hospital, some girls went to the leaders of the Propaganda Team to protest. When I returned, they asked me pointed questions about my absence. 'I don't care what the others do to me,' I wrote to my father. 'As long as I think it is worthwhile, no one can stop me.'

What really upset me was that the complaints made it harder to visit my father again during subsequent tours in Beijing. As a new recruit, I was not entitled to come home on leave during my first year's service. On the way back to base from Beijing, our motorcade often stopped at the famous Badaling section of the Great Wall for a short break. In those days, there were hardly any tourists, and the vast car park was always empty. I liked to sit on the battlements and stare towards Beijing. When would I go home again? When would I see my father and grandmother again?

After returning to base, I often wept with frustration, thinking of the troubles my family faced at that time. My father and grandmother were ill, and my mother still stranded in Yunnan with no prospect of return. My family needed me so much. What was the point of being parted from home again, and working for the army, especially in a job I cared nothing about? With no performing skills and no experience, I was useless here, and wasting my time and youth. At home, I could care for my family and study literature with my father, which now seemed like a beautiful fading dream.

Despite what I felt, I knew that I could not quit the army. My parents would be furious. They had tried their best to place their children in the army, hoping that we could find a future there. My father's supporters had championed my enlistment; they would be let down if I quit. For the sake of my own future too, I knew that I had no choice but to fight my way through every problem, and do what my assignments demanded.

When I left home for the armed forces, my mother had moved to Lijiang. During that period, she heard that Premier Zhou Enlai had given orders to rehabilitate disgraced officials if inquiries proved no charges, which should apply to her case. But in her university, the newly arrived PLA Propaganda Team decided that the priority was to 'graduate' the remaining students who had enrolled before the Cultural Revolution. Many of these had belonged to the rebel student forces formerly involved in persecuting suspect officials, so they were unlikely to cooperate in rehabilitating their own victims. After their 'graduation', most students were assigned to forest areas spread around Yunnan and neighbouring provinces. For a long time, they worked as forest labourers. The major improvement they enjoyed was that as graduates, they now received wages from the government.

After the students departed, only the staff were left: since the university had not found a place to settle, it was impossible to recruit new students. But now the rehabilitation of disgraced officials was postponed again, after the launch of a new campaign known as 'Purifying the class ranks' and supported by Mao Zedong. Its aim to clear class enemies out of the Party amounted to a continuation of the purge against new victims, this time mostly people of lesser Party rank, guilty of 'political problems' in their personal background. Several members of staff were arrested by the university authorities, including some professors accused of being foreign spies, having studied abroad some decades before. Interrogations often went on round the clock, and were attended by the 'revolutionary masses'. After days of constant pressure, most of the victims had to submit, often just before dawn. In a state of near-collapse, they just admitted every charge and hoped that the interrogation would stop.

Due to a shortage of staff to conduct the campaign, my mother and Lu Wen were assigned to guard a prisoner, the wife of a professor also arrested and jailed in a different place. My mother really hated this job, but she was not allowed to turn it down. This couple had a teenage daughter who was mentally handicapped. After her parents' arrest she was left alone at home. In the daytime, she often dressed up in her mother's clothes and walked around with an innocent smile, showing off her fashionable looks. At night, some vicious men often went to her home and sexually abused her. Every day, this imprisoned woman stood by the window of her cell, at the top of a small building, and watched her daughter wandering. She cried as she watched, perhaps because she realized what had happened to her daughter. The sight made my mother look away, and pierced her heart.

Soon after 'Purifying the class ranks', another national campaign was launched, known as 'Unearthing the 5-16 counter-revolutionary conspiratorial clique'. It purged many members of the rebel organizations for taking part in activities aimed at Zhou Enlai or other figures in the Party's new leadership. The '5-16 clique' was originally a rebel organization in a university in Beijing at the start of the Cultural Revolution, so the authorities in Yunnan thought that my mother's university should be the major focus of the campaign there, as it was the only institution that had moved from Beijing in recent years. They instructed the university to unearth the '5-16 clique' among its members.

As in previous campaigns launched during the Cultural Revolution, there was no clear criterion to identify the targets designated as the '5-16 clique', but this time it was the turn of Cao Lian and his allies to suffer, as the chief movers in the rebel organizations while the clique was active. For many members of staff who had experienced Cao Lian's bullying and lies, it was time to express their anger and resentment. Feeling erupted against him. By demand of the masses, he was arrested by the university authorities and denounced in various rallies. Weihe, his ally notorious as a thief, was lucky that he had already transferred to Anhui, his home province, to avoid the move to Yunnan. During the denunciation activities, Cao Lian was frequently beaten, by victims who failed to control their rage. 'Without the PLA Propaganda Team to protect him, Cao Lian might have been beaten to death at that time,' my mother told me many years later.

My mother was often summoned to denounce or beat Cao Lian. 'You suffered so much from Cao Lian,' they urged her. 'Why don't you take your chance for revenge?' But my mother would testify only to what she knew. Unlike Cao Lian with her, she would not invent accusations. In any case, she would never resort to violence herself. After all her suffering, what she wanted was justice, not revenge. By now, she recognized that almost everyone had become a victim of the Cultural Revolution, including those who had victimized others before. What was the Cultural Revolution for? When would the persecutions end? My mother felt more and more confused and disappointed by what was happening in China. At that time, her only hope was to be rehabilitated, and hence reunited with her family.

In fact, my mother's rehabilitation was already on the agenda at the university. Unlike my father, she was in the hands of outsiders, namely the PLA Propaganda Team. As servicemen, its members were on temporary assignments. Their careers were controlled by the army's command structure, not the university's, so their interests were independent from my mother's. Years of investigation had turned up no evidence against her. Now that Premier Zhou had given orders to rehabilitate disgraced officials, her ordeal should soon be at an end.

Just like my father's, my mother's rehabilitation was also made conditional on submitting a confession, which she hated but had to produce. She knew it was a sham, and utterly ridiculous. She had never done anything to harm the Party or the nation, and it was common knowledge inside the university that her crime was to have offended Cao Lian. Yet now she had no right to ask for justice, and had to acknowledge deserving whatever she had suffered. Soon after my mother offered her confession to the university staff, the Propaganda Team announced her rehabilitation.

Late in June 1971 my mother returned home, after almost two years of forced separation, but at once fell seriously ill. Five years of persecution, violence and damaging conditions had undermined her health. During her long spell in prison she had suffered from frequent stomach upsets caused by a deficient diet, and her cell was often very cold and damp. After the move to Yunnan, her stomach condition got worse, and often brought high temperatures. For a long time she was unable to eat, and even to sit down caused her terrible pain in her stomach, but she could not find a remedy. Neither of the areas she lived in had adequate medical services, and her symptoms went undiagnosed. At her colleagues' suggestion, she visited an army hospital near Lijiang where the doctors had some expertise in folk prescriptions, which sometimes soothed the pain, but it was far away from where she lived, and with no local transport available she had to walk for two or three hours every time.

After her return from Yunnan, my mother's health worsened. She spent most of her time in bed, drowsy with sleep and too weak to walk. Among the various doctors she saw in Beijing, one was Dr

Yang, in his seventies, and famous as an expert on traditional Chinese medicine. He worked from home, assisted by a number of apprentices, and his high-ranking patients included national and Party leaders and their wives. As Dr Yang's surgery normally did not open to the public, my mother was initially introduced by his former patient, General Dong Qiwu, the last Nationalist governor of Suiyuan province, the power base of General Fu Zuoyi. He got to know my parents after he followed General Fu to join the Communists at the end of the Civil War. Under the Communist regime, General Dong was given high social status, and later worked as Vice-President of the Chinese People's Political Consultative Conference, on a level with Baorhan, my best friend's father. During the Cultural Revolution, many celebrated political figures like Generals Fu and Dong, former high-ranking Nationalist officials now working for the Communist regime, enjoyed special protection from persecution because they contributed to the Party's political propaganda aimed at the Nationalist regime in Taiwan.

My mother's illness was eventually diagnosed as atrophic gastritis. (She also had damage to her back and legs inflicted during her imprisonment.) For a long time, she tried various treatments, but nothing would clear up her illness. As well as the doctors' prescriptions, friends recommended other methods. One that she tried was to drink three large mugs of cold tap water every morning on an empty stomach, and then go out walking for an hour. 'Finishing the first mug was okay,' she told me later, 'but the second was a strain, and the last mug often made me sick, especially because I couldn't stand the strong taste of bleach in the water.' Back in Beijing, her illness lasted for almost two years.

Shortly after my mother's return, my grandmother and my father suffered recurrences of their cardiac and hypertension problems, and went into hospital. By then Little Fourth, Second Uncle's youngest son, had had to leave. Without a resident's permit, he could not go to school or find a job in the capital, and was forced to return to the village in Manchuria where his parents lived in exile. After Little Fourth left, there was no one able to look after my grandmother in Beijing, so after her discharge from hospital she had to move to Third Auntie's family in Fuzhou.

From mid-September 1971, the name of Lin Biao suddenly disappeared from all official media, including reports on the official celebration of China's National Anniversary on 1 October. In the following month, there was no official explanation of the change, but among my colleagues there were rumours that Lin Biao had died while fleeing to the Soviet Union on 13 September 1971.

On 24 October, the Party's Central Committee informed the whole nation about the fate of Lin Biao. That day I wrote to my parents: 'Following urgent instructions from the Equipment Department, our recent tour was interrupted, as we were recalled to the base at once . . .' On 1 November, I wrote again: 'From today, all members of the base including our team start full-time political education [the start of the campaign against Lin Biao]. It will last for eight days while all production stops.'

By then, Lin Biao and his family were the targets of a national denunciation campaign. We learned that Lin Biao had been trying to seize power from Mao Zedong, and had staged an armed coup. As well as Lin Biao, his wife Ye Qun and their son, Lin Liguo, a young officer and high-flier who already controlled the air force, were also leading conspirators. It was said that they attempted to assassinate Mao in the period from August to September 1971, when he was touring around southern China to secure support from key Party, government and military leaders there. It seemed that Mao had got wind of Lin Biao's plan, and managed to escape assassination by frequent unexpected schedule changes. When Mao Zedong returned safely to Beijing on 12 September, Lin Biao saw that he had failed. In desperation, he decided to flee to the Soviet Union with his wife, son and a number of close companions. In the small hours of 13 September, they commandeered an air force Trident and took off in frantic haste. About two hours later, the plane crashed in the Undur Khan desert in Outer Mongolia: none of the passengers survived. During the following decades, there have been different versions of the story, but no way to confirm them. To this day, the truth cannot be known.

The nation was shocked by the news. The struggles within the Party's new leadership had not been made public. Only recently, Lin Biao had been Chairman Mao's closest comrade and best student, his chosen successor. All of a sudden he was accused of the ultimate sins: of attempting to stage a counter-revolutionary coup, and to assassinate Mao Zedong. Not long ago, many senior Communists labelled as traitors by Lin Biao had been persecuted. Now, he himself had died in flight to the Soviet Union, one of China's arch-enemies. What ironies history was revealing! What a farcical experience the Communist Party had been through!

For my parents, it was shameful that their well-tried Party and beloved Chairman had been deceived by Lin Biao. 'We hope that our Party and Chairman Mao can draw the proper lessons from this case,' they said in private, 'so that such a ridiculous situation will never happen again.' To their dismay, they soon found out that the Cultural Revolution continued. By Mao's account, Lin Biao represented the interests of the landlord and capitalist class, and aimed to restore capitalism in China, so his actions stemmed from the intensified class struggle between the proletariat and its enemies. During the campaign against Lin Biao, many colleagues told me privately that my father's ordeal was bound to finish soon. Unfortunately, their prediction was mistaken.

The downfall of Lin Biao had repercussions for his family and associates. In our base, the girl who was his great-niece was recalled from medical training in Beijing to work as a medical orderly, ending her dream of becoming a doctor. Fortunately, my parents had never asked Lin or his wife for help, or all their political troubles would have redoubled.

From spring 1971, our Literature and Art Propaganda Team made frequent tours of northern China, performing in Beijing, and in Hebei and Shanxi provinces. We made no profits, because publicizing Mao Zedong Thought came free to the audience, so the whole cost was covered by the military budget. For more than a year, we visited many cities, towns and villages. As well as entertaining our own and other branches of the forces, we put on shows for institutions, factories and local government workers. Sometimes we were also assigned by armoured forces headquarters to entertain their social or business connections. Among all the armoured forces divisions, our Literature and Art Propaganda Team had the best reputation. Our leading singers had fine voices, and we took pride in the orchestra. After the Cultural Revolution, a number of its talented members became well-known musicians in China, and performed on state television or radio. The musician who supervised our orchestra also became a famous conductor in the Beijing Film Studio Philharmonic Orchestra.

Venues for our performances varied from a magnificent concert hall in Beijing to makeshift open-air theatres in isolated mountain villages. Due to their remote locations and poverty, some villages we visited had no electricity supply, and we worked under gas-lamps. Wherever we went, we were hugely popular, especially in outlying mountain or rural areas where people longed for entertainment. For several years, even the 'model revolutionary plays' were not shown regularly, because theatre companies and mobile troupes were also engaged in political struggles. When entertaining troops, we often heard of soldiers walking more than ten kilometres to watch us. Sometimes, local people lined streets for miles to welcome us. One performance in a village's open-air theatre attracted more than ten thousand peasants. On another day, we visited an iron mine in the Tai-hang mountains. Far in advance, the temporary theatre, converted from a large canteen, was already overflowing. Apart from the mine's own staff and their families, there were local peasants who had walked for hours along mountain paths. Many had never been to a performance before. By demand of the crowd who were left outside, our leaders decided to stage an extra performance next day, which was watched by another huge audience.

The tour was a window for me: from it I saw different people, and learned a lot about society. One day, an unexpected visitor came to see me after our performance, an officer in the unit we had just entertained. In 1967, while stationed at armoured forces headquarters, he had been involved in persecuting my father. 'Please pass my apology to your father for what I did,' he said to me. 'As a naive young man, I was used to persecute him.'

On another day, we passed a military airfield in southeast Shanxi province, and found it covered by flames and smoke, with bursts of gunfire sounding. Our motorcade stopped, and everyone rushed to help put out the fire. When it was all over, we were shocked to hear that the fire had been set by a soldier with a grievance against his leaders. He had got hold of a machine-gun and several rifles, and kept shooting to deter fire engines or anyone else from approaching. When we arrived, he had just killed himself with the last bullet.

When touring in Hebei and Shanxi provinces, we often stayed in primitive accommodation, in areas known for their poverty and shortage of water. In a county town in Shanxi, for example, the taps ran for only a few hours every day. If we did not store water in advance, we would be unable to wash our hands and faces when removing our stage make-up. In another county town in northern Hebei province, there were no sanitary facilities where we stayed. Each morning we stood in the yard to brush our teeth, surrounded by curious local people. At the sight of our mouths foaming white with toothpaste, some local girls could not help giggling. Perhaps it was the first time in their lives that they saw toothpaste used. During the tours, it was usual for us not to have a shower or bath for several weeks, because hot water was not available. In cold conditions my hands got terribly rough and dirty without hot water to remove the greasy cosmetics. Another nuisance was filthy bedding: sometimes our sleep was invaded by armies of hungry bugs. But the nightmare for me was the appalling sanitation. In those days, indoor or flush lavatories were rare in many areas. Apart from the stink, the lavatories we used were terribly dirty, and the floors often covered with excrement and urine.

In contrast to the poor living conditions, we were treated to sumptuous feasts during the tours, mostly paid for by the host organizations. Sometimes, we could hardly believe their lavish hospitality. In a factory producing military equipment, each of our tables was served by several attendants whose task was to keep topping up empty bowls till we were crammed. All this over-eating made me and many of my colleagues put on weight – especially the girls. Some of our audiences burst out laughing when they heard dialogue complaining about starvation under the Japanese occupation, because each actress starving on stage looked so very well-fed.

During the tour, my singing did not improve, nor did my acting, so my performance was still limited to fifty-five seconds in a group dance. By now, I was getting more anxious about my future, and felt that I was wasting my energies, but for a long time I was not allowed to leave the Literature and Art Propaganda Team. Partly, it was due to my hard work and dedication to whatever additional jobs I was assigned to, so that I was regarded as a useful colleague. No matter how little interest I had in the team's activities, I always tried my hardest, knowing that otherwise I would be unable to obtain a good reference when the time came to leave, and might jeopardize my future in a new workplace. When I was put in charge of cosmetics, I kept the mirrors spotlessly clean, and the sponges for removing the make-up were thoroughly washed after use. In addition to the jobs assigned to me, I also volunteered for other work such as loading or unloading the heavy stage sets and props during the tours.

During intervals between tours, members of the troupe, except for those cast in major roles, were assigned to duties such as planting rice for the farms owned by the armoured forces. At that time, the base was carrying out massive construction work, and we were often detailed to move building materials such as bricks and sand. In those days, no machines were available to perform this sort of work. Very often, a group of three or four girls was ordered to load or unload a heavy truck. One of the hardest tasks was loading sand, which required us to stand on the ground and throw big shovelfuls two metres up into the truck. During the bitter cold of winter, we were sent to dig channels for central heating piping. Most of the time, my pickaxe rebounded from the frozen ground, and left only a graze on the surface. Soon, my palms were blistered and bleeding.

Although I could not sing, I was popular with my colleagues, as they were impressed by my resistance to hardships, cheerful nature and kindness to people. Though I tried to disguise my knowledge of classical culture, many colleagues gradually recognized and appreciated the education given by my father. In our private conversations, they also praised his integrity, and admired his novel. Hence, I was treated in a very friendly way.

Yet however much I enjoyed working with the Literature and Art Propaganda Team, I knew that this was not the right place for me. Once again, my father had to ask his supporters for help, but nothing could be done for some time. Then in April 1972, during the reorganization of the Propaganda Team, my request to leave was finally approved.

Chapter 20

From Medical Orderly to Army Doctor:
The Beginning of My Medical Career

(May 1972–September 1975)

By the time I left the Literature and Art Propaganda Team, the base where I was stationed had already stopped accepting female soldiers. I was reallocated to a hospital in the Armoured Forces 9th Division, the only section of the division that still recruited female staff. Established two years previously in the Nanjing Military Region, the division had been transferred to the Beijing Military Region shortly after the armed Sino-Soviet clash in 1969. Now its troops were stationed in southeast Shanxi province, and both the divisional headquarters and our hospital were located in Changzhi city, the administrative centre of Southeast Shanxi Prefecture. The previous autumn, our Propaganda Team had moved from Shacheng to the suburbs of Changzhi, so the city was not unfamiliar.

Though I had no qualifications, I was assigned as a medical orderly in the hospital's Outpatient Department. On 10 May 1972, I wrote to my parents: 'Today, I start work in the Treatment Room of my department, and my duties include providing services such as injections, and changing dressings for wounds . . .' Most jobs that should have been done by nurses were performed by medical orderlies. Ever since the hospital's foundation there had been an extreme shortage of qualified staff. In my department, for example, there was no nurse at all. Most of the nearly twenty staff were orderlies recently recruited. The few doctors we had also lacked adequate training, as they had either seen their courses cut short by the Cultural Revolution, or had never attended medical school at all. In China, there was no national registration for any professional qualifications. Normally, the hospital's Party committee proposed appointments onto its professional and administrative staff, which went higher up the ladder for approval.

Next day, I wrote to my parents again: 'Yesterday evening, I was informed by my department that I am to attend a course for training nurses, together with three other colleagues. The course is run by the Military Field Hospital No. 102, which is also stationed in Changzhi. It starts tomorrow and lasts for about two months . . .' At that time, the shortage of qualified staff afflicted medical institutions all over China. It was particularly severe in the armed forces, whose recent expansion demanded so many new hospitals. The Cultural Revolution had disrupted medical training for a long time, so there was no way to recruit enough qualified staff. The solution was for the military authorities at various levels to organize courses to train nurses or even doctors, in order to improve their own services. The Military Field Hospital No. 102 was a leading medical centre in southeast Shanxi, whose nursing courses, launched some years before, also provided vacancies to other local units. Since I could not do any nurse's job, my superiors sent me straight off to be trained.

'It is over a week since the course began,' I wrote to my parents on 20 May. 'Every day, we attend eight to nine hours of lectures. The students find them very hard to follow, even though many know a certain amount already. Compared with the rest, I am the least experienced, with the least medical knowledge, since I am the only absolute beginner. You can imagine how hard I have to work . . .' In my course, there were about thirty participants. Most were nurses, but a few junior doctors from local units also attended, as well as a head nurse from my hospital. The small number of medical orderlies enrolled in the course came mainly from my hospital.

'Last Tuesday we took the first exam, and I got the best result of all who took part, 93 per cent,' I wrote to my parents on 10 June. 'I was told that I was the only one who scored over 90 per cent. Our lecturers were very strict with their marking, . . .' All the lecturers in our course came from the Field Hospital No. 102, and were either experienced doctors or head nurses. From the very beginning, I enjoyed their teaching immensely.

'This Friday, we sat the final examination,' I told my parents three weeks later. 'Although the results have not been announced, I have a feeling from the lecturers' expressions that I did very well.' When the results came out a few days later, I found that this time I had 99 per cent, which was again the top performance. 'Our lecturers are amazed by my good results. What impressed them most was that I am a novice. Other participants are also full of praise for my intelligence and hard work, but I know that I can't let their praises go to my head . . .'

In fact, I had never expected such good results. Throughout the course, I felt that I was struggling every day to cope with the bombardment of completely new knowledge. Six years before, I had picked up some training at middle school, when I was assigned to run the health centre, but it did not help me now that whatever I had learned was long forgotten. I was no genius, so the only way to keep up was to work hard and spend almost all my spare time studying. Thanks to the good memory I inherited from my parents, I managed to memorize a whole lot of unfamiliar concepts and medical terminology in quick time.

'I have been back in my hospital for a month,' I wrote to my parents on 2 August 1972. 'By now, I can handle the daily work and nursing duty by myself. Recently, a patient's wound, whose dressing I had to change every day, healed nicely, and the duty doctor was very pleased. At the staff plenary meeting this week, my department head praised me again for my good work. In fact, these praises don't matter. What I'm really interested in now is to learn more knowledge and skills, to improve my work further . . .'

Despite all the praise I received, I often felt frustrated by my lack of qualifications, as my training was too short to equip me for all the jobs I dealt with. Formal training for nurses had taken about three years in the past, so no beginner could expect to qualify in the two-month course. But I could not refuse the jobs I was assigned, and nor could the others. To better my skills, I set out to teach myself, which was uphill work. Prevented by the Cultural Revolution, I learned very little science at school, so it was a struggle, and often a headache, to make sense of many topics essential to my work. But there was no supervision available, and no experimental facilities, so my self-education had to rely on reading. Soon, I built up a library of study materials based on books I bought or borrowed from colleagues. During that period, almost every letter to my parents mentioned my efforts to learn. I spent most of my weekends and holidays, and often stayed in my office till midnight after work, to carry on studying.

'We've been terribly busy,' I wrote to my parents on 21 April 1973. Most of our patients were troops from our division, but we also dealt with many local residents. 'Several months ago, a local patient brought me a bag of apples and pears, she felt so grateful for my services. Later, another patient brought thirty eggs. I tried to decline their gifts, especially since I know that local patients are often short of money, and eggs are very precious in this area. But they wouldn't listen and left their gifts behind. In the end, I insisted on paying for the gifts . . . A few days ago, an old woman patient brought a big packet of biscuits, which I declined. The following day, she came back with a beautiful notebook instead. I feel that I don't deserve my patients' warmth and kindness, as I do so little for them . . .'

By now, I was a minor celebrity in the hospital. After my excellent marks in the training course, my superiors felt that I had boosted our reputation among the local troops. Most of the staff in the hospital came from humble family backgrounds, and despite my father's political troubles they still viewed me as the daughter of a high official family. All the same, when I came back from the training course they soon found that I did not behave like many others with privileged backgrounds. They liked my friendly manner, and saw that I was eager to learn and dedicated to our work.

My will to improve myself convinced me that I must work harder than anyone else, and I volunteered for some of the drudge work that people avoided. Every morning, I tried to be the earliest to arrive, and started to do cleaning jobs at around six o'clock. In my hospital, each department had its own large plot where the staff produced vegetables for their own consumption in the canteen. The manure was human waste, and I was among the few who were willing to collect it from a big cess pit under a public toilet, and load it into containers. Afterwards, the stink clung to my skin and hair for days, no matter how thoroughly I washed.

The head of my department was an intelligent physician, known for his strictness, who looked for ability and commitment. Before my arrival, there had been clashes between him and some medical orderlies who came from well-connected families, so he had no respect for privileged backgrounds. But now my work convinced him that I was ready to hold a responsible position, and less than a year after my arrival I was put in charge of the department's Treatment Room, where the staff were all my seniors in working experience.

In April 1973, I was instructed to attend a training programme for obstetricians and gynaecologists. In recent years, my hospital had been seeking to provide an Obstetrics and Gynaecology service, for which it needed suitable personnel. I heard that many of our staff had asked to attend this programme, but none had been accepted. The proposal to send me was approved by the general management, as well as by my own department.

My progress at work did not remove the shadow of my father's political troubles, and it was these that delayed the approval of my application for Party membership. Among the armed forces, this was a crucial requirement both for promotion and for good training opportunities. In my hospital, everyone tried hard to join, but few were accepted. Normally, successful candidates had to perform exceptionally well at work, and be endorsed by the majority of their colleagues. Due to the strong competition among a large number of applicants, it was normal to wait for years to be admitted, and some unlucky ones would never succeed.

Soon after arriving at the hospital in May 1972, I submitted my application for Party membership, although I knew that the chances might be slim for a newcomer. In the previous year, I had joined the Communist Youth League in the Literature and Art Propaganda Team, which was a prerequisite for entry. Late in 1972, I received an unexpected visit from a sympathizer of my father's, an officer in the armoured forces headquarters in Beijing. 'I happened to hear from your superiors that your application had been turned down because of your father's political problems,' he said. 'In particular, people in your hospital don't know why he is still out of work.' According to the rules, I would not qualify for Party membership if my father was still in trouble, no matter how well I did my work. Since my division had only recently transferred to the Beijing Military Region, no one knew much about my father's record.

On 5 May 1973 I wrote to my father: 'Several days ago, I met the Political Commissar of our division's Logistics Department [my hospital's higher authority] by chance. Through him, I heard that my hospital had contacted a number of armoured forces leaders to inquire about your political situation, but had never received a reply. In the end, it was the headquarters Personnel Division [controlled by my father's supporters] that provided an official letter to prove your political innocence, so my application for Party membership has been accepted.'

My training took place in the civilian Changzhi City Hospital, whose obstetrics and gynaecological team was regarded as the best in southeast Shanxi prefecture. Rather than taking courses, I trained by the 'jin-xiu' procedure. In Chinese, the term often stands for 'advanced training', formerly practised among qualified personnel chosen for in-service training such as refresher courses, but my 'jin-xiu' was more like an apprenticeship. The term of my training was one year. Changzhi City Hospital attached me to a doctor who taught the skills and supervised my work, while my own hospital paid the costs and my living expenses.

On the registration form, my hospital authority stated that by the end of my 'jin-xiu' I was expected 'to be able to diagnose and treat common diseases of the female reproductive system, as well as to deliver babies and perform minor operations'. Ironically, I knew almost nothing about the human reproductive system, and had never witnessed a normal labour, but my superiors and I felt that the goal was not over-ambitious. In my department, a small number of medical orderlies already took on doctors' responsibilities. Among the former pupils at Ba-yi School, there were girls working as obstetricians and gynaecologists in various military hospitals, whose main qualification was a spell of 'jin-xiu' practice. In terms of academic ability and determination, I did not think that any of them was in an advanced position than me. Since they could do it, why shouldn't I?

At that time, there were many 'jin-xiu' trainee doctors in every department of Changzhi City Hospital, who came from all over southeast Shanxi, so some experienced doctors tutored several pupils. Most of the trainees had never been to a proper medical school before, and many were absolute beginners like me.

'Last Monday, my "jin-xiu" started,' I wrote to my parents on 5 May

1973. 'Everything is incredibly difficult for me, and I'm under high pressure . . . As a "jin-xiu" trainee, I have to work very hard, and be modest and careful with everyone in the department. In my spare time, I often help midwives and nurses in their jobs, so as to get more chances to learn what I need.'

At that time, most of the established rules and regulations previously observed in Chinese hospitals had been either abolished or changed, so there was little to prevent my involvement in all aspects of the department's work. I knew that after training I would be the only specialist in Obstetrics and Gynaecology in my own hospital, so as well as the course I was taking, I felt that I also needed skills in midwifery and nursing. My helpful manner and eagerness to learn were welcomed by members of the department, which was short of staff and faced a heavy workload. It was quite common to have so many women in labour arrive during the night that the delivery room overflowed and the later arrivals had to be delivered in the waiting room. When this happened, the department was in chaos, as all the other night staff, including nurses and sometimes even doctors, were called to give assistance. When I discovered how much I could learn on these busy nights, I found a bed in the department's small store room. Despite its uninhabitable condition – it was dark, damp, and infested by rats – I slept there every night. In any emergency, the duty staff could knock on my door, and I was ready to help within minutes.

'This is the most hectic week since my "jin-xiu" started,' I wrote to my parents three weeks later. 'Yesterday, I only got two and a half hours' sleep.' All week, I had been terribly busy with jobs that ranged from delivering babies to assisting with surgical operations or keeping notes on newly admitted in-patients. Except for sleeping, I spent almost all my time in the ward, the delivery room or the operating theatre, even when I was off duty. 'I'm glad to be so busy,' my letter continued. 'The doctors in the department often say: "If you want to learn, you've got to work hard," and I believe it. Dr Li is my supervisor. A graduate from Hebei

Medical University before the Cultural Revolution, she is regarded as one of the best obstetricians and gynaecologists in the hospital. When performing operations, she is very meticulous and thorough about every detail. Being an outspoken person, she is known for her strict discipline, and sometimes she can be quite tough when criticizing her trainees' performances. But I like her very much, and feel so grateful for her discipline . . .'

Right from the start of my training, Dr Li and I had got on very well. There was no set procedure with trainees, so my progress largely depended on my supervisor's efforts and teaching skills, as well as my ability to learn. So I was really lucky to have Dr Li, because she took every opportunity to teach me. Finding that I tried my best to memorize what she taught made her keener on providing more knowledge. When we were on duty together, she tried to find time to give me individual lectures on the basics of our field, and also to communicate her personal experience. Gradually, her lectures drew more listeners, who included many trainee doctors from other departments as well as several staff from her own. Later, Dr Li told her colleagues that of all her trainees, I was one of the best two in ability and achievement. The other was a university graduate who worked for Military Field Hospital No. 102, and had come for specialist O & G training several years before.

'For two weeks, I haven't set foot outside the hospital because I'm so wrapped up in work,' I wrote to my parents on 6 August 1973. 'Seven newly admitted in-patients were in critical condition with either massive postpartum bleeding or heart failure. During the emergency, I hardly slept for three nights, and the department staff were also exhausted. Now, all of the women are safe, including their newborn babies, more than ten lives altogether!' In those days, Dr Li's department often took in patients with critical conditions, most of them peasants from the Taihang mountain region, where poverty and inadequate medical services hindered diagnosis and treatment. By the time they reached Changzhi

City Hospital, lying on stretchers carried over long distances by a team of exhausted peasants, and wrapped in filthy duvets or blankets, they were often in critical condition.

'Through witnessing so many critical cases in such a short period, I gained some useful knowledge about how to deal with similar situations,' my letter continued. 'But I can't handle these cases on my own, nor can a number of doctors in this department. When they face serious problems, these doctors always ask for help from Dr Li or a few other more experienced doctors. Each night when Dr Li was called to emergencies I always followed her, and was amazed to see how capable and confident she was . . .' In spite of its high reputation, Dr Li's department also faced a shortage of qualified staff. A number of obstetricians and gynaecologists had been 'promoted' from midwives or nurses during the Cultural Revolution, without training as medical doctors. In recent years, many teenage girls had been recruited to work as nurses or midwives, even though their education had not passed middle school, and they often needed help from the duty doctors.

During my training, all the doctors in Changzhi City Hospital, regardless of their qualifications and previous professional status, were assigned to similar responsibility and held equal status. 'Doctor' became the most common form of address for staff who included nurses and midwives, which often caused confusion for patients. I often wondered how Dr Li and a few other experienced colleagues managed to survive their hectic schedules. On top of their own responsibilities, they were frequently called by their inexperienced or unqualified colleagues for urgent help, and since the staff were housed next to the hospital, they could be roused at any time of night, and even during weekends and holidays. Their accommodation was no better than the rest. Each family lived in one or two rooms, with no central heating, private lavatory, or other basic sanitation.

Yet despite their heavy workload and stressful lives, I rarely heard Dr Li and her experienced colleagues complain. This dedication must be attributed to their professional consciences, which caused them to put the interests of their patients before their own wellbeing. On the other hand, many who had been ranked as senior doctors or consultants in the past had suffered political sanctions at the start of the Cultural Revolution, as 'bourgeois academic authorities'. To avoid more accusations, they kept quiet about their current circumstances.

In those days, there was hardly any complaint from patients about the quality of services provided by doctors who lacked professional qualification. Perhaps it was hard to learn the truth, but even if they had known, I doubt that many patients would have worried. For thousands of years, doctors practising Chinese medicine were trained through apprenticeship, and the tradition still thrives in many areas. Therefore for many patients institutional training – even to practise Western medicine – was a foreign concept. Regardless of their background and qualification, our staff often received unconditional trust, as the majority of our patients came from rural areas. I was reminded of my former rural settlement, where the peasants often had enormous respect for education, and would ask us for help when someone fell ill, simply because we had attended school. At their request, we sometimes tried to judge their condition with our non-existent medical knowledge, and then provided them with tablets brought from home for our own needs. The most popular medicine was analgesics, as they believed that it could cure all their health problems. Each time, I marvelled at the gratitude the peasants expressed, and how much our little knowledge meant to them.

During my current training, I found that far from complaining, patients from rural areas always expressed satisfaction with their treatment in Dr Li's department. Again, it was not hard to see why. By now, a new primary health care system introduced into rural China under the collective economic structure, with 'barefoot doctors' working at village level, had been praised by the official media as a triumph of the Cultural Revolution. In theory, this system was supposed to provide peasants with free medical care from the collective. But in many rural areas, such as the Taihang mountains where I was working now, and the loess highlands where my rural settlement was located, the peasants lived in poverty, and the collective simply lacked the resources. The primary health care system was a fiction in such areas, so for the many peasants too poor to afford the most basic medication, any kind of medical support was enormously welcome.

In Yanchuan county, where I was 're-educated', one of the Beijing school-leavers later became a well-known self-taught local doctor. Due to its low charge, his practice attracted peasants from all over the county. It was said that he even performed more than 1,000 successful surgical operations, including appendectomy, because his patients could not afford to go to hospital. His operating theatre was a cave in his village, where the earthen walls and ceiling were lined with clean white sheets to keep off the falling dust. With no electricity, he worked by gas light, and his operating table was a single bed board placed across wooden benches. When he started to practise, he had to keep a textbook beside him, in case he needed to check procedures during the operation. His patients were hugely impressed. 'What a responsible doctor!' they enthused.

After the death of Lin Biao, Premier Zhou Enlai assumed greater responsibility for the everyday running of the Central Committee. Mao Zedong began to rely on him more than before, as his health was already declining. From late 1971, Zhou introduced a number of policies that aimed to improve the country's social and economic development. The most influential was speeding up the rehabilitation of politically disgraced officials. In April 1972, he was behind an editorial in the *People's Daily* which emphasized that 'long-tested revolutionary veteran cadres are valuable assets of the Party', and was seen as the first indication of Party approval for rehabilitating disgraced officials. Gradually, the names of numerous senior Communist figures reappeared in the official media,

as they came out of prison or returned from exile and were assigned to
various posts. The most important of these was Deng Xiaoping, purged
in 1966 as China's No. 2 capitalist-roader next to the disgraced
president Liu Shaoqi. In March 1973, Deng was reinstated as Vice-
Premier with the approval of Mao Zedong.

During that period, many of my parents' friends or former colleagues
also returned to Beijing from various locations, and spent a long time
waiting for rehabilitation, as my father did, or for career assignments. For
many rehabilitated high officials, new posts were hard to obtain, as the
ones they previously held were either taken, or had left Beijing. Over the
last few years, a great many institutions had been moved to the provinces
or reorganized, so senior posts were scarce in the capital. But these men's
wives often found work much faster, because many were middle- or low-
ranking cadres, and easier to place. While they waited, these jobless
officials referred to their own status as 'kao-bian-er-zhan', meaning standing aside. At that time, an ironic anonymous verse expressed their
frustration: '"Kao-bian-er-zhan" is a priceless status./ My wife goes out
to work/ And I do the cooking at home./ Hanging around the city every
day with a travel ticket,/ And then watching television at night.'

This was the only period I remember when my parents socialized frequently with their friends or former colleagues. During their reunions,
held in their various homes, they celebrated their survival from persecution, and expressed their anger at what they had suffered. Another key
theme was concern about China's political situation.

In August 1973, the Communist Party's Tenth Congress took place
in Beijing, and was organized in much the same mysterious manner as
the Ninth had been. By order of Mao Zedong, delegates were forbidden
outside contacts, and those with families in Beijing were not allowed
home. The Congress communiqué emphasized the continuation of the
Cultural Revolution. In the Party's revised constitution, a major change
was the deletion of Lin Biao as Mao's chosen successor. The Congress
was seen as a chance to redistribute power after Lin Biao, while Jiang

Qing's faction further developed its strength in the Party leadership. Kang Sheng became a vice-chairman, and so did Wang Hongwen, a leading rebel figure in Shanghai, and major ally of Jiang Qing. Another mainstay of Jiang Qing's faction, Zhang Chunqiao, joined the Standing Committee of the Politburo.

It was said that despite their growing power, neither Jiang Qing nor her allies were capable of replacing Zhou Enlai to manage the daily affairs of China and the Party, due mainly to their lack of competence, but also to their unpopularity, so they saw him as blocking their way forward. In particular, they disliked the policies he had recently introduced. They felt that by rehabilitating the victims of the Cultural Revolution he was undermining their own positions, and by restoring rules and regulations he was expressing his disapproval of what Mao and his radical followers had done during the Cultural Revolution.

As the struggles intensified between the camps of Jiang Qing and Zhou Enlai, Mao Zedong often stood by his wife, even though he still needed Zhou Enlai to run the country and the Party. Through various sources, my parents learned that misinformation from Jiang Qing and her associates often caused Mao to criticize the premier's work unreasonably. Late in 1973, Mao gave orders for the campaign to denounce Lin Biao, begun two years before, to extend to denouncing Confucius, claiming that both Lin Biao and the Nationalists were believers in Confucianism. All of a sudden Confucius, an ancient figure who lived more than two thousand years ago, found his ideology subjected to posthumous national denunciation. Prompted by Jiang Qing and her circle, China's media featured a spate of articles turned out by writing teams based in Beijing. In these, as well as in orchestrated public speeches by the Jiang Qing faction, often it was Zhou Enlai who was attacked by implication. Jiang Qing stressed that the objective was to denounce the 'big Confucian of our time inside the Party leadership'. Soon, it was clear to the nation that the purpose was to 'denounce Lin Biao, Confucius and Zhou Enlai'.

For the vast majority of Chinese, Zhou Enlai was the hope of the future. His influence had fostered improvements both in the economy and in many other fields. For my parents and many other revolutionary veterans, it was he above all who championed them inside the Party leadership. Without his efforts, the ordeals of many disgraced officials would not be over. Between themselves, my parents often commiserated over the political strain that Zhou Enlai faced, especially when they heard that he was suffering from cancer. During their dispute with Zhou Enlai, Jiang Qing and her colleagues often quoted a theory concocted by themselves: 'Veteran cadres are democrats, and democrats are capitalist-roaders.' It increased my parents' anxiety about their own and their country's future. 'If China fell into the hands of Jiang Qing's camp, sooner or later we would lose our heads,' my mother said. 'I'm not afraid of death,' my father answered, 'but after all these decades in the revolution, we never expected to end our lives like that. One day we may have to leave Beijing for the mountains, and fight as guerrillas against them.' In case they were needed, he asked my mother to prepare some peasant clothes. They also talked about building support in advance, for instance by making friends among peasants and workers from now on.

After the death of Lin Biao, there was gossip in the armoured forces about changes in my father's situation. I was told that his confession had already been approved, and also that he had turned down a job assigned to him. Nevertheless, it seemed that his outlook was improving. I did not know then that one significant reason for this was that Yibin, who recommended my father for Party membership in 1932, had withdrawn the false testimony against my father made under duress from the investigation team, and admitted recruiting my father. In reply to my repeated inquiries, my father wrote to me on 25 July 1973:

> Last autumn, I was unexpectedly summoned by the investigation
> team. I was informed about a recent Party document on the subject

of rehabilitating officials . . . according to this document, my rehabilitation must go through the following three steps: confession, acceptance by the masses, final conclusion. I replied that over the past years I have made public confession at least five times, and the masses have expressed their acceptance . . . Since October 1969, the conclusion of my case has been reported to the higher authority on three occasions. Why is my rehabilitation still required to go through the same three steps? I decided to write no more confessions. If asked, I would resubmit one of the former versions.

Concerning my decision, I had a number of visitors [his supporters or sympathizers in the armoured forces] who tried to persuade me to change my mind. I did not listen. Earlier this year, I was approached again by more people. As they pointed out, I would put myself into a negative position if I still refused. In the end, I agreed, but said that this time my confession would stick to the truth. In the past, many things I had to say were against my own will.

On 9 May this year, I read out my newly written confession at the plenary meeting of the headquarters Party members. After subsequent group discussions, a representative from each Party branch reported to the plenary meeting . . . The first speaker was a ganshi [junior political officer] who represented Party members of the Political Department. He objected to my confession by saying that it was more like a statement showing how good I am than confessing my problems. Later, I heard that several days before the plenary meeting, Mercy Ocean [deputy director of the Political Department] had briefed his staff about how to respond to my confession.

As soon as the first presentation was over, Mercy Ocean rushed onto the platform unexpectedly, and demanded to give an additional speech himself . . . From his briefcase, he took out a stack

of files collected over these years [as evidence against me], including many leaflets produced by rebel organizations during the
'Si-da' phase in early 1967. In his speech, he repeatedly emphasized the 'truthfulness' of his evidence, and swore that he has
never used fabricated accusations against me. By his account, my
family background is unclear, as I may come from a very rich
landlord family and one of my brothers is a 'big Bourgeois
Rightist'. He also said that in 1935, when our insurrection
against the Nationalists was defeated, I should have stuck to my
post for the local Communist underground. Referring to my
escape, he accused me of being a shameful deserter. You can
imagine, when the enemy came to arrest me under the 'white
terror', who would wish me not to escape? Only the Nationalists!
Mercy Ocean also repeated that I was a 'fake Communist', as he
disbelieved Yibin's confirmation of my Party membership. His
speech lasted one and a half hours, which was longer than my
own confession . . .

The next two speakers represented Party members in the
Command and the Logistics departments. Both of their speeches
only lasted a few minutes without clear points. I suppose this was
because they tried to change their prepared presentations in a
hurry [having heard Mercy Ocean's speech] . . . The last speaker,
representing the Department of Equipment, highly praised my
confession by saying that it was sincere and thorough. What an
extraordinary fellow!

At the end of the plenary meeting, I was asked to respond to
these comments, and my speech was very brief. First, I thanked
the speakers from all the Party branches. Without mentioning the
name of Mercy Ocean, I said that even I had no idea about the
'evidence' against me that I had heard today. If necessary, I would
like these charges clarified; otherwise we should just ignore them.
Afterwards, I heard that some participants were impressed by my

response . . . But others felt that I should not say anything negative about Mercy Ocean's attacks, as it showed that I was not open-minded.

On 3 July, I was summoned by the Party's Standing Committee of the Armoured Forces and informed about the final reports from Party members on my confession. Out of four Party branches at headquarters, only two expressed acceptance of what I said, while the others objected. I was told that my confession needed to be revised further, and then to be presented again to the masses so as to gain acceptance by the majority. Only then could the conclusion of my case be sent on to the higher authority for approval.

I replied that there was nothing more I could do, and I had my reservations about the comments made against me. I then asked for the comments obviously made under Mercy Ocean's influence to be deleted, and for the truth to be sought from the facts established during my rehabilitation. My request was refused. I was told that the masses would not agree with the statement that they were influenced by Mercy Ocean, so my request would cause resentment. I was also informed that many officers had developed doubts about Mercy Ocean's words, especially after his performance at that plenary meeting. They included those who started to work at headquarters after I was politically disgraced, and hence had no idea what I had been through. Members of the Standing Committee criticized me for underestimating the political consciousness of the masses, and said that they had reprimanded Mercy Ocean for his actions at the plenary meeting. Having failed to persuade me to make confession again, they asked me to spend some time considering their suggestion. And so my rehabilitation is still dragging on . . .

Shortly after returning from Yunnan, my mother was appointed deputy-director of her university's Political Work Section, which matched her former post as vice-secretary of the university Party committee. Her section's director was Ji Xian, the university's former Party secretary. Cao Lian was excluded from office after his rehabilitation. Considering the ill-feeling against him, the provincial authorities had to transfer him to another local institution. Despite her new appointment, my mother decided not to go back to Yunnan, as she had not recovered from her illness, and the family needed her. Permitted to remain in Beijing and manage the university's rear office, she had to start work while still convalescing.

The rear office consisted of less than twenty staff, whose chief responsibility was to look after the empty campus and its remaining equipment. The office also functioned as a reception centre, arranging accommodation, transport or travel tickets for the university staff when they returned on business from Yunnan. My mother's first impression of the campus was the riot of weeds. In the past, the university garden had been famous for its valuable, elaborately tended plants, kept mainly for purposes of teaching. Now, most of the exotic flowers and rare trees had disappeared, apparently transplanted into the private garden of Jiang Qing's new residence. The buildings were also extensively damaged. Before their departure to Yunnan some years before, many students had converted doors, desks or beds in classrooms or dormitories into big wooden crates to be used on the journey. Ever since then, these empty buildings had been locked, but scavengers had smashed hundreds of window panes to get inside the rooms and strip them bare.

Back in Yunnan, the university was stumbling in its quest for a permanent location. After my mother left, it arranged to move again from Lijiang to Dali, which had a suitable piece of land, but news of a leprosy epidemic around the new settlement started an exodus to Beijing. Within weeks, hardly anyone remained, and the first move to Dali was abandoned. Afterwards, most of the staff returned, but many who had originally brought their school-age children to Yunnan now left them behind in Beijing, because of concern about the uncertain future. Feeling sorry for their plight, my mother had them housed on the campus, and assigned an assistant from the rear office to make arrangements such as finding them places in local schools and providing meals in the staff canteen.

After further explorations, the university eventually found a site near Kunming, the provincial capital, which had originally belonged to the Chinese Academy of Sciences, and exchanged part of its campus in Beijing for the new location in Yunnan. By the late 1970s, the university had lost most of the land and buildings on its Beijing campus to various outside institutions, which demolished the swimming pool, garden and two-thirds of the nursery in order to build new facilities and accommodation. My mother said that the university would have had no grounds left in Beijing if her rear office had not fought against further erosion. In 1974, five years after the move from Beijing, the new campus opened in Yunnan, able at last to enrol new students and resume the teaching which had stopped eight years before.

'Although the rear office is very small, there are all sorts of problems your mother faces,' my father wrote to me on 21 April 1974. 'Anarchy prevails. Only a few of the staff are interested in doing their jobs, and hardly anyone listens to your mother. Every day when she comes home from work she seems exhausted and often sighs in frustration. She had only just recovered, but now she feels ill again. I am so worried about her situation. People like Cao Lian are quite common. I am concerned that in the future, she may run into political troubles again . . .'

At that time, the rear office was in fact headed by a representative of the PLA Propaganda Team from Yunnan, a junior army officer in his thirties, who came from a peasant background and had previously worked as a company political instructor. As the boss of an office in the capital, he relished his power and became arrogant towards my mother, knowing that she was regarded as an official who had 'committed mistakes'. Later, he had an affair with a divorced woman in Beijing, although he was married. When the relationship went wrong, he accused my mother of making trouble, because my parents had known the woman personally before the affair began. In fact they had both kept quiet about his affairs, but from then on he was my mother's enemy.

Because of this ill-feeling, my mother decided to leave the university, although she knew the problems that finding a new job might bring. With help from my father's former colleagues, eventually an institute in a government ministry showed an interest, and sent a member of its staff to her office to make inquiries – standard practice when officials changed jobs. Her Propaganda Team superior jumped at his chance to get even. Claiming to speak on behalf of the university authority, he alleged that my mother's political problems were not settled. As a result, the institute turned her down. Later, she found out that he had lied, but was helpless to call him to account. The PLA Propaganda Team was all-powerful in the university, and could not be challenged. There was nothing to do but to look for another chance to move.

In summer 1973, the municipal government in Beijing decided to offer a post to my mother. By then, the PLA Propaganda Team had withdrawn, and Ji Xian had been reinstated as the university's 'first hand'. As usual in China, my mother needed various documents from the university to carry out the transfer, such as a letter of consent and a formal reference. This simple procedure took her a year and a half to complete.

'Your mother's transfer was already agreed by the university, the provincial authority in Yunnan, and the municipal government in Beijing. But for more than a year after all these consents, the university refused the formalities,' my father wrote to me on 14 January 1975. 'This was due mainly to Shang, the vice-chancellor . . . His main reason was that your mother's leaving would give offence to those remaining in Yunnan, but the truth was that Shang disagreed with any decision made by Ji Xian . . . because he is contesting for power in the university with Ji Xian. Shang's resentment of your mother also comes from our failing to entertain him during his business trip to Beijing in 1973, which made him think that we looked down on him. In fact, we did plan to invite him, but he left Beijing in a hurry . . . We heard that in terms of character, Shang was no better than Cao Lian. Last summer when the leaders of the provincial education authority came to Beijing, I asked them again about your mother's transfer. Later, I was told that the provincial authority had tried again to persuade the university to complete the formalities. In order to hasten the procedure, I wrote personal letters to the university authority and to Ji Xian, so did your mother to Shang. Late last year we were finally informed that the procedure had gone through. We also heard that Shang, having failed to block your mother's transfer, gave instructions for some misinformation to be added to her university reference. Fortunately, his staff took no notice . . . After so much stress and strain, your mother has finally left the university, a place full of troubles. I feel enormously relieved . . .'

Two months later my father wrote: 'Originally your mother was offered a post as vice-secretary of the Party committee for the Beijing No. 2 Medical University. Since the formalities . . . lasted for nearly two years, the post was filled. Now, she has been appointed secretary of the Party committee for the Beijing Planetarium . . .' At that time, the Planetarium was engaged in an ambitious expansion programme ordered two years previously by Jiang Qing, whose aim was to make it the world's largest institution in its field. Completion was scheduled for October 1976, when the workforce would have doubled its current size. The status of the Beijing Planetarium in the Communist hierarchical structure was boosted from its original level, equivalent to county government, to prefecture level. To strengthen its leadership, my mother, who ranked equal to a prefectural governor, was appointed 'first hand'.

'This evening, a doctor in my department spoke to me on behalf of the Party branch,' I wrote to my parents on 5 May 1973. 'He said that there has been a lot of talk about me in our division, for instance saying that I was the No. I 'da-hong-ren' [Red Person – meaning the leadership's favourite member of staff] in the hospital. In the last few months, I have joined the Communist Party, and been elected as a model colleague as well as assistant secretary of the Communist Youth League Committee for the division's Logistics Department. In addition, I am now attending a programme to train as a medical doctor. I am told that no one else in our hospital has ever achieved so much in such a short time. I was warned to stay modest and level-headed . . . In fact, I have been terribly strained by the pressure of work and study, and have hardly noticed what anybody says . . .'

'Your achievement is a great comfort to your mother and me,' my father replied. 'In recent years, you have been determined to improve yourself through hard work, which is exactly what we expect from our children . . .' In his next letter I read: 'This morning, I went to the Army General Hospital to see doctors, and met two girls who asked after you. They are junior doctors, just graduated from universities. I recognized that they were former pupils of Ba-yi School, and their fathers worked with me in the 1950s. There are many more junior doctors in the hospital who have similar experiences to the two girls . . . I feel that you are different from them, as you have gone through some very tough experiences in your life. Now, you have grown up independently and developed unusual qualities of character . . . Everyone has their own way of life, but I think you have achieved much more than these young doctors. You have shown your ability to create your own future and no longer rely on your parents' influence. In contrast, many others would not have gone even a single step further if not for their parents' positions . . .'

In March 1973, a photograph of me at work with a colleague, taken by the division's photographers, was published by a number of influential newspapers, such as the national *People's Daily*, the *Shanxi Daily* (the mouthpiece of the provincial Party authority), and the official newspaper of the Beijing Military Region. The *People's Daily* could be regarded as the largest newspaper in the world, with a daily circulation of tens of millions, subscribed to by almost every office, workshop, village, school, shop and platoon in China. Our photo was featured in all these newspapers with the caption: 'Mu Aiping and Song Jianping of the Military Hospital No. 1864 practise acupuncture.' During that period, we two girls were often visited by photographers from my division, though more for our looks than our work, but the publication of our photo was like an official endorsement, and drew even more attention than before. During the following days, many patients walked around our hospital asking where the two 'famous girls' were.

On the night before our photo appeared in the *People's Daily*, Little Auntie had already heard about it from her neighbour, an editor in the official New China News Agency, but she could not believe it until she saw the paper the next morning. When my father saw the photo, he wrote me a cautionary letter: 'You mustn't be complacent about having your photo published. It is not achieved through your hard work, so there is no reason for you to be proud of yourself. On the contrary, you must be aware that there could be drawbacks, as you might become arrogant. People like Madam Tang are still around, and they might make trouble for you. You must be careful what you do. In future, you should try to stay out of the limelight . . .'

Considering my progress, my parents often felt grateful to the leaders of my division, especially to those in my hospital and department. Although none of them knew my parents personally, they treated me fairly, in spite of my father's political problems. 'It is due to their fairness that your good performances are recognized, and you are given so many opportunities to develop yourself,' my father wrote to me during that period. 'These leaders are the earliest guides in your revolutionary career, as well as good teachers and helpful friends, who are hard to find in life. You must listen to them, and never let them down . . .'

In summer 1973, I was elected as my hospital's only delegate to the Party Congress of the Armoured Forces in Beijing scheduled for the following autumn. This was a special honour because I was the only female delegate from the whole division, and also the youngest. I wrote to tell my father, and he replied on 24 August 1973:

> I am really concerned about what will happen . . . I don't think it will all be straightforward for you, as there are still opponents of mine at headquarters . . . Mercy Ocean might be involved in checking credentials, and would find pretexts to disqualify you as a delegate, though I think your division would protest . . . Another possibility is that some of my opponents might attack me again during the Congress . . . and you might be targeted too. If so, you mustn't panic, just try to stay calm and composed . . . Remember, if anyone tries to express their grudges against me by bullying my daughter in public, they would not make themselves popular with the masses . . . Normally, that sort of situation shouldn't happen, especially since Mercy Ocean was reprimanded at a high level for his attacks on me at the recent staff plenary meeting. But you must know that an unstable person is harder to predict . . .
>
> On the other hand, if you refused to be the delegate, your leaders and colleagues would feel you were letting them down . . . Even if your refusal was accepted, there would be speculation . . . It would be impossible to make public the real reason behind the change, so it would still reflect badly on your situation . . . [In any case] it has been decided that you represent the Party members of your hospital, so you have no choice but to accept the challenge . . . Life is full of complicated struggles which you have no way to escape. You just plunge bravely into them! . . .

A month later he wrote: 'Recently, I met the Political Commissar of your division's Logistics Department . . . I told him that your attendance at the forthcoming Party Congress might be contentious, considering the possible responses from my political opponents. His reply was very frank and brief: "People can differ about anything. Mu Aiping's position was approved by the Party Committee of our division's Logistics Department, so we don't care what the others said.'" Shortly afterwards, I was informed that for various reasons the Congress had been postponed, which solved the problem.

In April 1974, I completed the training programme and returned to my hospital. During the following months, I was often asked by colleagues or patients if I was ill. The heavy workload had started to sap my health, and I looked thin and pale. On top of my work in Obstetrics and Gynaecology, I was also on call for other tasks. The head of my department liked taking me as his assistant when he was asked to supervise or coordinate rescue operations by the regimental medical teams that came under our hospital's authority, or by other local military hospitals. Very often, I had to work all night during the rescue, but hardly had time to recuperate, as my own patients were waiting and no one could deputize for me. At the same time, I faced increasing responsibilities in the Communist Party and Communist Youth League organizations, since I was elected to join the Party branch in my department and to lead the Youth League in my hospital, in addition to the political jobs I already had. These unpaid administrative and political jobs took time and were physically taxing, as I often worked till midnight to prepare speeches or relevant documents.

I did not enjoy the administration and politics, and longed to devote my full-time energy to improving my medical knowledge and serving my patients, but I had no choice. At that time, people were encouraged to be 'you-hong-you-zhuan' (red and professional), combining revolutionary consciousness with high performance. To be 'bai-zhuan' (white and professional) – lacking revolutionary consciousness despite having high professional standards – was to embody bourgeois ideology. For the sake of my future, it was a label I had to avoid. In particular, I felt that these additional assignments displayed the confidence of my leaders and colleagues. Despite my father's political problems, I had been endorsed as 'you-hong-you-zhuan' by leaders at various levels in my division. If I refused their arrangements, I would let them down. On the other hand, having been nominated as a model member of staff, with extensive responsibilities, placed me in a unique position that brought further opportunities for medical training. Considering my parents' political circumstances, I had no fast track to a better future, and the only solution was to complete all the jobs assigned to me by working extremely hard.

In summer 1974, a severe epidemic of dysentery broke out among the hospital staff. At that time, our diet was poor, and consisted mainly of vegetables pickled in brine. Food in Changzhi had been terribly short for years, and the local government could not guarantee even to meet the rations. To make things worse, the canteen food was often badly cooked, in poor hygiene conditions. In summer, the terrible smell, greasy tables and unfresh food made me feel instantly queasy. Despite my hunger, I often left without eating.

During the epidemic, I became the worst-hit victim among the staff, as my health was already damaged by overwork. For almost three days I ran a high fever, and I passed out twice, despite all the hospital's treatment. On the advice of a visiting consultant physician from the Army General Hospital in Beijing, I was given an extra injection intended to lower my temperature, but the result was a disaster, as I turned out to be allergic to two major ingredients of the drug.

This happened exactly on my twenty-third birthday, 1 August 1974. Shortly after the injection, muscles in my body, legs and arms started twitching uncontrollably, and soon I felt driven out of bed as if by outside powers, desperate to sit up, stand up, and go outside at once to run and run . . . But as soon as I stood up I collapsed, and was too weak to move again. A patient who shared the same ward rushed out of the room screaming for help, and in seconds the ward was packed with nurses, doctors, and the director of the In-patient Department, who were soon joined by other colleagues. I was put back to bed, still tormented by the mysterious forces in my muscles, and nurses hung on to my limbs to keep me still. Looking at these familiar gathered faces, I begged: 'Let me out, please! Please! . . .' But no one spoke, and they all just stared at me anxiously. At last I fell quiet with exhaustion, and the crowd melted away, but as soon as I rested, my muscles started twitching again, and the madness returned.

From late afternoon to midnight, the In-patient Department was turned upside-down by the ebb and flow of nurses, doctors and various directors, none of them daring to order further treatment, as cases like my allergy were so rare that no one knew anything about them. In the middle of the commotion, the hospital's Political Instructor emerged from the crowd. 'Xiao Mu [Little Mu], you are a good comrade and I believe that you can beat the illness,' he announced. 'Chairman Mao taught us "Be resolute, fear no sacrifice and surmount every difficulty to win victory."' During the Cultural Revolution, Mao Zedong Thought was imposed all over the country, including the medical field, as the supreme controller, the 'invincible ideological weapon'. Heading each prescription was a printed quotation from Chairman Mao. 'Instructor, this isn't my fault!' I wailed. 'I can't control my body at all! I'm dying, please save me!' Eventually, it was the consultant from Beijing who decided to give me a general anaesthetic, which seemed to work. When I came to next morning, the symptoms had gone.

As my work progressed, my personal life became lonely. I was often too busy to socialize, even in my spare time. Colleagues jealous of my success turned unfriendly. Among my few female colleagues, I did not have any close friends, since I could not find anyone with similar experiences. In fact, I kept quiet about my past and my family's situation, for fear that my remarks might reach Beijing, and cause me and my father further troubles. Due to the rigid discipline enforced, I was not allowed to have a boyfriend, and had to distance myself from all male colleagues and patients.

In China, most members of the armed forces lived puritanical lives. Like me, nearly all of them were parted from their families for most of their service careers. The only exceptions were those with at least fifteen years' service or who ranked upwards from regiment commander, as they were entitled to bring their families along. Among the rest, married officers were only allowed a month's home leave each year. Sexual relationships outside marriage were forbidden, and so were any affairs between unmarried soldiers. As most members of the forces were at their physical peak, this rigid segregation could be oppressive. In my division, a young officer I knew committed suicide by throwing himself under a train. It was said that he was attracted to a female medical orderly in my hospital, but could not end his unhappy marriage. His petition for a divorce was rejected both by his wife, a peasant woman who still lived in his home village, and by the Party authority at his workplace.

In recent years, my hospital had seen many cases of illicit love affairs, which had damaged a number of careers. In addition to public condemnation, the culprits could face disciplinary charges, or lose their chance of training or promotion. Our leaders were zealous. Each day when mail arrived, the staff's personal letters went straight to the hospital authority. If an envelope roused any suspicion, the recipient would be summoned to the head office and ordered to read the letter out loud. This system sniffed out a number of secret affairs.

For the sake of my future, I saw no choice but to observe the puritan line. After my painful experiences at middle school, I often felt uneasy in male company. Come what may, I was determined not to suffer gossip again. So as not to draw attention, I dressed in baggy army uniform all the time, and hardly ever wore a new pair of shoes. My cold response to their approaches brought me a reputation as an unfeeling, arrogant girl among the young male officers I met.

My loneliness made me more homesick, and I missed my parents terribly, but I was far away, and home leave was twenty days in every three years. So I lived on my father's weekly letters, as my mother was busy with her job. My parents understood my feelings, and always encouraged me to persevere. Concerning my colleagues' jealousy, my father wrote: 'It is natural that everyone wants to be the winner. Since you have achieved so much, how could you prevent the others' jealousy? . . . Whatever happens, you must treat people generously.' About my feeling homesick: 'If I had my way, you would not be far from me. Of all my children, only you inherit my personal interests, and I have so much to teach you. But everything has been out of our control. Now, there is no suitable soil beside me where you can grow up, and you have found your own world. Just you keep trying to create a good future for yourself.' In answer to my loneliness, he sent information about the history of southeast Shanxi, and suggested that I visit Changzhi city and locate the historic sites. At my request, he copied my favourite classical poems for me. Sometimes his letters were like lecture handouts on special topics of mine, such as literature, history or writing techniques.

In November 1974, I was promoted to assistant doctor, the most junior medical position in the armed forces. After that, I was on call for the department, like the other doctors, in addition to my Obstetrics work. In a way, our work paralleled the functions of general practitioners in the West. When on duty, I had to treat all sorts of problems, and carried much more responsibility than my limited training justified. One winter evening, I failed to diagnose pneumonia in a baby patient. The boy was about to leave with his mother, when the hospital's deputy director, an experienced paediatrician, popped into my office by chance. He spotted the problem at once, and saved my patient, but I was feeling more and more anxious, afraid that sooner or later my incompetence would cause serious harm. I also found it hard to work on my own as an obstetrician and gynaecologist, since my training had been hasty and there was no one to consult.

These trials were not unusual. Many other doctors in my hospital lacked full training and had come through, or still faced, similar situations. Despite my leaders' unconditional trust, I was extremely unhappy about my professional incompetence, and knew that I needed a medical degree if I wanted to really help my patients.

Ever since starting work at the hospital, I had longed to go to university to study medicine, and had spoken to my superiors several times. They understood my reasons, but the problem was that the hospital had not been allocated a university place for several years. During the Cultural Revolution, the system of national enrolment by examination was abolished, and university places were allocated by the administrative system. The selection procedure was based on 'recommendation of the authorities and agreement of the masses' in their own workplace. In our division, candidates also needed membership of the Communist Party, together with at least two years of military service and an excellent record. As the hospital could not offer what I needed, several of my superiors suggested that I should find a university place through my family connections – in other words, through the back door. Knowing that my father was no longer in disgrace, they assumed that I could draw on his influence.

In those days, a considerable number of university places were siphoned off through corrupt administrative channels, and it was not uncommon for students to enter universities by pulling strings. But this was not an option for me, as my father was still not rehabilitated, and had no political power. In his letters, he always favoured using the official procedure. After my promotion, he began to realize how urgently I needed a proper medical course at university, but when he discussed my problem with his supporters in the armoured forces, they advised him not to worry too much. As a matter of course, sooner or later my hospital would be allocated a university place, and that would be my chance.

Through my father's letters, I knew that my only choice was to be patient. In June 1975, two university places for medical courses were allocated to my division. The next two months passed intolerably slowly, like waiting for the jury's verdict in a vital lawsuit. Despite all the confident assurances, there was no guarantee which way the choice would fall. These places were distributed by administrative bodies inaccessible either to my father or to his supporters, who were mostly medium-ranking officers with limited powers. All through the allocation, my dream could be destroyed in various ways. For example, the places might be allocated to regimental medical teams instead of to our hospital, as had happened in previous years. Or they might go to someone in the division whose family had the keys to unlock doors. Eventually, our hospital was informed about the allocation of a single university place, but my anxiety endured, because this opening soon attracted many applicants. Would my application be accepted? Could I pass the selection procedure? . . . I was already twenty-four. If I failed this time, I might never have a chance to go to university in my life. In particular, I could not afford to wait for several more years for the next allocation to my hospital. In my suspense, I often spent sleepless nights and could not eat. Then in late August 1975 the decision was made. I was awarded a place at the Third Military Medical University.

Chapter 21

Political Turbulence:
My University Life and
the Initial Clash between My Parents

(October 1975–July 1977)

I still remember the excitement of walking to class at university for the very first time. My eyes were moist with tears, and I kept on telling myself: 'At last, I made it!' For almost ten years, ever since that chaotic June of 1966 when my education had been halted by the Cultural Revolution, I had been clinging on, trying to outlast political persecution, humiliation, family separations and rural starvation. For this moment of return, I had sacrificed my life, submitted to the rigid army discipline, and lived like a puritan. For this moment I had endured dirt, stink and hard labour, and worked through countless nights, weekends and holidays . . . And now, here I was, a student, treading a university campus. My efforts had paid off! My longing to study had come true!

At that time, there were four medical universities run by the armed forces, each in a different region. Until the previous year, the Third Military Medical University where I studied had been a popular destination for 'back-door students', because of its location in Shanghai. It also took in overseas students from Vietnam, North Korea and

Cambodia, including the sons and daughters of leading figures in the Khmer Rouge. Shanghai was the most westernized city in China. Even during the Cultural Revolution, Shanghainese were better fed and better provided for than most other Chinese. When I enrolled, the university had just moved back to Chongqing, on the upper reaches of the Yangtze River, formerly Chiang Kai-shek's capital during the Sino-Japanese War. As compared with previous years, there was a drop in recruitment from the higher official families following the relocation.

During my university time, each academic year started from the beginning of September and ended in late July on the following year. There was no vacation within the academic year, so students only had a four week holiday in the summer between the two academic years. From the third year, students did not have any vacation even during the summer as their practical work started immediately. The only other short holidays allowed included Chinese New Year, but we only had three days and were not allowed to go home.

I was soon disappointed with the contents of our course. In the first year, almost half of it consisted of outright political indoctrination, which was not uncommon in higher education at that time. First, there was 'Learning from the People's Liberation Army' – several weeks of daily drills, like those for new recruits. Then came four solid weeks of camp and field training, when we had to route-march around mountain areas in the north of Sichuan province carrying bedding rolls and rifles on our backs. A few months later, we were sent to a local factory to work alongside manual workers for two weeks. This was 'learning from [industrial] workers', and it was followed by almost two months of 'learning from peasants' in a rural area far from the university. At intervals during these 'learning schemes', our studies were interrupted by full-time political indoctrination, one of them several weeks long.

Heavens! What was I here for? Why waste my time on so many unnecessary activities? I had been hard at work for many years. The Cultural Revolution, with its endless political campaigns, sometimes several at a time, had made full-time political indoctrination a routine in people's lives – hence the common saying: 'During the Nationalist time, too many taxes. Under the Communist regime, too many political meetings.' Now that I was a medical student, my priority was medicine, nothing else!

My feeling was shared by the other students. All of us had worked for the armed forces, and our various pre-university occupations included pharmacist, nurse, medical orderly, typist, switchboard operator, secretary and projectionist. Those who had worked as medical doctors, like me, accounted for only a small proportion. Among these 'worker-peasant-soldier students', the youngest had just turned twenty when the course started, while the oldest were nearing their forties. Educational levels varied from attendance at primary school to completing senior middle school. One of my classmates had enormous difficulties grasping how to add ½ and ⅓, simply because her whole pre-university education was two years at primary school. But one thing we all had in common: everyone longed to concentrate on medicine.

For the university authorities, however, the priority was to implement the radical education policies proposed by the Jiang Qing axis. It was the height of the power struggles between her camp and Zhou Enlai's. As Zhou's health was deteriorating, Mao Zedong appointed Deng Xiaoping to run the routine work of government and Party. In early 1975, Deng became the Party's vice-chairman, as well as first vice-premier and chief of the General Staff, which made him yet another threat to the goals of Jiang Qing and her faction. Perceived as representing the country's former administration, he had succumbed to their persecution during the Cultural Revolution. Once back in power, he pursued Zhou Enlai's policy of speeding up social and economic development, and soon faced fierce attacks from his opponents.

Late in 1975, a campaign was launched against Deng Xiaoping with Mao's approval. Mao was now in his early eighties, and in failing health. For outside communication, he relied on his nephew, Mao Yuanxin, a graduate of Feng-xin's university and now an ally of Jiang Qing. It was the information fed from her camp that convinced Mao Zedong that Deng's aim in restoring rules and regulations was to oppose the Cultural Revolution, which Mao could not tolerate.

In such a political climate, education became a battleground. Soon after our enrolment, Zhang Chunqiao, one of Jiang Qing's chief lieutenants, stated about education policy: 'I would rather have an illiterate labourer than an educated exploiter.' Hence, the university authorities had to promote indoctrination, or risk the charge of training the exploiters. We were told from the start that we must remember our duty to the educational revolution. As 'worker-peasant-soldier students', we must hold the field as masters, not surrender ourselves to 'bourgeois academic authority'; class struggle came before medicine. In any case, since the duration of our studies had been extended to nearly four years, compared with less than two in the recent past, we should not complain about the shortage of time to study medicine.

This cut no ice with the students, as we knew what mattered most for us. But we had no choice: no one could stop the tide of indoctrination. In our annoyance, the majority of students, including most of my classmates and me, did not return on time after the first summer holiday, in order to avoid part of the scheme of 'learning from peasants'. We argued that as 'worker-peasant-soldier students', we did not need such lengthy training, as we already belonged to the most revolutionary classes. During indoctrination, students had to take turns giving presentations to denounce the capitalist-roaders. It was common to hear identical contents, sentences or even paragraphs used by different speakers, as everyone just copied the articles published in the media.

As the new campaign developed, the written attacks on Zhou Enlai and Deng Xiaoping pumped out by Jiang Qing's camp grew both in number, length and incoherence. Very often, newspapers all over China were monopolized by the same article, which was also repeatedly broadcast on nationwide radio and television on the same day. During the broadcasts, our lectures and any other activities were interrupted, often for hours at a time. Gradually, students started to complain.

During indoctrination sessions, many read lecture handouts or other medical texts, ignoring the warnings from the university's political officers. Some simply slept, in a chorus of snoring. One day, a classmate nudged me and whispered: 'Look, it's the "son-in-law"!' Outside our lecture theatre window, a quiet and handsome man in his early thirties passed. He was a lecturer in Physiology. Through various stories circulating on campus, I had heard about his past experiences when selected as a candidate son-in-law for Lin Biao.

In the few years preceding the death of Lin Biao and his wife, the armed forces conducted a large-scale selection of possible marriage partners for their son and daughter, and this unsuspecting young lecturer was picked as a suitable candidate. By order of the university's higher authority, the General Logistics Department of the armed forces, he received a secret assignment to Beijing, with no questions asked and no one else to be informed. It was said that on his arrival, he was picked up from Beijing railway station by a Red Flag limousine. Since the 1960s, these luxury cars, which were black not red, and made in China, had replaced the Russian Zils as transport for top officials. Wherever they travelled, their passengers received VIP treatment. In Beijing, these limousines were often given the green light, especially when traffic was busy. Armed sentries guarding Party, military or government compounds would salute when the limousines passed, instead of stopping them for the usual security check.

The young lecturer was brought straight to a military compound, and was kept there for months, in a large house alone with heavy security, forbidden outside contacts. Most of his time he spent idly. What he did not know was that he was under secret observation by Ye Qun, Lin Biao's wife. She and her agents also tested his 'class struggle' skills, for instance requiring him to submit a paper denouncing the 'capitalist-roaders'. On a few occasions, he was taken to visit an exhibition, and found himself alone inside the hall, as all he did was strictly confidential. Apparently Ye Qun was not totally satisfied – perhaps his denunciation paper failed to meet her standard – so in the end he was sent back without an explanation. Furthermore, the university authorities were instructed not to allow him to marry, or even to have a girlfriend, without approval from upstairs. It seems that his name was still on the possibles list. After the death of Lin Biao, and details of this adventure were exposed, the lecturer faced difficulties in finding a marriage partner. His reputation suffered from his being considered as a suitable son-in-law to Lin Biao.

In the early morning of 9 January 1976, the Central People's Radio Station of China started to broadcast solemn music, which always signalled the death of some major Party figure. When the name of Zhou Enlai came over the campus loudspeakers, my heart sank, and our noisy dormitory building fell quiet. Tears covered many faces. The following days saw the biggest spontaneous popular response in the history of the People's Republic. Everywhere, slogans mourned or praised Zhou Enlai. Mourning halls were established all over the country, and grieving crowds queued to make their three bows in front of Zhou's portrait, their personal tribute to the beloved premier. In Beijing, Tian-an Men Square was a huge sea of wreaths, cut by a few narrow paths. The cypress trees around the square turned white, as if heavy with snow, where millions had tied their home-made tissue-paper chrysanthemums, mourning Zhou Enlai. The chanting of the Internationale mingled with heartbroken wails. In our campus, almost everyone wore a black armband with a white tissue chrysanthemum on their jacket. Zhou Enlai's portrait went up in offices and dormitories, and was surrounded by flowers. Sometimes, I was woken at midnight by a roommate sobbing: 'Premier, we will never be able to see you again!' And then all ten students in our dormitory wept together.

In recent years, Zhou Enlai's illness could not be kept a secret, but his death still shocked the nation. During the Cultural Revolution, he had fought to insulate the economy against being completely ruined by the endless political chaos, and was deeply concerned about his people's welfare. In sharp contrast with Mao's radical followers, he tried to protect and rescue many Communist officials from political persecution. Through various sources, more and more people knew that despite his services to the nation, Zhou Enlai was often unfairly treated by Mao Zedong. In my university, many students believed that his life was shortened by the political campaigns against him. Among Chinese, Zhou had became a hero and a saint, and his death made him an icon for the nation.

On 11 January 1976, the day that Zhou Enlai's body was cremated, millions of people lined the Avenue of Eternal Peace in Beijing where the funeral passed, among them my parents and many of their former colleagues. Alongside these veteran Communists, there were men and women of all ages and backgrounds – workers, peasants, servicemen, students, housewives, pensioners with walking sticks and children with their parents . . . They arrived in the early morning, and stood silently for hours in the bitter cold and wind. Few had met the premier personally, or received his help, but today, without any official decree or mobilization, they gathered spontaneously to say farewell. Heartbroken wails followed the progress of the hearse.

By contrast, however, many people felt angry about the responses of Jiang Qing and her allies. On television, she looked unmoved among the leaders of the country or Party who turned out to pay their respects to Zhou Enlai's body. What offended people most was that when everyone else bared their heads and mourned in silence, she kept her army cap on, which was viewed as a snub to the dead. In front of the television provided by the university for students, I heard furious shouts from the crowd around me: 'Who do you think you are?' and 'Stinking woman!' Never before had her unpopularity been so emphatically displayed. By order of Jiang Qing's camp, the media had to limit their coverage of the nationwide mourning that greeted Zhou Enlai's death. On 14 January

1976, the day before Zhou Enlai's memorial services, a front-page article in the *People's Daily* ignored the general grief and claimed that the
nation's chief interest right now was the campaign against Deng
Xiaoping. That day, the newspaper office received hundreds of angry
telephone calls protesting against these lies. Floods of protesting letters
followed, some of them using the title 'Mr Goebbels' to address the
editor-in-chief, recently appointed by Jiang Qing's camp.

After the death of Zhou Enlai, emotions erupted against Jiang Qing
and her faction. By now, she and her three key associates, Zhang
Chunqiao, Yao Wen-yuan and Wang Hongwen, were called the Gang of
Four. (Her long-time ally, Kang Sheng, had died of cancer in 1975.) In
my class, political indoctrination became a forum to attack the Gang of
Four, whom we regarded as major public enemies. It had been almost ten
years since the Cultural Revolution started, and people had lost patience
with the endless disruption. For me and many others, its spell was
broken, now that we saw what it meant in practice. More and more
people began to wonder what good the Gang of Four had done since
taking power.

During our stint of 'learning from [industrial] workers', I noticed that
many workers in the factory spent most of their working hours either
chatting or just hanging around the workshops. An hour before closing,
the place was almost empty, as most of the staff had left. It was March,
but the factory had not even met its February target. As employees in a
state-owned enterprise, the staff would be paid in any case. When their
managers requested higher output, many young workers told us: 'Who
cares? We'll soon be taking over!' On the day after we returned to university, the rebels completely stopped production. Around the same
period, many final-year students in my university had to stop their practical work because strife broke out between two rebel organizations in
their hospitals.

Sichuan province, where our university was located, is traditionally
known as 'the land of abundance' in China, due to its good climate and

fertile soil, but now it was child beggars who abounded on our campus. Barefoot and ragged, and carrying grubby baskets, they hung around the canteens at mealtimes, waiting for the leftovers. As members of the armed forces, we were adequately fed, and this alone was seen as a privilege by local peasants. In one busy street near our campus, starving peasants came to sell their children. One day, I saw a girl of two on sale for 50 yuan – about a month's salary for me. Her haggard mother had begged her way for days from their famine-stricken village. No natural disaster had caused this starvation. Its principal cause was the endless political chaos which had destabilized agricultural production. When they heard of such absurd remarks by the Gang of Four as 'We would rather have weeds with a socialist nature than capitalist crops', students at my university condemned them as 'rubbish'.

After Zhou Enlai's death, the Gang of Four lobbied hard to secure the post of premier for Zhang Chunqiao. At the same time, they intensified the campaign against Deng Xiaoping. But the new premier that Mao Zedong appointed was Hua Guofeng, who belonged to neither camp. In the 1950s, he had been the first Party secretary of Xiangtan, the prefecture where Mao's home village was located, and Mao liked him personally. The decision took people by surprise, but one thing it showed clearly was Mao's dissatisfaction with the Gang of Four. Despite his approving their campaigns against Zhou Enlai and Deng Xiaoping, in recent years he had warned Jiang Qing not to be too greedy for power. He also told others that her aim was to be chairman of the Communist Party. Mao should have realized that in using Jiang Qing to discredit Party colleagues he distrusted, he himself was being used by her ambitions. Through him, she had gained enormous power and wealth. He knew his wife's talent for mischief, and complained that she did not respect him or anyone else, she thought so highly of herself. Concerning her unpopularity, Mao said that people were just putting up with her as long as he lived, but in the future she would fall out with everyone.

Before the Qingming Festival of 4 April, a traditional occasion to show respect to the dead, the nation was swept again by spontaneous tributes to Zhou Enlai. Daily from late March, Beijing's main thoroughfares filled with crowds that marched or cycled towards Tian-an Men Square, carrying wreaths and portraits. Again, the square billowed with flowers and wreaths, and the cypress trees blossomed with white tissue chrysanthemums. The number of visitors peaked at two million in a day. The People's Heroes Monument, opposite the rostrum, was plastered with handwritten poems praising Zhou Enlai, and thronged by thousands busily jotting them down. Through various personal channels, these poems were soon circulated all over China.

Activities in memory of Zhou Enlai soon turned into a nationwide demonstration against the Gang of Four, with an outburst of slogans such as 'Whoever attacks Premier Zhou, their heads should be smashed!', or 'With our blood and lives, defend our beloved Premier Zhou!' In Shanghai, crowds roared: 'Down with Jiang Qing!' In Tian-an Men Square, speeches and poems condemning the Gang of Four were cheered and applauded.

At first, the Gang of Four tried to stifle people's activities through tactics like those they used after Zhou Enlai's death. Residents of Beijing were told that the Qingming Festival was a feudal custom that they should not follow, and were cautioned not to go to Tian-an Men Square. But they paid no attention. Then, the Gang issued orders to remove the wreaths, portraits, slogans and poems from the square at night, which brought emotional clashes between the furious crowds and the duty police. The tension in the square rose day by day, till on the evening of 5 April tens of thousands of armed police and militiamen were assigned to crush the demonstration. Next morning the square was empty, and there were reports that several hundred people had been arrested. There was no official news about the casualties, but I heard that after that collision, more than a hundred police were ordered to the square to clean bloodstains from the ground. The action was approved by Mao Zedong. It was said that information from Mao Yuanxin and other supporters of Jiang Qing convinced him that the events in the square were counter-revolutionary activities that had to be quelled.

On 7 April, an article produced by the Gang of Four, entitled 'A counter-revolutionary political event in Tian-an Men Square', was broadcast to the nation, which was the first mention of the incident in the official media. It was also announced that the Party's Central Committee had accepted Mao's proposal to remove Deng Xiaoping from all his posts, as Deng was accused of masterminding the counter-revolutionary campaign. Before that night, we were fascinated by the Tian-an Men Square demonstrations, which we heard about through various personal sources. But now, everyone was shocked by the brutality, as well as by Mao's decision to disgrace Deng Xiaoping again. Following the repression, our medical course gave way again to weeks of solid indoctrination, as the nation was forced to denounce Deng Xiaoping. We were instructed to report on our involvement in 'counter-revolutionary activities', including expressions of support for Deng Xiaoping or attacking the Gang of Four, and to inform against each other. With no pre-arrangement, none of my classmates replied.

In October 1975, when Deng Xiaoping was still in charge of the armed forces, my father was appointed Political Commissar of the Ba-yi (First of August) Film Studio in Beijing. This was the largest film studio in China, with a staff of one thousand four hundred, and was run by the General Political Department of the armed forces. The High Command of the People's Liberation Army includes the General Political, General Staff, and General Logistics departments.

My father's appointment brought much the same privileged status my family had enjoyed before the Cultural Revolution, and a large house in the centre of Beijing. It was located in Xi-jiu-lian-zi Hutong, one of the few streets in the capital where local households were presentable enough to be open to foreign visitors. Residents included the families of several army generals and celebrities such as Dr Mei Lanfang, the great Peking Opera Master, whose family had been our neighbours in the 1950s. Although Dr Mei had died in the early 1960s, his home was raided by the Red Guards during the Cultural Revolution. When my father first brought me to visit them in summer 1976, Madam Mei told me with pride: 'After all these years, we still survive!'

My father fell in love with the house the moment he saw it. It was a single-storey house, built in the early twentieth century by a wealthy merchant for his favourite concubine, surrounded by brick walls more than two metres high, and with a private entrance. Here he could keep his book collection away from prying eyes. Inside the entrance, there were several paved courtyards of different sizes, divided by arches and gates of brick and timber. The walls were decorated with beautiful carvings. As well as the kitchen, bathroom, lavatory and porter's room, there were about ten other rooms of various sizes, all of them modernized, but retaining some original features such as tiled floors and beautiful wooden decorations on the windows. In the winter, the studio provided coal, and a stoker to work in the boiler-room where our heating and hot water came from.

For the last five years, my father had been desperately looking for an alternative to the cramped accommodation where our family had been forced to live since 1970. That small apartment was located by the Western Hill, outside Beijing and with poor public transport. During my mother's illness after Yunnan, her regular visits to town to see her doctors were exhausting journeys that took at least two hours each way. Due to the lack of space, most of the books in my father's collection had to stay packed, and he always worried that they would be damaged by damp or insects. But without political influence, no change was possible. In China, there was no property market at all. Almost all the decent houses in Beijing were controlled either by various government offices or by the armed forces, and available only to their own personnel.

Beijing had suffered for years from an extreme shortage of houses, and the city's housing authority rarely had vacant accommodation.

During those difficult years, my parents visited many local authority offices in the city, and appealed to friends or former colleagues for help. Through a friend, they eventually found a small flat in Peace Street, in east Beijing, which eased my mother's journeys for treatment, but the family's book collection had to remain in Western Hill. To take care of the collections, they both made frequent trips between the two locations. For several months each year, the flat in Peace Street was very cold. There was no south-facing window, and the heating, controlled by a central boiler-room for the whole block, came on only from mid-November to mid-March. No other means of heating were available, so my parents spent a lot of time wandering around the city or visiting friends' homes, looking for sunshine or warmth. Each year, my father suffered from pneumonia brought on by the cold.

Often, as they walked along the Avenue of Eternal Peace, my parents asked each other: 'Will we ever have a house near here?' Now, here was their dream, built within walking distance of favourite places such as Tian-an Men Square, the Avenue of Eternal Peace, the Forbidden City, and even the China Book Store, in Liulichang Street. At last, my father could provide his family with warmth, space and comfort. In particular, he had his own study and library again, and room for his book collection. My parents paid to have the house redecorated, which was unheard-of in the armed forces.

Despite all these improvements, my father's political rehabilitation had yet to be completed. His diary records how members of staff unhappy with their work invaded his studio office and shouted that he was a 'capitalist-roader' from Deng Xiaoping's camp. In this new post, he was in fact demoted, as its rank was equivalent to deputy commander, and he had reached commander level in 1965. But the Party's decision was law, and he recognized Tang's hand at work.

By then, Tang and Ge, my father's leading persecutors, had also come through their political troubles. After his imprisonment a few years ago, Tang and his wife had started to build up their social connections again. Through the marriages of their son and daughters, they became kin to the defence minister (one of the ten Communist marshals), a deputy chief of the General Staff, and a deputy director of the General Political Department. In these high circles, they were the only couple I knew of who achieved such strong political connections through their children's marriages. After her elder daughter's marriage, Madam Tang would introduce her as 'our Marshal's daughter-in-law'. In view of these connections, the regional military authority had to be careful about any job it gave my father, who was seen as Tang's arch-enemy. Hence, it was impossible for my father to serve in the armoured forces again, and in other formations there were very few vacancies for men of his seniority. In any case, he believed that Tang and his wife would always try to block his promotion. When the General Political Department selected him to be Political Commissar of the Ba-yi Film Studio, and the regional leadership agreed, my father was obliged to acquiesce. As soon as he left, Tang regained his position as Political Commissar of the Armoured Forces.

The Ba-yi Film Studio was the last place my father had hoped to work for, since it was closely implicated in Jiang Qing's aim to control China's cultural field. In ten years, the leadership had been replaced six times, and hardly anyone wanted to risk being seventh. From the very beginning, my father recognized the danger. Since Jiang Qing knew all about what happened there, she could disgrace him again at any time. Both of my parents were politically opposed to what she stood for. During the demonstrations against the Gang of Four in 1976, they visited Tian-an Men Square several times, and were deeply impressed. 'This is the dawn of our country's new era!' said my father. 'And the hope of our people!' my mother agreed. They were shocked by the violence used to suppress the protestors. 'Such brutality only happened before under the warlords and the Nationalists,' my father commented. Afterwards, he acted to protect a number of those involved in the demonstration who were relatives of his studio staff.

The studio, although part of the armed forces, was organized more like a civil enterprise, so that much of my father's experience did not apply to his new situation. Like other cultural institutions in China, it was also in total confusion when he arrived, after years of anarchy and infighting during the Cultural Revolution. Wherever he went, even on his way to the canteen, he was often stopped by staff bringing troubles or complaints. Sometimes his workload kept him in his office overnight, and he only had a few hours of sleep. He suffered more often from high blood pressure, and developed additional symptoms of his cardiac problem. But he had to keep working, even when doctors in the studio's clinic urged him to take sick leave. When he eventually entered hospital, his staff took studio problems to his bedside.

My father was determined to clear up the mess, and he tried to improve the leadership by settling its differences, but his efforts were wasted. He was an utter outsider, who brought nobody with him except a few bodyguards from the Beijing Military Region. In contrast, there were various personal links between people in the studio and senior officers in the headquarters of the armed forces. Although he was the 'first hand' chief of the studio, he carried little weight. According to his diary, his decisions were often disputed, and the quarrels continued among the senior staff. Shortly after his arrival, some of his deputies started to lodge complaints against him over his head.

On the whole, my father's dilemma once again reflected his lack of personal connections in the armed forces. As a newcomer in the General Political Department, he was not backed by any particular faction, because he belonged to none of them. Therefore, he could not find the support he required, whereas those who disagreed with him could often invoke their personal connections. Throughout his revolutionary career, it had been his firm belief that a Communist should rely on the Party organization rather than on pulling strings, but now he paid the price for his belief. After nearly ten years of political persecution, this was a bitter conclusion.

The years of persecution changed my father. When she returned from Yunnan my mother found him always on edge. At home, his frequent fits of rage against his persecutors raised his blood pressure or brought on attacks of angina. Knowing that he could not afford such anger, my mother tried to play down his experiences. 'We are not the only ones to be purged during the Cultural Revolution,' she said. 'There are many who were in higher positions than us and did not survive, such as Liu Shaoqi and several marshals. Compared with them, we should feel that we got off lightly.' In fact, my mother suffered more violence and imprisonment than he did, but she always tried to leave it behind her. My father did not listen, and felt grieved by her lack of understanding.

During the process of my father's rehabilitation, the endless requests to revise his confession also incensed him. At the conclusion of his case, he insisted that his file should include a note to the effect that his persecution had been 'a conspiracy by someone with ulterior motives'. When his demand was turned down by the investigating team, he held out against signing the statement of rehabilitation which was requested as a formality, and this caused further delays. My mother understood his feelings, but considered his demand unrealistic, as no one would dare to endorse it. At that time, each rehabilitated victim had to accept the official formulation: 'There are some grounds for the persecution, but investigation reveals no evidence against the victim.' Since the leading figure in persecuting my father was Tang, with his strong connections, my father's demand was exorbitant. In his quest for support, he wrote to numerous military authorities, letters ten thousand words long, in which he refuted hostile accusations in detail. Writing them always revived his ordeals, and made his illness worse, but he just kept writing, days and nights, and swallowing tablets to control the angina. It hurt my mother to watch her husband undermine his health, and she tried to prevent him: 'The sky will be clear one day, and no one can distort history. Just be patient, please!' 'If everyone were like you, there would be no justice in the world!' my father retorted.

Throughout those years, when my father needed medical treatment sympathetic staff in the clinic of the armoured forces arranged for him to be admitted to a special ward for senior officers in one of the best military hospitals. The ward occupied a whole building of several floors, which provided a high standard of medical services, privileged living conditions, and round-the-clock security. My father's floor was for senior officers at the level of army commander. Like the others, my father had his own large room, with en-suite terrazzo-floored bedroom and tiled private bathroom. But most of the time, he was the only politically disgraced patient on his floor. When the doctors made their rounds, some would often bypass his door without entering, whereas in rooms where powerful patients lived they took their time, conducted careful examinations, and chatted cheerfully.

My father was bitterly hurt by the contrast. Often he rushed home to express his bitterness to my mother, and sometimes he refused to return, although he had not been discharged. Again, my mother tried to convince him not to take everything so hard. The senior staff in that department had grown-up children whose futures needed their support. With the right connections, their children could join the armed forces, possibly gain promotion, or a university place, or transfer to a better job. Why go out of their way to please my father, a man in political disgrace? But again, my father did not listen. He became increasingly sensitive about his surroundings. Things he had once shrugged off as trifles now upset him easily.

On my father's floor, many patients were his former subordinates, promoted during the Cultural Revolution. They were often escorted by their private staff, bodyguards, assistants or chauffeurs; my father was on his own and had to catch a bus when he went out. At mealtime, he could be alone in the patients' dining-room, while the others ate in their rooms, served by their private staffs. These experiences kept reminding him of his own unequal position, which he found hard to bear. He had been a proud man all his life, and always respected. Throughout the Cultural Revolution, only a tiny minority of senior officers were purged, while privileges grew among the military elite. For my father, this redoubled the sense of deep injustice that he felt.

My mother's situation was different. Before the Cultural Revolution, senior Communist officials already enjoyed fewer privileges than the military elite. In recent years, most of these officials had undergone political persecution, and their lives had changed fundamentally. In the early 1970s, a number of the Party's leading figures, such as Hu Yaobang, became customers of a public bathhouse in central Beijing, because the quarters forced on to them lacked basic sanitation. Public bathhouses were scarce, so they had to take bus rides each time, and sometimes queued for hours with ordinary people to have a bath. Of those who were still in power, few could keep up their privileged lifestyles. After Yunnan, my mother often met senior government figures on the bus, such as Madam Chen Muhua, once her fellow student in Yan'an, and now the deputy minister of Foreign Trade. Among civilian high officials, she did not feel particularly hard done by, because she was one out of many.

One day, my father asked my mother: 'Do you feel disgraced by having such an unlucky husband?' He was voicing his fear that she might look down on him. Nowadays she had to be very careful, as the slightest word or action could upset him. Inside the family, if anyone showed disagreement he would burst out: 'Nobody listens to me, because I am nobody now!' When his brothers or sisters visited our home, they would try to convince him not to brood about the past, but my father resented their concern. 'Everyone wants to get at me nowadays!' he grumbled to my mother. 'In the old days, they wouldn't have dared.' He had always been looked up to by his siblings, as the head of the 'revolutionary Mu family'. In his mind, it should be he who gave them advice, never the other way round.

After his children joined the armed forces, my father expected that we would make our way through hard work. He praised my progress, but he also criticized some of the others for their lack of achievements. I always thought that I had more than hard work to thank for my success, since I was fairly treated in my hospital and appreciated by my leaders, whereas my siblings' circumstances were often more affected by our father's political problems. In addition, since Feng-xin's and Aijun's units were stationed close to Beijing, there were more members with influential backgrounds, and more competition for promotion, or a place at university.

At that time, it was common in China for officials to use their positions to further their children's careers. While tens of millions of urban school-leavers toiled and starved in the countryside, the daughter of Mao Zedong and Jiang Qing was appointed deputy editor-in-chief of the *Liberation Army Daily*, the official voice of the armed forces, and later, chief of the Municipal Party Committee in Beijing. Before the fatal plane crash in 1971, Lin Biao's only son was promoted to a leading post in the air force while still in his mid-twenties. The Party elites were quick to follow these examples and none of their children went to the countryside. Many youngsters I knew had every step arranged, from recruitment into the armed forces to Party membership, accelerated promotion, or places to study their chosen subjects at university. They did not need to meet the official criteria, or offer qualifications. Sometimes, there was even no need for their parents to intervene in person: toadying subordinates knew what to do.

Before the Cultural Revolution, children were often told by parents and teachers that 'with a good command of mathematics, physics and chemistry, you can make a good living anywhere.' These three subjects were the basic requirements for enrolment in university science or engineering courses. But now, people said: 'Never mind about mathematics, physics and chemistry. It does more good to have a powerful father.'

For those outside the circle, there were barriers. One of my father's former colleagues was sent to a labour camp during the Cultural Revolution, so his children too were dispatched to the countryside. After his release, this man was still jobless and travelled around Beijing every day by bus or bicycle, scouring his social connections for openings for his children. Decades ago, he had lost an arm fighting the Japanese, and now he also suffered serious cardiac problems. During his searches he fainted several times. When he was too weak to walk, he sat on a bicycle and was pushed from place to place by his wife, to pursue his obligations. 'Our lives have been ruined,' he said to my parents. 'But our children are still young. We have to try our best to protect their futures from any more damage.' For the children of these jobless officials or officers, mere entry into the armed forces was not the end. Lacking political support, they were often assigned to dead-end jobs with no prospects of future improvement. In the words of a prevailing saying: 'With political power, you can have everything. Without it, you will have nothing.'

According to the rules, Feng-xin, as a university graduate, should have been promoted to company commander in the year after his enlistment. Instead, he spent two years working as a soldier, until my desperate father was forced to ask his supporters to intervene. Later, Feng-xin was transferred to another division of the armoured forces, where his position rose only to platoon leader. One day, his battalion commander visited our family and asked my father to help one of his relatives to move from a provincial unit to the Beijing Military Region – a difficult transfer, since it had to be approved by two sets of regional offices. Clearly, this officer wanted to exploit my father's connections in exchange for unbarring Feng-xin. My father disliked this idea, but he had to help his son, and asked some former colleagues for help. But this was not the officer's last request. Soon he was asking my father to procure flats in the centre of Beijing, or hundreds of tons of rationed petrol for his own needs. My father was shocked by such greed, and in any case these were fatuous requests, so Feng-xin's position remained unchanged.

Seeing no future in the armed forces, Feng-xin was inclined to quit, especially after his marriage in 1973. His wife worked in the west satellite suburb of Beijing, while Feng-xin's unit was stationed to the east. Because of his low rank, his wife was not entitled to join him, nor could he make regular visits home, so the young couple had to be parted for most of the time. But my father disapproved. Perhaps he felt that his son should be able to cope, considering what he had been through in his own youth. Feng-xin gave up his plan, but he was no longer interested in his job. Later, my father was furious when he discovered that Feng-xin was trying to spend more time with his wife, and blamed him for putting family before duty. To avoid being pressured, Feng-xin made fewer visits to my parents, which only annoyed my father more. The relationship between them was worsening.

After joining the armed forces, my other two brothers faced constant hard labour in harsh conditions. While they saw more and more of the senior officers' sons who had enlisted with them gaining promotion, studying at university, or being moved to better jobs, no improvements ever came their way. It was my younger brother, Feng-yuan, who found this harder to cope with, but his sulky expression displeased my father, who criticized him for shirking hardship and lacking determination. In his view his children should be just as tough, fearless and purposeful as he himself had been. He urged them to swallow their grievances, seeing that he had no political power to ease their path. But what he failed to recognize was that since Feng-yuan had rarely lived outside the circle of senior officers' families, their children were his fellows, and difficult to ignore. Failing to understand his sons, my father's solution of strict discipline and reprimands did not work. When he came home on leave, Feng-yuan's silent low spirits preyed on my father's nerves.

In 1974, Feng-an mentioned problems between my father and

Feng-yuan in a letter to Little Auntie: 'Baba is always strict with his children, but he overdoes his discipline, so that no one dares to tell him their true thoughts and feelings . . .' The letter was passed to my mother, but later my father came across it accidentally, and flew into a rage. 'How dare he speak ill of his father?' he shouted at my mother. 'Just because I'm a nobody now! He is not my son at all!' Bursting with rage, he wrote a twenty-page letter to Feng-an, rejecting his comments sentence by sentence and word by word, as if confronting his opponents. From then on, he refused to communicate with Feng-an again. On my mother's advice, Feng-an apologized later, but my father did not change his position.

In 1976, Feng-an left the army, again to my father's disapproval, as had happened with Feng-xin. But this time, my father could not change the situation, since the decision had been confirmed by Feng-an's unit. Out of the blue, he ordered Feng-an to go back to our rural settlement. 'If he returns to Beijing, I will go to live somewhere else,' he told my mother. 'I cannot stand living in the same city!' It was as if he had completely forgotten Feng-an's support during his hardest years. In the past, it had been Father who did his utmost to save his children from rural settlement. Now he was wishing hardships on his son! In Beijing, it had been every parent's wish to bring their children back to the capital. If Feng-an returned to the village, he might lose his residentship in Beijing permanently.

Due to our upbringing, my brothers had never been close to our parents, and little had passed between them. Having fallen out with his sons, my father treated them like strangers, and would hardly speak to them when they were around. These tensions distressed my mother. After all these years of suffering, what she longed for was a happy family life. But now, the family had lost its peace. As a wife and mother, she loved her husband as well as her children. Among the five children, she tended to give more attention to the two younger sons, since I was always favoured by my father, Aijun was my grandmother's pet, and

Feng-xin was older. Her special bond was with Feng-an, who resembled her in being reserved, humble and honest. He had always been a quiet boy, and no trouble to bring up. But now he was being treated unfairly, just because he was honest enough to express what he felt about my father. Feng-an was hurt, and that made my mother very upset.

My mother was in a deep dilemma. Her husband demanded her full loyalty and obedience, but she could not follow him unconditionally in dealing with their sons, since his way of disciplining them would only make matters worse. Her attempts to mediate failed, mainly because he refused to give ground. When she supported Feng-an's return to Beijing, my father blamed her for not standing by him. Afterwards, he would not let Feng-an live with him under the same roof. When my brothers were around, my mother always feared that the family gathering might be ruined by her husband's unpredictable moods. Very often, he would pick on some minor incident, and then rage at his sons. If my mother treated them fondly, she would be blamed afterwards for 'currying favour', and hence undermining his discipline. Considering his health, my mother tried not to argue, knowing that it would only make him angrier and bring on his hypertension and angina. Sometimes, she lamented to relatives: 'It seems just as if our sons were my own illegitimate children by another man!' She found that her husband was no longer the kind, broad-minded, reasonable person she had known.

At first, his new appointment put my father in better spirits. Although he rarely talked to his sons, his temper improved and the tension in the family reduced. But the remission did not last. Faced with insoluble problems in his work, he relapsed into the same forbidding temper, and the family suffered once again.

Now, one of my father's major targets was the 'stinking sons and daughters of the high officials', through which he voiced his resentment of his children. Indeed, he had always disliked this intolerant group, especially since the rise of the Red Guards. He never forgave these callous teenagers for the movement to 'Smash up the Four Olds', and the reign of violence in China, and it infuriated him when youngsters complained about suffering for their parents' political troubles. On 24 March 1973, he wrote to me: 'One of my former colleagues recently came out of prison, and found that his daughter refused to talk to him . . . She blamed her parents for not being revolutionary rebels, so that her future was ruined by their political problems . . . Her father was jailed for more than four years, and lost his position, but . . . what she cared about was her own future . . .' In his words, she and her contemporaries were a corrupt social group, who were arrogant, selfish and lived on their parents' power.

Since joining the armed forces, I had been away most of the time, and out of touch, but on my rare visits home I was upset by my father's attacks on his children, although I was still on good terms. What we had done as Red Guards was not entirely our own fault: we were teenagers, brainwashed by political indoctrination. What made us the sons and daughters of high officials? It was our parents' actions, not our personal choice. I understood his bitterness about the corruption initiated by senior officials and now endemic in society, but this had nothing to do with our family. As his children, what had we experienced during the Cultural Revolution? Over the years, what privileges had we received from him? Neither my siblings nor I had ever complained about the obstacles created by our parents' political disgrace. But I was hesitant to argue, as I knew what might follow. I loved my father dearly, and did not want to upset him.

On the morning of 9 September 1976, my father came home unexpectedly from work to look for my mother, who was out. He made no reply to my greetings, but roamed around in silence. Eventually, he stopped in front of me and said quietly: 'Chairman just passed away.' This was how I heard about the death of Mao Zedong.

When he reached his office that morning, my father was summoned to the General Political Department for an emergency meeting with other senior officers, where he was informed that Mao Zedong had died some hours ago. This made my father one of the handful of people in China to know the news, since the death was not announced until mid-afternoon.

My very first response to the news was: 'That is strange! The slogan "Long live Chairman Mao" [in Chinese, "Live ten thousand years"] has been shouted for so many years. In the end, he didn't manage even a hundred years!' I would never have expected to respond so mischievously to Mao's death. Until a few years ago, it frightened me to think that one day our Chairman would be gone, and China like a motherless child. In the days that followed his death, I did my best to join in the general grief, but often felt that it was not my real emotion, which was in contrast with the distress I experienced at the death of Zhou Enlai nine months before.

Having heard my response, my father was silent. Tears covered his face. 'Oh, Baba! You shouldn't cry for Mao!' I wanted to tell him. 'Just think how much you've suffered all these years! Without Mao, there would be no Cultural Revolution!' I wanted to remind him that not so long ago, during our private conversations, he had often blamed Mao for giving power to the Gang of Four. However, I kept quiet, confused by his tears. More than two decades later, my mother told me that Mao's death had come as no surprise, considering his fading health and age. What worried them most at the time was the future of the country. Since Mao's chosen successor, Hua Guofeng, was not thought strong or experienced enough to lead the Party, they feared that China would fall to the Gang of Four, with unthinkable effects. Compared with mine, their feelings were much more complicated. Mao had dominated their revolutionary careers. They had seen him guide their Party to victory over the Japanese and the Nationalists. He was the leader they had followed for most of their lives. They were deeply attached to him, and not impressed by my offhand response to his death.

In the afternoon of 9 September 1976, the radio told the nation: 'Comrade Mao Zedong, the esteemed and beloved great leader of our Party, our army and the people of all nationalities in our country, the great teacher of the international proletariat and the oppressed nations and oppressed people, Chairman of the Central Committee of the Communist Party of China, Chairman of the Military Commission of the Central Committee of the Communist Party of China, and Honorary Chairman of the National Committee of the Chinese People's Political Consultative Conference, passed away at 00.10 hours on 9 September 1976 in Beijing . . .'

My grandmother was back in Beijing, and living with our family again. When she heard the news, she burst into tears: 'Why should our Chairman Mao die and I be left alive? I would rather it was the other way round!' To her, my lack of grief was conscienceless. Until the end of Grandmother's life, Mao Zedong was like a living god in her heart. No matter how much our family suffered during the Cultural Revolution, she never complained about Mao, and only sighed: 'I can't understand why the Communists are always fighting each other.' Her powerful attachment was not uncommon among the majority of ordinary Chinese, who had no inside knowledge about the intra-Party conflicts. For several decades, Mao had been regarded as the nation's great saviour.

From 11 to 17 September 1976, Mao's body lay in state in the Great Hall of the People in Beijing. I felt so curious to see it that I postponed my departure to university. The ceremonies were not open to the general public, and all participants were security-vetted in advance. In Beijing, the limited vacancies were allocated to different organizations, which chose a small number of representatives from among their staff. Through armoured forces headquarters, I received permission to attend. When I came to Tian-an Men Square it was a hot afternoon, and a long silent queue stood outside the Great Hall of the People. The wait was long. Inside the hall, my first impression was the huge number of wreaths placed all around. The senders included foreign Communist leaders such as Kim Il Sung of North Korea, Enver Hoxha of Albania and Nicolae Ceauşescu of Romania. Mao's body was covered with the red flag of the Communist Party of China. To my surprise, he looked smaller than I always thought. The last time I had seen him in person was in winter 1966, standing up in his open-top limousine and waving to the crowd on the pavement, on his way to review the Red Guards. I was hugely impressed by his appearance and physical stature. Now, as people slowly passed his body, and many wept or wailed, once again I failed to produce any tears.

On 7 October 1976, my father was summoned to the General Political Department for another urgent meeting, and did not come home till midnight. My mother sat up waiting, and wondered what new shock was on its way. When he finally returned, the first words she heard were: 'Great news! The Gang of Four has been arrested! Our country is saved!'

Since the death of Mao, the Gang of Four's campaign to seize power in the Party and the country had reached its height. Officials in various institutions, provinces and military regions were mobilized to pledge their loyalty to the Gang of Four, and to write to the Party's Central Committee backing Jiang Qing as leader of the Party and the PLA. It was said that Wang Hongwei had ordered an enlarged official portrait, as he expected to become a national leader soon. Huge militia forces in Shanghai, the power base of the Gang of Four, were put on stand-by. Without official approval, Mao Yuanxin gave orders to move a division of the armoured forces from Manchuria, where he was based, to Beijing.

At this point, elder statesmen such as Marshal Ye Jianying and Li Xian-nian, allies of Zhou Enlai and Deng Xiaoping, decided it was time to arrest the Gang of Four, in a move supported by Hua Guofeng, and planned for the evening of 6 October. It was said that the whole operation took only one and a half hours, with no shooting and no casualties. The Gang was arrested. The Cultural Revolution was over.

When the names of Jiang Qing and her allies suddenly vanished from the media, only one explanation was likely, and private celebrations broke out among excited residents in Beijing. On 14 October, the arrest of the Gang of Four was announced to the nation. The response was universal and spontaneous. During the following days, jubilant crowds poured on to China's streets, singing and dancing, throwing firecrackers and waving colourful flags. Many shouted: 'Celebrate our second liberation!' (The first took place when the Communists took power in 1949.) Shops sold out of alcoholic drinks. At celebration banquets, the favourite food was crab, because the way crabs move symbolized the devious, threatening image of the Gang of Four. To take the image further, people buying crabs chose one female and three males. Through boiling the crabs and then breaking them into pieces, they expressed their long-repressed resentments against the Gang of Four.

I heard the news on my way back to university after a spell of 'learning from peasants'. During the two days' steamship trip, I only slept for five hours. Sitting on the deck alone, I forgot about the cold autumn rain and strong winds along the Wu and Yangtze rivers where we passed. My heart was a whirl of excitement. Since that chaotic summer of 1966, more than ten years separated the naive teenager from the young officer. The Cultural Revolution had brought extraordinary changes into my life and my parents', and I was no longer that fanatical pupil who utterly believed every word of Chairman Mao's. Compared with tens of millions in my generation, I could consider myself lucky, because most were still dispersed to their rural settlements. What would happen after the Cultural Revolution? It was beyond my imagination, but I believed that improvements would take place in the country as well as in my family, because I thought that things could not be worse than what we had come through.

My mother told me later that according to inside information, complaints against my father from his studio had already reached the Gang of Four. Another few months, and he would have been disgraced again.

For my mother, an immediate change was that the expansion of the Beijing Planetarium was revoked. Since her arrival the year before, she had seen no progress made there in any case. Before Mao's death, the country was already in serious economic difficulties, sharpened by the intensified power struggles. Jiang Qing's ambitious project was seen as an extravagance, and funding deliberately delayed. During the final years of Mao's life, his dissatisfaction with Jiang Qing was an open secret among high officials, and few took notice of her, so my mother concentrated on resuming the routine work of the planetarium, which had been halted for some time. Her efforts were praised by the municipal authorities, but her plan to resume the publication of the planetarium's journal was blocked by their cautions: 'You have to consider what you would do if you were instructed to publish articles denouncing Deng Xiaoping.' Now that the Gang of Four had lost, the Beijing Planetarium was back to its original position, which was a county-level enterprise. Since her post was now unnecessary, my mother decided to leave.

In my university, the authorities had no briefing from Beijing about education policies in the post-Cultural Revolution era, so our course arrangements hardly improved. In November 1976, we were informed to go to rural areas again for ten months of 'open-door schooling' (kai-men ban-xue), prolonging the Gang of Four's indoctrination. Immediately students covered the campus with big-character posters protesting against the decision. It had been fourteen months since our enrolment, and more than half of the time had been wasted on political indoctrination. Now that the Cultural Revolution was over, our studies should not be interrupted again. When our demand was rejected, all the students in my year launched a boycott. A few months ago, nobody would have dared: the boycott would have been condemned as a counter-revolutionary activity. But things were different now, and our action also won support from the teaching staff. Word reached us that similar actions were being staged in other military medical universities.

At first, the university authorities tried to put the conventional brakes on student action, such as calling general meetings to tell us off. When the vice-chancellor condemned the strike, all five hundred students in my year walked out in protest, and the platform faced an empty hall. To put more pressure on the authorities, the students wrote to the Party and military leadership. Normally, letters sent by ordinary people to these leaders seldom reached their desks, but we heard that through some students' personal connections, our letter went straight to Hua Guofeng, whose inquiry about our curriculum caused panic in the General Logistics Department. Three weeks into our strike, a deputy director of the department arrived from Beijing to negotiate. In the end, our demand was accepted. After more than a year at university, we were to do what we came for, and study medicine.

In July 1977, Deng Xiaoping regained all the leading positions in the Party, armed forces and government that he had lost the previous year. Later, the events in Tian-an Men Square were also rehabilitated, and the participants praised as heroes against the Gang of Four, rather than per-secuted as counter-revolutionaries. Under Deng's leadership, various new policies were introduced in education, among other areas. I still remember my excitement when I first heard that people in the profes-sional or academic fields must now spend five-sixths of their working hours doing their own jobs. There would be no more wasting my life on endless political indoctrination. Unlike the 'worker-peasant-soldier stu-dents' of previous years, we now faced various examinations, which was tough on everybody, since we had sat no entrance examination, and the traditional course had been shortened by a year.

In the new era, universities stopped enrolling 'worker-peasant-soldier students', and entry was based on the results of the all-China entrance examinations that resumed in 1977. Teachers and students could focus full-time on their subjects. Compared with the coming generation, the 'worker-peasant-soldier students' – who included everyone in my year – were viewed as under-qualified. Even before we graduated, teaching hospitals in my university were already considering replacing their 'worker-peasant-soldier' staff with future graduates enrolled after the Cultural Revolution. I was devastated by the change in our status. Getting into university had cost me years of unremitting work and deprivation. Once at university, we had fought to improve our education, and tried hard to make up the loss caused by the Cultural Revolution. Now, all our hard work to qualify as doctors was devalued even before our graduation! I wanted to apply for an entrance examination to start again, but was told that present-day students and graduates were not entitled to sit the resumed examinations. It seemed there was no altering our fortune. I regretted entering university in 1975, but how could I have known the upheavals that the next two years would bring?

Part Three
1975–June 1988

Who has passed judgement on the good and ill
You have wrought these thousand autumns?

extract from 'Kunlun – to the tune of
Nian Nu Jiao', composed by
Mao Zedong in October 1935

Chapter 22

Marriage and Politics:
In Confrontation with My Father
over My Wedding
(1975–August 1977)

To start this chapter, I have to take you back to early 1975, before I went to university. After my promotion to junior doctor in the Armoured Forces 9th Division, I was often questioned about my 'personal affairs' – in other words, whether I had a boyfriend, and specifically a fiancé. In China, such questions were natural, as people believed that 'men should get married while women should be married off'. As an officer, I was now eligible to settle my 'personal affairs'. At that time, most marriages were still arranged by the couple's parents, or through a go-between, because making friends of the opposite sex was not encouraged and there was little opportunity to socialize outside the workplace. In my hospital, all personnel, including those who were married but not entitled to married quarters, lived in dormitories located in the building where we worked. Without official permission, no one could leave the compound even for weekends or holidays, and all visitors had to be reported to the authorities, so it was not surprising that few could find a spouse without the help of matchmakers. Single officers like me always caught the eye of would-be matchmakers, perceived by the Chinese as benefactors, and praised by the Communists as people who cared for others.

In my division, the voluntary matchmakers who approached me included my patients and colleagues, some of them practically strangers. Someone would walk into my office and shut the door for privacy. After a few such visitors, I could sense their purpose even before they spoke. Since I did not have a boyfriend, various names of young officers from my division or other local units were put forward. I was expected to select one of these, as other people did, and then to attend a date which was arranged by the matchmaker. Afterwards, I could see the man on my own, and eventually marry him.

But I turned down all the names proposed, mainly on the grounds that it was too early for me to consider my 'personal affairs'. My mind was set on going to university, and sooner or later I expected to return to Beijing. For years, it had been my dream that one day I would live close to my parents, and share my father's interests in literature again. The officers recommended had enlisted outside the capital: marriage to any of these would mean either losing my dream of the future, or being parted from my husband, since few outsiders could obtain a residentship in Beijing or have their job transferred there.

At home, my parents also faced approaches from former colleagues, friends or relatives, and were given various names of high officials' sons as possible husbands. Father turned them down without even letting me know. Despite all this activity, my parents hesitated to ask me directly about my 'personal affairs'. In my family, such topics were not discussed in an open manner.

During my mother's imprisonment in the late 1960s, I had a crush on Drizzle, the son of Madam Dew (my mother's supporter in her university), and the feeling was mutual. When visiting his family to exchange my parents' messages, I found that he was exceptionally intelligent and knowledgeable, with a passion for military affairs. He was surprised to discover my knowledge of literature and history, interests we shared. But although we enjoyed talking together, we ventured no further. Having suffered so much from my relationship with Mighty China, I was scared to get close to a boy again, and Drizzle's politeness and respect made him equally restrained on his side. Later, both of us were dispatched to different rural settlements. In a long correspondence between his village in Inner Mongolia and mine in the loess highlands, we encouraged each other to cope with the hardship and shared our experiences. I enjoyed his letters immensely, attracted by his humour and moved by his caring manner towards me. But again, nothing we expressed exceeded friendship.

After I left my rural settlement, we went on writing until one day my father asked me about our relationship. It was in the winter of 1969, a year before I joined the army. In reply, I burst into tears, feeling terribly ashamed. The question revived the humiliations that I suffered in middle school, and never knew how to handle. 'Please leave me alone!' I wanted to say, but did not dare. I felt that no one could understand the pain I had endured. Shocked by my tears, my father stopped mentioning the topic of my 'personal affairs' for several years. I also stopped writing to Drizzle, and offered him no explanation. Desperate to be left alone in my private life, and to live quietly and peacefully, I thought that my only choice was not to get close to any male outside my family again.

In September 1973, I was unexpectedly summoned to Beijing for an urgent assignment: joining a team to arrange the funeral of my division's deputy commander, who had just died of cancer. I had never met him, and this was my first introduction to his family, including his only son, Great Peace, a young officer from a regiment in my division. After the funeral, I became a friend of the family, and was invited regularly to their home in the compound of the division's head office. Great Peace's mother was a kind, quiet, cultured woman, and the delicious food she always cooked for me was a wonderful treat, compared with the poor canteen diet. To find myself so cared for and appreciated reminded me of the pleasure my own family gave me. After the strict regime of my hospital, it was a joy to enter this relaxing, friendly atmosphere. Great Peace and I liked to talk. Brought up in provincial cities, he was fascinated by my inside knowledge of the capital's elites, and would listen for hours, sometimes joined by his two sisters. He was gentle, shy and sensitive, and four years my junior. I felt that he was like a younger brother.

In spring 1975 he sent me a letter – his first, so it took me by surprise. It said nothing special, but I sensed his affection, and that made it hard to reply. Did I love him or not? I had never thought about it. For years I had been told that love was an unhealthy feeling, a symptom of bourgeois emotion. With my history of painful experiences, I often felt embarrassed even to hear the word mentioned, as if I were colluding in a crime. For me, the feeling of being in love seemed so remote and incorrect that it might have belonged to another planet.

Several weeks passed, and I did not contact Great Peace or hear from him. Then on a quiet Sunday morning one of his friends, a young officer from his regiment, appeared in my office. I knew this visitor. He came from a high official family in Beijing, and his fiancée was a daughter of Marshal Liu Bocheng, several of whose children had attended the Ba-yi School. 'What has happened between you and Great Peace?' he asked at once. I did not know how to reply. 'Please let him know what you think,' said the visitor again. 'He has been ill because of your silence, and I felt sorry for his suffering.' In answer, I said that it was impossible for me to develop my relationship with Great Peace, because in Chinese society a husband should be older than his wife. Besides, at the moment I could not pursue my 'personal affairs', because my priority was to go to university. Afterwards, I wrote to Great Peace to deliver the message myself, and promised to keep up our friendship. When we met again in his home, both of us tried to avoid the subject of our relationship. In autumn 1975, I went to university in Chongqing, while Great Peace went to study philosophy at Beijing University. Before we left, we promised to write to each other.

On my way to university, I spent a few days with my parents in Beijing. After his long silence, my father asked again about my 'personal affairs'. Trying to keep calm, I mentioned what had happened between Great Peace and me. 'That is ridiculous!' he replied. 'How could such a young boy approach you?' Seeing his disapproval, I gave up the thought of a relationship with Great Peace. For many years, I had followed my father's instructions with deep love and unconditional trust, and was used to accepting his judgement. Instead, I asked him to look for a suitable man for me. In recent years, I had begun to recognize his changing character, and feared for our future relationship if he was unhappy about the man I found myself. I also thought that my parents would have better chances than me to find a suitable man in Beijing, since I was so far from the capital.

I told my father about my major criteria for a husband: ability, kindness, a good education and high moral standards. In particular, I was interested in the 'Chou-lao-jiu' (literally the 'Stinking Ninth Class') – university graduates enrolled before the Cultural Revolution. At that time, these people were often condemned as bourgeois intellectuals and classified next to the 'eight black' classes: landlord, rich farmer, reactionary, bad element, bourgeois rightist, renegade, enemy spy and capitalist-roader, the villains of the Cultural Revolution. But I liked them, and admired their educational attainments and intelligence.

Shortly after I left home for university, another candidate appeared. My father was approached by several officers in the armoured forces, recommending a young doctor called New Star, who worked in the headquarters' clinic. He was not a total stranger, because his father, Major-General Geng, and my father had known each other since the 1950s. My father regarded Geng as a decent person who had never involved himself in political persecution. My mother's response to the news was: 'I don't like children from high official families, and I'm not interested in making connections with people in higher social positions through marrying off our children.' My father disagreed. In his view, not only was Geng's rank the same as his own, but the two had joined the Communist Party in the same year, 1932. Nevertheless, Geng held a more senior post, and had been promoted to major-general before my father, with a higher salary grade. As Deputy Political Commissar of the Beijing Military Region, he had managed to remain safely in his post throughout the Cultural Revolution.

In November 1975, I received a letter at university from my father, which introduced New Star. He mentioned my mother's disapproval, and said that I should decide for myself. Knowing that New Star was one of the 'worker-peasant-soldier students', Father was concerned that I might not be satisfied with his educational background, but he also told me that my criteria were difficult to meet. My parents' social circle was mainly restricted to their friends and former colleagues. Most of their children were around my age, too young to have been educated as 'bourgeois intellectuals'. In Beijing, there was only a limited number of graduates enrolled before the Cultural Revolution, and my parents had not met any who were still single and without a girl-friend. According to the matchmakers, New Star had met me in 1973, when I was in Beijing for the funeral of Great Peace's father, and had fallen in love at first sight, but was too shy to approach our family for a long time. My father felt that such a deep affection recommended him, and I too was moved by the story, which reminded me of classical romances.

In my childhood, when our families were neighbours and sent their children to Ba-yi School, New Star had often visited us during school holidays. He was two years senior to me, and used to come with his elder brother, a classmate of Feng-xin's. He played with my brothers, and hardly spoke to my sister and me. After my father's transfer to the armoured forces in 1962, I seldom met the Geng brothers again. In 1968, he joined the armed forces, while Feng-an and I were consigned to the rural settlement. Now I had no idea what he was like, either in character or looks. My father was told that he was a decent man, and popular with his colleagues.

After several sleepless nights, I decided not to turn New Star down. I was attracted by the stories about him, and besides, this was the first man to be introduced to me by my father, the most trustworthy person in my life. At the age of twenty-four, I was getting more lonely in my private life. At university, I found that all girls of my age already had boyfriends. In China, staying single was socially unacceptable once past the recognized age of marriage, so my solitary status seemed odd. Until the arrest of the Gang of Four, no one could see an end to the Cultural Revolution, and I was sick of its effects. Marriage offered the prospect of finding a private territory where I could take refuge from the political chaos and share my feelings with a man I loved. With my agreement, my father gave my address to the matchmakers.

New Star's first letter, dated 26 December 1975, was very brief. He addressed me as 'Comrade Mu Aiping', and referred to the recent go-between activities as 'that matter'. I was asked to provide the following information: working and educational experience, personal character, interests, height, and place of enlistment. He also welcomed questions from me. I was disappointed by this letter, and especially by his handwriting. My parents always criticized my lack of interest in calligraphy at school, and I did not take trouble to improve my handwriting afterwards, but his was much worse than anyone else's I knew, and his style was clumsy compared with letters from my father, or friends such as Drizzle and Great Peace. Before replying, I wrote straight to my parents to complain. My father insisted that I should not judge a person by his handwriting only; it was moral qualities that mattered most. I accepted his advice, and tried to overcome my reservations when corresponding with New Star.

I learned from his letters that New Star's father came from a poor peasant family in the mountains of Jiangxi province in the south. In 1932, he joined the Red Army in a Communist base where his village was located. When his troops started the Long March in 1934, he was already political commissar for a regiment. Because of that, most members of his family were killed when the Nationalists occupied the abandoned base. The only survivors were Geng's two younger brothers, aged eight and twelve, who became street beggars for many years. When they grew up, they were conscripted into the Nationalist forces fighting the Communists. Later, one of them managed to escape, and was now a peasant in his home village. The other had been taken to Taiwan when the Nationalists lost the mainland, and had not been heard from since. New Star's mother came from Changzhi city, where my hospital was located. During the Sino-Japanese War, her father was killed by the Japanese as a member of the Communist underground. She went to Yan'an, and studied at the Chinese Women's University, in a class much junior to my mother's. Before the war ended, she married Major-General Geng, and then stopped working, like the wives of many other high officials.

I was touched by these stories of sacrifices to the revolution, and the pain endured in wartime, but what really moved me was the story he told me about his own suffering from political persecution. In early 1968, soon after entering the navy, New Star was imprisoned because his boss suspected that his father was in political trouble. He was interrogated, held incommunicado, and forced to do hard labour. One day, he saw his father's name on a long list of senior officials attending an event reported in the *People's Daily*, and cried because it meant that his father was safe. Within days, his ordeal was over. Later he was transferred to the Beijing Military Region where his father was posted. His story boosted my expectation that we could understand each other easily, since he too had come through difficult times.

When the country was grieving over the death of Premier Zhou Enlai in January 1976, New Star expressed his concern, and told me that he had written my name on a white tissue chrysanthemum and tied it on a cypress tree branch by Tian-an Men Square. I felt grateful for his thoughtfulness, and pleased to find more that we could share. In subsequent letters, he told me that good things were said about me in my division, and that the frankness I showed in my writing was exactly what he wanted, because he himself liked to be frank. When he said that the style of my writing and handwriting was very like my father's, I enjoyed the compliment.

Soon, our letters were getting longer and more frequent, our topics broader, and our tone more intimate. In all my life, this was the first time I had communicated so often with a man outside my family. Strangely, I did not suffer the anxiety that such contacts had caused me in the past. Now, I felt relaxed: there could be no questions asked by my father, and no threat of damage to my reputation. Among female students around my age, boyfriends were taken for granted. No one would condemn my conduct as 'shameful and indecent', or denounce me for 'being imbued with bourgeois ideas'.

Two months after our correspondence started, New Star confessed that sometimes his feelings towards me were hard to control. Although I tried to sound cool in my reply, I did not feel it. I was often too excited to sleep when his letters arrived, and couldn't wait to reply. When I wrote, I felt as if I was talking to him face to face, and my heart beat like any inexperienced young girl's. Although we had not met, I started to draw a picture in my mind with all the qualities that defined my ideal man. I believed he must be kind, caring, capable and hard-working. The photos he sent showed a tall, handsome man with a gentle manner. Gradually, my disappointment about his style and handwriting evaporated, and I lost my original regret that he did not belong to the 'Stinking Ninth Class'. When the university summer holiday was approaching, he started to discuss his plans for our careers and personal life, as if we had been close for many years. I showed no disapproval of his tone, as I thought that I was already in love with him.

More than two decades later, I read those letters again when preparing for this book, and could hardly believe how inexperienced and naive I was at that time, more like a teenage girl than a young woman in her mid-twenties. Since the age of fourteen, I had gone through experiences that should not happen to a teenager — becoming a rebellious Red Guard, defending my persecuted parents, exile and hardship in the countryside . . . On the other hand, I was still profoundly unsure of myself in human relations, having had so little taste of the ordinary patterns of life. During the last ten years, I had had few female friends, and little experience of boyfriends. In particular, my life had always been overshadowed by my dreadful experiences in middle school, which made me repress the romantic side of myself. Although it felt inhuman, I thought that my future gave me no choice. Now, my first closeness to a man — a paper closeness — immersed me completely in a fantasy about a wonderful husband.

On 29 July 1976, I went home for my first summer holiday. On the 30th, New Star visited me at home, and I was captivated by his handsome appearance and gentle manner, a perfect match for the picture in my mind. Although it was our first meeting, I did not feel too nervous, and treated him like a close friend. After that, he visited me at home almost every day, arriving at noon and leaving late afternoon. When he brought me birthday presents, I was moved again by his attentiveness. In my family, there was no birthday celebration for anyone. One day, he asked to kiss my cheek, and I agreed with pleasure. As his lips touched my skin gently, the muscles tensed and quivered in my cheeks. For Chinese, kissing is a very intimate contact. Apart from my father and Mighty China, he was the only man ever to have kissed me.

When I first visited New Star's parents, they served me Beijing roast duck, ordered specially from the famous Quan-ju-de Restaurant. During our meeting, I found Major-General Geng a quiet, caring person who treated me with respect. From various sources, I had heard stories about

Madam Geng's behaviour in the circle of high officers' families in Beijing. She had hardly worked at all after her marriage, and now held a low-level sinecure. New Star used to tell me that there was no comparison between his mother and mine, because my mother was a 'big cadre'. When we met, Madam Geng was polite and there was nothing off-hand in her manners.

In my family, New Star charmed my grandmother at once with his politeness and good looks, especially since she had known him as a child in the 1950s. My mother made few comments about him, but treated him warmly. Unexpectedly, it was my father who started to tilt against him. On the second week of my holiday, he told me that New Star should go to work instead of spending so much time with me, as he knew that New Star was not entitled to so much leave. On 28 July, the world's worst earthquake in the twentieth century had completely destroyed Tangshan, in northern China, an industrial city of more than a million inhabitants. Casualties were estimated at nearly half a million. The stricken area also included Beijing and Tianjin, and troops were badly needed to bring relief.

I tried to defend New Star, since I was completely attracted by him, and longed to see him every day. I only had four weeks' home vacation this year, and would not return till next summer. Knowing my father's authority in the family, New Star tried to please him, but it went wrong. One day, he offered to have a large army tent delivered, so that my family could use it for shelter in our courtyard if another earthquake should hit Beijing. My father refused, and snapped at me afterwards: 'How could I use military supplies for my own family's benefit?' I thought he was over-reacting, because these practices were not uncommon among senior officers' families. Gradually, my father began to refer to New Star as 'na-xiao-zi' ('that fellow') in his absence, which I felt was very rude. One evening, when I started to complain about the discomfort of sleeping in the courtyard at night – his precaution against a possible earthquake – he became suddenly furious and slapped my face to stop me. Since joining the army, this was my first experience of his violence and unreasonable behaviour. It really shocked me, but I did not dare to object.

I attributed my father's behaviour to jealousy. In the past, his influence had dominated my life, and now there was another man to share my feelings. 'Baba, you are too selfish!' I wanted to tell him. 'I'm twenty-five already, and this is the first time that I've had a proper boyfriend. I've always listened to you, and you yourself introduced me to New Star. Why are you so bad-tempered now?' Again, I did not dare to express my resentment. In order to avoid a clash, I tried not to mention New Star's name. Luckily, he was out at work most of the time, so their paths seldom crossed.

One evening at the end of August, the last day of my holiday, New Star came to say goodbye. When he arrived, my father was busy in his library, so I brought New Star straight to my room. A short while later, Father popped in unexpectedly. At the sight of New Star, his face filled with anger. Ignoring New Star's greeting, he left the room and slammed the door behind him. I followed him out. 'Baba, please listen. I didn't want to disturb you when he came. I was going to bring him to see you when you were free.' Father just pushed me away. Shocked by his manner, New Star left at once.

That night, the house turned deathly quiet, and no light was on except in my father's room. But I felt sure that everyone else was awake, as we wondered what would happen next. Suddenly, I heard Father's furious voice through the open window: 'How arrogant he is! He's only Geng's son! This is my home! And he goes straight to my daughter's room without a word to anyone else! Does he know that even in the whorehouse there are rules . . .' My mother came to my room, and sat by me in silence. Father raged for half an hour, while I wept uncontrollably. 'Mama, how could Baba treat me so badly?' 'You should have known your father's state of mind. After his political persecutions, he always suspects that people look down on him. Just lately, he's been upset because of his problems at work . . .'

In recent years, my father had lost his grip on his temper, and acted more and more unreasonably at home. By the end of the Cultural Revolution, all of his siblings and their spouses were out of political trouble, and some had even received promotion. During their visits, he tended to wear a cold expression all the time, and might not even greet them. They just had to swallow his rudeness. Considering his poor health, my mother also tried not to offend him. So the family just kept quiet whatever he did.

On my leaving day, I did not say goodbye to my father when he set off to work in the morning. On the way to the railway station, I still kept sobbing to my mother: 'I hate Baba! I will never forgive him . . .' This was the first time he had really hurt me. My mother had to stop me several times, in case our driver overheard. When the train started moving, I felt that my heart was broken. 'Over the last month, you have given me the happiest time in my life, and I experienced the most wonderful feeling for a human being,' I wrote to New Star on the trip. 'Unfortunately, our last meeting ended very sadly . . . I felt terribly sorry for you. Ever since we met, you have been so kind to me . . . Apart from my parents, no one else has ever been so caring and loved me so much. I have been thinking that from now on I must try my best to give you happiness, not only out of love but also in gratitude . . .'

The journey from Beijing to Chongqing took two days. On the second day, our train was stopped by the collapse of some tunnels ahead. I was over the moon when I heard it announced that passengers would be returned to where they started, as the repairs would take some time. Until that moment, I had been asking myself: 'Why don't I go back to Beijing?' I desperately wanted to see New Star again, to comfort him and apologize for what my father had done . . . And now, I was on my way!

My father seemed to have forgotten about his anger when he saw me again, and treated me as well as ever. During the two weeks before I left again, he took me to his studio several times, and arranged for me to watch the shooting of a film. Although I enjoyed the experiences, I thought of them as tricks to keep me away from New Star. Both of us tried not to mention his name, or the painful evening before my first departure. But what Father did not know was that he had pushed me still closer to New Star. And he could not take me to work every day.

During this period, I accepted New Star's request and gave my virginity to him. Soon after we first met, he had requested it repeatedly, and offered various reasons. He told me that he was going to join a medical team assigned to the earthquake area, and would be risking his life. He also said that my acceptance would amount to an engagement, since we had decided to marry in the future. Several times, he mentioned stories he had heard that many city girls in rural settlements had struck up sexual relationships with their male companions or local peasants, implying that my refusal concealed my no longer being a virgin. In all my life, this was the first direct approach for sex that I had faced. Drizzle and Great Peace had never touched me physically, or even held my hand, though both relationships had lasted several years. I still believed that sexual relationships outside marriage were wrong. For me, it was unthinkable to lose my virginity to a man who was not my husband. But my inexperience made it hard to say a straightforward 'No', so I resorted to various evasions, such as pretending not to understand what he meant, or trying to change the subject. These methods often helped me to deflect male admirers in the past, but they did not work now, as New Star kept renewing his request.

This time, I did not want to upset New Star again. I also wanted some way to retaliate against my father's unjust behaviour to us both. When it happened, I was terribly nervous, and racked with guilt. Despite my several years' work in gynaecology and obstetrics, I was still unbelievably ignorant about sex, avoided thinking about it in detail, and never discussed it with anyone, fearing that to do so was sinful. Although New Star took care of contraception, I was terrified of becoming pregnant. Several years ago, a pregnant student had nearly been expelled from my university. Thanks to the intervention of her boyfriend's father, a three-star general, she received a reduced punishment: to quit her course 'voluntarily'.

After what had happened, I recognized that I would never be the same. I had no alternative but to marry New Star. Now that I had lost my virginity, no other decent man would accept me as his wife. But the thought did not panic me, because I believed that I had made the right choice for my future husband.

When I returned to university, it was late September 1976. From then on, my father stopped writing to me. For years I had been used to his letters, which came almost every week. I knew that his job kept him too busy to write to me regularly, but I also recognized that a gap had emerged between us, and that made me anxious. The first month was particularly hard, as I joined other students to 'learn from peasants' in a remote mountain area in Sichuan. I only managed to escape part of the scheme by delaying my return to university, like many others did. About fifty female students shared a large room provided by the local people's commune, and slept on the cement floor. It rained every day, and our bedding was never dry. Almost every day, the commune's canteen dished up salted chilli, so hot that one small bite could burn all the way from my tongue to stomach. The region's poverty, remoteness and isolation often reminded me of my former rural settlement, but worst of all was the loneliness of being so far away from university and home, and forced to take part in meaningless indoctrination and hard labour.

During that period, writing to New Star became my greatest pleasure, and I looked forward to his letters every day. I missed him a lot. He had become the closest person in my life, and I looked to him for the understanding and encouragement that my father had provided in the past. Having lost my father's support, I found myself vulnerable and empty, too sensitive to my surroundings, and unstable in my feelings. But things did not turn out as I expected, as it was difficult for New Star to understand my deep affection for my father, and to appreciate the dilemma that I faced. In his letters, he criticized my 'petit bourgeois' sentimentalism, and showed little sympathy for my divided feelings. I was reminded of what I had heard before about his character: being cold and detached from everything. In the past, I had not taken it seriously, but now, I started to ask myself: what was he really like?

At the same time, I was troubled by the increasing campus gossip about New Star and me. Of five hundred students in my year, most had some connection to the Beijing Military Region or the General Political Department of the armed forces. Due to our fathers' positions, our relationship attracted great attention, especially among female students.

Despite my worries, I could not talk to anyone for fear of adding fuel to the gossip. In the past, I had only mentioned my 'personal affairs' to a girl in my year whom I trusted as a friend. But from the very beginning, stories were circulated about my relationship with New Star, many of them untrue and even malicious. After that, it became hard to trust anyone else again.

During the first summer holiday, New Star had suggested that we should marry next summer – my only home leave before my graduation. His chief reason was concern for his career, as he disliked his current job. His clinic in a military compound was overstaffed with doctors, who often enjoyed privileged status because they were relatives of armoured forces leaders. He was also fed up with the constant friction among the staff. In Beijing, clinics like his were known as 'cosy nests': they offered their staff an easy life, but little chance to develop. New Star told me some of his plans. For example, he wanted to attend a training course for military advisers, and have himself assigned to Third World countries. Through family connections, his application would be accepted, but he needed to get married first, as all such posts required it. At that time, working abroad was a prestigious opportunity, available only to a privileged few. These assignments were also very profitable, because a month's allowance abroad could come to several times one's annual salary. I had accepted his plan for marriage, because I wanted to advance his career. I was too captivated to question what he said.

But now I had second thoughts about marrying so soon. I wanted to know him more, and I was concerned about my father's attitude. At my suggestion, New Star made regular visits to my family after I returned to university, but his efforts to please my father did not work. The two had nothing in common. My father even blamed my mother for accepting presents that New Star brought to my family, and treated his guest with cold indifference. I felt that I owed him all my heart for the unfairness that he suffered, and tried to comfort him in my letters. But when I considered our marriage, the question remained: did I really know him well?

From early 1977, we started to argue in our letters, mainly about the timing of our wedding. I wrote suggesting that we needed to know each other better. He replied that there was no end to knowing a person, and we had reached a reasonable understanding. In his words, it was up to me whether we married next summer, but he also emphasised how much his job transfer and his prospects of improvement depended on my consent. I reminded him that my father might insist on me postponing the wedding until my graduation, as he wanted me to concentrate on my studies. New Star replied that if my studies mattered so much, why had I looked for a boyfriend while at university? Had I wanted to keep him available, for fear that no one would want me after graduation because I would be too old?

As summer approached, I grew more and more anxious about what I was to do. Since both of us were soldiers, both of us needed official permission to marry, and the approval procedure included political checks on the applicants' personal records and family background. Without approval, no couple could register their marriage. In our case the procedure should be straightforward, considering our backgrounds, but the formalities took time. I hesitated to tell my parents about our wedding plans, but without their consent I did not want to make an application.

New Star pressed harder. When he threatened to break up if I did not make a move, I was panicked. How could I cope with the social pressure? Our relationship was common knowledge in the circle of senior officers' families in Beijing. Doctors in the university's teaching hospital whom I had never met would ask about my progress with New Star, and several leaders and colleagues in my former division wrote to make the same inquiry. Our break-up would attract damaging speculations. In my experience, it was only women who lost when a relationship ended: they would either be blamed as the cause, or despised for having been abandoned. I had suffered enough from malicious gossip and rumours, and wanted a quiet private life.

But what dismayed me was the fact that I had lost my virginity to New Star: it made me feel powerless to oppose him. Although the Cultural Revolution claimed to destroy old traditions, it never touched the attitudes towards women's chastity. Through the history of a former Ba-yi pupil, I knew what would happen if we split. Some years ago, this girl had had an affair with a married colleague, and her life had been disgraced ever since. Wherever she worked, the story pursued her. Having lost her reputation, she had little chance of promotion or job training, and enormous difficulties in finding a marriage partner. Both her career and her personal life were severely damaged. I treasured my reputation, and was determined never to repeat the humiliation and discrimination I had suffered while at middle school. I had fought so long to create a good future for myself. Now I must protect what I had created.

I finally wrote to my parents asking for their consent to my marriage. My mother agreed. When prompted, my father wrote later: 'We don't want to interfere, so the decision is yours. But I am concerned about your possible changes after marriage, whether you can complete your studies, and keep your high aspirations and indomitable spirit . . .'

Having received his letter, I submitted my application to the university authority, which was like making a marriage announcement. Within days, the news had reached most students in my year.

Later, New Star told me that he never intended to break up, and had only made his threat to reverse my disagreement. I felt hurt by his trick. While the approval formalities progressed, we continued to argue, complain and blame one another in our letters.

Meanwhile, my father's work still troubled him. According to his diary, he still faced strong opposition among the studio's leadership. During the past campaign against Deng Xiaoping, he was accused of having sided with Deng. Now that the Cultural Revolution was over, he was attacked again for being aligned with the Gang of Four. To make things worse, he got no backing from the leadership of the General Political Department, no matter how hard he worked, and how much he achieved.

A national campaign had been launched against the Gang of Four, aiming to purge the remnants of the gang inside the Party, government and armed forces. Once again, a political initiative was used as a weapon in struggles for power. In the People's Liberation Army, the General Political Department became a major focus of the campaign. Jiang Qing's involvement in this department dated back to 1966, when she was invited by Lin Biao to convene the forum on literature and art for the armed forces. In 1975, Zhang Chunqiao, one of the Gang of Four, was appointed director of the department and after his arrest it continued to be run by deputy directors left over from his time. They therefore felt particularly vulnerable during the new campaign.

According to my father, some of his superiors feared that he knew too much about their role under Zhang Chunqiao. The Ba-yi Film Studio was one of the few institutions in the armed forces to which Jiang Qing always paid close attention. In the past, my father had shown his disagreement with instructions that came from her side. Knowing his outspoken character and commitment to Party principles, these deputies felt that he might give information against them, and decided to get rid of him. In his diary for 13 February 1977, my father wrote: 'A work team was assigned to the studio by the General Political Department.' During its mission, which lasted many months, the team's status was like an envoy's in imperial days, with power to investigate and sort out problems. Its presence showed official disapproval of my father's work, and placed him in a powerless position.

On 22 February 1977, my mother wrote to me: 'When reporting his work to leaders of the General Political Department ten days ago, your father was criticized again. He was very upset, and decided to return to the Beijing Military Region. Next day, he visited Major-General Geng [New Star's father] with his request. Geng made no objection . . . But two days later, New Star came to talk to me about obstacles to your father's posting in the region. It seems that Geng found it difficult to help.' At that time, Major-General Geng was in charge of senior appointments for the military region, which put him in a more powerful position than the other deputy political commissars. He was also one of the few leaders in the region who had worked with my father before the Cultural Revolution.

Soon after he consented to my marriage in April 1977, my father's view of Major-General Geng started changing rapidly. During the Cultural Revolution, Geng had overseen the cases of politically suspect senior officers. Many of the victims now rehabilitated blamed him for their misfortunes, and various other senior officers felt sidelined by him in their recent careers. At first my father dismissed these allegations, but as the stories accumulated, his previously good opinion of Geng began to waver, especially after his own recent experience. After nearly a decade of persecution, my father felt bitter, not only to have had to leave the Beijing Military Region, but to have been pushed into the minefield of the Ba-yi Film Studio. In contrast, Tang had regained his power in the armoured forces, and hangers-on of his like Mercy Ocean had been promoted. After all his lies and deceit, Tang had achieved his goal of displacing my father, and no one had paid for the injuries done to him. Considering Geng's key position in the region, my father felt that he must bear responsibility both for his past and for his present troubles.

My mother disagreed. She doubted that Major-General Geng would have joined or supported Tang. In her mind, Geng was a typical yes-man who would never oppose decisions made by others. This was why he could stay safe for so many years while the military leadership kept changing. New Star told me that his father was considered a 'lao-hao-ren' – one who tried never to give offence. My mother was not unfamiliar with such characters. She did not expect Geng to oppose a decision to persecute my father, once it was voiced by some powerful faction. Had he done so, he could not have survived the repercussions. Likewise, there was no surprise in Geng's compliance with the decision to assign my father to the film studio. Tang was too highly connected for Geng to dare offend him by offering my father a job in the Beijing Military Region. Nevertheless, she did not count Geng as a trouble-maker, because he did not initiate persecutions.

As summer approached, information reached military circles in Beijing about the reorganization of the armed forces. Restored to his position as chief of the General Staff, Deng Xiaoping appointed General Yang Yong, then commander of the Xin-jiang Military Region, as his deputy. Till the onset of the Cultural Revolution, General Yang had commanded the Beijing Military Region, and supported my father. When Yang's troubles started and my father was imprisoned, one of the charges laid against him was being Yang Yong's favourite colleague. It was said that during the years of General Yang's ordeal, President Kim Il Sung of North Korea tried to help him through diplomatic channels, and made a personal appeal to Mao Zedong. During the Korean War, General Yang was commander-in-chief of the 'Chinese People's Volunteers', and became a good friend of Kim II Sung. A few years back, shortly after General Yang was released, my father had visited him in Beijing and was warmly received. The news of his appointment heartened my father. He expected to be treated with justice by his former superior, and hoped for a last opportunity to improve his political career.

According to New Star, his father and General Yang were a pair of 'yuan-jia', natural opponents, and never got on well even during the Long March. Both were born in the same year, but Yang Yong had joined the Red Army two years earlier than Geng. Regarded as one of the most talented soldiers in the Red Army, Yang Yong was highly praised by Mao Zedong throughout the war. The two young commanders often quarrelled, and Geng resented what he saw as his rival's arrogance.

During the Cultural Revolution, General Yang suffered imprisonment, humiliation and torture. He was brought to many denunciation rallies, some of them held in Beijing's largest football stadium, the Workers' Stadium, and attended by more than one hundred thousand people. Next to him were other leading figures, such as Senior General Luo Ruiqing, chief of the General Staff before the Cultural Revolution. Senior General Luo was always carried in a big basket, due to a serious injury to his left leg, after he tried to commit suicide by leaping from the top of a building. Each of the victims wore a 'dunce's cap' – often a rubbish basket covered in white paper and inscribed with abusive slogans – and was forced into the 'jet-plane' position. On one occasion, General Yang found Major-General Geng sitting in the front row of the platform alongside the rally organizers, and joining the chant of: 'Down with the counter-revolutionary Yang Yong!' According to New Star, Yang Yong had never forgotten that picture. My father heard that before he took his new appointment, General Yang had openly expressed his resentment against Geng. If I married New Star, it could damage my father's standing with a potential ally.

Shortly before I returned home, my father said to my mother: 'We can't let our daughter marry Geng's son, you must help me to convince her.' My mother was shocked. Since I had never mentioned my misgivings about New Star, she only knew that we were deeply in love. Approval of our marriage had been granted. Relatives and friends had started to prepare wedding presents for us. 'It might be too late,' she replied. 'Why didn't you speak out earlier?' 'I didn't know Geng well before,' Father said. 'It isn't too late since they are still unmarried.' Mother just shook her head in disbelief. In her mind, I was a reasonable and very kind person with a strong character, not likely to bow to my father's wish. The strains between my father and Geng were a matter for the older generation, and ought to remain there. 'Why don't you believe me?' Father was getting angry. Mother did not argue, as she knew that he would not listen. Her views would only increase his anger and damage his health.

On 25 July 1977, I returned home for the second summer holiday. On the following two evenings, my father spent hours trying to convince me not to marry before finishing my course. I was surprised by what he said about the pressures in the studio, such as his feeling of 'du-re-ru-nian' – 'days wear on like years'. My mother had written about the problems he faced at work, but I had no idea that things were so desperate. He also talked about General Yang's appointment, and the possible risk to his relationship with the General if I married now. 'Please give me two years' extra time by postponing your wedding,' he pleaded, 'to give me the chance to improve my situation.' Even today, I can see his awkward expression, and the way he avoided my eye. Knowing his toughness and pride, I was moved by his manner, and felt sorry for his plight.

But on the other hand, I was not fully convinced by his words. Once the Cultural Revolution was over, I always thought that everything would turn out right, including my parents' political future. When so many purged officials were being rehabilitated, why did my father insist on the

political troubles he faced? Was he genuinely unlucky, or just too sensitive about his treatment? By now, I knew how touchy he could be,
through his clashes with my brothers and me. Also, it was hard for me
to believe that an honourable Communist like General Yang would
desert my father just because I married the son of his political opponent.
So I felt that my father might be exaggerating the harm that my marriage
might do. Nevertheless, I agreed to postpone my wedding, as I was
always willing to help my father. For my own sake too, I wanted a slower
tempo.

Following my return, New Star resumed his daily visits, using the
time off granted to a future husband. Now, he was gentle and caring
again. He looked very upset when I suggested that for the sake of my
studies we should wait, and I felt so sympathetic that I soon forgot my
earlier disappointment in him. Every day, he brought more news about
the pressures for him to marry. His parents expected to discuss the
wedding arrangements with me, but my father forbade me to visit
them. While New Star was considering postponement, we agreed to
tell his parents that I was ill and unable to visit them. Three days
passed, and they began to grow suspicious. Meanwhile, they were
receiving telephone calls inquiring about the wedding from their
friends, relatives and colleagues. One day, a group of New Star's colleagues embarrassed his parents by visiting their home in a minibus,
bringing presents and congratulations for our wedding. Afterwards, his
father told him furiously: 'Don't you dare to visit that family again!
They are intellectuals and look down on us country bumpkins!' New
Star told me that his father's education had stopped at primary school,
so he regarded my parents as intellectuals. Due to his anger, Major-
General Geng fell ill at work next day and was sent home urgently.

I felt caught between my father's demands and New Star's, especially
when I heard that my silence had caused his father's illness. But I still
tried to convince New Star to accept a postponement. On the fourth
day after my return, my mother inquired about my plans. 'Do you know

what will happen after your wedding is postponed?' she asked when I told her. 'Your relationship with New Star would be over, which is what your father hopes.' I immediately flared up in anger. Deeply hurt by the feeling that my father had cheated me, I decided to visit New Star's parents and discuss the wedding arrangements.

In the evening of 29 July, my father called me to his room. My mother was also there, and feeling apprehensive. After stalling for some time, he told me how he had changed his attitude: 'Geng is a bad man. I can't let my daughter marry into his family, so you must give up the idea. Also, I don't think that fellow is good enough for you.' That was the first I knew about his hostility to Major-General Geng. I was stunned, and then my anger grew. It was my father who had introduced New Star and told me that Geng was a decent person. Now it was him again who ordered me to break up on the eve of our wedding, because he now disliked Geng. If he felt that New Star was not good enough for me, why choose him in the first place? How could he behave so irresponsibly? Did he have any respect for my personal life?

I disagreed with my father's new view, because I had respect for Major-General Geng through my own contact. Therefore, I thought that Father's request was made purely to keep up his status with General Yang, which increased my anger further. Ever since the start of the Cultural Revolution in 1966, my personal life had been dominated by my parents' political circumstances. I was powerless to plan my future, or to enjoy a normal and happy family life. Now, a new era had started. My parents were rehabilitated. Why should my personal life still be sacrificed? From what my father said, it looked as if Major-General Geng might be out of favour soon, and that made it all the more unacceptable for me to split with New Star.

As the conversation continued, I struggled for words, and for control of my emotions. Finally, my father lost patience and asked me to make a choice: marry New Star or be his daughter. Faced with his threat, I lost control and poured out my resentment: 'Have you ever considered interests of mine? How could you mix my marriage with your politics? Do you want me to be a victim of your politics?' Under my tears and anger, my father's face turned pale, which panicked my mother and me, and she asked me to leave his room. That night, doctors from the studio's clinic were called in, to treat his high blood pressure and cardiac problems. I could not sleep that night, and made several attempts to see him again, which he refused. Next morning, there was no improvement in his condition, and he was admitted to hospital.

From that moment, I faced increasing pressure for a quick decision. My wedding was scheduled for 1 August 1977, my twenty-sixth birthday, but it was already 30 July when my father was admitted to hospital. They intended to keep him there for at least a month, but there were fewer than four weeks left of my summer holiday. New Star kept bringing me news about his family's preparations for the wedding. It was too late to change. At that time, the deepest worry I had was that he would break with me if I still insisted on postponement – a consequence I could not afford, having lost my virginity to him. Torn in these opposite directions, I cried to my mother to express my frustration. She understood, and thought that my father had withdrawn his demand, since he told her on his way to hospital: 'I won't intervene again. They will just do whatever they want.' On 31 July, Mother consulted our relatives in Beijing for advice; everyone said that we should get married and called my father's behaviour unreasonable. They suggested that my mother should attend our wedding on behalf of both my parents.

My father's diary for 1 August 1977 reads: 'Geng visited me in hospital this morning with his wife, telling me about the wedding scheduled in the afternoon . . . I don't want to intervene again, and will not attend the wedding either. She [my mother] arrived with the children, including that bad girl. Felt terribly irritated, and sent them [my siblings and me] out . . .' Years later, I discovered that since that day my father had called me 'that bad girl', 'that bad creature' or 'that girl' in his diary, rather than use my name. According to my mother, he said nothing against my wedding to Geng and his wife, and made no objection to the family's attending my wedding.

The wedding ceremony was simple. In the afternoon, members of the two families and their relatives, apart from my father and invalid grandmother, gathered for a dinner in Major-General Geng's house. It was a miserable occasion for me. As my father's favourite child, I had always dreamed that he would attend my wedding and share my happiness. But now, he was not there and I was not happy. I blamed myself for his illness, and felt guilty about having my wedding when he was in hospital. I kept wondering how to make it up in the future, because I loved my father dearly, so it was hard to focus on the wedding, and the hubbub all around me seemed remote. Much of my attention went to my mother, who was silent and subdued. When she left the crowd quietly, I followed and found her weeping alone in an empty room. 'I hope your father understands what I've been doing,' she said.

In his diary for 6 August 1977, my father wrote: 'She [my mother] came to see me this afternoon . . . I scolded her furiously. She colluded with that bad creature to trick me by sending me to hospital . . .' He accused my mother of plotting with me to send him to hospital to prevent his interfering in my marriage, and complained: 'When I was hovering between life and death, you took our children to enjoy the wedding celebration, and didn't mind at all about my health.' On that day, I also went to visit him. Out in the corridor I could only see my mother, as she sat in an armchair by the open door of his room. While his furious words poured out, she covered her face with her hands and remained quiet. Eventually she saw me standing in the corridor, and came out immediately: 'Your father is still angry. You'd better not see him at the moment.'

Several days later, I went to visit my father again with New Star, and found that he already had a visitor, one of his supporters in the armoured forces, who had acted as one of the matchmakers for my marriage. Ignoring our greeting, Father started a tirade against his persecutors. I remained quiet, so did New Star. The visitor tried to mediate by changing the subject, but it did not divert my father from his anger. After the visitor left, he went straight back to bed and said without looking at us: 'I don't want to see you again! Leave me alone! I asked you to give me two years of extra time by postponing your wedding. Why did you ignore me?' I burst out crying, but did not leave the room, expecting a chance to talk later. Without another word, he got out of bed and left the room. Half an hour later, a doctor arrived with my father's request for us to leave.

Chapter 23

'The Cart will find its Way round the Hill when it Gets There': Disappointment about My Marriage; My Mission to the Sino-Vietnamese War

(August 1977–July 1979)

'The General Political Department has appointed another Political Commissar for the Ba-yi Film Studio as "first hand" leader,' my mother wrote to me on 29 October 1977. 'This morning at half-past six, your father, together with other leaders from the studio, went to meet him at Beijing railway station.' Despite the new appointment, there was no notification of changes in my father's job, as if his existence was officially forgotten. Only five months later was he finally informed about his dismissal. I heard that his successor's previous post had been two or three grades lower than my father's. That day, my father's diary recorded: 'When we left the railway station, staff from the studio took the new Political Commissar's luggage to my car and asked me to get out. Without a car, I had to ask for a lift from the others to get back to the studio.'

A month earlier, my father had returned home, ignoring his doctors' advice, because he was fed up with staying in hospital. As his blood pressure was still unstable, doctors gave him sick leave for several weeks.

Before he recovered, his post had gone to the new arrival. Despite losing his job, he was still entitled to most of the benefits he previously received, such as his salary, house and private staff, but he still felt terribly bitter about the injustice he had suffered at the studio. Except during the Rectification Campaign and the Cultural Revolution, my father had always been valued by the authorities for his ability and political integrity. But at this post, he survived for less than two years, and his future in the General Political Department looked empty. He refused to accept such an end to his political career, and from October 1977 he began to look elsewhere. On 2 December 1977, his diary records: 'Sent the second letter to Yang Yong this afternoon.'

My mother was transferred from the Beijing Planetarium to the Chinese Academy of Sciences in October 1977. Her senior grade had hindered her from finding an appropriate post in Beijing. Vacancies were few, and being a woman made matters worse, as it was normal for men to be given priority. 'My job is still to be decided,' she wrote. 'Since I am a newcomer to the Academy, no one knows me well, so I only have temporary assignments at the moment. Your father and I have never had powerful connections. Wherever we worked, we have always started from the beginning, and immersed ourselves in hard work for the Party. That is our character.' Later, she was appointed deputy director of the Organization Department for the Academy's Party Committee.

As the new deputy chief of the General Staff, from autumn 1977 General Yang Yong started to reshuffle the leadership of the eight large military regions. I knew from New Star's letters that his father had applied for retirement. Major-General Geng was sixty-five, and had suffered from diabetes and cardiac problems in recent years. His senior rank entitled him to privileged living conditions from the Beijing Military Region after his retirement, and no reduction in salary. In China, Beijing was regarded as the best for almost everything – social infrastructure, municipal provision, living facilities, ancient and modern architecture – and the Party and military elites had automatic access to the city's leisure activities. Geng expected to spend his retirement there. Unexpectedly, his application was turned down. Instead, he was appointed as adviser in the Nanjing Military Region, a sign that he was out of favour. For senior officers, it was an unwritten law that transfer from Beijing to the provinces brought promotion, but Geng was passed over. The post of adviser, created in recent years for senior officers from the level of deputy army commander, was regarded as a sinecure, a transitional step before retirement. Considering his age, Geng would have no chance to transfer anywhere else after taking this appointment so he would have to retire in the Nanjing region, unable to return to Beijing because he would have no entitlements there.

According to New Star, his father owed his plight to General Yang Yong. In recent months, the military authorities had met to discuss leadership changes for the large military regions. Yang Yong stated that Geng was unsuitable to remain in the Beijing region, alleging his involvement in the purging of senior officers during the Cultural Revolution, and demanded his transfer. Before the announcement, Geng tried to have the decision changed through his high-level connections, so that he could take retirement in Beijing. Yang Yong refused all pleas, and reported to Deng Xiaoping that his proposal to transfer Geng had been passed.

When he told me about his father's new posting, New Star mentioned the possibility that we might follow his parents to the city of Nanjing, on the lower reaches of the Yangtze River. They wanted us with them, and if we agreed the Nanjing Military Region would arrange our job transfer. New Star had not decided, mainly because he feared that moving to Nanjing might make it very difficult to return to Beijing later on. He did not intend to spend the rest of his life living outside the capital. For me, Nanjing was simply too far from my parents. As a married officer living in a different region, I would only be entitled to a short leave once in every eight years to visit them, and that would give me hardly any opportunity to make peace with my father.

In mid-December 1977, I received an urgent telegram from New Star, calling me home because his parents were critically ill in hospital. Geng's plight had damaged his health, and hence his wife's. At New Star's request, I promised to talk to his father about our decision not to move to Nanjing. His parents' illness became my excuse to apply for leave from the university.

The day after my return to Beijing, I went to visit my parents and grandmother. My mother was still at work, and my father was in his study, so I went to Grandmother's room first. She was overjoyed to see me, and asked the maid to prepare my favourite food for supper, won ton soup. Eventually, I plucked up enough courage to enter my father's study, carrying a basket of fresh oranges from Chongqing as a gift – a rare treat in Beijing in those days. When he saw me, Father was speechless for a while, and made no reply to my greetings. Then his face changed. 'Get out! I don't recognize you as my daughter!' he said, without looking at me. 'Go to your father-in-law now, and don't come back to me again!' My face ran with tears, but I stayed, hoping for another chance to talk. So then he opened his door and called the maid to take me out, and the oranges too. When she heard what had happened, Grandmother just sighed, and tears came to her eyes. While I waited for my mother, I helped to prepare the won ton soup.

As soon as I left his room, my father phoned my mother at her office. 'Come back right now! That daughter of yours is home, she's trying to kill me with rage!' Mother rushed back in a panic. When she heard what had happened, she asked me to leave, for fear that my presence would cause more anger. 'Supper is ready. Please let our girl have some food first!' Grandmother begged. 'This is her home, and she has only just arrived.' My mother's tone was hopeless. 'You should have known that your father does not easily forgive people who have offended him.' It was snowing and dark outside when I left home.

My father was furious with my mother: 'Why did you go straight to your daughter instead of coming to me first?' Beside himself with anger, he condemned me for ingratitude and treachery, and included my mother for supporting me. She could not reply to his shouting, fearing to aggravate his illness, but her heart sank. 'Where is the caring and understanding Mu Xiang I have known for most of my life?' she asked herself. In later years, she often blamed the Cultural Revolution for destroying the harmony of her family, and traced the dreadful changes in my father to the long persecution he suffered.

Before I returned to university in January 1978, Little Auntie and her husband tried to mediate. They believed that my father's anger would cool, because he still loved me dearly. Ever since I was born, I had been his 'zhang-shang-ming-zhu' ('pearl in the palm'), the expression for a beloved daughter, so they thought that his hostility came mainly from his concern at losing face. At that time, Little Auntie was taking sick leave for her cancer treatment, so she managed to visit my father almost every day. When reminded how much I loved him, and how hurt I was feeling, he eventually stopped excoriating me whenever my name was mentioned, and his anger seemed to be melting, which gave Little Auntie and her husband cause to hope. They suggested that I should write to my father to apologize for quarrelling with him about my wedding. If only I could contrive to save his face, they might convince him to give ground.

When I was writing to my father, I reread some of his letters from previous years, remembering our closeness in the past. 'Those grievous years we spent together have been an unforgettable memory,' he wrote on 29 November 1974. 'I remember when you left for the rural settlement . . . In the early morning, you held my hands by the living room door to say goodbye. How innocent and naive you were at that time! How much anxiety and bitterness you had to bear . . . Afterwards, [through] reading your frequent letters . . . I recognized how valuable you are for the family. During the year you spent at home after returning from your village, your company brought so much pleasure to me. You took the whole responsibility of looking after me, cleaning my rooms and cooking for me. You . . . finished all the thick books I recommended, and discussed your reading with me. We went out together, walking round Beijing city, taking photos in Beihai Park . . . We bought some pears at a bus station, and a little peeling knife, and enjoyed the fruit in Jingshan Park . . . At dusk, we returned home to the Western Hill. After you left, I lost all interest in such outings. Last summer, I bound all your letters together, and read them through again . . .'

Now, I was writing to you again, dear Baba. I, too, would never forget those years. I wanted to let you know that my deep love for you was unchanged, and I was still willing to support you, look after you, and share your passion for literature. Did you know how important you had been and would be in my life? Now, all I wanted was your forgiveness.

Several hours after Little Auntie delivered my letter to my father, we met at her home. After a silent pause, she sighed 'I can't understand him,' and I knew that our efforts had failed. After all, my father still refused to forgive me.

Not till decades later did I discover how much my father hated me at that time. According to his diary, he had a sleepless night after seeing me, and composed several poems to voice his anger. In them, I was blamed for seeking higher status and comfort by my marriage. He regretted his 'misjudgment' in the past, and his high expectations. He also condemned Geng for bullying the weak and fearing the strong – his version of Geng's political behaviour during the Cultural Revolution. After the poems, he added: 'In the afternoon of 19 December 1977, that girl returned from Chongqing to visit her sick father-in-law. Several months ago, she made a tearful scene when I suggested delaying her wedding, which made me ill . . . She married on 1 August, intending to drive me to death, and I have been suffering from illness since. Comparing this with her manner to her father-in-law, I could not control my emotion, and succumbed to my illness again . . .'

On the day my letter came, my father also received a reply to his appeal to General Yang Yong. This letter was curt, and signed by Yang Yong's office, not by Yang himself. It rejected my father's request by stating that he must trust the Party; his job was a matter for the General Political Department. Father laid the blame on Yang Yong's response to my marriage. His diary for 24 December 1977 reads: 'Flower [Little Auntie] called, telling me about her conversation with that girl. The letter she wrote recalled many memories, which made me emotional again. But the more the past was mentioned, the more hurt I felt. At the moment, it is still impossible for me to see her again . . .'

In China, the saying for our marriage was 'men-dang-hu-dui' – 'the right door fits the right house', meaning that New Star and I were well matched in social and economic status. It seemed that we had all the advantages envied by millions in our generation: privileged backgrounds, Party membership, good occupations, and high status as young officers. In my university, everyone praised New Star's looks when they saw our photos. It seemed that I could not expect a better husband.

On the eve of our wedding, my mother asked me if I loved New Star. I burst into tears and said: 'I don't know.' During that stormy week before my wedding, I was in turmoil, overwhelmed by the troubles I faced. Pushed to a quick decision about the wedding, I had considered matters such as my career and reputation. I had even defended Major-General Geng against my father's judgement. The only question I did not take time to think about was whether I really loved New Star. When rebelling against my father's manipulation of my personal life, I never asked if I had made the right decision for myself. Both then and later, each time my mother and relatives asked about my main reason for marrying New Star, I answered: 'Because he has been so good to me.' I was captured again by his care and thoughtfulness during the days before the wedding, and full of sympathy for the way my father treated him. One reason that I could not confide was that my lost virginity gave me no other choice.

After the wedding, we only lived together for three weeks before I returned to university. Until my graduation two years later, the only time we met again was my brief return to Beijing due to his parents' illness. During our twenty days' honeymoon in Beijing, I was often in tears. I felt guilty about my father's illness, and feared that he would never forgive me for having my wedding while he was in hospital. At that time, New Star was the only person whom I expected to give me a shoulder to cry on, but I was disappointed by his response. He was annoyed by my father's disapproval, never agreed that our marriage damaged my father's relationship with General Yang Yong, and argued instead that my father had made his family the scapegoat for his failure to curry favour with Yang Yong.

During the honeymoon, I spent most days in my parents' house alone, and only returned to New Star's parents' house in the evening. I found that we had little in common. The long conversations I had so much enjoyed almost stopped, nor did we take an interest in each other's surroundings. My quick reappearance astonished the maid in my parents' house, a middle-aged woman, who told me: 'I've never seen a bride return to her parents' home alone in the early morning after her wedding.'

Now that we were married, I expected New Star's transfer to arrive – the reason he gave for marrying so fast. To my surprise, nothing happened. When I asked why, he always made excuses. I understood his difficulties in finding the proper job, but why had he insisted that his need to move quickly required us to marry in a hurry? If we were going to separate for nearly two years until I graduated, could he not have waited till then? He never gave me a satisfactory answer. In his words, he calculated that once I had lost my virginity, I would have to follow him rather than my father. Having observed other people, he had concluded that the way to catch the girl he fancied was to make love rather than just date her. How stupid and naive I was! Pressured into sex, then tricked into marriage, my own romantic fantasy entrapped me!

New Star also denied having fallen in love at first sight, the story that moved my father and me in the first place. Oh no! What had I done? Everything I thoroughly believed was untrue: his pose of love, his dangerous mission to the earthquake area, his job transfer, and his threat to break up if I refused his wedding plan . . . It was just as he said about my character: that I was too trustful of others. As a result, I had fallen out with my father, the most important person in my life, and my marriage had cost my family dear. My father was turning on everybody, and would not forgive my mother for attending my wedding. Knowing all this made it even harder to trust New Star again, and my resentment grew.

Likewise, shortly after the wedding New Star began to resent my not being meek and obedient, as his ideal wife would be. He complained that I was lazy at home, and that my love of reading was a hobby for 'stinking intellectuals'. My 'careless personal hygiene' often vexed him. Indeed, I have never seen anyone more obsessed with the subject. He refused to drink outside his home, even when visiting my family, except from his own mug, which he brought with him. Now, he hated to kiss me, for fear of contracting diseases. Before the honeymoon was over, I was already irritated by his frequent criticism of my 'dirty' behaviour at home, such as holding steamed buns with my fingers rather than with chopsticks.

Among many more disappointments for New Star was my 'overspending', for instance on writing paper for private letters. In his home, the bandages from his clinic functioned as ropes when he tied his belongings, and unused dressing pads became his cleaning rags. The house he lived in was provided to his father by the armed forces, and he had a well-equipped private bathroom for himself – a real luxury in China to this day. But he brought back wads of unused prescription forms from his clinic, in order to save money on lavatory paper. After the wedding, he was determined to keep our incomes separate, and never let me know how much he had saved. This was to prevent my spending too much money, he explained.

Yet despite my resentment, I did not lose hope for the marriage.

Many people I knew had also married in a hurry, and had just as little chance to get to know their spouse before the wedding. In the armed forces, unmarried officers were only allowed home on leave for twenty days in every second year, but many sought marriage partners at home, so it was normal for them only to meet their future spouses on leave, as arranged by their families, and then to marry on their subsequent leave. Most married officers only had permission for a one month visit home each year, and their spouses had only one month to visit them in their barracks. Therefore many couples had to endure ten months of separation each year. There was a saying, 'xian-jie-hun, hou-lian-ai' (first get married, then fall in love), and I thought that, despite an adverse situation, if both of us worked hard we might also get to know each other better. In the hope that I might discover some good features in him, and hence become happier with him, I tried to overcome my ill-feeling, and discussed our futures seriously.

Before my graduation, I was already concerned about our future careers. The end of the Cultural Revolution had initiated fundamental changes, and yesterday's 'Stinking Ninth Class' were now well respected for their educational attainments and skills. In contrast, the qualifications of the 'worker-peasant-soldier students' were devalued. In my university, staff with that background came under heavy pressures to upgrade. In a wave of career insecurity on campus, most of them worked very hard in their spare time, attending auxiliary training courses or preparing for various examinations, such as for postgraduate studies.

At the beginning of our relationship, I often asked New Star for professional advice, especially since he had already graduated and possessed several years' working experience. But now, as my studies progressed, I could easily spot his lack of training. As one of the earliest 'worker-peasant-soldier students', he had spent only two years on his course, the shortest ever in medical universities, and now regarded as a joke by some of our teaching staff, so he needed to realize what an inadequate medical training he had received, and how it might reflect on his career. Unless we worked hard to improve our qualifications, we would have to rely on family influence to stay in our profession, a solution I disliked, especially in view of our fathers' declining political positions. New Star was already close to thirty; it was high time to make his own efforts towards his future.

New Star took offence at my attitude, and called it 'petty bourgeois fanaticism'. During our arguments, he liked to attack me as 'petty bourgeois' or 'petty intellectual', terms used by Mao Zedong to disparage intellectual or professional backgrounds, as if we were still in that era.

Our letters were getting longer, sometimes six pages at a time, but now they seethed with arguments, quarrels, criticism and blame, erasing the romance and admiration that we used to exchange. But the more we argued, the less we found in common. It seemed that our differences defined us: on morality, attitudes to life and to people, personal interests and general mind-sets . . . And the lack of understanding made things even worse. In one letter, I suggested that more contact with people from the 'Stinking Ninth Class' might teach him something useful. His furious reply asked if I fancied some man from the 'Stinking Ninth'. His letters became unreasonable and insulting, with threats to compel me by violence if I argued in his presence. On 6 October 1977, just two months after the wedding, I wrote to him: 'You will never conquer me with violence! Never! Don't forget that I have my parents' blood, which makes me even stronger . . .'

'I could not get comfort or warmth from your letter,' I wrote on 24 November 1978. 'Honestly speaking, I don't look forward to your letters any more, or to my graduation, because I can't imagine how to live with you in future. There are too many problems between us . . . You'd better stop writing if you just keep cursing me. Your letters always upset me, and each time I take days to recover . . .' By then I had stopped writing to him regularly, fed up with the endless, fruitless quarrels.

New Star was entitled to a month of annual leave to visit his wife, with travel expenses provided, but I refused his repeated requests to visit, using my studies as an excuse, because I had lost interest in seeing him again. He tried to convince me that this was his final chance, because his transfer would soon come through, and leave would be harder to arrange in a new workplace. But now I was unmoved by his story, which was not unfamiliar. I expressed my disbelief about his transfer, and in fact it did not happen.

Eventually, I believed that the marriage had been a mistake for both of us, but clearly divorce was unthinkable. Under Chinese law, it was very unlikely to be granted without the consent of both parties, and I knew that New Star would regard my petition as a humiliating loss of face. In the old days, it was wives who were left by their husbands, never the other way round. Considering New Star's nature, I was afraid of retaliation, perhaps by spreading slanderous stories, if I initiated the divorce. And even if I managed to divorce, how could I bear the social stigma? Although divorce was not unusual among high Party circles, it was still not acceptable in society, especially for women, and the rare cases always attracted attention. I feared the damage to my reputation, and the impact on my career and personal life, because women suffered most. I was haunted by my ordeal in middle school.

For many years past, I had fought to defend my parents from political persecution, and coped with the hardships I faced, but the havoc in my private life was different: I could not tell how to sort it out. As New Star's wife, I found myself powerless to decide my future.

What a hell I had entered! Marriage did not bring me happiness. Just a few months after the wedding, my father lost his job and his approach to General Yang Yong was rebuffed. All the things I would not believe had come true. My mother and Little Auntie tried to convince me that Yang Yong's snub to my father also derived from other factors, such as Tang's hostile influence, and the lack of suitable vacancies. Though his work had been appreciated by Yang Yong, my father lacked personal contacts with him, and his approach in writing was ill chosen. 'Your father is too proud to pay personal visits to Yang Yong, or to flatter him, unlike others nowadays when asking favours from powerful figures,' Little Auntie commented. 'That makes it hard for him to get what he wants.' Nevertheless, I grew to believe that my marriage had done harm to my father's political career.

Two decades later, I wonder whether things might have happened differently had my parents adopted a different approach to forestalling the marriage. For example, they could have been patient and straightforward from the start, discussed their reservations about New Star with me, and suggested thinking through the relationship. As I trusted and respected them, I would have taken notice, and might have been more cautious. Unfortunately, my father's rudeness to New Star only pushed me further into the relationship. When I finally refused to defer the marriage, it was largely because I felt that he was putting his political career before my personal life.

I believe my mother regretted her own and my father's inadequate responses to their children. Neither of them had much experience of ordinary family life. When they left home to join the revolution, they were teenagers. As lifelong Communists, they always put the interests of the Party before their family's. After establishing their family, they had been engaged in busy and responsible jobs that left very little time for family matters. As a result, they paid hardly any attention to essential issues such as adjusting discipline over the long period of growing up, or finding ways to understand and communicate with their different children, each with different needs.

As graduation approached, my worries for my future intensified. Where was I going to work? How could I live with New Star? Ideally, I wanted to work in Beijing, and be close to my parents. For years they had been my oasis. No matter how severe the situation was, as long as I thought about my parents, there would be peace and hope. 'I often think back to the wonderful time I spent at home with those pleasant surroundings and books,' I wrote to them on 18 December 1972, before I went to university. 'Baba's talking to me was like showing magnificent pictures, which brought many beautiful dreams . . .' In the past, my brief spells at home had become real festivals in my life. My mother often joked: 'As soon as you're home, your father seems recovered from his illness.'

Now, all my years of hard work were about to reach their goal: soon after my graduation, I would be qualified as a medical doctor. But where was my oasis? My father had disowned me, and kicked me out of his house, so unless I lived with New Star I would be homeless. In China, accommodation was normally provided by people's workplace. Before I found a job, I had nowhere to live. Even if I could get one straight away, I had to join the long waiting list for accommodation, which could easily take years. As graduation neared, everyone was packing to go home, but I had no idea where to send my luggage to. I had no desire to live with New Star, but no alternative.

At university, my classmates used to joke about my suffering from 'lovesickness' because I lost weight rapidly after the wedding, and they thought that I was pining for New Star. For a long time, I could hardly eat or sleep, I felt so troubled. But I could not tell anyone the truth, for fear that it would reach the campus gossips. One day, I let slip to a female student that my marriage had been the biggest mistake in my life. Afterwards, my remark was passed on to New Star in Beijing, and he raised it several times in the following years. He seemed to know every-thing I did, despite the thousands of kilometres between Beijing and Chongqing.

In the university, students were divided by gender into squads that set the shape of our lives. For most of the four-year course, I shared a dor-mitory with nine other female students from my squad, and this collective way of living also extended to attending lectures, eating meals, and even going to cinemas or theatres. Among the female students, some showed intense curiosity in the others' personal lives, so I tried hard to keep mine private. I knew that almost all our mail passed through several other hands before it reached us, and though it was forbidden to open other people's letters, anyone could recognize the handwriting on the envelope. When reading his letters, and afterwards, I had to control my expression, so that no one would guess at my feelings.

During that period, I was growing more and more lonely and depressed. Since my siblings and I were not close, I could not lean on their support. Eventually, I quarrelled with my mother. In the past, I had sympathized with her difficult situation in the family, and felt grateful when she supported me over the wedding. But when I visited the house in the winter following my wedding, she asked me to leave, so as not to anger my father, and complained about the problems my wedding had caused her. I was left feeling deeply hurt, and abandoned by my family. I often felt suffocated by having no way to express my desperation, and I was losing control of my emotions. Back at the university that winter, I blamed my mother in several long letters for what she had done, and then stopped writing regularly. My angry letters often reduced her to tears, as she felt that she was unjustly treated by both sides in the confrontation between my father and me.

On 30 May 1978, I wrote in my diary: 'Life has been meaningless for me. It has lost its attraction, and the one narrow path remaining would lead me to death.' During that period, the idea of suicide came to my mind. If there was no end to the unhappiness in my life, I would rather die. But I refused to resign myself. For twelve years, I had weathered the disasters that afflicted my family and myself, so it was not my way to give up easily. I trusted the proverb 'che-dao-shan-qian-bi-you-lu' – 'the cart will find its way round the hill when it gets there': things will sort themselves out when the time comes. So I kept on telling myself that this was not the end of the world, I must wait and see. Even unaided, I could still find a future for myself. I focused on my studies, and often worked till midnight, which helped to take my mind off personal cares. In the final examinations, my mark was one of the highest.

In summer 1978, the headline news in all the national media was an anti-Chinese campaign in Vietnam. Almost every day, the major newspapers were crammed with appalling photos and reports showing how ethnic Chinese were being persecuted by the Vietnamese authorities. For months, a flood of refugees came pouring over the border into China. Having walked for days or weeks from their homes, many carried their few belongings, the old leaned on walking sticks, and the babies were held in the adults' arms. The refugees reported that they were no longer allowed to carry on their business or professions in Vietnam, and many had been forced to leave their homes and had their property and most other possessions confiscated. Objectors were arrested, jailed, or even tortured. The Chinese media also condemned the frequent trans-border incursions by Vietnamese troops, and the casualties and damage they were causing. Late in 1978 the Vietnamese launched a full-scale military attack on Cambodia against Pol Pot's Khmer Rouge regime, and occupied Phnom Penh on 7 January 1979. The Chinese government accused the Vietnamese of being an aggressor backed by the Soviet Union.

During that period, many people I met could not understand what had happened between China and Vietnam. Only a few years before, during the Vietnam War, the two countries had been on close terms, calling each other 'comrades and brothers'. Even during the chaos of the Cultural Revolution, China never ceased its support for Vietnam against the USA. Though suffering from widespread starvation, and endemic financial crisis, throughout the Vietnam War the Chinese government provided free economic aid, including rice and industrial products, as well as military equipment. All of a sudden, the 'comrades and brothers' were enemies, and ready to go to war.

In December 1978, Chinese troops near Chongqing started to move into the troubled border areas. Chongqing was involved in the

Sino-Vietnamese War from the very beginning, because of its closeness to Yunnan – together with Guangxi, one of the Chinese provinces on the border with Vietnam. On 14 February 1979, China declared war on Vietnam. The announcement shocked the whole nation, because it was China's largest military commitment since Korea in the early 1950s.

Several days after the war broke out, the students in my year were called to an urgent meeting where we learned that we were to be posted to the front. It happened in the evening, just a few hours after we finished our finals. By then, news had already reached the campus about the unexpectedly heavy casualties taken. The university's three teaching hospitals, with a capacity of over 1,600 beds, were already packed with wounded transferred from the front, and a number of the city's civilian hospitals had also been mobilized. We heard that another 8,000 wounded were still stuck at the front in Yunnan, waiting to be moved to the rear. In response to the strong demand for medical staff, about 500 graduates-to-be from my year were assigned to the front by the General Logistics Department.

We were told nothing in advance about the destination, length and nature of the mission, but everybody had to write a will, which would be left at the university. In mine, I named various members of my family, but not New Star, as beneficiaries. I did not mention any specific person as executor, since I felt that I was no longer attached to anyone in the world. 'Dear ones, I am not afraid of death,' I wrote. 'Please do not be too grieved if I die. My only wish is for you to have better lives in future . . .' When writing the will, I felt quite calm and relieved, because I had no regret about leaving the world, and death could only free me from the troubles I faced.

On 25 February 1979, we left Chongqing from a small railway station outside the city, which was already cordoned off by armed soldiers. During the two days' journey to Kunming, the provincial capital of Yunnan, I shared a goods wagon with about forty other female students. It had huge sliding doors on both sides, and the few windows were very small. Unless the doors were open, it was dark inside. Before the train departed, a university officer helped us to prise up a wooden floorboard in a corner, for use as a lavatory. At night, a kerosene lamp hung from the ceiling provided a flickering light.

For most of the journey, our train crossed remote mountain areas, and passed through countless bridges and tunnels. In China, building and maintaining the railway from Sichuan to Yunnan was often seen as a costly and unprofitable project, because many of the areas it served, such as Guizhou province, were known for their poverty, sparse population and harsh natural conditions. Since my childhood, I had heard it said of Guizhou: 'There is no single piece of flat ground larger than three fens [200 square metres], no clear sky that lasts more than three days, and no one with more money than three pennies.' During the Vietnam War, this railway played a vital role carrying aid and military supplies to Vietnam, Laos and Cambodia. Now, military trains carried troops, heavy weapons and vehicles in the same direction, but turned against Vietnam.

Once a day, our train stopped at a temporary military service station where we had a short break, with hot food, drinking water, and washing facilities. These halts were located in small towns where public buildings such as schools, government offices and even cinemas or theatres were converted into huge temporary canteens. The towns always thronged with troops in transit, and the service stations opened twenty-four hours every day. Wherever we went, we were the centre of attention, as very few servicewomen went to the front. Through the others we met in the stations, I learned that these troops came from various parts of southwest China. Some told me that they were bound for Cambodia to support Pol Pot's Khmer Rouge guerrillas, but had no idea how they would get to their jungle camps.

During the day, I loved to sit in the wagon, gazing through the open doors at the beautiful spring scenery of the Yunnan–Guizhou plateau. The further south we travelled, the more hills were covered by dense and colourful vegetation. Once in a while, a small village emerged out of nowhere, inhabited mostly by ethnic minorities. During the war, many of the villagers came to the railway every day and scavenged food thrown out from the passing trains. I was struck by the women's bright costumes, with their short close-fitting jackets and long wide pleated skirts. They reminded me of my happy childhood in the Ba-yi School. All through kindergarten, I became used to this style of dress, because I was often chosen to perform solo folk dances on special occasions, and I revelled in the camera-flash and applause. How happy I was at that time! How wonderful the world appeared! Even just four years ago, my life seemed full of hope and happiness. My family had been restored to privileged status, and I had achieved what I longed for: joining the Communist Party, promotion as an officer, and studying medicine at university. Now, it had all turned upside-down. The Cultural Revolution was over. Why did my ordeal continue?

At the front, I was assigned to Military Hospital No. 58, together with about twenty other female students. This was as close to the fighting areas as servicewomen were now allowed, about 200 kilometres away from the border with Vietnam. In the first few days of the war, some local female medical personnel had accompanied their units to Vietnamese territory and been captured there. Chinese forces had pursued and attacked the convoy that took these girls away, and eventually rescued them. After that, female servicewomen were kept out of the fighting areas. It was routine practice for hospital staff to assemble in the evening to listen to the headquarters' bulletin from the front. No one could say what might happen in the next few days. If Vietnamese troops crossed into China, our hospital's location could become a battlefield within hours.

When we arrived at the hospital, several all-male medical teams had already been dispatched to the fighting areas, so there were hardly any young male doctors left. The hospital had a capacity of 500 beds, but had admitted almost 1,000 wounded. The special ward where I worked had originally been established during the Vietnam War, to provide free treatment or convalescence for the Vietnamese wounded. Its staff included an officer who had previously worked as interpreter for these 'wai-bin', foreign guests. In those days, the ward had enjoyed privileged status, and was better equipped and supplied than those that dealt only with Chinese troops. These Vietnamese patients were also granted free trips to Kunming and other places, to visit specialists or go sightseeing and shopping. Their food allowance, also financed by the military budget in China, was several times higher than the ration for a Chinese patient.

From talking with my patients, I heard that many Vietnamese officers had received training in China during the Vietnam War, so that it was not uncommon now for opposing commanders to find that they knew each other personally. The Vietnamese were also familiar with the actual military strength of their opposition. When up against the Chinese 13th Army, they often gave ground because they knew that it was one of the most powerful forces in China. On the Chinese side, it was common knowledge that the Vietnamese 316A Division were crack troops. A number of its officers had once been privileged patients in the ward where I now worked. Most of the Vietnamese military equipment – weapons, vehicles and even uniforms – had been provided by China to fight against the USA. So my patients often lamented that having spent several billions of yuan (3.21 yuan equalled £1) on aid to Vietnam during the Vietnam War, China had armed an enemy.

My university colleagues and I worked as medical doctors, and were kept extremely busy from the day of arrival. At the busiest times, I was responsible for about sixty wounded. The daily routine inspection often took me a whole morning, and then I needed to write prescriptions, change dressings, and assist at surgical operations. Then when everything was over, I spent more hours updating my patients' medical records. Just to sit down properly for a meal or for a short break became a luxury. Apart from three or four hours' sleep every day, and snatching meals in the canteen, I practically lived in the ward.

The most hectic time was when an express train carrying wounded arrived, and I would join a team assigned to collect them at the nearest railway station, about 40 kilometres away. Since the trains only travelled at night, in case of air attacks, we had to get up in the small hours. When we arrived, before dawn, the station was already heavily guarded. In the area south of Kunming, including our own, the railway gauge was narrower than the general national standard, so the carriages I saw here were smaller than in most parts of China. Each of the express trains was converted into a mobile medical station, and camouflaged with branches. Inside most of the carriages there were two rows of narrow beds alongside each wall, with a single aisle just wide enough to walk through.

The moment the trains stopped, the reception squad went to work. Our orders were for the wounded to be transferred to the waiting vehicles within an hour. Since most of them could not walk, we always helped the stretcher teams of able-bodied soldiers to carry them. It was all I could do to manage my end of the stretcher. Just halfway through to the waiting vehicles, my arm muscles would start shaking uncontrollably, and I often feared that I might drop the stretcher. I learned from the others to hang a thick rope round my neck, with each end looped over a stretcher handle, so that my body took some of the strain. The return journey took almost two hours, because the fully loaded vehicles had to almost crawl over the bumpy mountain road. These vehicles were canvas-topped military trucks camouflaged with foliage. For lack of seating, everyone had to sit or lie on a layer of dry sand, about half a metre deep inside each truck, to reduce the discomfort to the wounded. Since many of the arrivals had too few warm clothes to protect them from the spring wind, they shivered with cold in the early morning. I often provided my own warm clothes, including the jacket I wore for the trip, to those most in need.

Through patients in my ward, I heard a lot of news about the front. A battalion commander told me that his regiment had been assigned to the spearhead position. At midnight on the day the war broke out, his unit crossed the Hong River, the border between China and Vietnam, in small boats. By the time the Vietnamese woke up, it was already four o'clock next morning, and the whole Chinese regiment had arrived. On the first day of the war, the Chinese side took heavy casualties, caused mainly by the Vietnamese artillery and by land mines, but the situation started to improve on the following day, especially when China's mine-clearing tanks went into action. The battalion commander had had his feet injured by shrapnel, despite the special shoes he wore, with steel-plated soles. During the Vietnam War, the Vietcong had become expert at using 'punji sticks', lengths of sharpened bamboo hidden in traps in the ground, against pursuing enemies. Now, all Chinese soldiers were issued with reinforced shoes.

Another casualty in my ward was a cheerful soldier not yet out of his teens. My colleagues and I nicknamed him 'Little Fatty', because of his plump cheeks and boyish smile. A former middle school pupil from a city in Henan province, he had joined the army less than a year before, and worked as a messenger because of his better education. During the first week of the war, his unit passed through many evacuated villages and small towns in Vietnam. Soon, the bag he carried was full of cameras looted from empty houses and intended as presents to his family or friends. Later, his company had its food supplies cut off for a week. When they resumed, the starving Little Fatty threw away all the cameras and stuffed his bag with food. The very next day he was injured, and then transferred back to China. He frequently grumbled: 'Had I known I'd be injured the following day, I would never have given up the cameras for food.'

My most painful memory is of a severely wounded soldier, Heaven Happiness, who came from a peasant family in Sichuan. He too was very young and had joined the army just a few months before the war. Flying shrapnel had pierced the back of his neck, paralysing his arms, legs and most of his body. Under fire from the Vietnamese, the Chinese rescue teams were unable to reach his position, so he lay in the muddy water of a paddy field for nearly two days without treatment. By the time he reached the hospital, his wound was infected, which delayed the removal of the shrapnel. When the operation eventually took place, it revealed damage to his spinal cord, which meant that he had little hope of recovering from the paralysis. I could not bring myself to tell him, but he recognized the truth through my silence. Afterwards, this young man became extremely quiet, which made me anxious. Despite my work load, I paid him more attention, and found time to talk to him regularly, trying to cheer him up. Due to his paralysis, he suffered from chronic constipation, but was too shy to complain. None of the conventional treatments worked, and in the end I decided to use my fingers to remove the solid matter. Using surgical gloves, I had to probe very gently, because some of the excrement had a rock-hard texture, whose sharp edges might damage the surrounding soft tissues. When it was done, almost two hours later, my face was damp with sweat, and his was bathed in tears.

Through working in the front, I saw many healthy young servicemen brought in permanently disabled, and some even died. As I began to understand that nothing in the world could be more cruel and bloody, and cause more human tragedies, than war, I longed to communicate with my father, and pass on what I thought. I found that his novel, *Autumn in Jinyang*, was popular with the wounded in my ward. Some of the staff expressed envy at my having such a writer for a father. Their friendly words were painful, since they only recalled our estrangement.

Having occupied several border towns in Vietnam, by mid-March 1979 the Chinese government had declared a cease-fire and withdrawn its troops from Vietnamese territory. According to the official media, China had taught the intended lesson to the Vietnamese aggressor. After the cease-fire, my companions and I stayed in the Military Hospital No. 58 for another month, until most of the wounded had recovered.

While waiting for trains back to Chongqing, we spent a week in Kunming, which was still full of troops in transit back to their barracks.

The local authorities provided us with comfortable lodgings and heavily subsidized food. In China, Kunming is known as the City of Perpetual Spring, with its many ancient temples, beautiful lakes, and the famous Western Hill. The Kunming Military Region organized sightseeing trips around the city, and films and shows in the evenings. Again, the female students from my university attracted strong attention for their rarity among the forces returning from the front. We were often exempted from buying tickets on buses, and given free admission to sightseeing spots.

The train to Chongqing was still made up of goods wagons, but the atmosphere was totally different. At each stop, we were given a welcome organized by the local authority. The platform was decorated with colourful flags, loudspeakers broadcast stirring music, and gongs and drums rang out. While huge crowds chanted slogans to welcome our triumphant return, we were ceremonially greeted by leading figures from the local Party committee, government and armed forces. The most impressive reception took place in Chongqing, organized by our university and the local authorities. From the front gate of the university, crowds lined both sides of the street for about a kilometre. Almost all the students and staff were mobilized, cheering and clapping, waving flags, and shouting slogans.

After the cease-fire, the government in Beijing assigned a large delegation, which included military leaders and provincial governors all over China, to entertain the troops returned from the war. The delegation also brought many of China's top singers, dancers and actors to give free performances to the troops. Soon, a wave of enthusiasm swept the nation, as authorities, institutions and enterprises at every local level started to organize their own displays of support. Letters from all over China flooded into the Military Hospital No. 58, together with shoals of parcels, with donations including food, clothes, shoes and stationery, contributed to show people's appreciation of the sacrifice made by the wounded to the nation. For several weeks after our return, we were bombarded with gifts, and invited to all sorts of entertainments in Chongqing. For the first time in my life, I was treated like a heroine.

On 27 July 1979, almost two months after my graduation, an article about our mission appeared in the *Liberation Army Daily*, China's second largest national newspaper, and mentioned my own work. Later, this article was transmitted nationally on the Central People's Broadcasting Station. But by then I was in no mood to enjoy the glory, caught up in the troubles that affected my life and my family's.

Chapter 24

Family in Turmoil:
My Parents' Marriage Crisis

(1978–1979)

Early in 1978, the General Political Department granted my father one year's leave to carry on his writing. After the Cultural Revolution, *Autumn in Jinyang* was reprinted, no longer condemned as a 'poisonous weed'. Bo Yibo, the former vice-premier, was rehabilitated, together with other members of the 'Renegade clique of sixty-one' formerly indicted by Kang Sheng and Jiang Qing. Bo Yibo became a senior statesman after 1978, and the anti-Japanese organization he headed during the Sino-Japanese War, the Alliance of Sacrificing Ourselves to Save the Nation, on which the stories in my father's book were based, was regarded as a revolutionary organization again. In response to readers' demands, my father's publisher urged him to write the continuation of his novel. When the Cultural Revolution started, he had finished the second volume, and nearly all of the third, but most of his manuscripts were lost when our house was repeatedly raided, so now he had to rewrite them.

He decided to continue his work in Taiyuan, the provincial capital of Shanxi, which was an important location in his book. It was twelve years since he had been summoned to Beijing urgently from Taiyuan in May 1966, and since then his writing had been interrupted by events. In Shanxi, *Autumn in Jinyang* had made his name well known. He knew a lot of leading figures there, since many had worked in the same Communist base before 1949, and most of the troops stationed in Shanxi were commanded by the Beijing Military Region.

'Your father left Beijing with a broken heart,' my mother told me nineteen years later. After losing his job in the film studio, the few posts he was offered were located in the provinces, and some were at a lower level, so he grew to believe that his rivals were still working against him, and turned down all of these assignments. Though he saw no future in the General Political Department, he had nowhere else to go. For months after he lost his job, he remained at home, and in a terrible mood, so my mother hoped that the move would help him to revive. Unfortunately, she was unable to accompany him, having only just started her new job at the Academy of Sciences.

Through my father's letters from Taiyuan, my mother knew that he was doing his best to concentrate on his writing, and the work was progressing. But as the news of his presence spread, his writing was interrupted by visitors, many of them local officials, the others passing through from Beijing. During these visits, he could not help dwelling on the political purge he had suffered for so long, and soon his peace of mind collapsed again. The act of excoriating his persecutors resurrected his blackest moods and wildest anger, and his wounded heart began to bleed again. During that period, he also visited several of the places where his guerrilla forces had been based during the Sino-Japanese War, and the reminder of those heroic times and his contribution to China and the Party redoubled the bitterness he felt about his treatment since the Cultural Revolution.

The investigation of Mu Xiang was completely unjust and wrong, so he must be rehabilitated, and all slander and libel removed. Those family members, children and former colleagues who were

affected by his political persecutions should also be cleared. The
Party Committee of the armoured forces should be held responsible for Mu Xiang's case, and apologize to him . . .

Excerpt from 'Decision to rehabilitate Comrade Mu Xiang'
by the Party Committee of the Armoured Forces in the
Beijing Military Region, 30 December 1978

This statement was not enough for my father. After all, no one was
found responsible for his persecution. Instead, Tang and Ge were also
regarded as victims of the Cultural Revolution, and also rehabilitated. For
my father, the injustice rankled more and more. For nearly half a century,
he had dedicated himself to his beloved Communist Party. Throughout
his revolutionary career, he had trusted it for fairness and justice. What
he had received was its opposite, and still no amends had been made.

Little Auntie told me later that before he left Beijing, my father often
swore to her that he would never stop fighting against injustice. As a lifetime revolutionary, he refused to give in, but what could he do? He was
unable to change anything, or to affect his persecutors, and Tang still
overshadowed his career.

'For more than ten years, I have suffered a great deal from the Evil
Tang,' my father wrote to my mother from Taiyuan on 12 July 1978. 'In
the past, I did not know Geng [New Star's father] well. Now, I recognized that my case was in his hands.' He wrote that Geng had set out to
oust him from the Beijing Military Region in 1975, in order to please
Tang. Nearly all his friends and former colleagues had advised him
against accepting the post in the Ba-yi Film Studio, and only Geng had
badgered him to take it. 'What he did was to push me into a living hell,'
Father wrote. 'How could he not know anything about the situation in
the studio? . . . How can I forgive him? He too should be held
responsible for the ten years of political persecution that I suffered . . .'

My father also condemned me in his letter: 'That girl's marriage was
another disaster . . . I only wanted her to postpone her wedding, but she

said that I victimized her . . . She made a tearful scene, and I almost died . . . When I was admitted to hospital, she got married straight away, like adding fuel to flames, trying to drive me to die . . . the only hope of improving my political situation was destroyed, because I was snubbed by Yang Yong . . . After all, it is me who becomes her victim! How could I forgive her? . . . Now, all my hopes and expectations have been destroyed, which is like a bolt from the blue, a deadly blow. I have already reached old age, what else could I expect? . . . It is the most painful regret in my life that my own beloved daughter threw herself into the arms of my enemy, and takes the foe for her father. How could I forgive her? How could I face those who also suffered from political persecution? My only choice is to make a clean break . . . When asked how many daughters I have, I have to say that I only have one . . .'

Since my father continued to condemn me, he could not forgive my mother either, because she had not backed him unconditionally. In the past, they had always stayed in tune, despite strains such as his troubled relationship with my brothers. When he came home from work, the first face he looked for was my mother's, and the two had remained in each other's confidence. Now, she was one more culprit responsible for his plight. Also, he interpreted my mother's support to me as a challenge to his authority in the family, which he could not tolerate. Therefore he accused her of betraying him, by shirking her duty and siding with their children. He claimed that she did not respect him, or take care of him. Gradually, his manner towards her hardened.

In my mother's view, my father deserved every sympathy for his ordeal, but she also felt that he should not brood on the bitterness of his past. After the Cultural Revolution, Deng Xiaoping had advised the members of the Communist Party to look ahead, if they wished to reunite the nation. Now, what the country needed urgently was to repair its damaged economy. It was Deng's ambitious plan that by the end of the twentieth century, China would develop from poverty to become a modernized economic power. He gave orders for the Party to concentrate its efforts on economic reform, rather than forever resurrecting past disputes. Hence, most victims of political persecution during Mao's era were reha- bilitated within a few years, and the Party took responsibilities for their ordeals, like what happened to my father. Therefore, there was no official investigation about any individual involvement in these persecutions, except for a few cases such as key accomplices of the Gang of Four or Lin Biao who were arraigned for their crimes. During the Cultural Revolution, a number of people who instigated moves against my parents later became victims themselves. After all the recent changes, it was going to be practically impossible to sort out the rights and wrongs of ten years of tangled disputes. My mother thought that even ignoring Tang's polit- ical connections, the way back to justice was closed, and trying to open it would only bring further disappointment.

She also felt that part of my father's pain derived from his personal character – he was too proud, too easily offended, and too concerned with saving face. If so, he would never find peace after all that had happened. Having been balked in his political career, in the end he had vented his resentment on members of his family. Before, he had seldom bothered about domestic affairs, and was kind at home. Now, my mother could hardly believe how unreasonable, narrow-minded and suspicious he had become to the rest of the family, including his own mother.

My father's troubles with his mother started halfway through the Cultural Revolution. In 1971, she moved to Fuzhou to live with Third Auntie's family, and later to Hangzhou, staying with First Auntie's family, since no one could look after her in Beijing. (My mother was still ill, having just returned from exile in Yunnan, my father had cardiac problems, and my siblings and I had joined the armed forces.) These two provincial cities were in the south of China, with a different climate from what she was used to in the north. She never adjusted to the greater humidity and the intense summer heat. In the winter, she suffered from cold in my aunts' unheated rooms, because only residents living north of the Yangtze River were entitled to rationed fuels for indoor heating. Despite her many layers of warm clothing, she still caught cold, which often developed into tracheitis and serious asthma, so she wanted to return to Beijing as soon as possible. In any case, she never felt at home when living with any of her daughters' families. By tradition, it was only sons, and especially the eldest son, who were responsible for supporting their parents.

My father was annoyed by his mother's demand, because his political ordeal was not over at that time, and he could not provide for her properly. After her return, he would never invite her to his little flat in Peace Street, imagining that she would look down on him for having to live in such poor conditions. As a last resort, my mother had to put Grandmother in a small flat in the empty campus where she was still in charge and could look after her more easily. But my father refused to join his mother, too proud to be housed by his wife. He stayed on his own in Peace Street, and only visited his mother at weekends. 'I returned to Beijing because I want to be with my eldest son,' she lamented, 'but he doesn't want to live with me.' Their separation lasted for two years, until my father started work at the Ba-yi Film Studio, and the house provided to him had plenty of room for my grandmother.

In recent years, my father often quarrelled with his mother, especially after he lost his job in the studio. He complained that she spent too much money, and refused to let his siblings send her pocket money. She had to stop wearing her new or smart clothes, which were mainly presents from her other children, because he rebuked her for being corrupted by a lifestyle too removed from the masses. She felt he asked too much, and often complained, which increased his resentment until he was disinclined even to speak to her. Before his departure to Taiyuan, he did not inform his mother about the trip, or any of his children, and did not wish her goodbye. When she looked out of her window and saw him leave, Grandmother wept that her son had forgotten his mother.

Unable to mend my father's deteriorating relationship with his family, now my mother found that she too was no longer trusted. In his altered state of mind, he felt insulted by criticism or advice from anyone in the family, which often induced his cardiac problems, so my mother felt obliged not to provoke him. Gradually, the gap between them widened. My father started to complain that his life resembled Tolstoy's later years, since there was no one in his family who understood him. He often lost his temper with my mother, claiming that she favoured their children over him. 'I have become the outsider of the family,' he said.

Several months after my father left, an employee of the China Bookstore called on my mother at home, collecting payments. The Cultural Revolution did not lessen the mutual support between my father and his friends in the store, and even reinforced it. During those upheavals, many of the staff refused to provide his investigators with details of his purchases, despite political pressure, and this helped him to safeguard his collection. Despite his own troubles, my father was also concerned for his friends. He provided financial assistance, and helped their children to leave their rural settlements.

When the China Book Store reopened in the early 1970s, my father became a regular customer again, and was treated with general respect, even before his privileged status was restored. The staff in reception often stood up, nodded and smiled when he went in or out. At the time when he was not entitled to a car, members of staff volunteered to deliver books that he was interested in or had just bought by bicycle after work. Before I went to university, each time I was home I used to accompany him to the book store, and help him carry back the books he bought. When our family moved to the latest house, his library and study were already too small. Soon, half of the living room was crammed with loaded bookcases, and more cases occupied spare bedrooms. His diary for 26 April 1974 reads: 'Bought 27 books today. What a pleasure!' On 11 June 1977: 'Bought books for 1,205 yuan this morning [a month's salary for a university graduate was about 50 yuan] . . . Returned to the store in the afternoon, and spent another 127.8 yuan.' This massive spending absorbed all of his income and much of my parents' savings. Thanks to my mother's income, the family managed to make ends meet without my father's salary.

The visitor from the China Book Store told my mother that during a recent trip to Shanxi, he had come across my father in a hotel located by a scenic spot nowhere near Taiyuan. He wondered if my mother knew a young woman my father was travelling with. He had mentioned the trip in a letter, though not this woman, but my mother did not give this news much thought. In more than thirty years of marriage, it was not unusual for them to endure long periods of separation, caused either by wars or by political persecution. Sometimes, they could not see each other for one or two whole years, but my mother had always trusted her husband. Now he was sixty-two. Since he had never been unfaithful even when they were young, why should my mother expect this to happen today? Despite their recent clashes, my mother was still deeply attached to her husband. No matter how his character changed, she always tried to understand him. With so much rage inside him, where else could he express it, if not to his own family? She expected that eventually he would compose himself, and once again become a kind son, a loving father, and a caring husband.

In summer 1978, she visited Father in Taiyuan for a week during a working trip. He seemed gloomy, and he was hypertensive, but he refused my mother's suggestion of returning to Beijing for a break, and to consult his doctors. When she came home, she was surprised to find a letter, posted before her arrival in Taiyuan, in which he tried to stop her visit. Twice before my father had been away from her in order to write. In 1959, he spent ten months writing *Autumn in Jinyang* in Beidaihe, the summer resort town on the Bohai Gulf. During that period, he was always asking my mother to visit him. In 1966, he phoned her frequently from Taiyuan, where he had just arrived, and pressed her to come over. But this time, when he had been gone for almost half a year, not only had he never invited her to join him, but he had also attempted to prevent her.

My mother could not help associating that unknown woman in Shanxi with my father's changed behaviour. During her visit, he had mentioned that the woman, whose name was Scarlet, was away in Beijing, sitting examinations for a postgraduate course in drama. Apparently she was a divorcee in her late thirties, only a few years older than my eldest brother, and worked as a clerk for the government agency for the preservation of cultural and historical antiquities in the province. During my mother's stay in Taiyuan, she had not taken much notice when a letter came from Scarlet, as she trusted her husband. But now she began to wonder what was happening. Later, she received another letter from my father, saying that he had finished the draft of his novel, and intended to stay longer in Taiyuan, researching ancient literature about the local-ity. He also mentioned that Scarlet had returned from Beijing after failing her examinations, and he wanted her as his assistant for the new project. My mother decided to see for herself what he was doing, and asked for a short leave from work.

As on his previous stay, my father was made welcome by the provin-cial authority as a guest of the 'Jiao-ji-chu', a reception centre reserved for the country's leaders and elites when they visited the province. The Communist regime divided China into thirty provinces, autonomous regions and great cities. Each has established an equivalent reception centre, which runs its own hotels, shops and transports, and employs a substantial staff. My father lived in Jinci town outside Taiyuan city, famous for its magnificent temple complex of the Tang Dynasty (618–907 AD), with ancient trees and a great spring located in the grounds. In 1937, when the Party assigned him to lead the anti-Japanese movement, he got to know Jinci town well, as a centre of his activities.

The huge compound where my father now lived comprised several grand buildings and a collection of sumptuous villas equipped with modern facilities and set in beautifully kept gardens. He chose a villa located in a quiet corner of the compound set aside for government ministers from Beijing or governors from other provinces. For most of the time, he was the only guest in the entire compound, but he shared it with armies of servants and security guards, whose duties included not only looking after the guests, but also keeping all the empty buildings and their surroundings ready for immediate occupation.

On my mother's second visit, Scarlet had already moved into the suite next door to my father. They worked in the same room, and strolled around the compound like a pair of inseparable lovers. My father also invited Scarlet to eat in the VIP canteen, where they shared the same table every day. Not only did he pay her food bills, which cost nearly 100 yuan a month, he also provided her with coupons for grain and cooking oil. At his request, my mother had to send him extra coupons, saved by the family at home, to meet Scarlet's consumption.

At the sight of my mother my father's face set, and he asked her: 'Why have you come back?' 'I want to help with your work,' she replied. 'You're no more use than a shop assistant,' he replied. 'How could you help with researching ancient literature?' Later, he accused her of going there to catch him out with Scarlet: 'Once, I thought you were great, but now I despise you . . . Another man would have divorced you already!' In Scarlet's presence, my father was often talkative and cheerful. One of their favourite topics was other people's extramarital affairs, which he refused to hear discussed in the past. Alone with my mother, his manner changed, as if towards a stranger. My mother was shocked by his transformation, and terribly hurt by his manner.

It seemed that my father met Scarlet through visiting her office, next to the compound. Her office was in charge of the preservation of historical and cultural antiquities. With his interest in culture and history, he often spent his spare time chatting to the staff there, especially since the Jinci town he stayed in was always quiet with few other places to visit. 'How wonderful *Autumn in Jinyang* is!' Scarlet enthused. 'I finished three hundred pages in one go — I couldn't stop reading.' Her compliments delighted my father. She also showed him two play scripts she had written, which impressed my father, even though no publisher or theatre had accepted them. A native Beijinger, she had studied play-writing in a drama school in Beijing shortly before the Cultural Revolution. My father was attracted by her knowledge of literature and good memory, and considered inviting her to adapt *Autumn in Jinyang* as a film script, a project he had harboured for many years. At that time, Scarlet was unhappy in her job, and desperate to return to Beijing permanently. Due to her humble background and lack of political connections, this was an elusive ambition, but she asked my father to draw on his own connections. She also told him that her brother, who had just entered university in Shanxi, wanted to transfer to another university. Normally, this was not possible, but he got what he wanted after my father made contact with the deputy provincial governor.

In recent years, my father had mentioned his wish for an assistant to my mother. After my marriage, he had lost hope for his political career, and his relationship with the rest of the family was deteriorating. That left his writing and his book collection. In addition to completing the four volumes of *The Billows*, he planned to base another novel on his experience of reorganizing the Nationalist troops handed over to the Communists by their commander at the end of the Civil War. Another book would deal with the plight of parents whose children were dispatched to rural settlements during the Cultural Revolution. He also planned to compile a catalogue of his book collection, and to carry out research on classical Chinese literature. His age and poor health might set a limit on so many ambitious plans, but although his rank entitled him to an assistant provided by the armed forces, he disliked the idea. Having no job himself, he was concerned that he would have no authority over an official assistant. At the film studio, he had taken an interest in a young actress, and tried to match her with my younger brother, hoping to make her his personal assistant after she married into our family, but they both rejected his initiative. Now, it seemed that my father had found his personal assistant, but my mother suspected that the relationship went well beyond his work.

In late December 1978, my father postponed his scheduled return again, and remained in Taiyuan for another month, till shortly before the

Chinese New Year. During the next few weeks, the VIP compound would stop hosting guests, while most of the staff went home for a long holiday. A few hours after his return, he talked to my mother seriously: 'I have tasted all sorts of human experiences in my life, so those like the relationship between mother and son, wife and husband or father and son have no meaning for me. I have reached my old age, so we just continue our relationship until the end of our lives . . . But you should not interfere in what I do . . . You should have known your place.' His words convinced my mother that her suspicions about Scarlet were true, and what her husband planned was to force her to accept the affair in silence.

On the eve of the Chinese New Year, my father became talkative again, telling his wife that as long as people's politics were correct, their private lives were up to them. For example, Nikita Khrushchev had asked in his memoirs: 'Who knows which woman was Lenin's real wife?' He also talked about the well-known extramarital affairs of Mao Zedong and various other leading Communists, as well as many celebrities in the field of literature and the arts. 'Since they can do it, why shouldn't I? It's not as if I lived in a feudal society, always watched by everybody else . . .' My mother was in tears. How could these words be spoken by a man who had been her faithful and loving husband for so many years, and who had often helped others to resolve their marriage problems? 'Can you have forgotten the deep love between us?' she asked him. 'Can you have forgotten the extraordinary years we have spent together for most of our lives?'

On the second day after the New Year, my father caught a cold. Although film studio doctors said that his condition was not serious, he insisted on going to stay in hospital. Due to his rank, he could enter hospital whenever he wanted, and for as long as he wished. This time, he was admitted by the Military Hospital No. 301, the general hospital of the People's Liberation Army, which has special responsibility for looking after China's statesmen and military elites. Eighteen years later, Deng Xiaoping died in this hospital having spent the last months of his life there.

My father's ward was located in the South Building, reserved for the military elite. Again, he occupied a large en-suite room on his own. Hospital regulations allowed visits only on a few afternoons in the week, and on Sundays. When my mother visited, she found Scarlet there several times. She had returned to Beijing, and was on loan by her workplace to a magazine. My father explained that Scarlet's visits were on behalf of their project. A few weeks later, my mother stopped finding her there, but she drew no conclusions from that.

During the next two months, my father would not hear of leaving hospital. One evening about nine o'clock, my mother received a phone call asking: 'Is Political Commissar Mu at home?' My father had vanished from the ward, and no one knew his whereabouts. This call alarmed my mother, because he was not home either, and she phoned back several times to ask for news. Around half-past ten, a nurse informed her: 'We just found him with that woman in the garden.' 'What woman?' my mother asked. 'The one who often comes out of hours.'

The South Building was kept guarded round the clock, so Scarlet was always stopped at the entrance when she arrived out of visiting hours. Sometimes she insisted that she needed to see my father for important work. For security reasons, visitors to the South Building were asked to fill in a form with brief personal details. Scarlet gave a false name, and false information about her workplace. When staff tried to check with my father, he answered: 'I don't know her name.'

My mother was deeply upset by what she heard, but still tried to save face for her husband, following the Chinese maxim that domestic shame should not be made public. 'I know that woman,' she said to the nurse. 'She does have important work with my husband.' The nurse was not impressed. 'What? Do they need to hug each other when they talk about their work?' Apparently a nurse had witnessed such a scene when she popped into his room for routine duties.

After that evening, the hospital buzzed with gossip about my father's relationship with Scarlet, and it soon reached military circles in Beijing.

He was criticized for breaking the hospital rules, and the hospital authorities complained to the General Political Department about his 'improper behaviour'. Under these pressures, on May Day 1979 he had to leave the hospital and go home.

In front of the family, my father kept quiet about this episode. To my mother, he claimed that the whole thing was a conspiracy cooked up by someone in the General Political Department: 'These people want to persecute me more, because they felt that losing me my job was not enough.' At the same time, he blamed my mother for 'collaborating' with the hospital to shame him in public. 'I have been terribly hurt by what happened,' she reminded him. 'Why would I want to get at you by collaborating with the hospital? It would do me no good at all to show you up in public.' But he never accepted her words.

In the past, my father had always treasured his time and worked hard at his writing and research, but after leaving hospital he was seldom at home. Almost every day, he left in the early morning and did not come back till after dark. Several times, the General Political Department phoned to summon him to meetings at headquarters, but no one at home knew his whereabouts. In desperation, my mother appealed to the Department to reassign him, in the hope that a new post would settle him down, but she was told that the scandal at the hospital made it difficult. Two years later, an officer in the General Political Department provided further information about events at that time: 'We believed that Mu Xiang and Scarlet had a dubious relationship . . . The Party organization talked to him formally, warning him to attend to this problem . . . Mu Xiang admitted that he was careless in some of his actions. In order to reduce tensions in his family, the Party organization sent Scarlet back to Shanxi through official channels.'

Shortly after Scarlet left Beijing, a letter she sent to our home showed how much she resented her treatment. It said that those 'high-ups' who were always making trouble for others might not see everything go the way they wished. Though the letter was addressed to both my parents, it was aimed at my mother. According to my father's diary several years later, Scarlet impressed her colleagues in Beijing as a formidable figure. My mother heard the same from Taiyuan. Scarlet meant what she wrote: the years to come took away everything my mother wished for in her life.

When Scarlet left Beijing, my father seemed disoriented, edgy and restless. When he came to himself again, my mother knew by instinct that Scarlet had returned.

In early June 1979, after my graduation, I met New Star in Nanjing, where he was staying with his parents. From there, we took a trip to visit my relatives. In addition to First Auntie and Third Auntie, my father's other sibling, Little Uncle, also lived in the south of China. He had left the armed forces, and now worked as director of the Public Health Bureau in Suzhou, one of the most beautiful and ancient cities in China. Having completed my studies, and my mission to the war, I felt utterly exhausted, and longed for a chance to relax. I hoped to recuperate on this holiday, ready to face the trials of finding work in Beijing, and my troubled relationship with my father.

Little Uncle's was the first stop on our trip, and we spoke in private about his visit to my family in Beijing some months before. When I heard about my parents' marriage crisis, I was devastated. Until that moment, it was the last thing I thought would happen to my parents. All through the Cultural Revolution, I was moved by the strength of their mutual love and concern. Without it, neither one of them could have survived the years of persecution. Indeed, I have seldom met a couple quite so deeply attached as my parents were. But now, all at once, my father had betrayed my mother for another woman. His behaviour had changed unrecognizably, and I felt myself partly to blame, because it was my marriage that had opened the breach between them.

I feared that my father's relationship with Scarlet would turn out badly. His selection of New Star as a partner for me had caused me to lose faith in his judgement. His privileged social positions had removed him from ordinary people for many years, and from contact with the younger generation. Since he did not know even his own children, how clear was his vision of Scarlet? According to my father, Scarlet was one of the few loyal friends he had ever had, and her place in his life could only compare with A-ying's, the great dramatist and veteran Communist whom my father had got to know through the China Book Store in the early 1960s.

During the Cultural Revolution, A-ying spent a long time in prison, and later suffered a serious stroke. After his release on bail, my father did his best to have him properly treated in Beijing. In 1972, I went to visit A-ying in hospital with my father while I was home on leave, and wept for his condition, for which my father often praised my tender heart. Before I met New Star, I often visited A-ying when I came home, and enjoyed his conversations with my father. In those days, A-ying lived in a porter's room by the entrance of a government accommodation compound, with no lavatory, kitchen or running water. In June 1977, soon after he was rehabilitated, he died of cancer, which was an enormous loss to my father. Several months later, Father lost his job in the Ba-yi Film Studio, and fell out with me over my marriage. He became increasingly lonely, and wrote touching poems and articles in memory of A-ying.

If my father saw Scarlet as somehow replacing A-ying, then I worried all the more about his judgement. He had known A-ying for nearly twenty years, they were similar in age, and shared common revolutionary experiences, and artistic and social levels. Scarlet came from a totally different background, and my father had only met her a year ago. It was hard to dismiss the likely role of fantasy in his responses to her. Through the history of my marriage, I knew how misleading that could be, and I could not bear to think about the consequences. At my father's age, if anything went wrong it might kill him.

During the rest of the trip, I often felt terribly depressed, but could not confide in New Star. Not only did I not trust him, I also knew that he would not provide what he had never had — the sympathy and comfort that I needed. It seemed that he did not mind what happened to me.

Just halfway through the trip, I was already sick of his constant complaints, and fault-finding, always over trivial matters. I started to pay no attention, and was often angered by his domineering manner, which led to frequent quarrels. On the way back to Nanjing, we had a public row in the train. When he left the compartment, two middle-aged men sitting opposite embarrassed me by asking: 'Do you go on like this at home?' They kindly advised me: 'So much quarrelling is not good for a couple's relationship.'

On the day we were due to leave for Beijing, New Star attacked me in his parents' home, following a quarrel, which was the first time he resorted to violence. I had always thought that the frequent threats expressed in his letters were just words that he meant to scare me. I was wrong! His assault left me trembling with rage. This was what marriage had brought me to! This was the future I faced! But who was to blame for that? It was me who had insisted on marrying him, so I must take the consequences. On top of this, I had to live with my guilt for my parents' marriage crisis. How could I cope with so much trouble?

I left New Star's parents' home alone, without telling anyone. For hours, I walked the streets of Nanjing, close to madness. When I was calm enough to think, I decided to return to Beijing on my own, as I could not forgive New Star's violence. I might have nowhere to stay there, if my father still shut me out, but I needed to know what was happening to my family. At the station, I discovered that I had come out without my train ticket, and had too little money to buy a ticket to Beijing. In Nanjing city, I did not know anyone apart from New Star's family, so I had to phone him from the station asking him to send some money. Soon after that, he and his mother arrived in his father's chauffeur-driven car. Instead of apologizing, he accused me of being a trouble-maker, and the cause of all our problems, and denied his assault. That started another quarrel, until Madam Geng intervened. She pressed me to go back with them, and in the end I did, but for most of his family this incident only confirmed New Star's claim about my unreasonable character and bad temper.

Back in Beijing, New Star attacked me again. It happened on my twenty-eighth birthday, 1 August 1979, which was a military holiday. We were staying temporarily in the empty house where his parents used to live, before the new occupants moved in. The house was surrounded by high brick walls, so the neighbours could not see, and there was nothing to restrain him. I had never experienced such violence in my life, and I felt outraged. I screamed and shouted and said anything that entered my head to express my rage and protest. Since I refused to keep quiet, and would not give in, his brutality worsened. Again and again, he slapped my face, punched and kicked my body, knocked me down and dragged me in and out of the house. Fearing that I was going to be killed, I picked up a broom to defend myself, but he wrenched it away and started to beat me with it. More than a head taller, and nearly twice my weight at almost 100 kg, he had total physical superiority. At times I could hardly breathe, and sweat drenched my face from the pain . . . He only stopped when a soldier assigned to look after the house arrived.

A week after my birthday, my mother accidentally learned about New Star's violence, which I had concealed. While I was having a nap in my parents' house after lunch, my clothes got disarranged, and she saw the bruising on my body. 'Oh no!' She burst into tears. 'How could he be so brutal?'

Till then, I had been reluctant to mention my disappointment with New Star, and especially his violence, to anybody else. I regarded it as private, and in any case, as it was my own insistence on the marriage that had damaged my family, I was afraid that no one would sympathize. In contrast, New Star made no secret of my ill-humour, and spread stories to my family about my 'disgracing' his family in the Nanjing Military Region by running away from his parents' home. In view of his gentle public manner, it was hard to disbelieve him, as it had been for me before I married him. For ten years and more, I had seldom been home, and had seen very little of most of my family, so they did not know me well, and it was easy for some of them to believe his words and suspect that I 'bullied' him.

Now that she had discovered New Star's violence, my mother talked to him seriously. Under her pressure, he promised not to beat me again, and apologized to me. But his promise lasted less than two months. I was brutalized again following a quarrel late one evening, while we were still staying in the empty house. This time, he tied my hands behind my back, and gagged me with a towel while he beat me, so that I could not shout for help, or escape, or defend myself. Afterwards, he went to sleep, and left me tied up and gagged outside the bedroom.

The worse New Star treated me, the more stubbornly I refused to surrender, and I grew to hate him. Sometimes, in interludes, he tried to please me, but the mere look of him often reminded me of his violence, and renewed my bitterness. My anger could be uncontrollable when he touched me physically. I refused to join him in the accommodation compound at armoured forces headquarters, saying that it reminded me of my family's ordeal during the Cultural Revolution, especially with Tang and his family still there. But what I did not tell New Star or anyone else was that I could not stand a life with New Star. Since he showed no intention of ending the marriage, divorce was impossible, but I could stay at my parents' all week, and only spend weekends with him. My father still refused to speak, but did not forbid me to stay, because he was wrapped up with Scarlet.

When I returned in July 1979, all my siblings were back in Beijing. Feng-xin was being transferred to a civilian job, discharged as part of the record reduction in China's armed forces ordered by Deng Xiaoping. Over the next few years, a million soldiers, about a quarter of the total, were to be shed. Feng-an was working for the Agricultural Film Studio, having graduated from the famous Beijing Film Academy. Aijun, my younger sister, had also finished a medical course and was working as an assistant doctor at a military clinic in the suburbs. About three years ago, my younger brother, Feng-yuan, had started an engineering course in a university in Beijing, as one of the last 'worker-peasant-soldier students'. My mother was also under transfer. The head office of the Chinese Academy of Sciences was reorganized in 1979, just two years after she joined it, so her department no longer existed. She expected to return to the Forestry University, which had just moved back from Yunnan. While she waited, she was mostly at home.

I felt deeply sorry for my mother, because she was completely unprepared for her marriage crisis, and the pain that it brought her. Since their marriage in 1945, my father had been a caring, loving husband, and open to her about everything. But now her world had come apart. My father's constant absences were torture, and drove her close to breakdown. She counted the hours till his return, and was often too distressed to do anything else. In front of her children and relatives, she could not help lamenting her husband's unfaithfulness, and complained about her fate. Throughout the Cultural Revolution, I never once heard her do that. Out of her deep attachment to my father, she still tried to save their marriage. When he came home, she hid her bitterness, greeted him warmly, and prepared his food with all her usual care. But nothing could stop my father's relationship with Scarlet. Sometimes, my mother lost control, or insisted on knowing what he was doing all day outside the house, which caused fierce rows between them.

Considering her good terms with my father's siblings, she looked to them for support. She visited Little Auntie frequently, and asked the others to come to Beijing so that she could discuss the matter with them. During my visit, Little Uncle had criticized my father's relationship with Scarlet to me, and First Auntie had suggested that my siblings and I should help my mother to save their marriage. But seeing the marriage failing, most of my father's siblings turned their backs on his wife, because he was their blood relation, and she was not. For them, my father was not only the respected eldest brother, but also the 'great red flag of revolution' for the Mu family. It was due to his influence that they had all joined the Communist revolution very young, and then distinguished themselves under the new regime. He was their pride. Since extramarital affairs were frowned on in society, they set out to protect his reputation. Despite the evidence that my mother could show them, they preferred to believe my father's claim that there was no affair with Scarlet at all, and he was a victim of his wife's unreasonable suspicions.

My father also managed to set most of his siblings against my mother personally, for instance by telling Little Auntie: 'Xu Jing said that you get involved in our family's business because you have eyes on our money.' For many years, my parents had helped Little Auntie financially, with generous contributions from my mother. Little Auntie's family income was lower than most of her siblings', and her disabled son was expensive to look after. It was my mother who bought her a wristwatch, sent her clothes and shoes, and paid part of the fees for a nanny. When TV was still a luxury in China, my mother bought Little Auntie a new set, which cost almost a year's wages for an ordinary Chinese. Yet now, Little Auntie swallowed my father's words, and turned against my mother. She campaigned on my father's behalf to win over their other siblings, and passed on everything she heard from my mother. Later, when my mother visited her, she asked her to leave and not come back.

My father also told his own mother that it was his wife who had kept them apart. Ever since my grandmother joined our family in 1951, my mother had regarded her as a substitute for her own mother, and the two had been deeply attached. But during the strife between my parents, my grandmother stood by her eldest son. All through her life, she had trusted him unconditionally, even as a child, so she would not hear him criticized. 'I know my son,' she used to say. 'He has never been interested in even talking to other women, so how could he be involved in an affair now?'

Because I knew the truth, and felt partly to blame for the crisis, I tried my best to support my mother. At that time, I had not found a job, so I had time to listen and talk, and to offer advice. Many of my father's siblings therefore accused me of giving way to personal spite, and trying to get even with my father for his opposition to my wedding. In the past, I had been Little Auntie's favourite niece, but now I felt unwelcome in her house. My grandmother too was angry because I stood by my mother.

When autumn came, I found that my father's approach to my brothers suddenly changed. In recent years, he had seldom talked to them unless he needed their assistance, say to rearrange his book collections or decorate the house. Now, he started to invite them home for individual talks. Feng-xin was still looking for a job, and often stayed in my parents' house, as I did. His own family lived in a satellite suburb of Beijing, whose sparse public transport made commuting a nuisance. Nearly every day, my father either came looking for Feng-xin or sent his bodyguard to fetch him. Each time, the conversation lasted for hours, sometimes till after midnight. Feng-an and Feng-yuan were also invited often, and talked at length. When my mother and I entered the room, silence would fall until we left.

Some of my father's siblings claimed openly that my brothers should be given powers at home, and it was right for my father to lean on his sons in a family emergency. They also insisted that Feng-xin, the eldest son, should take the lead among his siblings, and the married daughter – meaning me – should leave her parents' home and stop meddling in the family's affairs. Clearly, my father and his siblings intended to isolate my mother and me from the rest of the family. They knew that by winning over Feng-xin, my father could recruit his other sons. I heard later that during their talks my father apologized to his sons for neglecting them in the past, and promised his support from now on, whether to find them better jobs or accommodation, or to help them out with money.

Considering the state of the country after the Cultural Revolution, it struck me that it would have been difficult for anyone, let alone my brothers, not to succumb to my father's promises. In Beijing hundreds of thousands of exiled school-leavers had returned from their rural settlements and were desperate for jobs. After ten years of rural hard labour, they had grown from teenagers to adults. Many were over thirty, and had families. But their futures were at risk, since they had neither qualifications nor skills, and jobs were scarce. In terms of cash, the government provided almost nothing for the unemployed. Being jobless made it very difficult to find a place to live, and hence to qualify for many welfare services, such as free health care, because these benefits were mainly provided by the workplace, not by government offices. Apart from these former school-leavers, a massive amount of military personnel were also looking for civilian jobs, as disarmament proceeded. After several months of trying, Feng-xin still could not find a suitable job. Eventually, it was through my father that the Beijing Library, China's largest, took him on to its administrative staff.

Another major problem for China was the housing shortage. During the Cultural Revolution, construction work was held up for a decade in Beijing, while the population soared. The municipal housing authority had been starved of resources for years, and each workplace had a growing waiting list. It was not unusual for three generations to sleep in a single small room, as they could not find a second or a larger room. A common saying claimed: 'It's harder to find somewhere to live than someone to marry.' Feng-yuan, my younger brother, planned to marry in the following year, but could not find a place to live. He and his fiancée were still at university, and each one was entitled only to a single bed in an overcrowded dormitory, even after they married. My father promised to house them in a spare bedroom in the front courtyard after the wedding.

In autumn 1979, the government announced steep rises in the price of many staple goods, such as sugar, meat, fish and eggs. For more than twenty years, prices had been practically frozen, and many important items kept rationed and heavily subsidized. The transition from central planning to a free market under Deng Xiaoping's economic reforms was stoking up inflation. Since nationalization in the 1950s, most employees in China worked for the state or collective sectors. During the Cultural

Revolution, only one pay rise occurred. Now, inflation soon overtook the increase.

Concerned for the value of their savings in the bank, my mother suggested to my father that they should give some to their children now. My siblings and I were either married or about to marry soon, and our parents seldom offered financial help. My father had always raged at such suggestions, and sworn to give neither his property nor his privileges to his children. But now, his attitude had changed.

After so many years of rigid treatment, the emergence of a caring, loving father helped my brothers to forget their resentment. I have never known whether the idea of splitting my brothers from my mother and me came from my father or his siblings. Nevertheless, he got his way. In previous months, while Feng-xin and I were both spending time in my parents' house, we often talked, and shared similar views of my parents' situation. He also helped my mother when she needed it. Now, we hardly ever talked, and his manner towards me turned cold. In the past, my siblings had sympathized with my mother over my parents' marriage crisis; now, they started to distance themselves from both of us.

While preparing to write this book, I recognized that the change in my brothers' attitude to me came partly from their grievance in the past. Ever since I was born, my father had lavished his love and attention on me. In contrast, my brothers were often left out in the cold, which must have been hurtful. My siblings and I were not brought up together, and then we seldom met as adults, so there was little chance to grow closer.

In terms of winning over my brothers, my mother was outmatched by her husband. In our childhood, she was mostly an absentee parent, engaged in demanding work. During the Cultural Revolution, she was imprisoned and then dispatched to Yunnan. When she eventually came home, my siblings and I had already joined the armed forces. In the years when my parents had reserved their limited spare time for each other, my mother had little chance to forge close ties with her children. During my father's conflicts with my brothers, her efforts to mediate had antagonized both sides. Now, it was not difficult for the alliance of my father and his siblings to convince my brothers that she was an irresponsible mother, and my father a victim of her 'unreasonable suspicions'.

In late October 1979, a quarrel broke out between Feng-xin and me. For several weeks, the tension between us had been rising, in step with my disappointment over his altered manner. One lunch time, at the dining table, he started to tell me off for a trivial matter, which I saw as his pretext for hostility. When I answered back, he lost his temper and made a threatening gesture. My father left the table and returned to his room. In the end, it was my mother who rescued me.

I finally recognized my father's intention, namely to use his sons to do his fighting. I felt bitterly hurt. Till lately, he would never have allowed anyone to raise even a finger to me, his favourite child. Now I felt sure that he had prompted Feng-xin's hostility. It seemed that my father was no longer the kind and loving Baba I had known for most of my life. I could not help wondering what would happen in the future, as I doubted if his attitudes towards his sons had *really* changed, especially in the case of Feng-xin. In recent years, my father had proved capable of turning against anyone in the family whose least word or action offended him, and would never forgive them. In front of the family, he had seldom concealed his dislike for Feng-xin, and was often furious just to see him at home. How could he be so transformed? What was his real intention? Did he mean to wreck his family by dividing it? I found so many similarities to events in China during the Cultural Revolution, when Mao Zedong set his people and officials against each other in order to achieve his goals. Considering what the nation had suffered, I felt frightened for my family.

In the afternoon of my quarrel with Feng-xin, I moved out alone to the flat in Peace Street where my parents had lived during the Cultural Revolution.

Chapter 25

Military Hospital No. 263:
Working as a Medical Doctor;
the Exposure of my Troubled Private Life

(January 1980–June 1981)

Before I graduated, I had already heard about the overstaffing at military medical centres, especially in Beijing, the most popular goal for the sons and daughters of high officials. Most of them had entered university as 'worker-peasant-soldier students', and gone on to work as doctors. Military personnel received higher salaries than those in equivalent civilian jobs, even with the same qualifications and working experience.

Under the Communist regime, the recruitment procedure for jobs had little to do with competence or suitability. There were no advertisements or interviews, and China's military hospitals had to accept whoever was assigned from above. Since the major criteria for acceptance were political position and family influence, rather than the applicant's own qualifications or experience, it was almost impossible for anyone to work there whose family had no pull with the decision-making bodies. Now, my father and father-in-law were out of favour, so I had enormous difficulties in finding a job in Beijing. I knew that my father still had his 'face' – in other words, that he enjoyed respect among many former colleagues and subordinates. If he wished, he could still help me, as he had helped Feng-xin by contacting a former aide during the Korean War who now worked for the higher authority of the Beijing Library. But I had fallen out with my father, and stood by my mother, so I could not expect support. In the end, it was through an officer from the Logistics Department of the Beijing Military Region, a trusted follower of New Star's father, that I was given a job in Military Hospital No. 263, located in a suburb of Beijing, and just as overstaffed as all the rest.

I started work in early January 1980, more than half a year after my graduation. The rules required university graduates to spend their first year as interns in the hospital's main departments before they qualified as doctors, and I was assigned to the Department of Contagious Diseases. New Star was furious. He was afraid of contagious diseases, and on my first day at work he rang me at my office and condemned me for accepting the assignment. We did not see each other every day, and he had only just heard the news. He would not listen to my explanation, and flew into a rage. In front of my new colleagues, I had to keep calm. The more he swore and bellowed, the less I said. Several times, I hung up, but he kept calling back, and there was nothing to do but to listen to his flood of condemnations.

In my second month at the hospital, I was transferred to the Department of Obstetrics and Gynaecology, which was suffering from a temporary shortage of staff. Only three of its doctors were available, because the rest were on maternity leave. When it learned of my previous experience, the department pressed for my immediate transfer, so I became an exceptional case as a graduate who did not complete her internship.

There was a saying in Chinese medical circles that: 'Ophthalmology is the golden profession, surgery is the silver, and the messy work is Obstetrics and Gynaecology.' I suppose this was because ophthalmologists enjoyed pleasant working conditions compared with other specialists, and surgeons could shine with their skills, but an obstetrician and gynaecologist always dealt with blood and women's reproductive organs, which was seen as dirty work. I did not care about these prejudices, as I was deeply attached to my profession.

When I arrived, Dr Honest, the head of the department, signed a number of blank prescriptions for me. Officially, I was still an intern, not eligible to prescribe, even though I had already worked as a doctor five years ago, before I went to university. The hospital authority had to endorse Dr Honest's action, so that I could carry out my duties. In the 1950s it had been normal to see male obstetricians and gynaecologists in China, but now the profession was dominated by women. In his early fifties, Dr Honest was the only man in the department, and I often felt sorry for the handicap he carried there. According to the regulations, a witness must always be present when he examined or treated a patient. Sometimes, he could not work, because no one was free to assist him.

On my first day at work, I was assigned as duty doctor for the ward straight away, starting at eight o'clock in the morning until the same time next day. It was a stressful experience, especially when I was left alone at night in charge of all in-patients, newborn babies, and the delivery room. I was a newcomer not only to the department but also to the hospital, still finding my way around. If anything critical happened, it would take time to fetch help. The department was only a few years old. It had no senior doctors, so Dr Honest, the only consultant, was on stand-by for all the duty doctors, who were juniors. Though he lived in the staff accommodation compound, several kilometres away, he had no telephone link, because under the Communist hierarchical structure his position as head of our department equated to the rank of battalion commander, too low to rate a telephone at home. On that first night on duty, I consulted my textbook repeatedly about the in-patients' various conditions, trying to ascertain what I would do in an emergency. Fortunately, it was a peaceful night.

Like other parts of China, Beijing's birth rate had risen since the late 1970s, but the city's obstetrical services had stagnated. In civilian hospitals, the departments of Obstetrics and Gynaecology were over-loaded. Very often, two in-patients had to share a single bed during their short stay after giving birth. Hence, many pregnant women turned to their local military hospitals: though they might not be better equipped than the civilian hospitals, at least every patient had a bed. Although our hospital's mission was to look after local troops, most of my depart-ment's patients were local women.

Soon after I started work in my department, I gained a reputation among my colleagues as a jinx (Fang-jia). My duty seemed to coincide with crises, especially at night, such as a sudden rush of women in labour, pulling almost all the staff into the delivery room. Sometimes there were cases of difficult labour at night, which needed emergency operations, or a few in-patients' conditions became critical and required attention. When this happened, I had to organize everything on my own before Dr Honest was collected from home, and then we had to work all night. Many other doctors hardly ever ran into such problems, and so slept peacefully all night. So when I was on the night shift, the incom-ing nurses liked to joke: 'Bad luck! We're in for another hard night.'

But no matter how busy the night was, I could not rest next morning, because I had to look after my own in-patients, and take part in the scheduled surgical operations with my colleagues. This lack of sleep and heavy workload brought on arrhythmia, a condition I had never suffered before, but I had no chance to get a proper rest. When I was not on duty, I had to spend four hours a day commuting between home and the hos-pital, which involved changing buses twice each way, plus twenty minutes' walk between the nearest bus stop and the hospital.

I was happy in my job, because of the opportunities it gave to improve my professional experience. My patients' gratitude and my col-leagues' praise and respect brought me great satisfaction, and fortified me in my troubled private life. I would not lose hope for the future, because I was useful to society and enjoyed offering my knowledge and skills to help other people.

In September 1980, I qualified as a doctor, a position one step higher than assistant doctor. No examination was involved; the regulations only required completing the internship. The hospital submitted a proposal to the controlling authority, which was approved at once. I wonder what it contained, seeing that I did not complete the internship. My income did not rise, because salary levels for officers depended not only on their qualifications, duties or position, but also on their length of service, so I earned less as a doctor than several of the nurses in my hospital, who had greater seniority. But this did not bother me, and I had made good progress in repairing the damage to my career caused by my parents' political troubles. Most of my fellow doctors were around my age, and many were former pupils from the Ba-yi School. Due to their family background, most had been spared what I had endured during the Cultural Revolution. Ten years before, we had been opposites: while I was compelled to be a peasant, many of them had joined the armed forces and proceeded to study medicine. But now, I was glad to have caught them up!

Meanwhile, my parents' relationship worsened, and my siblings grew more hostile towards my mother and me, especially after I took over the flat in Peace Street. When they moved to their current house in 1976, my parents had decided to keep this flat, considering the housing shortage, and the possible needs of their children. Later, my father changed his mind and tried to give the flat to Scarlet, but my mother refused. He was furious, and at that point he preferred to leave the flat empty rather than pass it to any of his children. When I asked to move in, my mother made no objection, maybe for fear that the flat would otherwise fall into Scarlet's hands. But in my siblings' eyes, my mother's action was unfair. After all, New Star was already being housed by his workplace. My father and some of his siblings pumped up their anger, and especially Feng-xin's, who lived in a single room with his wife and daughter, in a flat they shared with another family. He had to spend hours commuting every day to his new job, and he demanded that I should move out from the flat.

Since I had left my parents' house to go to Peace Street after my quarrel with Feng-xin, there had been little contact between my siblings and me, and no chance for me to explain why I did not want to move in with New Star. In fact, New Star disliked this flat, and seldom came to stay. It was located in a massive block, one of hundreds built in this area during the early 1960s, and all alike. Its condition was very basic – grey cement floors with white walls, roughly painted, and no facilities to bath or shower. What New Star was really interested in was the luxurious house in the old part of Beijing that his parents used to occupy. After Major-General Geng took up his post in Nanjing, his wife was allowed to keep part of the house, because she was still on the staff of the Beijing Military Region. But she refused to make room for New Star, despite his request. New Star complained to me that she intended to get rid of him because she did not trust him. Madam Geng and her son were not close, despite the fact that she often joined him against me.

In April 1980, my family held a 'plenary meeting', chaired by Feng-xin. It came as a surprise to my mother, because it had never happened before. As her only supporter, I had become isolated from the family's affairs. No one informed me about the meeting, and I did not attend it. Nor did Aijun, who found an excuse to be absent when it took place. As well as my parents and brothers, Second Auntie, my father's younger sister, was also present. Right from the start, my mother was the only target of concerted attacks led by my father. He blamed her for staging continual rows at home, which disturbed his writing and damaged his health. Under this chorus of pressure, my mother had to agree to move in with me in Peace Street for a while, and asked for a couple of days to get ready.

After the meeting, my father became more hostile, intending to force my mother out as soon as possible. By then, he had banned her from entering their bedroom, as well as the study and library, which left her with the room in the front courtyard. Now he kept locking her into it. As my siblings were not around, she could not find anyone to help her get out, because the maid and my father's bodyguard were forbidden to open the door. Right from the beginning, the bodyguard had been drawn into my parents' marriage crisis. I heard that he had developed a close relationship with a local girl when he followed my father to Taiyuan in 1978. This was against regulations, but my father turned a blind eye. The bodyguard felt grateful, and took his side during our family troubles.

After my father's transfer to the Ba-yi Film Studio, the armed forces provided a maid instead of the family's chef. My father ordered her to stop calling my mother to table and preparing food for her, forcing my mother to visit the kitchen for food, till one day the tearful maid begged her: 'Aunt! please don't come to the kitchen again! The master won't let you eat here.' Worn out by humiliation and maltreatment, my mother left soon after the selective 'family meeting'. My father announced that his wife had abandoned her family, and walked out without saying goodbye.

The very next day, my father called his sons to a second meeting. 'Your mother has gone, and I need to get back to my writing,' he said. 'From now on, there's no need for you to come home again, or else my work will be disturbed. A while ago, I said that I would help you, but you must know that I now have neither a job nor political power, so it is difficult for me to help you change your jobs. My house is provided by the Ba-yi Film Studio, and I have to give it back when I next transfer, so don't expect to live here. And you don't need financial assistance, since you all have incomes of your own . . .'

My brothers could hardly believe their ears. It was Feng-yuan who suffered most from his father's broken promise. He was due to be married in summer, and he and his fiancée had even started to buy furniture. One of my father's reasons for forcing my mother to leave was that he had promised two rooms, including hers, to Feng-yuan. Now he advised my brothers to evict me from the flat in Peace Street, so that Feng-yuan could live there. Feng-yuan refused, but the Beijing housing shortage made it impossible to find a place, especially at such short notice, so in his desperation he turned to my mother. All she could do was to suggest that he should ask Little Auntie to intercede with my father. By then, the flat my grandmother had occupied in my mother's university had already been returned, and so had the others provided by armoured forces head-quarters, as they were too far out of town for any of my siblings. At that time, my father's siblings were still on good terms with my brothers, so Little Auntie agreed to help Feng-yuan. When she did, my father rebuked her furiously: 'You are my sister, why do you not stand by me?' She never dared to plead for Feng-yuan again.

Feng-yuan went on searching, but in vain. At the end of July 1980, a few days before the wedding, my three brothers visited my father again, trying to convince him to keep his promise to house Feng-yuan. Instead of listening, my father accused them of scheming with my mother to harass him. The negotiations lasted for hours and came to nothing. In the end, my father returned to his room, saying that he was too tired to continue. His rapid shift of ground in recent months had hurt my brothers, who felt cheated in the crudest way. Having used them to get rid of my mother, now he was getting rid of them. Insulted by his indifference today, they decided to ignore him, and started to arrange the rooms for Feng-yuan's wedding. It was the first time that my brothers had united to confront my father, and he was enraged. He rushed out of his room and shouted abuse, frantic to stop them. When things were reaching breaking point, a senior officer from the Ba-yi Film Studio arrived at the house to visit my father, and hence stopped the row. When he grasped the situation, he felt sympathetic with Feng-yuan, and suggested that my father should accept his sons' request, especially since the rooms were empty. Eventually, my father had to concede. The house belonged to the studio, so the officer's suggestion carried weight.

A few weeks later, on 26 August 1980, my mother returned to the house. Autumn was coming, and she wanted to collect her warm clothes, and various other belongings that she had not managed to take when she moved out four months before. As she arrived, she met my father coming out, but when she entered the living room she found that he had followed her. 'How dare you come back?' he stormed, and started to beat her, tearing her clothes and wrenching off her wristwatch. It was the maid who heard my mother's shout for help. Her arrival stopped the violence, but afterwards my father pushed his wife out into the street, and then locked the gate from inside.

My mother was close to a breakdown. She went straight to Feng-xin's office, and the sight of her bruised arms and torn clothes both shocked him into sympathy and redoubled his resentment of my father. He offered his support: 'Initially, my brothers and I agreed that you should stay away from the house for a while. That was four months ago, and it's time for you to return. When I have the time we'll take you home, and ask Father to give you back your watch.'

Many years later, my mother told me how much she regretted her hasty reaction that day. If she could have controlled her anger and behaved less emotionally, she might have handled the situation differently, and averted the tragedies that followed. Perhaps she might, but how could she, or any other human being, suffer such intimate disasters in detachment? In particular, there was no one who could help except her children.

In the early morning of 24 September 1980, I was nearing the end of my shift when the first incoming colleague approached. 'Do you know about what happened to your family?' she asked me quietly, and showed me yesterday's *Beijing Evening Post*, China's principal tabloid. Since our hospital was located in an outlying suburb, the newspaper never arrived until next morning.

I was stunned by what I saw. Splashed on the front page was a 'readers' letter' from 'The neighbours', headed 'Acting in Utter Disregard of Law and Discipline, Resorting to All Sorts of Vicious Tricks, and Extorting

Money: Xu Jing, Cadre of the Forestry University, Disgracefully Incited Her Sons to Beat up Her Husband'. This was the 'letter':

Xu Jing, cadre of the Forestry University . . . often deliberately attacks her husband (former Political Commissar of the Ba-yi Film Studio) by making trouble and spreading rumours, aiming to rob him of his salary and his income from writing. During this year's Spring Festival, when her husband asked for money to make a purchase she pretended to be generous and gave him a bankbook [equivalent to a cheque] for 1,000 yuan. To his embarrassment, when he went to cash the money, he found that this bankbook had been cancelled . . . Shortly afterwards, when her husband was critically ill, she removed all the family savings and valuables from their home.

Recently, Xu Jing resorted to brutality when she bribed her sons to loot her husband's book collection and the manuscripts of his novels. On the morning of 28 August, Mu Feng-xin, her eldest son and member of the Beijing Library staff, led a raid on his father. First they sent his bodyguard out by trickery, and the maid was forced to escape by climbing over the wall. Then they locked the gate from inside, cut the military telephone cables, and disconnected the doorbell. They resorted to the brutality practised during the Decade of Calamity [the Cultural Revolution], attacking their father from all sides, jostling and beating him. As a result, he suffered a relapse of his cardiac problem, and was in a critical condition. Fortunately, his former colleagues . . . rushed to the house, and the old man's life was saved.

Afterwards, many cadres and local residents were outraged, and asked the authorities to investigate. In particular, Mu Feng-xin ought to face criminal charges . . . and his mother should also be punished.

Years later, my mother recalled what happened between her, my brothers and my father on 28 August 1980:

When we arrived at the house, he and his bodyguard were busy packing books into big containers. He was worried that I would ask for a share when we divorced, and wanted to transfer most of the collection to secret locations. We thought that the bodyguard should not sit in on our family's business, so we made an excuse to send him out.

The boys started talking to their father: 'We've brought Mama back. Initially, it was agreed that she should stay away for a while, but several months have passed, and it's wrong for her to be away from home. Now that she's back, we hope that you two can live together peacefully.' Father said nothing, but sat in a chair, not looking at anyone. 'Please give Mama's watch back. She needs it,' the boys asked. There was still no reply. No one would budge, and Feng-xin was getting impatient: 'If you don't want to give Mama's watch back, you could give her yours instead.' He still kept quiet. Feng-xin eventually lost control and took off [my father's] watch, which put him in a rage. He jumped up from his chair, and started shouting abuse and screaming for help.

Meanwhile, the maid was panicked. She escaped from the house over the wall, because the boys had locked the gate to keep the bodyguard out. Then she and the bodyguard went to the local neighbourhood committee and reported a murder in progress. Soon, the police and some of the neighbourhood committee arrived, who were followed by officers from the film studio and the General Political Department, summoned by the bodyguard. While the boys and I were explaining what had happened, your father locked himself into his room, and started making telephone calls to his friends and former colleagues. 'They're trying to kill me and rob me. Please come and rescue me!' he shouted. The boys

were furious, afraid of his causing more chaos, but could not stop
him. In desperation, they cut the cables outside his room . . .

When I first read the so-called 'neighbours' letter', I could not believe
my eyes. I knew nothing about the incident described. During that
period, my duties had monopolized my time. I came home exhausted
and fell into bed, and my mother was frequently out, so we seldom
talked.

As a precaution at work, I had never spoken to anyone about my
parents' marriage crisis or my own unhappy marriage. Many of my colleagues had links to my family or New Star's, so my words could travel
far in the city's military circles. I also agreed with my mother that
domestic shame should not be public knowledge, especially since my
parents had been the pride of my life for so long. Before the exposure of
my family's griefs, I had become the envy of many colleagues, for reasons
including the status of my parents and father-in-law, my professional
qualifications and blossoming career. Some colleagues even joked: 'I
wonder what else you want out of life, since you have almost everything
that many others long for.'

The change was enormous, and instant. All of a sudden, my family's
troubles were the talk of the hospital, and causing a sensation in Beijing,
and soon in other parts of China. It was the first time that news about
top officials' family disputes had been reported by the media. For many
days afterwards, a stream of visitors came to see my father, and the street
outside the house was often blocked by their chauffeur-driven cars.
Some of the visitors even came from the provinces or other cities, rushing to call on my father, having read the *Beijing Evening Post*. Most of them
were moved by his tearful account of enduring his sons' brutality. He
would open his empty bookcases and say: 'Look, everything has been
looted, and I have nothing left.'

Unable to cope with the pressure, I asked for two days' leave and
locked myself up in the flat. There were plenty of knocks on the door,

but I did not reply, as I knew they came from strangers. My mother was away with my brothers and her friends, to confer about the problem. It was like the end of my world, and my heart was broken. I felt particularly distressed for my father. After all the strife between us, I found that I still loved him! If I closed my eyes, I saw him assaulted and calling for help. But how could I help? If my father were here, I could comfort him. If my mother and brothers were here, I could protest against what they had done to him. But now I was alone, and cut off from the family. I wanted to cry and scream, and felt choked with anger, pain and desperation.

I read the 'letter' again and again. Gradually, I began to recognize the style. Apart from my mother, no one was closer than me to my father's writing. I had been a keen reader of his novel since my childhood, and received his letters regularly for years. Despite the different contents, the letter published in the *Beijing Evening Post* resembled his writing in wording, sentence structure and expression . . . How I wished my judgement were wrong, but the more I read it, the more strongly I grew to believe that its author was my father, not 'the neighbours'.

In any case, the house was entirely surrounded by high walls, and the gate was always closed. And my family was not close to any 'neighbours', so how on earth could they suddenly know about private details such as the problem of the bankbook, which involved no one but my parents? This is my mother's account of the 'bankbook incident':

> After finding out that he gave money to Scarlet on his own, I decided to take charge of our bankbooks. That money was our savings together, which shouldn't be given away without my consent. At his request, I did give him a bankbook for 1,000 yuan to buy books. Later, I went to the bank to sort out our accounts, and found that the bankbook he had was still uncashed. Soon afterwards, he went to cash it, but was required to bring me too

for security reasons, because the bank clerk remembered my
enquiry. So he was furious. Despite my explanation and apology,
he accused me of deliberately cancelling the bankbook after giving
it to him . . .

From the time he went to Taiyuan in 1978 until my mother was
forced out in 1980, my father never paid a penny towards the family's
expenses, but still asked her for extra money. After I returned from university, my grandmother complained several times: 'My son earns good
money, but why do I have to live on my daughter-in-law's salary?' Since
he did not buy many books during that period, my mother often wondered where the money went. Later, she discovered that he had given
Scarlet 200 yuan when she went to Beijing to sit examinations, which
partly answered the question.

I also knew that before my mother was driven out, she was already
forbidden to enter many parts of the house, so how could she get access
to the family valuables, when they were guarded by my father and his
staff? When she was forced to go to Peace Street, my father had turned
their sons against her, I had been gone for several months, and Aijun was
unwilling to get involved, so she had to leave alone by taxi, taking only
two suitcases and a duvet with her.

When I reread the 'neighbours' letter', I saw that it did not name my
father, but said enough to indicate his social position and personal wealth,
mentioning his former post, his maid, bodyguard, and large income from
writing. In contrast, my mother was attacked by name, but described
merely as a 'cadre', which could cover a job as low as a secretary or junior
office clerk, so readers could easily assume that what she did to her husband was for economic reasons. This selective information allowed me to
sense intentions that no 'neighbours' were likely to have. I also knew that
in China, the press was under strict official censorship. Without authority,
it was impossible for any letter to be published on the front page of any
newspaper. Due to my father's position, in particular, no information

about his private life was allowed to be revealed, unless it was arranged by himself. As all these suspicions coalesced, I began to doubt the truthfulness of the story.

I felt particularly jarred by the comment published beside the 'letter' and headed 'What a Scandal':

The husband is critically ill, the money-making machine no longer valuable, so the curtain of the family's tenderness falls. The attachments of kinship are replaced by greed, warm greetings are replaced by verbal abuse, and care for family members is replaced by beating, smashing and looting. Xu Jing, a government cadre, led her sons into the scandal of seizing the 'estate'. Such bourgeois profit-before-everything behaviour was rare even in Balzac's *Human Comedy*, but happened in today's Beijing . . . Xu Jing and her sons should be condemned and punished.

Although the author used a pseudonym, this comment was supposed to convey the editorial view, but here again I sensed my father's voice. In the past, he liked to cite Balzac's *Human Comedy* when criticizing financial disputes in other families. Yet this comment was illogical. If my mother really regarded her husband as a cash machine, what did she gain by harming him physically? In his position, he would be entitled to a full salary with various privileged benefits as long as he lived, regardless of his health. Only in death would he be 'no longer valuable', and even then, my mother would inherit his estate, so what was the point of seizing the family property when her husband was 'critically ill'? The comment also referred to my brothers as 'her sons', not theirs, as if they had been fathered by someone else, which could easily bias readers' responses.

As I thought about the letter's implications, I felt increasingly dismayed. Was my father, whom I had not seen for over a year, really going mad? How did my mother cope with public denunciation from the man she still loved? By now, I had no doubt that my father was determined to destroy his own family completely.

One morning in December 1980, I was summoned unexpectedly by Dr Honest and another chief of my department, the Political Instructor. 'How is your relationship with your husband?' they inquired. I answered with surprise: 'It is OK.' 'If your husband proposed to divorce you, what would you do?' Now I felt embarrassed. 'Why do you ask?' I was lost for words. 'Of course, he's free to do so . . . Well, it is up to him . . .' The meeting took only a few minutes, and they would not say what had occasioned it. Next day, a colleague told me that the Party branch of my department, which was headed by the same two chiefs, had received a letter from New Star saying that he intended to divorce me.

By now, New Star and I were leading even more separate lives. Each time we met we soon quarrelled, and then spent at least two weeks apart. When we met again, we got along no better than before, and the pattern repeated itself, so reunions could be as short as a few days. It was obvious by now that we had almost nothing in common. To make matters worse, the tragic conflicts in my family kept reminding me of my role in the break-up of my parents' marriage, and intensified my guilt and regret for marrying him. The torrent of complaints and accusations that he set going with our marriage never stopped. Shortly before he wrote the letter to my department, we had finished a separation of nearly two months. Late one evening, he had come to stay with me in the flat in Peace Street when yet another quarrel erupted, and he walked out. He sent the letter proposing to divorce without informing me.

Under the Communist regime, it was normal for the Party to intervene in its members' private lives. One colleague of mine had to phone in on several occasions to excuse herself from work after being beaten by her husband the night before. The Political Instructor and other department chiefs had to rush to this doctor's home to mediate. But New Star's letter was a departure from the norm, as it was not mediation but divorce that he requested. By writing straight to my department, instead of contacting me or his own Party organization first, he was putting more pressure on me.

Soon, the hospital buzzed with rumours about my troubled family life. At that time, New Star was taking a training course at another military hospital in town, which had plenty of connections to my hospital, so comments he made could take as little as a day to reach my hospital, and then be passed to me. Every day brought reports that he was determined to divorce me, and accounts of his offensive remarks. 'Do you know how he has been abusing you to other people?' I was asked by friendly colleagues. 'He was really insulting.'

'New Star boasted about how violently he has treated you. He claimed he tied your hands and gagged you with a towel, and then he beat you . . . Is it true?' In the past, I had told no one outside my family about his brutality. Chinese society did not condemn domestic violence: wife-beating was viewed as a private matter, not to be interfered with. I never heard of any woman suing for divorce on the grounds of her husband's violence or mental cruelty. Since no one could help me to sort out my marriage problems, letting others know about my misery would only cause more gossip. I was too proud to admit to suffering violence.

'Have you heard how New Star gloated over your parents' marriage crisis?' I was asked again. 'He seems to enjoy your family's troubles . . .' This came as no surprise, as I knew that he disliked my father for treating him rudely in the past, trying to stop our marriage, and condemning his father publicly. He did not care how much my parents' marriage crisis distressed me, and took obvious pleasure in spreading stories about my father's relationship with Scarlet, so I had given up discussing family matters with him.

Despite all this activity, I did not hear directly from New Star till some days later, when he phoned me at my office and demanded that I follow his instructions and sort out the divorce without delay. He refused my suggestion that we should cool down first before we talked any further. Soon, his manner turned rough and he started to bellow. Though I tried to contain my anger in front of my colleagues, I had to hang up because I could not cope with his condemnations and there were patients waiting. But he rang back only a few minutes later, and in the end my work was interrupted for more than an hour.

I became the centre of attention at my hospital, now that my private life was on display. Inquisitive members of other departments used to approach my colleagues and ask: 'Who is this Dr Mu, the one whose husband wants to divorce her and whose parents are divorcing now?' Many of those who already knew New Star voiced sympathy with my situation, condemned his behaviour, and told me more about his reputation for dishonesty and bullying. 'What are you afraid of?' a colleague asked. 'With your looks, you'd have no trouble finding another husband. It would only improve your life!' Before they learned that I was married, some officers from local units tried to approach me through my colleagues.

At the same time, there were many who advised that I should do my best to save my marriage. 'You mustn't divorce,' I was told, 'or your reputation will be ruined for ever. Women are always the losers in a divorce.' I was fully aware of the social stigma that divorce imposed on women. Whether they admitted it or not, many Chinese were still influenced by the traditional saying, 'hao-nü-bu-jian-er-fu' – 'a virtuous woman cannot marry twice' – despite the decades of political campaigns, including the Cultural Revolution, which aimed to destroy such traditions. Even after they remarried, many women lived in the shadow of their past, classed as 'er-hun-tou', 'one who married twice', a derogatory term.

Although I had been longing to end my sorry marriage, I wavered now. Ever since my shaming in middle school, I had feared to repeat the experience, and believed that there was no future for a woman with a damaged reputation. Unwilling to lose what I had achieved through so many years of hard work and the sacrifice of my private life, I also felt deeply disturbed by the turmoil in my family, exposed by the *Beijing Evening Post* not long before. New Star was vindictive. I did not expect him to let me off easily if we divorced. Would I be strong enough to go through a hostile divorce, on top of the stress inflicted by my parents' marriage crisis?

After painful consideration, I eventually gave up the idea of divorcing New Star, and asked one of his colleagues, who had acted as our matchmaker before, to arrange a reconciliation. When New Star visited me again, I made no mention of his recent actions. His response was to tell me that I should apologize to him in writing, and promise never to oppose him again. I refused his demand, saying that it was unfair. Shortly after the reconciliation, he revealed accidentally that his intention in the divorce episode had been to 'teach me a lesson'. The discovery made me furious. This time, he had taken his tricks a step further, by damaging my general reputation. How I had let myself down by going through with our marriage!

In spring 1981, a large cut in staff numbers was planned to take place in my hospital under Deng Xiaoping's disarmament policy, and would focus on the surplus of doctors. Like other departments, mine already had more than twice its proper quota, but a steady flow continued to arrive in the hospital, most of them transferred from other military hospitals sited outside Beijing or in the provinces, attracted by the hospital's location. Normally, they came from politically influential or well-connected families, so they could not be rejected. For several months, the unprecedented staff reductions had been hotly discussed in the hospital, as people wondered what their futures held.

I believed that the cuts would not affect my job. Though qualified for less than a year, Dr Honest considered me as one of the two best members of his staff, and was impressed both by my professional knowledge and by my handling of difficult cases. Here I was grateful for my pre-university training in Obstetrics and Gynaecology in Changzhi City Hospital, and especially for the experience gained under Dr Li, my supervisor. Also, I was lucky that the Cultural Revolution ended during my second year at university, which transformed my medical training. The other colleague

favoured by Dr Honest was Dr Feng, whom I envied for her brilliant surgical skills. Apart from Dr Honest, we were the only two doctors in the
department with university training. Dr Feng was my age, but had graduated some years before I did, and her first name, Jinping, meant 'splendid
peace'. We two were known as the department's 'Two Pings', and regarded
as Dr Honest's 'zuo-bang you-bei', left and right arms.

At the end of the previous year, I had been elected as the model doctor
of the year by the staff of my department for my dedication to work and
the quality of my services to patients. In the hospital, I was praised for my
kind and helpful nature, and respectful manner towards others. Friendly
colleagues joked: 'There are only two people in our hospital that everyone
likes, and one of them is you.' I loved my work and surroundings, and my
whole focus was on improving my knowledge and qualifications.

My expectation was completely wrong. One morning in May 1981,
my department was informed that I was the only one in my department
scheduled to lose their job in the hospital's first list of staff cuts. A year
later, I heard how my fate had been decided from Swallow, a political
officer working for the hospital's leadership, the Party committee.

For several months, the members of the committee held a marathon
series of meetings to decide the first staff cuts, discussing each doctor
one by one. Very often, when a name was mentioned, a voice would rise
to say: 'I've just had a phone call from her [or his] father, saying that she
[or he] can't possibly go this time.' Or 'If we let her go, how will I
explain it to her parents?' And these names would not feature on the list.

In my hospital, many doctors came from powerful social backgrounds, with parents or in-laws who included a vice-premier, army
generals, government ministers, ambassadors, and leading figures in the
Beijing municipality. Others had personal links with the hospital authorities. It was said that the director paid special attention to one physician,
a girl in her mid-twenties, whose father was a middle-ranking officer
involved in decisions about the leadership of numerous military hospitals, including our own. Indeed, the hospital leaders were also concerned

about the effect of the cuts on their jobs. Some were nearing the end of their careers, and had to think about where they would spend their retirement, which was also up to their superiors. So for them it seemed expedient to please those members of their staff whose fathers could influence their future.

These staff cuts may have been the hardest task ever faced by the hospital management. Few people anywhere were willing to leave the armed forces. The move to the civilian sector always brought a sharp fall in salary, in my case probably by at least 20 per cent, even if I stayed in the same profession. Although the government and the military author-ities had promised to guarantee job opportunities to every officer who left the services, military doctors faced enormous difficulties in finding employment. Many of them came from the 'worker-peasant-soldier stu-dent' background now regarded as a substandard education, which made it almost impossible to find suitable jobs in civilian hospitals.

When my discharge was tabled, nobody spoke. My father and father-in-law were big names in the Beijing Military Region, but both were out of favour. Major-General Geng had been transferred to the Nanjing Military Region, and had no personal contacts in my hospital. Now that my family's turmoil had been put on display by the *Beijing Evening Post*, no one expected my father to look after my interests. It was Swallow who took the minutes at these meetings, and she felt anxious about the par-ticipants' attitude towards me. Although we were not friends, she felt that it would be unfair if I had to leave the hospital just because I had no family backing. In previous months, she had been assigned to report on staff performance to the hospital authority, so she knew how impor-tant I was to my department. Dr Feng was in her late pregnancy, and would soon start her six months' maternity leave. When Dr Honest went on holiday, I headed the department. Desperate to help my department and me, before my fate was decided Swallow found an excuse to suspend the meeting briefly.

'Please let Mu Aiping stay!' she pleaded with the committee during the break. 'Otherwise, her department's work will be badly affected!' But no one listened, and instead she was told off: 'You shouldn't interfere in the leadership's decisions.' 'Somebody has to go. If we kept Mu Aiping, who else could we let go?'

The decision shocked and angered many people in the hospital, especially in my department. Dr Honest and the Political Instructor protested at once to the hospital authority, and many other colleagues complained about the unfairness. But it seemed that no one could save me. I was told to stop working there and then, and Dr Honest was pressured into providing a reference for me on behalf of the Party branch of my department, as part of the leaving procedure. The managers were furious when they found that it contained two pages full of praise, and ended by asserting that 'Mu Aiping is a model for our department.' Dr Honest was summoned by the hospital's Political Commissar. 'Why have you written such a favourable reference?' he complained. 'How can she have no faults?' 'This reference is the view of our department,' Dr Honest replied. 'I have no right to change it on my own.' Later, Dr Honest told me that it was the first time he had confronted the hospital leadership face to face.

Shortly after I left, an in-patient, a local woman, died unexpectedly in my department, having just given birth to twins. Afterwards, her family demanded that her doctor should be charged with negligence. Almost every day, protesters gathered in front of the hospital's head office or inside my department's building, crying and shouting. They also prepared to sue the hospital. During the dispute, which lasted for months until an out-of-court settlement was reached, the department's work was frequently interrupted, and some of the hospital leaders had to hide when the crowd appeared. For nearly a year, my department had to look after the motherless twins, left behind by their family.

After the woman's deaths, the hospital authorities summoned the heads of all departments to an emergency meeting, to inform them about the case and alert them against negligence of duty. In reply, the Political Instructor of my department stated publicly: 'If Dr Mu were still here, this patient would not have died.' Dr Honest also told his superiors that he could not vouch for his department's standards, since Dr Feng was absent and I had been forced to leave. According to him, the only time he could sleep peacefully at night was when she or I were on duty, because he had faith in our work.

In June 1981, about a month after I had left, Dr Honest and the Political Instructor called at my home and asked me to return. I was told that the hospital authorities had changed their minds. 'Please keep quiet when you go back to work,' they advised. 'Don't ask for an explanation.' They were probably worried that I might offend the hospital chiefs by mentioning unfairness. For them, what mattered was to keep me.

Even today, I don't believe that the hospital changed its decision solely out of concern for patients' safety. During that period, there was increasing talk in military circles about my father's likely promotion after the recent appointment of Lieutenant-General Yuan Shengping as Political Commissar of the Beijing Military Region. A quarter of a century ago, he and my father had been close colleagues. Now that Lieutenant-General Yuan was 'first hand' leader of the military region, a number of senior officers who had hardly made contact with my father before paid visits to him in response to speculation about his probable return and promotion. I believed that this speculation must also have reached the hospital authorities, who had to take precautions in case my father really was promoted in the near future, and decided to help his children. Unfortunately, my father did not get his promotion, nor was he recalled to the Beijing Military Region. According to my mother, this was largely due to the publicity about their marriage problem, which damaged his reputation, especially because more and more people in military circles had heard about his relationship with Scarlet.

Chapter 26

New Hope:
The Birth of My Son

(June 1981–May 1982)

After the settlement of my marriage crisis, I began to think about having a child, partly in the hope of making up for the miseries I faced in my private life. In my hospital, I was known for my fondness for children, and colleagues and friends often expressed their surprise at the patience and kindness I showed towards their children. During my spare time, I liked to visit the hospital's kindergarten, and the sweets I brought made me a popular figure there, so people often joked that I should have a child of my own. In my hospital, most of the female staff around my age were already mothers. For Chinese, it seemed odd that I was not, since I was nearing thirty and had been married for several years. Some of my patients told me that in their localities mothers-in-law would complain if their daughters-in-law did not give birth within a year of marrying.

When I returned in June 1981, the hospital had started preparations to move to a new location, and would stop accepting patients soon. As the pressure of work would decrease until spring next year, I felt that it was a good time for me to have a child. New Star made no objection. He had blamed me in the past for not giving birth to a child so that he could enjoy a proper family life.

However, to have a child was not solely a decision for the parents. By then, the government had launched the one-child policy: women had to apply to their local authority before getting pregnant, as childbirth quotas were set in accordance with the government's population plan. Pregnancies outside the quota were liable to termination, and couples with 'non-plan' babies, born without official approval, faced stringent penalties – enormous fines that could be several times their joint annual income, or disciplinary charges imposed at work.

As procedure required, my hospital provided a letter supporting my application for inclusion in the childbirth quota. As well as our names, professions and workplaces, the letter specified our ages, duration of marriage, and childless status. As a rule, ours should have been a straightforward case, especially considering our age – New Star was thirty-two and I was approaching my thirtieth birthday. Unexpectedly, our application was denied by the local authority in the area where my flat was located, because neither of us were registered there. As members of the armed forces, we had no need to register for residence wherever we lived in China. I was told that since the number of childbirth allocations was based on the number of registered local residents, we did not qualify. Fortunately, the director of the local neighbourhood committee lived next to my flat, and was sympathetic. With her access to the local authority, she eventually helped me convince the officials to include me.

Before getting pregnant, another complication was to have my intrauterine device (IUD) removed. Under the government family planning policy, women were required to practise contraception after marriage, so I had the IUD inserted after leaving university. Now, removing the IUD was like announcing to my colleagues that I planned to have a child, because there was no way to keep the operation secret. I decided to have it done in my department. If I went to another medical institution, I needed an official letter from my hospital, otherwise no one would be allowed to operate.

A colleague performed the removal. Like many other family planning operations in China, such as abortion or IUD insertion, it was done without anaesthesia. I could not bear the agonizing pain and started to scream, which alarmed my colleague into halting the first operation. The second took place in the Army General Hospital, and was performed by a consultant. I tried my best to cope with the pain, fearing that otherwise the second attempt would also fail. When everything was over, my underclothes were drenched in cold sweat.

By late September 1981 I found that I was pregnant, but could not find New Star to inform him. Our quarrels had reduced, but we still lived apart most of the time. During his training course he stayed with his mother, though she often joined her husband in Nanjing. Sometimes we did not meet for weeks. He disliked the flat where I lived, and seldom invited me to his mother's place either. Eventually I ran into him at a friend's wedding party. Although we had not seen each other for weeks, he looked at me coldly and would hardly speak. When I told him about my pregnancy, I expected him at least to show concern about my physical condition. Instead, his reply was brief and distant: he was terribly busy, and had to deliver some videos to a high official family where many people were waiting to watch them with him. Soon after that, he hurried off.

I began to suffer from the sickness of early pregnancy, and the smell of cooked food turned my stomach. Then my arrhythmia problem started again, and I was losing my strength. One day I fainted in the flat, and came round lying alone on the cold cement floor. Sometimes I felt too sick to go to work, but had no one to look after me. My mother was frequently away, seeking support from my brothers or through her social connections, and most of my siblings and I were out of touch.

When New Star eventually called on me some time later, I was disheartened again by his indifference. He showed no concern about the sickness I was suffering, and would not agree to spend more time with me during my pregnancy. Instead, he suggested an abortion, which I angrily refused. Our conversation turned into a row, and he walked out.

Despite New Star's behaviour, I still kept hoping that he would eventually appreciate that I was pregnant with his child, and his manner would change. Sickness combined with loneliness and depression was making my life unbearable, and flooding my mind with weakness and incompetence. I was eager to talk to New Star again, to ask for the support that a husband gives his wife, and make him see that our future child and I both needed him, and it was difficult for me to shoulder the responsibility on my own. In China, the first pregnancy was regarded as a special event for families, and the mother much pampered at home. I too longed to be loved and cared for by my husband at this particular time.

I made several evening visits to his mother's house, hoping to see him again and to beg him for comfort, but he was always away. Sometimes I stood for hours under the dim light of the street lamps on the pavement outside, enduring the cold and wind, and then left in disappointment. One day in December, I finally got him on the phone. When I asked him to come and see me, he shouted: 'Go to your department if you're not feeling well! I'm not an obstetrician! It's not up to me to look after you!' I could not believe my ears, and burst out crying.

Meanwhile, my mother had run into unexpected difficulties in transferring from the Chinese Academy of Sciences to the Forestry University. When the Academy's head office was reorganized in 1979, she refused several offers to stay, and decided to return to the university, back from Yunnan since 1978. Many universities in Beijing had to move to the provinces under Lin Biao's No. 1 Directive in 1969, most of them for good, so it was extremely fortunate that the Forestry University managed to return, thanks to its major leaders, and especially Ji Xian, secretary of the university Party committee.

After the withdrawal of the PLA Propaganda Team in 1974, Ji Xian was reinstated as the university's 'first hand' leader, and faced rising demands from the staff to bring the university back to Beijing. Having moved to Yunnan against their will, many had left their families or children behind in Beijing, expecting to return sooner or later. The teaching staff found it impossible to apply expertise developed in the north of China to the southern region where Yunnan is located, with its enormous differences in natural conditions and vegetation. It frustrated them to realize that they were wasting their time and knowledge there. In Kunming, the provincial capital, there was already an established Department of Forestry in a local university, competent to meet the needs of Yunnan as well as several surrounding provinces. It was said that the provincial authority, when it agreed to accept the Beijing Forestry University in 1969, was mainly interested in the university's more advanced teaching and research equipment.

Before the Forestry University, a few others had already won release from provincial exile. One was the Beijing University of Agriculture, which had been stationed in northern Shaanxi. There, local residents had suffered for decades from endemic Kaschin-Beck disease, caused mainly by polluted drinking water, and this made the new arrivals particularly desperate to escape, for fear of contracting the disease. The leaders of the university spent years lobbying in Beijing, and eventually convinced the Party leadership to approve the university's return.

Encouraged by such cases, the Forestry University intensified its lobbying activities. For several years, its senior staff were either stationed in Beijing most of the time, or made frequent visits from Yunnan to offices in the central government or Party headquarters. Eventually, the case reached Vice-Premier Fang Yi, the head of the State Science and Technology Commission. With his approval, the university finally returned to Beijing, and many families ended long separations. The cost of the nine-year ordeal was horrendous, and covered mainly by the government budget, yet the Forestry University was only one of the hundreds or perhaps even thousands of similar cases traceable to the Cultural Revolution.

Ji Xian became popular on the campus for his efforts to restore the university, but that did not save him during a subsequent incident.

When the university returned, most of the campus was occupied by various other institutions, so it had to build temporary huts as offices or classrooms, and students lived in tents or huts on the sports ground, along with most of the staff and their families. Through various trans-actions, the university managed to retrieve most of its buildings, but those who clung on included a research institute of the Chinese Academy of Sciences, where Deng Xiaoping's daughter, Deng Nan, happened to work. The university leaders were deterred from further action by the prospect of Deng Nan pulling strings to help her institute. Another hold-out property was the largest teaching building on campus, now occupied by another research institute. In early 1980, a crowd of students acting on their own initiative broke into the building one evening and evicted the occupants. During that period, similar inci-dents happened in several other universities, and were reported by the Western media as anti-government student demonstrations. When these episodes were broadcast by the Voice of America, the Chinese authori-ties were furious. By order of the then premier, Ji Xian was sacked at once. Although he had taken no part in his students' action, he, as the 'first hand' leader, became the only one to be punished. His political career was over.

While Ji Xian was still in power, he wrote an official statement to declare: 'I endorse Comrade Xu Jing's return. With her knowledge of the university, her return will benefit our work.' But shortly afterwards, he reversed his decision without saying why. There was speculation on campus that he was pandering to supporters who had their eye on the post of vice-secretary of the university Party committee and feared that it might fall to my mother, who had held it about twenty years before. In response to this arbitrary change, she complained to the Forestry

Ministry, the university's higher authority, whose personnel director asked Ji Xian: 'Your statement accepting Xu Jing is still on record. Why have you changed your mind?'

Under pressure from the Forestry Ministry, Ji Xian took on my mother with reluctance, but over the next two months she did not receive her salary, or any official information about the terms of her post. Later, she heard that this was by order of Ji Xian. He also made an unexpected announcement at a plenary meeting of the university staff, appointing my mother as director of a university department, which in fact meant demoting her. She was not invited to the meeting, or given notice about the appointment. In desperation, she appealed for justice to the Forestry Ministry, whose staff were angry because they had not been consulted about her appointment. But before any settlement was reached, Ji Xian was removed from his post in reprisal for his students' action.

During that time my mother was offered several opportunities to work for the ministry's headquarters with a position equal to her previous grade, but she refused these offers, for fear that she might let the ministry down. The crisis in her marriage had disturbed her so much that she could not face the strain of starting a job in new surroundings. Working for the university was different, because she was familiar with the surroundings, and knew many of the staff. Her refusal seemed justified when soon afterwards my family's troubles broke in the *Beijing Evening Post*. After that, she was caught up in divorce battles for several years.

Ji Xian's successor, who came from outside the university, also refused to arrange a post for my mother, again without offering a reason. He and my mother were more or less equals in terms of their grades and revolutionary experience, except that she was more than ten years his junior. For this reason, she felt that he saw her as a threat.

As my pregnancy progressed, I kept expecting New Star's attitude to change, and looked forward to seeing him. If only he would show some concern, I could forgive his previous behaviour. A week passed, two weeks, one month, two months . . . He did not turn up, or make contact. As the New Year of 1982 approached, I thought that he might come to see me. I was wrong. Soon afterwards came the Chinese New Year, a traditional family occasion, but it brought no visit. Now I began to lose sleep, tortured by grief and disappointment. I was pregnant with his child, the only child that China's laws allowed. How could he care so little? When I saw how my colleagues and patients were cherished by their husbands during their pregnancies, I felt even more grieved by his indifference.

During these sleepless nights, I often looked back over my life. From the age of fourteen, I had come through endless ordeals: the humiliation I suffered at school as a naive pupil, years of persecution for my parents, hardship and starvation in the rural settlement . . . Then when my parents were finally rehabilitated, my estrangement from my father, my parents' marriage crisis, and my family divided . . . After all that, my own marriage had broken down and I could not tell how my career would develop . . . I had made some mistakes, but I believed that others might do the same in my shoes. For so many years, I had tried my best to work hard and be kind to others, and to stand up to unjust treatment when I met it. No matter how difficult the situation was, I would never surrender. But why did misfortunes still dominate my life? Why did I have to experience so much pain? The Cultural Revolution was over, but the ordeals continued in my life. I had passed my thirtieth birthday. How much more suffering remained?

Ever since the peace and happiness in my life was destroyed by the Cultural Revolution, I often had a feeling of being deeply wounded, as a consequence of what I went through. Despite the sociable and easygoing manner that I always showed to others, deep inside I actually felt bitter and lonely, especially when I was on my own. For the first several months after I moved to the flat, I was still jobless, and no-one in my family initiated any contact with me apart from my mother. I often locked myself into the flat without any contact with outside. After

some days of the 'self-imprisonment', I felt unbelievably strange about
my own voice when I started to talk to people again. Sometimes, I
thought that I was going to be driven mad by the incredible loneliness.
During that period, I started writing, which soon became my hobby. My
writing included short stories, novels and film scripts, which were based
on my own experiences. With no intention to publish them, I just felt
that through writing I could express my feelings, and hence relieve the
pain, sadness and anger in my mind.

Later, my mother moved into the flat, but it did not make life any
easier. Ever since I was born, my world had been my father's, as I was his
favourite child, and saw little of my mother. This was our first long
period of living on our own under the same roof, and it felt odd at the
beginning, especially with both of us locked in our different marriage
crises. After so many kinds of hardship, my mother seemed hesitant to
place her trust in others again, including her own children, and now I
could tell that her caution extended to me. During the family convulsions, my father and his siblings had accused her of buying her children's
support, but this was untrue, and in fact she kept her money away from
everyone. When we went shopping for food, she sometimes insisted on
our paying separate bills, and it upset me that she thought I might
exploit her. Now that I was pregnant, I was disappointed that she stayed
away so often, and when she was back she often left me to deal with the
household chores on my own, while she moped. Sometimes she kept to
her room for hours, writing long letters to my father. As she told me
later, they expressed concern for his welfare and hopes for reconciliation.
She regretted their separation and apologized for her share in it. I felt
that she was wasting her time, but she replied: 'He is my husband, and
I still love him.' Sadly, all these letters were returned unopened.

My mother often complained about my bad temper, because my
moods were no better than hers. Sometimes I felt close to a breakdown
under the strains of my private life, my heavy workload, the bias I suffered at the hospital, and bouts of sickness. It was not easy to maintain

control, especially when we clashed. On my mother's side, she was clumsy in handling her children, and attempts to improve the relationship did not work out as she wished. Misunderstandings too easily turned into quarrels. Afterwards, we might not talk for days at a time, or she would leave me alone in the flat.

The idea of ending my life returned again. Why go through endless troubles by staying in the world? During one sleepless night, I started to write a suicide note: 'I may already be in another world when people read this letter. All those who are going or have prepared to leave the world forever must have their minds full of words for the lucky survivors . . .' I wanted to write a long note to explain my decision. Since the anguish was too much to bear, I was afraid that if I did not unburden myself before I died, my soul would not rest in the next world.

I wrote for hours, and ignored the whistling wind outside our block. Suddenly, I felt the foetus moving. Although it had started some time before, my heart had never been so touched. It halted my pen and I burst into tears, and wept until no more tears would come. No, I could not die, because I was no longer on my own. I must be responsible for my future child, whom I had fought to bring to life. In a few months my child would be born. For the sake of my child, I must live, and never mind my troubles.

The dark sky was lightening, and the city began to wake up. Outside, the quiet was broken by the sounds of footsteps and bicycle bells. The pavements bustled with more and more peasant vendors arriving from outside town. They carried huge sacks, baskets or cages behind the saddles of their bicycles, crammed with goods such as grains, fresh vegetables, eggs or live chickens . . . A few years ago, a free market selling agricultural produce had sprung up along the pavements near our block, as a consequence of the shift from central planning to a market economy sponsored by Deng Xiaoping. This outdoor market was a huge success, because Beijing had been poorly supplied by the state-owned markets. Soon it became one of the city's largest autonomous markets, where many items rationed for decades could be bought, at a higher price.

In December 1978, the Communist Party decided that China's priority was economic development rather than the class struggle fostered by Mao Zedong and dominant for more than a decade. Deng Xiaoping's economic reforms were launched in the rural areas, and the collective economy created by Mao during the Great Leap Forward in 1958 was abandoned. Instead, agricultural production took place within individual households, and peasants were free to sell their produce. They welcomed the reforms.

In the new agricultural market near our block, the peasants made money and their customers found fresh and good quality products. Though the vendors were shabbily dressed, and many slept rough on the pavements to save money, they were no longer the quasi-serfs I was familiar with. Under the reforms, they were able to get rich through hard work. For the moment, they were a small minority among the 800 million peasants who made up 80 per cent of the population, but I believed that in the long run more and more peasants would be able to throw off the poverty and hunger that they and their ancestors had endured.

In recent years, I had also seen how many of the former rural exiles had created new lives for themselves in Beijing. At first, many of them had to take on whatever turned up in order to survive, such as selling hot tea on the pavement, since they had no skills and few employment opportunities. Instead of cups or mugs, they used rice bowls brought from their homes, like the tables and chairs they provided. Yet some of these tea-sellers became successful entrepreneurs, with several shops or other flourishing businesses. As the first generation raised in the People's Republic, many of us had gone through precarious lives. But we survived!

In the Peace Street area, there were at least a hundred huge apartment blocks, mostly housing government staff. When my parents first moved to the flat in the early 1970s, many blocks stood in darkness at night, because most of their occupants were consigned to labour camps, and their children to rural settlements. Now, these families had returned to peaceful lives, and this area was no longer a ghost town. Just six years ago, who would have foreseen that the Cultural Revolution would be over? Who dared to dream that so many improvements would happen?

The longer I thought about these positive changes around me, the more I revived. Eventually, I collected myself. The country's situation was improving, though slowly, and without much joy for me. I told myself that no matter how grim my life was, this was not the end of the world. As long as I did not give up, there was light in the future. I must ignore what I had suffered, and live as a strong person. From then on, I became cheerful and prepared to make my future baby welcome. The knitting I did included cardigans to fit various sizes from newborn baby to school age, as I thought that I might be too busy to produce them in the future, as a single parent. I rejected advice to terminate my pregnancy from colleagues concerned about my broken relationship, and told them that I would divorce New Star once my child was born.

I began to understand my mother. Several times I was woken up at midnight by her wailing in her sleep, a dreadful sound, voicing anger and pain so intense that I had only heard it once before, coming from my grandmother during the Cultural Revolution. Like her, my mother told me that she had had a nightmare, and said no more. But I could imagine how distressing these nightmares were, because such a wail could only happen when a person's soul was tortured, or her heart torn open. Poor mother! I should have realized how much you had suffered!

In my mother's personal life, nothing meant more than her marriage, especially because her childhood family life had not been happy. Throughout their marriage, she would do anything for her husband. For decades, she supported his career and let him spend most of their income on buying books. During the Cultural Revolution, she shared enormous risks to protect the collections. When our family moved into the current house, she pitched in to help the labourers they hired to refurbish it. Our neighbours were a high official family. Their maid laughed: 'You'll never catch our master's wife doing such dirty work.' Despite my mother's social position, she always felt like a vulnerable woman, and relied on her husband emotionally. After his cardiac problems started, she told friends that she did not know how she would manage on her own if he died before her.

Before the split, my paternal grandmother was always proud of having such a caring daughter-in-law, and their good relationship was well known among our neighbours and my parents' colleagues. In autumn 1976, she suffered a stroke that left half of her body paralysed. While she was in hospital, my mother visited her every day. She cooked her favourite dishes, fed her spoon by spoon, combed her hair, bathed her and helped with her toilet, which amazed the hospital staff.

Ever since I could remember, most of our visitors were my father's relatives, and their visits increased after the Cultural Revolution. Sometimes a second table had to be laid for meals. In addition to looking after her mother-in-law, this workload put a strain on my mother, but she carried on year after year. In contrast, her side of the family was excluded, except for occasional visits from Ning, my mother's second sister, and her children. Because my father was indifferent to her relatives, she seldom invited them, which caused Ning to accuse her of unfairness. Yet now, after all her sacrifices for him, and her years of befriending his relatives, the man she still loved had betrayed her. As a result she had lost the family she had treasured so much, and been driven from her home.

Due to her reticent nature, my mother hardly mentioned her pain to me, or the obstacles she faced at work. But now I began to see how desperately she needed support from others, just as I did, and feared that she too risked a breakdown. Sometimes she seemed confused. She had always dressed elegantly; nowadays she could forget to change for weeks. When she was tired, she just went straight to bed as she was, and did not mind when her bedding soon got dirty. I did my best to look after her, cooking her meals and changing her bedding. At that time, washing machines were rare in China, so I washed everything by hand. I also accompanied her to the local public bathhouse regularly, queuing for hours with local residents, since the flat had no bathing facilities.

My mother and I were getting closer. By spring 1982, our quarrelling had stopped. Instead, we enjoyed each other's company, and began to talk heart-to-heart, which never happened before. When I entered hospital for a while due to serious complications with my pregnancy, we both felt lonely and missed one another.

Shortly before the birth was due, New Star finally appeared, but offered no apology or explanation for his long absence during my pregnancy. I did not bother to complain, since I had made up my mind to divorce him in good time. A few weeks later he came again to say goodbye. His father was critically ill in Nanjing, and he was going to visit him. It was early May 1982, with only a few days to go, and I was on sick leave at home. For some months I had been suffering from high blood pressure, and terrible swelling from my feet to my upper body. Having no telephone in the flat, I was worried that if anything happened at night, I would have no way to send for immediate support. Being a high official, my mother was entitled to free telephone services at home. But since the flat was not inside the campus, the cost of installation was substantially higher. So the university was unwilling to pay for the extra cost, especially since she was jobless at that time. Due to shortages of telephone services, it was almost impossible for customers to get telephone installation at home through individual applications. I asked New Star to take me to my hospital before he left, so that I could stay in my department as an in-patient.

The birth was almost two weeks overdue, but there were no signs of labour starting. On 27 May 1982 a nurse made a routine check in the late afternoon, and I knew from her expression and repeated monitoring that something had gone wrong. 'Little Mu,' she said quietly, 'I'm afraid I'm picking up foetal distress.' My baby's heartbeat had become irregular, and I also felt more kicking than before, which confirmed the nurse's judgement. Soon the duty doctor hurried in. A few hours later, there was no improvement in my baby's condition, nor was there any sign of labour, despite some attempts at intervention. It was already late evening when Dr Honest, summoned from home, decided to carry out an emergency Caesarean section to save the baby. The regulations required a member of my family to sign a consent form, but there was nobody there from my family. New Star was in Nanjing, and by the time my mother could be fetched it would be too late. In desperation Dr Honest, as head of my department, had to sign the agreement, even though he would also be performing the operation.

I was given epidural anaesthesia, which is common for Caesareans, but my blood pressure dropped sharply. Within seconds I lost my vision and felt helplessly choked, as if falling out of control. 'Oh, Dr Honest, I'm dying . . .' I gasped these few words and blacked out. When I came round, the operation was still going on, and the first sound I heard was a baby's loud cry. 'Congratulations, Little Mu!' came the head nurse's cheerful voice. 'You've got a boy!' 'And naughty too!' another nurse joked. 'The first thing he did was to pee at my face . . .' While they joked and laughed, the baby was brought to me naked and feet first, which was routine procedure so that the mother could tell her baby's gender straight away.

Before I could snatch a glance at my baby's face, I was slipping again, this time due to the sharp rise in my blood pressure brought on by the drugs just used to bring me round. When it shot dangerously high, various other infusions were added to the drip. The result was another emergency. Soon after the injection, muscles all over my body started to twitch uncontrollably, and I realized that I had been given the allergenic drugs which had made me fall critically ill eight years before, in the hospital of the Armoured Forces 9th Division (the two allergenic drugs belonged to the promethazine and chlorpromazine families). When I told them the cause of my allergy, none of the staff there had any idea what to do, as they had never encountered it before. So all my previous symptoms took over again. I felt that I could not lie still, as if driven by mysterious powers, desperate to get down from the operating table, bolt outside and run and run . . . Tortured by the symptoms, I started to shout and thrash around with a new incision in my stomach, which rattled everybody, and especially Dr Honest. Soon, beads of sweat were rolling down his face, and he seemed on the point of collapse when his colleague, Dr Feng, who was assisting in the operation, relieved him and took charge. In order to stop me moving, they tied my arms and legs to the operating table, but I started to twist uncontrollably, till in the end it was only a general anaesthetic that saved me.

When I revived it was morning, and I was lying in my department's intensive-care ward, with Dr Honest sitting by my side. He seemed to have aged since my eyes closed, and looked pale and exhausted after staying up all night to keep an eye on my condition. 'How naughty you were, Little Mu!' he joked in the next few days. 'You almost scared me to death when I performed your Caesarean.'

The birth of my son caused a stir in the hospital. When they heard about my emergency operation, the night staff in many other departments kept popping in and out for news about my progress. The duty administrative officer organized emergency procedures such as sending vehicles to pick up Dr Honest from home or to collect blood supplies for me. Next morning, after the incoming staff heard the news that I had given birth to a handsome boy, visitors flocked to my ward from all over the hospital, some of them strangers to me. I knew this was due partly to my popularity, and partly to their sympathy for my circumstances. Normally, a new mother would be surrounded by her husband and family, and bathed in attention, but I had no one with me from my family. On the very night my son was born, my mother's feet were injured in an accident, and she could not leave the flat for many days.

I was full of joy when my son was brought to me on the morning after his birth. 'Now I have got you, my dear boy, I won't be lonely any more!' I murmured. 'I promise I shall give you a happy life.' At the suggestion of my best friend in the hospital, I named him Shan (meaning 'mountain'), wishing him a strong nature and a generous heart. Someone told me that a hospital administrative officer who knew my father personally phoned him to tell him about his grandson, but he hung up at once without a word.

A few days after the birth, New Star returned from Nanjing, as his father's condition was improving. Major-General Geng urged his son to return and look after me, and told him that he should treat me better, especially on this occasion. New Star was very pleased when he heard I had given birth to a son, and came to visit me in hospital. He told me that his father was also gladdened by the news, because the Geng family had an extra male descendant. From Nanjing, Major-General Geng phoned his home village in Jiangxi province, and asked his relatives to add his newborn grandson's name to the list of male family members presented before the ancestors' graves. When I thought about Little Mountain's future, I dropped the idea of divorce. Rightly or wrongly, I felt that it was too cruel for the little boy to grow up in a broken family.

Chapter 27

High Official Versus High Official: My Parents' Divorce

(September 1980–January 1984)

In September 1980, the same month that the *Beijing Evening Post* published the 'letter from the neighbours', my father sued for divorce, with this plaint to the Beijing Municipal Intermediate People's Court:

> I am a serviceman. My wife, Xu Jing [hereinafter called she], cadre of the Beijing Forestry University, has been trying to kill me for some time, which has severely damaged my physical and mental health, and put my life under serious threat. The details are as follows:
>
> Maltreating my aged and paralysed mother. She twice proposed to divorce me because I invited my aged mother and siblings to our home. She scoffed at my mother in order to get rid of her: 'All other old people live with their daughters. How could someone live with her son?' 'I want to divorce your son, so you'd better get out!' She often referred to herself as a widow. I let my mother live in a sunny room in our house, for which she often picked quarrels

with me. To my mother's face, she accused her of eating too much, and swore between her teeth: 'You'll come to a bad end!' So that my mother was often in tears.

Being hostile to my siblings. When my younger sister travelled a long way to visit my mother, she treated her coldly. When my nephew visited us, she did not allow the maid to cook for him. As a result, my siblings don't want to stay in our home when they come to Beijing.

Torturing me physically. She did not let me sleep for several nights, and used some shameless means, which I feel too embarrassed to describe, to make me ill. When I was on oxygen therapy at home due to my cardiac problems, she punched me violently over the heart, and beat me to the floor, and then back to my bed, not caring if I lived or died . . . She said to others: 'If he had died several years earlier, I might just about have missed him.' She wants me dead so desperately . . .

For a long time, she has libelled me maliciously, and attacked me for being involved in sexual affairs. Any woman who has contact with me is accused of having an affair. She goes to all sorts of lengths, such as making body searches, trying to wring confessions out of me, threatening and bugging. She has spread a lot of rumours, fabricated evidence and collected dossiers against me, and smears my name everywhere, intending to ruin my reputation and to cover her own ugly nature.

When I was away from Beijing to write, she took all my savings, about 25,000 yuan, together with 5,000–6,000 yuan in cash, which included my salary for over a year and my income from writing. And then she accuses me of giving money to some woman . . . Last year, I received some income from my writing again, which was cashed by her with an official letter she presented. During the night of the Chinese New Year, I was already suffering from a fracture to my left foot, but she knocked me down deliberately, so that the plaster was damaged. One day in spring this year, she threw a pair of scissors in my face.

In May this year, she caused me to fall critically ill again. While I was too sick to get out of bed, she arranged to have a whole truckload of valuable belongings removed from our home, and then abandoned the family of her own accord and has never returned . . .

In his plaint, my father also mentioned the episode of the bankbook, and the row he had with my brothers before Feng-yuan's wedding. Rather than admit that the row was caused by his breaking his promise to accommodate Feng-yuan, he claimed that his sons had been incited by his wife. In his account of the 'Family Conflict of 28 August' he repeated the allegations made in the 'letter from the neighbours', and described the assault he claimed that he suffered:

While he was beating me, the eldest one [Feng-xin] shouted: 'Give me a rope to tie him up!' Xu Jing sat outside, watching me being beaten and beaming with pleasure. 'Don't ask for any money back!' she said. 'I have given it all to the children.' She was shameless . . .

To conclude, my father wrote:

For many years, I have compromised and accommodated myself to her. Until last year, I still told her that I would not divorce her, and have tried my best to make up with her since. But things have gone against my wishes, as her tricks have turned more vicious, completely destroying any attachment between us. In her efforts to murder me she has used all sorts of illegal and evil methods, and even incited her sons to physical assault and murder . . . How evil she is! She has brought me to ruin. There seems no hope for any reconciliation, and the situation has worsened . . . So it is impossible for me to live with her in the same family. I am already over sixty, with limited time left. I would like to make a greater contribution to our Party, and write several more books. But under the current circumstances I can't even safeguard my life, so how can I carry on my work? Therefore I ask the court . . . please to pronounce my divorce from Xu Jing promptly, so that I may spend the rest of my life with my aged mother. As for the 30,000 yuan that she misappropriated, she has given the money to her sons and daughters to bribe and corrupt them, and it should all be returned . . . None of it belongs to Xu Jing, because she has always kept her money separately.

According to my mother, the first time that her husband mentioned divorce was in spring 1979, shortly after his return from the Military Hospital No. 301. 'I know that you are a good Communist, a good cadre and a good comrade,' he said to her privately. 'Through all these years of our lives together, you have also been good. Now, please let us get a divorce.' 'Since you think that we are a good couple, why do you want a divorce?' my mother replied. He did not answer. In China, extramarital affairs were disapproved of. If he admitted that his broken marriage was due to his affair with Scarlet, he might be held at fault in the divorce, a consequence he did not want to risk. Under the current marriage law in China, it was very unlikely for a divorce to be granted without mutual consent, so my mother's refusal was decisive. But now the situation had changed. In September 1980, the same month that my father filed for divorce, an updated marriage law relaxed restrictions for divorces. From then on, my mother's refusal could not block my father's plans.

In response to the lawsuit, my mother sent the court a detailed statement. This is how it ended:

The revolutionary family that we founded together is the fruit of our deep love, which has survived many ordeals and frustrations throughout more than three decades. We have had a happy and harmonious family life during the thirty-three years since we married. Only in the last year and a half have disagreements emerged between us, due to Scarlet's involvement. . . . I have made some mistakes in handling the matter. I would like to accept these lessons and to repair our relationship. Our thirty years of love go deeper than what has happened in a year and a half. . . . Tragedy must not befall our happy family. I want our children still to be proud of their revolutionary family. I want to go on looking after my aged mother-in-law until the end of her life, since we have lived happily together for three decades. I can't let the life of our innocent little granddaughter [Feng-Xin's daughter, my parents' only grandchild at that time] be overshadowed by her grandparents' divorce. Therefore I will try my best at any cost . . . to save our family. For so many years I have looked forward to the life I would spend with Mu Xiang on our retirement, hoping that we would help each other to leave some cultural legacy to future generations through our writings. Such a long-cherished wish must come true.

At the moment, Mu Xiang is not in a calm mood, so that he has spoken ill of me and acted inappropriately or mistakenly. That is understandable, considering his personal character and patriarchal behaviour at home. I hope that after a while, with help from our comrades, he will compose himself . . . In future, I will not disturb his work and writing, and will fully support him as I have always done in the past . . . I love him and our revolutionary family. I sincerely believe that he will be happy with me, and hence will achieve more in his career. Therefore, I strongly disagree with his divorce proposal.

Despite her husband's actions, my mother was still trying to save the marriage, as she treasured their love so dearly. If they divorced, my siblings and I would lose our parents' home, and her life would be lonely.

She also believed that my father could not enjoy a happy life no matter whom he lived with in the future, because it would be very difficult for anyone else to cope with his moods and patriarchal style.

In China, the judicial body consisted of the Junior People's Court at county level, the Intermediate and the Higher People's Courts at provincial level, and the Supreme People's Court at state level. Divorce proceedings normally start in the Civil Division of the Junior People's Court, but the litigation between my parents had to start in the Intermediate People's Court in Beijing, because the lower court was not authorized to deal with cases involving high officials.

The presiding judge was Mr Prosperity, a man in his forties, with a good reputation. A jury was also involved, but its opinions had little influence on the verdict. It was routine in divorces for the judge to try to mediate first, and to grant a divorce only when convinced that there was no possibility of reconciliation. At first, Judge Prosperity seemed a fair-minded man, spoke to my mother regularly, and treated her with respect. To rebut my father's accusations, she provided a great deal of written information, and always stressed her wish to save the marriage.

Within a few months, Judge Prosperity's manner towards my mother changed. His contacts became irregular, he showed impatience during their limited meetings, and several times I saw her weeping after them. 'He didn't listen at all,' she told me. 'He just kept telling me off for whatever I said.' After his change of attitude, Judge Prosperity denied that Scarlet had a role in my parents' marital troubles. In response to the evidence my mother provided, such as writings in which my father expressed his love for Scarlet or revealed their secret contacts and intimate relationship, the judge asserted: 'Mu Xiang has his own explanations for these things.' Later, he also said that it was unclear whether these documents were written by my father, but refused to consult a handwriting expert.

On 13 November 1981, my parents made their appearance in the only session of the court hearing. My father shouted abuse at my mother, and Judge Prosperity repeated that he could not accept the evidence she provided. 'We have investigated,' he told my mother. 'Scarlet has been looking for a marriage partner. She has found one, and is getting married soon. So your accusation about Mu Xiang's affair with her is simply untrue.' My mother retorted that whether or not Scarlet had found a husband did not affect her impact on the marriage. Again, she asked to have her evidence tested, but the judge told her bluntly: 'You should take responsibility for the breakdown of your marriage, because you don't understand your husband. You distrust him and hurt him.'

Judge Prosperity's change of tune reminded my mother of something he said during one of their meetings: 'In Beijing, Mu Xiang is an influential figure with many connections.' Had her husband influenced the court? It would have seemed unthinkable in the past, but now she had to accept the reality, since there were clues to confirm it. For example, a few days after the court contacted the university to investigate the case, the authorities there received a letter from my father accusing the official who had acted for the university of fabricating his evidence that my mother's good relationship with her husband was well known among her former colleagues. Only Judge Prosperity and a few other court officials had access to the court's investigation, and people at the university asked my mother: 'How could Mu Xiang know so quickly about what our official said?' Indeed, my father knew not only the details of the testimony but also the name of the official who provided it.

During that period, a retired deputy chief procurator in the Beijing Municipality volunteered to help my mother by passing her written response to my father's accusation to a leading member of the Intermediate People's Court of Justice. This retired official did not know my parents, but through her son, a former fellow student of Fengxin's, she felt sympathy for my mother. Shortly afterwards, this helpful woman received a letter from my father saying how bad his estranged wife was, and warning her not to interfere. My mother was puzzled:

'How could he be so well-informed about events in court?' Years later, when she had a chance to look at my father's diary during that period, the puzzle was solved. On 9 October 1980, the month after his petition started, he wrote: 'Snow's cousin is deputy director of the Intermediate People's Court of Justice.' Snow was a former wartime colleague of my father, now a senior officer in the armed forces. The deputy director of the Intermediate People's Court was Snow's female cousin, Junior Snow.

My father's diary for 4 January 1981 reads: 'Snow visited me tonight and said that Xu has written to the court every two or three days about the involvement of the third party in the marriage . . .' On 1 June: 'Junior Snow is a key person . . . Phoned Snow, and asked him to talk to his cousin . . .' A week later: 'Snow gave me details of his meeting with Junior Snow . . .' Ten days later: 'Snow told me about his visit to Junior Snow . . . She said that Xu has no intention to reconcile . . .' On 11 October: 'Snow told me on the phone what he heard from Junior Snow during his visit: (1) Prosperity [the Judge] will be instructed to pay close attention to the case; (2) no evidence was obtained from investigation in Shanxi [about his affair with Scarlet]; (3) the divorce will be approved; (4) I should not give up my demand to retrieve my money and books; (5) I should hurry the court more frequently; (6) the hearing is expected to be settled before the end of this year.' My father also met Junior Snow in person. He recorded in his diary for 15 June 1981: 'Met Junior Snow and the head of the Civil Division . . . Junior Snow was very polite . . .'

Snow was not the only outsider who backed my father during his divorce. In his diary he mentioned nearly a hundred names as influential supporters, half of them high-ranking officials such as army generals or former divisional commanders, and government ministers or prominent figures in the Beijing Municipality. Some were people my father had not known personally before, such as Wu Xinyu, deputy chairman of the Legal Committee of the National People's Congress, and Senior General Huang Kecheng, former chief of the general staff, whom he contacted through his closer connections. The rest of these names came from various backgrounds. Through an employee of the China Book Store, my father received support from one of her relatives with influence in both the Intermediate and the Higher People's Courts of Justice. Through an army doctor friend his appeal for support reached Ye Zilong, former chief steward and personal secretary of Mao Zedong, and now vice-mayor of Beijing, who sent his aide to the court to inquire about the case. My father kept in frequent touch with his connections, either by phone or in person.

According to my mother, most of these contacts offered their support because they trusted my father. He was known as a man of integrity, honest and kind to others, and many sympathized with him for what he had suffered during the Cultural Revolution. Not knowing what had really happened between my parents, it was hard for them to believe that my father might have an affair with another woman, so they were convinced that he was innocent, and my mother was at fault. Many also believed his story that his life was in danger from his sons who, prompted by his wife, had attempted to murder him. Some of these people knew my mother, but felt that they must stand by their friend.

'Then why did these people not help Father during the Cultural Revolution?' I asked my mother. 'Everyone must have known that he was innocent.' Her explanation was that people who were lucky enough to have avoided political troubles were unlikely to risk their own careers and families. But my father's divorce was not political. There was no risk or hardship in supporting him, and even if they happened to break the law they could rely on their positions or connections to protect them. Once they had moved to support him, they could not admit to being mistaken without losing face.

Another key supporter of my father was the retired Deputy Commander of the Beijing Garrison, known as Commander Calligrapher after his hobby. He got to know my father during the Anti-Rightist Campaign launched by Mao Zedong in 1957, when both of them held rank in the

Beijing Military Region. My father was in charge of examining cases of suspected Bourgeois Rightism for the region, and earned the gratitude of Commander Calligrapher by saving him from political persecution. In the early 1970s, after the death of Commander Calligrapher's wife, my father acted as matchmaker for his remarriage, which brought the two closer together. Knowing that I was my father's favourite child, Commander Calligrapher tried to match his son with me before I met New Star. In 1973 he arranged a meeting, which was awkward on both sides, since we had never met before, but especially for his son, who was tongue-tied for most of the time. Apparently he said afterwards that he felt like a poor man offered a precious stone that he liked a lot but could not afford. My father decided that this young man lacked confidence.

Despite Commander Calligrapher's best efforts, my father often used to criticize him, even in front of me, as a hanger-on for personal gain. It was said that before the Cultural Revolution he often visited the homes of leading figures in the armed forces bringing flowers that were planted and tended by his troops for his own use to curry favour. My father also disliked his putting on airs about his calligraphy. Yet now he became my father's right-hand man, kept busy throughout the divorce with manoeuvres that ranged from helping to plot the publicity campaign to housing my father's 'stolen' book collection. On 17 January 1981, my father noted in his diary: 'Drafting documents to the court . . . Calligrapher phoned. He did not sleep last night, considering ideas for me . . .' On 26 December 1982: 'Calligrapher phoned, saying that "e-fu" went to see Guan. Guan told him yesterday.'

As their conflicts intensified, my father often referred to his wife as 'e-fu', evil woman, in his diary, instead of by name, and called his sons 'ni-zi', unfilial sons. Guan was one of the most powerful women in China at that time, who also took sides with my father. By then there were two chief political factions that thrived under Deng Xiaoping, those of the former Beijing Municipality and of the former Communist Youth League, identified by their members' affiliations before the

Cultural Revolution. The widow of the former party secretary of Beijing Municipality, Guan was well connected to leading national figures who had been colleagues of her husband. She was influential in the municipality because most of its leading officials had either worked for her husband or were connected to her. Her husband's assistant in the 1950s, Chen Xitong, became mayor of Beijing in the early 1980s and then a member of the Politburo. (In the early 1990s, Chen Xitong shocked China through his involvement in a corruption case regarded as the most serious in Communist history. He was imprisoned in 1995, but the trial did not take place until 1998, allegedly because many leading national figures were implicated.)

During my parents' divorce, Madam Guan was appointed as a judge of the Special Court of the Supreme People's Court of Justice, for the public trials both of Jiang Qing and her close allies, and of the remaining heads of Lin Biao's faction. Some of them had spent nearly ten years in prison. Jiang Qing was sentenced to death, with a two-year stay of execution, so too was Zhang Chunqiao, her major ally, while the rest received prison sentences of sixteen to twenty years. Jiang Qing's sentence was reduced to life imprisonment in 1983. In 1991 she committed suicide. These trials became sensational events, broadcast almost daily on state television. Attention focused on Madam Guan as one of the few women judges on the platform, and her name became familiar to the public.

At the request of Commander Calligrapher, Madam Guan agreed to help my father. After that, my mother's case became hopeless. Having discovered Madam Guan's involvement, my mother tried to talk to her in person, but was refused. In desperation, she went to her office and waited there for hours, but when her opponent finally arrived she rejected my mother's request for her not to interfere with the arrogant claim that: 'We have nothing to talk about. The case is up to me.' Afterwards, she informed my father through Commander Calligrapher about my mother's visit.

In the circumstances, it was not surprising that Judge Prosperity pronounced against my mother. On 15 March 1982, just two months before the birth of my son, the court verdict stated:

> In the court's view, although they have been married for many years there have been frequent quarrels and fighting in recent years, due to Xu Jing's suspicions about Mu Xiang's affairs, which have caused the breakdown of the marriage. Xu Jing opposes divorce but is not keen to make efforts to reconcile. Having been through repeated mediation, Mu Xiang is determined to divorce. It would not be good for either of them if the marriage continued reluctantly, so a divorce should be granted . . . Under Articles 25 and 31 of the Marriage Law of the People's Republic of China, the following are the judgements: (I) Mu Xiang's divorce from Xu Jing is granted . . .

On 28 February 1982, two weeks before, my father had written in his diary: 'Snow phoned . . . He has heard from Junior Snow that the verdict has been authorized and printed . . . I will keep the books and she keeps the money. Tells me not to leak the information.'

My mother showed me the verdict in tears: 'More than forty years ago, I joined the Communist Party mainly because I hated the discrimination against women in the old society. How can I accept the injustice to me under the regime that I fought to establish? I would rather die!' Years later, she told me that by the end of the trial, she had lost hope of saving the marriage, but she could not accept the verdict, otherwise she would have no chance to clear her name. In spite of her husband's affair, the verdict found her guilty for the breakdown. Such an injustice she refused to swallow. So she decided to lodge an appeal with the Higher People's Court of Justice, the court of last instance in her case.

Before her appeal, I accompanied my mother to look for a lawyer, despite the complications with my pregnancy, as I feared that her grief was destroying her. It was during those days that I heard her wailing in the night. During the first trial, neither of my parents hired lawyers. The legal defence system had only recently been revived, and the role of lawyers was not fully recognized. I heard that judges sometimes ordered lawyers out of their courts, to stop them defending their clients. Nevertheless, my mother felt that she needed a lawyer for her appeal: at least she would have a voice to represent her.

In Beijing, legal services were provided mainly by the newly established Law Society, affiliated to the municipal Bureau of Justice. There we met the head of the Civil Division, Lawyer Elegance, a woman in her early forties, who agreed to represent my mother straight away. But next day she sent a message saying that on orders from above the Law Society was unable to take her case. My mother recognized her husband's hand at work, and was reminded of something a clerk had said during the previous trial: 'Xu Jing, what you've been doing is like solo dancing.' Indeed, she was on her own, while my father had his company behind him.

My father's diary for 8 April 1982 reads: 'Received a phone call saying that Xu has appealed, and her plaint was found today. It was written on 26th last month, and arrived in the court on 29th. I was offered a copy of it . . .' On 19 December 1982 he noted: 'Calligrapher phoned, to say that he told Guan all about the situation when she contacted him . . . Her manner still favourable.'

By now, my mother was convinced that the same fate would await her in the higher court unless she exerted influence of her own. She said to me: 'In the old China, the judiciary was dominated by the clients' money, but now it is controlled by political power!' It was true. The entire legal costs of the lawsuit, which lasted for over three years, came to 40 yuan each for hiring their lawyers, at a time when my mother's monthly income was close to 200 yuan and my father's over 300 yuan. In those days, both lawyers and judges were government employees.

My father's diaries during that period expressed his frequent concern that my mother would resort to her social connections. She knew many of China's most powerful women from her time in Yan'an during the Sino-Japanese War, as well as the wives of many leading figures in the Party, government and armed forces. On 30 August 1982, he wrote: 'It is confirmed that Zhang Yun has been involved [in supporting my mother].' Madam Zhang Yun was one of the famous Communist veterans, in charge of the Party's Central Discipline Inspection Commission, a powerful body. On 6 October he wrote: 'I hear that Kang Keqing has been involved . . .' At that time, Madam Kang Keqing, widow of Marshal Zhu De, was the country's most senior stateswoman. On 15 October: 'Trying to find out whether Chen Muhua has been involved . . .' Madam Chen Muhua was the vice-premier and then vice-president of the National People's Congress.

My father found that one of his estranged wife's strong supporters was Madam Wu Lan, director of the Department of Women's Affairs in the All-China Trade Union, who first met my mother in Yan'an in 1939. Wu Lan's ethnic background was Mongolian, but she was educated in Beijing during her childhood. My father had met her through my mother, and knew that she was an active figure in high official circles. His diary for 1 September 1982 reads: 'Tried to visit Wu Lan in the morning, but she was not in.' Several days later: 'Sent message to Wu Lan, telling that she should not intervene.' On 23 September: 'Calligrapher phoned, advising coercive measures against Wu Lan.'

With her helpful nature and warm heart, Wu Lan supported my mother spontaneously, and did not care about pressures from my father. Right from the start, my mother felt embarrassed to enlist her connections in a private matter, despite the obstructions she faced. It was Wu Lan who often encouraged her, cheered her up, and gave her ideas. Time and again she accompanied my mother to visit their former student friends from the Yan'an time, or others who could offer help. One place they visited many times was No. 22 Muxudi Avenue at the west end of Chang-an (Eternal Peace) Avenue, a luxury apartment block built in recent years to house government ministers. In high official circles it was known as 'Xiao Yang-jia Ling', Little Yang Hill. During the war, Yang Hill was the site of the Party's headquarters in Yan'an, where my mother worked after she graduated from the Women's University. Many residents at No. 22 also spent time in Yan'an during that period. Coincidentally, some members of my father's camp lived there too. At my mother's request, many of her friends and former colleagues offered support.

One day, Wu Lan asked my mother: 'Why don't you see Li Zhao? She and Comrade Yaobang invited me to dinner recently.' Li Zhao had been a fellow student in Yan'an, and her husband, Hu Yaobang, ranked next to Deng Xiaoping in China. The previous year, he had replaced Hua Guofeng, Mao Zedong's chosen successor, as Party Chairman. Before the Cultural Revolution, he had been General Secretary of the Communist Youth League, and his new position subsequently brought the faction of the former Communist Youth League into power.

My mother arrived at Hu Yaobang's residence without an appointment. According to practice, visitors to the country's leaders were supposed to make appointments in advance, except for those whose names appeared on special lists provided by the families themselves. My mother and Li Zhao were not close friends, so her name did not appear on the list, but Li Zhao received her at once, because she had read the news reports about her marriage problems, and felt very sympathetic. At the end of their meeting, Li Zhao suggested that my mother should send her a written account appealing for justice, which she would forward to Hu Yaobang.

Shortly after her visit, my mother was informed that Hu Yaobang had issued written instructions concerning the document she had provided, showing his sympathy and support and emphasizing that the vulnerable must be protected. He also gave orders for the case of my parents' divorce to be handled with justice and caution, especially considering their social positions and the long duration of their marriage. At the request of Hu Yaobang, my mother's document was forwarded to the Beijing Municipal government via various offices in the Party's Central Committee.

My mother's appeal set the Higher Court of Justice a dilemma. Behind my father stood prominent members of the faction of the former Beijing Municipality; on my mother's side stood Hu Yaobang, the leading figure in the faction of the former Communist Youth League. Caught between these two major political forces, the Higher Court could not afford to offend either. Their divorce became one of the few sensational cases in Beijing, rarely seen before in the history of Communist China. From now on, my father was no longer able to tamper with the trial unopposed. In his diary for that period, he often expressed resentment against Judge Calm, a senior judge who dealt with the case. On 31 July 1982, several months after my mother's appeal was lodged, he grumbled: 'Eventually got hold of Judge Calm on the phone. His manner was very bad. He spoke in a bureaucratic tone, and then hung up. I was furious . . .' On 22 June 1983: 'It was so difficult to get hold of Calm on the phone. He still talked about the same old stuff, such as how we should divorce in a peaceful way, and he didn't like me phoning him . . .'

Due to the support of Hu Yaobang, my mother's circumstances had improved a great deal. In contrast to Judge Prosperity, Judge Calm always listened patiently, and he re-investigated the case in response to the evidence she provided. He also visited my siblings and me to discuss my parents' situation. 'I really feel sorry for what has happened to your family, and deeply sympathetic with your mother,' he said when he visited me in the flat. 'But I must tell you that it is impossible for anyone to save your parents' marriage. You are the elder daughter, your mother will listen to you. Please help me to convince her to accept the divorce.' Judge Calm was in his forties, very polite, and a skilful communicator, but I could sense his frustration with the case.

The Law Society also agreed to provide a lawyer for my mother. Acting on orders, Lawyer Elegance represented my father, while her deputy, also a woman in her early forties, acted for my mother. Later, my mother asked her lawyer curiously: 'You and Lawyer Elegance work together in the same office. How can you represent the two sides of our divorce independently?' 'Different scripts,' her lawyer replied.

In addition to his social connections, my father also mobilized his siblings. On 27 July 1981, during the trial in the Intermediate Court of Justice, his diary records: 'Road suggested mobilizing everyone to write to the court.' Road is his youngest brother and my Little Uncle, who lives in Suzhou in south China. On 5 October 1982, after my mother's appeal to the Higher Court: 'Received a letter from Road with his correspondence to the court attached.' On 2 September 1982: 'Grace will visit the deputy director of the Supreme Court of Justice tomorrow with Guming . . .' Grace is his younger sister and my Second Auntie who lives in Xi'an. Guming's husband was the former 'first hand' leader of Beijing Municipality in the 1970s, now a government minister. Second Auntie got to know this couple during the Sino-Japanese War. Two days later, my father wrote: 'Grace and Flower visited the Higher Court of Justice this morning, and talked to the head of the Civil Division for two or three hours . . .' Flower was my father's youngest sister and my Little Auntie, the only one of his siblings who lived in Beijing.

Second Auntie seems to have played a very active role on my father's side. For many years, her efforts to please her eldest brother had not worked out as she wished, because he often criticized her flaunting the family's status, connections or wealth. My parents' marriage crisis made her a regular visitor, and she sometimes stayed in my father's house in Beijing for months, to back him up. She helped him win over my brothers, and recruited her connections in Beijing. One of her great contributions was to secure support from a senior officer in the General Political Department of the armed forces, whom she had known personally since the war. In the past, the department staff who dealt with the divorce had often shown sympathy for my mother. But after the trial started, their attitude changed. During the investigations, they denied the evidence my mother provided about my father's affair, such as the episode in Military Hospital No. 301, which they knew about.

According to my cousin, Little Fourth, his father, my Second Uncle, wanted nothing to do with my parents' divorce, but did not dare to turn his eldest brother down. So he tried not to visit my father during his working trips to Beijing until the day before he left, otherwise he would find himself sent to the court on lobbying duties, just as his other siblings when they came to visit.

Years later, Third Auntie told my mother that her solution to these errands was to while away time by strolling around Beijing, and then to tell him that the office was closed or the person in question not at work. But my father just kept sending her back to the court. When she finally met Judge Calm, Third Auntie said: 'I really feel sorry for my eldest brother's marriage problems, especially considering his rank as a high official . . .' Judge Calm interrupted: 'Xu Jing is a high official too.'

Of all my father's siblings, Third Auntie was the only one brave enough to raise a different voice. According to my father's diary, Commander Calligrapher ordered her to visit the court to demonstrate support for my father. On 17 March 1981, it records: 'Lotus [Third Auntie] . . . refused to write [to the court], saying that she did not know very much about what happened . . . Argued with her . . .'

For decades, my father's siblings had been proud to have my mother, a high official, as their sister-in-law. But after the 'Family Conflict of 28 August' in 1980, none of them dared to speak to her, even when they met in the street, except Third Auntie, who always showed her warmth and sympathy, and still called her 'my eldest sister-in-law' with respect. When her children travelled to Beijing, she always asked them to contact us. More than ten years later, she still expressed regret about the divorce when inviting my mother to visit her in Fuzhou. Her husband also said: 'Please believe that we are sensible people, and we know the truth.'

My mother's appeal lasted for nearly two years, though only one court hearing took place. This time my father got no chance to shout abuse. Based on evidence my mother provided and the court's investigation, Judge Calm plied him with questions about his affair with Scarlet, which he was unable to deny. Sometimes he answered: 'I can't remember.' When asked to identify his messages to Scarlet, he replied: 'I can't see the writing properly because of my eyesight problems.' Though Judge Calm did not persist, my father's embarrassment was clear to see.

In December 1983, the court issued its verdict. Due to the strong political backing on both sides, Judge Calm assumed a diplomatic, ambiguous tone:

> The court's own re-examination has not unearthed enough evidence to prove Xu Jing's suspicions about Mu Xiang's affair. But some of Mu Xiang's contacts [with Scarlet] did display a lack of consideration about the impressions conveyed to others, which deserve criticism . . .
>
> In the court's view, although they had many years of happy marriage, their relationship has deteriorated and they have separated due to Xu Jing's suspicions about Mu Xiang's affair. Although there are grounds for Xu Jing's suspicions, she sometimes acted impetuously and was unreasonable. Some of her radical responses caused the breakdown of the marriage, so that they are unable to live together. Repeated mediation has yielded no possibility of reconciliation, which shows that the marriage has really broken down. By the original verdict, the couple was granted a divorce, which is not in error and should therefore be upheld . . .

The verdict was delivered separately to my parents at their residences by the judge and their lawyers. Perhaps Judge Calm was concerned that my parents would reject his adjudication, and he might face an awkward situation if the verdict was announced in open court. Indeed, my mother was unhappy about the verdict, though it was an improvement on the previous one, but no further appeal was possible. In desperation, she wrote to the Higher Court of Justice to explain her disagreements:

(1) The judgement in the verdict contradicts the finding of the court hearing. Through the court hearing . . . it was clear that Mu Xiang should be held responsible for the breakdown of the marriage, which can be further proved through the 28 pages of transcription of the judge's remarks at the court hearing. But the verdict stated that the breakdown of the marriage was 'due to Xu Jing's suspicions about Mu Xiang's affair'.

(2) Judgements in the verdict are self-contradictory. It stated that Mu Xiang's contact with [Scarlet] 'deserve criticism', which is enough to show who should be held responsible for the breakdown of the marriage, and to justify my 'suspicions' or being 'unreasonable'. But the verdict still concluded that it was I who caused the breakdown. What sort of logic is that?

My mother also objected to the division of the family's property:

(1) The book collection was purchased and used by Mu Xiang and me together . . . But now, I am not entitled to a single item among the several tens of thousands of books, not even those provided to me by my own workplace for the needs of my work . . . I lodge a strong protest against the unfairness.

(2) Among the large items belonging to the family, Mu Xiang is entitled to all of those of higher value and quality, such as television set, refrigerator, Zeiss camera, hardwood desk, large rugs . . . Is this supposed to protect women's rights and privileges? I demand a share of these items.

(3) All the family's valuable belongings, including paintings and silver dollars, have been hidden by Mu Xiang. But the court has simply closed the case without trying to trace them, which is not correct. I will *reserve my rights forever to trace and retrieve these belongings.*

Since the start of the salary system in the early 1950s, most of my parents' incomes had been spent on their collections, so their savings accumulated mainly during the Cultural Revolution, when the China Book Store stopped trading. At her rehabilitation in 1971, my mother received arrears of pay for the previous four years, which accounted for most of the family savings. When she was forced out of home, she managed to bring about 13,000 yuan with her — less than half of the figure stated by my father. According to the verdict, she was now entitled to the money she brought with her, plus a few pieces of furniture, worth nothing compared with what my father kept. Even at that time, the family book collection was priceless, because many were original copies dating back to the Ming and Qing dynasties in the field of classical literature and history. Equally precious were the dozens of calligraphic works and paintings whose authors included great masters from the Song Dynasty to the present day, such as Huang Tingjian, Zheng Banqiao, Qi Baishi, Xu Beihong and Wu Changshuo. If they had to divorce, my mother argued that she must be entitled to half of all the family belongings. But my father had already transferred many of the books and art works into hiding, and the Higher Court of Justice was not interested in tracing them. It wanted to close the case as soon as possible.

My mother concluded her letter:

The Higher Court of Justice has done a lot of work on the case, and the hearing was fairly conducted. But the final verdict . . . is still based on unfair conclusions with various contradictions. Why has this happened? It is impossible not to attribute it to the intervention of 'higher authority'. In order to protect the dignity of our Party, to guard the sanctity of the law and the reputation of the Higher Court of Justice, I hope that staff working for the judicial bodies will be upright and stand by the law. They should let nothing prevent them from protecting the vulnerable, and hence showing justice to me, a woman over sixty and a nobody.

Shortly after the New Year in 1984, I accompanied my mother, together with Feng-an and Feng-yuan, to collect the share of family property awarded to her, from the house my father lived in. The many strangers present included staff from the Higher Court of Justice, the General Political Department and my mother's university, whose role was to carry out the division. Since October 1979, this was my first visit to the house that used to be my beloved home. It was like a nightmare to witness my family torn to pieces. My son was already one and half years old, but he had not seen and perhaps would never see his maternal grandfather in his life. Again and again, I asked myself: 'Why did this tragedy happen to my family? Who is to blame?' I longed to see my father and ask him not to leave the family who had been with him through so many difficult years, to hold on to him as I often had before, and tell him that I would do anything as long as our family could be saved. But my mother, brothers and I were shut out of the courtyard where my father lived, and he did not come out. He refused to talk to us for the last time.

In late 1983, before her battles against the divorce were finally ended, my mother retired. Her marriage problems had badly damaged her career. Since turning down her chances to work for the Ministry of Forestry in 1979, she had remained in her university, but without a post. Fortunately she was still entitled to her full salary, due to her position as a high official. In China, Communists with my mother's background are called the 'san-ba-shi' – the 'thirty-eight style' – because they joined the revolution in 1938, just after the Sino-Japanese War broke out, while the Party's membership spiralled. Before the Cultural Revolution, my mother was seen as a rising star among the 'thirty-eight style' intake. In 1961, still in her thirties, she was the youngest of the very few women at the top level of China's universities. But for more than two decades afterwards, her career stood still, due mainly to persecution under the Cultural Revolution, and later to the divorce battles that monopolized her time for almost five years.

In 1985, my father also officially retired, although he had held no

post since losing his job in the Ba-yi Film Studio in 1977. Like my
mother, he too had received full pay despite being jobless. Their divorce
also cost his career a great deal. Despite his campaign to justify his
actions, more and more senior figures in Beijing came to link his broken
marriage to his relationship with Scarlet, which hurt his reputation and
made finding a job even harder.

In China, the term for retirement by officials who joined the
Communist Party before 1 October 1949 was 'li-xiu', meaning to take
leave from work for rest; these pensioners could keep their salaries
intact, together with all their privileges. For later recruits, the term for
retirement was 'tui-xiu', meaning to quit work for rest; these were entitled to about two-thirds of their final salary on retirement. By the
1980s, most of the high officials who worked for the first generation of
the Communist regime had reached retirement age, but many tried to
stay in their posts, on the grounds that: 'With political power, you can
have everything. But without it, you will have nothing.' Some also argued
that ever since joining the Party they had followed Mao Zedong's slogan:
'Carry the revolution through to the end.' While the revolution continued, how could they abandon their posts?

Nevertheless, Deng Xiaoping was determined to replace the older
officials, and he offered them incentives. My father, on retirement, was
promoted to the level of deputy-commander of a 'bing-tuan', a large
military unit that combines several armies or about a dozen divisions.
Since the salaries of high officials from Grades 1–10 were frozen for
nearly thirty years, my father, being already at Grade 9, could not have
his pay raised, but he received a new car and a full-time chauffeur, and
kept the household staff who already worked for him. My mother also
received her final upgrade, and was promoted to Grade 11 in 1982.
When she retired, she was entitled to 1.5 extra months' salary per year,
with various other economic benefits such as free car services.

Chapter 28

Uncovering the Mystery of 'the Neighbours': My Mother's Battle to Clear Her Name; My Parents' Second Marriages

(September 1980–February 1986)

While she resisted my father's lawsuit for divorce, my mother had to fight another battle – to clear her name of the libel by 'the neighbours' printed in the *Beijing Evening Post*, which had badly damaged her and my brothers' reputations. Like me, she believed that there were no 'neighbours' at all, and that my father was behind the letter. Our views were shared by many others. A number of my mother's colleagues told her: 'I think that Mu Xiang may have been clever all his life, but this time he's been a fool. Apart from you and him, how could anyone else know so many details about what happened between you two? Who else could write that letter?' During the divorce proceedings, several leading officials in the university and in the Forestry Ministry told my mother that they had received letters from her husband repeating the accusations made in the letter to the *Beijing Evening Post*.

In my hospital, a number of colleagues also told me that the letter must have come from my father, and a common response was: 'None of these Lao-tou-zi ["old men" – the Communist veterans] are decent in their private lives! You should feel lucky that your father didn't have an affair before.' By now, Mao Zedong's sexual scandals were no longer a secret, and other statesmen such as Marshal Ye Jianying, President of the National People's Congress, and Li Xian-nian, President of China, were also notorious as womanizers. Very few of the Communist veterans involved in extramarital affairs divorced their wives, due partly to their concern for their children's welfare. But my father's case was different. In addition to his lawsuit for divorce, he also filed a suit to disown his children, which the court rejected on the grounds that it was impossible to cut these ties of blood.

Before the publication of the letter, my father had already told some former colleagues that he meant to make his family problems public. According to my mother, his purpose was to show that reconciliation was impossible and hence to pressure the court to grant a divorce. Immediately after the story hit the headlines, letters from all over China flooded into the newspaper's office. Most came from readers duped by 'the neighbours' letter', who therefore sympathized with my father and condemned my mother and brothers.

On the day after the letter was published, my mother visited the newspaper's head office to deliver a protest, which was supported by her university and the Forestry Ministry. It happened that the newly appointed 'first hand' leader of the university, Ji Xian's successor, had instructed his staff to do nothing for my mother, and my father had brought pressure to bear on the Forestry Ministry. Fortunately, colleagues dealing with my mother's case in both places were very sympathetic, especially since many were the university's graduates, or her supporters during the Cultural Revolution, so they ignored their bosses' warnings and tried their best to stand by my mother.

At the newspaper's head office, my mother discovered accidentally that the published 'letter' had not arrived by post, as they usually did. Since the newspaper management failed to account for its origins, they had to remain a mystery till she had a chance to consult my father's diary many years later.

Shortly before the letter was published, my father increased his contacts with a middle-aged woman called Mrs Pan, who had first visited my family in early 1980, introduced by a relative who knew my father. A clerk in the *Beijing Daily*, the official voice of the Municipality's Party Committee, she had written a film script, and was hoping for help to have it published or made into a film. A few days after the 'Family Conflict of 28 August' in 1980, she contacted a deputy editor-in-chief of the *Beijing Evening Post*, an acquaintance of Commander Calligrapher, with information provided by my father. It was this man who sanctioned the newspaper's investigation of the case.

On 5 September 1980, my father wrote in his diary: 'A staff reporter called Triumph from the *Beijing Evening Post* visited me this afternoon. Told him about what happened to me. He wanted to write an article.' Ten days after his visit, my father wrote in his diary: 'Triumph phoned to say that his article was finished, and then read it out to me . . .' Two days later: 'Originally, it was agreed that the article would be published in today's paper. But Calligrapher said that it would be postponed for one or two days.' On 20 September: 'It still hasn't been published today. Pan contacted the editor-in-chief and was told that the article was already finalized and would be published as soon as possible.' On the 22nd: 'Received a phone call from Triumph before supper, saying that it will be published tomorrow . . .' On the following day: 'It is published as the second front-page lead in today's *Beijing Evening Post* . . .'

My mother was determined to clear her name, but the court refused to accept her libel suit against the newspaper, asserting that it could only accept cases which had caused serious consequences, such as the victim committing suicide. Even if her lawsuit had gone ahead, she knew that my father would have tried his best to intervene. Her only chance was to force the *Beijing Evening Post* to re-investigate the story and so unearth the truth.

Eventually, the management of the *Beijing Evening Post* agreed a re-investigation, under pressure from the Forestry Ministry and my mother's university, but it was conducted by staff who had been more or less involved in the original story. On 4 May 1981, eight months after the 'letter' was published, the editorial board issued a report claiming that the only negative responses the newspaper had received had come from Xu Jing, her three sons and the Beijing Forestry University; apart from a single inaccurate word, the letter was based on true information, and served the positive purposes of promoting justice and enforcing law and discipline. The seven affidavits attached as appendices to this report were provided by Commander Calligrapher, four employees of the Ba-yi Film Studio, and my father's bodyguard and maid. Ironically, none of these statements came from our neighbours. My mother and brothers were also passed over by the re-investigation, even though they were the only others present during the incident.

My father's diary for 14 April 1981 reads: 'Calligrapher phoned in the afternoon, telling me how the re-investigation by the *Beijing Evening Post* came to see him in the morning . . .' In Commander Calligrapher's testimony, dated on the same day, he confirmed that on 28 August 1980, around 10 o'clock, Xu Jing had brought her three sons to beat up her defenceless husband. Mu Xiang had been beaten black and blue, at risk of his life: his body was covered with bruises. Finally, Commander Calligrapher concluded that the information reported in the letter had not gone far enough in depth and detail.

Another statement came from a film studio doctor who was dispatched to our house to rescue my father on 28 August. He had seen numerous bruises on my father's arms, and some cuts on his heels, but did not say what might have caused them. A few months after the re-investigation, an officer from the General Political Department of the armed forces told the newspaper what he saw when he was sent to our house that day. In his words, the cuts and bruises on my father's arms and legs were unlikely to have been caused by beating. Rather, they looked like the outcome of physical pushing and pulling between him and other people.

Since I was not present that day, my only information came from

Feng-an, and was later confirmed by my mother. He said that when Feng-xin failed to convince my father to return the wristwatch he had wrenched from my mother, he had finally lost patience and pulled it off Father's wrist. Straight away, my father jumped up from his armchair and started to butt his head against Feng-xin and shout abuse. I believed that my father was mad with rage because this was the first time his son had confronted him physically. In the past, it was he who used force, and none of his children would dare to raise a finger against him. Stunned by my father's reaction, Feng-xin held on to his head with no idea what to do next, and my two other brothers tried to take him back to his chair, hoping to calm him down. Instead he broke free and rushed to my grandmother's room, crying murder. Grandmother trembled with fear and her face turned grey. Panicked by the course of events, my brothers started to carry him back to his bedroom, fearing the shock to our crippled grandmother. It was a hot summer day, and my father had on a T-shirt, with slippers over bare feet. His struggles to get free left bruises on his arms. Earlier that day, he and his bodyguard had been busy loading books into crates to send them into hiding, and the cuts on his heels could have been caused by the many loose nails and splinters on the floor.

On the statement provided by a political officer from the Ba-yi Film Studio, my father noted three days after it was written: 'Information underlined with red pen is incorrect.' He included a page of corrections, one of them denying that he had torn off my mother's watch and claiming that she had deliberately left it behind, as a pretext to come back and loot his expensive Rolex.

My father's diary for 16 April 1981 reads: 'Talked to the bodyguard . . . He has written his testimony for the re-investigation . . .' This testimony, dated on the same day, provided a mass of details to corroborate 'the neighbours'' accusations against my mother. It also denied that my father had an affair with any woman.

The most far-fetched information came from the maid, who stated for example that my mother instructed her daughter to remove many of the family's belongings. My parents had only two daughters, and neither Aijun nor I knew about any 'looting'. The maid, a middle-aged peasant with little education, also mentioned the row my father had with my brothers before Feng-yuan's wedding, and claimed that my mother was present and egged them on. In fact, my mother was in the flat in Peace Street that day, and knew nothing about the clash until several days later. The maid alleged that my mother had intended to seize the family's wealth by inciting her sons to beat up and murder their father.

In her reply to the 're-investigation' report, my mother wrote: 'It is full of the words and tunes of "the neighbours", and I can see no sign of any real work done by the *Beijing Evening Post* . . . attacks against me by "the neighbours" are even a lot more malicious than those that originally appeared . . .' Having refuted the untrue accusations in the report, she pointed out: 'It is clear that "the neighbours" were in fact Mu Xiang himself together with a number of others who collaborated with him for personal gain . . . The *Beijing Evening Post* published their "letter" last year, and has now tried to use their words to prove that everything written was true, and hence to justify publishing the "letter" . . .' In conclusion she demanded that the case should be examined by the Party Committee of the Municipality.

My mother showed the report and statements to Zhang Dazhong, editor-in-chief of the *Beijing Daily*, with responsibility for overseeing the *Beijing Evening Post*. She did not know Zhang personally, but went to his home. 'What has the *Beijing Evening Post* done for the re-investigation?' she protested. 'If the "letter" was really written by our neighbours, why were none of the testimonies provided by them? Why was Mu Xiang allowed to inspect and alter the affidavits?' 'This is really disgraceful!' Zhang agreed. 'I will order a second re-investigation.'

My father noted on 3 July 1981: 'I hear that that evil woman has made complaints about the newspaper, and demanded another re-investigation. This time, it will be conducted by members of the newspaper's Party Committee . . .'

On 28 January 1982, nearly one and a half years after the 'letter' was published, the editorial board of the *Beijing Evening Post* issued a report based on the findings of the second re-investigation:

> In our unanimous view, it was inappropriate and incorrect that the *Beijing Evening Post* published this letter. There were also many problems about investigating the case before publication, from which the editorial board should draw a serious lesson.
>
> (1) Problems that happened between Comrade Xu Jing and her husband, Comrade Mu Xiang . . . were private family matters . . . which should not have been criticized publicly . . . But the *Beijing Evening Post* handled these matters crudely, and published the readers' letter even before confirming some facts, and so hurt Comrade Xu Jing by criticizing her by name.
>
> (2) While investigating the information provided by the letter, the paper's reporter only contacted some Ba-yi Film Studio personnel and Comrade Mu Xiang himself, but made no inquiries at the Forestry University where Comrade Xu Jing is based. In particular, Comrade Xu Jing, though criticized by name, was not contacted so as to check the facts or listen to her views. The work completely ignored the investigation procedure before an important article with critical views is published, so it was difficult to guarantee the facts . . .

An important finding of the second re-investigation was that the General Political Department of the armed forces had disapproved of publishing the 'letter'. In China, it was a routine, before reporting on an individual case, to consult the superiors of the party concerned. But Triumph did not inform the newspaper that the military authorities disapproved.

In reply to the new report, my mother demanded disclosure of 'the neighbours'' true identity and stressed how much damage had been done to her own reputation and the lives and careers of her children. Finally, she claimed:

(1) If the *Beijing Evening Post* really thinks that the publication of the 'letter' was wrong . . . please provide the Party Committees of the Forestry Ministry and the Forestry University, as well as the Municipality's Intermediate People's Court of Justice [where my parents' divorce was still being heard], with detailed written information about how the 'letter' was produced . . .

(2) Since the report admits that I was damaged . . . I strongly demand that the newspaper must give the same prominence . . . to clearing me of the accusations against me . . .

My mother's demand won support from the Chief of Propaganda in the Municipality's Party Committee, Madam Wang Dingkun: 'Xu Jing should be rehabilitated publicly in the newspaper.' Shortly afterwards, my father wrote to Madam Wang saying that 'as a former classmate of Xu Jing, you do not know how bad she has been in these years, so you should not help her'. In fact, Madam Wang had never been my mother's classmate. My father's diary for 4 August 1981 records: 'Calligrapher phoned at noon, urging me to write letters to destroy Wang Dingkun.'

Throughout the re-investigations, my father kept in regular touch with Triumph, Mrs Pan and some others on the newspaper who were involved with publishing the 'letter'. On 10 January 1982, shortly before the second report was issued, he noted: 'Triumph visited . . . telling me about the progress of the re-investigation.' On 4 September: 'Phoned Pan in the morning inquiring about the re-investigation. She promised to call me back in the afternoon. Felt anxious and failed to sleep at noon. Pan rang at 3 pm . . . saying that Triumph is under intense pressure.'

On 9 September 1982 the newspaper's editorial board reported the findings of its third re-investigation. By now, my mother had started her appeal to the High People's Court of Justice against the verdict on her divorce, and had been backed by Hu Yaobang, China's second in command. This report, substantially longer and more detailed than the previous two versions, admitted that the newspaper had learned the 'lesson of very bitter experience'. It listed several serious mistakes:

(I) From start to finish, we have never been clear about who 'the neighbours' were. So the 'letter' was in fact an anonymous letter, with an irresponsible attitude . . .

(2) The original investigation was biased, and did not consult the person criticized or the views of the Party Committee of the Forestry University . . .

(3) There were serious problems with the newspaper's procedure for sanctioning articles before publication. According to . . . Triumph, the 'letter' was examined in advance by the General Political Department of the armed forces, and was approved for publication. During the re-investigation, on 17 August 1981, staff from the newspaper were told by the General Political Department that the officer who dealt with this case did not read the 'letter' at all . . . He also expressed clear disapproval of publishing it . . . But Triumph has always claimed that this officer did examine the 'letter' and even made some alterations . . . [Triumph did not keep the copy with this officer's alterations], and finally agreed on publication. This problem needs to be further clarified . . .

Due to Triumph's involvement in the 'letter', the editorial board decided to give him an administrative disciplinary charge, and to impose a fine. It was agreed that the editorial board would make a public confession, as my mother requested, which would be published on the front page. A draft was provided:

On 23 September 1980, this newspaper published a 'letter' signed by 'the neighbours' complaining about a family dispute, together with a comment that criticized a cadre of the Forestry University, Xu Jing, and her eldest son, Mu Feng-xin, by name. Family disputes are complicated matters, which should not be criticized publicly in the press. When investigating the case before publication, we did not listen to the views of the persons criticized or of the Party Committee of the Forestry University. Some of the facts were also untrue. It was very inappropriate and incorrect to publish the letter. It is hereby confessed.

On 30 October 1982, shortly after the newspaper's report of the third re-investigation, my father wrote in his diary: 'Pan phoned, saying that the newspaper is going to publish a confession . . . Started to write to the editorial board and the Municipality's Party Committee immediately.' Next day: 'Continued the letters this morning . . . trying to stop the rehabilitation of that evil woman. Finished writing in the afternoon. Feeling anxious, extremely worried and indignant.' On 4 November: 'Wrote a short letter to the newspaper, exposing fallacies of that evil woman . . .' Five days later: 'Wrote the third letter to the Municipality's Party Committee, refuting the lies. Posted it in the afternoon.'

Later, I saw a copy of one of the letters my father wrote to the editorial board of the *Beijing Evening Post*, which was nearly ten thousand words long. He claimed again that the 'letter from the neighbours' was entirely based on fact, and extended his accusations against my mother and his children to me, claiming that I had several residences in Beijing, provided by my father-in-law, but still occupied the flat in Peace Street on my mother's instructions. This was completely untrue.

In answer to the report on the third re-investigation, my mother commended the newspaper's efforts and the enormous improvement made, but pointed out that the newspaper had known all along who 'the neighbours' were, but did not want to see 'them' unmasked. Concerning the draft confession, she complained that it did not apologize to her or her sons for the libels committed against them. The confession should admit that the original investigation had been biased, and the 'letter' published despite the disapproval of the military authorities. Finally, the confession should mention what steps the editorial board had taken to deal with its mistakes.

During the following years, the *Beijing Evening Post* came under pressure from both of my parents. My father's diary for 1 December 1982 reads: 'Pan phoned again, saying that the newspaper's confession is still to be published. Horrified . . . Phoned Calligrapher in the afternoon, asking him to intervene . . .' On 27 March 1984: 'Calligrapher phoned. Triumph told him on the phone that Deng Liqun has instructed the *Beijing Evening Post* to re-investigate the case, after that evil woman contacted the Party's Propaganda Headquarters . . .' Deng Liqun was the Party's Chief of Propaganda, responsible for overseeing the press. By then, my mother's appeal in the Higher People's Court of Justice had been heard. Since the verdict criticized my father's relationship with Scarlet, it strengthened my mother's position and won her more political support. On 13 April 1984, the *Beijing Evening Post* provided a revised draft confession, which included an apology to my mother and some other points she had asked for.

The newspaper's confession was never published, due largely to my father and his connections. On the other hand, my mother did not endorse the revised draft, which omitted several of her points. But this time, the newspaper did not reply to her objections. In fact, the board of the *Beijing Evening Post* was reluctant to admit to the public that it had mistreated my family, for fear of harming its own reputation, especially since some of its leaders had been involved in this episode on my father's side from the very beginning.

By the summer of 1984, my mother was really fed up with the endless battles which had dominated her life ever since her marriage crisis started in 1978. Although my parents were now divorced, my father seemed still tireless in his hostility, and his determination to prevent her from clearing her name meant that her battles would never cease. She was over sixty, and felt that her remaining time was precious. Nor could she forget her decades of married happiness, despite their painful sequel, so she was unwilling to spend the rest of her life in contention with her ex-husband. Knowing that if the newspaper's confession was published it would bring our family conflict back into the public eye, and worsen the social pressure on her children, in the end she decided to give up her battles with my father and the *Beijing Evening Post*.

After the 'Family Conflict of 28 August' in 1980, there were always four or five soldiers, in addition to the bodyguard, assigned to the house by the Ba-yi Film Studio at my father's request. He claimed that his life was in danger, because Feng-yuan still lived there, and his other sons and my mother had access to the front courtyard. Before these soldiers eventually left, my father insisted on having a lock and solid bar fitted on the gate between the front and back courtyards. Without a key, it was now impossible for anyone to open the gate from outside. The workmen who carried out the alterations laughed at their orders and wondered what the protection was for.

After that, the house was cut in two by a high brick wall and the locked gate, which split the family apart within the same house. Among my mother and her children, only Aijun was permitted to enter the back courtyard, the main part of the house. She was the youngest child, and still unmarried. Throughout my parents' marriage crisis, she tried not to get involved, for fear of being driven from her home. Although he did not fall out with her, my father regarded her as a spy planted on him by my mother, and this attitude was picked up and relayed by the maid, who often refused to cook for Aijun when she was home, and would shriek abuse if she went to the kitchen for food. Even when this bullying led to rows, my father showed no objection, and the woman treated Aijun worse and worse.

Shortly before the 'letter from the neighbours' appeared, Commander Calligrapher had spoken to Aijun and pressed her to take my father's side. 'I think both of my parents are good,' Aijun demurred. 'Your mother brought your brothers to beat up your father. How can you still support her?' 'I did not see them beat up my father,' she replied. 'Nor did I see him injured.' When her remarks reached my father, he was furious.

Aijun and her fiancé had scheduled their wedding for early 1981, so that she could escape my father's house as soon as possible. At the end of 1980, less than two months before the wedding, my grandmother called her to her room and told her tearfully: 'My child, you are grown up, and can support yourself. Please don't live here any more. This is not a good place.' My father was determined to drive Aijun out, and could not even wait for the two months to pass. My grandmother had to pass his message to her favourite grandchild because she did not dare to thwart her eldest son.

Next day, Aijun brought my mother the news. It broke her heart to see her younger daughter so upset, yet be unable to help. When I returned from work, I found mother suffering from high fever, with her lips covered in blisters, resulting from her anger and anxiety.

Aijun was allowed to collect her belongings from her room in the back courtyard, and my mother told her to look for the suitcase full of expensive silk and satin fabrics, accumulated over many years, which she had prepared for her daughters' weddings. In China, it was traditional for the bride's clothes and bedding to come from her family, while the bridegroom's family provided the couple's accommodation and furniture, and the wedding feast. Since I was still at university when I married, my mother had not given me these fabrics for my wedding. When forced out in spring 1980, she had to leave the suitcase behind. 'Now I will share the fabrics between you and Aiping,' she told Aijun. But what Aijun found was an empty suitcase, stripped like many others she saw.

When she collected her belongings, Aijun was watched by the maid all the time. On her way out, she met my father standing with Second Uncle in the back courtyard. Instead of saying goodbye, he began to accuse his 'unfilial sons and daughters'. 'Never pass the door of my house again!' he shouted. Aijun had always been Second Uncle's favourite niece, but now he did not dare even to greet her.

Among his five children, my father attended only Feng-xin's wedding, in 1973, before his change into a completely different person. In summer 1977, we fell out before my wedding. In 1978 his relationship with Scarlet in Taiyuan kept my father away from Feng-an's wedding. The weddings of my two younger siblings took place during the family turmoil. In 1980, my father broke his promise to accommodate Feng-yuan, which caused the general breach before Feng-yuan's wedding. And now he had evicted Aijun on the eve of her wedding!

Aijun's departure darkened my grandmother's life. She was eighty-six, already crippled after a stroke some years before, and also suffered from serious diabetes, heart problems and high blood pressure. Ever since joining our family thirty years ago, she had been deeply attached to my siblings and me, and watched us grow up. But now only my father remained, and he hardly talked to her. Feng-yuan still lived in the front courtyard, but she could not contact him. When my father was out, she sometimes hobbled to the locked gate with her walking stick, and watched the front courtyard through a narrow gap, hoping to see her grandson again. But soon the maid would find her, and shepherd her back to her room, scolding her because 'The master said that you are not to come to the gate.' Grandmother wailed: 'Am I a prisoner? What have I done wrong?'

Unhappiness and isolation wore down my grandmother's health, especially when the maid's unkindness worsened. One of her tasks was to look after my grandmother, but she often went out moonlighting to earn extra money, and left Grandmother unattended. When she saw Little Auntie, my father's only sibling in Beijing, Grandmother often wept and complained that she was bullied. Instead of providing care, the maid often scolded or screamed at her. Before being driven from home, Aijun had clashed with her on several occasions over her negligence and rudeness towards my grandmother. But now, my poor grandmother was defenceless. My father turned a blind eye to the maid's behaviour. Despite his mother's complaints and Little Auntie's frequent protests, he was unmoved.

One evening in 1981, my grandmother fainted under the maid's abuse, and her face turned blue. As a result, she was rushed to Military Hospital No. 301. When her condition stabilized, she sent a message to my father saying that she would not return unless the maid was sacked – which he refused. His petition for divorce had just begun, and so had the first re-investigation by the *Beijing Evening Post* of the 'letter from the neighbours', in which the maid backed my father. He could not afford to lose her support, for instance in providing false evidence against my mother and his children. As a result, my grandmother was discharged into Little Auntie's care.

On 14 July 1981, I wrote in my diary: 'Mama brought Feng-an and me to visit Grandmother at Little Auntie's home this morning . . . I was very upset. Due to my deep attachment, I could hardly tear myself away from her; as I might have no more chance to see her alive . . . Grandmother looked very thin, pale and weak. She often gasped for breath, and moved slowly . . .' That morning, Little Auntie and her husband were at work. Their family lived in a flat with only two small rooms, and Grandmother shared a room with Little Red, who was already eighteen. She was surprised to see us, but would only talk to Feng-an and me, and ignored my mother's greeting, obedient to my father and his siblings.

Having left the hospital, Grandmother was deeply hurt by her eldest son's attitude, and believed that without his consent, the maid would not have dared to bully her. What she could not bear was his decision to stand by the maid against his mother, when he refused to sack her. On the evening of 19 August 1981, Grandmother became unusually talkative, and kept telling Little Red about events of many years ago, such as how she insisted on sending her daughters to school despite objections from her mother-in-law and the local community. She also reminisced about her arrest by the Japanese, and her family's escape from pursuit, until gradually, her voice faded, and her speech became confused. Her face turned blue, and she panted for breath.

Little Auntie and her husband were alarmed, and went out to seek an ambulance. With positions in the Communist hierarchy equivalent only to county governor, they were not entitled to a telephone, so they had to reach a public telephone, and contact various local hospitals. When none could send an ambulance, they called a taxi. My grandmother had already lost consciousness, but was turned away by several hospitals that had no beds available, and died on the way to the next.

A few days later, when Feng-yuan told my mother about the sudden arrival of my father's siblings in Beijing, she knew that my grandmother had passed away. During the following days, I often saw her weeping in her room, and was moved by her attachment to my grandmother. Both of us thought that Grandmother would not have died had she still lived in my father's house. In recent years, she had had several similar attacks, but had been saved by the facilities in my father's place. As well as a telephone, he also had oxygen equipment. Due to his position, staff from the studio clinic were always on call, as were rescue teams from numerous military hospitals, and she could easily be hospitalized. In Little Auntie's less privileged home, there was no way for my grandmother to survive.

Shortly after my grandmother's death, Little Uncle and Third Auntie turned up in Feng-xin's office unexpectedly. On behalf of their siblings, they read out a statement in front of Feng-xin and his bosses, blaming him, his brothers and my mother for Grandmother's death. Next day, they sent similar allegations to Feng-xin's bosses. More than ten years later, my mother asked Third Auntie how she accounted for these actions. 'Please don't mention it again!' she replied. 'It was utterly embarrassing!'

Grandmother was cremated in Beijing, and her ashes buried beside my grandfather in North Forest Yard Village, in her home county. Like a fallen leaf, she eventually returned to her roots. The more I thought about her, the more I grieved for her final years. In all my life, I had seen few in her generation who could match her common sense and capability. Completely unschooled, she always impressed people with her intelligent conversation, sense of humour and open mind. It was she who supported all her sons and daughters in joining the Communists very young, despite the dangerous consequences for the family. She showed incredible courage in facing the enemy during the war, and my father's persecutors during the Cultural Revolution. To her family and friends, she never spared her love. My dearest grandmother, you deserved nothing but happiness in your family life, and should not have left the world with a broken heart.

After Aijun's removal, my father's next target was Feng-yuan and his family. With them around, it was difficult to effect the secret transfer of book collections, and my mother still had access to part of the house. My father's diary shows that during August 1980, the month before he sued for divorce, he was busy packing and transferring the collection, helped by his bodyguard. On 10 August: 'Visited Calligrapher . . . His basement is very spacious . . .' Four days later: 'The unfilial son [Feng-yuan] stayed home . . . no chance to move things out.' On 20 August: 'The unfilial son left by bicycle. Sent for a vehicle to carry two large wooden crates and four smaller ones to Calligrapher's place . . .'

When Feng-yuan graduated from university in summer 1980, my father wrote to high-ranking officers who were his former subordinates that Feng-yuan should return to his unit. Believing that his youngest son was still a serviceman, my father hoped that he would now be unable to live in Beijing, as his division was stationed in the north of Shanxi province. But it was too late. Feng-yuan had already arranged his demobilization, and obtained both his resident's card in Beijing and a job as a mechanical engineer in a factory. My father's fury caused the staff officer who dealt with Feng-yuan's demobilization to be dismissed from his job as a punishment.

It was not easy for Feng-yuan and his family to live in my father's house. From time to time, the water supply to the front courtyard was cut or the toilet blocked. By order of my father, the maid often stood outside their windows and bawled abuse. When my sister-in-law was home on maternity leave in summer 1981, her visitors heard the maid screaming. Several times, my father rushed into the back courtyard, irritated by the baby's crying, and shouted: 'Throw that terrible creature out!'

When Feng-yuan's son, Little South, was three months old, he began to attend the crèche in his mother's factory, because her official maternity leave was over. In China, women could not take breaks from work after childbirth. Since one wage was too low to support even a small family in the city, both wife and husband usually had to work full-time. Part-time work and job-sharing were unheard-of, and once a person left his or her job it was very hard to find employment again. Under the Communist regime, almost all jobs came from the state or collective sector. In order to work, you needed a 'quota' that was normally allocated by the government to certain categories, such as school-leavers, university graduates or ex-servicemen transferred to the civilian sector, but not to those who quit their jobs. New mothers must go straight back to full-time work.

In the crèche, Little South often suffered from illnesses passed on by other babies. Due to the staff's lack of training, often several babies would share the same bottle of milk, so if one suffered from diarrhoea, the rest would soon contract it. When Little South was able to sit properly, his parents often found a deep red mark imprinted on his bottom when he came home. All day long, he and the other babies of similar age were kept sitting on the pot, to save the staff the bother of changing nappies. Few of the parents dared to complain. Owing to the extreme shortage of child-care services, many felt lucky that their children had places at all.

The first winter in Little South's life was a harsh one. Only a few months old, he often caught cold through travelling on the overcrowded buses between his home and his crèche. Because his parents could not take time off to look after him, when he developed pneumonia he had to stay with his maternal grandparents, who lived in two small dark rooms with no indoor lavatory or kitchen, and only two small coal stoves for heating. Even at night, the baby wore many layers of clothes, and his ears developed chilblains.

Feeling sorry for Little South's plight, my mother volunteered to pay for a live-in nanny. She could not look after him herself, because she was busy fighting my father's petition for divorce and the libel in the newspaper. But no one outside the family dared to live in Feng-yuan's home, with its troubled situation. When I was pregnant with my son in winter 1981, I often brought Little South back to the flat during my sick leaves, to warm him in its centrally heated rooms. When bathing him, I found scabs caused by dirt on the delicate skin of his legs, because it was too cold to bathe him in his maternal grandparents' home.

As he grew up, Little South liked playing in the front courtyard, and often met my father passing through. But Father refused even to greet his grandson, and the little boy did not know who he was. At four years old, Little South complained to me: 'That old man in the back courtyard is so rude! He always bangs the gate on purpose when he sees me playing outside.'

During that period, my father sent several of his nephews, brought on visits by his siblings, to deliver messages asking Feng-yuan to move out. On these missions, they just chatted with Feng-yuan and his wife, reluctant to help my father but not daring to refuse his demand. A number of Feng-yuan's bosses also received letters or telephone calls from my father for the same purpose, but did not reply, especially since the factory had no housing for its staff.

On 5 December 1983, a few weeks before the final verdict on his divorce was issued, my father noted in his diary that he had found a means through the local Junior People's Court to sue his son. On 13 May 1984, five months after his divorce, his diary reads: 'Major aims at present are li-xiu and qu-ni' – taking retirement and driving out the unfilial son.

In autumn 1984, Feng-yuan was informed by the local Junior People's Court that my father had brought a lawsuit accusing him of threatening his life by remaining in his house. The judge who dealt with the case told Feng-yuan: 'I think this old man is mentally disordered. You would have no peace if you continued to live in his house.' In sympathy with Feng-yuan, the judge insisted that my father must find somewhere else for him and his family to live.

My father's treatment of Feng-yuan was criticized by the new body-guard who took over when the old one's term of service ended. This refusal to involve himself in our family dispute vexed my father so intensely that he ordered him to leave, and told the studio that his new bodyguard had tried to murder him. Later, this man wrote to Feng-yuan: 'I felt that your father, although a senior officer and famous novelist, was irresponsible and inhuman in dealing with his family . . . Considering your father's behaviour, I really felt ashamed to work for your family . . .'

Many people we knew said to us: 'What is wrong with this old man? He just spent years suing his wife, and now he starts another lawsuit against his own son.' People at the film studio said in disbelief: 'The bodyguard assigned to Mu Xiang is a decent young man and dedicated to his job. How can he be accused of murder? This old man must be mad.' But even today, my mother is not fully convinced. 'If your father had been mentally disordered, how could everything he did have been so well-planned and purposeful? He destroyed the family step by step, using all possible means, resources and connections, and let no one escape his clutches.'

While working on this book, I found a lot of accounts he wrote for the courts, the *Beijing Evening Post*, the military authorities and even his children's employers, containing accusations against us, many of them based on fabrications. For example, he spread stories that Feng-yuan had a criminal past, intending to prove what a danger he posed in his house. After the 'letter from the neighbours', one of my mother's former colleagues lamented: 'What on earth does Mu Xiang mean to do? If he doesn't care about himself or his wife, shouldn't he have thought about his children?' In every family I knew, it was the parents' wish to help their children. Only my father was so keen to bring them down.

When she looks back on those years, my mother has often sighed in disbelief: 'How could he have become so mean, narrow-minded and callous? Why did he treat his own family with the tricks he suffered himself during the Cultural Revolution?' Indeed, my father became a completely different person, stripped of his high integrity and his loving heart. Once so industrious in his career and honest to others, now he spent almost all his energy on hurting his wife and family. As long as it suited his purpose, he embraced what he detested before, even lying and forgery, and relied on those he once disliked. People he contacted during his divorce told my mother later that his crazed obsession with punishing his family caused many to try to avoid him. Losing his sense of how others perceived his actions, he often thought that he was a winner because he achieved what he intended.

After the divorce, my mother met a woman who sat on the jury for their case in the higher court. 'It was fortunate you divorced from Mu Xiang,' she said. 'You couldn't go on living with him, because he wouldn't get on with anyone . . . During the trial, he kept on phoning the court, talking on and on about how wicked you were. At first we tried to listen, but soon everyone was fed up. We couldn't believe that you, a veteran Communist and former university leader, could behave as badly as he claimed.'

A number of my father's relatives speculated that he might have been affected by dementia. At the start of my parents' troubles, Little Auntie noticed that my father, then over sixty, often unintentionally dramatized his life, as if living in illusions. Years later, Little Red told me that before he got rid of Feng-yuan my father often shook with fear when he heard his voice. Father's diary mentioned getting a heavy walking stick ready for self-defence.

I wonder why Father was so scared of his own children. Was it because his mind was ruled by his illusions? Was he eventually deceived by his own lies that his sons were murderous into treating them as enemies? Or was he afraid that his children would take revenge for what he had done to them? I believed that he did not know, or did not want to know, how his children thought. Despite their conflicts, I had no doubt that my brothers would never resort to violence. With a strict and successful father, it was difficult to develop their own strong characters. Growing up under his discipline, my siblings and I had always been law-abiding people. No matter what we endured from him, none of us ever considered retaliation, especially with the pressures we faced in our own lives and careers. By the time my parents divorced, all my brothers and I had changed jobs, mainly because our father's actions had damaged our positions. So we tried to steer clear of him, fearing his power to do more harm. Apart from Feng-xin, the rest of us were also under heavy pressure to improve our qualifications, because we had either been 'worker-peasant-soldier students' or had never studied at university. In recent years, we had therefore attended spare-time courses after work. By 1985, we all had children of our own, which made our lives even busier than before.

In contrast, my father had completed his career, and was entitled to ample privileges. For his campaigns against his children, he had plenty of time, energy and social connections, while we were almost powerless to protect ourselves. I began to regret being born into such a family, victims first of the Cultural Revolution, and then of our father's relentless pursuit. If this was the plight reserved for being a child of high officials, I would rather have been born into an ordinary family where I could enjoy a normal, peaceful life with plenty of love from my parents.

Many years later, one of my father's former subordinates tried to convince me to forgive him, blaming his treatment of his family on psychic trauma inflicted by incessant political troubles, depression and disappointment. From the start of my parents' marriage crisis, my father showed his disillusion with the Communist regime. In 1979, before their separation, when political dissidents established the famous 'Xidan

Democracy Wall' in Western Eternal Peace Avenue, my father was a regular visitor and made generous financial donations. Fearing for his safety, Little Auntie often warned him: 'Please stop visiting there. There are lots of plain-clothes police around who take photos secretly and keep surveillance.' But my father took no notice. When the short-lived Democracy Wall was banned, he told my mother angrily: 'The regime has changed! Which of the people in power still cares about the welfare of the ordinary people?' He also condemned the arrest of the famous dissident Wei Jingsheng, as a move to silence the people's voice. It shocked his former colleagues when he criticized the Party's leadership and corruption with remarks such as: 'These days, the Communists are worse than the Nationalists.'

Since my father was unable to change society, he may have turned his rage and disappointment against his family. During the last few years before I left, he often reminded me of a wounded lion. Anyone close to him could easily incur his bursts of anger, which could erupt at any time. Perhaps it was my father's disillusion with the Party that eventually destroyed his attachment to his family. Perhaps he came to see us as part of the Communist establishment, and a past he was determined to abandon. Making his wife and children suffer may have offered a way to relieve his own bitterness and anguish, and to avenge the humiliation, injustice and disappointment that he had endured. His aim was to detach himself completely, and to make a new life by fulfilling his literary career. That would make Scarlet the woman he chose to embody his new life in a second marriage.

Nevertheless, I am in no position to make sense of the unthinkable changes in my father, and nor is anybody else. In China, professional counselling, and therapy for psychic trauma, were not available. No record exists to prove any speculations about my father's psychological problems.

On 18 January 1984, just a few weeks after his divorce, my father mentioned in his diary that a former colleague had offered his services as a matchmaker, and provided four names as possible wives. In visits to his home, various other candidates were proposed. It seemed that my father, though nearing his seventies, was still marriageable, because of his social position, income, literary reputation and entitlement to privileges. The lengthening list contained candidates of various social backgrounds and ages, one of them the powerful Madam Guan, widow of the former Party secretary of Beijing, and a keen supporter during the divorce – 'No wonder,' my mother remarked when she heard about Guan's marital ambitions. It was said that my father replied: 'If I married Madam Guan, who would be the boss at home?' He also refused other candidates. It was Scarlet he wanted.

During his divorce, my father had been advised against marrying Scarlet by some of his sisters and by supporters such as Commander Calligrapher and Snow. To do so would prove my mother's allegation that the breakdown of the marriage stemmed from Scarlet, and they would lose face for standing by him. At that time, Father made no objection, claiming that Scarlet was going to marry someone else. But now that he had his divorce, there was no need to pretend. In any case, he explained: 'I have no other choice, because my relationship with her is written into the verdict.' Nothing could change his strong determination.

Scarlet was still single, and working in Taiyuan. My father's diary shows how often the two corresponded. He sometimes wrote to her every day, and she would phone as well as write. On 15 May 1984: 'Read again the more than ten of her letters that I have received in recent months. Felt a swell of emotion, difficult to control.' But during that period, troubles also surfaced. On 17 April 1984 he recorded: 'Received a letter from Scarlet this afternoon. She expressed some blame which I found hard to answer. Am terribly upset. I don't know what the future holds for me, and feel helpless to live in the world.'

As well as writing to Scarlet himself, my father mobilized various people to approach her, among them First Auntie. In mid-July 1984, she arrived in Beijing from her home in Hangzhou to prepare her match-making mission to Taiyuan. Father bought some sweets and cakes as gifts for Scarlet, and asked First Auntie to deliver them. On 8 August he noted: 'Glow [First Auntie] returned, and brought a letter from Scarlet which showed her displeasure with me.' On 2 October: 'Scarlet's letter arrived. Felt it hard to understand her expressions such as "the moon in the water" and "flowers in a mirror".' (In Chinese culture these are conventional images to express the idea that everything is an illusion.) The diary continues: 'In the past, she has disliked the concern that people around me showed me. Nor was she impressed by Glow. It is really hard to figure out what she thinks. I have to grit my teeth to bear my sadness . . .'

Despite all my father's approaches, Scarlet eventually turned him down, for reasons that invited speculation. By now, university graduates enrolled, like her, before the Cultural Revolution were no longer branded as bourgeois intellectuals or the 'Stinking Ninth Class', and their status had improved enormously under the new policies. So Scarlet's job had changed from office clerk to editing a literary periodical. Hence it was suggested that she no longer needed my father's position and influence. It was also said that my father had made his divorce such a high-profile case that Scarlet felt unequal to the pressures she would face if she married him. I think that even if Scarlet truly loved my father she might have been deterred from marriage when she saw how he treated my mother and his children during his divorce. Nevertheless, only she and my father knew exactly what happened between them.

In the end, my father was abandoned by the woman for whom he abandoned his own family. Having spent six years at war with his wife and children, he gained nothing but more disappointment and frustration. After all, he was left as an old and lonely man, and the new life he hoped to establish became an absolute illusion.

In summer 1985 we heard about my father's remarriage. His second wife, a divorcee, was a schoolteacher in Beijing and twenty-six years his junior.

In autumn 1985, my mother was coming close to a member of her university, Professor Zhong. In recent years, I had tried my best to look after her, and was prepared to carry on until the end of her life. But the time I could give her was limited, because of my work and my duties towards my son. Clearly, it was not in my power to reverse the growing loneliness that followed the collapse of her long, very close relationship with my father, especially after her retirement.

Though I knew that my mother felt lonely, I was disturbed when she told me that she wanted to marry Professor Zhong. It was not that I believed traditional sayings such as 'A virtuous woman cannot marry twice'. Rather, I feared for the family reputation. I had suffered enough from my father's relationship with Scarlet, and now my mother's remarriage might kindle more hostile gossip. In those days it was unusual for women of her age to marry again. When I voiced my objections, I started a quarrel that upset both of us very much. Afterwards, my mother dropped the subject, but I knew she was hurt by my lack of sympathy. I began to recognize that my mother's private life was her own, and my unreasonable attitude was also criticized by a number of my friends. I admitted to myself that I was a very unfree person, not brave enough to challenge social pressures. My personal life had been wrecked because I was always too concerned about my own or my family's reputation, and hesitated to make the right decision for myself. My mother should not suffer from my weakness. In winter 1985 I withdrew my objection to her remarriage. In February 1986 my mother married Professor Zhong.

Chapter 29

One Couple, One Child:
Press Officer for the State Family
Planning Commission
(1982–October 1987)

In autumn 1982, at the end of my maternity leave, I had a surprise message from New Star: the deputy minister of the State Family Planning Commission (SFPC), Mr Zhu, wanted to know if I was interested in working for him. I did not know Zhu personally, nor did my family. During New Star's in-service training, he had got to know Zhu's daughter, a physician at a military hospital. Through her colleagues who were former pupils of the Ba-yi School and had known me since my childhood, she heard of my reputation for being intelligent, hard-working and well-behaved, and passed these remarks to her father at a time when the Commission was desperately short of competent personnel.

At that time, I was seeking to leave the armed forces. Under the disarmament strategy, my department was due to be closed, and with my lack of family influence I could not see much hope in hanging on. As disarmament progressed, more and more people would have to leave the armed forces and look for good jobs in the civilian sector, which would only get more scarce in the future. So the sooner I changed places the better.

The SFPC, established just the previous year, was the youngest, smallest ministry under the State Council. In 1982, its head office had a staff of only fifty, compared with the several thousand maintained by longer-established ministries. At that time, it was rapidly expanding, and the large number of unfilled posts and greater prospects for promotion had attracted a mass of applicants. Deputy Minister Zhu had taken up his post only months before. A Communist veteran, he was selected in the late 1950s for training as the first generation of Party diplomats. Previously he had served as China's ambassador to countries in Africa and Europe. In the SFPC, he was in charge of foreign affairs, publicity and education. Owing to his background and experience, his manner was remarkably kind and gentle for a senior official of his rank.

When I decided to take up Zhu's offer, my hospital's management disapproved. 'Everyone knows that your department relies on the "two Pings" [Dr Feng and me],' a leading official told me, 'so we would be to blame if we let you go.' But I had made up my mind, determined not to miss this opportunity. I could not forget how desperate and frustrated I had felt the year before, when I was unexpectedly demobilized. At my request, the SFPC wrote formally to the Logistics Department of the Beijing Military Region to ask for my transfer. With the help of a senior officer in the department whose daughter was dating New Star's younger brother, I received permission to work on loan for the new State Commission.

In October 1982 I started to work for the SFPC, and was assigned to the Department of Publicity and Education. The first project that I was involved in was the National Family Planning Publicity Month, launched to enforce the one-child policy. It lasted from late December 1982 to Spring Festival (the Chinese New Year) in February 1983, in collaboration with several other ministries and national organizations, so as to mobilize all possible resources, and convey its message to every target group.

In November 1982 I attended a conference organized by the SFPC in

Beijing to pave the way for the publicity month. Bo Yibo, the former vice-premier and now an elder statesman, was invited as a keynote speaker. It was the first time I had met him, though his name had been familiar since my childhood, since the background of my father's novel was the Alliance of Sacrificing Ourselves to Save the Nation, headed by Bo Yibo during the Sino-Japanese War. (That is why his political persecution during the Cultural Revolution had also affected my father.) Bo Yibo had been one of the most handsome members of the wartime generation in Yan'an. Now he was in his mid-seventies, and his hair had turned white. What impressed me most was his sharp, outspoken speech. Among family planning workers he was a popular figure, because of his strong support for the birth-control policy. Conference delegates from Manchuria affectionately referred to him as 'our old man Bo'.

In December 1982, the National Family Planning Publicity Month opened with a high profile rally in the Great Hall of the People in Beijing, broadcast live to the nation on radio and television. The principal speakers included Madam Hao Jianxiu, Alternate Secretary of the Party's secretariat, who supervised Family Planning on behalf of the Central Committee. In the 1950s, Hao Jianxiu was praised as a labour model for the nation while a textile worker in Qingdao. She was chosen for leadership training, and hence attended courses to extend her previous limited education. Now, her post was one of the highest held by a woman in China, but she gave no sense of self-confidence, and gossip described her as incompetent. Despite her position, she lacked political power, and was treated as a token woman inside the Party leadership. I was surprised to learn that her speech was drafted by my department in the SFPC, and delivered word for word.

In the month after the rally, I was kept extremely busy every day. In order to run the campaign, each province, municipality and autonomous region had established a special office with a large staff, headed by the provincial Party leader and top governor. But in the SFPC, the daily work of coordinating the national campaign and liaising with each province occupied a team of less than ten in my department. One of my responsibilities was collecting information. Every day, mountains of post arrived from all over China reporting on progress. I had to read through these, and also to deal with the reports phoned in at least once a week by each of the campaign offices at provincial level. After collating the information, I wrote regular bulletins which were forwarded to the Party's Central Committee, the State Council, organizations involved in the campaign, and the provincial family planning commissions.

The publicity month was the largest, most ambitious campaign for birth control ever seen in China. Every day, a tide of publicity covered the whole country, and often made headlines from national to local levels. In cities, towns and many villages, all sorts of organized activities took place. Crowds thronged the streets to see the message danced, sung and acted by performers who included soldiers, factory workers, pensioners, and students from kindergarten to university. Doctors and nurses took to the streets, shopping centres and parks to spread knowledge of birth control methods or to provide health-care information for women and children. Many couples committed to the one-child pledge were visited at home and congratulated by local officials or their workplace bosses. For many years afterwards, slogans promoting the one-child policy became familiar sights on advertising hoardings all over China.

To a large extent, the powerful publicity for the one-child policy lifted the taboo on sex which had prevailed in China for thousands of years. In the past, the main chance for women to learn about childbearing came during their wedding preparations, often through whispers from already married women such as mothers or sisters. What they found out was sparse and unreliable. Some pregnant women were told that they should not practise sex in late pregnancy, otherwise the baby would be spotty through damage from sperm. Until recently, peasants in many areas knew nothing about contraceptive methods in common use for decades in the West. Reportedly some couples thought that condoms worked like herbs, the traditional, familiar medication, so they cooked up a soup with chopped condoms to prevent unwanted pregnancies. Having heard their complaints that the method did not work, local family planning workers insisted on the quality of the condoms, and replied: 'How could this happen? You can fill one with two litres of beer without bursting it.'

Under the national birth-control policy, childbearing became an open, approachable topic. In rural areas, the names of the couples granted permission to have a child were announced on their villages' public noticeboards, in just the same way that I found English local councils announcing their planning permissions to the community some years later. In each organization in urban areas, townships or districts, and every division of the armed forces, there was a special office charged with enforcing the one-child policy among their personnel, which included collecting information about pregnancies and even menstrual cycles, together with the means of contraception used or needed. When I worked for Military Hospital No. 263, married employees were required to keep these details regularly updated by filling in standard forms. At first, it was very embarrassing both to request and to collect such information, but once the ice was broken the procedure became a matter of routine.

In the early 1980s some peasants turned the free condoms provided by the government into colourful balloons, and then sold them to children in Beijing. After filling the condom with air, they pushed the closed end through to the open end, and tied both ends together to close the 'balloon', which therefore took the shape of a large apple, and was then painted with bright colours. The unusual shape and cheap price made them very popular with children. When I saw cheerful children brandish their colourful new toys, I often wondered if they knew what they were playing with.

After the publicity month, the SFPC urged me to sort out my transfer, and make myself a permanent member of staff. My hospital finally agreed, but said that I would have to find my own quota for residence in

Beijing. Members of the forces were not registered as local, and without the quota it would be impossible to settle in the city, where immigration was restricted. Only a small annual quota was allocated to the military, and in my hospital the few available had already gone. With so many staff cuts going on, there was a long queue waiting for next year's quotas, so my chance seemed very slim for the next few years. In desperation, I appealed to the deputy minister of the Ministry of Labour and Personnel, a former colleague of my mother's sister, whose ministry supervised the allocation of quotas to the armed forces. In spring 1984, after one and a half years of working for the SFPC, my transfer was finally completed, and my job became permanent.

In March 1983, shortly after the publicity month, Dr Qian Xinzhong, minister of the State Family Planning Commission, became the first recipient of the United Nations Population Award, together with Indira Gandhi, premier of India. After the announcement, I was assigned by my boss, the head of the Publicity Division, to interview Dr Qian and write an article. Till then I had never talked to Dr Qian, though he and New Star's father, veterans of the Red Army, had known each other since the early 1930s.

Dr Qian worked from home, rather than in his office in the SFPC. He lived in a beautiful house in one of the best areas of Beijing, by Houhai Lake, where several princes had their palaces during the Qing Dynasty. When I talked to him there, I was impressed by his cultivated manner, so unlike those of many other veterans. I learned that he had graduated from a medical school in Shanghai founded by Western missionaries before working as an army surgeon, and received professional training in the USSR during the Sino-Soviet 'honeymoon' period in the 1950s.

Dr Qian was quick to raise the subject of people who had 'let him down', and I realized at once that those he referred to were key members of the faction of the former Communist Youth League. Later, he even mentioned Hu Yaobang, leader of China's Communist Party, who headed that faction. According to Qian, his rivals had deliberately set out to accumulate bad news about the birth-control campaign and present it to the Central Committee, in order to deny his achievements. These confidences put me at a loss. As a newcomer to the SFPC, I had only heard that Dr Qian seemed not to get along with the first deputy minister, Wang Wei, a major member of the hostile faction, who had worked as Hu Yaobang's deputy before. I had heard it said that Qian sometimes made open complaints in the SFPC when provoked by Wang Wei's obstructions.

Dr Qian's choice of topics gave me great difficulties in writing up the interview. I could not mention his attacks on his political rivals, but not much else had been mentioned. After days of hard work I eventually finished the article, which focused on the inception of the United Nations Population Award and on China's birth-control programmes. At Dr Qian's request, I brought the draft to his home and read it to him. 'Very good article!' he applauded. 'You have an aptitude for writing which is unusual these days among young people.'

The article was published in the magazine run by the National Family Planning Association. A few days afterwards, Deputy Minister Zhu said when he met me: 'You shouldn't have written that article. Had I known about it in advance, I would certainly have stopped you.' Later, I heard that Dr Qian had instructed other departments in the SFPC head office to issue press releases promoting his award, but they had ignored his instructions, and only my department had put out an article.

Once I gained more insight into the SFPC, I began to understand Zhu's remarks. He did not belong to any side of the factional struggles in the SFPC, and did not want to see me involved. But the revelation came too late: my article had already been published. Since joining the SFPC, I had avoided trading on my connection with Zhu, and seldom mentioned my assignments to him. I knew very little about the high-level strife in the SFPC, and nothing at all about the response to Qian's request in other departments, so there was nothing to alert me to the possible political dimensions of my article. In fact, I did have misgivings about the assignment, after hearing Dr Qian accuse his opponents, but then I was politically inexperienced. Throughout my working life, I had been told that I should take whatever job my boss assigned me.

Some months after the United Nation's Population Award, Dr Qian Xinzhou was removed from his post as minister for the SFPC and replaced by his rival Wang Wei. Officially speaking, this was a routine change because Dr Qian was over seventy and due to retire. But foreign correspondents stationed in Beijing immediately contacted the SFPs, saying that Wang Wei was only a few years younger than his predecessor, and also over-age. They believed that it was not his age that cost Qian his job, but defeat in the struggle for power.

Shortly after the New Year of 1983, the death of General Yang Yong was announced to the nation. During the Korean War in the 1950s, he commanded the 'Chinese People's Volunteers'. It was said that Kim Il Sung, the Communist leader of North Korea, was in tears when he heard the news. 'I have lost a rare comrade-in-arms,' he lamented. New Star seemed relieved by the general's death. In 1977 his father, Major-General Geng, had fallen out of favour and found himself dispatched to the Nanjing Military Region. Over the years, New Star had blamed Yang Yong, Deng Xiaoping's deputy in charge of the armed forces, for his father's plight. Now there was hope for a change.

Early in 1982, after surviving his critical illness, Major-General Geng had applied to return for his retirement to Beijing, where he had worked for more than twenty years in the past, and where most of his family still lived. He was seventy, and had suffered from several diseases, the recent one caused by an allergy to broad beans, a staple plant in the Nanjing area. For the sake of his health, doctors advised him to leave this region. In those days, many of the military elite stationed outside Beijing also hoped to settle there after retirement. They knew that they had a better chance of maintaining their personal power if they retired in Beijing. But most of their applications were turned down for lack of suitable accommodation and other facilities. At first there had seemed no chance for Major-General Geng, but now things changed. Soon after the death of General Yang Yong, he was granted the permission previously refused.

From summer 1982, Major-General Geng spent most of his time in the capital before returning permanently in early 1984. During that period, he lived in a luxury hotel suite near Tian-an Men Square, provided free of charge through his connections in the Beijing Military Region, together with a Mercedes-Benz car and a full-time chauffeur.

Early one evening, a couple in their fifties called on Major-General Geng in his hotel suite. I was on my own in the living room, while Geng and his wife took a stroll after supper. The man was tall and strongly built, and talked in the distinctive accent of the Shandong Peninsula where my father came from. Though I had never met them before, he seemed to know me and greeted me warmly. Later, I learned that the couple were Chi Haotian and his wife. At that time, Chi Haotian was deputy chief of the General Staff, and regarded as a rapidly rising star among the military elite. I had heard about him through Little Uncle, who knew him personally. They had joined the Communist forces during the war from the Shandong Peninsula, and then worked for the 27th Army for many years. During the 1990s, Chi Haotian was promoted to General, the highest military rank when the military ranking system resumed after the Cultural Revolution, and became China's Defence Minister as well as a member of the Politburo.

According to New Star, his father had played a crucial role in Chi Haotian's career. The first time he had noticed Chi Haotian was during the late 1960s, when both were posted to Inner Mongolia. During that period, armed clashes were frequent on the northern frontier. In 1969, the north of China, including Beijing, was put on combat readiness in case of a Soviet invasion, with Inner Mongolia the front-line region. As a leading figure at front-line headquarters, Major-General Geng was in regular contact with Premier Zhou Enlai.

It was the height of the Cultural Revolution, when Mao and his radical followers were encouraging rebel elements to seize power from the establishment, and Major-General Geng's headquarters in Inner Mongolia was one of the many military institutions that faced direct attacks by the rebels. For several days, its compound was besieged by tens of thousands of local activists. Telephone lines were cut off, and all exits blocked. If nothing happened to stop it, the headquarters would soon be invaded and occupied. If that happened, confidential documents were likely to be seized, weapons looted, and many senior officers kidnapped. Eventually, the compound's whole military capability would be destroyed. Yet no one inside the headquarters dared to order armed resistance, for fear of being accused by Mao's radical followers of suppressing the revolutionary masses.

At this crucial moment Chi Haotian, then a deputy political commissar for an army division also stationed inside the compound, volunteered to lift the siege. At midnight he managed to get out by scaling the perimeter wall, with a team he picked for the mission. Disguised as members of the rebel organizations, they joined the hostile crowds. Soon he discovered that these rebels belonged to separate factions, and started to spread rumours among them, trying to set one against another. Within a few days, he successfully split the assailants. More and more rebels melted away, and eventually the siege ended.

Major-General Geng was hugely impressed by this performance. Several years later, it was largely at his recommendation that Chi Haotian was promoted to Deputy Political Commissar of the Beijing Military Region, and that began a steady ascent through senior posts in the armed forces, the government and the Party. He remained grateful for Geng's vital support in his career even when Geng was out of favour.

A few months after the visit by Chi Haotian and his wife, two more unexpected visitors came to see New Star's father. They were Major-General Tang and his wife, whom my father regarded as sworn enemies. Again, it was early evening, and I was chatting with New Star's parents. The meeting took both sides by surprise. It was the first time I had seen the two since 1970. Tang contrived an awkward smile, while his wife just pretended not to see me. As tension grew, New Star's mother took me to the room next door, but I could still hear the exchanges in the living room. After some small-talk, Madam Tang suddenly raised her voice and started to accuse 'people who loved to make trouble for others'. 'My husband is so honest and kind that he suffered a lot from political persecutions during the Cultural Revolution.' Madam Tang was getting emotional. 'Unlike someone else, who is always keen on stirring up trouble for others through his writing . . .' I knew the 'someone else' was my father.

New Star's parents did not answer this remark. Since my marriage, my father had never concealed the hostility he felt against Major-General Geng, which was no secret among the military elite. According to New Star, his father had told his family several times that he was innocent of what happened to Mu Xiang during the Cultural Revolution. Despite the divisions between the families, I had no grudge against Geng, who always showed me kindness and respect, and never referred to my father's accusations. But Madam Geng was different. Over the years, she told me several times that my marriage to her son would not have happened had her family known about my father's grievance. According to her, there had been no shortage of possible brides for New Star, since the family had been pursued by matchmakers bringing the names of girls from other senior officers' families.

I was shocked by this attack on my father. Nearly ten years since the end of the Cultural Revolution, Tang and his wife still could not eradicate its poison, just as my father could not. Yet why must Madam Tang vent her spleen on me? She must have known that my father had disowned his wife and children, so nothing she said to me would touch him. It seemed that she blamed her husband's plight on my father, but surely she knew that when Tang was purged during the Cultural Revolution my father had already suffered his political persecution and hence could not damage her husband. When would these vendettas disappear? This situation reminded me of a poem written by Mao Zedong in 1935: 'Who has passed judgement on the good and ill/ You have wrought these thousand autumns?'

In early 1984 Major-General Geng moved back to Beijing, and received temporary accommodation because construction work for his new residence would take several years to complete. Several of his senior contemporaries were granted the same permission, and became his neighbours. All were former prominent figures from large military regions outside Beijing, Red Army veterans who had taken part in the Long March in the 1930s and been promoted to major-general and upwards in the 1950s. The apartments converted for these families occupied the whole first floor of a block owned by the armed forces in the western suburbs of Beijing. Armed guards manned the entrance to this floor, and each family was provided with at least three full-time staff, usually a bodyguard, chef and chauffeur. A number of retired generals who had held higher positions than Geng also kept their personal assistants. A special office established by the General Political Department of the PLA supervised all these personnel.

I was not very pleased about Major-General Geng's new location. At that time, an institute run by the State Family Planning Commission, where many people knew me, rented the upstairs floor of this block. Till then I had tried hard to conceal my privileged background, but now it was no longer a secret. For most of the staff in the institute, as well as in the SFPC, the privileges enjoyed by New Star's parents and their neighbours were unheard-of. Aware of my relationship, several people expressed their disbelief to me that so few families could occupy an entire floor, especially since most were only couples, and their children lived elsewhere. For the entire institute, with nearly a hundred members of staff, one floor seemed space enough. Some people were also surprised to see the armed guard posted for these families, and asked me embarrassing questions such as: 'Do these families feel that workers from our institute threaten their safety?'

In early 1982, while pregnant with Little Mountain, I took entrance examinations for a part-time course in Chinese Language and Literature at the Beijing Radio and Television University, similar to Britain's Open University. By now, the qualification held by 'worker-peasant-soldier students' had been downgraded from 'Ben-ke', equivalent to a degree, to 'Da-zhuan', a university qualification through diploma courses, badly affecting pay, housing, promotion and perks. Shortly before I left the armed forces, employees with this devalued background were excluded from a nationwide pay rise in the civilian sector. Thousands gathered to protest at the headquarters of the State Ministry of Labour and Personnel. Because I still belonged to the armed forces, my salary did not suffer, but I sympathized with them, and felt strongly that we were not at fault for our background. During the Cultural Revolution, it represented the only way to resume an interrupted education and to study at a university, and many people I knew had founded successful careers on these beginnings. However, in spite of all objections the new policy was applied without exception to all who had come from this background.

During the 1990s, urbanites were no longer guaranteed lifetime employment: as the saying went, their iron rice bowl was broken by reforms in the political structure. As the state-run enterprises, institutions and government offices which were the main employers in China carried out wholesale staff cuts, more and more former students from the 'worker-peasant-soldier' background who had not improved their qualifications and skills faced dead-ends in their jobs. Acquaintances of mine became unemployed and struggled to find work again. Others had to take early retirement in their forties, and live on the meagre pensions provided by their workplace. When we met they were depressed and frustrated, and would grumble about the hopeless plight they faced. I sympathized deeply, knowing how many of them would have taken steps to improve their qualifications during the 1980s, had they seen what was coming.

Fortunately, I was able to grasp the urgency quite soon. In particular, ever since I was pregnant with him I had been determined to create a good future for Little Mountain and myself through my own efforts. I distrusted New Star, and never expected his support for myself or his son. Although the Cultural Revolution had cost ten years of my life, I was only in my early thirties, and felt that it was not too late to make up the lost time. Success in the part-time course I started would upgrade my qualifications to the level of a university degree. The armed forces did not offer a career, and my current medical background would not appeal to a civilian hospital, so I hoped that diversifying into Chinese Language and Literature would open more options for the future. Among hundreds of candidates in the district where I worked, my appearance drew attention during the entrance examinations, because I was the only heavily pregnant candidate. To my surprise I received one of the best results, and felt I owed thanks to the education given by my father.

The start of the course coincided with starting work at the State Family Planning Commission, and my duties required me to skip most lectures during the three and half years of study, because they often took place during working hours. At the beginning of each term, I tried to finish the assignments for the whole term as soon as possible, in case I could not find time to do the course work afterwards. Before examinations, I worked extremely hard for one or two weeks preparing for each subject, which meant getting up at two or three in the morning. This routine saw me through all my exams, sometimes with excellent results. One of my essays was chosen as the best submitted in the district. Several times, I had to sit exams unprepared for some subjects through shortage of time. Luckily, I just scraped through. In spite of the strain,

I never thought of giving up, and actually enjoyed the learning very much. In particular, I was delighted to find that the knowledge I gained was improving my work in the SFPC.

In March 1986, to pay tribute to model workers and high-performing areas, the SFPC convened a conference in Beijing which was attended by over 600 delegates from all over China. It had been several years in preparation, and a team of more than 200 members was assigned to conduct it. All the delegates and members of the working team were put up in a Beijing hotel at the SFPC's expense. Since the conference was regarded as a key occasion in the field of family planning, the SFPC leadership decided to launch a publicity campaign, and I was assigned to deal with the press.

Since spring 1983, I had been put in charge of press relations for the SFPC, and I established good contacts with the national press, based on mutual respect and support. Most of the correspondents I met were talented, dedicated people. Many had come through experiences like my own, such as hard labour in the countryside during the Cultural Revolution. Like me, they belonged to the first generation reared under the Communist regime. Now I was impressed by what they had achieved, and the confidence they showed in their own ability to create good futures for themselves. Most of them came from humble family backgrounds, so they had to achieve everything through their own efforts. In them, I saw hope for China's future.

At the same time, I also felt sorry for these correspondents because of the strict censorship they had to work under, and which I myself helped to enforce. They often expressed their frustration to me about the lack of freedom at work under the Communist regime, especially when reporting on politics and state policy. I heard that a famous correspondent from China's Central Television Station was told off by a leading government figure he interviewed, who was angered by his questions. 'I told you already that I can't give the answer!' this man shouted, on camera. 'How dare you ask again?' Afterwards, it was said that this correspondent was also reproved by his boss for 'offending' his interviewee, and was forbidden to present his programme for some time.

Certainly, I could not lift the censorship, but there were things I could do to help these reporters, such as feeding them regular information or suggesting safe subjects to report on. They welcomed this approach. When I first started working with the press, reporters often complained about Minister Wang Wei's uncooperative attitude, and a few transferred their anger on to me. Now they became friendly, and some even apologized for their past behaviour. I made a number of friends among them, and found myself invited to their homes and to social occasions. At this major conference, about fifty national press correspondents were invited, and each one briefed on the delegates they might be interested in interviewing. Again, my cooperation was welcomed. Some told me that the large press attendance reminded them of the annual conference of the National People's Congress, unusually large even at the national level.

The opening ceremony took place on 1 March 1986 in the Great Hall of the People, where the principal speaker was Wan Li, an elder statesman prominent in the faction of the former Beijing Municipality. At supper time that day, the *People's Daily* correspondent approached me in the hotel. 'I'm afraid I couldn't convince our deputy editor-in-chief to lead with Wan Li's speech tomorrow,' she told me anxiously. Minister Wang Wei had made this his special request. As the mouthpiece of the Communist Party, the *People's Daily* played a key role in conveying the leadership's message to the nation, and front-page coverage for Wan Li's speech would strongly signal the importance to the nation of the birth-control campaign.

In response to Wang Wei's demand, the deputy editor-in-chief claimed that it was too late to run the text of the speech next day. Each page had been finalized, and printing would start in a couple of hours. How could we possibly meet Wang Wei's demand? The largest, most influential newspaper in China need not take pressure from any government ministry.

Though the chances seemed slim, I had to talk to the deputy editor-in-chief myself, having no other option. It was already seven o'clock when he answered the telephone at home, and I tried my best to project a diplomatic, confident manner, not stressing the minister's will, but saying how encouraging it would be for family planning workers all over China to see the text of Wan Li's speech given pride of place in the *People's Daily*. I also expressed my gratitude for the long-term support that his newspaper had shown us. Eventually, he said: 'Please bring me the text immediately. I'll let you know my decision as soon as I've read it.' I travelled straight across Beijing to his office from the hotel, and had only just returned when he phoned to assure me that the text would make the headlines in the morning.

On the last day of the conference, I was summoned unexpectedly by Minister Wang Wei, who inquired about the coverage in the press. Our meeting was brief, but his expression showed his approval of my work. Press publicity had started in January, about two months before. A stream of reports promoting the SFPC's model workers and districts had appeared every day in newspapers and magazines, and on radio and TV throughout the country, often as headline news. In his closing speech to the conference, Minister Wang Wei praised the publicity breakthrough achieved by this occasion.

Chapter 30

No Right to Divorce, No Right to Love:
The End of My Marriage

(May 1982–October 1987)

During the first few months after Little Mountain's birth, New Star showed me more consideration, due partly to his father's criticism of his unreasonable behaviour during my pregnancy, and partly to his delight at having a male child. He told me several times: 'You are the heroine of our family, because you gave birth to a son.' But the improvement did not last. There were too many other issues that still divided us, in particular the basic differences in our character, principles and values.

By now, I had given up trying to persuade New Star to improve his qualifications: I knew that he would not agree. But to lessen his resentment of my studies, I tried my best to keep up the household chores. Since baby food was not on sale in those days, I also needed to prepare next day's lunch for my son in the evening, so that he could have proper food and his nanny could concentrate on looking after him when we were at work. It was often close to nine in the evening when I finished the housework and Little Mountain went to sleep. And then it was time for my studies.

New Star kept complaining about my studies, as he did not believe that hard work could promise a good future. To prove his case, he could cite any number of 'sons or daughters of high officials' whose family background propped up their achievements. Ever since the early 1980s, many of the so-called 'princelings', the children of the Party establishment, had climbed high in the Party, government or the armed forces. I could not change New Star's mind, especially since I myself had needed his father's connections to obtain my present job. But nor could he convert me to his view. Through my own experiences, I knew that if I wanted to achieve something, the only solution was to work hard. I did not want to live on political nepotism. Even if my father had stayed on good terms with his children, or if New Star's father had still been in favour, they belonged to the last generation; we could not rely on their support for the rest of our lives.

Had I been naturally submissive, I suppose that I might have been satisfied with such a husband. People in my hospital who had not seen his private face had expressed their reservations in the past. 'What more do you want from your husband?' they asked. 'Apart from his good looks and family background, he doesn't smoke or drink, and he's careful with money . . .' They might also be impressed by the gentle manner he displayed in public, just as I had been when we first met. But years of marriage had shown what he was really like, and the tactics he used in his efforts to control me had only enhanced my disappointment. Several times, he expressed his regret that he had failed to transform me into the ideal wife he expected. Perhaps he never asked himself how deeply his wife had been hurt by his violence and malice. I was not born to be a puppet, and my compromises could not last for ever. When I could not curb my anger or disapproval, a quarrel would follow, and often ended in violence.

Several months after the birth of Little Mountain, our quarrels intensified again, and his violence resumed. He was so much stronger that a single heavy slap to my face could knock me down, and often the spectacles I wore would fall and shatter on the concrete floor. As I was too shortsighted to go to work without them, I had to keep a spare pair in reserve. A few times, I tried to fight back, but only suffered more from his violence. Several times, I had to use make-up at work to cover the bruises on my face, and then invent excuses when people showed surprise because they knew I did not usually wear it. Before her remarriage, my mother lived with us in the flat in Peace Street, but she could not prevent my husband's violence. Sometimes she had to leave the flat in tears, because she could not stand to watch. After each row or beating, New Star would disappear for several weeks. When he returned there was no apology: it was as if nothing had happened. For the sake of my son, I had to swallow my anger, but this brought me neither his sympathy nor his respect. The quarrels went on, and I suffered his violence again.

As my feeling against him grew, it became unbearable to live with him. Sometimes I felt suffocated just to see him in the flat. I made various excuses to sleep on the floor of my mother's bedroom, and hence avoided sharing ours. My mother remarked several times that she had never seen another couple like us, and indeed I felt appalled myself to realize how desperately I craved not to live with him. But I had no right to divorce him. Now I had become a civilian, and he still belonged to the armed forces. Under Chinese marriage law, a divorce would not be granted without his consent. Since most members of the forces had to live apart from their families, the law took care to protect their marriages. I had to remain New Star's wife as long as he did not choose to end the marriage.

During that period, I often wondered what New Star really thought about the marriage. I did not believe that he loved me. According to him, I was lazy, dirty, incapable and extravagant, every other wife he knew was better, and he resented almost everything I did. He also resented my friends, and claimed that they were a waste of my time, because none of them could help to find me a job or a place to live. With his secretive character, he often complained that I could not keep my mouth shut, and he was not interested in introducing me into his social circle.

In November 1984 I was assigned to Manila, in the Philippines, to attend a two-week seminar organized by the United Nations. During the trip I got to know the delegation's English interpreter, Yale Lin. We had never talked before, but he was a friend of Feng-an's and knew something about my family background. He was only one year older than me, and known for his hard work and intelligence. The son of a humble family in Shanghai, he had been sent to Manchuria during the Cultural Revolution, and worked in the fields. Later he studied English as a 'worker-peasant-soldier student', but despite this unpromising background his fluency impressed many colleagues.

At that time, my life was at a low point. Condemned to an unhappy marriage, I needed to confide in someone who could understand me. Before the trip, I often talked to my best friend, a former hospital colleague, to express my frustration, sometimes sobbing on the phone for more than an hour. When I had to spend weekends with New Star, I made excuses to escape for a while by visiting friends. Now, in a foreign country, I could sense Yale's sympathetic interest, and we began to spend time together. It was my first trip abroad, and he enjoyed being my guide around the hotel and its locality. His wit and humour cheered me, and showed me ways to be more positive about my situation.

It took very little time for our closeness to cause rumours and gossip in the Chinese delegation of about twenty officials working in the family planning field. Some were put out that I, one of the few female delegates, should pay so much attention to Yale. Others disliked him personally, possibly offended by his outspokenness and intelligence. Another cause for their suspicion was my troubled relationship with my husband, which was no secret. Knowing that I was unhappy in my marriage, some might have thought that I was looking for comfort elsewhere. Ever since my childhood I had heard the traditional saying that 'gossip and rumours flourish outside a widow's door'. Now I began to believe that it applied not only to widows, but to any other woman who was unmarried or even unhappy with her husband. Many delegates were in their fifties, and still influenced by traditional ways of thinking. Some of them quickly spread stories about an affair.

In the tropical weather the favourite place for Yale and me was the hotel's outdoor swimming pool, which was overlooked by many rooms, including those occupied by our delegation. Soon some of our fellow delegates took to watching us swimming behind their closed curtains above. When we caught them peering, the narrow gap was hurriedly drawn shut. It was a farcical sight, and when I complained Yale would just laugh: 'Forget it!'

Back in Beijing, stories about my 'affair' were urgently passed on to our superiors by some of the delegates who described me 'naked and cuddling' by the swimming pool. In fact, we had not even held hands! For a government official, a sex scandal occurring during service abroad would result in serious disciplinary charges. Fortunately the deputy director of my department, Mr Han, felt that these stories were too tall to believe. The swimming pool was open to every guest, and there were always staff on duty. How could 'indecent conduct' be committed? 'These stories must be rumours,' he retorted to the informers. 'I don't believe that Little Mu would ever behave that way.'

After the trip to Manila, my enjoyment of Yale's company dwelled on my mind. There had been neither physical contact nor intimate conversation, yet I felt close to him due to our mutual understanding. I recognized that I had a crush on him. But my fondness for Yale did not make up for my unhappiness, as it brought still more frustration. Due to the allegations, I could not stay in regular touch with Yale, for fear of incurring more malicious lies.

I also worried about what would happen if New Star heard these stories. Before our marriage, he already condemned any contact with other men. When I told him about my escape from the countryside, he expressed his suspicion that the vice-chief of our production team, who took trouble to help me get away, had been involved with me. He did not believe that an innocent friendship could exist between men and women. After our marriage, I did as he wished and gave up my few male friends. The exception was Great Peace, the young officer I met in the 1970s when serving in the Armoured Forces 9th Division. Before I left for university in 1975, I agreed to remain his friend and keep in touch. After my wedding, troubled by the breach with my father and the setbacks in my marriage, I valued our friendship all the more. New Star claimed that it was partly his discovery that we still corresponded that provoked the violent beating he inflicted during the summer of 1979, after my graduation. In early 1980, unable to cope with more violence, I broke contact with Great Peace.

Knowing New Star's reactions, I feared that he would interpret my relationship with Yale as an extramarital affair if we kept up regular contacts. As a serviceman, New Star could accuse Yale and me of breaking the law by damaging his marriage, and take both of us to court. For weeks after my visit to Manila, I was tormented by the hope of seeing Yale again and the disgust I felt for New Star. Several times, I wept to my mother at night before going to his bed: 'This is hell, Mama! I hate him!' No one could help me, because I had no right to divorce my husband or to love another man.

In early 1983, New Star finally changed his job, as the armoured forces headquarters where he worked were also shedding staff under the disarmament policy. Using his father's connections, he managed to transfer to another clinic in town, run by the Logistics Department of the Beijing Military Region, and later got a two-room flat from his new workplace. In spring 1984 Little Mountain started kindergarten. It was one of the best in Beijing where it was difficult to get a place, and again Major-General Geng enlisted his connections. Shortly after his third birthday, Little Mountain was transferred with other children of his age from the day-care to the boarding department, and would only come home for weekends. The department was located next to Beijing Zoo, and on warm evenings the children were often taken for a stroll there free of charge. His dormitory was only a few hundred metres away from the giant panda house.

In December 1985 Little Mountain caught cold, and I took some days off work to look after him at New Star's flat. When he was recovering, I asked New Star to take my place for a day. Minister Wang Wei was to be interviewed by Western journalists, and wanted me there to assist him. Even when I showed him Wang Wei's written instructions, New Star still insisted I must stay at home. I tried to keep quiet, knowing what would happen if we quarrelled, but my silence only provoked him – he knew that I would not listen. When he threatened to beat me again, I took Little Mountain and returned to Peace Street. My mother looked after him for me while I went to work.

Over the years, I had grown deeply attached to the flat in Peace Street. During the Cultural Revolution, it was my parents' refuge from the pressures of the armoured forces and the ill will of their persecutors. I still remember the happiness, warmth and deep love that I experienced with my parents when I came home on leave from my unit. After my graduation from university, it also became a refuge for me, safe from our family conflicts, and it offered independence from New Star. Having received his new quarters, New Star urged me several times to give up the flat, but I made excuses to refuse and tried to spend most of my time there during the week so as not to bear his presence every day. Now that I was separated from him, the flat became home for me and my son.

Soon 1985 was over, and so was the winter. It seemed that spring arrived overnight. Within a few days, all the trees on the city streets turned green, and the blue sky looked brighter than before. Little Mountain also developed fast. He stopped crying when I left him at kindergarten on Mondays, and settled into his surroundings. When the kindergarten started a trial to teach young children English, he was fascinated by the new language. At weekends, he loved to recite his text-book to everyone he met: 'This is a pen. That is a book . . .' I was proud when his teacher told me that he was one of the best children in the English class.

I always felt excited on Saturday mornings, the last working day of the week, because I was going to collect my son, who was with me nowadays for most weekends and public holidays. Travelling home, he was happy and cheerful, like a bird just released from a cage. The way he enjoyed his new-found freedom reminded me of my childhood, and coming home from Ba-yi School. Like me, he too asked endless questions, which started as soon as we boarded the bus. 'Mama, why is the sky blue?' 'Why do birds have wings to fly but we don't?' 'Why do men have beards on their faces, but women don't? . . .' Very often, his questions made passengers laugh, which embarrassed him so much that he fell silent and hid his face. But a few minutes later, the questions flowed again.

At the outdoor free market on Peace Street, Little Mountain was fas-cinated by the live chickens and fish on sale. His favourite snack was roasted sweet potatoes, hot from the oven — a converted petrol drum — their soft light yellow flesh tender under the burnt peel. 'Tasty, tasty,' he would tell me, puffing away the steam. The street was full of the deli-cious smell, which reminded me how fast things changed in Beijing. When I was a child, the most familiar smells there came from the wood and coal that every family used for cooking and heating. And then, at the height of the Cultural Revolution, the smell of new-made paste filled the air, because the city was plastered with big-character posters and political slogans continually renewed by various rebellious organiza-tions. Very often, a layer put up just an hour before was already lost under another. When Little Mountain grew up, I looked forward to telling him stories about our country from my own experiences.

In recent years, my work for the State Family Planning Commission had been stressful. Sometimes I was given an urgent assignment in the late afternoon, or received a telephone call from the Ministry of Foreign

Affairs asking me to prepare information for the country or party leaders about China's family planning programmes for their impending state visits abroad. That evening or weekend, I had to draft the necessary documents as matters of urgency. After my separation from New Star, I often explained to Little Mountain that I had to write for 'Grandpa Wang', as children called Minister Wang Wei. Little Mountain had met Wang Wei, and been intimidated by his serious manner. When I was working, my son often stood by me and whispered: 'Mama, hold me, please!' I took him on my lap, and he stayed there till I finished. Sometimes his head lay on my shoulder and I could feel his soft breath. Gradually, it became his routine question: 'Mama, do you have to write for Grandpa Wang this weekend?'

From three years old, Little Mountain suffered from chronic tonsillitis. Almost every month in wintertime he came down with a high fever. If it happened in kindergarten his teacher notified my office and I hurried to fetch him home, and looked after him, sometimes with help from my mother, until he recovered. When I was too busy to stay away, I had to bring him to the office and keep him somewhere close while I worked. If the attack began at midnight on a weekend, I had to take him on my back to a local hospital for emergency treatment. My mother always worried about my safety, as these walks took thirty minutes in the dark, through empty streets, but I had no choice. The buses had stopped running by then, and it was hard to find a taxi. When the weather was bad, our journeys became an ordeal. I wrapped the boy in thick clothes and a warm coat to keep out the cold, covered his nose and mouth with a gauze mask, and struggled all the way against the howling wind. When I reached home again, I could hardly recognize myself in the mirror, under the layer of brown dust that covered my face.

No matter how many difficulties I faced, I became confident that I was able to bring up my son on my own, and seeing him develop was the greatest joy in my life. By now I had completed the course in Chinese Language and Literature, and my work was going well. In her new marriage, my mother was recovering from her sorrows, and visited me often. When I was away on working trips, she helped to look after her grandson at weekends.

Before my separation from New Star, my younger brother Feng-yuan and his family had moved into the Peace Street flat, as my father was set on evicting his youngest son, and the alternative accommodation he offered through the Ba-yi Studio was a single small dark room, with no lavatory, kitchen, running water or heating. Seeing these poor conditions, my mother suggested that they share this flat with me after she moved in with her husband. Little Mountain got on well with Feng-yuan's son, Little South, as both were of similar age. Among these prevalent only children, a common problem was loneliness at home, for lack of a sibling, so I was pleased that the boys could keep each other company. When Little South was not around at weekends, my boy used to grumble: 'I'm bored. I have no one to play with at home.'

By then, my relationship with Aijun and Feng-an had also improved and we saw each other regularly. For the first time since my wedding in 1977 I was enjoying life. But I knew that my newly-found peace would not last long, because New Star would not tolerate our indefinite separation. Perhaps he still expected that I would compromise again, as I had done before, but this time was different. I did not want to live with him any more. From time to time he made excuses to visit my son and me in Peace Street, expecting to be asked to stay for the weekend, but I turned him away. How long this separation would last, or what would happen to me next, I did not know. I had no right to end the marriage without New Star's consent, which meant that my fate was in his hands.

One evening in June 1986, I had two unexpected visitors: New Star and Zhu's daughter. Zhu had retired the year before from his post as deputy minister of the SFPC. Although I was still friendly with his daughter, her visit came as a surprise. It was a weekday, and Little Mountain was in kindergarten. In my room, my visitors sat in the armchairs near the door, while I kept as distant as possible, sitting on my bed. An awkward pause followed. I felt suffocated – my usual feeling with New Star in the flat. What was he here for? Why had he brought Junior Zhu?

'You two cannot go on like this for ever.' Junior Zhu broke the silence. 'You have been married for so many years. If there are problems between you, you should talk together frankly and sincerely.' As she was several years older, she often spoke like an elder sister. I heard a few days later that it was New Star who asked her to come.

'After you, Aiping,' he said at once. 'I'd like to hear what you think first.' He sat up straight, and adopted a considerate manner. I kept silent, taken by surprise but feeling instinctively that something unusual must have happened. 'This afternoon, the Party organization in my workplace contacted the State Family Planning Commission to discuss the problems of our relationship.' New Star finally came to his point. 'The matter is very complicated, and is taken seriously by your Party authority. The Party Committee in your head office has invited me for a talk tomorrow. Now I would like to hear about your ideas.'

I felt so stunned by what I heard that words failed me for a while, as I struggled to pull myself together, and not to show panic in front of New Star. 'I'm afraid that I don't have much to say,' I eventually managed to reply. 'We've been married for nearly nine years, and done nothing but quarrel. Since both of us are unhappy with the situation, we should have talked heart to heart about our problems. But I haven't, because I don't trust you. You are not honest with me, so I feel it is meaningless to talk . . .'

New Star felt insulted, and soon we were rowing again, which was awkward for Junior Zhu. During the argument he complained that I did not tell him anything about myself or my parents, and it was true. I had not even told him about their second marriages. After all that had happened between us, what was the point? It turned out now that he was also accusing me of having an affair with Han, the deputy chief of my department, and had prompted his Party branch to contact the SFPC to intervene. By his account, the affair had damaged his happy marriage.

Shortly after Wang Wei became the minister, Han had been in charge of my department. He and I got to know each other because he was the spokesman of the SFPC and I was his assistant. Twenty years my senior, he joined the Communist underground in the late 1940s, while a middle school pupil in Nationalist-occupied Shanghai. Under the Communist regime, he worked for the Supreme People's Procuratorate in Beijing, and seemed bound for success as a protégé of its chief, Zhang Dingcheng. During a political campaign in the early 1950s, his wife, and former comrade in the Shanghai underground, was labelled as a 'historical counter-revolutionary'. She lost her job, and was sent to a labour camp. Han was told officially that unless he divorced his 'counter-revolutionary' wife there was no bright future for him in the Supreme People's Procuratorate. But he refused to divorce her. 'I believed that my wife was innocent,' he told me. 'I never thought of leaving her, even when she was in deep trouble.' Throughout his wife's ordeal he gave her unconditional support, and brought up their children on his own.

I first heard Han's story from some colleagues, and was moved by his deep love for his wife. As I got to know him better, I was also impressed by his uprightness and courage. During the Cultural Revolution, he had left Beijing to join his wife in Hebei province, because she was banned from the capital. When Zhang Dingcheng was politically persecuted, Han, supposedly his favourite, came under heavy pressure to provide false evidence against him. When he refused he suffered imprisonment and torture. After the Cultural Revolution, Zhang Dingcheng was rehabilitated, but died a few years later. Still grateful for his colleague's loyalty, in his will he asked the Party's Central Committee to arrange Han's return to Beijing. This brought him to the SFPC, where he soon impressed Deputy Minister Zhu with his hard work and integrity and came to be seen as a member of Zhu's camp, just as I was.

After Zhu's retirement, Han and I faced similar problems: lack of backing from the top level of the SFPC. Although the post of director had been vacant ever since the establishment of my department, he had been running it, but remained in the post of deputy director. In addition to his department responsibilities, he also drafted many important documents for the SFPC, and prepared speeches for various leaders, among them Wang Wei's speech at the World Population Conference in Mexico in 1984 as head of China's official delegation. Due to the demands of his job, he often started work at two or three o'clock in the morning.

The more I knew Han, the more I respected him. I was also grateful for his enormous support and help in my work. Over the years, I got to know his wife and some other members of his family, and was sometimes invited to dinner with my son. In China, it was not unusual for people working in the same place to visit each other in their spare time, because there was little social life outside the working circle. Also, since many people lived in housing provided by their work unit, it was natural for neighbours to be colleagues. After the Cultural Revolution, Han's wife was politically rehabilitated. The persecution she suffered for almost twenty years had ruined her career and undermined her health, so she was retired with a small pension, and suffered from various illnesses. As my relationship with New Star kept on deteriorating, I could not keep it secret at work. Han was the leader of my Party branch, and listened with sympathy when I discussed it with him in the customary way.

For years I had hesitated to end the marriage, fearing that New Star would not readily let go. My fear proved true when the time came. Now that he recognized my determination to leave him, he felt publicly humiliated. Due to his privileged background, he was unused to opposition. As a married man, it would wound him to lose face because his wife had run away. Confident that his position as a serviceman gave him the upper hand under Chinese marriage law, he retaliated by accusing me of conducting an affair with another man, since in China it was usual to connect a broken marriage with adultery. He knew that Han and I were on good terms, and had worked together closely. Perhaps he was also confident about the power of a husband's words. He threatened to take

Han and me to court if the 'affair' did not stop, with a minimum sentence of two years in prison for damaging his marriage.

As a result of New Star's information, some officials from the SFPC head office were assigned to Military Hospital No. 263, my previous workplace, to investigate my conduct with men. Swallow, a political officer working for the hospital's Party committee, dealt with the inquiry. Five years ago, it was she who had stood by me when my name was first listed for redundancy. Now she was furious about New Star's accusation that I was notorious in the hospital for my promiscuous behaviour. 'That is utterly untrue,' she retorted. 'I swear by my Party membership that Mu Aiping never caused any gossip about her relationships with men when she worked for our hospital. She was known for her decency, hard work and popularity, and was respected by her colleagues and patients.' For a Communist official like Swallow, such an oath was the most solemn form of pledge. The SFPC investigation soon became the talk of the hospital, and many expressed their sympathy over New Star's unscrupulous treatment.

New Star also told the SFPC that he was going to the front line to fight in China's continuing confrontation with Vietnam. Frequent clashes were still taking place in border areas. Over the years, the whole nation had been mobilized to support the fighting troops, and those involved were treated as heroes. In New Star's words, he was ready to sacrifice his life for his country's sake, and simply wanted the Party to help him to sort out his marriage problem before he set out for the war. Through contacting another official in my department, he had the key to his flat taken away from me, saying that he intended to return the flat to his workplace as he was bound for the front. It seemed that his wishes were commands. But as had often happened in the past, none of his claims came true.

I had no way to know the details of New Star's allegations, because the head office Party Committee refused to tell me. Instead I was informed that as soon as I ended the separation, the investigation of my 'affairs' would cease. When the secretary of the committee informed me that New Star still loved me deeply, I could not believe my ears. If it were true, how could he explain what he had done to me over these years? I knew from experience how plausible New Star could make his stories sound, so it came easy for him to pose to observers as a heart-broken husband, his happy marriage ruined by his wife's affair. Perhaps they were ready to believe that I had initiated the trouble because it was I who had left my husband, which signalled my intention to divorce him. In particular, New Star had mobilized the Party organization in his workplace to make our marriage an official issue, which gave him lever-age with the SFPC officials.

In recent years, my marriage problem had ceased to be a secret in the SFPC. A well-meaning colleague once asked me frankly: 'Why don't you live in peace with your husband? As a woman, what else do you intend to do?' I sensed his disapproval of my attitude, and found out later that he was not alone in his view. In some people's eyes, I did not know my place as a wife, and lacked the meekness and obedience traditionally expected of women for thousands of years. For them, it was nonsense for a woman to judge the quality of her marriage.

At head office, I was the first female member of staff with marriage problems, which made me an easy target for gossip and rumours. After the trip to Manila, stories about my 'affair' with Yale had been circulated. Although there was no evidence to prove it, my reputation was damaged because my name was connected with a 'sexual scandal'. Had I been old or ugly, I might have been less vulnerable. Unfortunately, I was only in my early thirties, and regarded as attractive. Till lately I had been one of the youngest workers at head office. Comments from others about my 'good taste in clothes' did not help either. For a woman with a troubled marriage to be attractive to other men easily led to suspicions of trying to 'seduce' them. At the same time, my achievements at work and involvement in high-profile assignments also incurred jealousy, which made my situation even worse. New Star's visit to the SFPC caused some people there to accuse me of 'committing adultery' with my boss in order to further my ambitions.

One sympathetic colleague told me: 'Please don't take the campaign against you personally. You are only a scapegoat. Old Han is the real target.' Han's outspokenness and integrity had made him a number of enemies inside the SFPC who were followers of Minister Wang Wei, but he took no notice. In answer to warnings from sympathizers, he often replied: 'If you don't consider your personal gains or losses, you will be fearless.' Over the years, he did not conceal his appreciation of my work, or his low opinion of the competence of a few of his own officials aligned with Wang Wei. Because of these antagonisms and my troubled marriage, his 'relationship' with me had already been rumoured at head office even before New Star's official visit.

After the Cultural Revolution, politics offered little chance for undermining rivals, because large-scale political persecutions had ceased. Now, it was personal matters, such as sexual affairs or financial scandals, that became the weapons of choice in power struggles. I was surprised by New Star's knowledge about the infighting inside the SFPC, and the topics of gossip. To my knowledge, his only personal contacts there were Zhu and his daughter, whom I respected too much to suspect as likely sources. A number of friends had asked me: 'How is your husband so well informed? Is there anyone in the SFPC head office connected with him?' I had no way of knowing, but one thing clear to me was that the stories he spread had suited Han's rivals. I began to understand why it was that the Party Committee at SFPC head office had failed to stand by me. Even if sceptical about New Star's claims, these officials were bound to be cautious about offending Wang Wei's circle by showing support to me.

An official of the Party Committee told me clearly: 'We will not issue an official letter endorsing your divorce, even if you intend to divorce.' In China, people were required to provide an official letter from their workplace when registering their marriage or divorce, so the refusal of the letter meant that my divorce would be blocked. In recent years, Chinese society had begun to relax its attitudes towards divorce, but no such change had reached the SFPC, due largely to Minister Wang Wei's disapproval, though I heard that he himself had been divorced in the past.

Before my case there was only one SFPC colleague whose marriage problem had been made public. Stone was around my age, and came from a humble background. During the Cultural Revolution he was forced to leave Beijing with his family, because his parents were branded 'bourgeois capitalists'. After it ended, his record of hard work entitled him to enrol at a university. He needed permission from his workplace, a small firm in Hebei province, but he was told that his release depended on his marrying his boss's daughter. For the sake of his future, he had to accept. After graduation he was assigned to the SFPC, while his wife remained in Hebei province. It seems that she later complained to the SFPC that she and her husband were estranged, and he intended to divorce her. One day Stone was summoned by Wang Wei, who told him bluntly: 'I know you don't want to leave Beijing. If you don't make it up with your wife, I can send you back to Hebei just by a word to Xing Chongzhi.' Xing Chongzhi was the 'first hand' leader in Hebei province. Like Wang Wei, he belonged to the faction of the former Communist Youth League.

Apparently Stone was intimidated by Wang Wei's threat. He knew how hard it would be to return, once exiled from the capital again. When the SFPC started to house its staff, he was allocated a flat despite the many applications for limited resources. And then the SFPC helped to arrange a residence quota for his wife. For decades, hundreds of thousands of people had had to live apart from spouses who could not obtain permanent residence in Beijing. They would have envied Stone's wife, had they known how quickly she received the quota. One day, Wang Wei announced at a staff meeting: 'Good news! Stone's wife is pregnant.' I was not present, but when I heard about this remark I shook my head. I felt sorry for Stone and his wife, and especially for their future child. Recently Stone had told me how much he resented Wang

Wei's interference. After their baby was born, the couple separated. Years later, I heard that they were divorced.

No one would say that Wang Wei's meddling was wrong, because he represented the Party. Since the war, the Party had exerted its authority over marriage and divorce by giving or withholding its permission. But his staff's private lives seemed to hold a special interest for Wang Wei; I never heard of any other minister who intervened in individual marriage problems. This might hark back to his career in the Communist Youth League, where a major responsibility was to help youngsters to sort out their private lives, sometimes by matchmaking. During my time in the SFPC, Wang Wei and other senior figures made several general appeals for us all to help a single colleague to find a marriage partner. Perhaps he hoped to gain a reputation as a caring leader devoted to the welfare of his staff.

Soon after New Star's visit to the SFPC, I was summoned by Wang Wei to discuss my marriage. Compared with Stone's encounter, his manner seemed soft and polite, but I sensed his disapproval of my separation as he tried to persuade me to reconcile with New Star. 'This is my private life, and I have my reasons for the separation,' I replied. 'The Party Committee does not know what really happened between the two of us. How can they press me to reconcile with him?' Wang Wei also criticized my failure to 'behave carefully' in my contacts with Han, which meant that he was influenced by the rumours. When I warned him not to believe the allegations, because they were based on false information, Wang Wei seemed displeased by my refusal to listen.

What a dreadful summer I had in 1986! The campaign that New Star launched against me was outrageous. I heard that he burst into Wang Wei's office, demanding that the SFPC put a stop to my 'affair' with Han. Sometimes twice a week, I was summoned to the Party Committee at head office in response to his unexpected visits, often accompanied by officers sent at his request by his workplace Party authority to mediate between us. I might be confronted by nearly ten people at once – not only New Star, but also officials representing both sides' Party authorities. In front of everyone, he read out prepared public statements asking me to cease our separation. He promised me forgiveness if I would move back to his flat straight away.

On these occasions, I mostly sat on my own and kept quiet. In this marriage, it was New Star not I who had the right of divorce. If I stated my wish to divorce him, he would take his chance to turn the screw by forcing me to beg for his consent. Also, he would use it as evidence to prove his claim against me, since marital breakdown was seen as an outcome of adultery. I knew that each of these meetings was planned in advance, and that I was the only participant who had no idea of the agenda. Among the officials involved, the aim was to pressure me to end the separation, which would close the case and endorse their 'mediation'. Despite my distrust, I could not refuse to attend. I could not afford to offend these officials. With no prospect of support from elsewhere, anything that inclined them further towards New Star must be avoided.

Because I would not end the separation, the 'mediation' failed and I was blamed for 'lacking sincerity' towards reconciling with New Star. During that period, I repeatedly pleaded to SFPC officials dealing with my case: 'I have been working for the SFPC for years, why don't you believe me? I am a victim of the marriage, and in his power, why don't you support me? Do you know what really happened in my marriage?' But their reply remained unchanged: it was hard to disbelieve New Star's stories, because it was I who had left him. So the only way to demonstrate my innocence was to end the separation, and live with him again. That was impossible! In the past I had made many concessions, but they had not improved my situation, or our relationship. After that, I could not bear his presence any more.

During that summer, New Star also phoned me at work many times threatening to smash everything in my flat if I refused to surrender. He swore to friends of mine that he would either kill me or damage my face.

According to him he had followed me to and from work, trying to prove his accusations. Alarmed for my safety, my friends urged me to seek protection from the SFPC, but officials discounted the danger. 'He was just making threats,' I was told. 'No matter what comes between a couple, everything is settled as soon as they sleep together again.' They kept up the pressure to end the separation.

For several months, the SFPC was beset by New Star's visits. Dressed in their army uniforms, the appearance of him and his escort always caused a stir at head office. On my way to or from these meetings, I had to suppress my emotions, knowing that curious eyes observed me. As soon as I found a quiet corner, my tears just welled up, and I often felt choked by the cascade of anger and pain. But I had no time to express my feelings, only to dry my tears and hurry to my office. 1986 was my busiest year in the SFPC. Apart from my own responsibilities, I was a major organizer for several national conferences, and co-wrote three documentary film scripts introducing China's family planning programme, due for production next year.

In addition to my regular workload, I needed extra income to support my son. Although New Star had not stopped paying his share, he might withdraw his support at any time as our separation continued. Over the last two years, Little Mountain's kindergarten fees had doubled owing to high inflation, which cost almost my entire salary, but New Star's contribution did not change. As a single-child parent, I could claim part of the fees from my workplace, but the amount was not enough to enable me to keep myself as well as to cover other spending on my son. Fortunately I was hired by a number of influential magazines and newspapers as a regular contributor on China's family planning programme. This work paid handsomely – in some years more than my salary.

In summer 1986, the staff at SFPC head office had a routine health checkup, and I was diagnosed with low blood pressure and incipient heart disease. This came as no surprise. Lately I had often felt weak and terribly tired. Much of this problem was due to the long hours and pressures of my job — twelve-hour days with five hours' sleep were not unusual. But New Star's campaign played its part. How much more would I have to suffer from him? At times I felt driven close to madness. The idea of suicide haunted me again, and conflicted with fears for my son. For his sake I had to survive, no matter how long my ordeal lasted. During that period, my mother gave enormous support. Whenever I needed help, it was hers that came first. 'Please hold on,' she asked me many times. 'If you give up, who else can clear your name?'

One evening in early October 1986, I was alone in the first-floor flat. Due to New Star's threats of violence, I tried not to switch on a light or watch TV during evenings alone at home, so that he could not tell if I was in. But summer was over, the days were getting shorter, and the prospect of long dark evenings on my own was harder to bear. By six o'clock I could not help turning on the light, and started to write, voicing the loneliness, pain and anger I had to keep concealed.

Before long someone knocked at the door. My first reaction was to hide my writing and turn off the light. 'It must be New Star,' I thought, because no one was invited. I did not answer, and hoped that the caller would leave, but the knocking went on, louder and more and more impatient, which confirmed who was there. He started to pound and kick the locked door. Now and then, he would stop and rush to the front of the block, trying to see inside. When he returned, the banging and kicking resumed.

For more than half an hour, I sat in the dark with no idea what to do. Like a sheep waiting for slaughter, my body shook with fear and frustration. I knew that New Star would not give up until he got into the flat, but what would happen to me if he broke in? Did he intend to injure, kill me, smash everything inside, maybe to rape me? Who could help? The flat had no telephone. Feng-yuan and his family were out and I did not know when they would be back.

The banging and kicking redoubled. It sounded as if a heavy metal bar was being used. I knew that I could not hold out long, as the wooden door could cave in at any time. In desperation, I ran to the balcony and shouted for help. My neighbours had stayed silent till now, but they must have heard what was going on. Soon someone was talking to New Star outside the flat, which made him stop. When I opened the door, he forced his way in and searched each room as well as the balcony, claiming that I had a man in the flat. He checked under each bed, and ordered me to unlock every wardrobe, threatening that otherwise he would break them open himself and catch the 'man' who was hiding inside.

While New Star searched, the neighbours kept telling him: 'Please calm down. If you have any problem with Aiping, you should talk to her, not use force like this.' Hearing his accusations, some said in disbelief: 'You shouldn't make such claims without proof. We're her neighbours, and we've never seen any man visit her regularly.' New Star found nothing, but instead of apologizing for his behaviour he snapped at me: 'Why did you refuse to let me in? It only shows you have a guilty conscience.' He also told the neighbours: 'I've got evidence to prove what I said, because the man has admitted the affair.' 'Lies!' I shouted, and trembled with rage. New Star did not stay long, and when he left he took away everything he claimed belonged to him, including an electric iron, some mugs, and Little Mountain's suitcase. He also threatened to come back and dismantle fixtures he had helped to install when he lived in the flat, such as kitchen shelves and the washbasin in the lavatory.

That night, unable to sleep, I wrote a letter of nearly twenty pages to the head office Party Committee, describing New Star's intrusion and retracing the problems in our marriage. I ended by stating my determination to divorce him. Later I saw a memorandum on my letter written by a concerned official who suggested that the SFPC should inform New Star's workplace about his actions that evening, and ask his superiors to stop any further intrusions. In this official's words, it was time to let us end the marriage, and the question of New Star's sincerity when he prevailed on both sides' Party authorities to 'save his marriage' should be examined.

I believed that by now, officials in both our workplaces had developed doubts about New Star's claims, which had kept them busy all summer, pressuring me to end the separation. When they realized that he could provide no evidence at all to corroborate my 'affair' with Han, they began to pay attention to my words.

A few days after my letter was delivered, I received a telephone call at work from an SFPC Party official saying New Star wanted to see me. 'Please don't refuse to meet him. A tremendous change has happened.' In the Party committee's office, suddenly New Star assumed a caring, humble manner that might have belonged to a completely different person. When we were left alone in the room, he apologized for what he had done to me in recent months, admitted he was wrong, and begged forgiveness. He had never considered divorce, because he loved me and knew how much I meant to him. Seeing our marriage on the rocks, he was afraid that he would never find another wife like me . . . New Star's words were soft and sweet, but I just wept and wept. 'It's too late,' I eventually managed to reply. But he still asked me not to divorce him, saying that for the sake of our child we should try to repair the marriage. Now I was lost for words; I wanted the best for Little Mountain. In the end I told New Star that I needed time to think.

The following day, before sunrise, I was woken by a knocking on the door of the flat that also roused Feng-yuan in the next room. Neither of us answered, because we knew who it was. New Star had turned up the previous evening while Feng-yuan and I were having supper, expecting my reply to his request, and I had promised to contact him again when I made up my mind. Now he was back, this time sounding gentle and patient when he knocked, though no one answered. After a while he stopped, but soon came a clatter at my window. It was New Star again, throwing pebbles. I had to let him in, before he broke the glass.

He came into my room and asked me again for forgiveness, saying that he had spent a sleepless night, troubled by the prospect of losing me. 'You've won this time,' he said. 'What more do you want?' Then he

fell to his knees to show how sorry he felt. I lay on my bed, not looking and not replying. Suddenly he moved to get into my bed. Perhaps
he thought that my silence meant forgiveness. 'Leave me alone!' I
stopped him before he could touch me. After that, he kept on pleading
with me not to divorce him, but my reply remained unchanged: I
needed time.

Several days later I arrived in a city in Jiangsu province as co-organizer
of a high-profile conference. Minister Wang Wei attended, and would
give the closing speech. When he first saw me, he called my name warmly
from a distance. It was lunchtime, and the hotel dining hall was full of
delegates from all over China. Many curious eyes observed the object of
the minister's public attention.

I was surprised by Wang Wei's warm approach, as I knew that I did
not have his favour. In recent years I had often worked closely with him,
for instance as his aide for interviews with the foreign press. I was also
one of the few SFPC officials who had the honour to use his office on
their own. Several times, he called me in for urgent assignments, such as
drafting statements to the press. When he had meetings to attend he
would tell me: 'Stay here and don't go back to your office. I hope you'll
be done when I come back.' This made sense because I would have fewer
interruptions working in his office on my own. Although he needed my
assistance, I knew that my character did not appeal to him. Also, I had
been a target of head office gossip and attacks, which did not help, so
when we met he hardly spoke except on the subject of work. With those
outside his circle, he was always serious and remote.

'Congratulations, Little Mu,' Wang Wei began, after inviting me to sit
with him in a quiet corner of the dining hall. He had heard about New
Star's reversal, and assumed that my problem was over. Now that New
Star had apologized, I should forgive him and be reconciled. 'Oh no!' I
replied. 'It is too late to save our marriage after all he has done to me.'
My reply wiped the smile off Wang Wei's face. From then on his warmth
disappeared and his usual manner returned.

For years I had longed for divorce, and the time had come. If I made the request the SFPC would issue a letter permitting me to register my divorce. However, it was still not easy to take the final step, because of what might happen to Little Mountain.

New Star had claimed all along that if we divorced he would keep hold of our son. Through a friend, I consulted a judge in the local Junior People's Court concerning the procedure for custody. The first question I faced was: 'Have you found another man to marry?' When I said No it surprised him – 'Then what is the point of divorcing?' Through his questions I realized that even this judge believed that marital breakdown must be caused by adultery. Perhaps he thought, as many others did, that my plan to live alone after divorce was bizarre. Certainly his advice was that if I brought my case to court it was very unlikely that I could win, seeing that Little Mountain was a boy. Since the inauguration of the one-child policy, custody had become a major issue when the parents of these only children divorced, and already it was standard legal practice in the local courts to grant custody rights to the husband if the child was a boy. Otherwise the dispute might have no end, because the father would not readily let go, given the strong social bias towards sons.

When they saw how determined I was to keep Little Mountain, I was asked by various people, including the relevant SFPC officials: 'Who's going to want to marry you in future, a middle-aged divorcee with a child?' By then, I was approaching thirty-six, and people over thirty-five were regarded as middle-aged. When I said I was ready to be a single parent, I was warned how very hard it was for a woman to live alone in this society – a lesson my own experience had taught me. But nothing could be worse than what I had been through in marriage!

In weighing the decision to divorce, my only guide was my son's future. I carried very painful marks of my parents' divorce. My son was only four years old. Even if I gained custody, how could he bear the grief of the divorce? During that dreadful summer, I had seen how much the boy was affected by his parents' confrontations. He was growing more timid, insecure and susceptible. When he saw me cry at home, he too would cry, and the look on his face was terribly painful to me. My dearest child, it was I who fought to bring you into the world, but I could not provide a happy family because your father and I did not love each other. In your short life, you had seen so many quarrels and separations. You were too vulnerable to bear such a fragmented family life!

From autumn 1986 to spring 1987, I struggled to reach a decision. During this period, New Star kept visiting me, trying to win me round and full of promises. My determination wavered. For the sake of Little Mountain, should I not try again to save the marriage? On several occasions, I spent the night with New Star, but the sense of disgust that followed was unbearable. Meantime I found that he was still spreading stories about my so-called affair, with even more malicious fabrications. He told people that he was already divorced and asked them to seek marriage partners for him, though he claimed that teams of girls had already applied. When I heard that young women were visiting his flat, friends suggested that I should find out what they were doing there, but an SFPC official advised: 'Don't be silly! It makes no difference whether you catch him out or not. No one is interested in what has really happened between you both. The only way to save your reputation is to halt the separation, and then live in peace.' That was impossible advice!

Office of the Peace Street Area, Chaoyang District

This is to introduce Mu Aiping, cadre of the Commission, to proceed with the formalities of registering her divorce. Please receive her.

Salutations.

Head Office Party Committee

State Family Planning Commission

The above official letter, which functioned as permission to register my divorce, was issued at my request. It did not convey approval, but everyone knew that without official permission such letters would not be provided.

Along with the official letter from both workplaces, New Star and I had to submit our applications for divorce. New Star's application traced the breakdown mainly to our lack of mutual understanding before marriage. He also cited the long periods of separation, and frequent quarrels caused by our many differences in character. He made no mention of affairs, but emphasized that he was forced to accept my demand of divorce.

DIVORCE CERTIFICATE

No. 24

Mu Aiping (female), 36 years old, and New Star (male), 38 years old, have applied for a divorce. After examination, their application has been found to comply with the stipulations on voluntary divorce of the Marriage Law of the People's Republic of China, and they are hereby approved to register for divorce and granted this certificate . . .

The document was issued by the local district government on 22 October 1987. Since we never established a household, there were no common savings or property to divide. The only decision to be made was over the custody of our son. By now, New Star had waived his own demand, so I had my boy with me after all. As child support, New Star proposed the sum of 30 yuan per month, on condition that Little Mountain's name remained unchanged, otherwise the payment would stop.

My mother reminded me that New Star's payment should take

inflation into account. She was right. Ten years later, 30 yuan would buy a few chickens, while monthly incomes at New Star's level had risen from about 100 yuan in 1987 to more than 1,000 yuan. But New Star refused to raise his offer when I approached him, and since the registry office did not arbitrate disputes, our divorce would be settled in court if we disagreed. But the prospect of endless legal battles over child support was more than I could face. After ten years of antagonism I was exhausted, and longing for an end. I decided to accept New Star's offer, and to bring up my child on my own. My mother supported me: 'Even without his financial contribution, we will certainly give Little Mountain a good life, because he is our child.'

Shortly after my divorce, an official who handled my case in the SFPC gave me his verdict on New Star: 'He is a "da-shao-ye" [the spoilt son of a rich or powerful family]. For ages, who has dared to touch him, the son of Major-General Geng? So he has little notion of the effects of his actions, either on others or on himself. Even if their wives do have affairs, husbands normally keep quiet for fear of losing face. I've never seen anyone else kick up the fuss that New Star has.' This man was a former army officer, and better placed than his current colleagues to understand the privileged position enjoyed by New Star when his father was in power. His comments convinced me that he had doubted New Star's story from the beginning, though he kept quiet. When I was pressured to end the separation, he urged me several times to mind what I said to New Star in case we reconciled in future, which I took as a sign of sympathy.

While writing this book, more than ten years after the divorce, I began to see further into New Star's character. After all, he was the product of his upbringing. Had he not grown up in privileged surroundings, he might have been a different person. I was not the only victim of our marriage. Apart from painful experiences, in ten years of quarrels and repeated separations, what had either one of us gained?

I imagine that readers must often have wondered when reading this book: why did I not end the marriage earlier? By now, I hope that my experiences of divorce have provided an answer. Although divorce was a legal right in China, it took years to be socially accepted, especially when it was the woman who wanted the divorce. In the UK, one in four marriages ends in divorce. In 1980, the figure in China was one in 25. Many people I knew were trapped for years in their unhappy marriages. Any couple, but especially the woman, was bound to be deterred by an experience like mine. Referring to my divorce, the sympathetic SFPC official told me on one occasion: 'To my knowledge, you have experienced as much as a woman can suffer in China today.'

Chapter 31

'Heaven never Seals off all the Exits':
My Decision to Find a New Life;
the Death of My Father

(1987–June 1988)

Early in 1987, my department recommended my promotion to deputy head of my division, a post which had always been vacant. The proposal was turned down by the SFPC management, due mainly to my marriage problem, as I heard later. My personal reputation had been damaged by malicious gossip, and especially by New Star's allegations. For the sake of my career and reputation, I could not suffer the official decision in silence, so I was criticized for questioning a Party decision. I believed that one of the real reasons for blocking my promotion was my failure to defer to Minister Wang Wei. To my knowledge, no promotion could go through in the SFPC head office without his consent. He had taken no interest in me in the past, and when I ignored his advice to reconcile with New Star he may have felt that he lost face.

More generally, by refusing the Party's intervention in my private life and demanding the freedom of divorce, I was liable to be regarded as 'infected by bourgeois ideas'. In recent years, a political campaign had been launched to counter political and cultural influences from abroad, identified as 'Bourgeois Liberalization'. The start of the campaign often reminded me of the Cultural Revolution. In Beijing, numerous films, shows and publications were denounced and banned. Fortunately, these activities were soon called off, possibly for fear of impeding economic reform. Afterwards, the campaign against 'Bourgeois Liberalization' focused on political indoctrination inside the Party and government.

In such a climate, promotion was out of the question once I was labelled as 'infected by bourgeois ideas'. Ironically, at the same time some of my siblings and relatives accused me of having my mind 'too poisoned by the Communists' because they could not understand why I worked so hard at my job. In recent years, more and more people had become materialistic, and were only interested in work that brought personal gains. But I found it hard to change my attitudes, because I had been taught to work unselfishly for the Party, country and people, and felt guilty if I did not do my job properly.

Soon after my promotion was vetoed I met Forest, an official working for the Party's Propaganda Headquarters, at a conference in Beijing. We had worked together on a number of projects, because he headed a division that handled international publicity. He asked about my progress, and was surprised by my reply: 'That's not fair. In our place we have many officials less capable than you, but in higher positions.' This came as no surprise. Recently I had met Wang Wei's assistant on my way home after work, and he told me frankly: 'In fact, we are similar in capability and dedication. The difference is that I am rewarded for my work and you are not.' Wang Wei's assistant was about as old as me, a clever and hard-working former 'worker-peasant-soldier student'. Some years before, he had been promoted to divisional deputy head, equivalent to a county deputy governor. During the mid-1980s, it was not unusual in government ministries for officials of my age and background to be promoted to that level.

When Forest suggested that I should transfer my job to the Party's Propaganda Headquarters, I agreed at once. For years I had never considered leaving the SFPC, because the work was so suited to my education and experience, but my sense of injustice had sharpened. In particular, I was hurt by the lack of sympathy shown by the SFPC authorities during my divorce.

In line with common practice in job transfers, officials in the Party's Propaganda Headquarters contacted the SFPC declaring their intention to recruit me. By order of Wang Wei, the SFPC replied that it needed my services and could not let me go. Without permission, no transfer was possible. When we next met at work, Wang Wei told me that I should give up the idea of leaving. I believed that in his own interest he should not be keen on retaining me, though it was true that the SFPC would need time to replace me. I persuaded Forest to keep up his efforts, so he tried to bring pressure to bear through official channels to make my transfer possible.

A few weeks later, the Party's Propaganda Headquarters received an unexpected telephone call from SFPC head office. 'We don't want to keep Mu Aiping any more,' the caller said. 'You'd better send for her at once if you are still interested.' Forest's colleagues asked him: 'Why has the SFPC suddenly changed its mind? They're not in charge of us. Why should we follow their orders?' The SFPC's change of attitude also raised questions about its causes in the minds of Forest's boss and other officials. After this move by the SFPC, it was difficult for Forest to maintain their confidence in me, since they did not know me personally, and eventually my transfer was blocked.

I believed that Wang Wei was pleased to see me lose my chance, and so were my other ill-wishers. In the Communist hierarchy the Party's Propaganda Headquarters, being directly under the Central Committee, ranked higher than government ministries including the SFPC. In a place where my work was appreciated there was more prospect of promotion. After my problems with the SFPC, these people might have been worried in case I used my new position to even the score. Alternatively, they may have felt that they would lose face if a woman they had treated unfairly achieved success somewhere else.

Having failed to gain promotion and seen my transfer blocked, I was determined to leave the SFPC, but appropriate jobs were scarce, and even if I found an opportunity the SFPC could block me again. I could not simply quit, otherwise I would be left unemployed and with nowhere to go. In China there has been no social support for single parents. For the sake of my son and myself, I could not afford to take the risk. Instead I decided to distance myself by taking a postgraduate course. If the SFPC granted leave, I could keep my salary while I studied. Unfortunately I was already over thirty-five, the stipulated limit for postgraduate enrolment in China, so my only chance was to go abroad.

Because the United Nations and other international organizations offered financial support to China's family planning programmes, there were plenty of scholarships in the SFPC for training staff abroad, mainly in the West or Japan. In the past, my marriage problems had stopped me. In summer 1986, at the height of New Star's abusive campaign, my scheduled trip to Japan was cancelled by the SFPC. The rules that forbade certain groups to travel abroad, even on a brief working trip, applied not only to people with criminal or counter-revolutionary records but also to those with troubled marriages. When I learned about the decision, I made a strong protest against it. The ban could become a black spot on my record, usable as material evidence to strengthen New Star's allegations. This time I won. As compensation, I was given a chance to go to Hong Kong to attend a seminar, which counted as a mission abroad because Hong Kong was ruled by the British at that time. I heard that it was Wang Wei himself who gave the order.

The trip took place from December 1986 to January 1987, and I spent most of my spare time reading local newspapers or watching television. On my first visit abroad, to Manila, I had struggled to find my way around and communicate with local people because of my poor English. But in Hong Kong, Chinese was the major language. Very soon I discovered that the picture in my mind of the capitalist world was totally different from what I was seeing there. Ever since my schooldays

I had been told that under the capitalist system most people lived in utter misery, just as they did in China before the Communist regime. In recent years I had come to doubt that vision, as Deng Xiaoping's economic reforms brought greater contact with the outside world. Yet nothing could soften the shock of those weeks in Hong Kong when for the first time I saw how Chinese people living outside the control of the Communist Party enjoyed a much better life and far more freedom than they did in the mainland. All my political indoctrination had assured me that only the Communists could save China. Back in Beijing, the revelation kept me depressed for weeks. I often felt stifled, as if shut up in a small box, and burst into tears several times under the strain.

I was not the only one who suffered from the shock of foreign travel. One of my neighbours, a young official working for another ministry, told me that it took him almost a month to recover from his first trip abroad, a two-week visit to Australia. One of my friends, a very patriotic medical doctor who was nearly ten years older than me, spent a year in the UK as a visiting scholar in the 1980s. When she returned she spent months in deep shock and depression.

All of us loved our country and were proud to be Chinese. Nobody thinks that the capitalist system is perfect. What shocked us was the sudden revelation that what we had believed sincerely for most of our lives was actually untrue. The capitalist system was not as dark and evil as we were told. Unlike China, it respected and encouraged personal achievement through hard work. I was wounded by the feeling that I had been denied the truth for so many years.

From the late 1970s there was a widespread desire among young people to leave China in the hope of bettering their lives, mostly in the West or Japan. In the past I had not been affected, because I enjoyed my work and was unwilling to leave my family and country. But now I changed my mind, unhappy about my treatment in the SFPC and feeling helpless to change my situation. My trip to Hong Kong gave me broader perspectives on my future. In recent years the job market had started to change as the private economy soared. More and more foreign companies were opening offices in Beijing, and establishing joint ventures in China. Through taking a postgraduate course abroad I could further improve my educational qualifications and gain an adequate knowledge of English, which would open more options in the future, so that I need not rely on jobs offered by the state. Eventually I hoped to make a comfortable life for Little Mountain and myself, independent of Party control. As I brooded on the question, I often took heart from the famous proverb: 'Heaven never seals off all the exits.' I must never give up hope.

My bosses approved my application to study abroad, possibly to placate me, because I had expressed my determination not to go quietly after their callous treatment. In contrast, Han disapproved of my plan. In his view it amounted to 'ge-ren-fen-dou' – working hard for personal ambition – behaviour condemned for many years by Communist doctrine as 'bourgeois ideology'. Under Communism, people were supposed to bend to the Party's purposes, not to their own. Despite his record of achievement, Han too lost his chance of promotion, due largely to New Star's allegation about our 'affair'. His response was to tell people: 'If I put my own interests first, I would not have joined the Communists.' In recent years, more and more people had openly voiced their disillusion, offended both by the corruption and nepotism among the Party elite and by the injustice and lack of freedom in society. But Han would not have anyone attack the Communist Party to his face.

In his unconditional loyalty and unselfishness, my contacts with Han often reminded me of aspects of my father's character as I had known it in the past. Disillusion with the old society had caused them both to join the Communists very young, so the attachments were strong between them and the regime they had fought to establish. But the case was different for me, as it was for many others who grew up under the Communist regime. Told all our lives how wonderful this social system was, and how correct the Party had always been, our experience proved the reverse. Over the years, I had seen enough of how the Party's leaders and officials abused their powers for personal gain and mistreated truly dedicated Communists like my parents. I did not want to follow in their footsteps through pain and disappointment, and was determined to make my own choice for my life. Han was upset by my attitude, and told me: 'I appreciate your capability and the moral stand you take, but I can't tolerate your disbelief in the Communist Party.'

Early in 1987, massive student demonstrations in Beijing and other major cities demanded democracy and greater freedom for China. Alarmed by these symptoms of 'Bourgeois Liberalization', hard-liners in the Party leadership laid the blame on Hu Yaobang, who was known as a keen reformer, and removed him from his post as Party leader. In the past, Minister Wang Wei had not concealed his closeness to Hu Yaobang – they both belonged to the same political faction – and even displayed his portrait on his desk. Now the huge portrait disappeared. Articles appeared in the media finding fault with the implementation of birth-control policy under Wang Wei's ministry. In private conversations, several colleagues referred to the open criticism as the 'Anti-Wang Campaign'. Clearly his days in charge of the SFPC were numbered, now that the faction of the former Communist Youth League was in retreat.

Some friends tried to persuade me not to go abroad, saying that Wang Wei's forthcoming departure would bring changes in the SFPC. But I refused to trust my future to leaders I knew nothing about. I was also told that reform was on its way. The civil service, abolished under the Communist regime, would be restored, and employees rewarded for their work. But nothing could change my mind, especially because my time was running out. Even if political reform did move fast, it would take years to get things really changed. I was nearing my late thirties, and there was a long way to go if I wanted to create a new life for myself.

In September 1987 I attended an intensive English course, essential to prepare for my studies abroad. About fifteen years previously I had started to teach myself. It was during the Cultural Revolution, deprived of proper textbooks or any access to teachers. During my medical studies at university, our English course was crammed with indoctrination. I still remember the first few sentences in our textbook – 'Long live Chairman Mao! . . . Our Party is a great Party. We are loyal to the Party.' So my knowledge of English was poor, and the entrance exam for the course was a disaster. What with my demanding job and marriage problems, I had stopped learning English for years, and there was no time to revise. At the interview my confidence collapsed, I panicked, and failed even to answer simple questions like 'Where do you live?' Of course my application was rejected, but I decided to give it another try. Through my job, I happened to know an official in the Ministry of Foreign Trade who oversaw this training programme. When he agreed to support my application, I took his name card and went to see the director of the training centre, located in the Second Foreign Language Institute in Beijing. In trying for the first time in my life to use a personal connection to enter a course, I felt so utterly embarrassed that I brought my son along to boost my courage. With reluctance, the director finally agreed to accept me.

The one-year English course was designed for government officials, professional and academic people who were going to work or take post-graduate courses abroad. Most of them were ten years younger than me, with good educational backgrounds and better English, but many complained that the work was too intensive. The stress made several people ill, and some even struggled to finish. But I enjoyed the training thoroughly. Three months later the director was impressed by my progress when I joked to him in English at a party. Halfway through the course I had the highest exam marks in my class of nearly twenty, so I was treated as an exceptional case and promoted twice to higher classes where I still gained good results. In the end I was informed that two universities in the West had offered postgraduate places. By request of the SFPC, I accepted the offer from a British university.

On 20 May 1988 I found my mother and Aijun waiting when I came back from the English course in the late afternoon. 'The old man died today at home,' Aijun told me in tears. 'The old man' was the name the family had given my father since my parents' divorce. For a while, Aijun, my mother and I stared at each other and were speechless. It was too hard to express our feelings after so many years of family tragedy. My first reaction was: 'Oh no, it can't be true!' In my mind, my father was a tough and restless fighter. For more than half a century he had survived wars, the Cultural Revolution and divorce. He was only seventy-two, it was too soon to end his life. But it was true. Early that morning, my father left the world forever following a heart attack. That afternoon, Little Auntie's husband visited Aijun at work and brought the news. It was only now that we heard about my father's sorrows during his second marriage.

After my parents' divorce many names were put forward to my father as possible second wives by his friends and acquaintances. He settled on White, a schoolteacher and divorcee from Beijing who was twenty-six years his junior, and married her in 1985, soon after they first met. I heard later that it was mainly her enthusiastic approach that won him over, but I also believe that he must have been fond of her to marry. In terms of her age and university education she had some resemblance to Scarlet, the woman for whom he abandoned his whole family. By marrying her, perhaps he was trying to salve his disappointment after Scarlet turned down his proposal.

During my parents' divorce, my mother told Judge Prosperity of the Municipal Intermediate People's Court: 'Without his family, Mu Xiang will not have a happy life, no matter whom he marries.' Judge Prosperity replied: 'I don't think so. I've seen a number of high officials who divorced in their old age and then lived happily after remarriage to some young woman.' 'Mu Xiang is different,' said my mother. 'I know him better than anyone else.' Knowing his temperament, she believed that no one but herself and their children could cope with him, because we truly loved and respected him, and the solid ties between us had grown over years of our lives.

At first the remarriage seemed to go well. White treated my father with respect and worked hard to win his trust. Twice in less than two years he suffered heart attacks, and remained in Military Hospital No. 301 for several months. He was moved by White's efforts to look after him, and the attachment she showed. After the second heart attack he wrote a will:

> After my death there will be no mourning ceremony, such as paying last respects to my remains or publishing newspaper obituaries. . . . Instead of being cremated, my remains should be donated to medical institutions for the purpose of teaching or research, and my organs donated to patients for transplantation. My death can be reported only to my siblings and a few friends individually, but not to the children who were mothered by my ex-wife. . . . The collection of tens of thousands of books, which must neither be dispersed nor lost, will be donated to the state. . . . Domestic items are to be given to White, who can bring them with her if she remarries in the future. . . .

In China it was unusual to write a will. The topic of their death was a taboo that people tried never to mention, fearing to damage their luck. In any case, most of the population had almost nothing to bequeath. It was said that the will was requested by White because without it she was concerned that she would be unable to stand up to his five grown-up children when it came to dividing his legacy.

Home from hospital after his second attack, my father seemed crippled, and needed more day-to-day care than ever before. By then the four volumes of *The Billows* had been published, but he planned some more novels, and also wanted to produce a catalogue for his book collection and to do more research on classical Chinese literature. These had been long-term aims for many years, interrupted by the Cultural Revolution and then by his divorce. Now he worked furiously at home, as if racing against time.

Another concern was the fate of his book collection, built up over several decades, and absorbing much of the family income. These books had been part of his life, and helped him through the ordeals of the Cultural Revolution. In September 1986, less than two years before his death, he returned to Penglai, his home county — his first as well as the only visit since leaving fifty-one years ago. He received a warm welcome from the local authority, and was seen as the pride of his county, both as the area's only Communist general and for his achievements in literature. During his stay he spent a lot of time wandering around, looking for traces of his early years. Everything seemed changed. The town's surrounding wall had been demolished, and so had his old school. He tried to visit his secret meeting locations when working for the Communist underground half a century ago, but could not find them either.

It was during this visit that it occurred to my father to donate his book collection to his home county, and to have a building constructed to store it that would function as a public institute. He would contribute half of the building cost. In the past he had hardly bothered about supporting his family, because of my mother's good salary, but now he was his household's only source of income. In order to save money for the building, he tried to cut his everyday expenditure. Things that he used to take for granted, such as milk and fresh fruit, became rare luxuries. Yet the county's response to his proposal disappointed him, and nothing was resolved before his death.

After his second heart attack, my father started to complain to his relatives about his troubles with White. One day he found that some of his precious books were missing. Since his remarriage he had always locked his study and library, and kept the keys concealed. It was while in hospital after the second attack that he gave the keys to White, perhaps as a gesture of trust. Now she denied all knowledge of the books, but he did not believe her. Later he noticed the absence from his study of his bankbooks, which gave access to most of his savings, worth tens of thousands of yuan. Apart from himself, the only person who had a key and knew the location was White, who once again denied being involved. Determined to get his money back, my father asked various people for help. Under pressure, White finally returned the money which she already put into eight-year deposit accounts. 'What is she doing?' my father protested. 'Considering my age and health, I could die at any time before the eight years are up, and never be able to touch my money at all.' In his fury with White, I was told that he tore his will to pieces.

As their relationship worsened, White neglected her responsibilities at home, and they quarrelled more and more. After their marriage, my father had dispensed with his personal staff. It was said that this was at White's request, because she preferred to be on her own, but knowing my father I believed he must have readily consented. His nature was too private for him ever to have welcomed the presence of a live-in bodyguard or maid. Most of these servants were provided by the military, and were possible sources of gossip about his private life. The only exception came during his divorce, because he needed support from his bodyguard and maid. Now, White was often out, and left my father unattended. With no one to cook or shop for him, he often lived on instant noodles. Sometimes White did prepare food, but he refused it. When friends passed on rumours about White's affair with another man, it further increased his distrust.

Despite his misery, my father had little support outside his family. Having recently gone through five years of public battle for his divorce, he may have felt too embarrassed to have it known that his second marriage was also in trouble. Not only that, but those who had previously taken his side seemed reluctant to offer support. Perhaps they were tired of being enlisted in his troubles.

My father's siblings lived far away from Beijing, except for Little Auntie, but she died of cancer in September 1986. When her condition turned critical, her husband decided to inform my siblings and me. Since 1980, Little Auntie and her family had broken off with us, due mainly to my father's pressure. During her last years, she missed us very much, because the families had always been close, and she and I in particular. When her son, Little Red, phoned me at work with the news of his mother's grave illness I went straight to the hospital, but she was already in a coma and never regained consciousness. She died a few days later. During the arrangements for the funeral, my father warned her husband not to contact my siblings and me. Although he did not argue, afterwards he told Little Red: 'From now on, we don't listen to that old man any more.' At his suggestion my mother brought Aijun, Feng-an and me to pay our last respects before the cremation, but we could not attend the funeral because of my father's presence.

In the sadness of his failing second marriage, my father's attitudes towards his children started changing. Whereas in the past he would not hear us mentioned, now he just kept quiet when Little Auntie's husband deliberately talked about us during his visits. 'Should I bring the children to see you?' our uncle suggested several times, recognizing that he might have shed his hostility, but Father would never reply. His pride was in his nature. I suppose that having gone so far to let us down, he found it too hard to retreat.

Another factor might have been the agreement he made with White before their marriage, not to bring the children of their previous marriages into the family. When her first marriage ended White had gained the custody of her younger child, who was now at school, while the elder one lived with her ex-husband. In order to marry my father she had agreed to leave the child in her parents' hands, but since then she had tried to convince him to change the agreement. Knowing that I was my father's favourite, she suggested inviting me back, and then her child could also move in. But my father refused. Perhaps he was not interested in having White's children around.

During the last months of his life, my father finally admitted to a number of people that he missed his children dearly, especially me, and expected to spend the rest of his life with me after he heard about my divorce. I guess that by now he had recognized who really loved and respected him. Years later, I also heard that he regretted his separation from his children. He described being deeply upset by phone calls from me during which I just sobbed. These must have been hallucinations, because I had never made contact and had no idea about his situation. As for his expecting to see me, his relatives and friends did not know what to make of it, knowing how he had treated his family over these years, so none of his messages reached me.

What a sleepless night I spent. Stunned by sorrow and regret, I felt suffocated but was not able to cry. Since my parents' divorce, my father had been a hated figure in the family, and I had tried to forget him. Now, after all, I realized how much I still loved him. Nothing in my life had shocked me so profoundly as the news of his death. Nothing could hurt more than knowing it was so. Until this moment, I had no idea that we still loved each other so deeply, and how wretched and lonely he had been. But the truth came too late. Oh Baba, why did you leave the world in such a hurry? Did you know that I love you?

The following morning, Aijun and I went to Military Hospital No. 301 where my father's body was kept. We were told that in view of our family problems it had been officially decided to bar us from seeing our father. Aijun and I ran frantically around, looking for help. 'I must see my father today. No one must stop me.' I refused to be diverted. Eventually I came to the family planning office. In China these offices were established in most organizations, attached to the administrative body. Having heard that I worked for the State Family Planning Commission, the sympathetic officer intervened. In the mortuary we finally saw our father, the man we had ardently loved, and bitterly hated, over these years. This was my first meeting with him since 1979, but what I saw was his silent body. 'Baba, we are here. Please open your eyes and see us again!' Aijun and I wept uncontrollably.

My father was the third of the Mus to die in his generation. Second Uncle, the talented playwright, had left us the year before. After the

Cultural Revolution in 1976, Second Uncle was rehabilitated, but he found that his long persecution had destroyed his inspiration, which caused him great sorrow in his final years. In early 1987, he was diagnosed with terminal cancer of the oesophagus, and he died some months later. While researching this book, I saw published articles written by many of his friends, colleagues and relatives lamenting his death and praising his kindness and peaceful nature. Yet it was he who suffered most from persecutions in the family – an ordeal that started in the late 1950s and lasted nearly twenty years. Unlike my father, Second Uncle hardly ever complained, no matter how much he endured. During the Cultural Revolution, he was dispatched to a remote village in Manchuria, and lived like a peasant with his wife and youngest son for many years. I was told that when some local people needed money they would say: 'Let's borrow from Old Man Mu.' Although most of his limited money was never returned, he had no choice but to 'lend' it. To be labelled as a 'counter-revolutionary' deprived him of every right. I believe that his long periods of political persecution were a major cause of the cancer that killed him.

Second Uncle's wife arrived in Beijing on the day after my father's death. When she saw us, she said in tears: 'Your Second Uncle was too intimidated by your father, so he lost his last opportunity to see you.' In June 1987, less than a year before, Second Uncle had come to Beijing for treatment. He stayed in a hotel with his wife, and with help from Little Auntie's husband, Aijun and I arranged to visit him. Aijun had always been his favourite niece, because he did not have a daughter. As a child, she often called her exiled uncle 'Manchuria Baba'. We knew how ill he was, and that this might be our last chance to see him. But only a few days beforehand, we got a message from Little Red. Second Uncle could not meet us; he did not dare to offend my father. Three days after leaving Beijing, Second Uncle died.

The news of my father's death brought his remaining four siblings to Beijing. I felt awkward when we met, because only Third Auntie had kept in touch over the years. Clearly, they too were aware of the breach that had opened between us. Little Uncle explained: 'We could not refuse to support your father at the time of his divorce, otherwise he would have been left alone, and the consequence was unthinkable.' Little Uncle, did you think what your support would bring about? Like the others in his camp, you supported his abandoning the family that loved and sustained him for most of his life. The divorce did not make him any better, and in less than five years he was dead. I believed that my father would have lived had he stayed with my mother and their children.

My father's siblings were lodged in the guest house of the Ba-yi Film Studio, some way away from my father's house. When we met, they talked openly about their grievances against White. During the following years they told my mother more details about my father's unhappiness, in episodes such as the missing books and bankbooks. Recalling my parents' divorce, I felt that I could not quite rule out the possible bias in their accusations against White: they would always side with my father. While working on this book, ten years later, I saw a poem he wrote during his final months, revealing his unhappiness with White. I had no way to know the truth, since I had no contact with either. Nevertheless, the poem confirmed that my father's relationship with White was in trouble.

My father's siblings also held White responsible for his unexpected death, which happened in mysterious circumstances. Since his remarriage, my father had already suffered two heart attacks. Each time, Military Hospital No. 301 was informed of his condition immediately, and the ambulance and rescue team arrived within a quarter of an hour. This hospital has special responsibilities for the health of China's statesmen and military elite. Hence it had the very best equipment and a first-class, experienced staff, which saved his life on the previous two occasions. But when the third heart attack struck him, the hospital was not informed. Instead White seems to have contacted a local ambulance station that dealt with ordinary people, knew nothing about my father's circumstances, and lacked the appropriate equipment. But in any case, when the doctors arrived they found my father dead. While he was dying, White was the only person in the house.

It emerged that only days before his death, my father had demanded a divorce and brought White to the Municipal Intermediate People's Court of Justice. It was Saturday afternoon, a working day, but the court was closed to visitors, so he left in disappointment. Knowing my father, I believed that once he had made up his mind the decision was final. In contrast, White opposed the divorce, which would cost her almost everything she had gained through the marriage, in particular the privileged lifestyle and high income. Due to my father's position, even as his widow she would be entitled to considerable privileges. For example, she could continue to live in his house, and receive generous financial support for the children of her previous marriage. If my father was determined to divorce her, the only outcome that preserved all these benefits might be his death before the divorce was pronounced.

It seemed impossible for my father's siblings to solve the mysteries about his death, because White was alone at the time, and no one else could say what really happened. The bodies officially responsible for his welfare, such as the General Political Department of the PLA and the Ba-yi Film Studio, showed little interest in unearthing the truth. My father never had close political connections in either place, having worked there for less than two years with no political support. In addition, his troubled family life had been a headache for officers in both places ever since he started his campaign to divorce my mother, so few were willing to get involved again in further contentious disputes.

When he heard of my father's death, my little boy laughed. 'What? Who was my maternal grandfather?' It was the first he knew about having such a relation. What a coincidence it was, that both my son and I never met the maternal grandfathers who had shared the same city with us for many years. What was to blame for our family's tragedy?

I was in the final stage of my English training when my father died. For nearly a month I hardly slept in my sorrow. As soon as my eyes closed, there he was in front of me. I felt I was with him in the quiet hospital mortuary room where he lay in a container inside a huge freezer, his body wrapped in a pure white sheet. His short wiry hair had turned grey but was still thick. Why did he knit his eyebrows? He must be cold and lonely. Looking at his stern and silent face, I recognized how much disappointment, depression and anguish he had suffered.

Since his second marriage, I had heard about his heart attacks and knew that he was twice seriously ill. What could I do? I had no idea. Did he want to see me or not? I did not know. As a man of strong feelings, was he able to bear an emotional reunion after such a long separation? These questions created a dilemma. During his hospitalization the previous year I had sent him some ginseng and royal jelly – the traditional tonic in Chinese medicine – through my cousin, who promised not to mention my name. I expected his health to improve by the coming summer, and that I would be able to say goodbye before I went abroad. I was wrong, and the chance would never come again. It was the last mistake I made with you, my dearest father!

Baba, why did you leave the world in such a hurry? Why didn't you give me a chance to see you again? I would like to have told you that during the nearly ten years of our separation I experienced great ordeals in my life, but I did not give in. My inexperience and vulnerability led me to make mistakes, as so many do, but I never forgot the principles you taught me long ago, and always tried to be hard-working, honest and kind to others. Now I had ended my unhappy marriage, and looked forward to a new life . . .

Baba, did you regret what you did to your children and my mother? You were a lifelong fighter and a successful revolutionary, and few achieved what you did in all the fields of war, politics and literature. Why did you turn your family life into a disaster? No matter how much you had hurt us, I wished you a happy life after your divorce. For what you gave to China and the people, you deserved a happy ending. Why didn't you let me know how unhappy you were in your final years?

When I was still your sweet little girl, I liked sitting on your lap and playing horse-riding. You bounced me up and down, while I waved my arms and shouted: 'Charge! Down with the enemy!', imitating the revolutionary heroes in patriotic films I had seen. Suddenly the rocking stopped, you lowered your legs, and I lost my balance. 'Our hero is wounded,' you explained. 'Never! Never!' I shouted in disbelief. In my mind as a child, a revolutionary hero was invincible, untouchable. But now I have witnessed how badly a hero can be wounded. I knew that your heart was broken by the injustice and disappointment you endured from the society to which you had dedicated your life. You tried to avenge what you suffered, but what you achieved was the collapse of your own life. In your novels, the published epic of *The Billows*, almost all the major characters, presented as revolutionary heroes, are killed by the enemy. Did you use these stories to predict your own tragic end?

During these sleepless nights, I kept talking to my father until I was exhausted. But then I saw his face, and was woken by his voice: 'Help! Help! . . .' Again and again, I asked: 'Baba, what can I do?' I knew the pain of your dying without the presence of those you loved. You did not want to leave in such a hurry, because your ambitious plans remained to complete. In the final moments of your life, you must have desperately wanted to talk to us and leave your words. Given the chance, I would have shouted as I did during the Cultural Revolution: 'Baba, please hold out! I would fight to the death for you!' Now it was too late to do anything for you again. Who should I blame for destroying my beloved father, a person of integrity and intelligence? Who was responsible for ruining his life?

My family was reunited after my father's death. It was my first meeting with Feng-xin, my eldest brother, since our row in October 1979 when I moved out of my parents' house. In the past, I had thought I would never forgive him, but I found that my feelings had changed. Through the death of my father, I recognized how short our lives were, and how precious the family was. In recent years, Feng-xin had become an entrepreneur in Beijing, and was one of the first in China to own a private car. Little Red told me in admiration: 'How brilliant the children in your family are! With no support from your parents, you have all achieved so much.' During our reunion we all expressed forgiveness to my father for what he had done. I felt particularly sorry for my mother, because I found that she was still attached to him.

After my father's death, White produced his will, the one he had torn to pieces, but which was now the only legal document because no other could be found. No-one showed the will to my siblings and me, and we received nothing from his legacy, not even a piece of paper. We were only told that under the will's terms, we had no rights to his estate. Experts from national museums and art galleries were amazed by the mass of fine art treasures my father left. Among more than fifty thousand books, many are works of classical literature and history dating back to the Ming and Qing dynasties. The existence of such a private collection was regarded as a miracle in the cultural history of revolutionary China, and its value as priceless. The collection was donated to Penglai, his home county, to establish a museum.

In June 1988 the hearse brought my father's body to the crematorium, escorted by his siblings and his children. Dressed in a new army uniform, he travelled on one more journey. At the farewell, my siblings and I made three deep bows to pay our last respects. In front of his body, I murmured: 'Farewell Baba. Our love be with you forever.'

Epilogue

(July 1988–2000)

I had never thought that I would marry again. After my ordeal with New Star, it was not easy to decide to share my life a second time. But it eventually happened. In October 1995, eight years after the stormy ending of my first marriage, my wedding took place in a small town in England. The ceremony was very simple but I felt that I was the happiest person in the world, able to marry a man I trusted and loved. At the reception one of the guests, a close friend, delivered some unexpected news: I was to be awarded my PhD. In front of all the guests, I could not help shouting and jumping with delight. This was just as we Chinese exclaim: 'Shuang-xi-lin-men' – 'double happiness has visited the house.'

My husband and I settled in a picturesque English village. For the first time in nearly thirty years I found a proper home and a peaceful life. It was also the first time since leaving China seven years before that I was not troubled by financial difficulties. For many years I had suffered from frequent dreadful nightmares that left me awake in the dark in a cold sweat. Now the nightmares stopped, as I recovered from the traumas of the past. In my spare time I became a keen gardener and housekeeper, and enjoyed entertaining friends with my cooking. When I thought about what had happened to me, I often felt that it was too good to be true.

Despite all these causes for gladness, one sorrow remained: my son was still not with me. When I left China for the UK in July 1988, I had to leave six-year-old Little Mountain with my mother in Beijing. The reason was mainly financial. I was required by my workplace in China to surrender part of the scholarship I was awarded by a famous international organization. What they let me retain was not enough to keep both Little Mountain and myself while I studied. When I considered how lonely he would be, I almost gave up the idea of leaving China. Had I found a corner in my own country where I could live in peace with my son, I would never have endured such a separation. When I said goodbye to him, I promised that we would be reunited soon, as the master's degree course I was going to take only lasted for one year.

In April 1989 the death of Hu Yaobang caused a political storm in China. What happened some weeks later in Tian-an Men Square was watched around the world. The suppression of the students' demonstration was followed by an intensive political campaign. Once again continual political indoctrination became a routine feature of everyday life. Every government employee had to submit a written statement about their own involvement in the demonstration, which reminded me of my own experiences during the Cultural Revolution. Before my scheduled trip back to Beijing in October 1989 I was repeatedly warned by relatives, friends and even some former colleagues that I should remain in the West for the time being, as more and more people were deeply worried by the country's situation and no-one knew how long it would last. After several sleepless nights I decided to accept their advice. Instead of obeying instructions and returning at once, I started to work for a doctorate in the UK.

I can hardly describe how much I was disturbed by the thought of the possible consequences I would face. Shortly after reaching the UK I had been informed that I was to be promoted as soon as I returned to China. But now I decided to give up everything I had and remain in the West. Through various sources I heard that the SFPC was furious about my decision, which redoubled my concerns for myself and my family. For nearly two months, my mind was in a dreadful tangle. During the day I often just wandered around, bursting into tears in front of friends and acquaintances, unable to cope with the strain. At night, I felt lonely and depressed, swallowed by darkness. I ran a high fever, and my lips were covered in blisters for weeks . . .

The next few years brought many other problems. Without the consent of my workplace in China, my sponsoring body was unable to fund me to take a PhD abroad, so I had to seek other financial support. For a long time I had to live on the kindness of new friends made in the UK. Difficulties in collecting my research data from China caused more than a year's delay in completing my degree. Despite my excellent performances in English courses in both China and the UK, my English writing skills were so poor that just to write a simple note would take several hours. Some people raised doubts about my prospects for success with the doctorate. Over these years, a twelve-hour day became normal for me. The heavy workload and financial pressures gave rise to stress-related illnesses that could last for months at a time.

But the greatest torment I had to endure was the long separation from my family, and especially from my son. When deciding to remain in the West, I had hoped that Little Mountain could join me before long. Against my expectations, he was prevented from travelling abroad because my workplace in China refused to provide a letter supporting his application for a passport, which was officially requested, and my mother was similarly blocked. Likewise, no member of my family was able to attend my wedding in 1995. My own planned trips to China had to be cancelled because I was warned that I might face punishment for having remained in the West. After the events in Tian-an Men Square in June 1989, more restrictions were imposed on leaving the country, which deterred me from returning. I do not know how many sleepless nights I suffered, and how many tearful phone calls I made to my mother and Little Mountain. After our long separation, communication with my son was breaking down. The image and memory of his mother became blurred and my mother had replaced me. I was more and more troubled by feelings of deep guilt and sorrow for failing to provide my only child with love, and lived in hope of being reunited.

Late in 1993 I received a heartbreaking message. My son had been admitted to hospital in Beijing and diagnosed with lymphosarcoma – a cancer which has destroyed the health of many children. It was like the end of my world. After all these years of separation, I would never see my beloved son a healthy child again. How could such a disease strike a boy so seemingly strong, my only child who had given me the will to sur-vive these difficult years? Why didn't it come to me instead? For a long time, my heart was tortured by constant pain that I knew derived from what my son was suffering. My family warned me again to stay away, and promised to do their utmost to take care of him meanwhile. But the pain of our separation became more unbearable.

After my wedding in 1995, I at once planned my trip to Beijing, sure that the time for our reunion had come. Lately, the political situation had relaxed. To leave or enter China was getting easier. I was happily married, and my husband could provide the proper support. According to my family the boy had remained in hospital ever since his cancer was diagnosed, and his condition seemed stable. I contacted a charity in the UK which provides support for lymphosarcoma patients and their fam-ilies, to ask about arranging for my son's continued treatment when he joined me. We prepared a special room in our new home, and my hus-band was already looking forward to playing football with the boy. In my leisure time I loved to linger in my son's room, imagining how delighted he would be with the comfort and security I could finally provide. As he grew up, I hoped that he would understand the past, and the reason for my absence from his early life. From now on I would bring him up like any other mother, in a happy family.

> I just discovered that my dearest son has left the world already. He only survived about two weeks after his cancer was diagnosed in November 1993. For many years, I have been trying my best to create a good life for his future and was looking forward to our reunion. But he could not wait for it, my poor boy . . .

This was the letter I sent to a number of friends in January 1996, shortly before my planned return to China. After my wedding, information about Little Mountain suddenly stopped coming from my family, despite my repeated inquiries. I was panicked by the silence, and the question I dreaded even to think about eventually surfaced in my mind: 'Is my son still alive?' In answer to my appeals, one of my friends in China was no longer able to keep the truth away from me. From the hint she dropped in her letter, I finally recognized the cruel fate my son had suffered.

For days I lost any sense of what was happening around me, as if some part of me had gone. I could do little but cry. I kept asking myself: 'Why me? Why my Little Mountain?' It seemed like yesterday: when I first saw my son as a newborn baby, when he first called me 'Mama' with his sweet voice . . . How proud I felt, watching him walk for the first time. He held his nanny's hands, and toddled step by step. His face beamed with happiness which immediately lit up my life, and I found tears in my eyes . . . Over these years, it was the existence of my son that had given me the strength and courage to survive the endless troubles in my life. Now, when I was ready to repay his support and give him what I promised at his birth, a happy life, it was too late. He only lived in the world for eleven years. I should have realized that he was too vulnerable to cope with the life he endured as a little child. My poor boy, why did you not wait for me, so that I could hug and kiss you and let you stroke my hair again before you went to sleep, the way you loved to do since you were a baby . . .

I accepted the apologies made by my family and friends in China for those years of withholding the truth. Because my son's illness came so unexpectedly, everyone feared that his death would be more than I could bear to cope with, knowing how much my child meant to me. I began to understand why my family always made excuses to put off my trip to China after I heard about his illness. Once I was happily married, they thought that I would be stronger to cope with the cruel reality, and stopped telling stories about my son's hospitalization, expecting that the truth would eventually emerge . . .

Late in January 1996 I finally returned to China, and saw my mother and siblings again for the first time in over seven years. When I visited my son, I found a pile of cards in front of the box containing his ashes, which is stored in a cemetery in Beijing. These cards — sent for his birthday, Christmas and New Year, and with various cheering messages — had come from me in Britain after I was told about his illness in 1993. When writing them, I never thought that my boy had already left this world. During my stay in Beijing, Major-General Geng, his grandfather, also died. I was sorry that I could not say my farewells, because I still respected him and was grateful for his kindness in the past. At the same time, I also felt that his death might benefit my son. In the world where he now belonged, perhaps he would meet his loving grandfather, and then he would no longer be alone.

Since 1996, I have been back to China almost every year, and have been astonished by the enormous changes to the country. Beijing has become a vast construction site. I felt like a stranger in the place where I was born and spent most of my life. Sometimes I even got lost in old surroundings now unrecognisable. After my trip to Hong Kong in 1987, relatives and friends were delighted with presents like glue sticks, stockings or cigarette lighters. Now, foreign companies compete for China's opening market; their advertisements dominate the city. Almost everything that is sold in the West can be bought in China, and many items are even produced inside the country. By the end of the twentieth century, it has the largest mobile phone communication network in the world. The number of Internet connections has reached 9 million, and the figure is expected to double in 2000.

Rapid economic development has brought substantial improvements in people's lives, although there is still a long way to go. Most important of all, for the first time in history, there is no starvation for the majority of Chinese people. During my recent visits, I was particularly struck by the new professional and business elite, whose aspiration and achievements remind me of the people I saw in Hong Kong in 1987. The existence of this elite in China would be unthinkable during Mao's time. With the increasing new wealth, however, inequalities have grown. Huge numbers of job-seeking migrants from rural areas have flooded into the cities and many remain unemployed, living in appalling conditions. Since the state stopped guaranteeing life-time employment in urban areas (in the late 1990s) the number of urbanites living in poverty is soaring. Among the tens of millions who are unemployed or are in dead-end jobs, many are around my age – the so-called Red Guard generation. Their lack of qualifications and skills means there is little prospect of work in the future.

Today, people address each other as Mr, Mrs, or Miss, the honorific titles banned by the early Communist regime in favour of the revolutionary term Comrade. Among those who grew up in the post-Mao era, concepts such as 'class struggle' seem remote and unimportant. Memories of the Cultural Revolution belong to the older generation. No one is interested in the topic of revolution, or denouncing 'bourgeois ideology'. Instead they talk openly about money, cars, houses, fashion, stocks and shares. Prostitution, wiped out in the 1950s after the Communist takeover, has resurged, despite the government's efforts to eliminate it. Growing corruption, crime, and drug abuse have become serious threats to society. In response to these social problems, the government-run media has started to search for the immutable foundations of ancient Confucianism to improve social morality. After Mao's denunciations campaign against him and his ideology a quarter of a century ago, Confucius finally has been rehabilitated. The Communist dynasty has entered a completely new phase.

In today's China, divorce is no longer socially unthinkable. Just a few years after my divorce, several other members of the SFPC staff ended their marriages. One of them used to snub me and accuse me of 'indecency' during my divorce. It was said that in 1989, shortly after Wang Wei retired, the SFPC head office had the highest divorce rate of any government ministry. On my next visit to China in 1998, I heard that the national rate was one in four, exactly the same as in the UK. Seeing how many couples end their marriages peacefully now, my mother often regrets spending so much time fighting my father during their divorce: 'What was it for?' she sighs. 'In the end, what we achieved was to make both sides miserable.' I understand her feeling, but wonder what else she or my father could have done at that time. People are the products of the society they live in, including my parents, my siblings and myself.

My mother lives alone since my stepfather's death a few years ago, and her retirement life is quiet. My eldest brother, Feng-xin, still works as a businessman in Beijing. Feng-yuan, my younger brother, also a businessman, works in Shenzhen, the first special economic zone in China established after the Cultural Revolution. My second brother, Feng-an, has become an established cameraman in Beijing, and his films are shown regularly on China's Central Television channel. Aijun, my younger sister, works as a doctor at a clinic in the capital. My father's award-winning novel, *Autumn in Jinyang*, is still in print and sells in large numbers. It is regarded as a classic work about the Sino-Japanese War.

Before I came to the West in 1988, friends had already suggested that I should write about my experiences. 'It wouldn't be hard to find someone else in China whose experiences resemble some of yours,' they said.

'But it's almost impossible for anyone else to have gone through everything that you have.' Ever since I was a little girl I had dreamed of being a writer, under the powerful influences of my father and Second Uncle, whose work was known all over China, as well as of other famous writers whom I got to know through family connections. But I never imagined that my first book would be based on my own and my parents' lives. For many years I hesitated to begin. Exhausted and confused after my struggles during the Cultural Revolution, my unhappy marriage and my family tragedies, I needed time and space to put myself together again. Now the book is finished. The writing, although it brought many painful memories, has also helped me to know myself and my parents better, and to start to understand why and how these ups and downs could happen to us all. I hope that my Western readers will share my experiences with me, a person from a totally different world, and also gain an insight into what happened to China in the twentieth century.

Chronology

Year	General	Family/Author
1911	Qing Dynasty [ruled by the Manchu empire from 1644] collapses.	
1912	Dr. Sun Yat-sen's republic gives way to a short-lived new empire.	
1915	A collapse of central control in China.	
1916	Warlord government; wars (to 1928).	Father is born.
1917	Russian Revolution.	
1921	Establishment of the Communist Party in China.	
1923		Mother is born.

Year	General	Family/Author
1924	Great Revolution (to 1927): the first united front between Nationalists and Communists.	
1927	Chiang Kai-shek's coup against the Communists; establishment of the Nationalist government. Agrarian Revolutionary War (to 1937): Communists armed struggles against the Nationalists.	
1931	'Era of the Wang Ming Left-adventurism' (to 1935). Japan invades Manchuria.	
1932		Father joins the Communist Party.
1934	Long March of the Red Army, the Communist forces (to 1935).	
1935	Mao Zedong takes control of the Party. Japan invades north China.	
1937	Sino-Japanese War breaks out. Establishment of the Anti-Japanese United Front between Nationalists and Communists.	
1938		Mother joins Communist Party.
1939	The Nationalists' First Anti-Communist Campaign (to early 1940).	

Year	General	Family/Author
1940	The Nationalists' Second Anti-Communist Campaign (to 1941).	Mother works for Chairman Mao in Yan'an.
1942	Rectification Campaign (to 1945).	
1943	Rescue Campaign starts in Jin-Sui base.	Father is imprisoned.
1944		Mother is imprisoned; meets Father in the Communist concentration camp.
	Rescue Campaign ends	Parents are released.
1945	Japanese surrender. Nationalist military attacks against the Communists.	Parents marry.
1946	Nationalist-Communist Civil War breaks out.	Feng-xin is born.
1949	Communists take over Beijing. The People's Republic proclaimed. Nationalist-Communist Civil War ends.	
1950	China enters the Korean War.	Feng-an is born.
1951		Family moves to Beijing. I am born
1953	The Korean War ends.	Feng-yuan is born.
1954		I am sent to the Ba-yi school. Aijun is born.

Year	General	Family/Author
1957	Mao launches the 'anti-rightist' campaign.	
1958	Mao launches the Great Leap Forward.	
1959	Famine (to 1961). Mao purged Peng Dehuai for his criticism of the Great Leap Forward; the 'anti-rightist opportunists' campaign.	
1960	Split of China and USSR.	
1961		Father is Deputy Political Commissar of the armoured forces in Beijing; Mother is Party's vice-secretary of Beijing Forestry University.
1962	Mao's theory of class struggle developed.	Publication of Father's award-winning novel *Autumn in Jinyang*.
1965		Father's promotion to Political Commissar of the armoured forces.
1966	Mao launches the Cultural Revolution: Party leaders of Beijing Municipality are purged; Mao encourages youngsters to rebel against his political rivals.	Father is persecuted. Mother is denounced. I join the Red Guards for a few months.

Year	General	Family/Author
1967	Rebels' seizure of power from authorities all over China; arrests of military leaders.	Father is imprisoned, publicly humiliated, beaten. Father is released and reinstated. Mother is imprisoned.
1968	Mao send worker-soldier teams to educational institutions Mao instructs school leavers 'to be re-educated' by peasants.	Father is purged again; house arrest; interrogation. Mother is made to hard-labour. I am put into a camp for delinquents.
1969	Party's IX Congress. Lin Biao's No. 1 Directive: China is mobilised for war.	Feng-an and I are exiled to north of Shaanxi. Mother is exiled to Yunnan.
1970		I become a Peking Opera Singer.
1972		I become medical orderly.
1973	Deng Xiaoping returns to power.	I join the Communist Party.
1974		I become a medical doctor.
1975	Deng Xiaoping takes charge of the Party, government and military forces. National campaign against Deng by the Gang of Four.	Family regains a privileged status. I go to Medical school

Year	General	Family/Author
1976	Zhou Enlai dies. Deng is disgraced again. Mao dies; arrest of Gang of Four. The Cultural Revolution ends.	
1977	National campaign against the Gang of Four. Deng Xiaoping returns to power again.	I marry New Star.
1978	China's disarmament (to 1985).	Father goes to Tiayuan to write and meets Scarlet.
1979	Vietnam occupies Cambodia. Sino-Vietnamese War breaks out.	I work on the front line as an army doctor.
1980		I work as a doctor in Beijing. Mother is forced to leave home. Parents' marriage problems hit headline of the *Beijing Evening Post*.
1981	Hu Yaobang becomes Chairman of the Party. Political campaign against 'Bourgeois Liberalization'.	
1983	General Yang Yong dies.	Parents divorce
1985		Father remarries. My final separation from New Star.

Year	General	Family/Author
1986	Massive student demonstrations in China.	Mother remarries.
1987	Hu Yaobang is disgraced	Publication of the last volume of Father's tetralogy *The Billows*. I divorce New Star.
1988		Father dies. I win scholarship to Britain and leave China.
1989		Crushing of student demonstrations in Tian-an Men Square.

Index

Page numbers in *italics* refer to plates; and the following abbreviations are used: MA for Mu Aiping, MX for Mu Xiang, XJ for Xu Jing. Where appropriate, subheadings appear in chronological order.